MACHINE LEARNING AND DATA MINING:

Introduction to Principles and Algorithms

The ultimate goal of machine learning is knowledge.
The ultimate goal of human learning is wisdom.

ABOUT THE AUTHORS

Igor Kononenko studied computer science at the University of Ljubljana, Slovenia, receiving his BSc in 1982, MSc in 1985 and PhD in 1990. He is now professor at the Faculty of Computer and Information Science there, teaching courses in Programming Languages, Algorithms and Data Structures; Introduction to Algorithms and Data Structures; Knowledge Engineering, Machine Learning and Knowledge Discovery in Databases. He is the head of the Laboratory for Cognitive Modelling and a member of the Artificial Intelligence Department at the same faculty. His research interests include artificial intelligence, machine learning, neural networks and cognitive modelling. He is the (co) author of 170 scientific papers in these fields and 10 textbooks. Professor Kononenko is a member of the editorial board of *Applied Intelligence* and *Informatica* journals and was also twice chair of the programme committee of the International Cognitive Conference in Ljubljana.

Matjaž Kukar studied computer science at the University of Ljubljana, Slovenia, receiving his BSc in 1993, MSc in 1996 and PhD in 2001. He is now the assistant professor at the Faculty of Computer and Information Science there and is also a member of the Artificial Intelligence Department at the same faculty. His research interests include knowledge discovery in databases, machine learning, artificial intelligence and statistics. Professor Kukar is the (co) author of over 50 scientific papers in these fields.

MACHINE LEARNING AND DATA MINING:

Introduction to Principles and Algorithms

Igor Kononenko

Professor of Computer and Information Science
University of Ljubljana, Slovenia

Matjaž Kukar

Assistant Professor of Computer and Information Science
University of Ljubljana, Slovenia

Horwood Publishing
Chichester, UK

HORWOOD PUBLISHING LIMITED
International Publishers in Science and Technology
Coll House, Westergate, Chichester, West Sussex, PO20 3QL, UK

First published in 2007

British Library Cataloguing in Publication Data
A catalogue record of this book is available from the British Library

ISBN – 10: 1-904275-21-4
ISBN – 13: 978-1-904275-21-3

Cover design by Jim Wilkie.
Printed and bound in the UK by Antony Rowe Limited.

Table of Contents

Foreword

In the past two decades, Machine Learning (ML) has made, among the many areas of Artificial Intelligence (AI), probably the most significant progress, and has grown into a field of its own. In this period, many of its methods found their way into practical applications, and in many application areas are now routinely used. The wide spread and visibility of ML was accelerated by powerful new techniques, and also by the appearance of effective and user-friendly implementations of ML tools, including some excellent freely available platforms, such as Weka and Orange. All this has resulted in ML, together with its related areas of Data Mining, Knowledge Discovery in Databases, and Intelligent Data Analysis, becoming an effective tool for many other disciplines as diverse as engineering, medicine, biology, ecology, biochemistry and finance. In science, it is becoming part of general scientific methodology and is now used by scientists in interpreting experimental data and in formulating new scientific theories. ML is beginning to be taught outside Computer Science and is on the way to attaining a similar status as some other subjects of general importance, in the same way as it is, for example, useful to students of medicine and biology to learn the basics of statistics.

This book is written by two scientists who have made their own original contributions to the methods and applications of ML, one of the co-authors (I. K.) having been involved since its early stages. In my view, the main strength of this book is its breadth of coverage and wealth of material presented, without loss of depth. In this respect, the book is rather unique among the books on machine learning. The book covers a large majority of key methods, concepts and issues. The style of writing is terse and directly to the point.

In comparison with other books on ML, the following chapters seem to be particularly strong. Chapter 3 systematically introduces a repertoire of basic elements that are universally used as components of ML methodology. Chapter 6 gives an outstanding review of measures for attribute selection. Chapter 8 introduces constructive induction, a topic that is rarely covered in books. In Chapters 13 and 14 on the theory of ML, the book addresses deep theoretical questions of learnability.

This book will be useful reading both for beginners to the field, and even more so to people who have already done some work in ML, but would like to broaden their knowledge and are looking for reference to learn about yet unfamiliar topics.

Ivan Bratko

Preface

In learning, each day something is gained. In following the Tao, each day something is lost.

— *Lao Tse*

The book describes the basics of machine learning principles and algorithms that are used in data mining and is intended for students of computer science, researchers who need to adapt various algorithms for particular data mining tasks, and for education of sophisticated users of machine learning and data mining tools.

Machine learning has exhibited tremendous progress in the last two decades. Numerous systems for machine learning are nowadays available and the number of their applications in various fields, such as industry, medicine, economics, ecology, finance, and many others, is rapidly growing. Machine learning is used for data analysis and knowledge discovery in databases, data mining, automatic generation of knowledge bases for expert systems, game playing, text classification and text mining, automatic recognition of speech, handwriting, images, etc.

The basic principle of machine learning is modeling of available data. Results of various machine learning systems may be rules, functions, relations, equation systems, probability distributions and other knowledge representations. The obtained "knowledge" aims to explain the data and can be used for forecasting, diagnostics, control, validation, and simulations.

Several excellent books have already been written on machine learning and data mining, most notably (Mitchell, 1997; Witten and Frank, 2000, 2005; Hand et al., 2001; Alpaydin, 2005). The purpose of our book is to provide a thorough and yet a comprehensible general overview of the field. Our approach differs from other textbooks by providing several different points of view to machine learning and data mining, as reflected from the structure of the book:

- Besides defining the basic notions and overviewing the machine learning methods, Chapter 1 provides the historical overview of the field and an overview of the state-of-the-art data mining tools as well as established and emerging standards.

- Chapter 2 is the least formal and introduces the psychological and philosophical issues related to machine and human learning, intelligence, and consciousness.

- Basic principles of machine learning, described in Chapter 3, are the central issue and can be considered as the core of the book.

- The next three chapters divide the machine learning process into three basic components: the representation of knowledge (Chapter 4) defines the hypothesis space, Chapter 5 describes basic search algorithms that can be used to search the hypothesis space, and the attribute quality measures (Chapter 6) are used to guide the search.

- Chapters 7 and 8 add to the whole story formal and practical guidelines for preparing, cleansing and transforming the input data in order to get the most out of it with the available machine learning algorithms. Constructive induction, described in Chapter 8, has great potentials, however, in the past not many researchers or implementations considered it worthwhile. We believe that in the future, when more research will be devoted to this area, the advantages of constructive induction will be revealed and implemented in useful practical tools.

- The following four chapters use the principles and notions, described in preceding chapters, as building blocks in order to describe particular learning algorithms. Four chapters divide the field into four main approaches. Symbolic learning (Chapter 9) includes all approaches that result in symbolic and transparent knowledge representations. Statistical learning (Chapter 10), on the other hand, results in knowledge representations that are typically hard to understand and interpret by the end user. Artificial neural networks (Chapter 11) are inspired by biological neural networks. With respect to transparency of knowledge representation, artificial neural networks are much closer to statistical learning than to symbolic learning. Cluster analysis deserves a separate chapter (Chapter 12) as the task of clustering algorithms differs a lot from other machine learning tasks.

- The last two chapters introduce formal approaches to machine learning. Chapter 13 describes a mathematically and philosophically inspired problem of identification in the limit. The results of this formal theory provide the ultimate answers to philosophical questions which, however, are of modest practical use. On the other hand, the computational learning theory, described in Chapter 14, aims to provide theoretical answers to questions of more practical value.

In order to improve readability, we provide all the references in separate sections on further reading, that also contain chapter summaries. Obvious exceptions that naturally include references are, besides this preface, also historical Sections 1.3 and 1.4. We try to keep the text free of formal derivations. Where needed, we provide separate sections for formal derivations and proofs (Sections 6.3, 7.8, and 11.7). The diamond symbol $\Diamond$ in the text indicates that the proof of the assertion is omitted from the text and can be found at the end of the chapter in the corresponding section on formal derivations and proofs. Obvious exceptions are the last two chapters, where proofs can be found in the literature indicated in further reading. Those sections and chapters are intended for advanced readers. In the table of contents, advanced topics are indicated with * (moderately advanced) or ** (advanced). Appendix A defines some less known formal notions, which are occasionally used in the text.

Both authors have experience in teaching various parts of the material presented in this book, to undergraduate and postgraduate students. For the undergraduate course we suggest excluding sections and chapters marked with *: Section 3.4 (comparing performance of machine learning algorithms), sections related to inductive logic programming (Sections 4.2 and 9.5), Chapter 8 (constructive induction), Section 10.5 (support vector machines), Sections 11.3 and 11.4 (Hopfield's and Bayesian neural networks), as well as all sections and chapters marked with **. Optionally, Sections 9.3 (association rules) and 9.7 (Bayesian belief networks), and/or Chapter 12 (cluster analysis) can also be kept for the postgraduate course.

The book web page can be found at the address: `mldmbook.fri.uni-lj.si`, where all information and post-press corrections will be available. The readers' comments, suggestions and indications about errors in the text are welcome, and should be sent to either author's e-mail address: `igor.kononenko@fri.uni-lj.si` or `matjaz.kukar@fri.uni-lj.si`.

Acknowledgements

The book is the result of numerous years of active research in the field of machine learning. We are grateful to Professor Ivan Bratko for his pioneering efforts in establishing an outstanding machine learning research group in Ljubljana. We are grateful to the Faculty of Computer and Information Science for support, both during research and teaching. For long term collaboration in machine learning research we are particularly grateful to Matjaž Bevk, Zoran Bosnić, Ivan Bratko, Bojan Cestnik, Janez Demšar, Aleks Jakulin, Matevž Kovačič, Nada Lavrač, Uroš Pompe, Marko Robnik Šikonja, Luka Šajn, and Blaž Zupan. We thank Luka Šajn and Alan McConnell-Duff for proofreading the text, Jožica Robnik Šikonja for proofreading Chapter 2, Ivan Bratko and the anonymous reviewer for their comments and suggestions, and Bogdan Filipič, Marko Robnik Šikonja, and Blaž Zupan for their comments on earlier drafts of the book. Useful comments on various parts of the book were provided by several people. In particular, we thank Janez Demšar for his comments on Chapter 3, Aleks Jakulin for his comments on Chapter 8, Aristidis Likas and Eduardo Hruschka for their comments on Chapter 12, and France Dacar, Matevž Kovačič and Boštjan Vilfan for their comments on Chapter 13. The author of the "spider net" graphics from the book cover is a young artist and Igor's daughter Nina Kononenko. We thank also Francesca Bonner and Ellis Horwood from Horwood Publishing for their kind assistance and patience. Finally, we are grateful to our wives and children for their loving support and patience and to whom with all our love we dedicate this book.

Ljubljana, December 2006

Igor Kononenko and Matjaž Kukar

Chapter 1

Introduction

The time will come when we will have to forget everything we have learnt.
                                                    — *Ramana Maharshi*

Machine learning, a subfield of artificial intelligence, has shown tremendous improvements in the last 20 years. This is reflected in numerous commercial and open source systems for machine learning and their applications in industry, medicine, economics, natural and technical sciences, ecology, finance, and many others. Machine learning is used for data analysis and knowledge discovery in databases (data mining), automatic generation of knowledge bases for expert systems, learning to plan, game playing, construction of numerical and qualitative models, text classification and text mining (e.g., on the world wide web), for automatic knowledge acquisition to control dynamic processes, automatic recognition of speech, handwriting, and images, etc.

The basic principle of machine learning is the automatic modeling of underlying processes that have generated the collected data. Learning from data results in rules, functions, relations, equation systems, probability distributions and other knowledge representations such as decision rules, decision and regression trees, Bayesian nets, neural nets, etc. Models explain the data and can be used for supporting decisions concerning the same underlying process (e.g., forecasting, diagnostics, control, validation, and simulations).

We start with an overview and definitions of overlapping and frequently (mis)used buzzwords and acronyms, such as machine learning (ML), data mining (DM), knowledge discovery in databases (KDD), and intelligent data analysis (IDA). We continue with a short overview of machine learning methods and historical development of different directions in machine learning research: symbolic rule learning, neural nets and reinforcement learning, numerical learning methods, and formal learning theory. We describe a few interesting early machine learning systems, review typical applications and finish with an overview of data mining standards and tools.

1

1.1   THE NAME OF THE GAME

Why do we not, since the phenomena are well known, build a "knowledge refinery" as the basis of a new industry, comparable in some ways to the industry of petroleum refining, only more important in the long run? The product to be refined is codified human knowledge.

— *Donald Michie*

The main problem of contemporary data analysis is the huge amount of data. In the last decade, computers have provided inexpensive and capable means to collect and store the data. The increase in data volume causes difficulties in extracting useful information. The traditional manual data analysis has become insufficient, and methods for efficient computer-based analysis are now needed. Therefore, a new interdisciplinary field has emerged, that encompasses statistical, pattern recognition, machine learning, and visualization tools to support the analysis of data and discovery of principles hidden within the data. In different communities this field is known by different names: knowledge discovery in databases (KDD), data mining (DM), or intelligent data analysis (IDA).

The terms data mining (in the database community) and knowledge discovery in databases (in machine learning and artificial intelligence communities) appeared around 1990, but the term data mining became more popular in the business community and in the press. Frequently, data mining and knowledge discovery are used interchangeably.

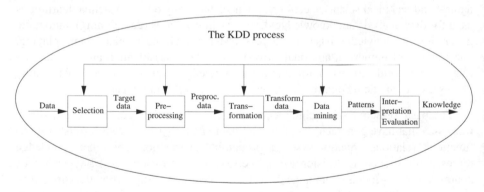

Figure 1.1: The process of knowledge discovery in databases.

KDD focuses on the knowledge discovery from data (Figure 1.1), including how the data are stored and accessed; how algorithms can be scaled to massive data sets and still run efficiently; how results can be interpreted and visualized; and how the overall man-machine interaction can usefully be modeled and supported. The KDD process can be viewed as a multidisciplinary activity that encompasses techniques beyond the scope of any particular discipline such as machine learning. Note that the KDD process uses data mining as one of its steps.

Data mining (DM) is an interactive and iterative process in which many steps need to be repeatedly refined in order to provide for an appropriate solution to the data analysis problem. Data mining standard CRISP-DM defines a process model that reflects the life cycle of a data mining project. It contains the phases (see Figure 1.2) of a data mining project and identifies relationships between them. The phases are cyclically iterated until some desired goal is reached. By comparing Figures 1.1 and 1.2 it is clear that basically they describe the same thing.

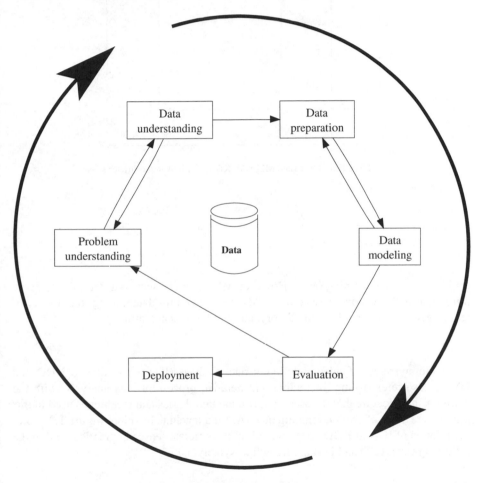

Figure 1.2: The cycle of a data mining process in the CRISP-DM standard.

The ambiguity whether KDD=DM arises from the fact that, strictly speaking, data mining (DM) covers the methods used in the data modeling step. This accounts both for visual methods as well as for methods that (semi)automatically deal with the extraction of knowledge from large masses of data, thus describing the data in terms of the interesting discovered regularities. Most automatic data mining methods have their

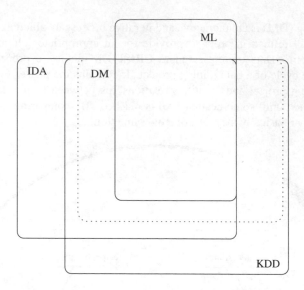

Figure 1.3: Relation between ML, DM, KDD, and IDA in the stricter sense.

origins in machine learning (ML). However, ML cannot be seen as a true subset of data mining, as it also encompasses other fields, not utilized for data mining (e.g. theory of learning, computational learning theory, and reinforcement learning).

A closely related field of intelligent data analysis (IDA) is similar to KDD and DM. It also refers to the interactive and iterative process of data analysis, with the distinguishing feature that the architectures, methodologies and techniques used in this process are those of artificial intelligence (AI) and machine learning. Figure 1.3 shows the relation of IDA to KDD, DM and ML in the strictest sense. In practice (and in the following text) KDD and DM are treated as synonyms.

There is a large intersection between KDD/DM and IDA. Both fields investigate data analysis, and they share many common methods. The main difference is that IDA uses AI methods and tools, while KDD/DM employ both AI and non-AI methods. Therefore, ML methods are in the intersection of the two fields, whereas classical statistical methods and on-line analytical processing (OLAP) belong to KDD/DM but not to IDA. Typically, KDD and DM are concerned with the extraction of knowledge from large datasets (databases), whereas in IDA the datasets are smaller.

1.2   OVERVIEW OF MACHINE LEARNING
METHODS

A learning machine, broadly defined, is any device whose actions are influenced by past experiences.

— Nils J. Nilsson

This overview is intended to give an impression of the field of machine learning. Therefore detailed explanations are omitted. The meaning of various terms mentioned in this section will become more familiar later in the book.

We differentiate machine learning methods with respect to how the obtained (induced) knowledge is used (see Figure 1.4): classification, regression, clustering, learning of associations, relations, and (differential) equations. Besides, machine learning is used in reinforcement learning within an iterative approach for optimization of value function approximation. Equation and reinforcement learning are not thoroughly discussed in this book, and are only described here for completeness.

1.2.1   Classification

Machine learning methods are most frequently used for classification. Let us suppose that we have an object, described with many attributes (features, properties). Each object can be assigned to exactly one class from the finite set of possible classes. Attributes are independent observable variables, either continuous or discrete. The class is a dependent unobservable discrete variable and its value is determined from values of respective independent variables. Machine learning methods are, among others, used for creation of *classifiers*. The task of the *classifier* is to determine the class to which the object in question should be assigned.

A typical classification task is medical diagnosis: a patient is described with continuous (e.g. age, height, weight, body temperature, heart rate, blood pressure) and discrete attributes (e.g. sex, skin discoloration, location of pain). The classifier's task is to produce a diagnosis – to label the patient with one of several possible diagnoses (e.g. healthy, influenza, pneumonia).

To determine the class, a classifier needs to describe a discrete function, a mapping from the attribute space to the class space. This function may be given in advance, or can be learnt from data. Data consists of learning examples (sometimes also called training instances) that describe solved past problems. For illustration let us again consider medical diagnostics. Here, solved past problems are medical records, including diagnoses, for all patients that had been treated in a hospital. The learning algorithm's task is therefore to determine the mapping by learning from the set of patients with known diagnoses. This mapping (represented as a function, a rule, ...) can later be used for diagnosing new patients.

Different classifiers represent mapping functions in many different ways. Most common classifiers are decision trees, decision rules, naive Bayesian classifiers, Bayesian belief networks, nearest neighbor classifiers, linear discriminant functions, logistic regression, support vector machines, and artificial neural networks.

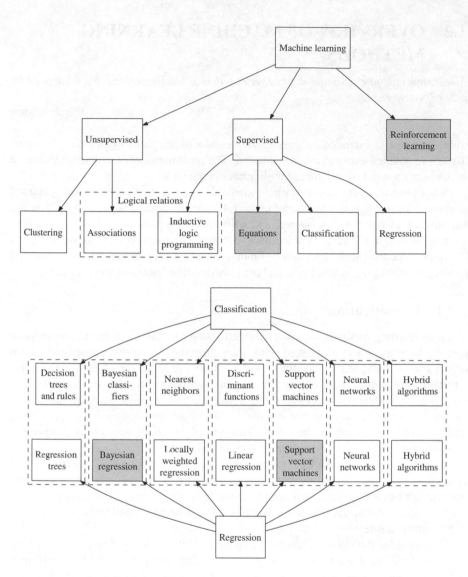

Figure 1.4: A taxonomy of machine learning methods. The methods not thoroughly discussed in the book are grayed.

Decision trees and rules. Algorithms for building decision trees and rules can select attributes and suitable subsets of their values according to their quality, and use them as building blocks of a conjunctive rule's antecedent. A consequent consists of one or more classes. When a new example arrives it is classified by applying a suitable rule.

For the given attribute A and its values $V_1 \ldots V_m$, decision trees and rules form conjunctive terms such as $A = V_j$ or $A \in \mathcal{S} \subset \{V_1, \ldots, V_m\}$. Continuous attributes are either discretized in advance or, even better, the terms like $A > x$, $A \leq x$, or

$x \geq A > y$, where $x, y \in \mathbb{R}$, are formed during learning.

Bayesian classifier. Given the attribute values of a new example, the task of the Bayesian classifier is to calculate conditional probabilities for all possible classes. The exact Bayesian classifier minimizes the expected error rate and is therefore optimal in this sense. As exact Bayesian classifiers are hard to come by (unless the learning data cover the complete attribute space and there is no noise), certain approximations and assumptions have to be used when calculating conditional probabilities.

The naive Bayesian classifier assumes conditional independence of attributes given the class. This (often very strong) assumption usually ensures reliable conditional probability estimations needed for classification, even from very small datasets. Implementations of the naive Bayesian classifier often assume that only discrete attributes are used; therefore continuous attributes need to be discretized in advance.

A generalization of the naive Bayesian classifier are *Bayesian belief networks*. They use acyclic graphs for modeling dependencies between attributes and the class. Conditional independence is implicitly assumed between nodes (attributes) that are not directly connected. A Bayesian network's topology can be given in advance (as a part of background knowledge for the problem), or can be learnt from data. Conditional dependencies are also learnt from data. Acyclic graph topology ensures efficient calculation of conditional probabilities for all classes. Bayesian belief networks can be used also for modeling probability distributions.

Nearest neighbors classifiers (instance-based learning). In its simplest form, the k-nearest neighbors classifier (k-NN) generates its knowledge base by storing all learning data. When a new example is presented for classification, the stored data are used to find a certain number (k) of most similar learning examples (nearest neighbors), according to some distance metric. The new example is labelled with a class, prevalent among its nearest neighbors. The number k is typically a small odd number (e.g. five or seven).

Discriminant functions. The task of the learning algorithm is to calculate coefficients for a discriminant function whose structure is fixed in advance. A discriminant function is actually a hypersurface, dichotomizing between two classes in the attribute space. As a hypersurface can be defined only in a continuous hyperspace, all attributes need to be continuous. If we have more than two classes, a separate hypersurface is necessary for each pair of classes. Discriminant functions can be linear, quadratic, polynomial, etc. In case of a linear discriminant function the corresponding hypersurface is a hyperplane dichotomizing between two classes. The hyperplane's (hypersurface's) coefficients are determined so as to minimize the classification error rate.

Frequently, Fisher's linear discriminant function is used. It assumes normal distribution of learning examples within each class. It maximizes the (Euclidean) distance between averaged examples from both classes. It accounts for potentially different class variances and finds an optimal classification boundary between classes.

Support Vector Machines (SVMs). SVMs were developed in the 1990s and are among the most accurate approaches to discriminant function classification. Due to their importance we discuss them separately. SVM is a multi-criterion optimization method:

- It maximizes the distance between support vectors and a dichotomizing hyperplane. Support vectors are learning examples that lie closest to the hyperplane and therefore define its *margin*. The method thus maximizes the margin as well.

- Since many classification problems are not linearly separable, SVMs implicitly transform the original attribute set to the much larger (possibly even infinite) attribute set by using kernel functions. The success depends mostly on a suitably chosen kernel function.

- Since every classification problem can be exactly solved by using arbitrarily complex discriminant functions, SVMs attempt to minimize the size of solution (the sum of attributes' weights).

- Although the transformation of attributes is nonlinear, some examples still get misclassified. SVMs therefore tend to minimize the number of misclassifications.

Completely satisfying all the above criteria is usually impossible, so a compromise needs to be found. Although SVMs use several optimization algorithms to optimize all criteria simultaneously, one still needs to appropriately weight the above criteria in order to obtain the best possible classification.

Artificial neural networks. Algorithms for artificial neural networks (ANNs) mimic biological neural networks by abstracting neural functions to a simple element (neuron), only able to summarize its input and normalize its output. Neurons are interconnected into arbitrarily complex artificial neural networks. For classification, most frequently feedforward multi-layered neural networks are used. Neurons are organized in a layered cascade: an input layer (corresponding to attributes), one or more hidden layers, and an output layer (corresponding to classes). The task of the learning algorithm is to determine weights on connections between neurons (used for calculating weighted sums in each neuron) in order to minimize the classification error rate.

For classification of a new example its attribute values are presented to the ANNs input neurons. These values are weighted according to the connections between neurons, and their weighted sums are calculated in each neuron in the subsequent layer of neurons. Normalized results in the output neurons determine the classification outcome (class).

Hybrid algorithms. Hybrid algorithms or their parts combine several different approaches by using their advantages and thus creating possibly superior learning algorithms. An example is the naive Bayesian classifier that has many nice features (speed, robustness, comprehensibility), and a sole problem – its naivety. It is often combined with other algorithms in order to – at least partially – avoid the effects of naivety:

- A locally naive (k-NN) Bayesian classifier is based on learning a naive Bayesian classifier on a set of k nearest neighbors of a new example. This reduces the naivety with respect to the original globally naive Bayesian classifier. Local classifiers are adapted to local distributions which implicitly account for attribute dependencies. The parameter k must be selected much larger than for ordinary nearest neighbor classifiers (e.g. $k > 30$) in order to provide sufficiently reliable conditional probability estimations.

- Clustering and the naive Bayesian classifier. For each class the learning examples are clustered (described later in this section) into several clusters. Each of them serves as a learning set for a separate new class. The number of obtained clusters is larger than the number of classes. The clustering algorithm should account for attribute dependencies and detect locally coherent subspaces, such that the naive Bayesian classifier can discriminate between them.

- The naive Bayesian classifier in the leaves of a decision tree. We may assume that the decision tree will account for dependencies among attributes, and split the original attribute space into subspaces where the remaining attributes are relatively independent. Such decision trees should be made smaller (by pruning) in order to obtain sufficiently reliable conditional probability estimations for the final naive Bayesian classification.

- The naive Bayesian classifier in internal nodes of decision trees. Instead of using original attributes to form splitting criteria, we can use a simple classifier in each internal node. Each node has for each possible class a corresponding subtree. A classifier learns from the training examples that belong to its node and assigns them to respective subtrees. The task of the subtree is to correctly classify learning examples that were misclassified in the previous node. A decision tree is built recursively until all examples are correctly classified or some other stopping criterion is fulfilled (e.g., number of examples becomes too small).

1.2.2 Regression

As in classification problems, in regression we have a set of objects (learning examples), described with several attributes (features, properties). Attributes are independent observable variables (either continuous or discrete). The dependent (target, regression) variable is continuous and its value is determined as a function of independent variables. The task of the *regressional predictor* is to determine the value of the dependent unobservable continuous variable for the object in question.

Similarly to classifiers, a regressional predictor implements a continuous function mapping from the attribute space to prediction values. This function can be given in advance or learnt from previously solved problems (a learning set). The task of the learning algorithm is therefore to determine a continuous function by learning from the learning set. This function can later be used for predicting values for new, previously unseen examples.

Regressional predictors differ with respect to the representation of regressional function. Most common regressional predictors (regressors) are linear regression, regression trees, locally weighted regression, support vector machines for regression, and multi-layered feedforward neural networks for regression.

Regression trees. Algorithms for building regression trees are similar to algorithms for constructing decision trees. According to their quality, they choose attributes and subsets of their values for building the node-splitting criteria. Tree nodes stand for attributes, tree branches (edges) for attribute values (conjunctively combined), and leaves for consequents of the prediction rules that map from the remaining (non-used) attributes to the prediction value. Discrete and continuous attributes are handled within internal nodes much in the same way as in decision (classification) trees. In terminal nodes (leaves) we have a continuous function. It is usually assumed that all the remaining attributes are continuous. Most frequently, single point functions (the mean value of dependent variable of the corresponding subset of learning examples), or linear regression functions are used.

Linear regression. A linear regression function assumes all attributes to be continuously-valued and suitably normalized. It also assumes the existence of a linear relationship between dependent and independent variables. The learning algorithm needs to determine the coefficients of the linear function in order to minimize the sum of squared (or absolute) errors of regressional predictions evaluated on learning examples. Either analytical solution or iterative optimization may be used. The result of learning is a hyperplane that for each example determines the value of the dependent variable. The error for a given example is its distance from the hyperplane in the dependent variable's axis.

For non-linear problems a series of linear functions or nonlinear parts included in the functional expression can be used.

Locally weighted regression. Locally weighted regression is the nearest neighbors algorithm adapted for regression, such that linear regression function is calculated from the new example's nearest neighbors. Linear regression is thus adapted to the local properties. Besides linear regression, the average value of nearest neighbors or some other simple function can be used – we cannot afford to use complex functions due to the small number of neighbors.

Support vector machines for regression. Since SVMs perform implicit transformation of the attribute space by utilizing kernel functions, there is no need to introduce nonlinearities for description of the hypersurface. SVMs can be easily adapted for solving regressional problems. A margin around the regressional hyperplane is defined such that correctly predicted learning examples lie inside it. Support vectors determine the margin. SVMs aim to minimize the margin as well as minimize the prediction error on learning examples. As is the case with SVM's for classification, the criterion function needs to be optimized with respect to the prediction error of the regressional variable as well as with respect to the complexity of the criterion function (measured with magnitudes of weights for implicitly generated attributes).

Artificial neural networks.   For regression, as well as for classification, multi-layered feedforward networks are commonly used. Simple calculation elements (neurons) are organized in a layered cascade: an input layer (corresponding to attributes), one or more hidden layers, and an output layer with a single neuron (corresponding to the regressional variable). The task of the learning algorithm is to determine weights on connections between neurons (used for calculating weighted sums in each neuron) such that the regressional error is minimal.

Hybrid algorithms.   As for classification, hybrid algorithms combine several differ-ent approaches by using their advantages and thus creating possibly superior learning algorithms. Strictly speaking, locally weighted regression is of this kind, combining linear regression with nearest neighbors. The same holds for the use of linear regression (or other simple methods) in the leaves of regression trees. The rationale here is that regression trees should partition the attribute space finely enough for a simple regressor to work well. Such regression tree should be made smaller (by pruning) in order to allow enough examples for simple regressors.

1.2.3 Logical relations

Logical relations can be considered a generalization of discrete functions. As opposed to functions, there is no single dependent discrete variable (class), and all variables (attributes) are treated equivalently. Sometimes, some variables have unknown values, and we want to predict them. In other cases, all the variables have known values and we want to check if the relation holds for this particular set of values. According to the expressive power of the language used for describing learning examples and logical relations, we differentiate between *learning associations* and *inductive logic programming*.

Associations.   We speak of associations when the propositional (with attributes) data description is used, such as in classification and regression, the only difference being the absence of the dependent variable. Each variable may in turn be considered as independent (its value is given), or dependent (its value is not given). Because of the absence of an explicitly defined dependent variable, association learning is often considered *unsupervised*, together with clustering (to be described later).

A straightforward approach to association learning is to break the problem into a learning problems, a being the number of attributes. In each new problem, one attribute is taken as a target (dependent) variable, whereas others are treated as independent variables. The type of the learning problem (classification or regression) depends on the type of the attribute (discrete or continuous). Two approaches to association learning are associative neural networks and association rules.

- Associative neural networks are artificial neural networks where every neuron can serve both as input and output. Each neuron represents one attribute. Neurons are mutually interconnected with two-way connections, so that the signal can travel in either direction. The signal value is multiplied by the weight of the connection. Each neuron calculates its own weighted sum of the incoming connections. This (normalized) sum represents the attribute value. In an associative neural network the initial state is determined by the given attribute values. After the initial set-up, all neurons start calculating their outputs asynchronously and in parallel. This process goes on until the outputs of all neurons cease changing. Thus the unknown values of the attributes are calculated.

  The task of the learning algorithm is to set the weights on connections between each pair of neurons. According to the utilized learning algorithm we speak of Hopfield and Bayesian neural networks. Hopfield neural networks are based on correlation of the state activity of neurons. Bayesian neural networks use in every neuron the naive Bayesian learning rule for calculation of the weighted sum. Similarly, its learning rule calculates the conditional probability of activity of each neuron given the states of other neurons.

  Associative neural networks are frequently used for pattern recognition when only partial data are known, and the missing part needs to be reconstructed. For example, in face recognition only a part of the face can be seen. Another use is in combinatorial optimization problems, where parameters (attributes) compete with each other in the sense that higher values of one may result in lower values of others. Associative neural networks tend to find a compromise – a locally optimal combination of parameter values.

- Association rules are similar to classification rules. They differ in the consequent, where instead of class any attribute may occur. The antecedent is made of conjunctively connected terms, built from other attributes. The aim of learning association rules is to find new interesting relations between attributes. They may contribute to (human) knowledge of a certain problem and give insight about regularities in data. The task of the learning algorithm is to find all association rules that are both accurate and interesting.

  Association rules have originally been used in *market basket analysis*. With their help the merchants can plan the arrangement of items on the shelves in their shop. For example, a rule may say, that there is a high probability that a customer, buying flour, sugar, and nuts, will also buy eggs.

Inductive logic programming. In inductive logic programming (ILP) the first-order predicate calculus is used as a description language. It is usually limited to Horn clauses with negation, or equivalently, to Prolog expressions. A learning problem is described with the background knowledge (a set of relations, or Prolog programs) and with sets of positive (true) and negative (false) facts (examples) for a target relation. The task of the learning algorithm is to derive the target relation (a Prolog program) covering as many as possible positive and as few as possible negative examples. ILP can be considered as a process for discovering systems of logical equations.

In practice, inductive logic programming is used for solving geometrical and spatial problems, such as structure prediction of chemical compounds, gene expression determination in functional genomics, spatial planning and subspace recognition, and static and modeling problems in machine engineering.

1.2.4 Equations

When modeling real-world problems, we often have to deal with measurements of different, related and mutually dependent processes. By learning systems of equations we aim to explicitly describe these dependencies. The same system of equations may as well be used for simulation and forecasting. We usually deal with real-valued (continuous) variables, numerical relations, and dependencies. In contrast to this, ILP is concerned mostly with logical variables, relations, and dependencies.

When learning systems of equations, their structure may either be given in advance in the form of background knowledge, or the learning algorithm needs to derive from data the structure of equations as well as their corresponding coefficients. For modeling dynamic systems that change continuously through the time, systems of partial differential equations need to be derived. The task of the learning algorithm is to derive a system of equations that is both simple (in terms of equations) and accurate (with respect to input data).

Equation discovery is frequently used in meteorology for modeling weather systems, in ecology for modeling biological subsystems, and in machine engineering for modeling technical and dynamical processes.

1.2.5 Clustering

Unsupervised learning is different from classification and regression since only description of examples with attributes is given, without the supervising (target) variable. Clustering is the most popular of unsupervised learning methods. The task of the learning algorithm is to determine coherent subsets (clusters) of learning examples. Clustering is frequently used in natural sciences, econometrics, process analysis, psychological and sociological research.

The number of clusters may either be given in advance as a part of the background knowledge, or determined by the learning algorithm. Its task is therefore to determine a relatively small number of coherent clusters, that is, subsets of similar examples. The choice of the (dis)similarity measure is the most important part of the background knowledge, and of utmost importance for successful and meaningful clustering. Most popular approaches to clustering are:

- Hierarchical clustering. In agglomerative (bottom-up) hierarchical clustering, each example initially forms a separate cluster. At each step of the algorithm, the most similar clusters are amalgamated, thus forming a tree of clusterings (dendrogram). Frequently, pairwise amalgamation is used, leading to binary trees. Amalgamation continues until all examples belong to a single cluster. Finally, the learning algorithm or the end user, selects the most suitable clustering level from the constructed tree. In divisive (top-down) hierarchical clustering, all examples initially belong to a single cluster. The number of clusters is incremented at each step of the algorithm by dividing an existing cluster into (usually, two) sub-clusters. The process continues until a suitable number of clusters is obtained.

- Partitional clustering. Initially, the number (c) of required disjoint clusters needs to be known. Given a criterion for measuring adequacy of a partition of examples into c clusters, the algorithm searches for optimal partitions of examples. The process starts with an initial clustering (frequently obtained by randomly selecting c examples), and a set of transformations for changing a partition into another partition. The learning algorithm (e.g., iterative relocation algorithm) modifies a partition until no allowable transformation would improve the given criterion of partition adequacy.

1.2.6 Reinforcement learning

Reinforcement learning deals with the problem of teaching an autonomous agent that acts and senses in its environment to choose optimal actions for achieving its goals. The agent receives information about the current state in the environment and performs actions to change it. Each time the agent performs an action, he may also get a positive or a negative reward (punishment). A reward is not necessarily a result of the latest action, but may be an effect of a (sometimes very long) series of actions. Since rewards are often indirect and delayed, learning is difficult and slow. A learner may be conservative and use only the knowledge it already has, or it might experiment with new, rarely used actions to obtain the knowledge of new situations.

The learner's task is to learn from indirect, delayed rewards, how to choose sequences of actions that maximize the cumulative reward. Usually, the fastest solution (in terms of the number of actions) is preferable. Therefore, the weighting of accumulated rewards is often chosen so that immediate rewards are most important.

A commonly used approach to reinforcement learning is *Q learning*. This is a form of reinforcement learning in which the agent iteratively learns an evaluation function over states and actions. It can be employed even when the learner has no prior knowledge of how its actions affect the environment.

Reinforcement learning is frequently used for controlling dynamic systems (robot control, crane control), solving various optimization problems, and game playing (chess, backgammon, various card games).

1.3 HISTORY OF MACHINE LEARNING

It is virtually impossible to find an "original" idea that was not present earlier in the scientific literature. When the need for an idea is in the air, the idea is usually discovered by several groups simultaneously.

— *James A. Anderson*

Developing and experimenting with machine learning algorithms started simultaneously with the introduction of early electronic computers. Even in the beginning, several fundamentally different approaches were studied, such as symbolic rule learning, neural networks, reinforcement learning, genetic algorithms, numerical methods, and formal learning theory. Other subfields, such as equation discovery, constructive induction, and inductive logic programming appeared later and will not be discussed in this section. In this and a subsequent section we make an exception and give references, while throughout the book we list references only in the "Further reading" sections at the end of each chapter.

1.3.1 Symbolic rule learning

Learning rules via decision trees

The origins of symbolic rule learning go back to the early 1960s. Hunt et al. (1966) had developed a system called CLS (Concept Learning System) for learning decision trees from examples. Their basic motivation was to simulate human behavior. They presented extensive experimental evaluation of different variations of their system and a comparison to human learning. They experimentally proved that there exist many human learning strategies, at least one of them being similar to that of their CLS system. They had to deal with several fundamental problems, specific to each learning algorithm:

- dealing with unknown values of attributes,
- dealing with inapplicable values of attributes,
- evaluating and dealing with costs for obtaining attribute values,
- selecting the "best" of logically equivalent rules,
- estimations of classification accuracy, dealing with prior probabilities of classes and a-priori classification probability,
- definition of rule simplicity,
- incremental learning and windowing,
- heuristic estimation of attribute's quality, including information gain and χ^2 statistics,
- continuous and ordered discrete attributes,
- dealing with multi-valued (non-binary) discrete attributes,
- statistical reliability of rules and their parts.

CLS had also been used for generating diagnostic rules in medical problems. It was a mixed success: although CLS had helped the physicians to organize and analyze collected data, no new previously unknown rules were found.

CLS was an inspiration for Quinlan (1979) to develop his system ID3 (Iterative Dichotomizer 3). It was designed for building rules from large (for that time) collections of data. It was used for automatic building of rules for determining whether a position in a chess endgame is a winning or losing position. The initial dataset consisted of 1.4 million positional descriptions, however with a more suitable attribute definition this was reduced to approximately 30,000 descriptions. ID3 built a decision tree with 334 nodes. After the tree was reviewed, a new set of attributes was defined, yielding 428 descriptions of unique positions. The final decision tree had only 83 nodes and had correctly classified all 1.4 million possible positions. Experiments with ID3 had also shown an important advantage of decision trees – comprehensibility – that makes them visually appealing to problem experts. For this purpose decision rules can easily be extracted from the tree by reading off the paths from the root node to all the leaf nodes.

ID3 had strongly influenced other systems for building decision trees and rules, including ACLS (Paterson and Niblett, 1982), Assistant (Kononenko et al., 1984; Cestnik et al., 1987), C4 (Quinlan, 1986) and C4.5 (Quinlan, 1993). Independently, Breiman et al. (1984) had developed a system CART that is based on similar ideas.

Direct learning of decision rules

In parallel with decision tree learning, the algorithms for direct rule learning were developed. The first practical system was AQ11 (Michalski and Chilausky, 1980) that was successfully used for diagnosing diseases of soybeans. This successful experiment has heavily influenced many later algorithms and applications. AQ11 was followed by the series of AQ-type algorithm, e.g. AQ15 (Michalski et al., 1986). There are several descendants of the AQ algorithms, most well-known being CN2 (Clark and Niblett, 1987b,a; Clark and Boswell, 1991).

1.3.2 Neural networks

Donald Hebb is by many considered the father of artificial neural networks. In his book "The Organization of Behaviour" (1949) he introduced a notion of a simple rule for changing the strength of connections (synapses) between biological neurons. There exist many neurophysiological confirmations that this is the basic learning rule in the brain. The rule states that the strength (conductivity) of the synapse is proportional to the simultaneous activity of both connected neurons. Such a rule requires only local information. Locality of information was a common motive in the development of algorithms for learning neural networks.

The first significant step in the development of artificial neural networks took place in 1957 when Rosenblatt introduced the first concrete neural model, the two-layered perceptron (Rosenblatt, 1962). Perceptrons use a basic delta learning rule, and can solve linear classification problems. Minsky and Papert (1969) have shown that the basic delta rule cannot be used to solve nonlinear problems. This result was a cold shower for neural networks enthusiasts, and has significantly choked research efforts. At that time, the use of the multi-layer perceptron – MLP, a variation of Rosenblatt's original perceptron model that contained multiple layers – was complicated and unpractical due to the lack of a suitable learning algorithm.

The interest in neural networks again increased after Hopfield's work on associative neural networks (1982; 1984). Unlike the neurons in MLP, the Hopfield network consists of only one layer whose neurons are fully interconnected with each other. Since then, new versions of the Hopfield network have been developed. The Boltzmann machine (Hinton and Sejnowski, 1986) has been influenced by both the Hopfield network and the multi-layered perceptron.

The application area of neural networks remained rather limited until the breakthrough in 1986 when a general backpropagation algorithm for learning multi-layered perceptrons was introduced. It was independently invented by several researchers, but made popular by a seminal work by Rumelhart et al. (1986b), published in the book edited by Rumelhart and McClelland (1986).

Adaptive resonance theory (ART) was first introduced by Cohen and Grossberg (1983). The development of ART has continued and resulted in a neural network model ART I (Carpenter and Grossberg, 1987a) and the more advanced ART II (Carpenter and Grossberg, 1987b) and ART III (Carpenter and Grossberg, 1990) network models.

Radial Basis Function (RBF) networks were first introduced by Broomhead and Lowe (1988). Although the basic idea of RBF was developed 30 years ago under the name "method of potential function", the work by Broomhead and Lowe opened a new frontier in the neural network community.

A unique kind of network model is the Self-Organizing Map (SOM) introduced by Kohonen (1982). SOM is a certain kind of topological map which organizes itself based on the training input patterns. SOMs are used for clustering, visualization, and abstraction (i.e., for unsupervised learning).

1.3.3 Reinforcement learning

One of the first successful experiments with machine learning were Samuel's (1959) programs for playing checkers. They played by performing a look-ahead search from each current position. They used what we now call heuristic search methods to determine how to expand the search tree and when to stop searching. Samuel used two main learning methods, the simplest of which he called *rote learning*. It consisted simply of saving a description of each board position encountered during play together with its backed-up value determined by the *minimax* procedure. The result was that if a position that had already been encountered were to occur again as a terminal position of a search tree, the depth of the search was effectively amplified since this position's stored value cached the results of one or more searches conducted earlier. Samuel found that rote learning produced slow but continuous improvement that was most effective for opening and end-game play, but did not perform well in middle-game.

The second learning method, the *learning by generalization* procedure, is based on reinforcement learning (Section 1.2.6). It learns by modifying the parameters of the

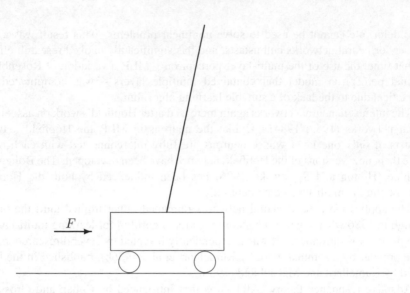

Figure 1.5: A dynamic pole-cart system.

function used for position evaluation (the value function). Samuel's program played many games against another instance of itself and performed a backup operation after each move. A backup was made to the value of each on-move position after a move by each side, resulting in a second on-move position. Samuel fixed the weight of the most important feature, the piece advantage feature, which measured the number of pieces the program had relative to how many its opponent had, giving higher weight to kings, and including refinements so that it was better to trade pieces when winning than when losing. Thus, the goal of Samuel's program was to improve its piece advantage, which in checkers is highly correlated with winning. In contrast to the rote-learning version, this version was able to develop a good middle game but remained weak in opening and end-game play.

Michie and Chambers (1968) are pioneers in learning to control dynamic systems. Their system BOXES had learnt to control a simple nontrivial dynamic system (a pole and a cart). The cart is movable along tracks of limited length. The pole is connected to the cart with a single joint; its axis being perpendicular to the plane defined by the middle of the tracks and the pole (see Figure 1.5). Additionally, the system is constrained by using discrete time.

The controlling task was to push the cart left or right with a constant force so as to keep the pole from falling down.

The BOXES learning algorithm partitions the state space into regions according to how each dimension of the space is discretized. The main idea of the BOXES algorithm is to define a discrete space of all possible situations. For each situation (a box - thus the name of the algorithm), the system should find an appropriate decision, i.e. whether to push left or right. The state space is partitioned into boxes according to how each dimension of the space is discretized. In the pole and cart problem, there are four dimensions, one for each state variable (position and velocity of the cart, angle and angular velocity of the pole).

The algorithm starts with randomly selected decisions that were changed after each fall of the pole. In time, the system has learned to successfully control the cart without the pole falling for 10,000 simulated time intervals (200 seconds). BOXES has strongly influenced many later approaches to learning to control dynamic systems with reinforcement learning, inductive learning, and neural networks (Urbančič and Bratko, 1993).

1.3.4 Genetic algorithms

Some researchers had experimented with combining reinforcement learning with stohastic search algorithms, such as *genetic algorithms*. Bagley (1967) had used reinforcement learning combined with genetic algorithms in the problem of learning strategies for a three-pawn game on a 3×3 chessboard. This was also a pioneering work in genetic algorithms. It became more widely known and recognized with the classic book by Goldberg (1989), accompanied with the development of fast computers. However, the basis of contemporary research of genetic algorithms was already provided by Holland (1975).

Genetic algorithms belong to the class of stochastic search methods. Whereas most stochastic search methods operate on a single solution to the problem at hand, genetic algorithms operate on a population of solutions. To use a genetic algorithm, potential solutions to the problem must be encoded in a structure that can be stored in the computer. This structure is called a chromosome. The genetic algorithm starts with a population of chromosomes and applies crossover and mutation to individuals in the population to generate new individuals. It uses various selection criteria so that it picks the best individuals for mating (and subsequent crossover). The objective (fitness) function determines how good each individual is. The evolution continues generation after generation, until certain fitness criteria are met.

The basic genetic algorithm, as described above, is very simple. Since the algorithm is separated from the problem representation, searches of mixed continuous/discrete variables are just as easy as searches of entirely discrete or entirely continuous variables.

From genetic algorithms, an entire field known as *evolutionary algorithms* has evolved. This is a group of problem-solving algorithms which use computational models of some mechanisms of evolution as key elements in their design and implementation. A variety of evolutionary algorithms have been proposed. Besides genetic algorithms, the major ones are evolutionary programming (Fogel, 1995), evolution strategies (Schwefel, 1981), classifier systems (Holland, 1986), and genetic programming (Koza, 1992).

1.3.5   Statistical methods

Nilsson (1965) describes statistical methods based on linear, piecewise linear and quadratic discriminant functions. He describes the basic notions of the naive Bayesian classifier, and contemplates the problem of reliable approximations of probabilities with Laplace's law of succession. A formal definition of the naive Bayesian classifier as well as a comprehensive analysis of the Bayesian view to decision making was described already by Good (1950; 1964).

K-nearest neighbors methods were proposed more than fifty years ago in the earliest experiments in pattern recognition (Cover and Hart, 1967). However, due to their need for computing power and especially for large and fast memory, the approach was not really popular until recently (Aha et al., 1991). Faster and cheaper computers, as well as advances in parallel processing, have recently enabled these methods to be more widely used.

1.3.6   Formal learning theory

Gold (1967) has extended both the theory of recursive functions and the theory of computability in order to build the foundations of formal learning theory (Osherson et al., 1986). The definition of learnability is analogous to the definitions of logical provability and computability.

The former definition is based on Gödel's (1931) theorem on incompleteness of the first-order logic. It states that in first-order logic there exist formulae that cannot be proven to be either true or false. The latter definition is due to Turing's (1936) theorem on the undecidability of the universal language. It states that there is no algorithm (Turing machine) that would, for any given input algorithm and input data, be able to calculate the result in a finite number of steps (Hopcroft and Ullman, 1979; Jeffrey, 1981).

Although formal learning theory does not have significant practical consequences, it is interesting as a theoretical background for machine learning for addressing mathematical and philosophical questions, such as what functions are describable and what functions are the limits of logical reasoning as opposed to intuitive mind. The latter issue is discussed in the next chapter, while the formal learning theory is reviewed in more detail in Chapter 13.

Gold's formal learning theory was a foundation for the first inductive logical programming system MIS – Model Inference System (Shapiro, 1981).

1.4   SOME EARLY SUCCESSES

In general, people are better qualified for art than for science. The former mostly belongs to them, the latter to the world.

— *Johann Wolfgang Goethe*

1.4.1   Automatic Mathematician

Lenat (1983) introduced an experimental system called Automatic Mathematician (AM) implementing *theory driven discovery*. It turned out that it could model a remarkable selection of cognitive activities as search in which the program is guided by a large collection of heuristic rules. Initially AM was given the definitions of 115 simple set-theoretic concepts. Each concept was represented internally as a data structure with a couple of dozen of "empty spaces" – slots. AM used a collection of 243 heuristics for guidance, as it tried to fill in those blank slots. These heuristic rules may be described as a tool for selecting a path in a state space that is most likely to lead to a promising solution for a given goal (best-first search).

From the initial 115 concepts and 243 heuristics, AM managed to discover the basic mathematical operations such as addition, multiplication, and their inverses. Multiplication was discovered in different ways: as multiple additions, Cartesian product, and the length of the list where each element was replaced with another list.

Following this, AM discovered the concept of divisibility and noticed that some numbers have a number of divisors. One of AM's built-in heuristics tells it to explore extreme cases. Its first attempt was to find all the numbers with '0' divisors, but found none, then one divisor (found 1) and two divisors. Before creating a new concept of prime numbers, it listed all the numbers with three divisors, for example 4. The reason that the prime number concept was noted is due to AM's "Look for something interesting" heuristic. Other interesting heuristics were "Matching is interesting" and "For interesting operators, define also inverse operators". AM had achieved similar successes in planar geometry.
Lenat defined the discovery process as follows:

1. New knowledge can be discovered by using heuristics.
2. New knowledge needs new heuristics.
3. New heuristics can be discovered by using heuristics.
4. New knowledge needs new representations.
5. New knowledge representations can be discovered by using heuristics.

AM had successfully fulfilled the first criterion. But as soon as it exhausted its specialized domain knowledge, AM wasn't able to continue discovering in proper directions and improve its knowledge. It even stopped working after a few hours, since it would invariably modify something important out of existence.

1.4.2   EURISKO

Lenat's later work was EURISKO (1984), which attempted to overcome AM's failures by discovering new heuristics, thus partially fulfilling criteria 3 and 5 from the previous section. EURISKO treated heuristics as knowledge and modified them during learning by using other heuristics. In this aspect EURISKO was not a success, as the task of discovering new heuristics proved to be too complex. It was also shown that AM had a bias toward learning concepts in number theory. Lenat and Feigenbaum (1987) described the reasons for the failure with the fact that the ultimate limitation was not what was expected (CPU time), or hoped for (the need to learn new representations), but rather the need to have a massive fraction of consensus reality already in the machine.

However, EURISKO turned out to be a huge success in other aspects. It won a national war-game tournament (Traveller), a complex game where players need to construct a battle fleet containing tens of different ships with various armament. EURISKO parsed the rule book – several hundred pages of detailed descriptions, such as how extra armor changes the vulnerability and maneuverability of ships – and played 10,000 simulated battles with itself. It came up with some unorthodox designs for a battle fleet. One strategy allowed damaged ships to commit suicide to increase fleet maneuverability, and another deployed pesky flotillas of lightly armed ships. EURISKO humiliated all its opponents for two years in a row; then the organizers forbid computer programs to compete.

Another success of EURISKO was in designing integrated circuits (ICs). From basic structures it created a new structure that could perform two different tasks, thus improving the design of ICs. EURISKO applied the following heuristic: "If the structure is useful, try to make it more symmetric". Since IC design is a complex process, designers tended to produce simple structures meant to perform a single task only, and did not even try to build a structure that could perform two different tasks (Michie and Johnston, 1984).

1.4.3   DENDRAL and META-DENDRAL

The DENDRAL Project was initiated in 1965 by E. Feigenbaum, J. Lederberg and B. Buchanan (Lindsay et al., 1993). DENDRAL began as an effort to explore the mechanization of scientific reasoning and the formalization of scientific knowledge by working within a specific domain of science, organic chemistry. DENDRAL used a set of knowledge-based or rule-based reasoning commands to deduce the likely molecular structure of organic chemical compounds from results of past chemical analyses and mass spectrometry data. The program took almost 10 years of combined efforts from world-class chemists, geneticists, and computer scientists. In addition to rivaling the skill of expert organic chemists in predicting the structures of molecules in certain classes of compounds, DENDRAL proved to be fundamentally important in demonstrating how rule-based reasoning could be developed into powerful knowledge engineering tools.

DENDRAL led to the development of other rule-based reasoning programs, including META-DENDRAL, developed by Buchanan and Mitchell in 1978 (Dietterich, 1982). This inductive program was an early attempt to break the knowledge-learning bottleneck, as it automatically formulated new rules for DENDRAL to use in explaining data about unknown chemical compounds. Using the plan-generate-test paradigm, META-DENDRAL has successfully formulated rules of mass spectrometry, both by rediscovering existing rules and by proposing entirely new rules. Its use resulted in a number of papers published in the chemistry literature.

The development of META-DENDRAL had produced several contributions to ideas about learning and discovery. These ideas suggest: that induction can be automated as a heuristic search; that, for efficiency, search can be broken into two steps–approximate and refined; that learning must be able to cope with noisy and incomplete data; and that learning multiple concepts at the same time is sometimes unavoidable.

1.4.4 Model Inference System

Shapiro's Model Inference System (MIS) was the first system to infer from examples logic programs consisting of definite clauses (Shapiro, 1981). It was mainly intended for incrementally learning Horn clauses – Prolog programs (Bratko, 2000). MIS performed a breadth-first search of the space of all possible clauses, ordered by θ-subsumption. Its learning examples described the correct and incorrect instances of the target relation. Besides learning examples, MIS also used additional relations as a background knowledge, used for synthesizing the target relation. During learning, MIS generated new potential instances of the target relation and asked the user to confirm whether the generated instance belongs to the target relation, or not.

For example, let the target relation be append(S1,S2,S). It is true, when the list S can be obtained by the concatenation of lists S1 and S2. MIS was presented 56 facts, both correct and incorrect ones, such as the following:

```
append([], [a], [a])                        correct
append([a,b], [c,d,e], [a,b,c,d,e])         correct
append([a], [], [])                          incorrect
```

From 56 facts MIS synthesized the correct Prolog definition of the relation:

```
append([], X, X).
append([A|X], Y, [A|Z]) :- append(X,Y,Z).
```

MIS had successfully synthesized many recursive relations and rules, such as that for addition and multiplication of whole numbers. Besides synthesizing new Prolog programs, MIS could also be used for debugging existing programs. This required the user to correctly answer many questions asked by MIS during the debugging process.

The success of the MIS system has introduced a new field of machine learning, that of inductive logic programming – ILP (Lavrač and Džeroski, 1994). Because of the huge (non-polynomial) search space, MIS (and several other ILP systems) are suitable only for learning short relations (theories). A lot of research was necessary to make ILP algorithms useful in practice.

1.5 APPLICATIONS OF MACHINE LEARNING

Omnipotence is not knowing how to do every thing, but simply doing all things. There is no need to translate it into language.

— *Alan Watts*

This section describes some typical application areas for machine learning methods, as well as a few examples of successful applications.

1.5.1 Diagnosing the production process

In most production processes there are small deviations from the normal course of events. The important deviations are those that cannot be anticipated by the controller (or the controlling system) because of partially incomplete knowledge (model) of the underlying production process. Machine learning methods can, from the periodical observations (measurements) of the production process, synthesize a process model that can be used for forecasting in the future. Here, the suitable choice of the measured parameters is of the utmost importance. If the process engineers are unsure what parameters to select, it is best to select as many as possible and leave it to the machine learning algorithm to select the important ones.

Paper mill

In a Swedish paper mill they were trying to solve the problem of large amounts of crumpled (wrinkled) paper. Since several analyses had not produced any results, they decided to apply machine learning methods. Before that, a series of measurements of different production parameters were taken.

The process outcome (percentage of wrinkled paper) was discretized and decision trees were built from the collected data. Immediately it became obvious that a single parameter consistently occupied the root node of the decision tree. This parameter had the heaviest influence on the amount of wrinkled paper. If the value of the parameter was held within a certain interval, the amount of wrinkled paper was significantly lower than before.

In the production process the engineers started to observe the critical parameter and maintain its values in the pre-defined interval. This resulted in significantly reduced amounts of wrinkled paper and substantial savings in the production process.

Steel plants

In steel plants, measurements of the liquid steel are used to assess the steel quality and its future uses. The correct assessment is very important, as it influences the steel plant's income. Steel quality assessment is usually carried out by seasoned experts.

Because experts are not always readily available (weekends, vacations, illness), and the production process must not stop, suboptimal decisions have been made in the past. From the past expert's assessments, a decision tree was constructed and evaluated. It turned out that on the independent data set it performed even better than experts. An expert system was developed and put to routine production use.

1.5.2   Medical diagnosis

In contemporary medicine, the foundation of successful treatment is the correct diagnosis. The diagnosis is put forward by the physician, according to the patient's signs, symptoms and diagnostic test results (lab tests, x-ray, ultrasound, and other image modalities). A problem similar to diagnostics is prognostics, where the physician forecasts the course of the disease.

Based on the records of the patients who had been treated in the same hospital for the same (or similar) disease, machine learning methods can be used to induce knowledge (trees, rules, ...) that can be used for diagnosing (or prognosing) new patients. The induced knowledge may be used as an explanation for given diagnoses, and provide insight into the diagnostic problem. Tools based on induced knowledge are also used to assist medical students and inexperienced physicians.

Breast cancer

In the oncological clinic the physicians wanted to improve prognostics of patients treated for breast cancer. Physicians were aware of the unreliability of their prognoses. They collected medical records for about 300 patients with confirmed prognoses after a few years. The data was used with machine learning methods in order to produce classifiers that could prognose the outcome of the treatment in different times after operation.

It turned out that none of the attributes, collected immediately after operation, were relevant for prognosis. Physicians were using these attributes for their prognoses as relevant, and therefore their prognoses were even worse than the simplest majority classifier that accounts only for prior probabilities of prognoses and ignores the patient data.

1.5.3   Risk evaluation of insurance and loan applicants

When dealing with personal, real estate, and personal property insurance, the agents try to assess whether the insurants present too large a risk for the insurance company. For this purpose they use data collected from different forms and other documents filled-in by applicants. For making their decisions, agents use their experience and incomplete knowledge of the applicant. Given a database of insurance clients and their subsequent monetary claims, machine learning methods are used for generating knowledge for risk assessment and applying it on new clients.

Banks use similar criteria for approving loans to their clients, when the clients are found to be reliable enough to pay back their loan by instalments. Clients are evaluated according to their personal and business data, collected by the bank accountant. Problematic loan-takers are those for whom it cannot be reliably decided whether the loan shall be granted, or not.

Loan approval

A bank was using statistical methods for risk assessment of their clients asking for a loan. The loan was granted when the client's risk factor was above a certain (pre-determined) threshold, and rejected when the assessment was below another pre-determined threshold. Problematic (undetermined) clients were those with risk factors between those thresholds. Their applications were subsequently evaluated by financial experts who also made the final (dis)approvals. The bank decided to use machine learning for evaluation of problematic clients. They had collected about 1000 descriptions of problematic clients, together with experts' decisions and the final outcome – whether the loan was paid off, or not. The data was used for building decision rules. On an independent testing set, the rules outperformed the experts by correctly classifying two thirds of test examples. Besides classification, the rules were also used for explaining why certain loans were not approved. The rules were subsequently used as a part of routine work in this bank.

1.5.4 Image classification

Advances in digital image acquisition have resulted in tremendous amounts of images stored in computers and in the WWW. This caused growing needs for image search, clustering, classification, and recognition. Since manual image processing is next to impossible, there is a growing need for automated methods. Machine learning methods can be used for image classification. For this purpose, images are parameterized (described with a set of numerical parameters) in advance. Representation of images with attributes can be used for classification, clustering, object recognition, and symbolic image description. This approach is heavily dependent on a good description with attributes, that is, on the chosen parametrization.

GDV images

When recording human fingertips with the Kirlian gas discharge visualization (GDV) camera, the resulting images of coronas are of special shape if the person is in an altered state of consciousness (for example during meditation, bioenergetic or homeopathic healing session, when exercising breathing techniques, when he or she has taken some drugs or alcohol, when he or she has some psychological problems). Until recently, the recognition of special corona shapes that indicate the altered state of consciousness was performed manually by experts. Developers of the Kirlian camera wanted to automate the recognition process. Corona images of people in normal and altered states of consciousness were parameterized using various numerical parametrization algorithms. Numerical descriptions of images were then used for machine learning. The derived classifiers were more accurate than human experts. The Russian company decided to install the classifier into the commercial system for parametrization, visualization and analysis of corona images.

Astronomic images

For the purpose of creating and maintaining a catalogue of astronomic objects, until recently astronomers had to review manually large numbers of images to discern galaxies from stars and other objects (e.g satellites). Nowadays, there is nothing unusual in processing huge image databases, consisting of hundreds of terabytes of data. In the mid-1990s, researchers from the Jet Propulsion Lab at the Californian Technical University (Caltech) developed a system SKICAT which uses decision trees for classification of objects from astronomic images. Decision trees have yielded more than 90% classification accuracy, thus significantly speeding-up the process of object classification. Most of the astronomic catalogue, consisting of 50 millions of galaxies, and more than 2 billion stars, had been created automatically.

1.5.5 Predicting the structure of chemical compounds

In pharmaceutics, discovering and improving active substances represents the majority of the research. In hundreds of laboratories, tens of thousands of chemists spend their time synthesizing and testing new substances. Predicting the substance's activity in advance based on its structure would significantly speed up the emergence of new drugs. In this problem the natural representation of knowledge – as well as of the problem itself – are logical relations. The representation with attributes is usually too weak and therefore inappropriate.

Drug activity

King et al. used an inductive logic programming (ILP) system GOLEM for modeling *activity* of drugs' compounds based on the knowledge of their structure, activity of their parts, and their known chemical properties. Activity is a bounded real number and is usually modeled with statistical methods. Compared to them, GOLEM achieved slightly better accuracy, and much better comprehensibility of derived rules, describing the chemical properties of compounds.

Proteins

Proteins are polymers built from 20 different L-alpha-amino acids. They have a specific three-dimensional shape. The sequence of amino acids is the primary structure of the protein, whereas its three-dimensional shape is the secondary structure. Predicting the protein's secondary structure based on its primary structure is an unsolved problem, one of the most difficult from molecular biology.

Since proteins are sequences of different length with spatial relations between their elements, representation with attributes is inappropriate for this problem. Usually, the first-order predicate calculus is used instead.

Muggleton used an inductive logic programming (ILP) system GOLEM for predicting the secondary structure of proteins based on their primary structure and background knowledge about physical and chemical properties of sequence parts. His approach to learning was iterative, meaning that derived relations were used as a part of background knowledge in the next iteration. The achieved classification accuracy was 80%, beating the previous best result of neural networks (77%). Besides that, the rules derived by GOLEM were much more comprehensible to experts than the neural network's weights.

Functional genomics

King et al. developed an autonomous robotic system "Robot Scientist" which aids in execution of experiments and testing of hypotheses in functional genomics. Robot Scientist plans and executes experiments: it mixes different chemicals, measures the resulting parameters, and analyses them. The results of the experiment are forwarded to the machine learning system *ASE-progol* (the successor of the ILP system *Progol*; ASE = Active Selection of Experiments). It induces the rules to guide the planning of experiments. This is a key step in the process because the space of all possible experiments is much too large, so the number of experiments needs to be limited. The system has performed comparably to expert geneticists.

1.5.6   Game playing

When playing nontrivial games, such as chess or go, the space of all possible game trees is so huge that it cannot conceivably be fully searched for an optimal strategy. The search space is simply too great; even much faster computers than those we have nowadays would not help. Therefore, all game-playing strategies are heuristic, building upon expert players' knowledge. In game playing computers have one important advantage over humans: a tremendous speed of analyzing positions several moves ahead. Sometimes, the speed alone is sufficient to allow the computer to equal, or even beat the best human players. In 1997 the program-computer system Deep Blue managed to beat the chess world champion Kasparov. Deep Blue built upon the computing power as well as on a huge database of historic chess games.

While in chess there are on average a few tens of legal moves from one position (the branching factor), there are several games where the number of legal moves goes in several hundreds. In such cases, searching the game space is hopeless even for the fastest computers. Therefore, either the masters' knowledge of the game-playing must be suitably encoded (being next to impossible for complex games), or the program must learn how to play the game.

TD-Gammon

One of the most impressive game playing applications of learning is Tesauro's TD-Gammon for the game of backgammon. TD-Gammon required little backgammon knowledge and yet learned to play extremely well, close to the level of the world's strongest grandmasters. The learning algorithm in TD-Gammon was a straightforward combination of the reinforcement learning (using the TD(λ) algorithm) and nonlinear function approximation using a multi-layer neural network trained by the backpropagation algorithm. In backgammon, the branching factor is very high (usually, several hundreds of moves are possible). The game also has a stochastic nature because of the dice throwing. This renders usual search methods less effective, but is especially suitable for reinforcement learning.

TD-Gammon was developed in several phases. Each phase was improving on the structure and the size of the neural network from the previous one. Initial versions of TD-Gammon were using only a plain board encoding (number of white and black pieces at each location) as input. In later versions, a set of handcrafted features, deemed important by experts, was also added. This included pre-computed information such as the probability of being hit, or the strength of a blockade. In the final version (TD-Gammon 3.0) the neural network consisted of 80 hidden neurons. TD-Gammon 3.0 had played one and a half million games with itself before the learning process converged into a local optimum. The final version of TD-Gammon also included a 2-ply search in making its move selection. These added features made TD-Gammon the first computer program to attain strong master level play, equaling the world's best human players.

Tesauro was able to play his programs in a significant number of games against world-class human players. Based on these results and analyses by backgammon grandmasters, TD-Gammon appeared to be at the playing strength of the best human players in the world. In the long run, TD-Gammon may play even better than grandmasters, because of the possible human player's weariness and preferences for certain strategies. TD-Gammon has also changed the way the best human players play the game. It learned to play certain opening positions differently than was common among the best human players. Based on TD-Gammon's success and further analysis, the best human players now play certain positions as TD-Gammon did.

1.6 DATA MINING TOOLS AND STANDARDS

You are free, and that is why you are lost.

— Franz Kafka

As machine learning and data mining have matured, they are used both in experimental as well as in commercial applications. Machine learning (ML) and data mining (DM) models generated by ML and DM applications are often used as components in other systems, including those in customer relationship management, enterprise resource planning, risk management, and intrusion detection. In research, ML and DM are used for analysis of scientific and engineering data.

1.6.1 Data Mining standards

Employing common data mining standards greatly simplifies the integration, updating, and maintenance of the applications and systems containing the models. Established and emerging standards address various aspects of data mining, such as:

- models for representing data mining and statistical data,
- cleaning, transforming, and aggregating attributes used as input in the models,
- interfaces and APIs for linking to other languages and systems,
- settings required for building and using the models,
- processes for producing, deploying, and using the models,
- standards for analyzing and mining remote and distributed data.

Model and data representation

- The Predictive Model Markup Language (PMML) is an XML standard being developed by the Data Mining Group (`www.dmg.org`) with strong commercial support. PMML represents and describes data mining and statistical models, as well as some of the operations required for cleaning and transforming data prior to modeling. PMML aims to provide enough infrastructure for an application to be able to produce a model and another application to apply (consume) it simply by reading the PMML XML data file.

- The Common Warehouse Metamodel (CWM) developed by the Object Management Group (`www.omg.org`) standardizes a basis for data modeling commonality within an enterprise, across databases and data stores. It includes meta-models for relational, record, and multidimensional data; transformations, OLAP, and data mining; and warehouse functions including process and operation. Meta-data are used for specifying model building settings, model representations, and results from model operations, along with other data mining-related objects. Models are defined through the Unified Modeling Language (UML).

Standard APIs

To facilitate integration of data mining with application software, several data mining APIs have been developed.

- The SQL Multimedia and Applications Packages Standard (SQL/MM) includes a specification called SQL/MM Part 6: Data Mining, which specifies a SQL interface to data mining applications and services. It provides an API for data mining applications to access data from SQL/MM-compliant relational databases. It is a collection of SQL user-defined types and routines to compute and apply data mining models.

- The JDM (Java Data Mining) was developed by the Java Specification Request-73 (JSR-73). It defines a pure Java API supporting the building of data mining models and the scoring of data (using the previously built models), as well as the creation, storage, and maintenance of and access to data and meta-data supporting the data mining results. The JDM standard takes into account the CWM as well as the PMML and SQL/MM standards.

- The Microsoft-supported OLE DB for DM defines an API for data mining for Microsoft-based applications. OLE DB for DM was especially noteworthy for introducing several new capabilities, variants of which are now part of other standards, including PMML. OLE DB for DM was subsumed by Microsoft's Analysis Services for SQL Server.

Process standards

- The Cross-Industry Standard Process for Data Mining Special Interest Group, an industry organization, developed CRISP-DM (see Figure 1.2) to define a data mining process that applies across diverse industry sectors. The process is designed to make large data mining projects faster, less expensive, and more manageable by breaking the process down to manageable phases. It consists of checklists, guidelines, tasks, and objectives for every stage of the data mining process.

WWW standards

- The semantic Web includes the open standards being developed by the World Wide Web Consortium (W3C) for defining and working with knowledge through XML, the Resource Description Framework (RDF), and related standards. RDF can be thought of informally as a way to code triples consisting of subjects, verbs, and objects. The semantic Web can in principle be used to store knowledge extracted from data through data mining systems.

- Data webs are Web-based infrastructures employing Web services and other open Web protocols and standards for analyzing and mining remote and distributed data. In addition to standard Web protocols, some data webs also use protocols designed to transport remote and distributed data, such as the Data Space Transport Protocol (DSTP), developed by the National Center for Data Mining at the University of Illinois at Chicago and standardized by the Data Mining Group.

1.6.2   Data Mining tools

In the beginning, machine learning applications were used exclusively as research tools. Typically they were highly specialized and parameterized, requiring a machine learning expert (typically the author) to handle them efficiently. As the field has matured, machine learning tools were adapted for use with database management systems, and the term data mining was coined. With time, more and more tools were made more user-friendly and adapted for commercial use.

Nowadays there exist at least a hundred different data mining tools and suites, both commercial and free (open source), so a thorough overview is next to impossible. Data mining tools can be divided into three groups concerning their origin. In the first group there are mostly commercial tools that originate from database management systems. In the second group there are tools that have their origins in classical data analysis (statistical) tools, both commercial and non-commercial. In the third group we find traditional free research tools, mostly open sourced, but well documented and sufficiently user-friendly.

Database-originating tools

These tools and applications have been developed in close cooperation with database vendors. They are very useful for business applications because they are well integrated with database management systems, and provide additional levels of security since data does not leave the database during data mining. They also support most data mining standards. Their drawback is typically a limited number of machine learning and data mining techniques available. Typical representatives are:

- IBM was the first large database vendor to include data mining capabilities in its products in the mid-1990s. IBM's product, Intelligent Miner for Data offers the latest data mining technology and supports full range of mining processes, from data preparation to mining and presentation. It includes data mining methods for classification, clustering, and learning associations.
  www.ibm.com/software/data/iminer/fordata

- Oracle Data Mining provides GUI, PL/SQL-interface, and JDM-conforming Java interface to methods such as attribute importance, Bayesian classification, association rules, clustering, SVMs, decision trees, and more.
  www.oracle.com/technology/products/bi/odm/index.html

- Microsoft had first added data mining capabilities (although only on a small scale) to its SQL Server in 2000. They have made a lot of improvements with Microsoft SQL Server 2005, as it thoroughly supports both data mining and OLAP. Implemented methods include decision trees and regression trees, association rules, sequence clustering, time series, neural networks, Bayesian classification. They can also be extended by the third-party algorithms.
  www.sqlserverdatamining.com

Statistics-originating tools

These tools originate from classical statistical (data analysis) applications. Therefore they offer numerous classical data analysis methods, as well as modern data mining algorithms. While they cooperate well with databases, they are not integrated with them, and typically work in a client-server model, with data storage and access handled by remote database management systems. In this group we find both commercial and non-commercial (open source) applications.

- SPSS Clementine is a visual rapid modeling environment for data mining. It offers advanced statistical and data mining methods, including decision

tables, decision trees, classification rules, association rules, clustering, statistical modeling, linear models, and many others.
`www.spss.com/clementine`

- Statistica Data Miner is a comprehensive, integrated statistical data analysis, graphics, data base management, and application development system. Its data mining capabilities consist of several thousands of analytic, graphical, and data management functions and an exhaustive collection of data mining and machine learning algorithms including SVM, clustering, classification and regression trees, generalized additive models, neural networks, automatic feature selection, k-nearest neighbors, and association rules.
`www.statsoft.com/products/dataminer.htm`

- SAS Enterprise Miner is an integrated suite which provides a user-friendly GUI front-end to SEMMA (Sample, Explore, Modify, Model, Assess), a process model similar to CRISP-DM. Implemented data mining methods include decision trees, neural networks, memory-based reasoning, linear and logistic regression, clustering, associations, and time series.
`www.sas.com/technologies/analytics/datamining/miner`

- S-PLUS and Insightful Miner. S-PLUS is a language and tool for data analysis, data mining, and statistical modeling. Insightful Miner is a big-data workbench for building predictive analysis applications. Implemented methods include decision and regression trees, linear and logistic regression, several types of neural networks, the naive Bayesian classifier, Cox proportional hazard models for censored data, clustering, and ensembles.
`www.insightful.com/products/iminer`

Open source tools

Tools from this group have typically started as proprietary research tools. They require some more efforts from end users, however they are well documented and represent a cutting edge in machine learning and data mining.

- MLC++ is a portable machine learning library in C++. It provides general machine learning algorithms that can be used by end users, analysts, professionals, and researchers. The main objective is to provide users with a wide variety of tools for data mining and visualization. Implemented algorithms include the naive Bayesian classifier, various decision trees, decision tables, decision rules, k-nearest neighbors, various neural networks, and more.
`www.sgi.com/tech/mlc`

- Orange is a component-based data mining software. It includes a range of preprocessing, modeling and data exploration techniques. It is based on C++ components, that are accessed either directly, through Python scripts, or through the graphical user interface. Data mining algorithms include association rules, classification and regression trees, clustering, function decomposition, k-nearest

neighbors, logistic regression, the naive Bayesian classifier, and SVM.
`www.ailab.si/orange`

- Weka is a collection of machine learning algorithms for solving real-world data mining problems. It is written in Java and runs on almost any platform. Weka contains tools for data pre-processing, classification, regression, clustering, association rules, and visualization. It may easily be extended by developing new machine learning schemes.
`www.cs.waikato.ac.nz/ml/weka/index.html`

- R is a language and environment for statistical computing and graphics. It is an open source project similar to S language. There exist many (free) data mining add-on packages, including decision and regression trees, Bayesian classification, SVMs, k-nearest neighbors, neural networks, and many other.
`www.r-project.org`

1.7 SUMMARY AND FURTHER READING

You can't talk to hole-in-the-corner scholars about the Way, because they are constricted by their doctrines.

— Zhuang Zi

- Machine learning and data mining are two parts of the same story: extracting useful information (and knowledge) from collected data. While machine learning focuses more on development of data modelling techniques, data mining is more application-oriented.

- Machine learning methods can be divided into supervised and unsupervised. Supervised methods can be further divided according to the type of the supervising variable: for continuous variable we speak of regression and for discrete of classification. The most popular classification methods are decision trees and rules, Bayesian classifiers, nearest neighbor classifiers, discriminant functions, support vector machines and neural networks. The most popular regression methods are linear and locally weighted regression, regression trees, support vector machines and neural networks. Unsupervised methods are divided into clustering and association rules.

- The history of machine learning goes hand-in-hand with the advent of computers. Soon after computers became reasonably accessible, different machine learning techniques began to appear: symbolic rule learning, neural networks, reinforcement learning, genetic algorithms, statistical learning. Historically, machine learning methods have been successfully employed in various difficult problems, such as game playing, circuit design, medical diagnostics, financial and industrial applications, astronomy.

- There exist several emerging standards for machine learning and data mining: for model representation (e.g. PMML), for process standards (e.g. CRISP-DM), for standardized application programming interfaces (e.g. JDM).

- Plenty of commercial and open-source machine learning and data mining tools are nowadays available. Most popular commercial tools originate either from database products (IBM Data Miner, Oracle Data Mining) or statistical programs (SPSS Clementine, S-PLUS and Insightful Miner, SAS Enterprise Miner). Popular open source data mining tools (Weka, Orange) mostly originate from academic or research institutions.

Fayyad and Uthurusamy (1996) and Brachman and Anand (1996) contemplated on knowledge discovery in data(bases) and data mining. Lavrač et al. (1997) were the first to explicitly explore relations among KDD, DM, IDA, and ML. The CRISP-DM project (www.crisp-dm.org) is a serious, well founded, and well received approach to standardizing guidelines for the data mining process and knowledge discovery in databases.

Early systematic documentation of ML research is a series of books edited by Michalski et al. (1983, 1986), Kodratoff and Michalski (1990), Michalski and Tecuci (1994), and Michalski et al. (1998). A thorough collection, edited by Shavlik and Dietterich (1990) gives most of the important early ML research articles.

Pioneering work in learning decision rules and trees from examples has been carried out by Hunt et al. (1966). Decision trees have become popular with the early work of Breiman et al. (1984) and Quinlan (1979) and their successors (Paterson and Niblett, 1982; Kononenko et al., 1984; Cestnik et al., 1987; Quinlan, 1986). Quinlan (1993) is a good reference for decision trees. Decision rules have gained in importance by the work of Michalski and Chilausky (1980), and its later variants (Michalski et al., 1986; Clark and Niblett, 1987b,a; Clark and Boswell, 1991). An excellent book by Breiman et al. (1984) provided the foundation for many approaches to symbolic learning.

A good general introduction to neural networks is a textbook by Haykin (1998). It gives a thorough overview of both supervised and unsupervised neural networks. Kohonen (2001) gives an even more detailed treatment of unsupervised neural networks, introduced by himself (1982). Anderson and Rosenfeld (1988) had compiled a comprehensive collection of significant early papers on artificial neural networks.

Bernardo and Smith (2000) provide a thorough introduction to Bayesian theory and decision analysis, including probabilistic graphical models, data mining, information retrieval and machine learning. Kononenko (1989b; 1991a; 1991b) discusses several Bayesian approaches to machine learning and their extensions.

Sutton and Barto (1998) present in their book a complete, though gentle introduction to reinforcement learning. Goldberg (1989) is a general reference for genetic algorithms.

Nilsson (1965) documented early stages of discriminant analysis. An excellent book by Vapnik (2000) describes the state of the art methods, mostly support vector machines.

Osherson et al. (1986) provide a detailed description of the formal learning theory and its results. Kearns and Vazirani's excellent book (1994) is a comprehensible reference to foundations of computational learning theory. Everitt et al. (2001) and Gordon (1999) are good general references for clustering.

Applications described in Section 1.5 are presented in more detail in the following papers. Tesauro (1992, 1995) has developed the highly successful program TD-Gammon that played the game of backgammon at the grandmaster level. Fayyad (1995) was the first to use machine learning (decision trees) for classification of objects from astronomic images within the SKICAT project. King et al. (1992) and Muggleton (1992) used an inductive logic programming (ILP) system GOLEM for modeling the activity of drugs' compounds and predicting the secondary structure of proteins based on their primary structure. King et al. (2004) had developed an autonomous robotic system Robot Scientist for automatic planning and execution of experiments in functional genomics.

The application in the paper mill was developed with the Assistant professional system (Kononenko et al., 1988). The development of an expert system for a steel plant is described in (Lavrač et al., 1986). The problem of predicting the recurrence of breast cancer was first described in (Kononenko et al., 1984), and later became a popular benchmark data set, available at ML repository (Hettich et al., 1998). The loan approval application is described in (Witten and Frank, 2000) and the recognition of altered states of consciousness with GDV images is described in (Kononenko et al., 2004).

Chapter 2

Learning and Intelligence

Trying to understand yourself is like trying to bite your own teeth.

— *Alan Watts*

In this chapter we define learning and discuss its relation to intelligence and artificial intelligence. Then we analyse in some detail natural learning. We relate learning and intelligence to consciousness and finally provide the motivation for machine learning.

2.1 WHAT IS LEARNING

Learning denotes changes in the system that are adaptive in the sense that they enable the system to do the same task or tasks drawn from the same population more efficiently and more effectively the next time.

— *Herbert A. Simon*

2.1.1 Definition of learning

Learning can be defined by the following general situation: we have a system – the learner – that has (wishes) to perform a certain task. At the beginning the performance is poor. With practice, by imitating the teacher or by trial and error, the performance gradually becomes better. "Better" may mean faster, more accurate, cheaper etc., depending on the task. Practising, imitating the teacher, and repeated trial and error is called *learning*.

The learner has *learned* to perform the task, if he or she can repeat the task equally well without relearning. To be able to repeat the task equally well the system – learner – has to transform. The process of transformation due to learning is called *knowledge acquisition*.

Knowledge is defined as an interpretation of the information contained in data. Knowledge can be either given in advance (for example inherited or pre-coded), or is

37

the result of learning. It can be correct or wrong, correct but useless, incomplete, etc. Any data with a given interpretation can be considered as knowledge. However, in practice only useful knowledge is interesting, i.e. knowledge that enables the system to perform better when solving tasks from the given problem domain.

Learning takes place in almost all living beings, the most obvious in humans. Learning by a living system is called *natural learning*; if, however, the learner is a machine – a computer – it is called *machine learning*. The purpose of developing machine learning methods is, besides better understanding of natural learning and intelligence, to enable the algorithmic problem solving that requires specific knowledge. Often such knowledge is unknown or is used by a limited number of human experts. Under certain preconditions, by using machine learning algorithms, we can efficiently generate such knowledge which can be used to solve new problems.

Even the whole natural evolution can be regarded as learning: with genetic crossover, mutation and natural selection it creates better and better systems, capable of adapting to different environments. For our purpose, only learning in a single system is interesting. However, the principle of evolution can also be used in machine learning to guide the search in the hypothesis space through the so called *genetic algorithms* (see Section 5.9).

2.1.2   Artificial intelligence research

When we exclude consciousness the reasoning is transformed into mathematically predictable activity based on information, available in advance.
— Mortimer Taube

Learning, knowledge and intelligence are closely related. Although there is no universally accepted definition of intelligence, it can be roughly defined as follows:

Intelligence is the ability to adapt to the environment and to solve problems.

In the definition itself we have learning – adaptation. In order to solve problems one obviously needs knowledge and the ability to use it.

A long term goal of machine learning research, which currently seems unreachable, is to create an artificial system that could through learning achieve or even surpass the human intelligence. A wider research area with the same ultimate goal is called *artificial intelligence*. Artificial intelligence (AI) research deals with the development of systems that act more or less intelligently and are able to solve relatively hard problems. These methods are often based on imitation of human problem solving. AI areas, besides machine learning, are knowledge representation, natural language understanding, automatic reasoning and theorem proving, logic programming, qualitative modeling, expert systems, game playing, heuristic problem solving, artificial senses, robotics and cognitive modeling.

In all AI areas machine learning algorithms play an essential role. Practically everywhere one has to include learning. By using learning techniques, the AI systems can learn and improve in perception, language understanding, reasoning and theorem proving, heuristic problem solving, and game playing. The field of logic programming is also highly related to inductive logic programming that aims to develop logic programs from examples of the target relation. In qualitative modeling, machine learning algorithms are used to generate descriptions of complex models from examples of the target system behavior. For the development of an expert system one can use machine learning to generate the knowledge base from learning examples of solved problems. Intelligent robots inevitably have to improve their procedures for problem solving through learning. Finally, cognitive modeling is practically impossible without taking into account the learning algorithms.

2.2 NATURAL LEARNING

Unknowing is either wisdom or the lack of knowledge.

— Osho

Humans learn throughout the whole life:

- newborn learns to look, to listen, to distinguish the voices and faces of mother and father from other people;

- baby learns the meaning of words, the connection between sight and touch, and various moving skills like grasping of objects, crawling and sitting;

- child learns to walk, to speak words and later sentences, to ride a bicycle, to swim etc;

- pupil learns to read, write and calculate, trains in abstract reasoning, logic inference, in understanding and speaking foreign languages, in memorizing;

- schoolgirl assimilates new, more or less general descriptive knowledge, improves in logic and abstract reasoning, learns heuristics for problem solving;

- student through learning restructures her knowledge, assimilates new specialized descriptive knowledge, learns special heuristics for specific problem solving, learns to explore and trains in hypothesis testing;

- at work we learn our profession, with experience we improve our performance and broaden our knowledge.

We learn practically every day, which means that our knowledge is changing, broadening and improving all the time. Besides humans, animals also learn. The extent of the ability to learn depends on the evolutive stage of species. Some researchers have succeeded even to train worms.

   Investigation and interpretation of natural learning is the domain of *the psychology of learning* and *educational psychology*. The former investigates and analyses the principles and abilities of learning. On the other hand, the latter investigates the methods of human learning and education and aims at improving the results of the educational process. Educational psychology considers attention, tiredness, forgetfulness, and motivation to be of crucial importance for a successful educational process and carefully takes into account the relation between teacher and learner, and suggests various motivation and rewarding strategies. All those are of great importance for human learning, however, much less important for the (contemporary) machine learning.

2.2.1 Innate and learned

Education's purpose is to replace an empty mind with an open one.

— *Malcolm S. Forbes*

One of the basic questions, addressed by the psychology of learning, is the distinction between innate and learned knowledge. This question is important also for machine learning researchers: what kind of background knowledge (program) is necessary or sufficient for efficient and successful machine learning.

Many a skill of animals is innate and not learned. For example, grain pecking is innate to chickens and practice has no influence on its success. The age, however, is important due to growth of the body into its final (adult) form, on which learning has no influence. This ripening process can have periods when learning is possible and necessary for the subsequent organism development. For example, rats, reared in an environment where they could not learn to grasp and push objects, are later unable to construct nests even if they are pregnant and have available building material.

Innate skills are called *instincts*. Even with humans instincts play a significant role. A child has an innate inclination towards learning and learns spontaneously. The innate ripening process is necessary for certain forms of human learning. However, learning itself is crucial for human existence, while with many animal species this is not the case. In fact, the higher the evolutive stage of species, the more important is the role of learning. A higher final level of the learning capability of species implies slower learning in childhood. For example, primates spend much more time on perceptual learning than simpler species.

Human newborns have certain innate recognition abilities such as, for example, the ability to distinguish faces from other objects. However, most of perception is yet to be learned, especially seeing and hearing. When blind-born persons gain their eyesight after an operation, the sight disturbs them and they can't use it. Only after training can they start to recognize figures, faces etc. Their ability to use eyesight is even worse than with newborns – this can be explained by the loss of innate abilities during growing up.

Therefore, a living organism has certain innate abilities that determine its learning abilities and also its intelligence. For example, a worm has 13 neurons and a bee has about 900 neurons which suffice to remember a relatively long path from the beehive to a pasture. Animals learn to solve simple tasks as quickly as humans do. On the other hand, solving harder problems can be learned only by the most evolved species. For example, a gorilla was successfully trained to understand more than one thousand words – the typical vocabulary of a teenager.

Table 2.1 lists the physiological abilities of the human brain (we could say the

number of all neurons	10^{11}
number of neurons in the cerebral cortex	2×10^{10}
number of impulses per neuron	10 impulses/sec
speed of information flow through channels	30 bits/sec
number of chemical reactions in the brain	$10^5 - 10^6$/sec
number of synapses per neuron	10^4
number of all synapses	$10^{14} - 10^{15}$
number of skin pain points	1.2×10^6
number of fibres in an optic nerve	1.2×10^6
short term memory	7 pointers (addresses)
long term memory – synapses alone	$> 10^{15}$ bits
speed of the long term memory access	2 secs
optimal outside temperature	$18°C$
number of different aminoacids	20
aminoacid chain length	several thousands
potential number of different proteins	$> 20^{1000}$
genetic code	$> 10^9$ bits = 1G bit
number of produced protein molecules	15.000/sec/neuron

Table 2.1: Physiological abilities of the human brain.

"hardware"). The respectful hardware insinuates a conclusion that the quantity causes a qualitative leap in intelligent behavior.

2.2.2 Memory

The proofs from numerous sources indicate that the brain might memorize just every experience.

— Peter Russell

One of the fundamental conditions for successful learning is the ability to memorize. This can be illustrated with patients who, due to certain brain damage, have lost the ability to store new experiences in the long term memory. Such a person is not even able to remember the experience from a few minutes ago. If the experience is repeated the patient considers it as a novel one. Such people behave in the same way all life through. Their knowledge does not change through time, for them the time stopped at the moment of their brain damage. Even ten years later they still think that they are ten years younger and are each time very surprised when they notice that their environment has changed and their colleagues look older. Their reactions are the same again and again. They are like computer programs which always for a given input return the same answer.

The human brain is composed of a huge number of neurons (see Table 2.1). Neurons are interconnected with synapses which transmit the impulses between neurons. Besides receiving impulses from some neurons and transmitting them to other neurons, each neuron participates in various activities. There is a lot of neurophysiological evidence that those activities are the basis of memory:

Creating new connections between neurons: structural changes in the brain appear all life through. By creating new connections and dying off the existing ones the relations between the neurons are changed, and consequently also the functioning of the brain.

Changing the connection strengths on the synapses: the connection strength affects the permeability of the synapse for impulses, transmitted from one neuron to another. By changing the connection strength the frequency of impulses is changed, which in turn affects the activity of the receiving neuron.

The same basic principle is used in artificial neural networks, which is one of machine learning subareas, described in Chapter 11. If biological neurons were very simple processors (as is usually the case with artificial neurons, which are able to sum up the input impulses and, in case that a certain threshold value is exceeded, send the impulses forward to other neurons), and if the only memory mechanism was the connection strength, then the brain would have enough capacity to memorize everything one can experience in one hundred years!

Protein construction: a neuron produces 15,000 protein molecules per second. The combinatorics of different aminoacids enables practically an unlimited number of different proteins (see Table 2.1). It was experimentally confirmed that the memory can be transferred between different animals even of different species (for example from trained to non-trained rat and even from trained rat to non-trained fish) by extracting the proteins from the brain of a trained animal and infusing them into the brain of a non-trained animal. Without any training the receiver "learns" the same behavior as the trained animal.

The possibility of transferring the memory between different species indicates that the protein code is universal. It is already well known that the genetic code is universal, i.e. the same for all living beings, although there exist small deviations – dialects of the genetic code.

We may say that the abilities of the human memory are indeed unlimited. Researchers agree that a person can memorize just every experience from the lifetime. However, the addressing of the memory is problematic, i.e. recollecting of memorized facts is not always easy and sometimes seems impossible. On the other hand, in special states of consciousness, such as deep relaxation or under hypnosis some people are able to recollect details from their experiences that happened many years ago, even from early childhood. Also, people with photographic memory can recollect all the details from scenes they saw many years ago. For example, they are able to recollect from their childhood a picture with some text on the wall and they are able to read from that picture although, at the time they saw the picture, they were not able to read.

An extreme example is a Russian journalist Solomon Shereshevski, named also "Mr. S". His main problem was how to forget. He was able to recollect every detail from his life. When asked to describe what he was doing, for example on October 13 five years ago, he thought for a while and then asked: "At what hour?" On one occasion he had read a string of several hundred meaningless syllables and recollected it without a mistake. Several years later he was still able to recollect it.

The most difficult task for ordinary people is to recollect data which cannot be related to other known data – in fact, the address of that data in the memory is missing. Due to its associative nature we say that the brain is an associative memory and is content-addressable. That is why we are better at *recognition* than at recollection or *reconstruction* of known concepts, images, melodies etc. Some types of artificial neural networks are also content-addressable and exhibit in some aspects similar behavior to that of the brain (see Chapter 11).

One of the memory features is its rationalization. We quickly "forget" the details of a concept, a picture, or an event, however, the basic outline and the idea are kept in memory. Such a rationalization is a basis for *generalization* where the memory covers a series of similar situations that differ in details. Learning algorithms for artificial neural networks are based on similar principles.

2.2.3   Types of natural learning

Memorizing is something else than learning.

— *Peter Russell*

Many researchers were trying to define types of natural learning and were searching for a basic type, from which all types originate. Most frequently, the types of learning are classified according to the learning complexity, the learning material, and the learning strategy.

With respect to the **complexity of the learning process** we differentiate the following learning types:

Imprinting: the simplest form of learning appears when a certain knowledge is imprinted in the learner's memory and after that the knowledge does not change any more. Hatched ducks, for example, follow their mother duck until they grow up. If, however, in the moment they are hatched they see somebody else (a dog or a human), they will follow him/her instead.

Conditioning and associating: most psychologists consider *conditioning* a primary learning type. The experiments of Russian psychologist Pavlov with dogs are well known. The training of dogs was simple: each time the bell rang they received food. Soon, only the sound of the bell was enough to provoke the salivation. With conditioning a conditional reflex emerges (besides innate reflexes which are unconditional). It appears as an association between various mechanical or mental sensations and/or their reactions.

Probabilistic learning: the learner is asked to select the correct outcome, however, the process of outcomes is stochastic. Therefore, the correct outcome can be predicted only with a certain degree of probability. Experiments showed that, for example, if one outcome has probability 70% and the other probability 30%, the learners tended to select the former outcome in 70% of cases and the latter in 30% of cases. This gives an average prediction accuracy of $0.7^2 + 0.3^2 = 58\%$. Note that the strategy of selecting always the most probable outcome would give a better (in this case the best possible) accuracy of 70%.

Memorizing: this is a relatively simple type of learning, although memorizing of large amounts of data is typically problematic. Simplistic memorizing without any understanding of the meaning does not require additional mental activities. However, this kind of learning is hard just because during the learning no associations with known concepts are created. For computers, on the other hand, this kind of learning is trivial.

Learning by trial and error: the learner starts from an initial state and in each turn chooses from a set of alternatives (actions, directions, moves, decisions) and changes the current state in order to achieve the goal state. At the beginning, the selection of alternatives is more or less a random process of trial and memorizing the outcome. By practising, the learner acquires the ability to select more promising alternatives. A typical example is searching for an exit from a labyrinth. Rats, for example, after several trials learn to find an exit from the labyrinth without any mistakes. Memory has a crucial role in this process. In more complex tasks, however, the logical reasoning becomes essential.

Somewhat different is the learning of motor skills, for example riding a bicycle. The learner also learns by trial and error, however, the "reasoning" is subconscious – we can hardly speak of logical reasoning here, although a learned reaction (reflex) can be considered a kind of selection among alternatives or a (subconscious) logical conclusion.

Imitation: in this case the learner first observes someone who is solving the same or a similar task, and then imitates him/her in order to solve the given task. For example, dogs and cats learn more quickly to solve tasks, such as jumping over obstacles, if they are allowed to watch other animals solving the same kind of tasks. For solving more complex problems the observation does not help, however, it can help more developed species, such as monkeys. When imitating complex procedures the learner has to understand the situation and incorporate the causal reasoning. Humans are the most powerful imitators.

Learning by understanding and insight: this is the most demanding kind of learning. It requires memorizing, abstract (symbolic) thinking, logical reasoning, and causal integration which leads to problem understanding. The insight comes suddenly, when the learner discovers the solution by integrating the relationships in a given problem situation. To some extent, higher developed species are able to learn by understanding and insight; by far the most qualified for that kind of learning are humans.

As regards **the learning material** we differentiate the following learning types:

- sensorial learning,

- learning of motor skills, and

- semantic (textual) learning.

In all kinds of learning there appears a *spontaneous generalization*. In sensorial learning the learning material is generalized to similar sensations. For example, if we learn to react to the sound of a given frequency, we will react to all similar sounds – the closer the frequency is to the learned one, the stronger is the reaction. During learning of motor skills with one part of the body the skill will generalize also to other parts of the body. For example, the learned reactions with the right hand will be transferred to some extent also to the left hand and even, to lesser extent, to the legs. In semantic learning the learned reaction generalizes to phonetically and semantically similar words (synonyms). Again, the more similar the word is, the stronger is the reaction.

There appears also an inverse process – *differentiation (specialization)*. By conditioning one can train animals to differentiate similar sensations which otherwise cannot be differentiated by initial generalization. By differentiation the reactions specialize to certain kinds of sensations. If, however, the sensations are too similar (e.g. too similar frequencies, colors, heights, shapes, times etc.) the learning fails with animals as well as with humans.

Learning of *concepts* is of special importance. Concepts are classes or categories of objects, events, experiences or notions, which can – due to particular reasons – be treated in the same way, or have certain common characteristics. Usually (but not necessarily) we associate with each concept a unique name. Concepts can be more or less concrete/abstract and more or less simple/complex (e.g. conjunctive and disjunctive concepts). We learn concrete (less abstract) concepts more easily. It is also well known that humans more easily learn conjunctive than disjunctive concepts (the same is also true for machine learning).

Most of children's learning consists of acquiring existing concepts. Typically, a teacher provides (positive) examples and (negative) counterexamples and a partial description of a concept. This kind of learning from examples is also a basic kind of machine learning, called also *inductive* or *empirical learning*. Only rarely does the learner have to create new concepts, which is of course a much harder task. In machine learning there is also occasionally a need to generate a new concept. Such learning is called *constructive learning* or *constructive induction* (see Chapter 8).

During learning one searches for a solution in the space of possible hypotheses (models, theories, solutions). Learners use different **search strategies** which are also used in machine learning (see Chapter 5):

Breadth first search: with this strategy the human learner systematically and exhaustively searches the space of all consistent hypotheses, i.e. descriptions of the target concepts that correspond to all encountered positive learning examples and do not correspond to any of the encountered counterexamples (negative examples). In machine learning exhaustive search is typically too inefficient, however, breadth first search can be used as a basis for more advanced search techniques. An example of (inefficient) implementation of breadth first search is the MIS system for inductive logic programming, described in Section 1.4.4. Exhaustive search makes good use of all available information. It returns the optimal hypothesis by using the minimal number of learning examples and counterexamples. The use of this strategy for humans is hard and tiresome, and for computers it is complex and inefficient due to combinatorial growth of the search space.

Depth first search: with this strategy the human learner sequentially puts, verifies and modifies the hypotheses until a dead-end is reached, then it backtracks to the beginning and puts another hypothesis. Such learning is for humans relatively simple, however, it does not guarantee finding the optimal hypothesis and usually requires more learning examples. Similar findings hold also for machine learning algorithms.

Conservative focusing: the first positive learning example is used as an initial hypothesis. The learner is modifying the hypothesis by systematically changing one variable, until a consistent hypothesis is obtained (i.e. it corresponds to all positive examples and does not correspond to any of the negative examples). Such a strategy can be used also in machine learning.

Focused guessing: the first positive learning example is used as an initial hypothesis. The learner is modifying the hypothesis by changing several variables at once. This strategy is related to stochastic search strategies (see Section 5.8), where the algorithm starts with a randomly selected hypothesis and, in order to improve it, modifies several variables at once in the stochastic manner.

It is interesting that humans use the above strategies consciously or subconsciously. In the subconscious learning it is often the case that the trained person, who is able to correctly differentiate positive examples from counterexamples, is not able to describe the target concept and is also unable to explain the process of differentiation of positive and negative examples. This phenomenon appears with experts in a given domain, who have great difficulties in describing the knowledge they use in their work. For the development of expert systems (computer programs, that are able to solve hard problems in a given domain), experts should provide a description of the knowledge base. If the experts are not available, or if they are not able to describe their knowledge, we can use machine learning to automatically induce the knowledge base from examples.

2.3 LEARNING, INTELLIGENCE, CONSCIOUSNESS

Identity between human and machine is not achieved by transferring the human characteristics to the machine but rather by transferring the mechanical limitations to the human.

— Mortimer Taube

As already stated, intelligence is defined as *the ability to adapt to the environment and to solve problems.* Nowadays, most of the researchers agree that there is no intelligence without learning. Learning alone, however, is not enough. In order to be able to learn, a system has to have some capacities, such as sufficient memory capacity, ability to reason (processor), ability to perceive (input and output) etc. These abilities per se do not suffice if they are not appropriately integrated or if they lack appropriate learning algorithms. Besides, for efficient learning one needs also some initial knowledge – background knowledge, which is inherited in living systems. By learning, the abilities of the system increase, thereby intelligence also increases. An oversimplification gives the following equality:

intelligence = hardware + background knowledge + learning + ?

Opinions of various scientists and philosophers are not convergent as to whether hardware, background knowledge, and learning suffice for (artificial) intelligence. Defenders of the opinion that natural intelligence is the only possible intelligence disagree with their opponents who claim that it is possible to create the intelligent machine.

2.3.1 Amount of intelligence

Knowledge is important, however, much more important is its beneficial use. This depends on human mind and heart.

— Dalai Lama

The systems cannot be strictly ordered with respect to the amount of intelligence because we have to consider various types of intelligence (abilities): numerical, textual, semantical, pictorial, spatial, motor, memorial, perceptive, inductive, deductive etc. Lately, even emotional intelligence has become widely recognized. Some authors describe more than one hundred types of human intelligence. A system (a human or a machine) can be better in some types of intelligence and worse in others. When speaking of artificial intelligence we do not expect an intelligent system to be extremely capable in only one narrow aspect of intelligence, such as for example the speed and the amount of memory, the speed of computation or the speed of searching the space or (almost optimal) game playing – nowadays computers in each of these aspects already have very advanced capabilities. We expect an intelligent system to be (at least to some extent) intelligent in all areas which are characteristic for human problem solving. It seems that we need an integration of all different types of intelligence into a single sensible whole (a kind of supervisory system) so that during problem solving it is possible to switch appropriately between different types of intelligence. Anyway, most of the speculations about artificial intelligence do not take into account yet another level: consciousness (which seems to be a good candidate for the supervisory system).

2.3.2 Consciousness

When you remove all thoughts, what remains is pure consciousness.

— Ramana Maharshi

Self awareness, differentiation of self from others, awareness of your own problems, tasks and your own (ethical and moral) responsibilities – all these are related with consciousness, however, what consciousness is by itself is much harder to define. Nowadays scientists from various fields study various aspects of consciousness: psychologists, psychiatrists, neurophysiologists, physicists, biologists, chemists and biochemists, computer scientists, philosophers etc. At the annual International Conference on Consciousness Studies in Tucson, Arizona hundreds of scientists from all over the world each year try to clarify at least some aspects of consciousness. Over the years it has become clear that no one really knows how to define consciousness. In recent years, they have also invited to the conference people that study and practice various spiritual techniques and meditation. It seems that consciousness is highly subjective while science, by definition, is struggling to be objective. The relation between science and spirituality is described in more detail below in Section 2.3.6.

Some quantum physicists relate consciousness with the collapse of the wave-function which is used to describe the probability distribution of all possible states of the observed system (for example a set of particles). When the measurement takes place the wave function collapses, and from all possible states one particular state appears as real – the result of the measurement. The great mathematician John von Neumann, who provided a rigorous mathematical foundation of quantum mechanics, believed that only the human consciousness can collapse the wave function. The eminent Nobel prize-winning physicist Eugene Wigner writes: "It follows that the quantum description of objects is influenced by impressions entering my consciousness ... It follows that the conscious being must have a different role in quantum mechanics than the inanimate measuring device." The famous physicist John Wheeler has taken this one step further. According to him the entire universe can emerge into true physical existence only via observation of the consciousness!

Therefore, the quantum principle of non-determinism of state "until the measurement" could actually mean "until the measurement, performed by a conscious being". By this principle the reality is not determined until a conscious observer measures it. If confirmed, this hypothesis could clarify many currently unexplained phenomena, such as telepathy, precognition, tele-kinetics and clairvoyance. Most researchers still assume the materialistic explanation of consciousness – they assume (note that this is only an assumption), that consciousness appeared in a certain stage of evolution and is the result of a complex (hard-wired) system such as the human brain.

| | self awareness ||
mental content	YES	NO
YES	wakefulness	dreaming
NO	meditation	dreamless sleep

Table 2.2: States of consciousness.

With humans we differentiate several states of consciousness. One possible classification is provided in Table 2.2. Note that the boundaries between the waking state, dreaming and dreamless sleep are fuzzy. For example, while dreaming one can be self-aware (lucid dreaming). Besides, we do not know if a dreamless sleep exists at all, because when we do not remember any dreams we cannot be sure that in fact there was no dream.

Functions of the human consciousness can be further divided into several levels: pure consciousness (without mental content, which in Table 2.2 corresponds to meditation), super-consciousness or altered state of consciousness (corresponds to special abilities, such as clairvoyance, telepathy etc.), normal consciousness (waking state – mental content depends on our attention), subconsciousness (corresponds to all mental processes, which we are not aware of, but in principle we could become aware of them with the appropriate focus of attention), and unconsciousness (which most probably corresponds only to the dead body).

2.3.3   Limits of symbolic computability

It is impossible to teach the truth.

— Osho

Theory of computability reveals that only a tiny (one could say a negligible) part of all problems, which can be formally described, can be algorithmically solved. The number of all different algorithms is countable infinity $\aleph_0$ which is equal to the cardinality of the set of all natural numbers: $|\mathbb{N}| = \aleph_0$. However, the number of all problems is uncountable infinity $\aleph_1$ which is equal to the power of the set of real numbers $|\mathbb{R}| = \aleph_1$ (in fact, the uncountable infinity corresponds to the power of the powerset of a countably infinite set: $2^{\aleph_0} = \aleph_1$). Therefore, the number of all problems is so huge that almost none of them are algorithmically solvable.

Nowadays, the science uses the following formal symbolic languages for describing (modeling) reality:

- mathematical logic,
- programming languages,
- recursive functions, and
- formal grammars.

All these formalisms have equivalent expressive power and they all have equivalent limitations: they can partially describe the phenomena in the discrete world (discrete functions), and practically a negligible part of the continuous world (continuous functions). Therefore, if the world is indeed continuous, then most probably it is undescribable by any of the formalisms which we are able to use with our (rational) mind. This would implicate that any knowledge that can be reached by science, described in books or by teachers, cannot be ultimate, as it is always only an approximation of the reality.

Note that the number of all rational numbers (fractions) is the same as the number of all natural numbers: $|\mathbb{N}| = |\mathbb{Q}| = \aleph_0$ (we can assign to each rational number a unique natural number and vice versa). The set of rational numbers corresponds to the *discrete world*, while the set of all real numbers corresponds to the *continuous world*. The names here are suggestive: rational numbers correspond to the world, reachable by our rational mind, while real numbers correspond to the reality which is much more rich and is *in principle unreachable to rational mind!*

In all the years since the very beginning of electronic computers, we cannot notice any crucial progress towards the ultimate goal of creating an intelligent machine by using machine learning algorithms. Anyway, we can mention some important steps:

- Lenat's Automatic Mathematician, described in Section 1.4.1,
- great successes of computers in playing complex games, such as checkers, backgammon, and chess,
- artificial neural networks for modeling the cognitive processes in the brain,
- several successes in generating new and beneficial knowledge from data.

But the principal limitations for programming languages and other formalisms, described above, that stem from the computability theory, hold also for any ML algorithm, no matter how advanced and complex it may be. As mentioned in Section 1.3.6 and described in detail in Chapter 13, the strict limitations are posed by the theory of learnability. The latter is derived from the computability theory – the machine learner is necessarily an algorithm. As it may be expected, all the limitations for computability hold also for learnability.

2.3.4 Possibility of artificial intelligence

Morality and intelligence are learnable.

— *Anton Trstenjak*

Practically all research of artificial intelligence methods has attempted to develop systems that behave intelligently and are able to solve relatively hard problems. The developed methods are often based on imitating the human problem solving. As a long-term goal we are interested in whether computer intelligence (capability) can indeed achieve or even exceed the human intelligence. Important aspects for understanding the abilities of artificial intelligence are the impact of learning on intelligence, the speed of problem solving, the principal limitations of algorithms, and the imitation of intelligent behavior:

Impact of learning on intelligence: by learning, the capability of the system increases, therefore also its intelligence increases. Human intelligence is dynamic and is changing throughout the whole life, mostly increasing. However, when determining the amount of intelligence one has to take into account numerous different types of intelligences, mentioned in Section 2.3.1.

Faster is more intelligent: adaptation to the environment and problem solving are better (more efficient) if they are faster. Therefore, intelligence is highly related to speed and time. All tests of intelligence are timed as are all examinations. Therefore, we can conclude, in that sense, that faster computers are more intelligent than slower ones, that parallel processing is more intelligent than the serial one, etc.

Limitations of intelligence: if humans were equivalent to a computer algorithm then all the limitations posed by the computability theory would hold also for humans – this would have a strong impact on the abilities of human intelligence. If, however, we assume that humans are stronger "machines" than (digital) computers (for example continuous and not discrete machines) then the human activity is undescribable. The consequence of this assumption is that it is impossible to describe algorithmically an artificial intelligent system which would completely reproduce the human behavior.

Imitating intelligent behavior: nowadays the technology of movies, multimedia, computers, robots, and virtual reality is very convincing and suggests that it is possible to imitate everything and induce the sensation of reality.

Therefore, if we omit the consciousness, a machine can in principle be intelligent enough (for example by huge amount of memory, containing the solutions to all possible situations) to induce the sensation of artificial intelligence. If we also add extraordinary processing abilities (super parallelism with super-fast processors), algorithms for efficient search of huge spaces, and machine learning algorithms that would enable online improvements of algorithms and heuristics, then such a machine could rightly be named "intelligent" – it could outperform the humans in many if not all "practical" tasks. Of course, such a machine still lacks consciousness.

2.3.5   (Im)possibility of artificial consciousness

If you understand others you are intelligent.   If you understand yourself you are enlightened.

— Lao Tse

In principle, we are able to determine (detect or objectively measure) any system that has certain learning capabilities and that has a certain level of intelligence. Opposed to learning and intelligence, consciousness is much different. It is necessarily related to subjective experience and any objective observer has no means to verify it. Although nontrivial, it is objectively possible to determine the ability to learn, the amount of acquired knowledge, the ability to (intelligently) adapt to the environment and solve problems. Various tests of intelligence are able to measure only specific types of intelligence and the results are typically only partially reliable. On the other hand, in principle it is not possible to verify the consciousness of the system. Whether a (biological or artificial) system is conscious or not is known only to the system itself – in the case that it is conscious. An observer from outside has no way to verify it. You can speak about consciousness only if you yourself are conscious and if you assume that systems, similar to you, are also conscious. Any conscious system can be imitated with an unconscious system to arbitrary (but always incomplete) resemblance, therefore any objective observer can be fooled.

In the following we speculate about some interesting viewpoints. A system can be more or less intelligent but without consciousness (such as a robot or in an extreme case a human zombie) or a system can be conscious but much less intelligent (such as less intelligent people or animals). Consciousness seems to be fundamentally related to the following notions: life, intelligence, and free will.

Consciousness = life? Humans are conscious, dogs and cats are conscious (typical claims of pet owners), and even amoeba may be conscious to some extent. Nowadays science is still not able to explain the origin of life. According to materialistic assumption, life appeared by chance (which is highly improbable) or it is a result of the complexity and selforganization of the matter. Another theory states that life came out of space (aminoacids on the meteors), but then we have to ask, where and how those aminoacids were created. By vitalistic assumption, on the other hand, life was created by a higher force – a universal consciousness.

More intelligence enables higher level of consciousness? Although consciousness is not objectively verifiable nor measurable we can speculate that with greater capabilities, i.e. greater intelligence, a higher level of consciousness can be achieved – we can assume that less developed species are less intelligent than more developed ones. Of course, you can have obvious counterexamples: have a super intelligent system (for example a highly intelligent man) and remove consciousness (such as brain washing or simple blindness with his or her own ego), you can obtain a highly intelligent system (for example a fanatic or an extremely avaricious man for money or power) that is not conscious of his or her actions. If we paraphrase: a child (in the sense of lack of consciousness) is playing with a nuclear bomb. The consequences can be catastrophic.

Consciousness implicates free will? If a system only reacts to outside stimuli then its responses are determined and unconscious. A conscious system can by itself, without any outside cause or stimulus, decide for an action (and not reaction) which means that it has free will. Various researchers and philosophers still argue whether free will exists at all, however, it seems sensible to assume that if consciousness exists then free will also exists.

SCIENCE	SPIRITUALITY
scientists	mystics
logical, rational mind	intuitive mind, inner sense, heart
objectivity	subjectivity
measurable, describable	nonmeasurable, undescribable
describing reality	conscious sensing, awareness of reality
how?	why?
studies matter	studies consciousness
life appeared by chance	life is chance
doubt, verification	faith
logic, experiments, statistics	relaxation, meditation, ceremonials
analysis, differentiates, parts	synthesis, joins, whole
discrete, rational world (Q)	continuous, real (R), irrational world
objective, indirect experience	subjective, direct experience
theory, approximation of reality	practice, reality itself
active, violent free will	passive, harmonious free will
subordination, control	cooperation
taking, profit, ego	giving, sharing
separation, space-time dimension	all is one, spectral dimension
causality, thinking of past and future	no causality, now!
knowledge	wisdom
Scientific theories: quantum, relativity, thermodynamics, evolution ...	Spiritual virtues: love, humility, compassion, patience, courage, sincerity ...
Scientific branches: mathematics, physics, chemistry, biology ...	Spiritual movements: yoga, tao, zen, sufism, institutional religions, new age ...

Table 2.3: Relation between science and spirituality.

2.3.6   Science and philosophy

Science without faith is lame, religion without science is blind.

— Albert Einstein

This section outlines the relation between science, which tends to be objective and therefore limited to the rational (logical) mind, and spirituality, which tends to be subjective and primarily uses intuitive mind (heart). Both science and spirituality search for the truth, but use completely different tools and interpret their results on completely different grounds. We follow the above statement of Albert Einstein and argue that science (objectivity) and spirituality (subjectivity) are complementary to each other and that we need both. Table 2.3 presents the main contrasts between science and spirituality. Science models empirical data: derives a model (hypothesis, theory) which describes measurements and, if the model describes the data accurately, reliably and repeatedly, it is eventually accepted to be a (natural) law. If new measurements (which can be more accurate or measured under different conditions) deviate from the current knowledge, the laws are changed/broadened in order to correspond to them. Science limits itself with objective principles and admits only the rational mind, which is limited, as described in Section 2.3.3, with symbolic representation/computability/learnability (although, of course, scientists during creative research also use intuition which is most probably undescribable). Science is interested in HOW nature operates and is not concerned in WHY the universe exists and what is the purpose of life. Due to ignorance of the latter two questions many scientists (unfoundedly) assume that the universe and life appeared by chance and that there is no deeper purpose of existence.

On the other hand, spirituality is mainly concerned with the purpose of life. In all traditions, spiritual movements and religions, from the east and the west, we can find the same basic issues:

- the purpose of life goes beyond the materialistic world;

- everything that exists is one, originates from the same source and serves the same purpose - the separation is only an illusion of the rational mind, the true reality is always NOW;

- the truth is undescribable and unreachable to the logical mind, it is necessary that everyone tries to feel it by him or herself by direct subjective experience;

- the purpose of life is learning, the goal is to overcome the limitations of ego, to directly and subjectively recognize the truth and to attain wisdom;

- spiritual life is based on cultivation of spiritual virtues, such as unconditional love, compassion, faith, humility, patience, tolerance, simplicity, spontaneity, modesty, courage, sincerity, forgiveness etc.

Spirituality is necessarily subjective and uses intuitive mind, inner sense – the heart. Various relaxation methods, meditation and spiritual ceremonials tend to calm down the rational mind, to eliminate thoughts, in order to enable the direct sense of reality and to widen one's consciousness.

Philosophy (in the original sense of the word) uses both science and spirituality, objective and subjective experience, in order to achieve the balance and harmony between rational and intuitive mind, between head and heart. True philosophy deals with both questions, how the universe operates and why it exists and what is the purpose of life. Great philosophers and sages from all cultures remind us that we need both, rational and intuitive mind. As the Dalai Lama has stated: "We need education and the sense of moral ethics – these two have to go together."

Intelligence is the capability that artificial systems are gaining, and in the future they will continue to gain more and more capabilities. However, consciousness has deeper meaning and purpose, it is necessarily connected with the ethics of life. Intelligence without heart is unconscious intelligence, able to demolish and destroy the environment and itself. Artificial (and natural) intelligence is a tool which can be beneficially used or abused, the responsibility remains on your consciousness and conscience.

2.4   WHY MACHINE LEARNING

The appropriate relationship between human and machine is complementarity and broadening and not imitation.

— *Mortimer Taube*

Humans always wanted to know themselves better and to create systems that would exceed human abilities. Cognitive modeling is intended to investigate and explain cognitive processes in the human brain. Nowadays it is impossible to explain cognition without learning and most cognitive models include various learning algorithms.

Human learning seems extremely slow: twenty years of education is necessary for a Master of Science (M.Sc.) to start to learn his or her profession at work. Only after the next ten or twenty years is enough experience gathered for us to have an expert in a narrow problem domain. Such experts are not able to simply transfer their knowledge and experience to their younger colleagues. Besides, an expert has all human weaknesses: can be forgetful, is regularly tired, effectiveness depends on current mood, motivation, weather, state of health etc.

One of the principal purposes of the development of machine learning has already been mentioned: automatic generation of knowledge bases for expert systems. An expert system is able to help human experts with their work and in exceptional cases can even replace them (at least temporarily, for example when an expert is absent, ill etc.). For expert systems we require that they are able to explain and argue their decisions. Only then can a user trust such a system and transfer to it (less) important decisions. For successful complex specialized problem solving a knowledge base is needed. It can be developed "manually", by examining the existing literature and interviewing available human experts. This is typically tiring, time consuming, non-consistent, unreliable, and sometimes even impossible. Another possibility is the automatic generation of the knowledge base by inductive learning algorithms. It is well known that while experts can hardly depict rules which they use during a problem solving, they can easily provide examples of solved problems. The descriptions of solved problems can be obtained from archives and from stored records in the documentation. Descriptions of problems, solved in the past, can be used for machine learning of rules which can serve as a knowledge base for an expert system.

Of course, one has to be careful with automatically derived knowledge bases. Such a knowledge has to be checked and evaluated. Most often the accuracy on unseen (testing) cases is evaluated. It is sometimes essential that automatically derived rules be transparent and understandable. We usually need to correct and/or adapt the rules and iteratively repeat the learning phase by appropriate modification of learning examples, also by changing the description language.

Expert systems have all the advantages that hold for computers: they are never

HUMAN	COMPUTER
forgetful	reliable, repeatable
needs rest	can work without stopping
hardly transfers knowledge	trivially transfers knowledge
limited exact memory	huge exact data bases
high speed associative memory	needs exact address
slow exact processing	extremely fast exact processing
efficient parallel processing	mostly sequential processing
wide commonsense knowledge	narrow specialized knowledge
learns from errors	repeats the same error
dynamic knowledge	static knowledge

Table 2.4: Comparison of humans and computers.

tired, available 24 hours per day, 365 days per year, they are reliable, provide replicable results, the knowledge base is trivially transferrable to other computers, and they can consult huge data bases, collected in the past.

In spite of the obvious advantages, expert systems cannot and in the (near) future will not replace human experts. The comparison of human and computer characteristics is sketched in Table 2.4. Although computers can with extremely high speed manipulate huge amounts of data with mathematical accuracy, they by far do not reach the wideness of human knowledge and the intelligent and common sense access to the huge human memory. Due to enormous parallelism in the brain, humans are able far more quickly and with a surprising ease to solve certain kinds of problems which nowadays computers are not able to solve, or the solution would be much too slow.

A major advantage of humans is that they are flexible and they dynamically change and improve their knowledge. That is why we need to develop advanced machine learning systems. With appropriate algorithms we need to make our computers more flexible and adaptable to new situations and problems. Therefore, even algorithms themselves will be in the future dynamic and will gradually change with learning. However, we have to be aware that the behavior of such systems may be unpredictable and that we have to include the mechanisms for verification and control. Some researchers predict that intelligent systems will even have to "lie" in order to achieve optimal performance in critical situations (when immediate action is needed and there is no time to argue with the user). Such a system is hard to master and there always has to exist the possibility of complete control of the system.

2.5   SUMMARY AND FURTHER READING

Intellect separates, locates and compares details by searching mutual contrasts;
Wisdom unites and joins apparent opposites into one uniform harmony.

— *Sri Aurobindo*

- Practising, imitating the teacher, and repeated trial and error is called *learning*. The process of transformation due to learning is called *knowledge acquisition*. Learning by a living system is called *natural learning*; if the learner is a machine – a computer – it is called *machine learning*.

- *Intelligence* is the ability to adapt to the environment and to solve problems. *Artificial intelligence* research deals with the development of systems that act more or less intelligently and are able to solve relatively hard problems. A living organism has certain innate abilities that determine its learning abilities and also its intelligence.

- One of the fundamental conditions for successful learning is the ability to memorize. There is a lot of neurophysiological evidence indicating that the following activities are the basis of *memory*: creating new connections between neurons, changing the connection strengths on the synapses, and protein construction. Researchers agree that a person could memorize every experience from the lifetime.

- With respect to the *complexity of the learning process* we differentiate the following *learning types*: imprinting, conditioning and associating, probabilistic learning, memorizing, learning by trial and error, imitation, and learning by understanding and insight. Learners use different *search strategies* which are used also in machine learning: breadth first search, depth first search, conservative focusing, and focused guessing.

- If the world is continuous, then most probably it is *undescribable* by any of the symbolic formalisms which we are able to use with our (rational) mind, and the same holds for computers. Important aspects for understanding the abilities of artificial intelligence are the impact of learning on intelligence, the speed of problem solving, the principal limitations of algorithms, and the imitation of intelligent behavior.

- We expect an intelligent system to be (at least to some extent) intelligent in all areas which are characteristic for human problem solving. Most of the speculations about artificial intelligence do not take into account yet another level: *consciousness*. Consciousness is highly subjective, while science - by definition - is struggling to be objective.

- Consciousness is necessarily related to *subjective experience*, and any objective observer has no means to verify it. Consciousness seems to be fundamentally related to the following notions: life, intelligence, and free will.

- Scientists use the rational mind in order to indirectly and objectively study matter and to derive *knowledge*. Mystics use the intuitive mind in order to directly and subjectively study consciousness and to attain *wisdom*. Both science and spirituality search for the truth. They are complementary to each other and we need both.

A classic introductory book on the psychology of learning is (Borger and Seaborne, 1966). A thorough overview of human learning and memory is given by Anderson (1995), while educational psychology is described by Driscoll (1994). Descriptions of neurophysiological brain properties are documented in (Buzan, 1977; Changeux, 1986; Lausch, 1972; Michie and Johnston, 1984; Russell, 1979; Schauer, 1984). Russell (1979) and Buzan (1977) describe several interesting and surprising phenomena of the human brain and give several references on experiments with animal learning. Sacks (1985) describes anomalies of human behavior after certain brain damages. The important neurophysiological evidence that synapses are the basis of the brain memory was reported by Hebb (1949). The huge capacity of the human memory is discussed by Russell (1979) and more formally by Kohonen (1984). Cognitive modeling with artificial neural networks is described in a book edited by McClelland and Rumelhart (1986). Emotional intelligence became popular through books by Goleman (1997).

The classic philosophical books by opponents of the possibility of artificial intelligence are (Dreyfus, 1972; Taube, 1961). More recent discussion on this topic is by Penrose (1989), Searle (1992), and Sloman (1992). Another collection of papers is edited by Gams et al. (1997). The theory of computability is thoroughly described in excellent books by Hopcroft and Ullman (1979) and Manna (1974). Einstein (1940) discusses the relation between science and religion. An excellent classic book on relation between quantum physics and spirituality is (Capra, 1983). Some aspects are further discussed by Wallace (2000), Kononenko (2002), and in a collection of papers edited by Lorimer (1998). Karl Pribram (personal communication, 2006) pointed out that the rational mind operates in the space-time dimension while the intuitive mind, which most people use only occasionally and sporadically, operates in the spectral dimension. Besides numerous jewels in classical spiritual literature, nowadays masterpieces include books by Eckhart Tolle (1997) and Nisargadatta Maharaj (1973). The annual International Conference on Consciousness Studies takes place at the University of Arizona in Tucson: www.consciousness.arizona.edu. A huge amount of experimental work has been done by the Institute of Noetic Studies, www.noetic.org and published by *Journal of Scientific Exploration*.

Michie and Johnston (1984) warn against the unpredictability of complex systems and claim that in certain critical situations expert systems of the future will have to lie to the user.

Chapter 3

Machine Learning Basics

Man and computer are capable of achieving together what neither of them can alone.
— Hubert L. Dreyfus

In this chapter we look at the basic principles that guide the design of machine learning systems, such as the principle of simplicity (formalized as the minimum description length principle), the principle of multiple explanations, and principles for the evaluation of learned hypotheses. We explore some basic building blocks used in machine learning algorithms, such as probability estimation and performance evaluation. We finish with a review of techniques for combining machine learning methods.

3.1 BASIC PRINCIPLES

Machine learning is a precondition for the intelligent system.
— Alan M.Turing

In this section we define machine learning as data modeling. We explore the minimum description length principle (MDL) which states that the shortest hypotheses that explain the learning data are also the most probable. We discuss the much less known, and seemingly opposite principle of multiple explanations which for prediction suggests using all possible hypotheses. Finally, we review different approaches for estimating probabilities from data. Among other things they imply that the more reliable hypotheses are those that explain more data.

3.1.1 Learning as modeling

As described in Chapter 1, learning is any modification of the system that improves its performance in some problem solving task. The result of learning is knowledge which the system can use for solving new problems. Knowledge can be represented

59

in many different ways: it can be a set of memorized previously seen examples, an algorithm for solving certain problems, or a set of instructions for efficient problem solving. When dealing with machine learning systems we will often distinguish between the *learning algorithm* and the *execution algorithm*. The learning algorithm generates new knowledge (or modifies existing knowledge) from the set of learning data and background knowledge (if any). The execution algorithm uses the generated knowledge for solving new problems. The generated knowledge is often called the *model*. The model should always conform to the background knowledge and learning data.

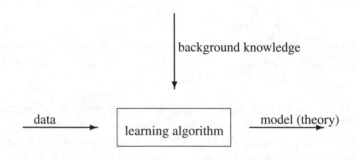

Figure 3.1: A machine learning algorithm.

In machine learning all input data (statements) are supposed to be true, and the model is a formula from which we can (to a certain extent) derive the input data. The model is therefore an abstraction of data. Instead of the word *model*, the words *hypothesis* and *theory* are frequently used throughout the book.

Machine learning can be defined as describing or modeling the data. Inputs to the machine learning system are a set of learning data and background knowledge. The output is is a description (model, hypothesis, theory) that describes and explains the data and background knowledge together (see Figure 3.1). Background knowledge is most often a space of possible models, and an optimality criterion. The learning algorithm therefore searches for a model that satisfies the given optimality criterion. Background knowledge may also consist of an initial hypothesis (an approximate solution) and a set of heuristics for guiding the model search.

Machine learning can therefore be treated as an optimization problem. Given a solution (model) space, and an optimality criterion, the model satisfying this criterion is sought. The criterion value depends upon the current model, background knowledge, and learning (modeled) data. Since the solution (model) space is usually very large (often infinite), the search for optimal solutions is not feasible and therefore we search for best suboptimal solutions.

Model types

There exist several different types of models, and therefore different kinds of machine learning problems.

Discrete functions. Their domains are finite, unordered sets of values. The dependent variable is called the *class* and its value the *class label*. The problems where target models are discrete functions are called *classification problems*. When the function is learnt it is used for classification of new examples (determining the value of a dependent variable given the values of independent variables). Often the obtained function returns not only a single value (a class label), but a set of values. Its elements may be weighted; usually with their probabilities. We therefore deal with functions mapping from the problem space into a multidimensional continuous space. For example, a medical diagnostic rule maps a patient state to a set of possible diagnoses with respective probabilities.

Many decision problems, diagnostic problems, control problems, and prediction (forecasting) problems can be formulated as classification problems. Typical examples include medical diagnostics and prognostics, weather forecasting, diagnostics of industrial processes, classification of products according to their quality, and dynamic system control.

Continuous functions. Their domains are potentially infinite ordered real-valued sets. The dependent (target) variable is called the *regressional variable*. The problems where target models are continuous functions are called *regressional problems*. As in classification problems, automatically generated target functions are used for determining the value of a dependent variable given the values of independent variables.

Many decision and prediction (forecasting) problems can be formulated as regressional problems. Typical examples include time series forecasting, controlling dynamic systems, and determining the influence of different parameters on the value of the dependent variable. Besides determining the value of the target function, *confidence intervals* are often required in regressional problems. A confidence interval quantitatively describes the reliability of proposed problem solutions.

Relations. Automatically built relations are used either for determining whether a given object tuple is an element of a relation, or as a function, where one or more parameters serve as dependent variables. Relations are more general than functions, and the space of possible relations is significantly larger than the space of possible functions. Relational learning problems are therefore more demanding with respect to finding suboptimal solutions, quantity of learning data, and background knowledge. Relations may be either continuous (equation systems), or discrete (logical relations). Examples of relational learning include learning the structure of chemical compounds, learning properties of geometric objects, and determining general (hidden) regularities in databases.

3.1.2   Minimum description length principle

It is vain to do with more what can be done with fewer.

— William of Ockham

Nature is pleased with simplicity, and affects not the pomp of superfluous causes.

— Isaac Newton

Make it as simple as possible – but not simpler!

— Albert Einstein

When searching the space of possible hypotheses conforming to input (learning) data and background knowledge, the task of the machine learning algorithm is to find "the best" hypothesis. This is why we need criteria to measure the quality of hypotheses. A well known criterion is the Occam's razor principle. It states that the simplest explanation is also the most reliable. As we will see later in this section, the Occam's razor can be generalized to the minimum description length (MDL) principle, or equivalently, to the principle of maximum hypothesis probability.

Different criteria are used for different learning problems, and can be combined with each other. Some well-known criteria are:

- maximizing the prediction accuracy,
- minimizing the expected cost of prediction errors,
- minimizing the hypothesis' size,
- maximizing the hypothesis' fitness to the input data,
- maximizing the hypothesis' comprehensibility,
- minimizing the time complexity of prediction,
- minimizing the number of parameters (attributes) required for prediction,
- minimizing the cost for obtaining parameters (attributes) required for prediction
- maximizing the hypothesis' probability according to the background knowledge and input (learning) data.

The last criterion – *maximizing the hypothesis' probability* – is the most general, and satisfies most of the above criteria. It can be shown that on average over all possible prediction problems, the most probable hypothesis maximizes the prediction accuracy. For a given (maximal) prediction accuracy, the most probable hypothesis is also the smallest in size, and has the best fit to the input data. Since the hypothesis is the smallest, it is in this sense also the most comprehensible, uses a minimal number of parameters (attributes), and ensures the quickest prediction. When the costs of prediction errors (misprediction costs) and costs for obtaining parameters are uniform, the remaining two (cost sensitive) criteria are also satisfied.

Let $\mathcal{H}$ be the set of possible hypotheses, $H \in \mathcal{H}$ a hypothesis, B the background knowledge, and E input (learning) data. Ideally, when probabilities $P(H|E, B)$ of all hypotheses are known, given the background knowledge and input data, one needs to find the hypothesis that maximizes the conditional probability:

$$H_{opt} = \underset{H \in \mathcal{H}}{\mathrm{argmax}} \left\{ P(H|E, B) \right\} \tag{3.1}$$

Unfortunately, prior and conditional probabilities are usually unknown, and therefore the above criterion is substituted with various heuristic criteria. For this purpose, the *minimum description length* (MDL) principle – essentially equivalent to the criterion of maximal hypothesis probabilities – is frequently used. Let $P(H|B)$ be the (prior) probability of hypothesis H given the background knowledge B. Let the amount of information $I(H|B)$, necessary for determining whether the hypothesis H is true, given the background knowledge B, be defined as:

$$I(H|B) = -\log_2 P(H|B) \ [bit] \tag{3.2}$$

Analogously, we define the conditional amount of information $I(H|E, B)$, necessary for determining whether the hypothesis H is true, given the background knowledge B, and input data E as:

$$I(H|E, B) = -\log_2 P(H|E, B) \ [bit] \tag{3.3}$$

We can rewrite (3.1) as

$$H_{opt} = \underset{H \in \mathcal{H}}{\mathrm{argmin}} \left\{ I(H|E, B) \right\} \tag{3.4}$$

Since by the Bayes' theorem it holds that

$$I(H|B, E) = I(E|H, B) + I(H|B) - I(E|B) \tag{3.5}$$

and since $I(E|B)$ is constant, the criterion (3.4) can be rewritten as

$$H_{opt} = \underset{H \in \mathcal{H}}{\mathrm{argmin}} \left\{ I(E|H, B) + I(H|B) \right\} \tag{3.6}$$

By this optimality criterion we search for the hypothesis that minimizes the sum of its description length and the length of input data description given the hypothesis. In fact, the criterion aims to find a trade-off between the hypothesis size $I(H|B)$ and the size of its error $I(E|H, B)$.

The problem of minimizing the description length of a data set can be reformulated in the communications theory context as follows. The *transmitter* has to transmit to the *receiver* a description of a certain data set through the communication channel. The channel is binary - it can transmit only zeros (0), and ones (1). The message length is the number of bits needed for binary data encoding. We assume that the transmitter uses optimal data encoding. The receiver, however, must be able to decode the message. This means that the receiver must either know the decoder in advance, or the transmitter must encode the decoder and send it along with the data description, thus further enlarging the message size. The task of the transmitter is to minimize the overall message length.

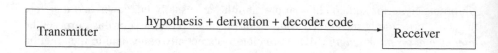

Figure 3.2: A communication channel.

The transmitter can either directly encode the data and send them to the receiver, or it can encode the data model (hypothesis) as well as derivations of original data from the hypothesis (see Figure 3.2). If the model and the data derivation can together be described more tersely than the plain data, the hypothesis is *compressive*:

$$I(H|B) + I(E|H, B) < I(E|B) \qquad (3.7)$$

For checking this criterion, probabilities $P(E|B)$ do not need to be known; it is sufficient to know the data description length $I(E|B)$. It can be estimated by assuming some (sub)optimal encoding scheme. We have to be satisfied with suboptimal coding, because the problem of determining the optimal code is not computable.

By the minimum description length criterion the only acceptable hypotheses are the compressive ones. In the worst case the original data set can be used as a trivial model.

The optimal hypothesis is short ($I(H|B)$), but conveys enough information to derive original data with minimal additional information ($I(E|H, B)$). For derivation we assume that both transmitter and receiver possess the background knowledge B. If the receiver does not have the background knowledge B, it is made a part of input data E.

3.1.3   Incremental (on-line) learning

Nature never says whether the guesses are correct. Scientific success consists of eventually offering a correct guess and never deviating from it thereafter.

— *Osherson et. al., 1986*

A basic – batch – learning algorithm (Figure 3.1) assumes that all learning data are available at the beginning. An alternative scenario is that the learning algorithm receives input data sequentially. After encountering each input datum the learning algorithm modifies its hypothesis (model) so as to suit both older data and the current datum (see Figure 3.3).

The learning process where the learner modifies its hypothesis each time after receiving new data is called *incremental* or *on-line* learning. The simplest incremental algorithm rejects the previous hypothesis every time a new input datum is received,

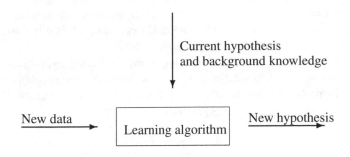

Figure 3.3: Incremental learning.

and immediately builds a new hypothesis from scratch. We will not discuss such algorithms. The task of a truly incremental algorithm is to find a minimal necessary modification of the current hypothesis so as to suit all hitherto received input data. Sometimes, incremental algorithms "forget" some portions of older input data, and therefore new hypotheses can be contradictory to older data. Forgetting is beneficial in cases when the target problem is changing dynamically, thus changing the optimal hypothesis as well.

It could be expected that the incremental learning process converges to the optimal hypothesis for a given problem, and that after some time, the hypothesis won't change in spite of new input data. Unfortunately, the learning algorithm *never* knows whether the optimal hypothesis has been learnt, because at any time new data can be contradictory to the current hypothesis. In practice, however, often after some time new input data cease to improve the current hypothesis.

3.1.4 Principle of multiple explanations

If more than one theory is consistent with the observations, keep all theories.

— Epicurus

For each particular model find what its prediction is and then weight its prediction with the probability of that model, and the weighted sum of those predictions is the optimal prediction.

— Peter Cheeseman

The Occam's razor principle is well known and frequently used in machine learning systems, mostly in a sense of favoring simpler (shorter) hypotheses. The *principle of multiple explanations* is less known. It says that all hypotheses consistent with input data are to be kept. This principle is seemingly contrary to the Occam's razor principle, however it turns out that both principles supplement each other. We use the Occam's razor principle for searching for a single best (on average) hypothesis, or for a set of relatively good hypotheses. It is therefore used in the learning phase for guiding the search On the other hand, by the principle of multiple explanations we achieve best results by suitably combining all generated hypotheses. It is therefore used in the executing phase for directing an execution algorithm.

Execution algorithms often utilize a single (most optimal) hypothesis. Let the $\mathcal{R}$ be a set of possible problem solutions, and $s \in \mathcal{R}$ one particular problem solution. Let $P(s|H)$ be the probability of the solution s if the hypothesis H is correct. The solution, offered by the optimal hypothesis is given by

$$s_{opt1} = \operatorname*{argmax}_{s \in \mathcal{R}} \left\{ P(s|H_{opt}) \right\} \tag{3.8}$$

However, this is not the optimal solution! The principle of multiple explanation suggests using all possible hypotheses. We can do it formally by weighing each theory's solution with its probability. An optimal execution algorithm uses all hypotheses that are probable enough:

$$s_{opt} = \operatorname*{argmax}_{s \in \mathcal{R}} \left\{ \sum_{H \in \mathcal{H}} (P(s|H)P(H|E,B)) \right\} \tag{3.9}$$

The Occam's razor principle helps to eliminate hypotheses with negligibly low probability $P(H|E,B)$. But the problem of probability approximations for $P(H|E,B)$ used in (3.9) still remains.

Note that if the combination of hypotheses is interpreted as a single best hypothesis, we face an apparent contradiction to the principle of multiple explanations. However, now the space of possible hypotheses is vastly enlarged: if the original space contained n possible hypotheses, the new space contains at least 2^n hypotheses (a power set). If we also take into account all possible probability distributions over hypotheses, the space is even larger. In the new hypothesis space the optimal hypothesis coding and the minimum description length criterion change accordingly.

3.1.5   Estimating probabilities

Probability is in fact a more precise description of the common sense.

— Pierre-Simon Laplace

In machine learning we often deal with probability estimation. The probability of some event is either given in advance and is therefore a part of the background knowledge, or it must be estimated from data. In the latter case, estimations are often based on small sets of data, and may not be reliable.

The probability of an event is estimated from its relative frequency measured on a learning set. Optimality of the probability estimation depends on the assumed prior probability distribution. Frequently, the *beta* distribution $\beta(a, b)$ is used. Its density $p(x)$ is defined as:

$$p(x) = \begin{cases} \frac{1}{B(a,b)} x^{a-1}(1-x)^{b-1} & 0 \leq x \leq 1 \\ 0 & otherwise \end{cases} \quad (3.10)$$

$a > 0$ and $b > 0$ are the parameters of the distribution, and $B(a, b)$ is the beta function defined with:

$$B(a, b) = \int_0^1 x^{a-1}(1-x)^{b-1} dx \quad (3.11)$$

Parameters a and b can be interpreted as the number of successful (a) and the number of unsuccessful (b) outcomes of $a + b$ independent experiments. If random variable P has $\beta(a, b)$ distribution, then its expected value is

$$E[P] = \frac{a}{a + b} \quad (3.12)$$

that exactly corresponds to the relative frequency of successful experiments (a successful and $a + b$ total). If the prior probability distribution is $\beta(a, b)$, and our learning data consist of s successful experiments, and n total experiments, then the number of successful experiments is a random variable R distributed as $\beta(a + s, b + n - s)$. The probability p of a successful experiment is estimated by taking the expectation on R:

$$p = E[R] = \frac{s + a}{n + a + b} \quad (3.13)$$

Relative frequency. If the prior probability distribution is $\beta(0, 0)$ then (3.13) is the *relative frequency*:

$$p = \frac{s}{n} \quad (3.14)$$

The problem of using the relative frequency is that extreme probability estimations 0 and 1 frequently occur when the size of the data set is small. With a small number of experiments n it can easily happen that the number of successful experiments $s = 0$, or $s = n$. Such probability estimations are overly pessimistic for $s = 0$, or overly optimistic for $s = n$, and are better avoided. If we have enough data (say, $n > 100$), then the relative frequency is a reliable probability estimation.

Laplace's law of succession. If the prior probability distribution is $\beta(1, 1)$, corresponding to the uniform prior probability distribution, we get *Laplace's law of succession*:

$$p = \frac{s + 1}{n + 2} \quad (3.15)$$

This estimation is more cautious than relative frequency, and ensures that for every $n > 0$, and $0 \leq s \leq n$ it holds that $0 < p < 1$. The basic Laplace's law of succession can be used only when two outcomes are possible (success and failure). It can be straightforwardly generalized to handle multiple (k) outcomes:

$$p = \frac{s+1}{n+k} \tag{3.16}$$

The drawback of this estimation is that it adopts an often unrealistic assumption of uniform prior probabilities. For many machine learning applications this is not acceptable.

***m*-estimate.** If we set $m = a + b$ and the prior probability of the observed event is $p_0 = a/(a+b)$, we get the m-estimate:

$$\begin{align} p &= \frac{s+mp_0}{n+m} \tag{3.17} \\ &= \frac{n}{n+m} \cdot \frac{s}{n} + \frac{m}{n+m} \cdot p_0 \tag{3.18} \\ &= \frac{1}{n+m} \left(n \cdot \frac{s}{n} + m \cdot p_0 \right) \tag{3.19} \end{align}$$

From (3.19) we can see that the m-estimate is composed of the relative frequency weighted with n (total number of experiments), and of the prior probability estimate p_0 weighted with the parameter m. The value of m can be interpreted as the number of experiments that support the prior probability estimate.

The m-estimate is reasonably flexible. It allows for choosing a suitable prior probability p_0 and its weighting with parameter m. If there is no prior knowledge on estimating p_0, Laplace's law of succession can be used. Parameter m can be varied according to the background knowledge. In practice, $m = 2$ is frequently used.

It turns out that both the relative frequency and Laplace's law of succession are special cases of the m-estimate. If we set $m = 0$ we get the relative frequency. If we set $m = 2$ and $p_0 = 1/k$, with k being the number of possible outcomes, we get Laplace's law of succession.

3.2 MEASURES FOR PERFORMANCE EVALUATION

If you shut your door to all errors, truth will be shut out.

— Rabindranath Tagore

When a machine learning algorithm is used in a given domain for building a theory (hypothesis,model), we want to estimate how successful the automatically built theory will be for solving new problems (i.e., we want to estimate its quality). We call particular problems *problem examples*, or simply *examples*. In classification problems we want to know how successful the generated theory will be for classification. In regression problems we wish to know how precise the predicted values will be, and what is their confidence level. For logical relations we want to estimate the percentage of new tuples (example problems) for which it will be correctly determined whether they belong to a certain relation.

For quality estimation of automatically generated theories we split the available data (with known correct solutions) into two subsets: a *learning set* and a *testing set*. The learning set is available for theory generation (learning), whereas the testing set is used for quality estimation (Figure 3.4).

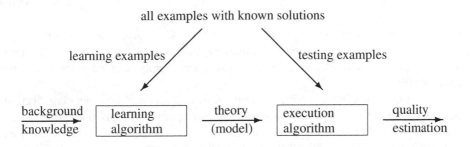

Figure 3.4: Quality estimation for automatically generated theories (models).

Sometimes the quality of a generated theory cannot be estimated by counting (in)correct problem solutions, but rather the problem has to be treated as a whole. Such problems are decision problems and game playing, where the success or failure can be determined only after a sequence of individual problem solutions has been executed. Similarly, when controlling dynamic systems, information of the success is provided only after a lengthy controlling process.

In this section we review only those quality measures that are based on singular problem solutions. For estimating the quality of classification algorithms, the following measures are frequently used:

- classification accuracy and confusion matrix,
- misclassification cost,
- Brier score, information score and margin (utilizing estimated class probabilities),
- sensitivity, specificity, ROC curves, precision and recall.

For estimating the quality of regression algorithms the following measures are most frequently used:

- mean squared error,
- mean absolute error, and
- correlation coefficient.

Last but not least, we will discuss the relation between bias and variance in machine learning.

3.2.1   Classification accuracy and confusion matrix

The solution of each particular classification problem is a single class out of several (m_0) possible classes. Classification accuracy and confusion matrix are frequently used to evaluate the quality of classifier's solutions. Success of classification problem solutions is measured with *classification accuracy*. It can also be used for relational problems under the assumption that the relation membership is a two-class problem. Classification accuracy is defined as a relative frequency of correct classifications

$$Acc = \frac{n_{corr}}{n} \cdot 100\% \tag{3.20}$$

with n being the number of all possible examples for a given problem, and n_{corr} the number of correctly classified examples by the current theory. The classification accuracy can be interpreted as a probability that a randomly selected example will be correctly classified.

In real-life problems it is virtually impossible to determine the exact classification accuracy because correct classifications of all examples are simply not known. Also n is often large, if not infinite. Classification accuracy is therefore estimated from an independent testing set of solved examples, if available. Let n_t be the number of testing examples. The classification accuracy is estimated with:

$$Acc_t = \frac{n_{t,corr}}{n_t} \cdot 100\% \tag{3.21}$$

The testing set of examples must be independent of the learning set. Similarly, on the learning set the classification accuracy is estimated with:

$$Acc_l = \frac{n_{l,corr}}{n_l} \cdot 100\% \tag{3.22}$$

This is an optimistic estimation (upper bound) of the classification accuracy. It is not difficult to build theories that achieve $Acc_l = 100\%$. It is sufficient to remember all learning examples and their (correct) solutions. Such theories perform well only on the learning set, and their Acc_l is usually a very poor estimation of the actual classification accuracy. Theories with $Acc_l \gg Acc_t$ *overfit* the learning set. Many machine learning algorithms require special techniques to prevent overfitting.

The lower bound of the classification accuracy is estimated with the *majority class*. The majority class is the most frequent class in the whole example space. Since the distribution of classes in example space is usually not known, it is estimated from the learning set. Let $n(C)$ be the number of learning examples from class C, and n the number of all learning examples. The lowest acceptable classification accuracy (the *default accuracy*) can be trivially achieved by classifying all examples into the majority class:

$$Acc_m = \max_C \left\{ \frac{n(C)}{n} \right\} \cdot 100\% \tag{3.23}$$

Surprisingly, a really miserable classifier can achieve an even lower classification accuracy. For example, in a medical problem of breast cancer prognosis, the majority

Correct class	Predicted as			Total
	C_1	C_2	C_3	
C_1	12.3	2.4	8.5	23.2
C_2	5.5	58.7	2.1	66.3
C_3	0.0	2.0	8.5	10.5
Total	17.8	63.1	19.1	100.0

Table 3.1: An example of a confusion matrix (its elements are percentages).

class has an 80% prevalence. Many classifiers achieve the classification accuracy lower than 80%. The reason for this anomaly is that most parameters (attributes) describing the patient are irrelevant for prognosis. If they are not detected and treated as irrelevant by a machine learning algorithm, their use makes the classification more or less random, weighted with prior class probabilities. Since the prior probabilities are $P_1 = 80\%$ and $P_2 = 20\%$, the random classification accuracy is $P_1^2 + P_2^2 = 68\%$.

The classification accuracy is an average over all classes and therefore does not tell anything about distribution of correct classifications. If we are interested in classification accuracy for each class in particular, a confusion (misclassification) matrix is a better choice. In Table 3.1 an example for a three-class problem is shown. Diagonal elements of the inner 3×3 table are percentages of correct classifications. The sum of each row is a prior probability of the respective class, and the sum of each column is the percentage of all examples that were classified in the respective class. The difference between the two sums illustrates the classifier's bias for or against the class.

3.2.2 Misclassification costs

In some problems the costs of misclassifying examples from some class may be much greater than the costs of misclassifying examples from other classes. In medicine, a wrong diagnosis for a risky patient is usually a much more serious mistake than a wrong diagnosis for a non-risky patient. In classification problems with unequal misclassification costs the main quality criterion is an average misclassification cost. Let $n_t(i, j)$ be the number of test examples belonging to the class C_i and classified into the class C_j by the given theory. The total number of correctly classified test examples is therefore:

$$n_{t,corr} = \sum_{i=1}^{m_0} n_t(i, i) \tag{3.24}$$

where m_0 is the number of classes.

For a given cost matrix $\{Cost_{i,j}\}$ it usually holds $Cost_{i,i} = 0$, $i = 1, ..., m_0$. A cost matrix is not necessarily symmetric; there are no restrictions on $Cost_{i,j}$ and $Cost_{j,i}$. The average misclassification cost is given by

$$Cost_t = \frac{\sum_{i,j} \left(Cost_{i,j}\, n_t(i, j) \right)}{n_t} \tag{3.25}$$

3.2.3   Class probability estimation

Instead of a plain classification (a single assigned class), many classifiers give the class probability distribution. When computing the classifier's accuracy, most often the classification to the most probable class is assumed. However, such an approach ignores the rest of available information from the class probability distribution.

Ideally, a quality estimation measure should account for both prior and posterior class probability distributions. The *Brier score* and the *margin* use only posterior class probability distributions, whereas the *information score* uses both.

Brier score.   Let m_0 be the number of classes, c_j the correct class for the j-th testing example, and $P'_j(c_i)$, $i = 1 \ldots m_0$ the posterior probabilities returned by the classifier. The ideal target distribution is

$$P_j(C_i) = \begin{cases} 0, & C_i \neq c_j \\ 1, & C_i = c_j \end{cases} \tag{3.26}$$

The Brier score estimates the dissimilarity between the actual and ideal target distributions, averaging over all n_t testing examples:

$$Brier = MSE_P = \frac{1}{n_t} \sum_{j=1}^{n_t} \sum_{i=1}^{m_0} \left(P_j(C_i) - P'_j(C_i) \right)^2 \tag{3.27}$$

This is a mean squared error of the predicted class probability distribution. Ideally, if a classifier always predicts the correct class with probability $P'_j(c_j) = 1$, the Brier score is 0. On the other hand, if it always predicts an incorrect class with probability 1, the Brier score is 2 (1 for wrong classification for the correct class, plus 1 for wrong classification for the incorrect class). The classifier's quality is therefore estimated as $1 - Brier/2$.

Information score.   As stated before, an ideal quality estimation should account for both prior class probabilities as well as for posterior class probabilities, returned by the classifier. For example, classifiers typically achieve the classification accuracy about 80% for breast cancer recurrence prognosis, and 45% for primary tumor localization. Apparently, classifiers are much more successful in the first problem. However, in the first problem there are only two classes versus 22 in the second problem. In the breast cancer prognosis the majority class is 80%; it is only 25% in the primary tumor localization. A classifier that achieves 80% in the first problem is basically useless, because this result can be achieved trivially by the simple majority classifier ($Acc_m = 80\%$). On the other hand, 45% in the second problem is quite a success.

The difficulty of a classification problem can be estimated as an expected amount of information needed for classification of a single example. This measure is called a *class entropy*. The prior probability of the class C_i is estimated with its relative frequency

$$P(C_i) = \frac{n(C_i)}{n} \tag{3.28}$$

The amount of information necessary for determining if an example belongs to the class C_i is

$$H(C_i) = -\log_2 P(C_i) \quad [bit] \tag{3.29}$$

The entropy of all classes is the average information:

$$H(C) = -\sum_{i=1}^{m_0} \left(P(C_i) \log_2 P(C_i) \right) \tag{3.30}$$

C is the dependent variable with possible values (domain) $C \in \{C_1, \ldots, C_{m_0}\}$. The larger the entropy, the more difficult the classification problem. $H(C)$ has its maximum at $\log_2 m_0$ when all classes are equiprobable:

$$P(C_i) = \frac{1}{m_0}, \quad i = 1, \ldots, m_0 \tag{3.31}$$

$H(C)$ has its minimum at 0 when all learning examples belong to the same class:

$$P(C_k) = 1, \quad \text{and} \quad P(C_i) = 0, \quad i \neq k \tag{3.32}$$

The information score is a measure that accounts also for prior class probabilities. Let c_j be the correct class of the j-th testing example, and $P'(c_j)$ the posterior probability for the same example, as given by the classifier. The average information score is defined as follows.

$$Inf = \frac{\sum_{j=1}^{n_t} Inf_j}{n_t} \quad [bit] \tag{3.33}$$

and

$$Inf_j = \begin{cases} -\log_2 P(c_j) + \log_2 P'(c_j), & P'(c_j) \geq P(c_j) \\ -(-\log_2(1 - P(c_j)) + \log_2(1 - P'(c_j))), & P'(c_j) < P(c_j) \end{cases} \tag{3.34}$$

If the posterior probability of the correct class is higher than its prior probability, the obtained information is correct and therefore the information score is positive. Such an information score can be interpreted as: the prior information, necessary for correct classification minus the residual (posterior) information.

If the posterior probability of the correct class is lower than its prior probability, the obtained information is incorrect and therefore the information score is negative. Without the leading minus sign it can be interpreted as: the prior information, necessary for incorrect classification minus the residual (posterior) information necessary for incorrect classification.

The difference between classification accuracy and information score is best illustrated with the following (real-life) example. Consider two possible classes $C = \{C_1, C_2\}$ with prior probabilities $P(C_1) = 0.8$ and $P(C_2) = 0.2$. For a given testing example the classifier returns the following posterior probabilities: $P(C_1) = 0.6$ and $P(C_2) = 0.4$. If the correct class is C_1, the answer is correct by the classification accuracy criterion, and incorrect by the information score criterion, as its information score is negative, and therefore the provided answer is misleading. On the other hand, if the correct class is C_2, the answer is incorrect by the classification accuracy criterion, and correct by the information score criterion, as its information score is positive.

For an ideal classifier that always returns the probability 1 for the correct class, the average information score equals the entropy. Entropy is therefore an upper bound for the information score. For a trivial *default classifier* that returns for every example the prior probability distribution, the information score is equal to 0. This is the lower bound for a sensible classifier's performance.

For comparing the learner's performance between different problems it is sometimes useful to normalize the information score with entropy. Thus we get a *relative information score*:

$$RInf = \frac{Inf}{H(R)} \cdot 100\% \qquad (3.35)$$

Margin. Margin is a simple measure that partially deals with probabilistic classification. It is defined as a difference between the posterior probability of the most probable class and the posterior probability of the second most probable class. Margin is usually used for measuring the classifier's *reliability* – the larger the margin, the more reliable the classifier's decision. For example, the classification into the first class is more reliable if the class probabilities are 0.9 and 0.1 than if the class probabilities are 0.6 and 0.4. Of course, the margin does not account for prior class probabilities.

For discriminant functions, the classification's reliability is given by the distance from the separating hyperplane: the larger the distance, the more probable the classification to the class that lies on that side of the separating hyperplane. The larger the margin around the hyperplane that does not contain any learning examples, the more reliable is the discriminant function. Support vector machines are actually founded upon an algorithm for maximizing the margin.

3.2.4   Performance evaluation for two-class problems

In many problem domains the prevalent problem types are two-class problems, where we have to decide for or against some category (e.g. the patient is or is not ill, the client does or does not represent a risk, the purchase is or is not promising, ...). Examples from the first class are called *positive examples*, whereas examples from the second class are called *negative examples*. Performance analysis is performed on elements of the *confusion matrix*, described in Table 3.2.

Sensitivity and specificity. Two frequently used performance measures are *sensitivity* and *specificity*. They are calculated from the four basic quantities, elements of the misclassification matrix for two-class problems (Table 3.2).
Sensitivity is a relative frequency of correctly classified positive examples:

$$Sens = \frac{TP}{TP + FN} = \frac{TP}{POS} \qquad (3.36)$$

correct class	classified as		$\sum$
	P	N	
P	TP	FN	POS=TP+FN
N	FP	TN	NEG=FP+TN
$\sum$	PP=TP+FP	PN=FN+TN	n = TP+FP+FN+TN

P – positive class; POS – number of positive examples
N – negative class; NEG – number of negative examples
n – total number of examples
TP – number of true positive examples
FP – number of false positive examples
TN – number of true negative examples
FN – number of false negative examples
PP – number of predicted positive examples
PN – number of predicted negative examples

Table 3.2: A confusion matrix representing (mis)classification quantities for two-class problems.

Specificity is a relative frequency of correctly classified negative examples:

$$Spec = \frac{TN}{TN + FP} = \frac{TN}{NEG} \qquad (3.37)$$

Classification accuracy is therefore:

$$Acc = \frac{TP + TN}{TN + FP + FN + TN} = \frac{TP + TN}{n} \qquad (3.38)$$

Sensitivity and specificity are frequently used in medical terminology for assessing the quality of diagnostic tests. If, in some medical problem (e.g. diagnosis of a certain illness), the laboratory test has a sensitivity of 0.85 and a specificity of 0.95 this means that:

- if the patient is ill, then the test will confirm[1] the illness with probability 0.85
- if the patient is not ill, then the test will with probability 0.05 wrongly proclaim the patient as ill.

Researchers and practitioners often try to maximize the sensitivity of a test while setting some lower bound for the acceptable specificity. It is trivial to achieve the sensitivity of 1.00 simply by classifying all examples as positive. This gives sensitivity 1.00 and specificity 0.00. It is equally trivial to achieve the specificity of 1.00, again simply by classifying all examples as negative. This gives sensitivity 0.00 and specificity 1.00.

---

[1]Note that this does not mean that for the patient classified as ill the probability of illness equals 0.85; this corresponds to the notion of precision, described below.

ROC curve. When searching for an optimal classifier we are interested in a relation between its sensitivity and specificity. They can be simultaneously depicted in a ROC (Receiver Operating Characteristic) curve. ROC curve analysis is a classical methodology that originates from a signal detection theory. A ROC curve displays a relation between sensitivity and specificity for a given classifier (Figure 3.5). On a horizontal axis we have a false positives ratio (equivalent to 1-specificity), whereas on the vertical axis we have a true positives ratio (sensitivity).

Here we must mention the differences between various types of classifiers. If a classifier always predicts only a single class label, we can get only a single point on a ROC curve. If a classifier for each class returns its score (or equivalently, its probability), it is called a *scoring classifier*. For each example x, a scoring classifier outputs scores $f(x, +)$ for a positive, and $f(x, -)$ for a negative class (the scores don't need to be normalized). Scoring classifiers can easily be converted to *ranking classifiers* by calculating the likelihood of an example x being positive

$$f(x) = f(x, +)/f(x, -) \tag{3.39}$$

The value of $f(x)$ can be used to rank examples from most to least likely positive. For ranking classifiers it is easy to produce an entire ROC curve by varying a decision threshold. The usual threshold is 0.5, i.e. an example is classified into the class whose probability exceeds 0.5.

By changing the threshold we traverse along the ROC curve. The threshold 0.0 means that all examples are classified as negative. All negative examples are therefore correctly classified, and all positive examples incorrectly classified. This gives sensitivity 0.0 and specificity 1.0; it is depicted as the point in the bottom left part of Figure 3.5. On the other hand, the threshold 1.0 means that all examples are classified as positive. All negative examples are therefore incorrectly classified, and all positive examples correctly classified. This gives sensitivity 1.0 and specificity 0.0; it is depicted as the point in the top right corner of Figure 3.5. A diagonal connecting these two extreme points (a dotted line in Figure 3.5) characterizes random (knowledge-free) classifiers using different thresholds. Useful classifiers are found only in the ROC space above the dotted line. An ideal classifier with both sensitivity and specificity equal to 1.0 would be found in the top left corner. The closer to the ideal point the ROC curve comes, the better the classifier.

When comparing two classifiers, we can claim that one is better than another if its sensitivity and specificity are both not less than that of the other classifier's. In other cases it is undecidable which one is better.

But if we can draw the ROC curves for both classifiers by continuously changing the threshold from 0 to 1, the quality of the classifier is reflected in the area under the ROC curve (AUC). The classifier with larger AUC is the better one.

AUC has also a statistical meaning. Its value is equal to the value of the Wilcoxon-Mann-Whitney test statistic. It is also the probability that the classifier will score a randomly drawn positive example higher than a randomly drawn negative example.

Changing the threshold while drawing the ROC curve corresponds to changing the misclassification costs for positive and negative examples. ROC curves can therefore be used for the misclassification cost analysis as well.

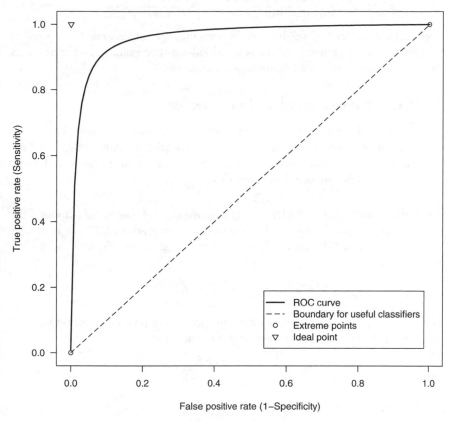

Figure 3.5: A typical ROC curve.

Recall and precision.   In information retrieval (searching for important documents), frequently used measures are recall and precision. The definition of recall equals that of sensitivity:

$$Recall = \frac{TP}{TP + FN} = \frac{TP}{POS} \tag{3.40}$$

Precision estimates the portion of correctly classified examples that were classified as positive (retrieved important documents against all documents marked as important).

$$Precision = \frac{TP}{TP + FP} = \frac{TP}{PP} \tag{3.41}$$

For scoring classifiers we can, by changing the threshold, obtain a precision-recall curve with properties similar to that of the ROC curve.

Another frequently used measure in information retrieval is the F-measure :

$$F = \frac{2 \cdot Recall \cdot Precision}{Recall + Precision} = \frac{2TP}{2TP + FP + FN} \tag{3.42}$$

All three measures (recall, precision, and F measure) do not account for a possibly huge number of true negatives – correctly classified negative examples – because they are not relevant when searching for important documents.

3.2.5   Performance evaluation in regression

In regressional problems it is unreasonable to use classification accuracy. The reason is simple – in most problems it would be 0 as we model continuous-valued and not discrete functions. More appropriate measures are those based upon the difference between the true and the predicted function's value.

Mean squared error.   The most frequently used measure of quality for automatically built continuous functions (models) $\hat{f}$ is the *mean squared error (MSE)*. It is defined as the average squared difference between the predicted value $\hat{f}(i)$ and the desired (correct) value f_i:

$$MSE = \frac{1}{n} \sum_{i=1}^{n} (f_i - \hat{f}_i)^2 \tag{3.43}$$

Because the error magnitude depends on the magnitudes of possible function values it is advisable to use the *relative mean squared error* instead:

$$RE = \frac{n \cdot MSE}{\sum_i (f_i - \overline{f})^2} \tag{3.44}$$

where $\overline{f}$ is an average function value:

$$\overline{f} = \frac{1}{n} \sum_i f_i \tag{3.45}$$

The relative mean squared error is nonnegative, and for acceptable models less than 1:

$$0 \le RE \le 1 \tag{3.46}$$

$RE = 1$ can be trivially achieved by using the average model $\hat{f}_i = \overline{f}$ (Equation (3.45)). If, for some function, $RE > 1$, the model is completely useless. An ideal function is $\hat{f}_i = f_i$ with $RE = 0$.

Mean absolute error.   Another frequently used quality measure for automatically built continuous functions (models) $\hat{f}$ is the *mean absolute error (MAE)*. It is defined as the average absolute difference between the predicted value $\hat{f}(i)$ and the desired (correct) value f_i:

$$MAE = \frac{1}{n} \sum_{i=1}^{n} |f_i - \hat{f}_i| \tag{3.47}$$

Since the magnitude of MAE depends on the magnitudes of possible function values it is often better to use the *relative mean squared error*:

$$RMAE = \frac{n \cdot MAE}{\sum_i |f_i - \overline{f}|} \qquad (3.48)$$

where $\overline{f}$ is defined as in Equation (3.45). The relative mean absolute error is nonnegative, and for acceptable models less than 1:

$$0 \leq RMAE \leq 1 \qquad (3.49)$$

$RMAE = 1$ can also be trivially achieved by using the average model $\hat{f}_i = \overline{f}$.

Correlation coefficient. The correlation coefficient measures the statistical (Pearson's) correlation between actual function values f_i and predicted function values $\hat{f}_i$ for a dependant (regression) variable:

$$R = \frac{S_{f\hat{f}}}{S_f S_{\hat{f}}} \qquad (3.50)$$

where

$$
\begin{aligned}
S_{f\hat{f}} &= \frac{\sum_{i=1}^{n}[(f_i - \overline{f})(\hat{f}_i - \overline{\hat{f}})]}{n-1} \\
S_f &= \frac{\sum_{i=1}^{n}(f_i - \overline{f})^2}{n-1} \\
S_{\hat{f}} &= \frac{\sum_{i=1}^{n}(\hat{f}_i - \overline{\hat{f}})^2}{n-1} \\
\overline{f} &= \frac{1}{n}\sum_i f_i \\
\overline{\hat{f}} &= \frac{1}{n}\sum_i \hat{f}_i
\end{aligned}
$$

The correlation coefficient is bounded to the $[-1, 1]$ interval. 1 stands for perfect positive correlation, -1 for perfect negative correlation, and 0 for no correlation at all. For useful regressional predictors, only positive values of correlation coefficients make sense:

$$0 < R \leq 1 \qquad (3.51)$$

As opposed to the mean squared error and the mean absolute error that need to be minimized, the learning algorithm aims to maximize the correlation coefficient.

3.2.6 Bias and variance

As described in Section 3.1.2 there is a trade-off between complexity and accuracy of the hypothesis that is determined by the MDL principle (Equation (3.6)). This trade-off can also be shown by decomposing the total hypothesis' error in an error originating from the learning algorithm (bias) and an error originating from the learning data (variance).

Machine learning algorithms aim to approximate the target function. The quality of an approximation depends on both the learning algorithm and the learning data. When using real-world data it is unreasonable to expect that the hypothesis will be absolutely correct, and therefore we almost always have to deal with errors. The sole exceptions are either artificial or trivial problems with complete information (learning data). The hypothesis' error is usually estimated for a particular (unlabelled) example, or for a set of (unlabelled) examples.

Let t be the unknown correct value we wish to predict, and $\hat{t}$ the actual predicted value. For a fixed learning algorithm the predicted value depends only on the learning set of examples. If we run an algorithm on different learning sets, we get different predicted values $\hat{t}$. An expected prediction $E[\hat{t}]$ is the mean predicted value of all possible learning sets of a fixed size. Because $E[\hat{t}]$ depends on the learning algorithm, the difference to the true t is defined as the *bias* of the learning algorithm:

$$Bias(t) = E[\hat{t}] - t \tag{3.52}$$

Bias generally depends on the value t we wish to predict. The learning algorithm is unbiased if its bias is 0. Bias is a systematic error that cannot be avoided unless the learning algorithm is changed (e.g. by altering the hypothesis space, by changing the searching algorithm, or by using multiple learning methods such as boosting (Section 3.5.3) or bagging (Section 3.5.3)). Because the value t is unknown, the bias cannot really be calculated. However, it can be empirically estimated on artificial data with known t, or on large datasets by using some form of cross validation (Section 3.3.3).

For a particular example the hypothesis predicts the value $\hat{t}$ which is generally diffcrent from $E[\hat{t}]$, that again depends on the learning set. *Variance* is a measure of the algorithm's sensitivity to the learning set:

$$Variance(\hat{t}) = E[E[\hat{t}] - \hat{t}]^2 \tag{3.53}$$

Variance does not depend on actual values of t. It can therefore be estimated by multiply sampling the learning set, generating hypotheses, and calculating the variance of predictions $\hat{t}_i$. If we have several algorithms with the same bias, the one with the smallest variance should be chosen.

The total prediction error is therefore composed of bias (systematic error of the learning algorithm), and variance (error originating in learning examples). Error is given as the difference between the actual value t and the predicted value $\hat{t}$. It is usually estimated with the mean squared error $E[(\hat{t} - t)^2]$ that equals to the sum of squared bias and variance as shown in the following derivation:

$$E[(\hat{t} - t)^2] = E[(\hat{t} - E[\hat{t}] + E[\hat{t}] - t)^2] \tag{3.54}$$

Since t is constant, $E[t] = t$, and $E[E[\hat{t}]\hat{t}] = E[\hat{t}]^2$, we get

$$E[(\hat{t} - t)^2] = (E[\hat{t}] - t)^2 + E[(E[\hat{t}] - \hat{t})^2] \tag{3.55}$$

or equivalently

$$E[(\hat{t} - t)^2] = Bias(t)^2 + Variance(\hat{t}) \qquad (3.56)$$

The expected error is therefore composed of both bias and variance. Unfortunately, they are opposed to each other, so a compromise between them needs to be found. If we wish to minimize the variance, we need to simplify the hypothesis by reducing the number of its parameters. An extreme case is a constant prediction: the hypothesis always predicts the same value. Its variance is 0, however its bias may be arbitrarily large. On the other hand, if we wish to minimize the bias, we need to enlarge the hypothesis space by increasing the number of parameters. This frequently leads to overfitting of the learning examples. It means that the hypothesis is highly dependent on the learning examples and therefore its variance is high. Generally, the more parameters we have, the worse their estimations are, and therefore the variance increases.

3.3   ESTIMATING PERFORMANCE

I trust the trustworthy, I also trust the untrustworthy. This is the real trust.

— Lao Tse

To estimate the performance of a learning algorithm, or the quality of the learned hypothesis (model), we test the hypothesis on an independent (testing) set of examples. The estimation is reliable if the testing set is large enough. Otherwise, the learning-testing process (Figure 3.4) needs to be reiterated several times. In this section we describe some basic techniques for estimating the quality of hypotheses: estimation of the quality and its reliability in terms of the standard error and the confidence interval. For a repeated learning–testing process we describe methods for cross validation and multiplication of learning examples. Finally we review techniques for comparing the quality of different machine learning algorithms.

3.3.1   Reliability of quality estimations

When the testing set of examples with known values of dependent variable is large enough, the learning-testing process from Figure 3.4 is performed only once. A hypothesis is built on a sufficiently large learning set; its quality estimated on a sufficiently large testing set. For estimating the quality Q, one of the methods described in Section 3.2, averaged over all n_t testing examples, is used.

$$Q = \frac{1}{n_t} \sum_{j=1}^{n_t} Q_j \qquad (3.57)$$

For estimating the reliability of the quality estimation Q the *standard error* is used:

$$SE(Q) = \sqrt{s^2/n_t} \qquad (3.58)$$

with s^2 being the variance of quality measured on the testing set:

$$s^2 = \frac{\sum_{j=1}^{n_t}(Q_j - Q)^2}{n_t} \qquad (3.59)$$

The standard error is interpreted as the mean error for a given quality estimation measure with n_t testing examples. It can be rewritten as follows:

$$Quality = Q \pm SE(Q) \qquad (3.60)$$

As the standard error follows the standardized normal distribution, the more exact interpretation is that this is a confidence interval with the confidence level of approximately[2] 0.68. The actual quality therefore lies on the interval $[Q - SE(Q), Q + SE(Q)]$ with probability 0.68. By increasing the number of testing examples n_t, the standard error SE decreases.

The definition of standard error from Equation (3.58) is valid only for measures that are estimated with an average over all n_t testing examples. For other measures, standard errors need to be derived individually. For example, for relative mean squared error RE (Equation 3.44) the standard error is calculated as follows:

$$SE(RE) = RE\sqrt{\frac{1}{n}\left(\frac{s_1^2}{E^2} - \frac{2s_{12}}{s^2 E} + \frac{s_2^2}{s^4}\right)} \qquad (3.61)$$

with E being the corresponding mean squared error (Equation 3.43) and s^2 its variance:

$$s^2 = \frac{1}{n}\sum_{i=1}^{n}(f_i - \overline{f})^2 \qquad (3.62)$$

s_1^2, s_{12}, s_2^2 are calculated as follows:

$$s_1^2 = \frac{1}{n}\sum_{i=1}^{n}(f_i - \hat{f}_i)^4 - E^2 \qquad (3.63)$$

$$s_{12} = \frac{1}{n}\sum_{i=1}^{n}\left[(f_i - \hat{f}_i)^2(f_i - \overline{f})^2\right] - s^2 E \qquad (3.64)$$

$$s_2^2 = \frac{1}{n}\sum_{i=1}^{n}(f_i - \overline{f})^4 - s^4 \qquad (3.65)$$

3.3.2 Confidence interval

The *confidence interval* is a generalization of the standard error. First we choose a significance level α (say, 0.05 or 0.01) and a corresponding confidence level $1 - \alpha$ (say, 0.95 or 0.99). The confidence level is interpreted as the probability that the actual

---

[2]0.68, or more exactly 0.6826895, is not a magic number. It is the area under the density function of the standardized normal distribution between $(\mu - \sigma) = -1$ and $(\mu + \sigma) = +1$.

quality (that was estimated by Q) actually lies on the specified interval $[Q-x_\alpha, Q+x_\alpha]$. The standard error is just a special case of a confidence interval where the confidence level equals to $1 - \alpha = 0.68$. For a given confidence level we calculate a half-sized interval x_α:

$$x_\alpha = z\left(\frac{\alpha}{2}\right) SE(Q) \tag{3.66}$$

$z(\cdot)$ is an interval size for (error) values that are standardized and normally distributed. For example, for $\alpha = 0.05$ the value of $z(\alpha/2) = z(0.025) = 1.96$. In this case we can claim with probability 0.95 that the actual quality estimation averaged over all possible sets of examples lies in the interval $[Q - x_{0.05}, Q + x_{0.05}]$. For the standard error, $x_{0.32} = SE(Q)$, or equivalently, $z(0.16) = 1$.

3.3.3 Cross validation

When the total number of learning examples is small it is unreasonable to deprive the learning algorithm of a set of examples that are to be used for testing. Although all examples are used for learning, the automatically generated theory (model) still needs to be evaluated. What can we do in such a situation? As described in Section 3.2, estimating the quality on the learning set itself may yield only a poor estimation. A better approach is to use a *leave-one-out* method. By this approach one new theory is built for each available learning example. Each particular example is excluded from the learning set and all other examples are used for learning. The learned theory is used for solving the excluded example. The process is repeated for all examples, and the quality of the theory built from all available examples is estimated as the average quality of leave-one-out theories. We therefore estimate the quality of the final theory as the average of different theories. Because their learning sets are very similar, the theories are also very similar, both in performance and in meaning.

In many problems, the leave-one-out method may be too time-consuming. If we have n examples available, $n + 1$ theories need to be built (n for leave-one-out evaluation and one final theory built from all examples). A leave-one-out method can be generalized to the "leave $\lceil n/k \rceil$ examples out" method, better known as *k-fold cross-validation*. The number k determines the number of theories that need to be built for quality evaluation. The set of learning examples is split into k (approximately) equally sized subsets. For each particular subset a theory is built by using a union of all other subsets for learning. The obtained theory is used for solving examples from the given subset. The quality of the final theory, built from all available examples, is estimated as the average quality of k theories. In practice, $k = 10$ is most frequently used. The leave-one-out method is therefore a special case of cross validation where $k = n$.

In classification problems *stratified cross validation* is frequently used. It is very similar to the basic cross-validation, with one important addition: the subsets are built so as to preserve the original class distribution in all subsets. This guarantees that both learning and testing sets will have approximately equal class distributions.

For all kinds of cross-validation (including the leave-one-out method) we can use the formulae for standard error and confidence interval as described in Section 3.3.1.

We must, however, be aware that those estimations are of heuristic nature, as we do not really test the final theory, but estimate its quality from several different theories built on slightly smaller learning sets.

3.3.4 Bootstrap methods

When the total number of examples is very small (less than 50 examples) all described evaluation methods, even the leave-one-out method, become unreliable. This is due to the small absolute number of testing examples. We get a more reliable quality estimation by repeating 2-fold cross-validation several times (each time by randomly splitting the examples into two equally sized subsets). Typically, the process is repeated 100 times. It has been shown that, for a quality estimation of the final theory (built from all available examples), an average quality estimation of a hundred 2-fold cross-validations is more reliable than the leave-one-out method. It is, however, less reliable for problems with small actual errors (e.g., classification accuracy more than 90% in classification problems).

In statistics, a *bootstrapping* method has been developed. It excels for estimating the quality of theories (models) built upon small sets of examples. By this approach the following process is repeated 200 times. From the set of n examples we randomly select n examples with replacement. On average, the learning set consists of only 63.2% of original examples (some are represented several times). The model is built with n selected examples, and evaluated on examples not contained in the learning set (on average, 36.8%). The average quality over 200 repetitions is a pessimistic quality estimation for a model built on all original examples. The estimation is pessimistic because on average only 63.2% of examples are used for learning. The error estimated by this approach is usually denoted as e_0.

The final error estimation is a linear combination of an optimistic error e_ℓ of the model (built and tested on all available examples), and a pessimistic error e_0:

$$e = 0.368 \cdot e_\ell + 0.632 \cdot e_0 \tag{3.67}$$

Instead of e_0 an error estimation obtained by a hundred two-fold cross-validation runs may be used.

3.4 *COMPARING PERFORMANCE OF MACHINE LEARNING ALGORITHMS

If one wins everybody else has to lose. Is that entertaining at all?

— *Marlo Morgan*

As machine learning algorithms are applied in different problem domains it is sometimes desirable to choose the best one for a given problem. We therefore compare the performance of learning algorithms (the quality of the generated models). When comparing the algorithms, there are several pitfalls to be avoided. The first and most frequent mistake that some authors make is that they tune the parameters of their machine learning algorithm until the best classification accuracy on the testing set is achieved. They publish their results and compare them with results of other competing algorithms (with pre-set parameters). Such a comparison is obviously unfair. Setting the parameters of all algorithms should be performed before testing the algorithms on an independent testing set. For setting the parameters, the learning set would need to be split into the true learning set, and a separate *validation set*, used for optimizing the parameter values. The algorithm's parameters can be tweaked until best results are achieved on the validation set. When testing the algorithm's performance on an independent testing set, it is strictly forbidden to change the parameters in order to improve the results! Otherwise, the obtained performance estimation is overly optimistic.

The estimated algorithm performances may be used for comparing the algorithms and choosing the best among them. If the performance differences are small, the comparisons may be unreliable – especially if standard errors are relatively high. Therefore, appropriate significance tests for comparing performance differences need to be used. Algorithms may be compared according to several different scenarios:

Scenario 1: two algorithms on a single problem domain;

Scenario 2: two algorithms on multiple problem domains;

Scenario 3: several algorithms on multiple problem domains.

For each scenario we assume either that:

- the number of available labelled examples is sufficiently large in order to use an independent testing set without significantly reducing the learning set and thus potentially diminishing the algorithm's performance. For example, if several thousands of examples are available, we can easily afford a few hundreds of testing examples. This is usually sufficient to compare several algorithms. Their performance is thus estimated as an average performance on an independent testing set.

- the number of examples is relatively small. For performance estimation some form of cross-validation is used. Usually, this is 10-fold stratified cross validation, or leave-one-out testing. In either case, performance is estimated by averaging the performance over all testing examples. In k-fold cross-validation the averaged performance estimations for each testing fold can also be used for comparing two algorithms on a single problem domain.

3.4.1   Two algorithms on a single domain

Methods for comparing the performance of two algorithms on the same problem (domain) form the basis for performance comparison techniques. Mostly they have rather solid foundations in statistics and are usually well analyzed and widely accepted.

	Significance levels α		
Statistics	0.05	0.01	0.001
$t(9)$	2.262	3.250	4.781
z	1.960	2.576	3.291
$\chi^2(1)$	3.841	6.635	10.828

Table 3.3: Typical critical values for statistics: t with 9 degrees of freedom, z and χ^2 with one degree of freedom.

Cross-validation

For k-fold cross-validation, when comparing two algorithms (A_1 and A_2) on exactly the same folds, a corrected, one-tailed paired t-test is used. The t-test is used because the number of folds is usually small ($k < 30$). It is one-tailed because we are interested in finding the better algorithm.

The standard t-test is performed as follows. For all k folds, the performance difference between two algorithms is calculated:

$$diff_i = \widehat{Perf_1} - \widehat{Perf_2} \qquad i = 1,\ldots,k \qquad (3.68)$$

For $\widehat{Perf_1}$ and $\widehat{Perf_2}$ we assume that they follow the normal (Gaussian) distribution. The null hypothesis (that we wish to reject) is that both algorithms achieve the same average performance ($\overline{diff} = 0$). The average performance $\overline{diff}$ and its standard deviation s are calculated as below:

$$\overline{diff} = \frac{1}{k}\sum_{i=1}^{k} diff_i \qquad (3.69)$$

$$s = \sqrt{\frac{1}{k-1}\sum_{i=1}^{k}(diff_i - \overline{diff})^2} \qquad (3.70)$$

The comparison order of algorithms is chosen so that $\overline{diff} \geq 0$. The experimental statistic

$$t_{exp} = \frac{\overline{diff}}{s}\sqrt{k} \qquad (3.71)$$

follows the Student t distribution with $k-1$ degrees of freedom. For a given confidence level $1 - \alpha$ the null hypothesis (both algorithms achieve the same performance) is rejected if $t_{exp} > t(\alpha, k - 1)$. This criterion holds for the one-tailed test; for the two-tailed test a value of $t(\alpha/2, k - 1)$ would be used. Typical α values are 0.05, 0.01, or 0.001. For $k = 10$ typical critical values of $t(\alpha, k - 1)$ are shown in Table 3.3.

The use of standard t-test for any form of cross-validation is not entirely correct, as it assumes independence of experiments. In cross-validation, learning sets and therefore experiments are not independent! A *corrected t-test* addresses this anomaly. The only difference to the original t-test is that in Equation (3.71) the factor $\sqrt{k}$ is replaced with the reciprocal squared root of its inverse plus the ratio between numbers of testing (n_t) and learning (n_l) examples for each step cross-validation:

$$t = \frac{\overline{diff}}{s\sqrt{\left(\frac{1}{k} + \frac{n_t}{n_l}\right)}} \tag{3.72}$$

As in k-fold cross-validation with n examples it holds

$$n_t = n/k \tag{3.73}$$

and

$$n_l = n_t \cdot (k - 1) \tag{3.74}$$

we finally get the corrected t-test statistic:

$$t = \frac{\overline{diff}}{s\sqrt{\left(\frac{1}{k} + \frac{1}{k-1}\right)}} \tag{3.75}$$

The corrected t-test has several nice properties that can be further emphasized by repeating cross-validation several times (e.g. 10 times 10-fold cross-validation).

In an undesirable case when the two compared algorithms do not use the same data splits, a different statistic is used:

$$t = \frac{(\overline{Perf}_1 - \overline{Perf}_2)}{\sqrt{(s_1^2/k) + (s_2^2/k)}} \tag{3.76}$$

Here, $\overline{Perf}_j$ is the average of $\overline{Perf}_{ji}$, the average performance of a j-th algorithm in the i-th experiment (data split):

$$\overline{Perf}_j = \frac{1}{k}\sum_{i=1}^{k} \overline{Perf}_{ji} \qquad j = 1, 2 \tag{3.77}$$

$$s_j = \sqrt{\frac{1}{k-1}\sum_{i=1}^{k}(\overline{Perf}_{ji} - \overline{Perf}_j)^2} \tag{3.78}$$

Leave-one-out testing and sufficiently large independent testing set

For leave-one-out testing, or when a sufficiently large testing set is available, a one-tailed z-test is used, as in both cases the total number of testing examples is relatively high ($n_t = n$). The only difference to the t-test is that the number of experiments (data splits) k is replaced with the number of examples n, and that the statistic is normally distributed. Hence, the letter z will be used instead of t.

$$z_{exp} = \frac{\overline{diff}}{s}\sqrt{n} \tag{3.79}$$

For a given confidence level $1 - \alpha$ the null hypothesis (both algorithms have the same performance) is rejected if $z_{exp} > z(\alpha)$ (for the two-tailed test the value of $z(\alpha/2)$ would have been used). Critical values of $z(\alpha)$ for $\alpha \in \{0.05, 0.01, 0.001\}$ are shown in Table 3.3.

For classification problems, where the classification accuracy is compared, an even more sensitive *McNemar's test* can be used. Because the classifier's answers are either correct or incorrect, a *binomial distribution* can be used. Let A_1 and A_2 be the two compared classifiers, n_{21} the number of examples correctly classified by A_1 and incorrectly classified by A_2, and n_{12} the number of examples correctly classified by A_2 and incorrectly classified by A_1. McNemar's test uses the following statistics:

$$s_M = \frac{(|n_{12} - n_{21}| - 1)^2}{n_{12} + n_{21}} \tag{3.80}$$

Again, the null hypothesis is that both algorithms have the same performance. If the null hypothesis holds, the denominator of s_M has a very small value (it approaches to 0). The s_M statistic is distributed according to the χ^2 law with one degree of freedom. If the null hypothesis holds, s_M has an average value of 1, and a standard deviation of approximately $\sqrt{2}$. So, if the null hypothesis holds, we have $P(s_M > \chi^2(\alpha, 1)) \leq \alpha$ (see critical values in Table 3.3).

Bonferroni correction

If many comparisons of different algorithms (e.g., for different parameter settings) are performed on the same problem domains, there is an increasing probability that the winner will be determined purely by chance, although an ordinary statistical test confirms its supremacy. Similarly, when comparing two algorithms on several problem domains, a result on one problem may be significant by chance alone. In such cases, an ordinary statistical test (e.g. *t*-test) has to be complemented by the *Bonferroni correction*. It is however, very conservative, and significantly reduces the strength of the underlying tests. The null hypothesis is rejected only if the differences are relatively large.

For a given significance level α, and N independent experiments on the same data, the expected number of outcomes significant purely by chance is $\alpha \cdot N$. The Bonferroni correction therefore requires a more stringent significance level α_B for actually achieving the original significance level α. If an experiment is repeated N times with results being significant with α_B, then the significance levels of a series of N experiments equals to

$$\alpha = 1 - (1 - \alpha_B)^N \tag{3.81}$$

From this we get

$$\alpha_B = 1 - (1 - \alpha)^{\frac{1}{N}} \approx \frac{\alpha}{N} \tag{3.82}$$

For example, if 100 experiments are performed ($N = 100$), and the required significance level is $\alpha = 0.05$, the Bonferroni correction requires $\alpha_B = 0.0005$.

Although the Bonferroni correction is very simple, it reduces the power of tests, thus making the testing procedure very conservative. In practice it is often better to use more powerful tests for comparing two, or more algorithms on several domain problems.

3.4.2   Two algorithms on several domains

For comparing the performance of two algorithms (A_1 and A_2) on several domain problems, a nonparametric *Wilcoxon signed rank* test is used. It ranks the absolute performance differences between the two algorithms on D domain problems. Let d_i be the performance difference between two algorithms on the i-th domain problem, $i = 1 \ldots D$.

$$d_i = Perf_{1,i} - Perf_{2,i} \qquad (3.83)$$

If the number of domains with $d_i = 0$ (both algorithms perform equally) is odd, one of those domains is ignored in further computations. Differences are ranked in decreasing order according to their absolute values. When several differences are equal, their average rank is assigned to all of them. For example, for differences in Table 3.4 we

difference	0.0	0.5	1.7	-1.3	0.0	1.0	0.0	-1.0
rank	–	5	1	2	6.5	3.5	6.5	3.5

Table 3.4: An example of differences and ranks for the Wilcoxon signed rank test. The non-whole numbers represent average ranks for absolutely equal differences.

first remove the first difference (odd number of equal results), and then we calculate the ranks. The ranks of positive and negative differences are separately summed up. To both sums, half of the sum of zero-difference ranks is added.

$$R^+ = \sum_{d_i > 0} \text{rank}(d_i) + \frac{1}{2} \sum_{d_i = 0} \text{rank}(d_i) \qquad (3.84)$$

$$R^- = \sum_{d_i < 0} \text{rank}(d_i) + \frac{1}{2} \sum_{d_i = 0} \text{rank}(d_i) \qquad (3.85)$$

When the number of domains is small ($D < 30$) the T statistic (3.86) is used for computing critical values:

$$T = \min\{R^+, R^-\} \qquad (3.86)$$

Its critical values are tabulated in most general statistics handbooks. For our example from Table 3.4, with $D = 8$ and $\alpha = 0.05$, we have $T = \min\{16, 12\} = 12$. The null hypothesis (both algorithms achieve the same performance) would have been rejected for $T \leq 3$.

For larger number of domains ($D \geq 30$) the z statistic is used:

$$z = \frac{T - \frac{1}{4}D(D+1)}{\sqrt{\frac{1}{24}D(D+1)(2D+1)}} \qquad (3.87)$$

It approximately follows the standardized normal distribution. Therefore, for significance level $\alpha = 0.05$ the null hypothesis is rejected if $z < -1.96$.

3.4.3   Several algorithms on several domains

For comparison of several (k) algorithms it is necessary, due to the increasing number of comparisons ($k \cdot (k-1)$), to compare the algorithms on as many domain problems as possible. To reduce the number of comparisons, it is best to focus on a particular (e.g., a newly developed) algorithm, and compare it with all others, thus reducing the number of comparisons to $k-1$. When comparing each algorithm to all others, the number of comparisons is considerably larger thus increasing the danger of some differences being significant by chance alone. Therefore, the tests need to be more conservative and consequently their strength is reduced.

When comparing several algorithms on several domains, a *non-parametric improved Friedman test* can be used. It is a non-parametric equivalent of a two-way ANOVA. The Friedman test ranks the algorithms for each dataset, the winning algorithm getting the rank 1, the second best the rank 2, and so on. In case of ties, average ranks are assigned. Let k be the number of algorithms to compare, and D the number of domain problems. Let r_i^j be the rank of j-th algorithm on the i-th dataset. The Friedman test compares average ranks of algorithms

$$R_j = \frac{1}{D} \sum_{i=1}^{D} r_i^j \tag{3.88}$$

The original Friedman statistic

$$\chi_F^2 = \frac{12D}{k(k+1)} \left(\sum_{j=1}^{k} R_j^2 - \frac{k(k+1)^2}{4} \right) \tag{3.89}$$

is distributed according to χ_F^2 with $k-1$ degrees of freedom, when D and k are big enough (as a rule of thumb, $D > 10$ and $k > 5$). For smaller numbers of algorithms and domains, exact critical values have been computed. As the original Friedman statistic has been shown to be too conservative, it is better to use an improved statistic

$$F_F = \frac{(D-1)\chi_F^2}{D(k-1) - \chi_F^2} \tag{3.90}$$

that is distributed according to F-distribution with $k-1$ and $(k-1) \cdot (D-1)$ degrees of freedom. Its critical values can be found in most general statistics books. For example, for 14 domains ($D = 14$), four algorithms ($k = 4$) and significance level $\alpha = 0.05$ the null hypothesis is rejected if $F_F > F(3, 39) = 2.85$. If the null hypothesis (all algorithms achieve the same performance) is rejected, we continue with testing which pairs of algorithms differ significantly.

If each algorithm is compared to all others, a *Nemenyi test* can be used. On the other hand, if one particular algorithm is compared to all other algorithms, a *Bonferroni-Dunn* test can be used. Both tests reject the null hypothesis (that the two compared algorithms A_1 and A_2 achieve the same performance) if the difference of their average ranks ($\overline{R_{A_1}}$ and $\overline{R_{A_2}}$) is greater or equal to the critical difference CD:

$$|\overline{R_{A_1}} - \overline{R_{A_2}}| \geq CD = q_\alpha \sqrt{\frac{k(k+1)}{6D}} \tag{3.91}$$

test	Number of classifiers								
Nemenyi	2	3	4	5	6	7	8	9	10
$q_{0.05}$	1.960	2.343	2.569	2.728	2.850	2.949	3.031	3.102	3.164
$q_{0.10}$	1.645	2.052	2.291	2.459	2.589	2.693	2.780	2.855	2.920
Bonferroni - Dunn	2	3	4	5	6	7	8	9	10
$q_{0.05}$	1.960	2.241	2.394	2.498	2.576	2.638	2.690	2.724	2.773
$q_{0.10}$	1.645	1.960	2.128	2.241	2.326	2.394	2.450	2.498	2.539

Table 3.5: Critical values of q_α for Nemenyi and Bonferroni-Dunn tests (several algorithms on several domain problems).

The difference between Nemenyi and Bonferroni-Dunn tests is only in the choice of critical values q_α (see Table 3.5).

3.5 COMBINING SEVERAL MACHINE LEARNING ALGORITHMS

More than with friends we learn tolerance with our enemies.

— Dalai Lama

The *minimum description length principle* (Section 3.1.2) requires from the learning algorithm to find a trade-off between the hypothesis' complexity and its accuracy. A hypothesis needs to be as simple as possible and yet provide a good data model. On the other hand, the *principle of multiple explanations* (Section 3.1.4) requires the prediction algorithm to use many considerably different hypotheses consistent with the data. A learning algorithm should consider both criteria and generate several different hypotheses (models) during the learning phase. There are two possibilities:

- Hypotheses are generated by different learning algorithms on the same data. In a classification problem we could, for example, learn a naive Bayesian classifier and a multi-layered neural network, store learning examples for a k-nearest neighbors algorithm, and calculate a discriminant function using the SVM method.

- Hypotheses are generated by the same algorithm either by running it with different parameter settings or by variating its learning set. Popular general methods from this group are *bagging* and *boosting*; for decision trees frequently *random forests* are used.

When several hypotheses are built they need to be combined into the final hypothesis (classifier or regressor) by the principle of multiple explanations. As the conditional hypothesis probabilities $P(H|E, B)$ from Equation (3.9) are usually not known, some suitable method for combining hypotheses needs to be used. In the following sections we review some popular approaches to hypothesis combination.

3.5.1 Combining predictions of several hypotheses

Combining predictions of several hypotheses has gained considerable popularity in machine learning, especially in classification problems. As the approaches used in classification and regression are considerably different, they are reviewed separately.

Classification

In classification, predictions of different classifiers can be combined in several ways:

Voting: each classifier gives a vote for a particular class; the example is labelled with the class label that has received most votes.

Weighted voting: each classifier contributes a class probability distribution (or normalized scores). A class probability acts as a weight; the example is labelled with the class label that has the greatest sum of weights.

Reliability-weighted voting: the reliability of a particular prediction is estimated with some method (e.g., with transduction (Section 3.5.4)), or the overall classifier's reliability is estimated (e.g., with cross validation). Reliability estimations are subsequently used as weights in weighted voting.

Bayesian voting: each classifier contributes a class probability distribution. A naive Bayes formula (Equation 9.11) is used to calculate combined probabilities for all classes. In the formula, each classifier is treated as a discrete attribute (the conditional class probability given the classifier equals to the probability provided by the classifier). As in all naive Bayesian calculations, independence of attributes (classifiers) is assumed.

Stacking: this approach requires a separate validation set. Classifications of validating examples are used as attributes for meta learning. The task of the learning algorithm is to use single predictions for predicting the correct class. The combination function is therefore not given in advance, but learnt from data. Although for such a meta learning approach any learner can be used, it has been shown that simple learners perform best in practice (because of higher bias they reduce overfitting).

Locally weighted voting: For a new example that needs to be labelled (classified), k nearest neighbors from the learning set are selected. For each classifier, an average (local) performance is determined by using the selected k examples for testing. Classifications for the new example are either weighted with their local performance, or only the best local classifier is used.

Dynamic choice of classifiers: As for a locally weighted voting, k nearest neighbors from the learning set are selected for each new example that is to be labelled. Each classifier contributes the class probability distributions for a new example and for its k nearest neighbors. Then, some measure is used to calculate distances between probability distributions of each of the k neighbors and the new example. Frequently, the Kullback-Leibler divergence is used for this purpose. Let m_0 be the number of classes and p and q two probability distributions. The Kullback-Leibler divergence is calculated by

$$KL(p, q) \;=\; -\sum_{i=1}^{m_0} p_i \log_2 \frac{p_i}{q_i} \tag{3.92}$$

Only those neighbors for which the distance does not exceed some pre-defined threshold are used for further computations. With a given threshold let the number of nearest neighbors with similar class distributions be $l \leq k$. On the remaining set of l learning examples the classifier's performance is estimated. Note that l may vary between classifiers as the probability distributions may be considerably different. When classifying new examples, classifications are either weighted with their local performance, or only the best local classifier is used.

In practice, the most frequently used combination method is weighted voting. However, some studies show that the best results are obtained by using the naive Bayesian combination.

Regression

In regression, a straightforward approach for combining regressional predictors is to average their predictions. Usually, a weighted average is used. For each predictor, its weight is either a reliability of a particular prediction estimated with some method (e.g. transduction (Section 3.5.4)), or an overall predictor's reliability is estimated. As in classification, meta learning of a combination function (stacking) can also be used in regression.

3.5.2 Combining algorithms

In the previous section we have reviewed how learning algorithms can be combined in parallel. They are run independently; only their predictions are somehow combined. A combination function may be fixed, or learned by a meta learner from algorithms' predictions on a validation set.

Learning algorithms can also be combined sequentially: the first algorithm learns the target function, the second learns to predict errors of the first, and so on. An ordered chain of hypotheses is built; each (except the first one) predicts errors of the previous hypothesis. Because of possible overfitting, chains of length 2 are mostly used in practice: an algorithm that predicts the target values and an algorithm that tries to correct its errors. It is important to supply the correction algorithm with learning examples from a separate (validation) set; otherwise overfitting may quickly occur.

In principle, sequential, parallel and meta learning can be arbitrarily combined. Thus we can get algorithm networks with different topologies. A well known approach to combine a multitude of simple base algorithms (threshold functions) into a complex structure are *artificial neural networks* (Chapter 11). Because of dangers of overfitting, and preferences for simple and transparent hypotheses, complex combinations of different base learning algorithms are rarely used in practice.

3.5.3 Bagging, boosting and random forests

Bagging, boosting and random forests are *ensemble learning algorithms.* Their common property is that they generate ensembles of base classifiers and ensure their diversity by providing them with different sets of learning examples.

Bagging. The term *bagging* is short for *bootstrap aggregating.* Bootstrap (Section 3.3.4) is a method for replication of learning examples when the learning set is small. In bagging, a series of different learning sets is generated. When the total number of learning examples is n, each new learning set is generated by n-times randomly (with replication) selecting an example from the original learning set. Some examples may therefore occur more than once, and some examples may not occur in a new learning set (on average, 36.8% of examples). Each newly generated learning set is used as an input to the learning algorithm. Thus we get a series of potentially different hypotheses that are used for predicting the value of a dependent variable by combining all generated hypotheses.

Bagging excels especially when unstable base algorithms with high variance are used, such as decision or regression trees. Bagging is robust, as increasing the number of generated hypotheses does not lead to overfitting.

Boosting. Boosting is a theoretically well-founded (see Section 14.8.3) ensemble learning method. Its basic idea is to weight learning examples according to how difficult they are. It assumes that the base learning algorithm is able to deal with weighted learning examples. If this is not the case, weighted learning examples are simulated by sampling the learning set similarly as in bagging. The only difference is that the probability of selecting an example is not uniform, but proportional to its weight.

Boosting requires several iterations of the learning process. In the first iteration the learning algorithm builds a hypothesis from equally weighted learning examples (each example's weight is equal to 1). A hypothesis predicts the value of a dependent variable (the class label) for each learning example. Afterwards, all the weights are adjusted. For examples with correct predictions, weights are decreased, and for examples with incorrect predictions, weights are increased.

The most frequently used approach for weighting of examples is as follows. Let e be the (normalized) hypothesis' error on a particular learning example. The example's weight is adjusted by multiplication with $e/(1-e)$. Lesser errors therefore yield lesser weights. After all weights have been adjusted, they are normalized so that they sum up to n (for n learning examples).

The following iterations of the learning process therefore focus on difficult learning examples. The process is reiterated until the overall error f becomes sufficiently small or large, the latter meaning that the remaining difficult examples are not solvable. Such (last) hypotheses are rejected as they do not contribute any useful knowledge. Also rejected are hypotheses with overall error f too close to 0, as they tend to overfit the learning data. The remaining hypotheses form an ordered chain.

All the remaining hypotheses are used for final predictions. Each hypothesis' prediction is weighted with its performance (e.g., classification accuracy) on a weighted learning set used for its generation. Accurate hypotheses therefore carry more weight. For voting, a weighting scheme $-\log(f/(1-f))$ is frequently used, with f being a hypothesis error on the corresponding weighted learning set.

Boosting frequently yields better performance than bagging. Contrary to bagging, it can also be used with stable base learning algorithms which have small variance. Sometimes, however, overfitting can occur. In such (rare) cases, the performance of a combined hypothesis is worse than the performance of a single hypothesis.

Random forests. Random forests are intended to improve the predictive accuracy of tree-based learning algorithms. Originally, they were developed exclusively for improving decision trees but can also be used for improving regression trees. The basic idea is to generate a series of decision trees that limit the selection of the best attribute in each node to a relatively small subset of randomly chosen candidate attributes. If the number of attributes is a, a typical number of candidate attributes is $\lfloor \log a \rfloor + 1$. This number can also be 1, meaning a completely random attribute selection in each node of a decision tree. The size of the forest (the number of generated trees) is normally at least 100, but can be considerably higher.

Each decision tree is generated from the whole learning set, and is subsequently used for classification of new examples by the uniform voting principle. Each decision tree gives its vote for the class label to the new example. All votes together form a class probability distribution.

The random forests method is robust as it reduces the variance of tree-based algorithms. Decision trees combined in a random forest achieve the classification accuracy of the state-of-the-art algorithms. The downside of the method is the incomprehensibility of its decisions, as interpreting the combined answer of the set of 100 or more decision trees is rather difficult (the same problem also plagues bagging and boosting).

3.5.4   Transduction in machine learning

Machine learning builds upon *inductive reasoning*, that is learning from particular (learning examples) to general (output hypothesis). On the other hand, in *deductive reasoning* a generated hypothesis is used to predict the value of the dependent variable for each new example. Inducing a hypothesis and using it for deduction is therefore an intermediate step in predicting the value of a dependent variable. In *transductive reasoning*, when solving a given problem, one avoids solving a more general problem as an intermediate step. The basic idea behind this principle is that, in order to solve a more general problem, resources may be wasted or compromises made which would not have been necessary for solving only the problem at hand (e.g., function estimation only on a given point). This common-sense principle reduces a more general

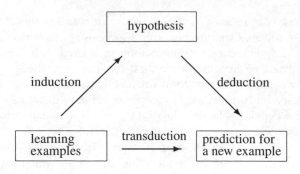

Figure 3.6: Different forms of reasoning in machine learning.

problem of inferring a hypothesis valid on the whole input space (inductive inference) to the problem of estimating the predictions only at given points (see Figure 3.6). An illustrative example for transductive reasoning is lazy learning by the k-nearest neighbors method: the learning algorithm does not generate a hypothesis but only stores learning examples (see Section 10.1.1).

The transduction principle is frequently utilized in a reverse direction by including new (unlabelled) examples into the learning set. As each new example's label (value of a dependent variable) is unknown, an example has to be suitably labelled in order to run a learning algorithm to generate a *transduced* hypothesis. There are several varieties of this approach:

- All possible labellings are exhaustively tried out; afterwards the best labelling (and thus the best hypothesis) is chosen according to some criterion, (e.g., MDL). Obviously, this approach can only be used when the number of labels is finite (e.g., for classification).

- An initial hypothesis is generated from the original learning set. It is used to label new examples; newly labelled examples are included into the training set and a new hypothesis is generated. The process is repeated until there are no significant changes in example labels between two consecutive steps. The final hypothesis determines the labelling of new examples.

- It is sometimes desirable to evaluate the quality of a single prediction instead of the overall quality of a predictor (as described in Section 3.2). A hypothesis is induced from the learning set and used to label a new example. The newly labelled example is included in the learning set, and another, transduced hypothesis is induced. It is used to label the new example with the transduced label. The difference (distance) between induced and transduced labels (or probability distributions, if available) is evaluated as a quality estimation (or reliability of the original prediction). Different distance metrics can be used in classification, and normalized Euclidean distance in regression.

predicted class

$\downarrow$

actual class $\rightarrow$ $\begin{bmatrix} 0 & 1 & 2 \\ 2 & 0 & 3 \\ 2 & 6 & 0 \end{bmatrix}$

Figure 3.7: Sample cost matrix for a three-class problem.

- Transductive reliability estimation (as described above) can also be used for correcting predictions. The direction (sign in regression) and the magnitude of reliability estimation (a distance between induced and transduced predictions) indicate the necessary correction of the prediction.

3.5.5 Cost-sensitive learning

In classification problems it is often necessary to minimize misclassification costs instead of error rates. Most learning algorithms do not account for misclassification costs, although many can be adapted for this purpose.

The cost of misclassifying an example is a function of both the actual (true) class and the predicted class. It can be represented as a *cost matrix* $Cost_{i,j}$ with rows representing actual (true) classes, and columns representing predicted classes (Figure 3.7).

$$Cost_{i,j} = \begin{cases} \geq 0, & \text{for } i \neq j \quad \text{cost of misclassifying an example} \\ & \qquad\qquad \text{from "class } C_i\text{" to "class } C_j\text{"} \\ 0, & \text{for } i = j \quad \text{cost of correct classification} \end{cases} \qquad (3.93)$$

When all misclassification costs are equal, we have a *uniform* cost matrix:

$$Uniform\ cost_{i,j} = \begin{cases} 1, & i \neq j \\ 0, & i = j \end{cases} \qquad (3.94)$$

Cost-sensitive learning is frequently used in imbalanced classification problems where one or more classes are sparsely represented. For example, in a two-class problem, one class might have the prevalence of $P_1 = 0.99$ against $P_2 = 0.01$ for the second one. Most learning algorithms would generate a trivial hypothesis (a *majority classifier*) that would classify all examples into the first class. Frequently, the minority class is actually the subject of analysis, so the majority classifier is not what is desired in this case.

Changing misclassification costs is equivalent to changing weights of examples belonging to different classes. In a two-class problem, a ROC curve can be generated for an arbitrary classifier by varying misclassification costs, thus changing the ratio between specificity and sensitivity. To get a smooth curve, averaged results (e.g., by stratified cross validation) are used for each sensitivity-specificity ratio.

The cost matrix serves as an additional input to the learning algorithm. If an algorithm cannot explicitly account for misclassification costs, several approximate approaches can be used, as described below.

Minimizing conditional risk: The simplest way to account for misclassification costs is to minimize a conditional risk for classification. If, when classifying a new example, the classifier returns a probability distribution $P = \{p_i\}$ for classes $i = 1 \ldots m_0$, an optimal classification is defined so as to minimize the conditional risk:

$$Risk_j = \sum_{i=1}^{m_0} p_i \cdot Cost_{i,j} \tag{3.95}$$

Weighting learning examples: Another simple way to force an algorithm to account for misclassification costs is by forcing an algorithm to use suitably weighted learning examples. Learning examples, belonging to the class whose misclassification is more expensive, get proportionally higher weights. As an algorithm is designed to minimize the error rate (maximize classification accuracy), the larger weights of examples from more expensive classes force the algorithm to minimize the misclassification cost.

Similarly to boosting, this approach assumes that a learning algorithm is able to deal with weighted examples. If this is not the case, weighted examples are emulated by replicating learning examples proportionally to their weights. If for example, in a two-class problem, the misclassification cost (weight) ratio is $1:20$, each example from the second class is replicated 20 times.

Exact weights can be calculated only in two-class problems. For multi-class problems, weights can be set proportionally to expected misclassification costs (3.96). P_i is a prevalence (prior probability) of the class C_i.

$$E[Cost_i] = \frac{1}{1 - P_i} \sum_{j \neq i} P_j Cost_{i,j} \tag{3.96}$$

Relabelling learning examples: To get an optimal classification that minimizes the conditional risk (3.95), an algorithm has to account for it. This can be achieved by relabelling learning examples. For each learning example a class probability distribution $P = \{p_i\}$, $i = 0 \ldots m_0$ is produced, either with the algorithm alone or with other methods (e.g., bagging or boosting). If necessary, the example's class label is altered so as to minimize the conditional risk (Equation 3.95). This method relabels the low-cost examples that lie in the vicinity of the decision frontier for high-cost examples. It is thus better to misclassify some low-cost examples in order to ensure correct classification of high-cost examples. The final classifier is built from the relabelled learning set.

3.5.6   Function imitation

Some difficult problems can be adequately solved only by using rather complex learning algorithms and knowledge representations. The downside of complex methods such as support vector machines, or neural networks, is their untransparency and unintelligibility of their results. In order to improve the comprehensibility, function imitation can be used.

First, the best (complex) algorithm is used to solve a problem and to build a suitable model (a hypothesis). The model is used to label new examples that are produced by randomly generating their attribute values (according to their distribution in the learning set). New examples are generated, labelled and included into the new learning set. Eventually, the learning set grows large enough to use a more transparent learning algorithm (e.g., decision or regression trees) that learns to imitate the original model. Although increasing the number of new examples causes the model complexity (e.g., decision tree size) to increase simultaneously, we expect that the new model will remain more transparent and comprehensible than the original one.

3.5.7   Classifiers for regression and regressors for classification

It is sometimes necessary, or even advantageous, to solve regressional problems with classification algorithms. For this purpose, the values of a dependent (prediction) variable are discretized into a reasonable number of intervals. Each interval represents a discrete class value. Learning examples constructed from values of independent variables and labelled with appropriate interval index form a new classification problem that can be solved by an arbitrary classification learning algorithm. For predicting the value of the original (continuous) dependent variable, the classifier's answers (interval indices) are mapped to continuous values. Since the classifier's answer can be treated as the class probability distribution[3], a probability-weighted average of classes (interval midpoints) can be used for prediction.

Although some information is lost when an independent variable is discretized, this works advantageously in noisy problems. Since discretization partially removes the class noise, this may help the classifier to achieve better results (smaller MSE) than regressional learners.

Sometimes, the reverse process – applying a regressional algorithm to solve a classification problem – is also useful. If the original classes are ordered, or there are only two classes, their indices can be used directly. If not, a classification problem is split into several two-class problems using either of the following methods:

- For each class c, a two class problem is built, consisting of classes c and $\bar{c}$ that is a union of all other classes.

- A binary class hierarchy is built either by a problem expert, or by some clustering methods (Chapter 12). Each node in the hierarchy where two subclasses are joined is treated as a new two-class classification problem.

---

[3]For the rare cases where this is not the case, a probability distribution can be obtained in combination with other methods, e.g. bagging (Section 3.5.3).

- An error-correcting output code scheme is used (see Section 3.5.8).

For use with regressional learning algorithms, the two classes are relabelled with 0 and 1, respectively. Predicted values are mapped back to discrete classes by using a threshold (typically 0.5) for discretization. If the predicted value is larger than the threshold, class 1 is predicted; otherwise class 0 is predicted.

By changing two-class problems into regressional problems, additional flexibility is introduced in the problem space. Since a regressional predictor can predict any value from the $[0, 1]$ interval and not only the values 0 and 1, it may sometimes achieve better classification accuracy than classification learners.

3.5.8   Error-correcting output codes

Multi-class problems can be solved by combining several binary (two-class) classifiers via *error-correcting output codes*. In multi-class problems classes are encoded with fixed-length bit strings (codes) that split the problem into several subproblems by maximizing distances between class codes. For the code length ℓ, the original (multi-class) problem is transformed into ℓ binary (two-class) subproblems. Each of the binary subproblems merges the original classes encoded with 0 in the first class, and those encoded with 1 in the second class.

A sample error-correcting output code for the five-class problem is shown in Table 3.6. The code is represented in a matrix $W_{i,j}$. Each row i corresponds to one class, each column j to one binary classifier. The code splits the original classification problem into 15 two-class subproblems. Each subproblem is solved by using its own classifier. Answers of all 15 classifiers are merged into a bit string. The final classification is produced by finding a row that is most similar to the obtained bit string in terms of bit differences (Hamming distance). For example, a bit string S = 100011011000111 differs from C_1 and C_2 in 7 bits, from C_3 in 3, from C_4 in 11, and from C_5 in 9 bits. The most suitable answer is therefore C_3. If the combined classification is correct, the code has managed to correct three wrong bits (binary classifications).

Class	Classifier														
	1	2	3	4	5	6	7	8	9	10	11	12	13	14	15
C_1	1	1	1	1	1	1	1	1	1	1	1	1	1	1	1
C_2	0	0	0	0	0	0	0	0	1	1	1	1	1	1	1
C_3	0	0	0	0	1	1	1	1	0	0	0	0	1	1	1
C_4	0	0	1	1	0	0	1	1	0	0	1	1	0	0	1
C_5	0	1	0	1	0	1	0	1	0	1	0	1	0	1	0

Table 3.6: Sample error-correcting output code for the five-class problem.

A good error-correcting output code must have the following two properties :

Row resolution: each row must be as different to other rows as possible in order to maximize the number of bits (errors) it is able to correct. In Table 3.6 the minimal (and also the maximal) difference between each pair of rows is 8 bits. This ensures the correction of at most four errors.

Column resolution: each code bit stands for one two-class classification problem. All two-class problems must be uncorrelated; therefore all columns must be different. And, since complementing a column keeps a two-class problem intact (by relabelling the classes we get the original problem), each column must also be different from any of the other columns' complements. The level of correlation between two-class classification problems is minimized by maximizing the difference between the columns (and their complements as well). Columns consisting of all ones or all zeros are not useful because they represent a trivial classification problem. In Table 3.6 each column differs from all other columns and their complements in at least one bit.

The number of useful different columns (excluding the complements and trivial columns) equals to $2^{m_0-1} - 1$ for m_0 classes in the original problem. Error-correcting codes are therefore meaningful only for $m_0 \geq 4$, as for $m_0 = 3$ we get only three useful columns that cannot repair any errors.

For a particular classification a code string S is constructed, $S = \{S_j\}$ where S_j is a class index (0 or 1) given by the j-th classifier. This notion is easily extended to probabilistic classifiers that return a class probability distribution $P_j = \{p_j(0), p_j(1)\}$ by taking probability of a class 1 for S_j ($S_j = P_j(1)$).

A new example is classified in the class corresponding to the row in the error-correcting output code matrix that is most similar to the code string S containing the answers of all two-class classifiers. For probabilistic classifiers the distance between the code string S and a row i in a code matrix $W_{i,j}$ is calculated as follows:

$$D_i(S) = \sum_{j=1}^{k} |S_j - W_{i,j}| \qquad (3.97)$$

or equivalently

$$D_i(S) = \sum_{j=1}^{k} |p_j(1) - W_{i,j}| \qquad (3.98)$$

Thus we do not require to explicitly set a bit (a class index) for each classifier. If this were the case, the answers $P_j(1) = 0.51$ and $P_j(1) = 1.0$ would have been treated equivalently.

It is interesting to compare the approaches for combining predictions of several hypotheses (Section 3.5.1) with the error-correcting output codes. Both approaches try to obtain useful information from as many different classifiers as possible. By the former approach each classifier predicts the same function; the final prediction is obtained by voting or some other methods. By the latter approach each classifier predicts as different a function as possible in order to reduce the level of correlation between classifiers.

3.6   SUMMARY AND FURTHER READING

Bigotry tries to keep the truth safe in its hand with a grip that kills it.

— *Rabindranath Tagore*

- Every kind of machine learning results in some knowledge extracted from available data. In machine learning, knowledge is often represented as a model (hypothesis, theory) of data.

- There exist two fundamentally different families of learning algorithms: batch and incremental. In batch learning algorithms, all learning data is supposed to be available from the start, so the generated model always reflects all the available data. In incremental (on-line) algorithms, data arrives sequentially, and the generated model is modified after each received datum.

- Minimum description length (MDL) is an important principle in machine learning. It can be used for design and guidance of learning methods. The MDL principle determines a trade-off between complexity and accuracy of the model. The total hypothesis' error can be decomposed into an error originating from the learning algorithm (bias) and an error originating from the learning data (variance).

- A crucial part of most machine learning is the probability estimation. The simplest method – relative frequency – is only rarely appropriate because of the relatively small numbers of corresponding data. It is often beneficial to use advanced methods, such as Laplace's law of succession or m-estimate.

- Performance of a learning algorithm is often assessed by utilizing a separate testing set. When the number of available examples is relatively low, various sampling techniques, such as cross validation and bootstrap methods are used.

- In classification problems, most performance measures are based on the matrix of (mis)classifications (confusion matrix). Besides the simple classification accuracy, advanced and probability-based measures such as Brier score, information score or margin can be used. They often provide better performance assessment.

- Two-class problems are among the most common, and therefore for them several specially developed performance measures exist, such as recall and precision, sensitivity and specificity, and ROC curves.

- In regression problems, performance measures are based on a magnitude of difference between the actual and the predicted value. Commonly used measures are mean squared error, mean absolute error, and correlation coefficient.

- There are several pitfalls to avoid when comparing performances of machine learning methods. Blind application of statistical tests is therefore not recommended. Different techniques should be used for comparing two methods on a single problem, two methods on several problems, and several methods on several problems. In spite of their lower strength, non-parametric statistical tests are preferred to parametric ones, as they utilize fewer underlying assumptions.

- Machine learning methods are frequently combined in order to obtain a better-performing method. Popular approaches include different kinds of voting schemes, stacking, bagging, boosting, and random forests.

Many basic principles used in machine learning were known in other scientific areas far before the advent of computers. For example, the Occam's razor principle and the principle of multiple explanation have their respective origins in medieval and classical Greek philosophy.

The famous Greek philosopher Epicurus (341 – 270 BC) was the first to propose what later became known as the *principle of multiple explanations*: "If more than one theory is consistent with the observations, keep all theories". As another famous Greek philosopher and poet Lucretius (94 – 51 BC), one of the primary sources for Epicurean doctrines, vividly states: "There are also some things for which it is not enough to state a single cause, but several, of which one, however, is the case. Just as if you were to see the lifeless corpse of a man lying far away, it would be fitting to state all the causes of death in order that the single cause of this death may be stated. For you would not be able to establish conclusively that he died by the sword or of cold or of illness or perhaps by poison, but we know that there is something of this kind that happened to him."

The words of the medieval English philosopher and Franciscan monk William of Ockham (1285-1349) "pluralitas non est ponenda sine neccesitate" or "plurality should not be posited without necessity" have long since become known as Occam's razor. It was a common principle in medieval philosophy and was not originated by Ockham himself, but because of his frequent usage of the principle, his name has become indelibly attached to it.

In more recent times, Solomonoff (1964, 1978) has unified the seemingly opposing Occam's razor principle and Epicurus' principle of multiple explanations to one elegant, formal, universal theory of inductive inference, which initiated the field of algorithmic information theory. He was also the first to put forward the general idea to use compressed data for prediction. Rissanen (1978, 1993), inspired by Solomonoff's idea of ultimate effective compression of data, formulated the minimum description length (MDL) idea. Following his work, Li and Vitanyi (1993) have formulated the ideal MDL.

Machine learning has been heavily influenced by ideas that were exploited in statistics, for which (Chase and Bown, 1986) is a good introductory textbook. Learning as modeling is actually an approach taken from statistical data analysis, although in machine learning, restrictions on model types are considerably more relaxed. However, it should be noted that both in statistics and machine learning the use of the word *model* is intuitively just the opposite of that in formal logic (Lloyd, 1984).

Similarly, probability estimation, especially from small datasets, was studied in statistics for several centuries. It has been shown that – especially for very small datasets – relative frequencies are too optimistic, and more conservative approaches should be used. Niblett and Bratko (1986) thoroughly analyzed the use of Laplace's law of succession in machine learning and extended it (from the original form applicable only to two-class problems) to handle multi-class problems as well. Cestnik (1990); Cestnik and Bratko (1991) further extended their approach to parameterized probability estimation by introducing the m-estimate, which was independently derived also by Smyth and Goodman (1990).

For measuring the model performance, several evaluation measures have been invented in scientific areas that have historically dealt with collections of data, e.g. in sociology, psychology, medicine, biology, information retrieval. Many have been adopted for use in machine learning and often they are considered roughly equivalent to each other. Lately, however, it has been shown that alternative, and often better measures can be invented, such as the Brier score (Breiman et al., 1984) and the information score (Kononenko and Bratko, 1991), as well as measures based on ROC curve analysis (Egan, 1975; Provost et al., 1998; Provost and Fawcett, 2001).

In regressional problems, there is significantly less confusion about performance measures. They are mostly variations of error means such as the mean squared error, the mean absolute error, and the relative mean squared error (Breiman et al., 1984).

For performance evaluation on small datasets, cross-validation and stratified cross validation are used. Diaconis and Efron (1983) have shown that for really small datasets bootstrapping works better than any form of cross-validation (including the leave-one-out testing).

When testing the significance of performance differences between machine learning algorithms, we come to more shaky ground. Historically, well known statistical tests have been used for this purpose. It has been shown that due to certain properties of experimental results obtained from machine learning algorithms (results should not be treated as independent) it is improper to use basic tests for this purpose. Several possible solutions have been proposed. Salzberg (1997) proposes using the Bonferroni correction; this however seriously diminishes the power of an underlying test. Other authors have proposed specialized tests: Dieterich (1998) has proposed McNemar's test, Nadeau and Bengio (2003) and Bouckaert and Frank (2004) have proposed a corrected t-test. Demšar (2006) presents a comprehensive overview of this topic. He advocates the use of non-parametric tests, and especially the improved Friedman test (Iman and Davenport, 1980).

For combining the answers of several classifiers, the combined answer is either the "best" single answer, or some kind of weighted vote (Smyth and Goodman, 1990; Kononenko and Kovačič, 1992; Woods et al., 1997; Giacinto and Roli, 2001). Advanced general methods for combination of classifiers include boosting (Schapire, 1990), bagging (Breiman, 1996), and random forests (Breiman, 2001). Dietterich and Bakiri (1995) have combined several binary classifiers via error-correcting output codes in order to reliably solve multi-class problems.

Vapnik (1995, 1998), has made popular the transductive approach, that in order to solve a particular problem, one should avoid solving a more general problem as an intermediate step. It has been further refined and applied by Gammerman et al. (1998), Vovk (2002), Joachims (1999), Kukar and Kononenko (2002), Kukar (2003, 2006) and

Bosnić et al. (2003); Bosnić and Kononenko (2005).

Pazzani et al. (1994) as well as Turney (1995) have provided the motivation for treating relevant problems as cost sensitive and thoroughly analyzed the problems of cost sensitive machine learning. Kubat and Matwin (1997) have researched similar methods for imbalanced problems. Several authors have proposed modifications of existing algorithms in order to make them cost sensitive (Kukar and Kononenko, 1998). Domingos (1999) has proposed a general method for making the algorithms cost-sensitive; it is, however, rather complicated and time-consuming. There exists a comprehensive on-line library of resources devoted to cost sensitive learning (`bibliographies.apperceptual.com/cost-sensitive.html`), created and maintained by Peter Turney.

Chapter 4

Knowledge Representation

Currently we are unable to introduce to the information theory any element that would tell us about the value of information for the human. This exclusion of the human factor is a serious limitation that enables one to treat the information as a measurable quantity.

— *Mortimer Taube*

In the usual supervised machine learning, the learning algorithm receives as input the background knowledge and the learning data. It then searches its hypothesis space and returns the final hypothesis as a result. It is therefore necessary to efficiently represent the background knowledge, the input data and the hypothesis space in order to allow for efficient usage and generation of new knowledge. During the learning process some learning algorithms produce dynamic knowledge that is subsequently used for solving new problems, and this new knowledge must be efficiently represented as well. While searching the hypothesis space, an algorithm uses *operators* for moving through the search space, i.e., for modifying the current hypothesis (or the set of current hypotheses).

Different kinds of knowledge are represented in different ways. Most frequently, the following types of knowledge representation are used:

- propositional calculus,

- first-order predicate calculus,

- discriminant and regression functions, and

- probability distributions.

In the following sections each of the above knowledge representation types is discussed in more detail.

4.1 PROPOSITIONAL CALCULUS

Syntactic analysis is impossible without an agreement about the meaning of the sentence.

— *Mortimer Taube*

In mathematical logic, propositional (sentential) calculus is a formal deduction system whose atomic formulae are propositional variables. Propositional calculus is frequently used for representation of:

- learning examples in classification and regression problems

- hypotheses in symbolic learning of classification and regression rules.

4.1.1 Representation with attributes

In classification and regression problems the representation with attributes is by far the most common representation. An attribute (sometimes also called a feature) is a variable with a specified domain (a set of allowed values). It represents some property of an example. Each learning example is described with a vector of attributes. Attributes can be discrete (nominal or ordinal) or continuous, and their number (a) is given in advance. Representation with attributes is defined by:

- a set of attributes: $\mathcal{A} = \{A_0, \ldots A_a\}$;

- for each discrete attribute A_i: a set of allowable values $\mathcal{V}_i = \{V_1, \ldots, V_{m_i}\}$;

- for each continuous attribute A_i: an interval of allowable values $\mathcal{V}_i = [Min_i, Max_i]$;

- the dependent (target) variable is by definition represented with A_0:

  - in classification problems A_0 is a discrete attribute (class C with values $\{C_1, \ldots, C_{m_0}\}$;

  - in regression problems A_0 is a continuous attribute.

- each example is described with an attribute vector $t_l = \langle v_{0,l}, v_{1,l}, \ldots, v_{a,l} \rangle$; its value of the dependent variable is given by $c_l = v_{0,l}$;

- the set of learning examples is a set of attribute vectors $\mathcal{T} = \{t_1, \ldots t_n\}$.

4.1.2 Attribute properties and dependencies

Attributes have various properties important for their usage in machine learning and data mining:

Noisy attribute: is almost every attribute in real data. Some attribute values may be wrong because of measurement or typographical errors.

Incomplete attribute: is an attribute where for some examples some attribute values are missing. Learning algorithms should be able to handle the missing values.

Besides the properties of individual attributes, dependencies between attributes (independent variables) and the dependent variable are also important:

Random attribute: is an attribute unrelated to the dependent variable and is best ignored because it may disturb the target concept.

Redundant attribute: is an attribute whose information content is completely contained in another attribute. A trivial random attribute is a copy of another attribute. Such attributes are also best ignored.

Correlated attribute: is an attribute whose information contents are partially contained in another attribute or a set of attributes. The more correlated the attributes are, the more interdependent they are, and the more redundance we get.

Strongly interdependent attributes with respect to the dependent variable:
When strong interdependence with respect to the dependent variable exists among attributes, the target function is difficult to determine, since each attribute's importance is detectable only in the context of other attributes. In classification problems (discrete target functions) the strongest interdependence with respect to the class is a *parity function*. Its simplest manifestation is a binary XOR function; its negation (equivalence) is equally difficult. We have two binary attributes, A_1 and A_2, and a binary class:

		XOR	equivalence
A_1	A_2	$A_1 \neq A_2$	$A_1 = A_2$
0	0	0	1
0	1	1	0
1	0	1	0
1	0	0	1

Each attribute by itself conveys absolutely no information about the class. This causes troubles for most machine learning algorithms. The parity problem is a generalization of XOR function to more than two attributes. The more attributes participate in the parity function, the more difficult the problem is. However, there exist algorithms (such as ReliefF, described in more detail in Section 6.1) that can efficiently cope with difficulties of this kind.

How surprising the dependencies between the attributes and the class can be is best shown by an example, known as the *Simpson paradox*. Let A and B be two different treatments. Each treatment was used to treat a group of 100 patients. The results of the treatments were as follows:

Treatment	Successful	All
A	50	100
B	40	100

Treatment A is seemingly better than the treatment B. However, when looking at the attribute *Age* (Table 4.1) the situation is turned completely upside down. Both in the group of the younger patients and in the group of the older patients treatment B is better than treatment A. If the relevant data (in our case age) is not accounted for in data analysis, the results by themselves may lead to wrong conclusions.

	Treatment		
Age	A	B	Total
Older	2/10	30/90	32/100
Younger	48/90	10/10	58/100
Total	50/100	40/100	90/200

Table 4.1: Success of two treatments with respect to the patient age (number of successfully treated/number of all treated).

4.1.3 Classification, regression and association rules

Classification and regression rules are usually made of two parts: a conditional part (antecedent) and an unconditional part (consequent). Such rules are often called *decision rules*. Usually, the antecedent is a conjunction of propositions T_i, and the consequent includes the proposition T_0.

$$T_{i_1} \wedge T_{i_2} \wedge \ldots \wedge T_{i_l} \Rightarrow T_0 \tag{4.1}$$

If the attribute A_i is discrete, the propositions are formed like $T_i = (A_i \in \mathcal{V}_i')$, where $\mathcal{V}_i'$ is a subset of allowed values for A_i: $\mathcal{V}_i' \subset \mathcal{V}_i$. If the attribute A_i is continuous, the propositions are formed like $T_i = (A_i \in \mathcal{V}_i')$, where $\mathcal{V}_i'$ is a sub-interval of the interval of the allowed values for the attribute A_i: $\mathcal{V}_i' = [Min_i', Max_i']$, $Min_i' \geq Min_i$, $Max_i' \leq Max_i$. In regression problems, the interval in the consequential proposition is sometimes reduced to a single point $Min_0' = Max_0'$. In classification problems, the consequential proposition may include only one value: $|\mathcal{V}_0'| = 1$.

Rule representation can be generalized by allowing other logical operators in the antecedent (instead of restricting them to conjunction). They may include disjunction, negation, equivalence, and others. Such a generalization considerably enlarges the hypothesis space, and thus heavily increases the complexity of the learning algorithm.

An important generalization of the consequential proposition is such that the value of dependent variable is not exactly determined. In classification problems, class probability distributions are used for this purpose: $\{P(C_j), j = 1 \ldots m_0\}$. In regression problems, inexact solutions can be represented with confidence intervals by requiring a strict inequality $Min_0' < Max_0'$, or with probability distribution densities. This approach is also useful in classification when dealing with learning examples where the class cannot always be reliably determined. In such cases a probability distribution provides more information than labelling an example with the most probable class. Considering the fact that the dependent variable is actually just another attribute, we can, if any attribute's value is not known for sure, represent it with a probability distribution (for discrete attributes), or with a conditional probability density distribution (for continuous attributes).

Association rules are a generalization of classification rules to problems where not only the target variable (class), but also the associations between attributes are of interest. The consequential part of the rule therefore does not include the proposition about the target variable T_0, but an arbitrary conjunction of propositions:

$$T_{i_1} \wedge T_{i_2} \wedge \ldots \wedge T_{i_l} \Rightarrow T_{j_1} \wedge T_{j_2} \wedge \ldots \wedge T_{j_k}$$

In practice, $k > 2$ is only rarely used.

4.1.4   Generality of rules

For the purpose of defining the concept of generality, we introduce two relations between rules: "more general" $\prec$ and "less general" or "more specific" $\succ$. We say that the rule p_1 is more general than the rule p_2 if p_2 can be derived ($\models$) from p_1:

$$p_1 \prec p_2 \Leftrightarrow p_1 \models p_2$$

For example, the following holds

$$(a \Rightarrow c) \prec (a \wedge b \Rightarrow c) \tag{4.2}$$

since by the definition of implication ($\Rightarrow$) it holds that

$$(\neg a \vee c) \models (\neg a \vee \neg b \vee c) \tag{4.3}$$

However, among the following pairs of rules, neither the relation "more general" nor the relation "more specific" can be defined:

$a \Rightarrow c$ and $b \Rightarrow c$
$a \wedge b \Rightarrow c$ and $a \wedge d \Rightarrow c$
$a \Rightarrow c_1$ and $a \wedge b \Rightarrow c_2$

Thus the relation $\prec$ only partially orders the set of rules. In terms of rule generality, we are interested only in the input space covered by the rule and have no interest in the consequent. Therefore, we can compare only the conditionals part (antecedents) of the rules:

$$(P \Rightarrow \_) \prec (P' \Rightarrow \_) \Leftrightarrow P' \models P \tag{4.4}$$

In such a case we say that the condition P *covers* the condition P'. Obviously,

$$(a \Rightarrow \_) \prec (a \wedge b \Rightarrow \_) \tag{4.5}$$

since it holds that

$$a \wedge b \models a \tag{4.6}$$

Learning examples can be viewed as a very specific rule that consists of as many propositions in the antecedent, as is the number of attributes. It is said that the rule *covers* the learning example if the learning example satisfies the antecedent of the rule. The rule *correctly covers* the learning example if the rule for the given example correctly predicts the value of the independent variable.

4.1.5   Operations on rules

Two basic operators for learning symbolic rules are generalization and its reverse, specialization. The antecedent of a rule, formed as a conjunction of propositions, can be *generalized* in several ways:

- one or more propositions are omitted from the conjunction in the antecedent;

- in the proposition that checks for the membership of a discrete attribute's value to a subset of allowed values, the subset is expanded by including one or more additional attribute values;

- in the proposition that checks for the membership of a continuous attribute's value to a given interval, the interval is expanded by increasing the upper bound or by decreasing the lower bound.

In a relaxed rule structure where, besides conjunction, other operators are allowed (negation, disjunction), there are additional possibilities for generalization (e.g., replacing conjunction with disjunction, disjunctive inclusion of additional propositions).

The antecedent of a conjunctive rule can be *specialized* by using the reverse operators of those used for generalization:

- one or more propositions are conjunctively appended to the antecedent;

- in the proposition that checks for the membership of a discrete attribute's value to a subset of allowed values, the subset is reduced by excluding one or more attribute values from the subset;

- in the proposition that checks for the membership of a continuous attribute's value to a given interval, the interval is shrunk by decreasing its upper bound or by increasing its lower bound.

When the antecedent part of a rule is altered, the consequent part changes according to the new coverage of learning examples. In classification problems, the probability distribution of classes is changed; in regression problems, the confidence interval is changed.

4.1.6   Hypothesis space

In symbolic rule learning the hypothesis space $\mathcal{H}$ is defined as the power set of all possible rules. The following properties of hypotheses are important:

Consistency: a hypothesis H is *consistent* if for each rule $r \in H$ it holds that it correctly predicts the class value for all learning examples covered by the antecedent of the rule r.

Completeness: a hypothesis H is *complete* if every learning example is covered by at least one rule $r \in H$

4.1.7   Decision and regression trees

A *decision tree* is a special case of a set of decision rules. A decision tree (see Figures 4.1, 9.1, and 9.1) consists of internal nodes – corresponding to attributes, edges – corresponding to subsets of attribute values, and terminal nodes (leaves) – corresponding to class labels. Each path starting in a tree root (topmost node) and ending in a tree leaf corresponds to a decision rule. The conditions (pairs of attribute names and corresponding sets of attribute values) evaluated in each internal node are conjunctively connected. Each decision tree can readily be converted to as many rules as there are leaves in the tree. However, not every set of decision rules can be converted to a decision tree. If leaf labels are continuous, such a tree is called a *regression tree*.

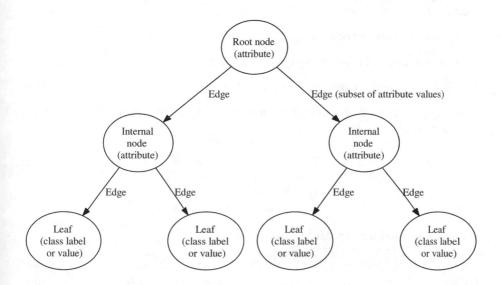

Figure 4.1: A schematic representation of a decision or regression tree.

Knowledge representation with decision or regression trees can be generalized by evaluating in each node an arbitrary function of several attributes instead of a single attribute. For example, in regression trees terminal nodes (leaves) often consist of linear functions of subsets of attributes. Such (polythetic) trees offer more flexible knowledge representation than the usual (monothetic) trees, unfortunately often at the cost of comprehensibility and transparency.

If each internal node has at most two successors, such a tree is called a *binary tree*. Every decision or regression tree can be converted to a binary tree.

4.2 *FIRST ORDER PREDICATE CALCULUS

The only benefit of logic is that it liberates the human from logic and directs him or her towards faith which leads to the holy understanding.

— Mikhail Naimy

In mathematical logic, the predicate calculus is a formal system used to describe mathematical theories. The predicate calculus is an extension of the propositional calculus, which is inadequate for describing more complex mathematical structures. Grammatically speaking, the predicate calculus adds a predicate-subject structure and quantifiers on top of the existing propositional calculus. A subject is a name for a member of a given group (set) of individuals, and a predicate is a relation on this group.

As opposed to the propositional calculus, the first order predicate calculus can be used for describing objects (examples) as well as:

- relations between objects

- universally and existentially quantified variables.

The first order predicate calculus therefore allows for:

- more compact description of learning examples and hypotheses. For example, a set of rules

$$
\begin{aligned}
A_1 = 1 \ \wedge \ A_2 = 1 &\ \Rightarrow \ A_0 = 1 \\
A_1 = 1 \ \wedge \ A_2 = 0 &\ \Rightarrow \ A_0 = 0 \\
A_1 = 0 \ \wedge \ A_2 = 1 &\ \Rightarrow \ A_0 = 0 \\
A_1 = 0 \ \wedge \ A_2 = 0 &\ \Rightarrow \ A_0 = 1
\end{aligned}
\tag{4.7}
$$

  can be rewritten in predicate calculus as

$$
A_0 \Leftrightarrow (A_1 = A_2)
\tag{4.8}
$$

- description of recursive rules of potentially infinite length. The first order predicate calculus can therefore describe hypotheses that cannot be described in the propositional calculus. For example, a first order hypothesis

$$
\begin{aligned}
f(0) &= 1 \\
f(X) &= X \cdot f(X - 1)
\end{aligned}
\tag{4.9}
$$

  cannot be described in the propositional calculus.

In machine learning and data mining only a subset of the first order predicate calculus is used, because of its reduced algorithmic complexity. Usually, the representation is limited to Horn clauses including negated literals. Such clauses are equivalent to clauses in the *prolog* programming language. A research field in machine learning that deals with learning theories in a subset of the first order predicate calculus is called *inductive logic programming* (ILP).

4.2.1 Prolog programming language

Prolog stands short for *programming in logic*. Prolog is a programming language considerably different from usual procedural languages. Prolog programmer uses a natural language description of the problem and specifies *what* needs to be done, instead of developing an algorithm that specifies *how* to do it. Contrary to programming in procedural languages, prolog programming is about translating the problem description (what has to be done) from natural language to a formal definition. A prolog program therefore defines the problem to be solved, but does not specify *how* to solve it. This task is left to the prolog interpreter.

Prolog language is made solely of a subset of first order predicate logic, also called Horn clauses with negated literals. Horn clauses are of the form:

```
If condition 1 and condition 2 and ... condition N hold,
then the conclusion holds.
```

The above statement is rewritten in prolog as follows:

```
conclusion :-
    condition1,
    condition2,
    ...
    conditionN.
```

Such a statement is called a prolog *rule*. Its conclusion (consequent) is called a *head*, and its conditional part (antecedent) is called a *body*. A *fact* is a special case of a rule that has an empty body ($N = 0$). Rules and facts describe relations between objects that appear in a prolog program.

Prolog is an interactive language, aiming at communication with the user. A user establishes a dialogue with the prolog interpreter by creating a list of prolog clauses (both rules and facts) representing a program. After that, the interpreter can be queried about the truth of certain statements. If they can be inferred from the given program by the prolog interpreter, they are confirmed to be true. Programming in prolog is therefore based upon describing relations between objects, and not describing algorithms which would specify how the tasks should be performed. The execution of a prolog programme is actually a deduction of statements in a query given the list of facts and rules in a prolog program.

Prolog programming

A classical example of prolog programming are family relations:

```
child(tea,lily).
child(leo,lily).
child(lily,ana).

parent(X,Y) :- child(Y,X).
```

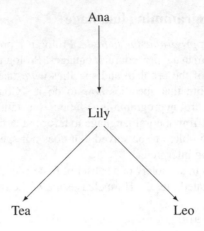

Figure 4.2: The family relations tree.

Relations from the above program are depicted in Figure 4.2. Our prolog program consists of four clauses: three facts and one rule. The facts state that Tea and Leo are Lily's children and that Lily is Ana's child. The rule says that somebody (X) is someone's (Y's) parent, if someone (Y) is somebody's (X's) child. Because of prolog syntax requirements, personal names are written in small letters, and variables in capital letters (X and Y). Since each name corresponds to exactly one person (prolog object), personal names are *constants*. On the other hand, *variables* can represent any object (person) for whom the programmed relation is valid. Variables are *universally quantified* in the head, and therefore *existentially quantified* in the body (conditional part) of the clause.

When the prolog interpreter is run, it normally prompts with

```
?-
```

and waits for commands. The first command is to read commands from the file `example`, where our family relations program is stored:

```
?- consult('example').
```

as soon as the prolog interpreter finishes reading clauses from the file, we can place questions (say, "Is Lily Ana's child?", and similar).

```
?- child(lily,ana).
yes
?- child(lily,leo).
no
```

```
?- child(X,ana).
X = lily
yes
?- child(tea,X).
X = lily
yes
?- child(X,Y).
X = tea
Y = lily;
X = leo
Y = lily;
X = lily
Y = ana;
no
?- parent(X,lily).
X = ana
```

To each question, prolog answers `yes` or `no`, and also explains what values the variables should have for a positive answer (so that the relation holds). Prolog execution is actually proving under what conditions (if any) some relation holds. Our last question is actually a request to prolog interpreter to prove the statement that X is Lily's parent. The prolog interpreter answers that the statement is true when X = `ana`, that is, that Ana is Lily's parent.

4.2.2   Inductive logic programming

In *inductive logic programming* (ILP) the task of the learning algorithm is to induce, given the background knowledge B, a set of positive learning examples E^+ and a set of negative examples E^-, as simple a target relation (hypothesis) H as possible, covering all positive learning examples $e \in E^+$ and no negative example $e \in E^-$.

$$\forall e \in E^+ : B \wedge H \models e \qquad (4.10)$$

$$\forall e \in E^- : B \wedge H \not\models e \qquad (4.11)$$

Learning examples are presented as a set of facts. The set of positive learning examples E^+ consists of m-tuples that are elements of the target relation of arity m. The set of negative learning examples E^- consists of m-tuples that are not elements of the target relation.

Background knowledge is a set of relations that can be used by the learning algorithm for inferring a definition of the target relation. In background knowledge, a relation is given either *extensionally*, as a set of facts not including any variables, or *intensionally*, as an ordered set of prolog clauses.

A hypothesis space $\mathcal{H}$ is a set of all possible definitions (possible prolog programs) of the target relation. The concepts of hypothesis completeness and consistency, as well as relations more and less general ($\prec$ and $\succ$) are defined exactly the same as for the propositional calculus.

Let us illustrate ILP by an example. Let the target relation be
predecessor(X, Y). A set of positive learning examples E^+ consists of the
following facts:

```
predecessor(akel, andrej).
predecessor(andrej, boris).
predecessor(boris, miha).
predecessor(akel, boris).
predecessor(akel, miha).
predecessor(andrej, miha).
```

A set of negative learning examples E^- consists of the following facts:

```
predecessor(akel, akel).
predecessor(andrej, akel).
predecessor(boris, andrej).
predecessor(boris, akel).
predecessor(miha, boris).
predecessor(miha, akel).
```

The given background knowledge B consists of the relation $parent(X, Y)$, here
presented extensionally:

```
parent(akel, andrej).
parent(andrej, boris).
parent(boris, miha).
```

An ILP learning algorithm can use the given learning examples and background
knowledge to infer a correct definition of the target relation:

```
predecessor(X, Y) :-
    parent(X, Y).
predecessor(X, Y) :-
    parent(X, Z),
    predecessor(Z, Y).
```

4.2.3   Operations on predicates

The first order predicate calculus uses the same basic operations for transforming the
hypothesis space (generalization and specialization) as the propositional calculus. A
rule in the first-order predicate calculus is generalized with the following operations in
the body (antecedent) of the rule:

- one or more literals are omitted from the body of the rule,

- one or more constants are changed to (existentially quantified) variables,

- if the same variable can be found in several literals it is renamed in one or more appearances.

A *literal* is either an elementary proposition or its negation. These generalizations take into account that all variables in a rule are universally quantified (meaning that the variables in the body of the rule are actually existentially quantified – by the definition of implication). For example, let us consider relations `lover(X)` and `loves(X,Y)`. Since it holds

$$\forall X : lover(X) \models lover(peter) \models \exists X : lover(X) \tag{4.12}$$

therefore it also holds

$$(\forall X : lover(X)) \prec lover(peter) \prec (\exists X : lover(X)). \tag{4.13}$$

Since, on the other hand

$$\begin{array}{lll} (\forall X, \forall Y : lover(X) & \leftarrow & loves(X,Y)) \\ (\forall X : lover(X) & \leftarrow & \exists Y : loves(X,Y)) \end{array} \equiv \tag{4.14}$$

therefore it holds

$$\begin{array}{lll} (\forall X : lover(X) & \leftarrow & \exists Y : loves(X,Y)) & \models \\ (\forall X : lover(X) & \leftarrow & loves(X,judy)) & \models \\ (\forall X : lover(X) & \leftarrow & \forall Y : loves(X,Y)) \end{array} \tag{4.15}$$

and

$$\begin{array}{lll} (\forall X : lover(X) & \leftarrow & \exists Y : loves(X,Y)) & \prec \\ (\forall X : lover(X) & \leftarrow & loves(X,judy)) & \prec \\ (\forall X : lover(X) & \leftarrow & \forall Y : loves(X,Y)). \end{array} \tag{4.16}$$

A rule in the first-order predicate calculus is specialized with reverse operations in the body (antecedent) of a rule:

- one or more literals are appended to the body of the rule,

- one or more variables are changed to constants,

- if several different variables can be found in the body, some of them are renamed using the names of other existing variables.

Two forms of generalization frequently used in ILP are *least general generalization* and *inverse resolution*.

Least general generalization or shorter *lgg* is used to infer a literal t in the body of the clause. A new literal must be *just enough* specific to be more specific than two given literals t_1 and t_2:

$$t \succ t_1 \text{ and } t \succ t_2 \tag{4.17}$$

This of course means that the clause containing the literal t in the body is more general than the two clauses that instead of t contain literals t_1 and t_2.

$$lgg(t_1, t_2) = t \tag{4.18}$$

Least general generalization of the two literals in the body of the rule is defined with the following four rules (V is a newly introduced variable):

1. $lgg(t, t) = t$
2. $lgg(f(s_1, ..., s_n), f(t_1, ..., t_n)) = f(lgg(s_1, t_1), ..., lgg(s_n, t_n))$
3. $lgg(f(s_1, ..., s_m), g(t_1, ..., t_n)) = V$
4. $lgg(V, t) = V$

All newly introduced variables (V) are existentially quantified.

Inverse resolution uses the inverse substitution, similarly to the way resolution uses the substitution. How resolution works is best illustrated with an example. Given a clause

```
mother(X,Y)  :- female(X), parent(X,Y).
```

and facts

```
female(mary).
parent(mary,tim).
```

resolution may infer from the clause and from the first fact by substitution $\{X/mary\}$ the following intermediate clause:

```
mother(mary,Y)  :- parent(mary,Y).
```

The next resolution step uses the substitution $\{Y/tim\}$ together with the intermediate clause and the second fact to infer the following fact:

```
mother(mary,tim).
```

As a contrast, inverse resolution may start with a positive learning example

```
mother(mary,tim).
```

using the fact

```
parent(mary,tim).
```

from the background knowledge it may infer the clause without any substitution

```
mother(mary,tim) :- parent(mary,tim).
```

By using inverse substitution $\{\mathtt{tim/Y}\}$ we obtain the intermediate clause

```
mother(mary,Y) :- parent(mary,Y).
```

The next inverse resolution step may use the intermediate clause and the fact

```
female(mary).
```

to infer (without any substitution) the clause

```
mother(mary,Y) :- parent(mary,Y), female(mary).
```

or by using inverse substitution $\{\mathtt{mary/X}\}$ the final clause

```
mother(X,Y) :- parent(X,Y), female(X).
```

4.3 DISCRIMINANT AND REGRESSION FUNCTIONS

That which we call a rose by any other name would smell as sweet.
— *William Shakespeare*

Discriminant functions are used for solving classification problems by implicitly describing boundary surfaces between separate classes (values of the independent variable) in a-dimensional space, where a is the number of attributes. Let $V = \langle v_1, \ldots, v_a \rangle$ be a vector of attribute values for all attributes $A_1, \ldots, A_a$. For each class C_k, $k = 1 \ldots m_0$, a separate discriminant function $g_k(V) = g_k(v_1, \ldots, v_a)$ with a arguments is required. It maps each example from a-dimensional space to a real number. A boundary surface between classes C_i and C_k is defined with

$$g_i(V) - g_k(V) = 0 \qquad (4.19)$$

Discriminant functions therefore define $m_0(m_0 - 1)/2$ boundary surfaces between all different pairs of classes. The task of the learning algorithm is to find functions g_k, $k = 1 \ldots m_0$, as simple as possible, so that for each learning example

$$\begin{aligned} t_j &= \langle c_j, v_{1,j}, \ldots, v_{a,j} \rangle \\ j &= 1 \ldots n \end{aligned} \qquad (4.20)$$

it holds that the function value corresponding to the correct class of this example $c_j = C_i$ is greater or equal to function values for all other classes $C_k, k = 1 \ldots m_0, k \neq i$:

$$g_i(v_{1,j}, \ldots, v_{a,j}) > g_k(v_{1,j}, \ldots, v_{a,j}) \qquad (4.21)$$

Regression functions are used for solving regression problems by mapping an example description to an approximation of value v_0 of the continuous target variable A_0:

$$g(v_1, ..., v_a) = v_0'$$ (4.22)

By definition, the value v_0' should be such that $v_0' \approx v_0$. A single regression function defines a regression hypersurface in $(a + 1)$-dimensional hyperspace. The task of the learning algorithm is to derive function g, as simple as possible, that approximates the target values, as precisely as possible.

If symbolic rules are not involved in any part of the learning process, it is – by definition of discriminant and regression functions – normally assumed that all attributes are continuous. Under this assumption, binary (two-valued) discrete attributes are acceptable, however multi-valued discrete attributes are not, unless their values can be ordered in a meaningful way. If this is not the case, each value of a discrete attribute is replaced by a new binary attribute.

In practice, most frequently used discriminant and regression functions are

- linear functions,

- squared functions,

- Φ functions,

- neural networks.

4.3.1   Linear functions

Linear functions form a linear combination of attribute values

$$g(V) = w_1 v_1 + w_2 v_2 + ... + w_a v_a + w_{a+1}$$ (4.23)

Linear discriminant functions therefore define boundary hyperplanes

$$G_{ij}(V) = g_i(V) - g_j(V) = 0$$ (4.24)

so that

$$(w_{i,1} - w_{j,1})v_1 + ... + (w_{i,a} - w_{j,a})v_a + (w_{i,a+1} - w_{j,a+1}) = 0$$ (4.25)

If, in a classification problem, for a given set of learning examples there exists a consistent set of boundary hyperplanes, we say that the classes are *linearly separable*. The task of the learning algorithm is to determine, for each class c_k, a vector of weights

$$W_k = \langle w_{k,1}, ..., w_{k,a+1} \rangle$$ (4.26)

When solving regression problems, a linear regression function defines a regression plane in $(a + 1)$-dimensional hyperspace. Regression problems that can be adequately solved with linear regression functions are called *linear problems*.

4.3.2   Square and Φ functions

Square functions are of the form

$$g(V) = \sum_{j=1}^{a} w_{jj} v_j^2 + \sum_{j=1}^{a-1} \sum_{k=j+1}^{a} w_{jk} v_j v_k + \sum_{j=1}^{a} w_j v_j + w_{a+1} \quad (4.27)$$

Each square (discriminant or regression) function has $(a+1)(a+2)/2$ weights to be determined by the learning algorithm.

Φ functions are a generalization of linear and square functions to arbitrary functions that can be expressed as a linear combination of parameters calculated from the original a attributes:

$$\Phi(V) = w_1 f_1(V) + w_2 f_2(V) + ... + w_M f_M(V) + w_{M+1} \quad (4.28)$$

The more complex functions are used, the larger the number (M) of parameters is, and the more difficult the learning process becomes. By increasing the number of parameters, we obtain complex functions that are prone to overfitting learning examples, and are therefore not useful for predicting target values for new examples, either in classification or in regression problems. The minimum description length (MDL) principle suggests finding a set of discriminant or regression functions as simple as possible for reliable prediction of the target values of new examples.

4.3.3   Artificial neural networks

Artificial neural networks are built of small, independent building blocks – artificial *neurons*. Artificial neurons are abstractions of biological neurons. Their limited functionality is implemented as a weighted sum of input signals x_i that is subsequently transformed with a threshold function f into an output signal. An output signal x_{out} may be active (1) or inactive (0 or −1). Figure 4.3 shows an artificial neuron that computes the function.

$$x_{out} = f\left(\sum_i w_i x_i + w_{bias}\right) \quad (4.29)$$

A threshold function f may be implemented as a basic (step) threshold function (shown in Figure 4.4):

$$f(x) = \begin{cases} 1 & x > 0 \\ -1 & x \le 0 \end{cases} \quad (4.30)$$

More frequently than the step threshold function, a sigmoid function

$$f(x) = \frac{1}{1 + e^{-x}} \quad (4.31)$$

(shown in Figure 4.5) is used because it is continuous and continuously derivable.

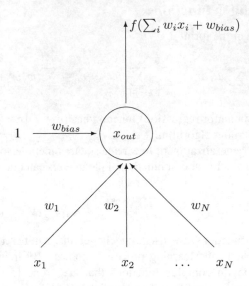

Figure 4.3: An artificial neuron (N is the number of incoming synapses).

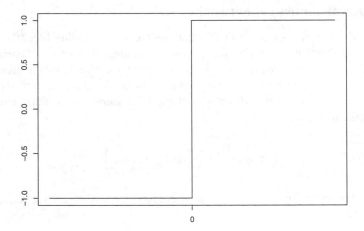

Figure 4.4: The basic step threshold function.

Artificial neural networks connect neurons in various topologies. Because of practical considerations, the most frequently used topology is the *layered* one, and the most popular neural networks are the feedforward multilayered artificial neural networks.

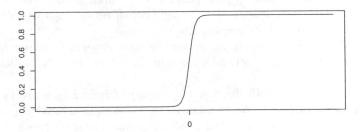

Figure 4.5: The sigmoid threshold function $f(x) = \frac{1}{1+e^{-x}}$.

In layered topologies, neurons are grouped into several layers: an input layer, an output layer, and zero or more hidden layers. The input layer forwards input signals to all neurons in the next layer. Every neuron in a hidden layer receives exactly one signal from each neuron from the previous layer and forwards its output signal to each neuron in the next layer. Finally, output signals of the output layer are outputs of the neural network (Figure 4.6).

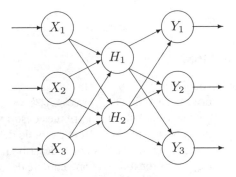

Figure 4.6: A three-layered feedforward neural network consisting of three input neurons, two hidden neurons and three output neurons.

Connections between neurons are also called *synapses*. Each synapse is associated with a weight that multiplies the signal transmitting through the synapse. The matrix of all synapse weights defines the function that is calculated by the neural network. The task of the learning algorithm is to set the weights so that the neural network calculates the desired target function. In the execution phase, for classification problems each output neuron calculates a discriminant function that corresponds to one particular class. Output neurons compete with each other, the one with the highest output signal value wins, and the class for a given input is determined by the winning neuron. For regression problems, there is only a single output neuron, and its output signal approximates the values of the target function.

A special case of a multi-layered network is a two-layered network without any hidden layers. Two-layered networks are used for solving linear classification and regression problems.

In practice, most frequently three- and four-layered feedforward networks are used. It can be shown that four-layered feedforward networks can approximate any target function with arbitrary precision. The number of input neurons is determined by the number of continuous attributes. Discrete attributes are handled as described in the beginning of this section. The number of output neurons is one for regression problems, or equal to the number of classes for classification problems.

The number of hidden layers and hidden neurons determines the modelling capabilities of a neural network. By increasing both numbers we increase the network's capabilities simultaneously with the number of weights that need to be set by the learning algorithm. This increases the difficulty of the learning process as well as the danger of overfitting the learning examples. The task of the learning algorithm is therefore not only to set the weights so as to approximate the target function, but also to do so with as small a neural network as possible.

4.4 PROBABILITY DISTRIBUTIONS

A hair divides what is false and true.

— *Omar Khayyam*

4.4.1 Bayesian classifier

Let us define the following quantities:

$P(C_k)$ — prior probabilities of classes C_k, $k = 1, \ldots, m_0$

$V = \langle v_1, \ldots, v_a \rangle$ — the vector of values of attributes describing an example

$d(V)$ — the classifier mapping from example description V to the class

$t(V)$ — the true class for an example described with V

$P(V)$ — the prior probability of an example described with V

$P(V|C_k)$ — the conditional probability of an example described with V given the class C_k

Bayesian classifier $d_B(V)$ is defined as a classifier that minimizes the probability of misclassification over all possible classifiers

$$\forall d(\cdot) : P(d_B(V) \neq t(V)) \leq P(d(V) \neq t(V)) \tag{4.32}$$

The average classification accuracy for the Bayesian classifier is given by

$$Acc_B = P(d_B(V) = t(V)) \tag{4.33}$$

By its definition, the Bayesian classifier is given by

$$d_B(V) = \operatorname*{argmax}_{C_k} P(C_k|V) = \operatorname*{argmax}_{C_k} P(V|C_k)P(C_k) \tag{4.34}$$

and therefore its average classification accuracy is

$$Acc_B = \sum_V \max_{k \in \{1...m_0\}} \{P(C_k|V)P(V)\} \tag{4.35}$$

Theoretically, the Bayesian classifier is the best classifier that any learning algorithm can produce. However, since prior and conditional probabilities are not known, they can be only more or less accurately estimated from learning examples. If two learning algorithms are compared, the one that more closely approximates the Bayesian classifier is the better of the two.

4.4.2   Learning examples as probability distribution

The simplest approximation of a probability distribution is a dynamic approximation $P(C_k|V)$ from stored learning examples. Lazy learning algorithms that store learning examples and use them as a knowledge base, can for each new example dynamically produce a probability distribution from stored learning examples. In practice, two fundamentally different approximations of probability distributions are used:

K-nearest neighbors: for each new example described with V the algorithm searches for K nearest (most similar) examples in the stored set of learning examples. A relative distribution of these examples is used to estimate the probability distribution $P(C_k|V)$. This estimation may also be weighted with distances to each of the K nearest neighbors.

Density estimation: the algorithm uses a pre-defined *kernel function* g that defines the influence space of each learning example so that it decreases with distance. For a new example a probability distribution $P(C_k|V)$ is determined by calculating for each learning example $t_i, i = 1...n(C_k)$, labelled with class C_k a relative density:

$$P(V|C_k) = \frac{1}{n(C_k)} \sum_{i=1}^{n(C_k)} g(V - t_i) \tag{4.36}$$

All learning examples affect the final density estimation, however their influence is determined by the kernel function g according to their distance to the new example described with V.

4.4.3   Naive Bayesian classifier

The naive Bayesian classifier assumes the conditional independence of attributes with respect to the class. It can be derived using the Bayes rule:

$$P(C_k|V) = P(C_k)\frac{P(V|C_k)}{P(V)} \tag{4.37}$$

Assuming the conditional independence of attribute values v_i given the class C_k

$$P(V|C_k) = P(v_1 \wedge \ ... \ \wedge \ v_a|C_k) = \prod_{i=1}^{a} P(v_i|C_k) \tag{4.38}$$

with a single application of the Bayes rule we get

$$P(C_k|V) = \frac{P(C_k)}{P(V)} \prod_{i=1}^{a} P(v_i|C_k) \tag{4.39}$$

With another application of the Bayes rule

$$P(v_i|C_k) = P(v_i)\frac{P(C_k|v_i)}{P(C_k)} \tag{4.40}$$

we get

$$P(C_k|V) = P(C_k)\frac{\prod_{i=1}^{a} P(v_i)}{P(V)} \prod_{i=1}^{a} \frac{P(C_k|v_i)}{P(C_k)} \tag{4.41}$$

The factor

$$\frac{\prod_{i=1}^{a} P(v_i)}{P(V)} \tag{4.42}$$

is independent of the class, so by omitting it we get the final expression

$$P(C_k|V) = P(C_k) \prod_{i=1}^{a} \frac{P(C_k|v_i)}{P(C_k)} \tag{4.43}$$

The task of the learning algorithm is to use learning examples to approximate probabilities (both unconditional and conditional) on the right-hand side of the Equation (4.43). Knowledge stored in a naive Bayesian classifier is therefore represented as a tabular approximation of prior class probabilities $P(C_k)$, $k = 1...m_0$, and of conditional class probabilities $P(C_k|v_i)$, $k = 1...m_0$ given value v_i of attribute A_i, $i = 1...a$.

4.5   SUMMARY AND FURTHER READING

We do not stop playing because we grow old, we grow old because we stop playing.
— Oliver Wendell Holmes

- Different machine learning methods require different types of knowledge representation, such as propositional calculus, first-order predicate calculus, discriminant and regression functions, and probability distributions.

- Propositional calculus is used for representation of learning examples in classification and regression problems, as well as for representation of hypotheses in symbolic learning of classification and regression rules.

- First order predicate calculus is used for describing objects (examples) as well as relations between objects and universally and existentially quantified variables. Only a subset of the first order predicate calculus (limited to Horn clauses with negated literals) is normally used in machine learning, because of its reduced algorithmic complexity.

- Horn clauses are equivalent to clauses in the prolog programming language. They are used for describing learning examples in inductive logic programming (ILP). In ILP the learning task is to induce, given the background knowledge, a set of positive learning examples and a set of negative examples, as simple a target relation (hypothesis) as possible, covering all positive learning examples and no negative examples.

- Discriminant functions are used for solving classification problems by implicitly describing boundary surfaces between separate classes (values of the independent variable) in a multi-dimensional space. Similarly, regression functions are used for solving regression problems by assigning to the example description an approximate value of the continuous target variable. Commonly used discriminant and regression functions include linear functions, squared functions, Φ functions, and neural networks.

- Probability distributions are used for representing the generated knowledge in several machine learning methods, such as nearest neighbors, density estimation, and Bayesian classifiers.

Hand et al. (2001) discuss dependencies among attributes and provide a most thoroughly illuminating example known as the Simpson paradox. Bratko (2000) and Kononenko and Lavrač (1988) describe the prolog programming language and how it is related to the first order logic. Lavrač and Džeroski (1994) describe inductive logic programming in general, and least general generalization and inverse resolution in particular. Rumelhart et al. (1986a) is a classical reference for multi-layered feedforward networks. A book by Bernardo and Smith (2000) is a good general reference to Bayesian theory in general, and Bayesian classification in particular. Beaumont (2004) provides a comprehensible introduction to probability theory. Naive Bayesian classifiers are analyzed and extended by Kononenko (1991b). Nearest neighbor methods are described in much detail by Aha et al. (1991). Wand and Jones (1995) give a comprehensive review of kernel functions and density estimation methods.

Chapter 5

Learning as Search

The willing finds the way. The unwilling finds an excuse.

— Arabian proverb

This chapter outlines the basic search techniques which are used by various machine learning algorithms to *search the hypothesis space*. In order to search the space of hypotheses, learning algorithms use various *operators* that enable different transformations of the hypotheses. Let H_i be the initial hypothesis and let the set of all successors H_s of current hypothesis H be denoted with $\{H_s \mid H \longrightarrow H_s\}$. Here $\longrightarrow$ denotes an application of any of the applicable operators which transforms the current hypothesis into one of its successors. We say that (successor) hypothesis H_s is *derived* from (current) hypothesis H. The hypothesis space $\mathcal{H}$ is defined with a set of all hypotheses that can be derived from the initial hypothesis by repeatedly and sequentially applying (possibly different) operators:

$$\mathcal{H} = \{H \mid H_i \xrightarrow{*} H\}$$

The star ($*$) indicates zero or more applications of operators. We introduce also the evaluation function q that evaluates the quality $q(E, B, H)$ of the hypothesis H with respect to evidence (a set of learning examples) E and background knowledge B. The task of the (ideal) learning algorithm is to find the hypothesis $H_0 \in \mathcal{H}$ that maximizes the quality function:

$$H_0 = \underset{H \in \mathcal{H}}{\mathrm{argmax}}\, q(E, B, H)$$

For example, consider the space of all possible if-then rules when learning a classifier. Learning consists of searching the space of all possible *condition parts* of if-then rules. A condition part is a conjunction of attribute-value pairs. Each condition part together with learning examples uniquely determines the conclusion part of the rule – a class probability distribution. An initial hypothesis may be an empty rule (the most general rule) or a rule that corresponds to one learning example (the most specific rule), or any conjunction of a randomly selected subset of (attribute=value) pairs. An operator may be a conjunctive addition of an attribute-value pair to the condition part of the rule (specializing the rule). Another operator may be a deletion of an (attribute=value) pair from the condition part of the rule (generalizing the rule). The initial hypothesis and two kinds of operators, together with the learning set of examples, uniquely determine the space of all possible rules. In the next chapter we show that an appropriate quality function (q) is the so called J-measure (defined with Equation 6.10).

As another example consider a continuous space of all possible feedforward multilayered artificial neural networks with one hidden layer. The number of input and output neurons is determined with the target learning task (the number of attributes and the number of classes). The number of neurons in the hidden layer, however, has to be determined with the learning process. Each layer of neurons is fully connected with the next layer of neurons. Each connection has an associated weight – a real number (that is why the space is continuous). Besides selecting a topology, the goal of the learning process is to determine the values of all weights. An initial hypothesis may be a network with an overly large number of hidden neurons and with each weight randomly set to a relatively small real number. A possible operator is a small change in one of the weights. If the weight becomes (close to) zero, the associated connection is deleted. If all the incoming connections to a hidden neuron are deleted, the neuron is removed from the network. Therefore, the initial hypothesis with the weight-change operator determines the space of all possible networks. As a quality function (q) we can use any function that measures the difference between the actual and the target output of the network for each learning example (the smaller the difference, the better the hypothesis).

Machine learning algorithms use various strategies for searching the hypothesis space. Basic strategies are:

- exhaustive search,
- bounded exhaustive search (branch and bound),
- best-first search,
- greedy search,
- beam search,
- local optimization,
- gradient search,
- simulated annealing, and
- genetic algorithms.

A single ML algorithm can combine several search strategies. In the following sections we provide brief descriptions with pseudocodes for some variants of basic strategies.

5.1 EXHAUSTIVE SEARCH

The secret of the success is that we tackle the problem with our whole being.

— *György Polya*

The simplest search method is *exhaustive search* that evaluates each hypothesis in the hypothesis space and returns the best one. However, if the space is too huge the search may stop before the whole hypothesis space is searched. In the algorithm pseudocodes we verify such situations with function "time-expired" – it returns *true* if no more time is available to proceed the search process.

5.1.1 Breadth-first search

A basic exhaustive search strategy is the *breadth-first* search. The search begins with immediate successors of the initial hypothesis, i.e hypotheses that are derived from the initial hypothesis by a single application of an applicable operator. Then the search continues with successors of those hypotheses, then with successors of successors, etc. The hypotheses whose successors have already been derived are called expanded (otherwise unexpanded). The pseudocode is given in Algorithm 5.1.

Algorithm 5.1 Breadth-first search.

INPUT: Set of examples E; Background knowledge B; Initial hypothesis H_i;
OUTPUT: Best hypothesis found;

hypothesis H_0; { currently best hypothesis }
hypothesis H, H_s; { current hypothesis and its successor }
hypothesis H_m; { best successor }
list of hypothesis Open; { unexpanded hypotheses }
list of hypothesis Successors; { successors of the current hypothesis }

$H_0 = H_i$;
Open = $[H_i]$; { list with one element }
while not empty(Open) **and not** time-expired **do**
    H = head(Open); { first element of Open }
    Open = tail(Open); { list without first element }
    Successors = $\{H_s | H \longrightarrow H_s\}$;
    Open = conc(Open,Successors); { concatenation }
    $H_m = \mathrm{argmax}_{H_s \in Successors} \, q(E, B, H_s)$;
    if $q(E, B, H_m) > q(E, B, H_0)$ **then** $H_0 = H_m$; **end if**;
end while;
return(H_0);

The main problem with breadth-first search is that its space-complexity grows exponentially with the depth of the search tree where the depth is equal to the number of successors between the initial hypothesis and the current hypothesis.

5.1.2 Depth-first search

Another basic strategy is the *depth-first search* which has a linear space complexity with respect to the search depth. The idea is to recursively expand the first successor until a dead-end (either no successors or maximum depth $MaxD$) is reached and then to backtrack to the last expanded hypothesis and continue with the next of its successors. The pseudocode is given in Algorithm 5.2.

Algorithm 5.2 Depth-first search.

INPUT: Set of examples E; Background knowledge B; Initial hypothesis H_i;
Depth limit integer MaxD;
OUTPUT: Best hypothesis found;

hypothesis ***Depth***(E, B, H_i, MaxD);
   { hypothesis H_i; – current hypothesis }
  hypothesis H_0; { currently best hypothesis }
  hypothesis H_s; { successor of the current hypothesis }
  hypothesis H_m; { best successor }
  list of hypothesis Successors; { successors of the current hypothesis }

  if MaxD = 0 **then** return(H_i) **else**
    $H_0 = H_i$;
    Successors = $\{H_s | H_i \longrightarrow H_s\}$;
    for $H_s \in$ Successors **do**
      $H_m = $ ***Depth***$(E, B, H_s, \text{MaxD}-1)$;
      if $q(E, B, H_m) > q(E, B, H_0)$ **then** $H_0 = H_m$; **end if**;
    end for;
    return(H_0);
  end if;

The problem with depth-first search is that the depth of the search has to be limited in advance because the algorithm cannot detect eventual cycles (or infinite branches) in the hypothesis space. This limitation can prevent the algorithm from finding best hypotheses.

5.1.3 Iterative deepening

A compromise between breadth-first and depth-first searches is *iterative deepening*. It simulates the breadth-first search by starting with a depth-first search with depth limit set to 1 and then iteratively increasing the depth limit (see Algorithm 5.3). Iterative deepening has no problems with cycles and has linear space complexity with respect to the search depth. The price of both advantages of two basic algorithms is the increase in time complexity with respect to the breadth first search – already searched parts of the hypothesis space are searched all over again and again.

If the search space is finite and if the set of operators guarantees no cycles then it

---

Algorithm 5.3 Iterative deepening.

INPUT: Set of examples E; Background knowledge B; Initial hypothesis H_i;
OUTPUT: Best hypothesis found;

    hypothesis H_0; { currently best hypothesis }
    hypothesis H_m; { best hypothesis of one iteration }
    integer MaxD; { current depth }

    $H_0 = H_i$;
    MaxD = 1;
    while not time-expired **do**
        $H_m = \textbf{\textit{Depth}}(E, B, H_i, \text{MaxD})$; { see Algorithm 5.2 }
        if $q(E, B, H_m) > q(E, B, H_0)$ **then** $H_0 = H_m$; **end if**;
        MaxD = MaxD + 1;
    end while;
    return(H_0);

---

is safe to use a depth-first search without depth limit. Unfortunately, in most practical problems the search space is too large to be exhaustively searched, often it is even infinite. Therefore, in most of the cases the exhaustive search is completely useless. Consider the learning problem with ten binary attributes and two possible classes. The hypothesis space consists of all binary functions of 10 arguments, which gives the following number of hypotheses:

$$2^{2^{10}} > 10^{300}$$

Even the extremely efficient algorithm which would expand one thousand billions (10^{12}) of hypotheses per second would spend over 10^{280} years to search the whole space! Therefore, in most of real world problems the algorithms are able to search only a modest subset of the whole hypothesis space.

5.2 BOUNDED EXHAUSTIVE SEARCH (BRANCH AND BOUND)

All too easily we construct mental prejudices which later hinder understanding instead of making it easier.

                                        — Werner Heisenberg

The bounded exhaustive search is a more useful variant of exhaustive search which uses the following ideas:

- a successor operator "$\longrightarrow$" partially orders the hypotheses – this guarantees that algorithms do not cycle;

- besides (heuristic) function q we introduce another (heuristic) function $maxQ$ that estimates the upper bound of the quality of all successors that can be derived from the current hypothesis H:

$$\forall H_s, H \xrightarrow{*} H_s : maxQ(E, B, H) \geq q(E, B, H_s)$$

- if the algorithm previously encountered a hypothesis H_0 which has a better estimate than the upper bound of successors of the current hypothesis H:

$$q(E, B, H_0) \geq maxQ(E, B, H)$$

then there is no need to expand current hypothesis H (the set of all successors derivable from H is thus eliminated from the search process).

Therefore the estimates q and $maxQ$ enable one to reduce the search space by discarding unpromising branches. This is why we call this search strategy also "branch and bound": when a hypothesis is expanded (branch) the unpromising successors are discarded (bound). Note that if q and $maxQ$ are sound (they don't "lie") then the bounded exhaustive search guarantees the optimal solution. In practice it is often necessary to use heuristic (unsound) functions q and $maxQ$ in order to efficiently reduce the search space. Although such functions do not guarantee optimal solutions they can efficiently guide the search towards acceptably good solutions.

The following example is an application of the basic idea. When learning a conjunctive rule from examples we can partially order the hypothesis space with an operator that introduces the relation "more specific" (inverse operator is "more general"). The initial hypothesis H_i is the empty hypothesis that covers all learning examples. With specialization (adding a conjunctive condition) we can derive from H_i any conjunctive rule.

A simple hypothesis quality evaluation function can be defined as follows:

$$q(E, B, H) = \begin{cases} generality(H) & \forall e \in E : B \wedge H \models e \\ -\infty & \exists e \in E : B \wedge H \not\models e \end{cases}$$

If the hypothesis is inconsistent with learning examples then it has the worse estimate (second line). If it is consistent (first line) then the more general the hypothesis, the better is the estimate. Note that for conjunctive rules this criterion corresponds to the criterion of smaller rule complexity – shorter rules will have a better estimate. Therefore, if we find a consistent rule we can safely discard all more specific rules – their quality is necessarily worse:

$$\forall e \in E : B \wedge H \models e \Rightarrow \forall H_s, H \xrightarrow{*} H_s : q(E, B, H) \geq q(E, B, H_s)$$

Therefore, for a consistent rule H it holds $maxQ(H) = q(H)$.

5.2.1   Bounded breadth-first search

The bounded exhaustive search based on the breadth-first strategy is depicted in Algorithm 5.4. The breadth-first search even with branch and bound improvement suffers from typically unacceptably high space complexity.

Algorithm 5.4 Branch and bound based on breadth-first search.

INPUT: Set of examples E; Background knowledge B; Initial hypothesis H_i;
OUTPUT: Best hypothesis found;

   hypothesis H_0; { currently best hypothesis }
   hypothesis H, H_s; { current hypothesis and its successor }
   hypothesis H_m; { best successor }
   integer MaxD; { current depth }
   list of hypothesis Open; { unexpanded hypotheses }
   list of hypothesis Successors; { successors of the current hypothesis }

   $H_0 = H_i$;
   Open = $[H_i]$;
   while not empty(Open) **and not** time-expired **do**
      H = head(Open); { first element of Open }
      Open = tail(Open); { list without first element }
      if $maxQ(E, B, H) > q(E, B, H_0)$ **then**
         Successors = $\{H_s | H \longrightarrow H_s\}$;
         Open = conc(Open,Successors); { concatenation }
         $H_m = \mathrm{argmax}_{H_s \in Successors}\, q(E, B, H_s)$;
         if $q(E, B, H_m) > q(E, B, H_0)$ **then** $H_0 = H_m$; **end if**;
      end if;
   end while;
   return(H_0);

Algorithm 5.5 Branch and bound based on depth-first search.

INPUT: Set of examples E; Background knowledge B; Initial hypothesis H_i;
Currently best hypothesis H_0; (Initially $H_0 = H_i$)
OUTPUT: Best hypothesis found;

hypothesis ***BBDepth***(E, B, H_i, H_0);
   { hypothesis H_i; – current hypothesis }
   hypothesis H_s; { successor of the current hypothesis }
   list of hypothesis Successors; { successors of the current hypothesis }

   if $q(E, B, H_i) > q(E, B, H_0)$ **then** $H_0 = H_i$; **end if**; { better hypothesis }
   if $maxQ(E, B, H_i) > q(E, B, H_0)$ **then** { do not discard successors }
      Successors = $\{H_s | H_i \longrightarrow H_s\}$;
      for $H_s \in$ Successors **do** $H_0 = $ ***BBDepth***(E, B, H_s, H_0); **end for**;
   end if;
   return(H_0);

5.2.2   Bounded depth-first search

As the depth of the search is implicitly limited with function $maxQ$, it is often better to use the depth-first search instead of the breadth-first search, especially if the appropriate selection of operators guarantees the hypothesis space without cycles. The bounded exhaustive search based on the depth-first strategy is depicted in Algorithm 5.5.

5.3   BEST-FIRST SEARCH

Method is a trick which has been used twice.

— György Polya

The best-first search is an improvement of the bounded exhaustive search based on the breadth-first search. The idea is to always expand the most promising unexpanded hypothesis H_{max}:

$$H_{max} = \operatorname*{argmax}_{H} [maxQ(E, B, H)]$$

This way we use function $maxQ$ to guide the algorithm towards more promising

---

Algorithm 5.6 Best-first search.

INPUT: Set of examples E; Background knowledge B; Initial hypothesis H_i;
OUTPUT: Best hypothesis found;

> hypothesis H_0; { currently best hypothesis }
> hypothesis H_{max}, H_s; { current hypothesis and its successor }
> hypothesis H_m; { best successor }
> list of hypothesis Open; { unexpanded hypotheses }
> list of hypothesis Successors; { successors of the current hypothesis }

> $H_0 = H_i$;
> Open = $[H_i]$;
> **while not** empty(Open) **and not** time-expired **do**
> > $H_{max} = \operatorname{argmax}_{H \in Open} maxQ(E, B, H)$; { best in Open }
> > Open = Open$\setminus \{H_{max}\}$;
> > **if** $maxQ(E, B, H_{max}) \leq q(E, B, H_0)$
> > > **then** Open = []; { empty list – discard all candidates }
> > > **else**
> > > > Successors = $\{H_s | H_{max} \longrightarrow H_s\}$;
> > > > Open = conc(Open,Successors); { concatenate }
> > > > $H_m = \operatorname{argmax}_{H_s \in Successors} q(E, B, H_s)$;
> > > > **if** $q(E, B, H_m) > q(E, B, H_0)$ **then** $H_0 = H_m$; **end if**;
> > > **end if**;
> **end while**;
> return(H_0);

---

parts of the hypothesis space. The sooner we find a relatively good hypothesis H_0, the stronger the pruning of the "branch and bound" principle will be:

$$q(E, B, H_0) \geq maxQ(E, B, H) \Rightarrow \forall H_s, \ H \xrightarrow{*} H_s : \ discard \ H_s$$

Therefore, the best-first search is in general more efficient than the basic branch and bound algorithm. However, the problem of the space complexity remains – the algorithm has to store all unexpanded hypotheses, which in most cases implies an unacceptable exponential space complexity. The pseudocode is provided in Algorithm 5.6. As in many practical problems a heuristic function $maxQ$ is used (which does not guarantee the upper bound of the quality of the successors), we sometimes call the best-first search also *heuristic search*. The efficiency of the best-first (as well as bounded exhaustive) search depends heavily on the power of functions q and $maxQ$. Note that the ideal sound function $maxQ$ will guide the algorithm directly towards the best hypothesis which, when found, will prune off all unexpanded hypotheses.

5.4 GREEDY SEARCH

We are aware of the presence of superintelligent beings as much as the mouse that gnaws a book is aware of its message.

— Jacques Bergier

Greedy search is called also the best-only search or the hill climbing. The greedy algorithm uses function max_1, that takes into account the quality of the hypothesis itself and the quality upper bound of its successors:

$$max_1(E, B, H) = \max \left(maxQ(E, B, H), q(E, B, H) \right)$$

In each step we keep only the best successor H_{max} of the current hypothesis H and "greedily" discard all the others:

$$H_{max} = \operatorname*{argmax}_{H_s, \ H \longrightarrow H_s} max_1(E, B, H_s)$$

H_{max} becomes the new current hypothesis and the process is repeated until the current hypothesis becomes better than any of its successors:

$$q(E, B, H) > max_1(E, B, H_{max})$$

The final current hypothesis is returned as the solution (see Algorithm 5.7).

Greedy algorithms often search not only inside the hypothesis space $\mathcal{H}$ but rather in a superspace $\mathcal{D} \supset \mathcal{H}$ that contains also partial hypotheses. The search principle in $\mathcal{D}$ is the same except that instead of function max_1 we use max_2 that estimates the quality upper bound of successors of partial hypothesis D:

$$\forall H_s, D \xrightarrow{*} H_s, H_s \in \mathcal{H}, D \in \mathcal{D} : \ max_2(E, B, D) \geq \hat{q}(E, B, H_s)$$

Algorithm 5.7 Greedy search.

INPUT: Set of examples E; Background knowledge B; Initial hypothesis H_i;
OUTPUT: Best hypothesis found;

    hypothesis H_0; { current hypothesis }
    hypothesis H_s; { successor of the current hypothesis }
    hypothesis H_{max}; { best successor of the current hypothesis }
    list of hypothesis Successors; { successors of the current hypothesis }

    $H_0 = H_i$;
    repeat
        Successors $= \{H_s | H_0 \longrightarrow H_s\}$;
        $H_{max} = \text{argmax}_{H_s \in Successors} \, max_1(E, B, H_s)$; { best successor }
        if $max_1(E, B, H_{max}) > q(E, B, H_0)$ **then** $H_0 = H_{max}$; **end if**;
    until $H_0 \neq H_{max}$;
    return(H_0);

For example, when learning consistent rules, every inconsistent rule is only a partial hypothesis and only rules that are consistent with all learning examples are candidates for the final hypothesis. However, in order to find consistent rules one has to search the superspace that includes also inconsistent rules.

Greedy search is very efficient but of course in most applications it does not guarantee optimal solutions. However, for huge search spaces greedy search is often an acceptable compromise and is typically the first thing to try.

5.5 BEAM SEARCH

Everybody has to find the truth by him or herself.

                       — Socrates

Beam search is a generalization of the greedy search. Instead of updating one most promising (partial) hypothesis (referred to as current hypothesis), beam search updates M most promising (partial) hypotheses. M is referred to as the beam size. In one step the algorithm expands all M current hypotheses and from all the successors, including current M hypotheses, selects M most promising. This process is repeated until we cannot get a better hypothesis (see Algorithm 5.8). By increasing the beam size M we increase the size of the searched space and therefore the time complexity. With $M = 1$ we get the basic greedy algorithm.

Algorithm 5.8 Beam search.

INPUT: Set of examples E; Background knowledge B; Initial hypothesis H_i; Beam size M;
OUTPUT: Best hypothesis found;

   hypothesis H; { current hypothesis }
   hypothesis H_s; { successor of the current hypothesis }
   set of hypothesis Beam; { current M hypotheses – current beam }
   set of hypothesis Beam1; { new M hypotheses – new beam }
   list of hypothesis Successors; { successors of the current hypothesis }

   Beam1 = $[H_i]$;
   repeat
      Beam = Beam1;
      Successors = $\{H_s | H \longrightarrow H_s, H \in \text{Beam}\}$;
      Beam1 = M best hypotheses from set Beam $\cup$ Successors;
   until Beam = Beam1;
   return($\text{argmax}_{H \in Beam}\ q(E, B, H)$);

5.6 LOCAL OPTIMIZATION

The path of a thousand kilometers starts with one step.

— Lao Tse

Local optimization differs from the greedy search in the following:

- Initial hypothesis $H_i \in \mathcal{H}$ is randomly generated.

- Local optimization usually searches only in the space of hypotheses $\mathcal{H}$ (and not in the space of partial hypotheses).

- The number of available operators for generating the successors is usually larger than with greedy search.

The idea of the local optimization is to start with a randomly generated hypothesis which is subsequently locally optimized by using a greedy algorithm with a given set of operators. The complexity of the algorithm depends on the operator set size. The algorithm is stochastic in the sense that the result depends on the randomly generated initial hypothesis. However, we repeat the whole process several times, subject to the time limit, each time with another randomly generated initial hypothesis. The result is the best hypothesis found in different trials. The flexibility and efficiency of local optimization makes it one of the most promising search techniques in many search problems.

5.7 GRADIENT SEARCH

The country that needs many physicians and lawyers is rotten.

— *Plato*

When searching the space of hypotheses we assume that the number of successors of each hypothesis is finite. This most often holds for discrete spaces. However, when the space is continuous, it has to be discretized in one way or another in order to make the search feasible.

Gradient search is a variant of local optimization for continuous spaces. Instead of using a set of operators and searching for most promising successors, the idea is to use the gradient of the quality function:

$$q'(E, B, H) = \frac{dq(E, B, H)}{dH}$$

The current hypothesis is changed in a direction which locally maximizes the function value. If the hypothesis is parametrized (determined) with p: $H = H(p)$, then the hypothesis should be modified by changing the parameter value in a direction that maximizes the derivative $q' = dq/dp$. As we do not have discrete operators, we need an additional numerical parameter η to determine the step size:

$$p = p + \eta \frac{dq(E, B, H(p))}{dp}$$

We continue the search by repeatedly updating the derivative and appropriately modifying the current parameter value (which determines the current hypothesis). The process terminates when the improvement of the hypothesis quality falls below the prespecified threshold ε (see Algorithm 5.9).

Algorithm 5.9 Gradient search.

INPUT: Set of examples E; Background knowledge B; Step size η; Improvement threshold ε;
OUTPUT: Value of parameter p that maximizes the hypothesis quality;

    parameter p_0; { current parameter value }
    parameter p_{new}; { new parameter value }

    p_{new} = random_parameter;
    repeat
        $p_0 = p_{new}$;
        $p_{new} = p_{new} + \eta \times dq(E, B, H(p_{new}))/dp$;
    until $q(E, B, H(p_0)) > q(E, B, H(p_{new})) + \varepsilon$;
    return(p_0);

5.8 SIMULATED ANNEALING

Good and evil do not exist. Exist only closer to and farther from One.

— Plotinius

Simulated annealing is a generalization of the local optimization. The basic idea stems from thermodynamics. Boltzman's law states that the probability that an atom is in a certain state with energy E_i is proportional to:

$$e^{-E_i/T}$$

where T denotes the *temperature*. Therefore, the probability of the states with minimal energy is larger for smaller temperatures. A (sub)optimal state (for example a regular crystal) corresponds to the state with low energy. In order to achieve a state with as low as possible energy it is necessary to heat the material and then slowly cool it. If cooling is too fast we get a less optimal state (irregular crystal). The slower the cooling, the larger the probability of the optimal state.

This idea can be used in combinatorial optimization by introducing the probabilistic behavior into the local optimization algorithm. The successor of the current hypothesis will not be selected deterministically but rather stochastically. The better the evaluated successor's quality, the larger the probability of selecting it. By introducing parameter T for the temperature we can control the level of randomness. Higher temperature implies more random movement in the search space. Lower temperature implies more deterministic behavior. With $T = 0$ the algorithm becomes completely deterministic and equivalent to local optimization.

In the following we describe a basic variant of simulated annealing and an advanced variant, called Markovian neural networks.

5.8.1 Basic algorithm

The basic algorithm (see Algorithm 5.10) starts with a random hypothesis and at the beginning at high temperatures stochastically searches the hypothesis space. From the successors of the current hypothesis H, it randomly selects one successor H_s. If the quality of the successor is greater than that of the current hypothesis:

$$q(E, B, H_s) > q(E, B, H)$$

then H_s is accepted with probability $P = 1$, otherwise it is accepted with probability, proportional to its quality and inversely proportional to the temperature:

$$P(H_0 = H_s) = e^{(q(E,B,H_s)-q(E,B,H))/T}$$

The temperature is slowly decreased until it becomes negligible (practically zero). The slower the cooling, the larger the space searched by the algorithm and the larger the probability of finding an optimal state. Usually the following geometric rule is used for cooling:

$$T = \lambda T, \quad \lambda < 1$$

Algorithm 5.10 A basic variant of simulated annealing.

INPUT: Set of examples E; Background knowledge B;
Maximal and minimal temperature T_{max}, T_{min}; Cooling factor λ;
OUTPUT: Best hypothesis found;

    real T; { current temperature }
    hypothesis H_0; { current hypothesis }
    hypothesis H_s; { successor of the current hypothesis }
    hypothesis H_{max}; { best successor of the current hypothesis }
    list of hypothesis Successors; { successors of the current hypothesis }

    H_0 = random_hypothesis;
    $T = T_{max}$;
    repeat
        H_s = random_successor(H_0);
        if random(1) $< e^{(q(E,B,H_s)-q(E,B,H))/T}$ { random(X) – random number $\in [0, X]$ }
        then $H_0 = H_s$;
        end if;
        $T = \lambda T$;
    until $T \leq T_{min}$;
{ local optimization }
    repeat
        Successors = $\{H_s | H_0 \longrightarrow H_s\}$;
        $H_{max} = \mathrm{argmax}_{H_s \in Successors}\ q(E, B, H_s)$; { best successor }
        if $q(E, B, H_{max}) > q(E, B, H_0)$ **then** $H_0 = H_{max}$; **end if**;
    until $H_0 \neq H_{max}$;
    return(H_0);

When T becomes close to zero, the algorithm finishes with deterministic local optimization.

5.8.2 Markovian neural networks

A variant of simulated annealing that is computationally more complex but in general gives better results is the *Markovian neural network*. The name comes from its ability to be implemented on a parallel – neural network-like – hardware and the algorithm is based on Markov chains. The idea is that the process of successor selection uses more information and is therefore not completely random as it is with basic simulated annealing. Markovian neural networks take into account the quality of (a finite subset of) all successors. Better successors have a higher probability of being selected (see Algorithm 5.11).

If there is at least one successor better than the current hypothesis, then we exclude

---

Algorithm 5.11 Markovian neural networks algorithm.

INPUT: Set of examples E; Background knowledge B;
Maximal and minimal temperature T_{max}, T_{min}; Cooling factor λ;
OUTPUT: Best hypothesis found;

    real R, Q, Sum; { for throwing a dice on the interval [0,1] }
    real T; { current temperature }
    hypothesis H_0; { current hypothesis }
    hypothesis H_s; { successor of the current hypothesis }
    hypothesis H_{max}; { best successor of the current hypothesis }
    list of hypothesis Successors; { successors of the current hypothesis }
    integer i; { index of Successors }

    H_0 = random_hypothesis;
    $T = T_{max}$;
    repeat
        Successors = $\{H_s | H_0 \longrightarrow H_s \land q(E, B, H_s) > q(E, B, H_0)\}$;
        if empty(Successors)
          then Successors = $\{H_s | H_0 \longrightarrow H_s \lor H_s = H_0\}$;
        end if;
        R = random(1); { throwing a dice; random(X) – random number $\in [0, X]$ }
        $Q = 0$;
        $i = 0$;
        { normalization of probabilities }
        Sum = $\sum_{H_s \in Successors} e^{(q(E,B,H_s) - q(E,B,H_0))/T}$;
        while $Q < R$ **do** { searching the best successor }
            $i = i + 1$;
            $Q = Q + [e^{(q(E,B,Successors[i]) - q(E,B,H_0))/T}]$/Sum;
        end while;
        H_0 = Successors[i]; { selected successor }
        $T = \lambda T$
    until $T \leq T_{min}$;
  { local optimization }
    repeat
        Successors = $\{H_s | H_0 \longrightarrow H_s\}$;
        $H_{max} = \text{argmax}_{H_s \in Successors}\, q(E, B, H_s)$; { best successor }
        if $q(E, B, H_{max}) > q(E, B, H_0)$ **then** $H_0 = H_{max}$; **end if**;
    until $H_0 \neq H_{max}$;
    return(H_0);

---

all the successors that are worse than the current hypothesis. :

$$P(H_0 = H_s) = \frac{e^{(q(E,B,H_s)-q(E,B,H_0))/T}}{\sum_{H_l,H_0\to H_l,q(E,B,H_l)>q(E,B,H_0)} e^{(q(E,B,H_l)-q(E,B,H_0))/T}}$$

If, however, all the successors are worse than the current hypothesis, one of them is selected randomly but the probability of the selection is proportional to the successor's quality. In the latter case the set of successors is augmented with the current hypothesis itself:

$$P(H_0 = H_s) = \frac{e^{(q(E,B,H_s)-q(E,B,H_0))/T}}{\sum_{H_l,H_0\to H_l \vee H_l=H_0} e^{(q(E,B,H_l)-q(E,B,H_0))/T}}$$

As in simulated annealing, the temperature is decreased in each iteration. At the end, when the temperature reaches the lower bound, the local optimization is performed.

5.9   GENETIC ALGORITHMS

Random mutations implicate absurdly long periods necessary for the evolution of living beings.

— *Werner Heisenberg*

Genetic algorithms are based on the idea of evolution and natural selection. One hypothesis corresponds to one *subject*, coded with a string of symbols, called *genes*. A genetic algorithm starts with a randomly generated set of subjects – hypotheses – called a *population* or a *generation*. In each iteration the current population stochastically generates the next population. The following genetic operators, stemming from biological genetics, are used:

- reproduction: the better the subject (hypothesis), the greater the probability that it will contribute its genetic code for successors;

- crossover: each successor is generated from two (randomly but proportionally to their quality) selected subjects from the current population, called parents; a successor is created with an appropriate combination of randomly selected parts of gene strings from both parents;

- mutation: randomly selected genes of the successors randomly (with small probability) change their values.

5.9.1   Basic algorithm

Usually, genetic operators in each iteration follow the following order (see Algorithm 5.12):

1. Reproduction: each subject from the current generation is copied into the temporary generation in the number of copies, proportional to its quality. As the number of subjects in each generation is limited, a certain number of worse

---

Algorithm 5.12 Genetic algorithm.

INPUT: Set of examples E; Background knowledge B; Number of generations G;
Number of examples in a population n; Probabilities of crossover and mutation P_c, P_m;
OUTPUT: Best hypothesis found;

  real R, Q, Sum; { for throwing a dice on the interval [0,1] }
  array[$1..n$] of hypothesis H; { current population }
  array[$1..n$] of hypothesis HS; { next population }
  integer i, j, k, l, j_1, j_2, cross; { indices }

  { initial population }
  for $j = 1$ **to** n **do** H_j = random_hypothesis; **end for**;

  for $i = 1$ **to** G **do** { G generations }

    { reproduction }
    for $j = 1$ **to** n **do**
      R = random(1); { throwing a dice; random(X) – random number $\in [0, X]$ }
      $Q = 0$;
      $k = 0$;
      Sum = $\sum_l q(E, B, H_l)$; { normalization of probabilities }
      while $Q < R$ **do** { searching for the selected parent }
          $k = k + 1$;
          $Q = Q + q(E, B, H_k)/$Sum;
      end while;
      $HS_j = H_k$; { selected parent }
    end for;

    $H = HS$; { new population }
    { crossover }
    for $k = 1$ **to** round($n \times P_c$) **do**
        j_1 = round(random($n - 1$))+1; { first parent }
        j_2 = round(random($n - 1$))+1; { second parent }
        cross = round(random(hypothesis_length-1)+1); { crossover point }
        HS_{j_1} = crossover(H_{j_1}, H_{j_2},cross); { first successor }
        HS_{j_2} = crossover(H_{j_2}, H_{j_1},cross); { second successor }
    end for;
    { mutation }
    for $j = 1$ **to** n **do**
      for $k = 1$ **to** hypothesis_length **do**
        if random(1) $< P_m$ **then** $HS_j[k]$= random_value; **end if**;
      end for;
    end for;

    $H = HS$; { new population }
  end for; { G generations }

  return(argmax$_{H_j} q(E, B, H_j)$);

---

subjects are "extinct" (the number of their copies in the temporary generation is zero). Let n be the number of subjects in each population and let $\mathcal{P}$ be the current population. The expected number of copies contributed by subject H equals:

$$\frac{n \cdot q(E, B, H)}{\sum_{H_s \in \mathcal{P}} q(E, B, H_s)}$$

2. Crossover: in the temporary generation two subjects (parents) are randomly selected and one (or more) crossover points in the genetic code is randomly selected. From two parents two successors are created: the first successor is constructed from the gene string of the first parent from the beginning of the string to the crossover point, and from the gene string of the second parent from the crossover point onwards. The rest of the genes (of the second parent from the beginning of the string to the crossover point, and from the gene string of the first parent from the crossover point onwards) are used for the construction of the second successor. If there is more than one crossover point, during construction of a successor at each crossover point the parent that contributes the genes is switched. The crossover is performed $(n \times P_c)$-times, where P_c is a user defined parameter – the crossover probability.

3. Mutation: with small (user defined) probability P_m each gene in each successor randomly changes its value. The mutation probability is usually very small and has no significant influence on the algorithm success.

A key part of the use of any genetic algorithm is the selection of an appropriate subject coding. The more appropriate the coding for the selected way of crossover, the better the performance of the genetic algorithm. The user predetermines the values of the following parameters:

- G – the number of generations (iterations),

- n – the number of subjects in a population,

- P_c – the probability of crossover, and

- P_m – the probability of mutation.

5.9.2   Genetic algorithms in machine learning

Genetic algorithms can be used in any (sub)problem that requires optimization in a large search space. When developing a ML algorithm one has to solve such subproblems like feature subset selection, parameter tuning, constructive induction, and of course the hypothesis learning itself.

Feature subset selection is one of the key issues in data mining and is described in Section 7.7.1. For searching the exponentially growing space of all possible subsets of features (attributes) we can use a genetic algorithm. A solution is a subset of features. The obvious encoding scheme for subjects is a string of bits (genes), each corresponding to one of the features. The value 0 indicates that the corresponding feature is excluded from the set and the value 1 indicates that it is included. A less trivial part is defining an appropriate evaluation function. Typically a performance measure is used that evaluates the success of the target ML algorithm when using the given subset of features. This is the most time consuming part of the search, as for each subject in each generation the target ML algorithm has to be run on a subset of learning examples and its result appropriately tested on the validation set of examples.

Parameter tuning is an important part of most ML algorithms. Due to huge time complexity it is often most appropriate to use a greedy-like search. As parameter values are often real numbers the gradient search is most often used. However, in some cases the whole learning process is reduced to parameter tuning and in such cases one can apply also more complex, genetic-like search techniques. To code the real numbers we can use the binary representation of the numbers. In such a representation the importance of bits depends on their position in the code. If this is not appropriate, we can apply various transformations of bit strings into numbers.

In neural networks, when the structure of the network is fixed, the learning process has to find the optimal values of synapses' weights (see Chapter 11). The most popular backpropagation algorithm uses the gradient search. More general local optimization is implemented by re-learning, each time from a different randomly generated initial state. On the other hand, a genetic algorithm can, in some cases, lead to better results which can compensate for the increased time complexity of the search process.

Constructive induction aims to construct new attributes from existing ones (see Chapter 8). Typically a set of operators is given in advance and one has to construct new attributes from existing ones using various operators. Genetic algorithms can be used to search the huge space of possible new attributes. Like in feature subset selection, the most complex part of the search is the evaluation function which evaluates the quality of newly generated attributes.

Hypothesis learning is itself an optimization problem. The learner has to select the best hypothesis from a typically huge space of all possible hypotheses. Therefore, genetic algorithms can be used to search the target hypothesis space.

For example, when learning decision rules, one rule corresponds to one subject. An appropriate coding scheme is as follows. For each attribute and also for the class variable a string of bits is used where each bit corresponds to one value of that attribute. For the class variable each bit corresponds to one class. If the attribute bit value is 0 the corresponding attribute value is excluded from the condition part of the rule, and if the bit value is 1, the corresponding attribute value is included. If all bits for some attribute are set to 0, the attribute is excluded from the condition part of the rule. The bit string for the class variable represents the conclusion part of the rule (which must not be excluded).

Another example is learning logical relations in inductive logic programming. The hypothesis space in this case is a (huge) set of all possible logic programs. Each logic program can be represented as a tree. In order to use genetic algorithms, genetic operators have to be adapted for the tree like representation. For example, crossover can be implemented by exchanging the subtrees of the parent subjects.

5.10 SUMMARY AND FURTHER READING

We do not live for the body, however, without the body we cannot live.

— *Seneca*

- The *hypothesis space* is defined with a set of all hypotheses that can be derived from the initial hypothesis by repeatedly and sequentially applying (possibly different) operators. The task of the (ideal) learning algorithm is to find the hypothesis that maximizes the *quality function*.

- The space-complexity of *breadth-first search* grows exponentially with the depth of the search tree. *Depth-first search* cannot detect eventual cycles (or infinite branches) in the hypothesis space. *Iterative deepening* has no problems with cycles and has linear space complexity. In most practical problems the search space is too large to be exhaustively searched.

- If the problem space has certain properties the non-exhaustive search process may still be able to guarantee the optimal solution. The *branch and bound* algorithm uses a function that estimates the upper bound of the quality of all successors that can be derived from the current hypothesis.

- The idea of the *best-first search* is to always expand the most promising unexpanded hypothesis. The algorithm has to store all unexpanded hypotheses, which often implies an unacceptable exponential space complexity. In many practical problems for the branch and bound and for the best-first search, a *heuristic function* is used which does not guarantee the upper bound of the quality of the successors.

- *Greedy search* in each step keeps only the best successor of the current hypothesis and "greedily" discards all the others. Greedy search is very efficient but, of course, in most applications it does not guarantee optimal solutions. *Beam search* is a generalization of the greedy search by keeping a set (beam) of most promising hypotheses.

- *Local optimization* in each iteration starts with a randomly generated hypothesis which is subsequently locally optimized by using a greedy algorithm with a given set of operators. *Gradient search* is a variant of local optimization for continuous spaces where the gradient of the quality function can be used to guide the search.

- *Simulated annealing* starts with a random hypothesis and at the beginning at high temperatures stochastically searches the hypothesis space. After each step the temperature is decreased and the search becomes more deterministic.

- *Genetic algorithms* are based on the idea of evolution and natural selection. They start with a randomly generated set of subjects – hypotheses. In each iteration the current population stochastically generates the next population by using genetic operators, such as reproduction, crossover, and mutation.

- Genetic algorithms can be used in any (sub)problem that requires optimization in a large search space. When developing a ML algorithm one has to solve optimization subproblems, such as feature subset selection, parameter tuning, constructive induction, and the hypothesis learning itself.

Descriptions of basic search techniques, such as the greedy search, backtracking (the depth first search), the breadth-first search, branch and bound, local optimization, and the best first search can be found in general books on algorithms, for example by Cormen et al. (1990) and by Neapolitan and Naimipour (1996) and in an outstanding classical book by Aho, Hopcroft and Ullman (1983). The best-first search is most often implemented in $A*$-like algorithms, described in most textbooks on artificial intelligence, for example by Bratko (2000). Simulated annealing was first introduced by Kirkpatrick et al. (1983). Later many variants were developed. The one described in this book, Markovian neural networks, was developed by Kovačič (1991). A nice overview of stochastic search methods, together with genetic programming, is described by Jacob (2003).

A good general book on evolutionary computing is by Eiben and Smith (2003) and on the use of genetic algorithms in data mining the book by Freitas (2002). The genetic algorithms research goes back to Holland (1975) and became popular in machine learning due to a seminal book by Goldberg (1989). The early description of various uses of genetic algorithms in ML is described by De Jong (1990) and later for rule induction (Vafie and DeJong, 1994) and multistrategy learning (de Garis, 1994). The early use of genetic algorithms for inductive logic programming and qualitative modeling is described by Varšek (1991). Research results, applications and theoretical studies on genetic programming are collected by Kinnear (1994), Angeline and Kinnear (1996), and Langdon et al. (1998).

Chapter 6

Measures for Evaluating the Quality of Attributes

Human inventions do not appear by chance.

— *Werner Heisenberg*

One of the crucial tasks in machine learning is the evaluation of the quality of attributes. For this purpose a number of measures have been developed that estimate the usefulness of an attribute for predicting the target variable. We describe separately measures for classification (which are appropriate also for relational problems) and for regression. Most measures estimate the quality of one attribute independently of the context of other attributes. However, algorithm ReliefF and its regressional version RReliefF take into account also the context of other attributes and are therefore appropriate for problems with strong dependencies between attributes.

In this chapter we use the symbol $\Diamond$ to indicate that the proof of the assertion can be found at the end of the chapter in Section 6.3. Let us refresh the representation of examples with attributes. It is defined with:

- a set of attributes A = $\{A_0, \dots, A_a\}$, where a is the number of attributes;

- each discrete attribute A_i has a set of m_i possible values $\mathcal{V}_i = \{V_1, ..., V_{m_i}\}$;

- each continuous attribute A_i has an interval of possible values $\mathcal{V}_i = [Min_i, Max_i]$;

- the dependent variable is given with the target attribute A_0: for a classification problem it is a discrete attribute (class) C with values $\{C_1, ..., C_{m_0}\}$, for a regressional problem it is continuous;

- one learning example (training example) is a vector of values of all attributes, including the target attribute: $t_l = \langle v_{0,l}, v_{1,l}, ..., v_{a,l} \rangle$ (for classification we refer to class with $c_l = v_{0,l}$);

153

- a set of n learning examples is given with a set of vectors $\mathcal{T} = \{t_l, l = 1...n\}$

6.1 MEASURES FOR CLASSIFICATION AND RE-LATIONAL PROBLEMS

Hard problems in life always begin as simple.

— Lao Tse

The basic task of the learning algorithm during the search of the hypothesis space is to evaluate either the utility (quality) of each attribute for the given learning problem, in case of representation with attributes, or the utility of each candidate literal, in case of relational representation (i.e. representation using the first order predicate calculus). Here we use the representation with attributes. The use of measures for evaluating the utility of literals in relational problems is analogous to estimating the utility of binary attributes.

Measures for guiding the search in classification and relational problems, described in this section, are:

- information gain,
- Gain-ratio,
- distance measure,
- weight of evidence,
- minimum description length (MDL),
- J-measure,
- χ^2 and G statistics,
- orthogonality of class distribution vectors (ORT),
- Gini-index and
- ReliefF.

6.1.1 Impurity functions

Basic measures for evaluating the utility of attributes in classification problems (or utility of literals in relational problems) are impurity measures. Let $C_1, ..., C_{m_0}$ represent possible classes (values of discrete attribute A_0). An *impurity measure* is defined as function ϕ of probability distribution $P(C_k) \geq 0, k = 1...m_0, \sum_k P(C_k) = 1$, with the following properties:

1. ϕ has single maximum, when $P(C_k) = 1/m_0, k = 1...m_0$.

2. ϕ has m_0 minima: $P(C_k) = 1, P(C_l) = 0, l = 1...m_0, l \neq k$.

3. ϕ is symmetrical (insensitive to the order of arguments).

4. ϕ is concave: $\frac{\partial^2 \phi}{\partial P(C_k)^2} < 0, k = 1...m_0$.

5. ϕ is continuous and continuously derivable.

The quality of discrete attribute A_i with a set of possible values $\mathcal{V}_i = \{V_1, ... V_{m_i}\}$ is defined as the expected *decrease of impurity* when the attribute value is known:

$$q(A_i) = \phi(P(C_1), ..., P(C_{m_0})) - \sum_{j=1}^{m_i} P(V_j)\phi(P(C_1|V_j), ..., P(C_{m_0}|V_j)) \quad (6.1)$$

Prior probabilities of classes $P(C_k)$, attribute values $P(V_j)$, and conditional probabilities of classes given the value of the attribute $P(C_k|V_j)$ are estimated from the distribution of learning examples.

The quality of attribute has the following properties (proofs can be found in Section 6.3.1):

Nonnegativity: $q(A_i)$ cannot be negative:

$$q(A_i) \geq 0$$

and is equal to 0 when prior and posterior distributions are equal:

$$q(A_i) = 0 \Leftrightarrow \forall j \, \forall \, k : P(C_k) = P(C_k|V_j)$$

$\diamondsuit$

Maximum: $max(q(A_i)) = \phi(P(C_1), ..., P(C_{m_0}))$
$\diamondsuit$

Increasing the number of attribute values: If we transform attribute A_i with m_i values into attribute AN_i, so that value V_{m_i} is replaced with two possible values VN_{m_i} and VN_{m_i+1}, then it holds:

$$q(AN_i) \geq q(A_i)$$

$\diamondsuit$

This property implies that by increasing the number of values the estimate of the attribute quality also tends to increase. Therefore the estimate of the quality q is biased to overestimate attributes with more values. In practice this property is undesirable, also because the reliability of probability approximations is lower for attributes with more values. To overcome this problem various normalizations are needed that take into account the number of attribute's values.

6.1.2   Measures based on information content

Most measures used in ML are based on information content. The *amount of information* (measured in bits), necessary to determine the outcome X_j of an experiment, is defined as a negative logarithm of its probability:

$$I(X_j) = -\log_2 P(X_j)$$

The average *amount of information*, necessary to determine the outcome among m disjoint possible outcomes X_j, $j = 1...m$, $\sum_j P(X_j) = 1$, is called *entropy* of an outcome:

$$H(X) = -\sum_j^m P(X_j) \log_2 P(X_j)$$

Entropy is an impurity measure (the proof is provided in Section 6.3.2).
◊

In the following the base of the logarithm is always 2 and will be omitted. Let us introduce the following notation:

n	–	the number of learning examples,
$n(C_k)$	–	the number of learning examples from class C_k,
$n(V_j)$	–	the number of learning examples with j^{th} value of the given attribute A,
$n(C_k, V_j)$	–	the number of learning examples from class C_k and with j^{th} value of A.

The corresponding probabilities are approximated with relative frequencies (alternatively, a more sophisticated approximation can be used, such as Laplace's law of succession or the m-estimate, see Section 3.1.5) from the learning set:

$$
\begin{aligned}
p_{kj} &= n(C_k, V_j)/n \\
p_{k.} &= n(C_k)/n \\
p_{.j} &= n(V_j)/n \\
p_{k|j} &= p_{kj}/p_{.j} = n(C_k, V_j)/n(V_j)
\end{aligned}
$$

We define the following entropies:
H_C – class entropy:

$$H_C = -\sum_k p_{k.} \log p_{k.}$$

H_A – entropy of attribute A:

$$H_A = -\sum_j p_{.j} \log p_{.j}$$

H_{CA} – entropy of joint event class–attribute value:

$$H_{CA} = -\sum_k \sum_j p_{kj} \log p_{kj}$$

$H_{C|A}$ – conditional class entropy given the value of attribute A:

$$H_{C|A} = H_{CA} - H_A = -\sum_j p_{.j} \sum_k \frac{p_{kj}}{p_{.j}} \log \frac{p_{kj}}{p_{.j}}$$

$$H_{C|A} = -\sum_j p_{.j} \sum_k p_{k|j} \log p_{k|j}$$

Note that since H is nonnegative it follows that $H_{CA} \geq H_{C|A}$.

Information gain

Standard attribute quality measure is information gain, which is obtained if entropy (H) is used as impurity function ϕ in Equation (6.1). It is defined as the amount of information, obtained from the attribute, for determining the class:

$$Gain(A) = H_C - H_{C|A} \qquad (6.2)$$

Information gain is also referred to as *mutual information* due to its symmetry:

$$H_C - H_{C|A} = H_C + H_A - H_{CA} = I(A;C) = H_A - H_{A|C} = I(C;A)$$

Information gain has the properties of the attribute quality function (6.1):

$$Gain(A) \geq 0$$

$$max(Gain(A)) = H_C$$

$$Gain(AN) \geq Gain(A)$$

where attribute AN is obtained from attribute A by replacing one of its values with two possible values. The latter property is undesired. Therefore, in the following, we introduce two normalized versions of information gain.

Gain-ratio

The gain-ratio is defined as information gain, normalized with the attribute entropy:

$$GainR(A) = \frac{Gain(A)}{H_A} \qquad (6.3)$$

The normalization eliminates the problem of overestimating the multivalued attributes, however, the gain-ratio overestimates attributes with small attribute entropy H_A. Therefore, when estimating the quality of attributes with the gain-ratio, the safe procedure is to take into account only attributes A_i with above average information gain:

$$Gain(A_i) \geq \frac{\sum_{j=1}^{a} Gain(A_j)}{a}$$

Distance measure

Distance measure, written in the form of proximity, is defined as information gain, normalized with joint entropy H_{CA}:

$$1 - D(C, A) = \frac{Gain(A)}{H_{CA}} \qquad (6.4)$$

A measure D(C,A) is a distance, because it is:

1. nonnegative: $D(C, A) \geq 0$

2. equal to zero only for identical events: $D(C, A) = 0 \Leftrightarrow C = A$

3. symmetric: $D(C, A) = D(A, C)$

4. it fulfills the triangular inequality: $D(C, A_1) + D(A_1, A_2) \geq D(C, A_2)$

The proof can be found in Section 6.3.3.

$\diamondsuit$

Function (6.4) satisfactorily overcomes the problem of multivalued attributes and, contrary to the gain-ratio, is not problematic for small values of the denominator (H_{CA}).

Weight of evidence

Plausibility of an outcome X_k is defined as the logarithm of probability ratio:

$$\log odds(X_k), \qquad odds(X_k) = \frac{P(X_k)}{P(\overline{X}_k)}$$

where $P(\overline{X}_k) = 1 - P(X_k)$. Plausibility can have any value from the interval $(-\infty, \infty)$. *Weight of evidence* of outcome Y_j for outcome X_k is defined with:

$$WE(X_k|Y_j) = \log \frac{odds(X_k|Y_j)}{odds(X_k)}$$

The weight of evidence can have any value from the interval $(-\infty, \infty)$. *The average absolute weight of evidence* of outcome Y for X_k is defined as follows:

$$WE(X_k|Y) = \sum_j P(Y_j) \left| \log \frac{odds(X_k|Y_j)}{odds(X_k)} \right|$$

This measure is nonnegative. It is used for evaluating the quality of attributes in binary classification problems. Let attribute A have m possible values. The quality estimate is:

$$WE_k(A) = \sum_j^m p_{\cdot j} \left| \log \frac{odds_{k|j}}{odds_{k\cdot}} \right|, \qquad k = 1, 2$$

where k is the class index. It holds $WE_1(A) = WE_2(A)$.

A straightforward generalization can be used for evaluating the quality of attributes in multi-class problems:

$$WE(A) = \sum_k p_k \cdot WE_k(A) \tag{6.5}$$

The average absolute weight of evidence is appropriate for evaluating multivalued attributes – it demonstrates an acceptable bias with respect to the number of attribute values.

MDL

Following the minimum description length principle (MDL), we can define the quality of attribute as its compressivity. Let us define the problem of data transmission through the communication channel. Both, the sender and the receiver have access to the domain definition – they know the number of values m of the given attribute A and the number of classes m_0. They also have access to the value $v^{(l)}$ of attribute A for each learning example t_l. But only the sender knows the correct classes of examples. His task is to send the shortest possible message containing the classes of all examples to the receiver.

The sender has two options: The classes can be either explicitly coded, or the attribute A is used so that classes are separately coded for each value of the attribute. The former case requires that the message contains also the class probability distribution, so that the receiver can decode the classification; in the latter case, however, each value of the attribute corresponds to different class distribution. Therefore, the latter case requires that the message, besides classification, contains a class probability distribution for each attribute value.

The number of bits, required to code the classes of n examples with the given class probability distribution can be approximated with $H_C \times n$ plus the number of bits, required to code the class distribution. The number of different possible distributions of n examples over m_0 classes is equal to:

$$\binom{n + m_0 - 1}{m_0 - 1}$$

(splitting the interval $1...n$ into m_0 subintervals, some of them can be empty, is the same as splitting the interval $1...n + m_0$ into m_0 nonempty subintervals; there are $n + m_0 - 1$ possible boundaries from which $m_0 - 1$ has to be selected).

Therefore, the number of bits, required to code the classes, is given with:

$$Prior\_MDL_1 = nH_C + \log\binom{n + m_0 - 1}{m_0 - 1}$$

The estimate of the number of bits for coding the classes, given the values of the attribute A, is the sum over all attribute values:

$$Post\_MDL_1(A) = \sum_j n(V_j)H_{C|j} + \sum_j \log\binom{n(V_j) + m_0 - 1}{m_0 - 1}$$

$$Post\_MDL_1(A) = nH_{C|A} + \sum_j \log\binom{n(V_j) + m_0 - 1}{m_0 - 1}$$

The quality $MDL_1(A)$ of attribute A is defined as the compressivity of attribute, i.e. as the length difference of code without using attribute values and the code with using them. The quality is normalized with the number of learning examples:

$$MDL_1(A) = \frac{Prior\_MDL_1 - Post\_MDL_1(A)}{n}$$

$$= Gain(A) + \frac{1}{n} \left(\log \binom{n + m_0 - 1}{m_0 - 1} - \sum_j \log \binom{n(V_j) + m_0 - 1}{m_0 - 1} \right) \quad (6.6)$$

The above quality measure uses coding, based on H_C. This coding is optimal only for an arbitrary number of codewords (in our case one codeword corresponds to one learning example). If, however, the number of codewords (learning examples) is known in advance, we can apply more optimal coding. The number of all possible classifications of n learning examples is equal to:

$$\binom{n}{n(C_1), ..., n(C_{m_0})}$$

Therefore with optimal coding we obtain:

$$Prior\_MDL = \log \binom{n}{n(C_1), ..., n(C_{m_0})} + \log \binom{n + m_0 - 1}{m_0 - 1} \quad (6.7)$$

and

$$Post\_MDL(A) = \sum_j \log \binom{n(V_j)}{n(C_1, V_j), ..., n(C_{m_0}, V_j)} + \sum_j \log \binom{n(V_j) + m_0 - 1}{m_0 - 1}$$

Finally, the quality of the attribute is defined with:

$$MDL(A) = \frac{Prior\_MDL - Post\_MDL(A)}{n}$$

$$MDL(A) = \frac{1}{n} \left(\log \binom{n}{n(C_1), ..., n(C_{m_0})} - \sum_j \log \binom{n(V_j)}{n(C_1, V_j), ..., n(C_{m_0}, V_j)} + \right.$$

$$\left. + \log \binom{n + m_0 - 1}{m_0 - 1} - \sum_j \log \binom{n(V_j) + m_0 - 1}{m_0 - 1} \right) \quad (6.8)$$

This measure is most appropriate for estimating the quality of multivalued attributes. Its advantage is also in the detection of useless attributes: if $MDL(A) < 0$ then the attribute A is non-compressive and therefore useless for theory construction (unless it is useful in combination with other attributes – see ReliefF algorithm below).

J-measure

Measures like information gain, gain-ratio, distance, weight of evidence, and MDL are defined to evaluate the quality of an attribute as a whole. In practice we sometimes need to estimate the quality of a single attribute value. A naive trial to adapt the quality measure (6.1) would give the following measure:

$$q_1(V_j) = \phi(P(C_1), ..., P(C_{m_0})) - \phi(P(C_1|V_j), ..., P(C_{m_0}|V_j))$$

Such a measure has two significant shortcomings:

- it can be negative and

- does not differentiate between permuted distributions, for example:

$$P(C_1|V_j) = P(C_1), P(C_2|V_j) = P(C_2), ..., P(C_{m_0}|V_j) = P(C_{m_0}) \Rightarrow q_1(V_j) = 0$$
and

$$P(C_1|V_j) = P(C_{m_0}), P(C_2|V_j) = P(C_{m_0-1}), ..., P(C_{m_0}|V_j) = P(C_1) \Rightarrow q_1(V_j) = 0$$

A more appropriate measure that overcomes these two shortcomings is J-measure. It can be derived from information gain as follows:

$$\sum_{j=1}^{m} J_j = Gain(A) \tag{6.9}$$

where m is the number of values of attribute A. The appropriate measure, stemming from the above equality, is

$$J_j = p_{\cdot j} \sum_{k} p_{k|j} \log \frac{p_{k|j}}{p_{k\cdot}} \tag{6.10}$$

The proof of equality (6.9) can be found in Section 6.3.4.
◇

J-measure can be used to evaluate the quality of a single attribute value or the quality of a whole decision rule. Due to Equation (6.9) it can be interpreted as the expected amount of information, obtained from condition j, for classification. In fact it evaluates the information content of the condition (indicated with index j), which can be either a single attribute value (V_j) or a conjunction of several such conditions.

J-measure has the following two advantageous properties (the proofs are in Section 6.3.4):

Nonnegativity: $J_j \geq 0$
◇

Upper bound: $J_j \leq 0.53 \; bit$
◇

In addition, the following statistic approximately follows the χ^2 distribution with $m_0 - 1$ degrees of freedom (m_0 is the number of classes):

$$2nJ_j \ln 2 = 1.3863 \; nJ_j \tag{6.11}$$

where n is the number of learning examples. Therefore, J-measure can be used to verify the statistical significance of difference between prior ($p_{k\cdot}$) and posterior ($p_{k|j}$) distribution. The test can be used to evaluate the significance of a single attribute value or the significance of a whole decision rule.

6.1.3   Some other measures

Statistics χ^2 and G

Measures that use χ^2 distributed statistics are calculated with the following formula:

$$P(X_0)_D = \int_0^{X_0} p(x)_D dx \tag{6.12}$$

where $p(x)_D$ is a chi-square distribution with D degrees of freedom and X_0 is the statistic value for the given attribute. Standard algorithms are available for calculation of (6.12).

If we want to evaluate the quality of attribute A_i, we can use statistics χ^2 and G. Both are approximately χ^2 distributed with $(m_i - 1)(m_0 - 1)$ degrees of freedom, where m_i is the number of values of attribute A_i and m_0 is the number of classes.

Statistic χ^2 is defined with:

$$\chi^2 = \sum_k \sum_j \frac{(e(C_k, V_j) - n(C_k, V_j))^2}{e(C_k, V_j)}, \tag{6.13}$$

where $e(C_k, V_j)$ is the expected number of examples from k-th class and with j-th attribute value if we assume the independence of attribute and class:

$$e(C_k, V_j) = \frac{n(V_j)n(C_k)}{n}$$

Statistic G is the generalization of statistic $2nJ_j \ln 2$ from Equation (6.11):

$$G = 2nGain \ln 2 = 1.3863n \times Gain \tag{6.14}$$

Statistics G and χ^2 are used for testing the significance of difference between the prior class distribution (before using attribute A_i) and posterior one (after using attribute A_i). However, they are not appropriate for comparing the quality of different attributes.

Orthogonality of class distribution vectors

Orthogonality ORT of class distribution vectors is a measure for evaluating the quality of *binary* attributes. Let $\vec{V}_j = \langle p_{1|j}, ..., p_{m_0|j} \rangle$ be a vector of class distribution for j-th value of the binary attribute A, $j = 1, 2$. The attribute quality is defined as one minus the cosine of the angle between two vectors:

$$ORT(A) = 1 - cos\theta(\vec{V}_1, \vec{V}_2) = 1 - \frac{\vec{V}_1 \cdot \vec{V}_2}{\|\vec{V}_1\|\|\vec{V}_2\|} \tag{6.15}$$

$\vec{V}_1 \cdot \vec{V}_2$ represents the dot product:

$$\vec{V}_1 \cdot \vec{V}_2 = \sum_k p_{k|1}p_{k|2}$$

and $\|\vec{V_j}\|$ is the vector length (Euclidian norm):

$$\|\vec{V_j}\| = \sqrt{\sum_k p_{k|j}^2}$$

The measure has the following nice properties:

Symmetry: $ORT(A)$ is symmetrical with respect to classes.

Bounds: $0 \le ORT(A) \le 1$
The vectors have nonnegative coordinates, therefore the angle between them cannot exceed $90°$.

Minimum: $Gain(A) = 0 \Leftrightarrow ORT(A) = 0$
Both measures achieve minimum when $\vec{V_1} = \vec{V_2}$.

Maximum: $H_{R|A=V_1} = 0 \wedge H_{R|A=V_2} = 0 \Rightarrow ORT(A) = 1$
If the attribute ideally differentiates between the classes ($Gain(A) = H_R$) then $ORT(A)$ achieves maximum.

Relation to information gain: $ORT(A) = 1 \nRightarrow Gain(A) = H_R$
For ORT, to achieve maximum, it suffices that it ideally differentiates subsets of classes:

$$\left(\forall k \in [1...m_0] : \exists j \in \{1,2\} : (p_{k|j} = 0 \wedge p_{k|3-j} \ne 0)\right) \Rightarrow ORT(A) = 1$$

On the other hand, for information gain, to achieve maximum (H_R), the attribute has to ideally differentiate all the classes.

The use of ORT is limited to binary attributes. If we want to use it for multi-valued attributes, all the attributes have to be binarized (see Section 7.3). The binarization of attributes implicitly solves the problem of overestimating the multi-valued attributes.

Gini-index

Prior Gini-index is defined as follows:

$$Gini\_prior = \sum_k \sum_{l \ne k} p_k.p_{l.} = 1 - \sum_k p_{k.}^2$$

Prior Gini-index is an impurity measure (the proof is in Section 6.3.5).
$\Diamond$

The quality $Gini(A)$ of attribute A is defined with Equation (6.1) by replacing ϕ with $Gini\_prior$, i.e. we have a difference between prior and expected posterior Gini-index:

$$Gini(A) = \sum_j p_{.j} \sum_k p_{k|j}^2 - \sum_k p_{k.}^2. \tag{6.16}$$

$Gini(A)$ has properties, stemming from Equation (6.1):

A_1	A_2	A_3	C
0	0	0	0
0	0	1	0
0	1	1	1
0	1	0	1
1	0	0	1
1	0	1	1
1	1	0	0
1	1	0	0

Table 6.1: Example learning task.

Nonnegativity: $Gini(A) \geq 0$

Maximum:
$$Gini(A) = Gini\_prior \Leftrightarrow \forall j : \exists! k : p_{k|j} = 1$$

Increasing the number of attribute values: $Gini(A)$ at most increases. This property is undesired – $Gini(A)$ overestimates multi-valued attributes.

6.1.4 ReliefF

All measures described so far evaluate the quality of an attribute independently of the context of other attributes. Equivalently, they assume independence of attributes with respect to class. We call them "myopic" measures because they cannot detect the information content of an attribute that stems from dependencies between attributes. A small example learning task, provided in Table 6.1, illustrates the problem of attribute dependencies. We have three binary attributes, two possible classes, and eight learning examples. The correct target rule

$$T = (A_1 \neq A_2)$$

does not contain the third attribute. However, myopic measures (all measures, described so far) would estimate attribute A_3 as the most important and would consider the other two attributes irrelevant:

$$Gain(A_1) = GainR(A_1) = 1 - D(A_1, R) = WE(A_1) = ORT(A_1) = Gini(A_1) = 0$$

and the same for attribute A_2. The reason for not detecting the importance of attributes A_1 and A_2 is their strong mutual dependance. If we evaluate each independently of the other, they both seem completely irrelevant for the given classification problem.

The context of other attributes can be efficiently taken into account with algorithm ReliefF. Let us first describe a simpler variant, called RELIEF, which is designed for two-class problems without missing values. The basic idea of the algorithm, when analysing learning examples, is to take into account not only the difference in attribute values and the difference in classes, but also the *distance* between the examples. Distance is calculated in the attribute space, therefore similar examples are close to each other and dissimilar are far apart. By taking the similarity of examples into account, the context of all the attributes is implicitly considered.

The basic algorithm RELIEF (see Algorithm 6.1) for each example from a random subset of m ($m \leq n$) learning examples calculates a nearest example from the same class (nearest hit H) and a nearest example from the opposite class (nearest miss M). Then it updates the quality of (each) attribute with respect to whether the attribute differentiates two examples from the same class (undesired property of the attribute) and whether it differentiates two examples from opposite classes (desired property). By doing so, the quality estimate takes into account the local ability of the attribute to differentiate between classes. The locality implicitly takes into account the context of other attributes.

Algorithm 6.1 Basic algorithm RELIEF; function diff is defined with Equation (6.17).

INPUT: n learning examples I described with a attributes; Sampling parameter m;
OUTPUT: for each attribute A_j a quality weight $-1 \leq W[j] \leq 1$;

    integer inst, att, l; { indices }
    array[1..a] of real W; { quality weights }
    example M, H; { nearest miss and nearest hit }

    for att = 1 **to** a **do** W[att] = 0.0; **end for**;
    for l = 1 **to** m **do**
        randomly pick an example I[inst];
        find its nearest hit H and nearest miss M;
        for att = 1 **to** a **do**
            W[att] = W[att] − diff(att,I[inst],H)/m + diff(att,I[inst],M)/m;
        end for;
    end for;
    return(W);

For (each) attribute A_{att} function *diff(att,Instance1,Instance2)* in Algorithm 6.1 returns the difference of attribute values of two examples:

$$diff(i, t_j, t_k) = \begin{cases} \frac{|v_{i,j} - v_{i,k}|}{Max_i - Min_i}, & A_i \ is \ continuous \\ 0, & v_{i,j} = v_{i,k} \wedge A_i \ is \ discrete \\ 1, & v_{i,j} \neq v_{i,k} \wedge A_i \ is \ discrete \end{cases} \qquad (6.17)$$

Quality estimations W can also be negative, however, $W[A_i] \leq 0$ means that attribute A_i is irrelevant.

In fact RELIEF estimates the following difference of probabilities:

$$\begin{aligned} W(A_i) \ &= \ P(diff(i, \cdot, \cdot) = 1 | \textit{two nearest examples from the opposite classes}) \\ &- \ P(diff(i, \cdot, \cdot) = 1 | \textit{two nearest examples from the same class}) \quad (6.18) \\ &= \ P(diff(i, \cdot, \cdot) = 0 | \textit{two nearest examples from the same class}) \\ &- \ P(diff(i, \cdot, \cdot) = 0 | \textit{two nearest examples from the opposite classes}) \end{aligned}$$

If we omit the nearness condition we get a function, which is closely related to Gini-index. We call it (myopic) RELIEFm:

$$Wm(A_i) = constant \times \sum_j p_{\cdot j}^2 \times Ginim(A_i) \tag{6.19}$$

where $Ginim(A)$ is highly related with $Gini(A)$ from Equation (6.16):

$$Ginim(A) = \sum_j \left(\frac{p_{\cdot j}^2}{\sum_j p_{\cdot j}^2} \times \sum_k p_{k|j}^2 \right) - \sum_k p_k^2. \tag{6.20}$$

The proof is provided in Section 6.3.6.

$\Diamond$

The only difference of $Ginim(A)$ to $Gini(A)$ is that instead of factor:

$$\frac{p_{\cdot j}^2}{\sum_j p_{\cdot j}^2}$$

in Equation (6.16) we have:

$$\frac{p_{\cdot j}}{\sum_j p_{\cdot j}} = p_{\cdot j}$$

However, the crucial difference between myopic RELIEFm in Equation (6.19) and $Gini(A)$ is in the factor in front of $Ginim$ in Equation (6.19):

$$\sum_j p_{\cdot j}^2$$

This factor represents the prior probability that two randomly selected examples have the same value of the given attribute. The factor implicitly normalizes the RELIEF's quality estimates with respect to the number of attribute's values. While $Gini(A)$ overestimates multi-valued attributes, RELIEF (and also myopic RELIEFm) has no such undesired bias.

Basic RELIEF is able to evaluate the quality of continuous and discrete attributes, which are highly interdependent. For example, for very hard parity problems of arbitrary order, where the learning examples are described with an additional number of irrelevant attributes, RELIEF is able to detect a subset of relevant attributes. The time complexity[1] is $O(m \times n \times a)$, where a is the number of attributes, n the number of learning examples and m is a user defined parameter. For calculation of each nearest hit and miss we need $O(n \times a)$ steps. Greater m implies more reliable evaluation of the attributes' qualities but also greater time complexity. If we set $m = n$ we get the most reliable quality estimates and the highest time complexity. This is often unacceptably slow, therefore, for large n, we set $m \ll n$, typically $m \in [30...200]$.

A more realistic variant of RELIEF is its extension, called ReliefF (see Algorithm 6.2). Original RELIEF was designed for two-class problems without missing values and is quite sensitive to noise. ReliefF is able to deal with incomplete and noisy data and can be used for evaluating the attribute quality in multi-class problems:

---

[1]For definition of O-notation see Section A.2 in the appendix.

Algorithm 6.2 ReliefF.

INPUT: n learning examples I described with a attributes and labeled with m_0 classes;
Probabilities of classes $p_{c.}$; Sampling parameter m;
Number k of nearest examples from each class;
OUTPUT: for each attribute A_j a quality weight $-1 \leq W[j] \leq 1$;

    integer inst, att, kk, t, c, cc, l; { indices }
    array[1..a] of real W; { quality weights }
    array[1..k,1..m_0] of example M; { nearest misses and hits }

  for att = 1 **to** a **do** W[att] = 0.0; **end for**;
  for l = 1 **to** m **do**
  randomly pick an example I[inst];
  for $t = 1$ **to** m_0 **do**
    find k nearest examples M[kk, t] from class C_t, $kk = 1..k$;
    $c = \arg_{cc}(C_{cc} = c_{inst})$; { class of I[inst] }
    for att = 1 **to** a **do**
      for kk = 1 **to** k **do**
        if $t = c$ { nearest hit? }
          then W[att] = W[att] – diff(att,I[inst],M[kk, t])/$(m * k)$;
          else W[att] = W[att] + $p_{t.}/(1 - p_{c.})*$ diff(att,I[inst],M[kk, t])/$(m * k)$;
        end if;
      end for; { kk }
    end for; { a }
  end for; { t }
  end for; { l }
  return(W);

Missing attribute values: ReliefF can use also incomplete data. For that purpose we generalize function *diff* to calculate the probability that two examples have different values of the given attribute. We have two possibilities:

- one of examples (t_l) has an unknown value of attribute A_i:

$$diff(A_i, t_l, t_k) = 1 - p_{v_{i,k}|c_l}$$

- both examples have unknown attribute values:

$$diff(A_i, t_l, t_k) = 1 - \sum_{j=1}^{m_i} \left(p_{V_j|c_l} \times p_{V_j|c_k} \right)$$

Noisy data: The most important part of algorithm RELIEF is searching for the nearest hit and miss. Noise (mistake) in class and/or attribute value significantly affects the selection of nearest hits and misses. In order to make this process more reliable in the presence of noise, ReliefF uses k nearest hits and k nearest misses and averages their contributions to attributes' quality estimates. k is a user defined parameter with typical values $k \in [5...10]$. This simple extension significantly improves the reliability of quality estimates.

Multi-class problems: Instead of k nearest hits and misses, ReliefF searches for k nearest examples from each class. The contributions of different classes are weighted with their prior probabilities. In Algorithm 6.2 the weighting factor is $p_{t.}/(1 - p_{c.})$. The class of an example is c, while t is the class of its nearest miss. The factor is therefore proportional to the probability of class t, normalized with the sum of probabilities of all classes, different from c.

6.2 MEASURES FOR REGRESSION

Nature does not allow the wise to have wishes or ambitions, nor does it allow the foolish to get rid of them.

— *Sri Sri Ravi Shankar*

In regression the quality of attributes can be evaluated using the following measures:

- expected change of variance,
- regressional ReliefF, and
- minimum description length principle (MDL).

6.2.1 Change of variance

Instead of impurity measures, which are used in classification problems, in regression problems the *variance* of the continuous target (regression) variable is used. It is defined as the mean squared error:

$$s^2 = \frac{1}{n} \sum_{l=1}^{n} (c_l - \bar{c})^2$$

where $\bar{c}$ is the mean of the target variable over all n learning examples:

$$\bar{c} = \frac{1}{n} \sum_{l=1}^{n} c_l$$

Variance is closely related to Gini-index, which is an impurity measure. If in the binary classification problem one class is transformed into value 0 and the other into value 1 of the regression variable (the discrete class variable is transformed into a continuous one), we get the following equality:

$$Gini\_prior = 2s^2$$

The proof is provided in Section 6.3.7.

For evaluating the quality of attribute A_i we use *the expected change of variance*:

$$ds^2(A_i) = \frac{1}{n} \sum_{l=1}^{n} (c_l - \bar{c})^2 - \sum_{j=1}^{m_i} \left(p_{\cdot j} \frac{1}{n(V_j)} \sum_{l=1}^{n(V_j)} (c_{j,l} - \bar{c}_j)^2 \right) \qquad (6.21)$$

The continuous value of the target variable for the l-th learning example with the j-th value of attribute A_i is denoted with $c_{j,l}$, while $\bar{c}_j$ denotes the mean of these values over all $n(V_j)$ examples with j-th value of attribute A_i:

$$\bar{c}_j = \frac{1}{n(V_j)} \sum_{l=1}^{n(V_j)} c_{j,l}$$

The expected change of variance behaves similarly to the expected change of impurity (Equation (6.1)):

Nonnegativity: $ds^2(A_i) \geq 0$

Maximum: $max(ds^2(A_i)) = \frac{1}{n} \sum_{l=1}^{n} (c_l - \bar{c})^2$

Increasing the number of attribute values: If we change attribute A_i with m_i values into attribute AN_i, so that value V_{m_i} is replaced with two possible values VN_{m_i} and VN_{m_i+1}, then it holds:

$$ds^2(AN_i) \geq ds^2(A_i)$$

6.2.2   Regressional ReliefF

Like most of the attribute quality measures, defined for classification problems, the expected change of variance is also a myopic measure. When estimating the quality of an attribute it does not take into account the context of other attributes. In this section we develop a non-myopic measure for regression by appropriately adapting algorithm ReliefF.

In regression problems the target variable is continuous, therefore nearest hits and misses cannot be used in a strict sense as in algorithm ReliefF. RReliefF (Regressional ReliefF) uses a kind of "probability" that two examples belong to two "different" classes. This "probability" is modeled with the distance between the values of the target variable of two learning examples.

In Section 6.3.6 it is shown that (myopic and non-myopic) RELIEF calculates the following:

$$W(A_i) = \frac{P_{samecl|eq\_val} P_{eq\_val}}{P_{samecl}} - \frac{(1 - P_{samecl|eq\_val}) P_{eq\_val}}{1 - P_{samecl}} \qquad (6.22)$$

For estimating the quality in Equation (6.22) we need the (posterior) probability $P_{samecl|eq\_val}$ that two (nearest) examples belong to the same class provided they have the same attribute value, and the prior probability P_{samecl} that two examples belong to

---

Algorithm 6.3 RReliefF – Regressional ReliefF.

INPUT: n learning examples I described with a attributes;
Sampling parameter m; Number k of nearest examples;
OUTPUT: for each attribute A_j a quality weight $-1 \leq W[j] \leq 1$;

    integer $inst, att, kk, l$; { indices }
    integer N_{dC}; { "class" difference count }
    array[1..a] of real W; { quality weights }
    array[1..a] of real $N_{dC \wedge dA}$, N_{dA}; { "class"-attribute and attribute difference counts }
    array[1..k] of integer M; { indices of nearest examples }

    set all N_{dC}, $N_{dA}[att]$, $N_{dC \wedge dA}[att]$, $W[att]$ to 0;
    for $l = 1$ **to** m **do**
    randomly pick an example $I[inst]$;
    find indices $M[kk]$ of k nearest examples, $kk \in [1..k]$;
    for $kk = 1$ **to** k **do**
    { index 0 in *diff* corresponds to target (regression) variable }
    $N_{dC} = N_{dC} + diff(0, I[M[kk]], I[inst])/k$;
    for $att = 1$ **to** a **do**
    $N_{dA}[att] = N_{dA}[att] + diff(att, I[M[kk]], I[inst])/k$;
    $N_{dC \wedge dA}[att] = N_{dC \wedge dA}[att] + diff(0, I[M[kk]], I[inst]) \times$
       $diff(att, I[M[kk]], I[inst])/k$;
    end for; { att }
    end for; { kk }
    end for; { l }
    { for each attribute calculate the value of (6.23) }
    for $att = 1$ **to** a **do**
    $W[att] = N_{dC \wedge dA}[att]/N_{dC} - (N_{dA}[att] - N_{dC \wedge dA}[att])/(m - N_{dC})$;
    end for;
    return(W);

---

the same class. We can transform the equation, so that it contains the probability that two examples belong to different classes provided they have different attribute values:

$$W(A_i) = \frac{P_{diffcl|diff}P_{diff}}{P_{diffcl}} - \frac{(1 - P_{diffcl|diff})P_{diff}}{1 - P_{diffcl}} \qquad (6.23)$$

Here P_{diff} denotes the prior probability that two examples have different attribute values, and P_{diffcl} denotes the prior probability that two examples belong to different classes.

Algorithm RReliefF has to approximate the probabilities in Equation (6.23). The details are provided in Algorithm 6.3. The algorithm calculates the "frequencies":

- N_{dC} – sum of "probabilities" that two nearest examples belong to different classes;

- $N_{dA}[att]$, – sum of "probabilities" that two nearest examples have different attribute values;

- $N_{dC \wedge dA}[att]$ – sum of "probabilities" that two nearest examples belong to different classes and have different attribute values.

Finally, from the above "frequencies", it calculates the attribute qualities $W[att]$ using Equation (6.23).

The time complexity of RReliefF is equal to that of basic RELIEF, i.e. $O(m\, n\, a)$. The most time consuming operation is searching for k nearest examples. We need to calculate n distances which can be done in $O(n\, a)$ steps. Building the heap requires $O(n)$ steps and k nearest examples can be extracted from the heap in $O(k \log n)$ steps. In practice this is always less than $O(n\, a)$.

Both algorithms, ReliefF and RReliefF, calculate the quality of attributes according to Equation (6.23), which represents a unified view on the attribute quality estimation – in classification and regression.

6.2.3   MDL in regression

In order to use the minimum description length principle (MDL) in regression we have to determine an appropriate coding of real numbers, which can be used for coding the values of the target variable, the values of continuous attributes and the prediction errors. Coding has significant influence on the behavior of MDL estimate. Because, in principle, the coding of an arbitrary real number requires an infinite code, we have to bound the precision with a fixed number of decimal places. In such a way the real numbers can be coded like natural numbers.

When coding the value of the target variable (or the value of a continuous attribute), all possible values have the code of equal length, defined with:

$$\log_2 \frac{Interval}{Precision} \tag{6.24}$$

It is obvious that the selection of precision influences the code length.

On the other hand, when coding the error, the desired code property is that smaller numbers (lower error) have shorter code length. The Rissanen code can be used for that purpose:

$$Rissanen(0) = 1$$
$$Rissanen(n) = 1 + \log_2 n + \log_2(\log_2 n) + ... + log_2(2.865064...)$$

The sum is limited to positive summands. The idea of the code is that for coding the number n we need $\log_2 n$ bits, for coding the length of the code, we need another $\log_2(\log_2 n)$ bits, etc.

When the appropriate coding is selected, the attribute quality can be estimated in the same manner as in classification (Equations (6.6) and (6.8)). Instead of class distribution we code the mean value of target variable using Equation (6.24) and for each learning example the deviation (distance) from the mean value using Equation (6.25).

6.3　**FORMAL DERIVATIONS AND PROOFS

Reason can answer questions, but imagination has to ask them.

— *Ralph Gerard*

6.3.1　Properties of the attribute quality

Attribute quality, defined with

$$q(A_i) = \phi(P(C_1), ..., P(C_{m_0})) - \sum_{j=1}^{m_i} P(V_j)\phi(P(C_1|V_j), ..., P(C_{m_0}|V_j))$$

where ϕ is an impurity function of a given class distribution, has the following properties:

Nonnegativity: $q(A_i)$ cannot be negative:

$$q(A_i) \geq 0$$

and is equal to 0 iff prior and posterior distributions are equal:

$$q(A_i) = 0 \Leftrightarrow \forall j \, \forall \, k : P(C_k) = P(C_k|V_j)$$

Proof. We have

$$P(C_k) = \sum_j P(V_j)P(C_k|V_j)$$

and

$$\frac{\partial P(C_k)}{\partial P(C_k|V_j)} = P(V_j)$$

The first derivative of function q is equal to 0 when $P(C_k) = P(C_k|V_j)$:

$$\frac{\partial q}{\partial P(C_k|V_j)} = \frac{\partial \phi(P(C_1), ..., P(C_k), ..., P(C_{m_0}))}{\partial P(C_k)} P(V_j) -$$

$$-P(V_j)\frac{\partial \phi(P(C_1|V_j), ..., P(C_k|V_j), ..., P(C_{m_0}|V_j))}{\partial P(C_k|V_j)}$$

As ϕ is concave, it holds:

$$\frac{\partial^2 \phi}{\partial P(C_k)^2} < 0, \quad k = 1...m_0$$

It follows that the second derivative of function q in point $P(C_k) = P(C_k|V_j)$ is positive:

$$\frac{\partial^2 q}{\partial P(C_k|V_j)^2} = \frac{\partial^2 \phi(P(C_1), ..., P(C_k), ..., P(C_{m_0}))}{\partial P(C_k)^2} P(V_j)^2 -$$

$$-P(V_j)\frac{\partial^2 \phi(P(C_1|V_j), ..., P(C_k|V_j), ..., P(C_{m_0}|V_j))}{\partial P(C_k|V_j)^2}$$

$$\frac{\partial^2 q}{\partial P(C_k|V_j)^2} = -C(P(V_j)^2 - P(V_j)) \geq 0$$

Therefore, in point $P(C_k) = P(C_k|V_j)$, function q has minimum.　　　　□

Maximum: $max(q(A_i)) = \phi(P(C_1), ..., P(C_{m_0}))$.

Proof. Function reaches its maximum when the attribute ideally differentiates the classes:

$$\phi(P(C_1|V_j), ..., P(C_k|V_j), ..., P(C_{m_0}|V_j)) = minimum, \quad j = 1...m_i$$

i.e. when $P(C_k|V_j) = 1$, $P(C_l|V_j) = 0, l = 1...m_0, l \neq k, j = 1...m_i$. □

Increasing the number of attribute values: If we change attribute A_i with m_i values into attribute AN_i, so that value V_{m_i} is replaced with two possible values VN_{m_i} and VN_{m_i+1}, then it holds:

$$q(AN_i) \geq q(A_i)$$

Proof. The derivative of function $q(AN_i) - q(A_i)$ is equal to 0 when $P(C_k|VN_{m_i})=P(C_k|VN_{m_i+1})=P(C_k|V_{m_i})$, $k = 1...m_0$. Because of

$$P(C_k|V_{m_i}) = \frac{P(C_k|VN_{m_i})P(VN_{m_i}) + P(C_k|VN_{m_i+1})P(VN_{m_i+1})}{P(V_{m_i})}$$

it holds also:

$$\frac{\partial P(C_k|V_{m_i})}{\partial P(C_k|VN_{m_i})} = \frac{P(VN_{m_i})}{P(V_{m_i})}$$

Therefore the derivative of $q(AN_i) - q(A_i)$ is equal to:

$$\frac{\partial(q(AN_i) - q(A_i))}{\partial P(C_k|VN_{m_i})} =$$

$$P(V_{m_i})\frac{\partial\phi(P(C_1|V_{m_i}), ..., P(C_k|V_{m_i}), ..., P(C_{m_0}|V_{m_i}))}{\partial P(C_k|V_{m_i})}\frac{P(VN_{m_i})}{P(V_{m_i})} -$$

$$- \frac{\partial\phi(P(C_1|VN_{m_i}), ..., P(C_k|VN_{m_i}), ..., P(C_{m_0}|VN_{m_i}))}{\partial P(C_k|VN_{m_i})}P(VN_{m_i})$$

The second derivative is positive:

$$\frac{\partial^2(q(AN_i) - q(A_i))}{\partial P(C_k|VN_{m_i})^2} = CP(VN_{m_i})\left(1 - \frac{P(VN_{m_i})}{P(V_{m_i})}\right) \geq 0$$

This means that in point $P(C_k|VN_{m_i}) = P(C_k|VN_{m_i+1}) = P(C_k|V_{m_i})$, $k = 1...m_0$, the function reaches its minimum. □

6.3.2 Entropy is an impurity measure

Let us have m disjoint possible outcomes X_j, $j = 1...m$, $\sum_j P(X_j) = 1$, of an experiment. Entropy of an outcome, defined as:

$$H(X) = -\sum_j P(X_j) \log_2 P(X_j)$$

is an impurity measure.

Proof.
1. Maximum:

$$H(X) = - \sum_{j}^{m-1} P(X_j) \log_2 P(X_j) - \left(1 - \sum_{j}^{m-1} P(X_j)\right) \log_2 \left(1 - \sum_{j}^{m-1} P(X_j)\right)$$

$$\frac{\partial H}{\partial P(X_k)} = - \log_2 P(X_k) - \log_2 e + \log_2 \left(1 - \sum_{j}^{m-1} P(X_j)\right) + \log_2 e$$

The first derivative is equal to zero when $P(X_k) = 1/m$.
The second derivative is always negative:

$$\frac{\partial^2 H}{\partial P(X_k)^2} = - \log_2 e \left(\frac{1}{P(X_k)} + \frac{1}{\left(1 - \sum_j^{m-1} P(X_j)\right)} \right) < 0$$

2. Minimum:
$$H(X) \geq 0 \wedge H(X) = 0 \Leftrightarrow (P(X_j) = 0 \vee P(X_j) = 1)$$

3. H is symmetric.
4. H is concave.
5. H is continuous and continuously derivable. $\square$

6.3.3 Distance measure

Measure
$$D(C, A) = 1 - \frac{H_C + H_A - H_{CA}}{H_{CA}} \tag{6.25}$$

is a distance.

Proof.

1. Nonnegativity: $D(C, A) \geq 0$
   It holds:

   $$D(C, A) = 1 - \frac{Gain(A)}{H_{CA}} = \left(1 - \frac{H_C}{H_{CA}}\right) + \left(1 - \frac{H_A}{H_{CA}}\right)$$

   Nonnegativity holds since $H_{CA} \geq H_A$ and $H_{CA} \geq H_C$.

2. Equal to zero for identical events: $D(C, A) = 0 \Leftrightarrow C = A$
   The property follows from:
   $D(C, A) = 0 \Leftrightarrow H_C + H_A = 2H_{CA}$
   $H_{CA} \geq H_C$
   $H_{CA} \geq H_A$
   $H_{CA} = H_C \Rightarrow H_{A|C} = 0$
   $H_{CA} = H_A \Rightarrow H_{C|A} = 0$

3. Symmetry: $D(C, A) = D(A, C)$ is obviously true.

4. Triangular inequality: $D(C, A_1) + D(A_1, A_2) \geq D(C, A_2)$
   Let us rewrite function D as follows:

$$D(C, A_1) = \frac{H_{A_1|C} + H_{C|A_1}}{H_{A_1 C}}$$

Firstly, we show the following inequality:

$$H_{C|A_1} + H_{A_1|A_2} \geq H_{C|A_2} \tag{6.26}$$

Due to $H_{C|A_1} \geq H_{C|A_1 A_2}$, we can write:

$$H_{C|A_1} + H_{A_1|A_2} \geq H_{C|A_1 A_2} + H_{A_1|A_2} = H_{CA_1|A_2} \geq H_{C|A_2}$$

Secondly, we prove the following:

$$\frac{H_{C|A_1}}{H_{CA_1}} + \frac{H_{A_1|A_2}}{H_{A_1 A_2}} \geq \frac{H_{C|A_2}}{H_{CA_2}} \tag{6.27}$$

¿From $H_{CA} = H_{C|A} + H_A$ we get:

$$\frac{H_{C|A_1}}{H_{CA_1}} + \frac{H_{A_1|A_2}}{H_{A_1 A_2}} = \frac{H_{C|A_1}}{H_{C|A_1} + H_{A_1}} + \frac{H_{A_1|A_2}}{H_{A_1|A_2} + H_{A_2}} \geq$$

$$\geq \frac{H_{C|A_1}}{H_{C|A_1} + H_{A_1|A_2} + H_{A_2}} + \frac{H_{A_1|A_2}}{H_{C|A_1} + H_{A_1|A_2} + H_{A_2}} =$$

$$= \frac{H_{C|A_1} + H_{A_1|A_2}}{H_{C|A_1} + H_{A_1|A_2} + H_{A_2}}$$

To complete the proof of Inequality (6.27) we use Inequality (6.26):

$$\frac{H_{C|A_1} + H_{A_1|A_2}}{H_{C|A_1} + H_{A_1|A_2} + H_{A_2}} \geq \frac{H_{C|A_2}}{H_{C|A_2} + H_{A_2}} = \frac{H_{C|A_2}}{H_{CA_2}}$$

Finally, we use the Inequality (6.27) to obtain the triangular inequality. By swapping C and A_2 in (6.27) we get:

$$\frac{H_{A_2|A_1}}{H_{A_2 A_1}} + \frac{H_{A_1|C}}{H_{A_1 C}} \geq \frac{H_{A_2|C}}{H_{CA_2}} \tag{6.28}$$

By summing Inequalities (6.27) and (6.28) we obtain the triangular inequality:

$$\frac{H_{A_2|A_1} + H_{A_1|A_2}}{H_{A_2 A_1}} + \frac{H_{A_1|C} + H_{C|A_1}}{H_{A_1 C}} \geq \frac{H_{A_2|C} + H_{C|A_2}}{H_{CA_2}}$$

$\square$

6.3.4   J-measure

J-measure, defined as

$$J_j = p_{\cdot j} \sum_k p_{k|j} \log \frac{p_{k|j}}{p_{k\cdot}} = \sum_k p_{kj} \log \frac{p_{kj}}{p_{k\cdot} p_{\cdot j}}$$

has the following properties:

Relation with information gain: $\sum_j J_j = Gain(A)$

Proof.

$$Gain(A) = H_C + H_A - H_{CA} = \sum_k \sum_j p_{kj} \log p_{kj} - \sum_k p_{k\cdot} \log p_{k\cdot} - \sum_j p_{\cdot j} \log p_{\cdot j}$$

From

$$\sum_k p_{k\cdot} \log p_{k\cdot} = \sum_j \sum_k p_{kj} \log p_{k\cdot}$$

and

$$\sum_j p_{\cdot j} \log p_{\cdot j} = \sum_j \sum_k p_{kj} \log p_{\cdot j}$$

we get the required equality:

$$Gain(A) = \sum_j \sum_k p_{kj} \log \frac{p_{kj}}{p_{k\cdot} p_{\cdot j}} = \sum_j J_j$$

$\square$

Nonnegativity: $J_j \geq 0$.

Proof. Let us rewrite J-measure as follows:

$$J_j = p_{\cdot j} \left(\sum_{k=1}^{m_0-1} p_{k|j} \log \frac{p_{k|j}}{p_{k\cdot}} + \left(1 - \sum_{k=1}^{m_0-1} p_{k|j}\right) \log \frac{1 - \sum_{k=1}^{m_0-1} p_{k|j}}{1 - \sum_{k=1}^{m_0-1} p_{k\cdot}} \right)$$

¿From this we get the partial derivative:

$$\frac{\partial J_j}{\partial p_{x|j}} = \log \frac{p_{x|j}}{p_{x\cdot}} + \log e - \log \frac{1 - \sum_{k=1}^{m_0-1} p_{k|j}}{1 - \sum_{k=1}^{m_0-1} p_{k\cdot}} - \log e$$

The above expression is equal to 0 when:

$$\forall k : \; p_{k|j} = p_{k\cdot}.$$

In this point it holds also $J_j = 0$. We conclude the proof by showing that this point is the minimum of J_j:

$$\frac{\partial^2 J_j}{\partial p_{x|j}^2} = \frac{1}{p_{x|j}} + \frac{1}{1 - \sum_{k=1}^{m_0-1} p_{k|j}} > 0$$

$\square$

Upper bound: $J_j \leq 0.53 \, bit$

Proof. Because the derivative of J_j is equal 0 also in the case, when for some $k_0 : p_{k_0|j} = 1$ and $\forall k \neq k_0 : p_{k|j} = 0$, this point represents a function extreme. Therefore the upper bound can be estimated with:

$$J_j \leq p_{\cdot j} \left(\min \left\{ \max_k - \log p_{k\cdot}, \; - \log p_{\cdot j} \right\} \right) \leq -p_{\cdot j} \log p_{\cdot j} \leq 0.53 \, bit$$

In the above derivation we used also the Bayesian equality:

$$\frac{p_{k|j}}{p_{k.}} = \frac{p_{j|k}}{p_{.j}}$$

and for $p_{k_0|j} = 1$ we have also

$$\log \frac{1}{p_{k_0.}} = \log \frac{p_{j|k_0}}{p_{.j}} \leq \log \frac{1}{p_{.j}}$$

$\square$

6.3.5 Gini-index

Prior Gini-index, defined as:

$$Gini\_prior = \sum_k \sum_{l \neq k} p_{k.} \cdot p_{l.} = 1 - \sum_k p_{k.}^2.$$

is an impurity measure.

Proof.
1. Maximum:

$$Gini\_prior = -1 - \sum_k^{m_0-1} p_{k.}^2 - \left(1 - \sum_k^{m_0-1} p_{k.} \right)^2$$

$$\frac{\partial Gini\_prior}{\partial p_{k.}} = -2p_{k.} + 2\left(1 - \sum_k^{m_0-1} p_{k.} \right)$$

The first derivative is equal to 0 in point: $p_{k.} = 1/m_0$
The second derivative is (always) negative:

$$\frac{\partial^2 Gini\_prior}{\partial p_{k.}^2} = -2 + 2(-1) = -4 < 0$$

2. Minimum:
$$Gini\_prior \geq 0 \wedge Gini\_prior = 0 \Leftrightarrow \exists! k : \; p_{k.} = 1$$

3. $Gini\_prior$ is symmetric.
4. $Gini\_prior$ is concave.
5. $Gini\_prior$ is continuous and continuously derivable.

$\square$

6.3.6 RELIEF and Gini-index

The quality estimate of attribute A_i by algorithm RELIEF is given with:

$$
\begin{aligned}
W(A_i) \;=\; & P(\mathit{diff}(i, \cdot, \cdot) = 0 | \textit{two nearest examples from the same class}) \\
- \; & P(\mathit{diff}(i, \cdot, \cdot) = 0 | \textit{two nearest examples from the opposite classes}) \quad (6.29)
\end{aligned}
$$

If we omit the nearness condition we get a (myopic) RELIEFm:

$$Wm(A_i) = constant \times \sum_j p_{.j}^2 \times Ginim(A_i) \qquad (6.30)$$

where $Ginim(A)$ is given with:

$$Ginim(A) = \sum_j \left(\frac{p_{.j}^2}{\sum_j p_{.j}^2} \times \sum_k p_{k|j}^2 \right) - \sum_k p_{k.}^2. \qquad (6.31)$$

Proof. By omitting the nearness condition in Equation (6.29) we get:

$$Wm(A_i) = P(\text{diff}(i, t_j, t_k) = 0 | c_j = c_k) - P(\text{diff}(i, t_j, t_k) = 0 | c_j \neq c_k)$$

where c_x stands for the class of learning example t_x.

Further, let:

$$P_{eq\_val} = P(\text{diff}(i, t_j, t_k) = 0)$$
$$P_{samecl} = P(c_j = c_k)$$

and

$$P_{samecl|eq\_val} = P(c_j = c_k | \text{diff}(i, t_j, t_k) = 0)$$

By using the Bayesian rule we get:

$$Wm(A_i) = \frac{P_{samecl|eq\_val} P_{eq\_val}}{P_{samecl}} - \frac{(1 - P_{samecl|eq\_val}) P_{eq\_val}}{1 - P_{samecl}} \qquad (6.32)$$

By using the following two equalities:

$$P_{samecl} = \sum_k p_{k.}^2.$$

$$P_{samecl|eq\_val} = \sum_j \left(\frac{p_{.j}^2}{\sum_j p_{.j}^2} \times \sum_k p_{k|j}^2 \right)$$

we finally get:

$$
\begin{aligned}
Wm(A_i) &= \frac{P_{eq\_val} \times Ginim(A_i)}{P_{samecl}(1 - P_{samecl})} \\
&= \frac{\sum_j p_{.j}^2 \times Ginim(A_i)}{\sum_k p_{k.}^2.(1 - \sum_k p_{k.}^2.)} \\
&= constant \times \sum_j p_{.j}^2 \times Ginim(A_i) \qquad (6.33)
\end{aligned}
$$

$\square$

6.3.7   Variance and Gini-index

If in the binary classification problem one class is transformed into value 0 and the other into value 1 of the regression variable (the discrete class variable is transformed into continuous one), we get the following equality:

$$Gini\_prior = 2s^2$$

Proof.

$$Gini\_prior = p_{1.}p_{2.} + p_{2.}p_{1.} = \frac{2n(C_1)n(C_2)}{n^2}$$

$$\bar{r} = \frac{n(C_1) \times 0 + n(C_2) \times 1}{n} = \frac{(C_2)}{n}$$

$$s^2 = \frac{1}{n} \sum_{l=1}^{n} (c_l - \bar{c})^2$$

$$= \frac{1}{n} \left(\sum_{l=1}^{n(C_1)} \left(0 - \frac{n(C_2)}{n} \right)^2 + \sum_{l=1}^{n(C_2)} \left(1 - \frac{n(C_2)}{n} \right)^2 \right)$$

$$= \frac{1}{n} \left(n(C_1) \left(\frac{n(C_2)}{n} \right)^2 + n(C_2) \left(\frac{n(C_1)}{n} \right)^2 \right)$$

$$= \frac{n(C_1)n(C_2)(n(C_1) + n(C_2))}{n^3} = \frac{n(C_1)n(C_2)}{n^2} = \frac{Gini\_prior}{2}$$

□

6.4   SUMMARY AND FURTHER READING

The difference between truth and fiction: fiction has to make sense.

— Mark Twain

- One of the crucial tasks in machine learning is the evaluation of the *quality of attributes*. For this purpose a number of measures have been developed that estimate the usefulness of an attribute for predicting the target variable.

- Useful attributes decrease the *impurity* of the target variable. Basic impurity measures for classification are *entropy* and *gini index*, and *variance* for regression. The corresponding quality measures are *information gain* and *gini index gain* in classification, and the *change of variance* in regression. All these measures overestimate attributes with many values.

- Measures with most appropriate bias with respect to the number of attribute values, are the *Distance measure* (obtained by normalizing the information gain), the *average absolute weight of evidence* (can be derived from information gain by replacing the entropy change with the weight of evidence), and *MDL*. MDL is able to detect useless – non-compressive – attributes.

- *J-measure* is derived from information gain. It evaluates the quality of a single attribute value or a single classification rule. It can be used to verify the statistical significance of the attribute value or the classification rule.

- Most measures estimate the quality of one attribute independently of the *context of other attributes*, therefore such measures are *myopic*. However, algorithm ReliefF and its regressional version RReliefF take into account also the context of other attributes and are therefore appropriate for problems with strong dependencies between attributes, such as XOR.

- The basic idea of various variants of algorithm *RELIEF* is to take into account not only the difference in attribute values and the difference in classes, but also the *distance* between the examples. Distance is calculated in the attribute space, therefore similar examples are close to each other and dissimilar ones are far apart. By taking the similarity of examples into account, the context of all the attributes is implicitly considered.

- In order to use the basic idea of RELIEF in regression, RReliefF (Regressional ReliefF) uses a kind of "probability" that two examples belong to two "different" classes. This "probability" is modeled with the distance between the values of the target variable of two learning examples.

- In order to use the minimum description length principle (MDL) in regression, we have to determine an appropriate *coding of real numbers*. When coding the value of the target variable (or the value of a continuous attribute), all possible values have the code of equal length. On the other hand, when coding the error, the desired code property is that smaller numbers (lower error) have shorter code lengths.

Many attribute evaluation measures for classification are based on *information theory*, developed by Shannon and Weaver (1949). The use of information gain for attribute quality estimation was proposed by Hunt et al. (1966) and became popular with Quinlan's (1979) ID3 algorithm. Quinlan (1986) introduced Gain-ratio which is widely used for generating decision trees with the most popular algorithm C4.5 (Quinlan, 1993). Rajski (1961) defined the distance measure. Mantaras (1989) proposed the use of distance measure in machine learning and described the proof for triangular inequality from Section 6.3.3. Good (1950) defined *plausibility* as the basis for the weight of evidence measure, which was introduced to the ML community by Michie (1989). J-measure was proposed by Smyth and Goodman (1990), Fayyad (1991) introduced ORT measure. An excellent classic book by Breiman et al. (1984) thoroughly analyses Gini-index and shows its relation to variance, described in Section 6.3.7.

The minimum description length principle and the coding of numbers in Equation (6.25) was introduced by Rissanen (1993). MDL principle is thoroughly analysed and discussed in the well-known book by Li and Vitanyi (1993). Suboptimal (Equation (6.6)) and optimal (Equation (6.8)) variants of MDL measure were introduced by Kononenko (1995).

White and Liu (1994) proposed statistics χ^2 and G for evaluating the attribute quality, however, Kononenko (1995) showed that these statistics are inappropriate for distinguishing attributes of different quality. Standard algorithms for evaluating Equation (6.12) are described by Press et al. (1988).

The starting point of non-myopic attribute evaluation measures was the description of the basic algorithm RELIEF by Kira and Rendell (1992a; 1992b). Its extension ReliefF was introduced by Kononenko (1994) who showed also the relation with Gini-index (described in Section 6.3.6). Regressional variant RReliefF was developed by Robnik-Šikonja and Kononenko (1997). The same authors (2003) provide thorough analysis and discussion of different variants of RELIEF. Another measure, Contextual merit (CM), based on nearness of examples, is described and related to RELIEF in Kononenko and Hong (1997).

Chapter 7

Data Preprocessing

Keen intelligence is two-edged. It may be used constructively or destructively. Intelligence is rightly guided only after the mind has acknowledged the inescapability of spiritual law.

— *Sri Yukteswar*

Various machine learning algorithms or their parts significantly differ in the representation of learning examples. This chapter first reviews methods for representation of complex structures with attributes, and then deals with approaches for transforming the representation of learning examples, such as:

- discretization of continuous attributes,
- fuzzy discretization of continuous attributes,
- binarization of attributes,
- converting discrete attributes to continuous, and
- dealing with missing and unknown attribute values.

Towards the end of the chapter we review some methods for visualization, both of input data and of results of machine learning, and techniques used for dimensionality reduction of the attribute space. Constructive induction, another important approach for transforming representation of learning examples, is described in Chapter 8.

7.1 REPRESENTATION OF COMPLEX STRUCTURES

The mind can never recognize neither create the beauty.

— *Eckhart Tolle*

The representation of learning examples with attributes (in propositional calculus) is

181

described in more detail in Section 4.1.1, together with properties and dependencies of attributes. In this section we review methods for describing complex structures (texts, images, graphs) with attributes. Complex structures can be naturally represented with the first-order predicate calculus. If we use a representation where the number of attributes is equal for all learning examples and fixed in advance, we must necessarily be satisfied with inexact representations that summarize some important properties of complex structures.

7.1.1   Representation of text documents

Recent developments in information technologies and popularization of the Internet have considerably increased the number of accessible text documents. Searching for important documents by hand is a virtually hopeless task. Searching for relevant documents (information retrieval) can benefit from machine learning and data mining techniques. However, for this purpose the learning examples (text documents in this case) must be appropriately described.

A frequently used approach for describing text documents is a *bag of words*. Each word is an attribute by itself, and for a given document its value is a frequency of the word in the document. Since the number of words (and therefore the number of attributes) can be over 10^5, the number of words is usually reduced by omitting conjunctions (e.g., "and", "or", "also"), separator words, very common words (e.g., "is") and some general words that convey no information about the document. Also, instead of complete words, only their stems are used, e.g. instead of words beaten, beatable, beating, beater, only the stem *beat* is used. Thus, all conjugations and declinations, and sometimes even synonyms, are treated as the same word.

Although the described approaches can considerably reduce the number of attributes (words in the bag), their number can still be very high. At the same time, many of the words are bound to have their count equal to 0. Huge numbers of attributes imply the use of a highly efficient machine learning algorithm. For the purpose of text classification, most frequently the naive Bayesian classifier and support vector machines (SVM) are used. Both are very efficient and often produce the best results in terms of predictive performance.

7.1.2   Representation of images

Similarly to text documents, images also need to be described with numerical features (attributes) in order to allow for efficient image recognition, classification, and search. Most frequently, images are *bit images*, consisting of *pixels*. For image description (parameterization) either general or specialized methods are used:

First and second order statistics.   First order statistics are calculated from probabilities that, when selecting a random image pixel, it has certain properties. The values of these statistics depend only on individual pixels and are independent of the neighboring pixels. Attributes that are derived from the first order statistics include the average image brightness and its standard deviation, entropy, and various moments.

Second order statistics are calculated from probability estimations that, when randomly selecting two equidistant image pixels, the two pixels have certain chosen properties. Attributes that are derived from the second order statistics include contrast, homogeneity, correlation, and variance.

Principal component analysis. The principal component analysis (PCA) is an algebraic procedure that converts a larger number of possibly correlated variables (attributes) to a smaller number of uncorrelated variables, named *principal components*. PCA is a rather popular approach for image parametrization. Each image is described as a linear combination of eigenvectors. PCA aims to find principal components from the distribution of eigenvectors in the learning set.

Attributes derived by association rules. Association rules can be used to describe relations between image pixels, similarly to describing relations between attributes (see Section 4.1.3). Each association rule consists of a conjunction of conditions in both the antecedent and the consequent part. In images, conditions constrain the pixel properties in the vicinity of the starting pixel. Thus the association rule statistically describes relations between neighboring image pixels.

Tailor-made image description. For each domain problem a specialized image description can be constructed with the use of appropriate background knowledge. Such attributes (e.g. the noise level, shape and brightness coefficients, the brightness deviation, the number of separated image fragments) can be more useful (informative) than the general attributes.

7.1.3   Representation of graphs

Many difficult problems can be naturally represented with directed and undirected graphs. Graphs may describe temporal ordering of events (e.g., for project planning), or various relations between objects (e.g., links between hypertext documents, such as HTML documents on the Internet). To describe graphs with attributes, their general properties need to be extracted, such as:

- the number of nodes and edges in the graph,
- the average number of incoming edges for each node (in-degree),
- the average number of outgoing edges for each node (out-degree),
- minimal, maximal, and average lengths of (acyclic) paths in the graph,
- average properties of object represented by the nodes,
- the number of cycles in the graph,
- average properties of pairs of objects represented by connected nodes.

Besides general properties, each graph can also be described with specialized attributes, describing the problem depicted by the graph.

7.2 DISCRETIZATION OF CONTINUOUS ATTRIBUTES

God, grant me the serenity to accept the things I cannot change, courage to change the things I can, and wisdom to know the difference.

— *Reinhold Niebuhr*

Many machine learning and data mining algorithms can deal only with discrete attributes. Therefore, continuous attributes need to be discretized either in advance, or during the learning process. Discretizing a continuous attribute means splitting (breaking) an interval of allowed values to a finite number of disjunct sub-intervals that are subsequently treated as discrete attribute values. By each discretization of an attribute some information is lost, since the attribute values from the same interval cannot be distinguished any more. However, discretization can also be advantageous, especially where some practically important interval boundaries can be used (resulting in more comprehensible knowledge), and where for noisy attributes some noise tolerance can be gained. For discretization purposes, an algorithm must sensibly determine

- the optimal number of intervals and
- optimal boundaries for each interval,

so as to maximize the attribute utility for a given classification or regression problem. In the following, we review only discretization methods for classification problems, as approaches for regression are similar, although less commonly used.

Utmost care is needed for choosing a suitable number of intervals. More intervals imply smaller loss of information, but also less reliable estimations of probability distributions within intervals. On the other hand, fewer intervals imply a greater loss of information, but also more reliable estimations of probability distributions within intervals. The number of intervals may be determined manually, or automatically with a suitable heuristic function.

7.2.1 Types of discretization

In practice, two greedy approaches to discretization are used: a *bottom-up* and a *top-down* approach. In both cases learning examples are first ordered according to the attribute values.

In the bottom-up approach discretization starts with as many intervals as there are learning examples. Subsequently, two adjacent intervals, most similar with respect to class probability distributions, are joined. The process is repeated until the quality $q(A)$ of the discretized attribute A stops increasing, or there are only two intervals left. The time complexity[1] of the bottom-up approach is $O(n^2)$, n being the number of learning examples.

In the top-down approach discretization starts with a single interval. In each step, one boundary is chosen (the number of intervals is incremented by one) so as to maximize the quality $q(A)$ of the discretized attribute A. The process is repeated, until the quality $q(A)$ of a discretized attribute stops increasing. The time complexity of the top-down approach is in the worst case also $O(n^2)$. However, since the number of intervals k is typically $k \ll n$, the time complexity is usually in the range of $O(kn)$.

7.2.2 Controlling discretization

In discretization, candidates for interval boundaries are only boundaries between examples that belong to different classes. The formal proof and justification of this statement are provided in Section 7.8. ◇

For controlling the discretization of a continuous attribute, any measure for the attribute quality can be used. However, we must be aware that the expected reduction of an impurity function q by including new boundaries increases. This is a consequence of the fact that a discrete attribute's importance increases if the number of its values is incremented. Therefore functions that prefer multi-valued attributes, such as information gain and Gini index are not suitable for discretization. Instead, functions that do not overestimate multi-valued attributes should be used, such as distance measure $1 - D$, MDL or ReliefF (see Section 6.1).

7.2.3 Fuzzy discretization

For a discretized attribute, a boundary between two intervals is actually a boundary between two decisions. The usual – hard – discretization does not distinguish between the values that lie closer to, or farther from an interval boundary. For example, if an attribute is discretized with boundaries 0.00, 0.30 and 1.00, we get two intervals: $[0.00, 30]$ and $[0.31, 1.00]$. Thus, attribute values 0.31 and 1.00 are treated in the same way, whereas 0.30 and 0.31 are treated differently, although they lie much closer to each other.

This obvious drawback of hard discretization may be mitigated by using soft or fuzzy discretization of continuous attributes. In *fuzzy discretization* a boundary is not a single point, but a probability distribution that models uncertainties of an attribute value belonging to each side of the boundary. Generally, each learning example has, for a newly discretized attribute, its values given as a distribution of memberships to different intervals. Hard discretization is represented by a simple step distribution (Figure 7.1(a)). For fuzzy discretization, different monotonous distributions may be used. Figures 7.1(b) and (c) give two examples of fuzzy discretization.

Instead of using fuzzy interval boundaries, one can also fuzzify the continuous attribute's values. Each attribute value is thus represented not by a single point on a real line, but by its most probable value, and a probability density function

---

[1] For definition of O-notation see Section A.2 in the appendix.

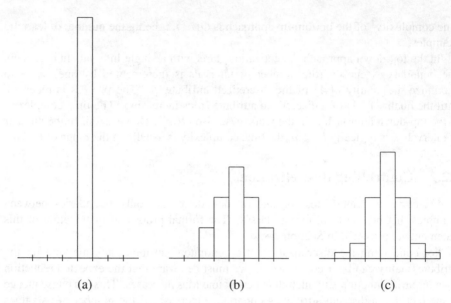

(a)   (b)   (c)

Figure 7.1: A hard (a) and two different fuzzy discretizations (b) and (c) for a given attribute value.

that monotonically decreases with the distance from the most probable value. The attribute is discretized with hard interval boundaries. To an example, each value of the discretized attribute is assigned with probability proportional to the area under the attribute's probability distribution within the corresponding interval.

7.3 ATTRIBUTE BINARIZATION

Freedom is not worth having if it does not include the freedom to make mistakes.
— Mahatma Gandhi

Several machine learning algorithms were originally designed to work only with binary-valued attributes. Also, many machine learning algorithms build binary decision trees. In both cases, all attributes are *binarized*, that is, each attribute is transformed into several binary attributes.

When building a binary decision tree, a single best binary attribute is chosen as the splitting criterion in each node. There are several reasons for building binary decision trees:

- Building binary trees increases the possibility of smaller and thus more optimal decision trees:

  - Several different values of a multi-valued attribute may yield similar or even identical subtrees (the replication problem). With binarization, similar subtrees may be unified into a single subtree.

- Binary splits of the learning set reduce the danger of shattering the data into too many small subsets. Each decision and probability estimation is thus more reliable.

- Some measures of attribute quality (e.g., information gain and Gini index) overestimate multi-valued attributes. By using binarization this problem is elegantly avoided.

- Some measures of attribute quality (e.g., ORT) work only with binary attributes.

For binarization of continuous attributes, only the first step of top-down discretization is performed since only a boundary that maximizes the attribute's quality is needed.

For binarization of multi-valued discrete attributes there are two possibilities:

- For each value of the original attribute A a new binary attribute is generated by joining all other values into another value. The number of new binary attributes is equal to the number of original attribute values m_A.

- The number of generated binary attributes is the number of possible different splits of attribute values into two disjunct subsets. If an original attribute has m_A values, we get

$$\frac{1}{2} \sum_{k=1}^{m_A-1} \binom{m_A}{k} = 2^{m_A-1} - 1 \tag{7.1}$$

new binary attributes.

The latter approach is more general, however it is too time consuming when the number of original attribute values is even moderately large. Except in very special cases (e.g., for two-class problems), for which efficient algorithms exist, inexact algorithms are used that provide acceptable, but sub-optimal solutions for binarization.

7.3.1 Two-class problems

For two-class problems we can, for an arbitrary impurity measure, determine the optimal binarization of an attribute A with m_A original values, in linear time $O(m_A)$.⋄

Let attribute values $V_j, j = 1 \ldots m_A$ be ordered with respect to increasing conditional probabilities of the first class:

$$P(C_1|V_1) \le P(C_1|V_2) \le \cdots \le P(C_1|V_{m_A}) \tag{7.2}$$

The quality of a binarized attribute A (with two values, corresponding to disjunct subsets of original values) is therefore

$$q(A) = \phi(P(C_1), \ldots, P(C_{n_0})) - \sum_{j=1}^{2} P(\mathcal{V}_j)\phi(P(C_1|\mathcal{V}_j), \ldots, P(C_{n_0}|\mathcal{V}_j)) \tag{7.3}$$

It can be shown that Equation (7.3) has its maximum where for the two subsets $\mathcal{V}_j, j = 1, 2$ it holds

$$\mathcal{V}_1 = \{V_1, \ldots, V_l\}, \quad \mathcal{V}_2 = \{V_{l+1}, \ldots, V_{m_A}\} \tag{7.4}$$

for some l: $0 < l < m_A$. For two-class problems it therefore suffices to review only $m_A - 1$ splits of attribute values instead of all $2^{m_A-1} - 1$.

7.3.2 Multi-class problems

For multi-class problems as well as for two-class problems, where impurity measures are not to be used, a greedy algorithm (Algorithm 7.1) for searching a (sub)optimal binarization can be used.

Algorithm 7.1 Greedy binarization.

INPUT: A bag of attribute values with corresponding class labels.
OUTPUT: Two sets of values, corresponding to two new binary values.

    Choose an attribute value that maximizes its quality, if treated as a binary attribute, and assign it to the set S_1
    Assign all other attribute values to the set S_2.
    repeat
        if there exists a value $V_2 \in S_2$ that, when moved to S_1, improves the attribute's quality
        then
            move V_2 from S_2 to S_1
        end if
        if there exists a value $V_1 \in S_1$ that, when moved to S_2, improves the attribute's quality
        then
            move V_1 from S_1 to S_2
        end if
    until the quality of binarized attribute ceases to improve

---

7.4 TRANSFORMING DISCRETE ATTRIBUTES INTO CONTINUOUS

Though man's ingenuity for getting himself into trouble appears to be endless, the Infinite Succor is no less resourceful.

— Lahiri Mahasaya

Several machine learning methods, most notably those originating from statistical techniques, cannot deal with discrete attributes and therefore implicitly assume that all attributes are continuous. Such methods are different regression models, discriminant functions, and also neural networks.

    A two-valued attribute can always be treated as a special case of a continuous attribute. One value is treated as 0 and another as 1. Thus they can be ordered, and used in arithmetic operations and functions.

If the values of the multi-valued discrete attribute can be ordered (i.e. the attribute is *ordinal*), they can be enumerated and treated as continuous values. Otherwise, a multi-valued attribute with m values is transformed into m binary attributes (as described in Section 7.3.2), each subsequently treated as a continuous attribute. The downside of this approach is a potentially large number of interdependent new attributes.

7.5   DEALING WITH MISSING VALUES

The true wisdom of an old man is to include death in his life and working plan as the ultimate peak of his life and work.

— *Anton Trstenjak*

In real-life data mining problems there is often the case when values of some attributes are missing. Missing values can either be ignored, supplanted by the most probable attribute value, or treated with a probability distribution of attribute values. For calculating the probability of a given attribute value, usually conditional probabilities given the class, are used for discrete attribute A_k:

$$P(V_j | C_k), \quad j = 1 \dots m_k \tag{7.5}$$

For continuous attributes, conditional probability distributions given the class are used. To determine the most probable attribute value, machine learning algorithms can be used. They learn to predict the missing attribute value from all other attributes and the class label. Thus we get as many learning problems as there are attributes with missing values. Alternatively, maximum likelihood algorithms such as the *EM algorithm* see Section 12.5.2) can also be used to fill-in the missing values.

7.6   VISUALIZATION

And the more you become aware of the unknown self - if you become aware of it - the more you realize that it is inseparably connected with everything else that is.

— *Alan Watts*

Because of the nature of their brain, humans tend to process visual information much quickly than numerical information. This is why data visualization is of great importance both in data preparation and interpretation, for discovering important relations, for quality assurance and quality control in machine learning and data mining in general. Data visualization is actually a transformation of the raw data into a more presentable (and understandable) shape. Although different visual representations appeal to different individuals, there exist some general principles for data visualization.

In data mining and machine learning it is important to suitably prepare the learning data, and – according to the knowledge about the data – to devise a suitable learning approach. This means that data has to be reviewed, ordered, and transformed in the most appropriate format for the learning task. While problem experts are invaluable for data preparation and problem definition, nevertheless a data mining expert has to get familiar with data properties and quality. For this purpose, different visualization methods are frequently used.

However, data to be used for learning are not the only thing worth visualizing. Results of machine learning algorithms – both intermediate and final – must also be comprehensibly interpreted and discussed with problem (domain) experts, who are often unfamiliar with advanced computer techniques and representations. This is where visualization techniques are of exceptional use, presenting complex concepts in easily understandable pictures. Visualization may considerably simplify the dialog with the expert, as well as speed-up the interpretation and evaluation of the produced results, models or hypotheses.

7.6.1   Visualizing a single attribute

For visualization of discrete attributes, most frequently histograms are used. They depict relative frequencies of attribute values. Thus, a histogram is actually a probability distribution of attribute values. However, histograms are useful only for visualizing discrete attributes; continuous attributes have to be discretized first. For visualization purposes, equidistant discretization is usually preferred in order to preserve the scale of the original attribute. By studying the probability distribution of the attribute, one can possibly detect curious anomalies, indicating either particular domain properties, errors in data, or specific data encoding. Figure 7.2 shows an actual example of the histogram of a continuous attribute. The histogram shows an extraordinarily high number of examples with attribute values close to 0. In this (real-life) case it turned out that this was a consequence of data encoding, where missing (unknown) values were encoded as 0, that is otherwise a perfectly valid attribute value.

Figure 7.3 shows how histograms can be converted to density estimation plots. The smoothing factor depends on the problem domain and should be chosen with care.

7.6.2   Visualizing pairs of attributes

When visualizing pairs of attributes, we are especially interested in their mutual dependence. For this purpose, a *scatterplot* visualization technique is used. An example of visualizing the (almost linear) relation between two attributes is shown in Figure 7.4.

If one of the attributes is time, a *time plot* can be drawn. Time plots can show interesting properties of attributes. Figure 7.5 shows an unexpected step-like growth of children's weight with respect to the time. It turned out that this unexpected result was a consequence of sloppy weight measurements. Children were weighed with their clothes on, both in winter and in summer. Since in winter the weight of clothes is much larger than in summer, this causes the step-like weight growth, that has actually nothing to do with children's actual weight gain.

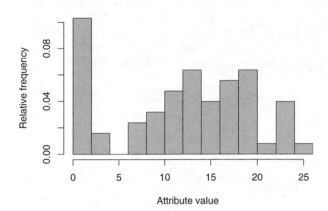

Figure 7.2: A histogram of a single continuous attribute. Note the unusually high number of values near 0.

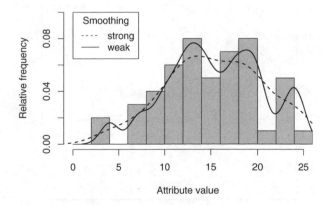

Figure 7.3: A histogram and two different density estimations of a single continuous attribute (the same as in Figure 7.2, with anomalous encoded values (0) removed).

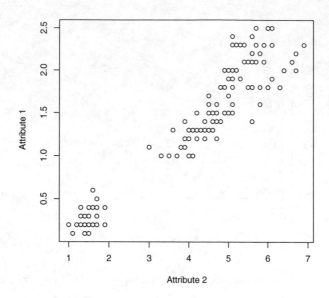

Figure 7.4: A scatterplot depicting an almost linear relation between two attributes.

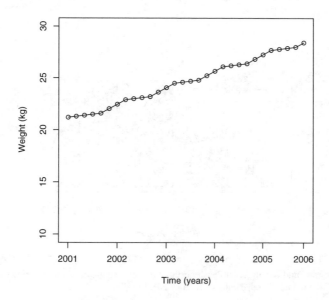

Figure 7.5: An example of the time plot.

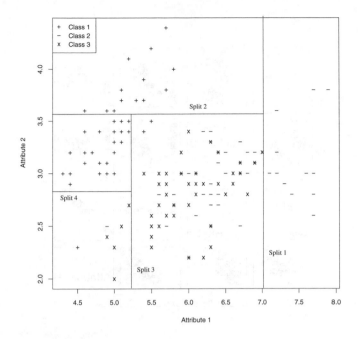

Figure 7.6: A scatterplot depicting results of decision tree learning in a three-class problem.

In classification problems, sometimes dependencies between two attributes and the class attribute are visualized. In this case, a scatterplot is composed of different symbols representing classes so that all points belonging to the same class are labelled with the same symbol. Figure 7.6 depicts a scatterplot for a three-class problem. Different classes are represented with different symbols (+, − and ×).

7.6.3   Visualizing several attributes

Several attributes can be visualized by depicting their pairwise dependencies in a scatterplot matrix – a matrix of pairwise scatterplots with empty diagonal elements (Figure 7.7). While this is not a true visualization of the complete attribute space, it often provides useful information, since in most cases pairwise dependencies are what is of greatest interest.

Alternatively, all attribute values can be visualized at the same time for given examples. Their values are depicted on a vertical axis. An attribute is therefore a vertical line. Each example has its attribute values connected with a broken line. From such a *parallel* plot it can be seen how strongly attributes are correlated, whether there exist some similar subsets of examples, and the degree of correlation between subsets of examples. An example of parallel plot depicting four continuous attributes is shown in Figure 7.8.

Yet another visualization technique – *star glyphs* – represents learning examples with stars. Each star spike corresponds to an attribute value – the larger the attribute

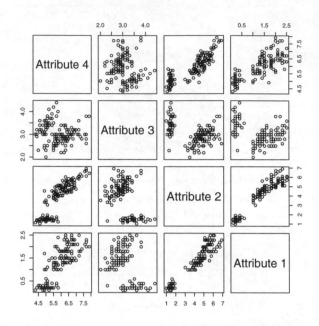

Figure 7.7: A scatterplot matrix depicting pairwise dependencies between attributes.

value, the longer the spike. Adjacent spikes are connected with a straight line. Therefore, similar examples are represented with similar stars. An example of a star glyph plot is shown in Figure 7.9.

Psychovisual approaches, such as Chernoff faces take advantage of the natural familiarity and recognition of human faces. Here, attribute values determine the features of the face, such as: height of face, width of face, shape of face, height of mouth, width of mouth, curve of smile, height of eyes, width of eyes, height of hair, width of hair, styling of hair, height of nose, width of nose, width of ears, height of ears. Figure 7.10 visualizes the same examples as Figure 7.9.

Besides explicit visualization of attribute dependencies with respect to actual attribute values, dependencies between attributes can be calculated in advance over all learning examples, and subsequently visualized. Such a *global* visualization of attribute dependencies is described in Section 8.1.

7.6.4   Visualizing results of machine learning

Machine learning results can be visualized as a set of hypersurfaces in a-dimensional space, where a is the number of attributes. Hypersurfaces discriminate between examples from different classes. It is easiest to visualize the hypersurface's projections into two-dimensional subspaces, and examine the curves that dichotomize between different classes. An example of decision tree class boundaries is shown in Figure 7.6.

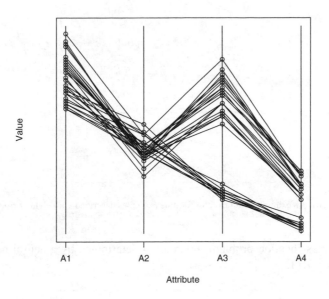

Figure 7.8: An example of a parallel plot depicting values of four continuous attributes (A1-A4) for 30 examples.

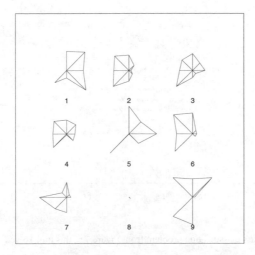

Figure 7.9: An example of a star glyph plot for nine examples described with eight attributes.

Figure 7.10: An example of a face plot for nine examples described with eight attributes.

For the same classification problem, boundaries determined by a neural network are shown in Figure 7.11.

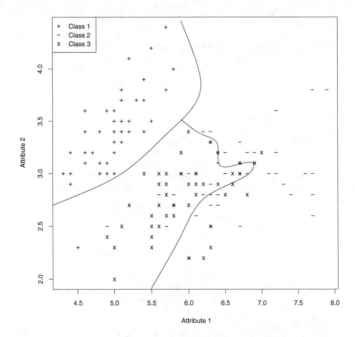

Figure 7.11: A three-class classification problem from Figure 7.6, this time solved with a neural network.

In regression problems, the result of learning is a hyper surface in a $(a + 1)$-dimensional space, a being the number of attributes, and an additional dimension

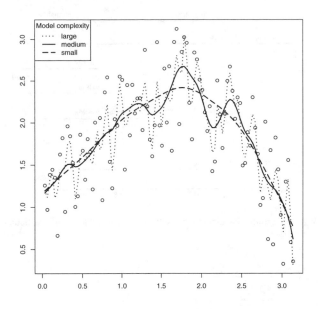

Figure 7.12: A relation between model complexity and its performance (ability to fit the data).

reserved for the regressional variable. In two dimensions it is therefore possible only to visualize the regressional values in dependence of a single attribute. Figure 7.12 depicts results of three regressional models of different complexity, evaluated on the same data. The figure clearly shows a compromise between the regressional model's complexity and its ability to fit data.

Besides visualizing the results of the learned model, it is often beneficial to visualize also the structure of the learned model. Visual representation of the learned decision or regression tree may be interactive in describing the tree structure on several different levels of detail. For example, each node can be expanded with a mouse click, displaying the number of learning examples, class distribution, and estimated attribute quality.

When using a model to solve new problems (e.g., to make class predictions for new examples) it is often useful not only to predict the class value, but also to transparently describe why such a value was predicted. With respect to the types of models they produce, different algorithms offer different explanations of their results. For the naive Bayesian classifier an explanation is a sum of information scores for each separate attribute (see Equation (9.14)). Such an explanation is visualized with a histogram of information scores. It helps in determining the attributes that decidedly impact the final result, and provides insight into the classification process.

A modified naive Bayesian classifier that uses odds instead of probabilities (similarly to Bayesian neural networks, described in Section 11.4, Equation 11.11) can

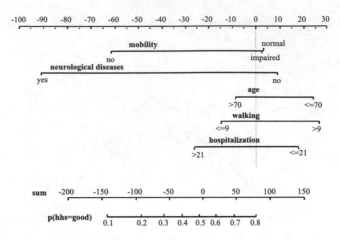

Figure 7.13: A nomogram, visualizing a naive Bayesian classification of a particular example.

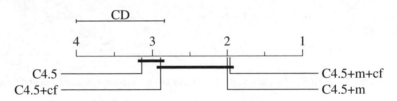

Figure 7.14: Visualization of significance of performance difference for several machine learning algorithms.

be visualized by nomograms. Figure 7.13 depicts a calculation of probability for class "good" $P(hhs = good)$ across the sum of attribute scores. For each attribute its score on a scale from -100 to 30 (for this example) is shown. Each attribute value contributes its score to the total sum that determines the odds and thus the class probability. An unknown attribute value does not contribute to the final sum of scores.

When comparing the performance of different machine learning algorithms, different statistical tests can be used (Section 3.4). To determine how significant the performance differences are, one has to review a table of test results for all pairs of machine learning algorithms. This, however, is a tedious, unrewarding work. Such a table can be visualized, as shown in Figure 7.14. This figure compares four variants of the popular C4.5 decision tree learners. The upper part of the figure depicts a critical value for performance difference CD for the Nemenyi test (Equation 3.91). C4.5 variants whose performances differ insignificantly are connected with a bold line. This clearly depicts for which algorithms their performance is more or less significantly different. From the figure it is clearly visible that the original C4.5 significantly differs from both C4.5+m and C4.5+m+cf. On the other hand, the variant C4.5+cf is not significantly different from any other variant.

7.7   DIMENSIONALITY REDUCTION

Nothing in the world makes people so afraid as the influence of independent-minded people.

— *Albert Einstein*

Advances in data collection and storage capabilities during the past decades have led to an information overload in most sciences. Researchers working in domains as diverse as engineering, astronomy, biology, remote sensing, economics, and consumer transactions face huge quantities of observations and simulations on a daily basis. Such datasets, in contrast with smaller, more traditional datasets that have been studied extensively in the past, present new challenges in data analysis. Traditional statistical methods break down partly because of the increase in the number of observations, but mostly because of the increase in the number of variables associated with each observation. One of the problems with high-dimensional datasets is that, in many cases, not all the measured variables are important for understanding the underlying phenomena of interest. While certain computationally expensive novel methods can construct predictive models with high accuracy from high-dimensional data, it is still of interest in most applications to reduce the dimensionality of the original data prior to any modeling.

7.7.1   Feature subset selection

In order to allow for efficient machine learning and data mining, it is often advantageous to select an optimal subset of attributes (features). Feature subset selection is necessary when there are too many attributes or the set of attributes consists of irrelevant, random, redundant, or correlated attributes that may degrade the learning performance. The desired subset of attributes should optimize some criterion (e.g., the hypothesis compressiveness or the classification accuracy). Because the number of possible feature subsets (2^a, where a is the number of features or attributes) is usually too large, heuristic approaches are used to select a (sub)optimal set of attributes.

The simplest and quickest method for feature subset selection is *filtering*. By this approach the attribute quality is estimated with a chosen function (e.g., MDL or (R)ReliefF), and k best attributes out of total a attributes are selected. The number k may either be chosen in advance, or determined dynamically by counting the number of attributes whose quality exceeds some threshold value.

A more advanced, but much slower method is *internal optimization*, also called a *wrapper* approach. For this purpose, a machine learning algorithm is used in conjunction with internal cross validation (i.e., cross validation without testing examples). Learning examples are divided into a temporary learning and a temporary testing set in order to estimate the optimization criterion. Learning is repeated with different parameter settings (in this case, different subsets of attributes) until a (local) optimum is found.

Usually a greedy approach is used for searching the space of feature subsets. If a set of attributes is relatively small, more advanced methods can be used. Most frequently, *forward search* and *backward search* are used:

- Forward search starts with an empty set of attributes. In each subsequent step it proceeds by adding either a random attribute (faster) or an attribute that optimizes some criterion (slower), and accepts the addition if the new feature subset improves the optimization criterion.

- Backward search starts with the complete set of attributes. In each subsequent step it proceeds by removing either a random attribute (faster) or an attribute that optimizes some criterion (slower), and accepts the addition if the new feature subset improves the optimization criterion.

- Mixed search starts with a random set of attributes. In each subsequent step a new attribute can be added (as in forward search), or an existing attribute removed from the set of attributes (as in backward search).

In all cases the process is repeated until the optimization criterion cannot be further improved.

7.7.2   Feature extraction

In feature extraction we are interested in finding new features (attributes) that are calculated as a function of the original features (attributes). In this context, dimensionality reduction is a mapping from a multidimensional space into a space of fewer dimensions. It is sometimes the case that analyses such as regression or classification can be carried out in the reduced space more accurately than in the original space. More formally, the dimensionality reduction problem can be stated as follows: given the a-dimensional random variable $\mathbf{x} = (x_1, \ldots, x_a)$ find a lower dimensional representation of it, $\mathbf{s} = (s_1, \ldots, s_k)$ with $k < a$, that captures the content in the original data, according to some criterion. The components of $\mathbf{s}$ are sometimes called the hidden or latent components. Different fields use different names for a multivariate vectors: the term "variable" is mostly used in statistics, while "feature" and "attribute" are alternatives commonly used in data mining and machine learning.

Dimensionality reduction without loss of information is possible if the data falls exactly on a smooth, locally flat subspace; then the reduced dimensions are just coordinates in the subspace. More commonly, data is noisy and there does not exist an exact mapping, so there must be some loss of information. Dimensionality reduction is beneficial if the loss of information due to mapping to a lower-dimensional space is less than the gain due to problem simplification.

Dimensionality reduction methods can be classified as linear and nonlinear. Linear methods attempt to find a globally flat subspace, while nonlinear methods attempt to find a locally flat subspace. As is the case with other problems, linear methods are simpler and more completely understood, while nonlinear methods are more general and more difficult to analyze.

Linear techniques result in each of the $k \leq a$ components of the new variable being a linear combination of the original variables:

$$\mathbf{s} = W\mathbf{x} \qquad (7.6)$$

where W is a $k \times a$ linear transformation weight matrix. When expressing the same relationship as

$$\mathbf{x} = A\mathbf{s} \tag{7.7}$$

where A is a $a \times k$ mixing matrix, the new variables $\mathbf{s}$ can also be called the hidden or the latent variables. In terms of an $n \times a$ observation matrix (dataset) X, we have

$$A = WX \tag{7.8}$$
$$X = AS \tag{7.9}$$

There exist a plethora of dimensionality reduction methods, most popular being the principal component analysis (PCA), the independent component analysis (ICA), the factor analysis, and random projections. Most dimensionality reduction methods assume that all attributes are continuous. If this is not the case, they should be transformed as described in Section 7.4.

7.7.3   Principal components analysis

Principal components analysis (PCA) is a linear transformation that chooses a new coordinate system for the data such that the greatest variance by any projection of the data set lies on the first axis (then called the first principal component), the second greatest variance on the second axis, and so on. PCA can be used for reducing dimensionality in a dataset while retaining those characteristics of the dataset that contribute most to its variance by eliminating the later principal components (by a more or less heuristic decision). The remaining characteristics may be the "most important", but this is not necessarily the case.

PCA has the speciality of being the optimal linear transformation for keeping the subspace that has the largest variance. However, this comes at the price of a rather great computational requirement. As opposed to some other linear transforms, PCA does not have a fixed set of basis vectors, but its basis vectors depend on the particular data.

Assuming the zero empirical mean (the empirical mean of the distribution has been subtracted from the data set), the principal component $\mathbf{w}_1$ of a dataset X can be defined as:

$$\mathbf{w}_1 = \underset{\|\mathbf{w}\|=1}{\operatorname{argmax}} E\left\{ \left(\mathbf{w}^T X\right)^2 \right\} \tag{7.10}$$

With the first $k-1$ components, the k-th component can be found by subtracting the first $k-1$ principal components from X:

$$\hat{X}_{k-1} = X - \sum_{i=1}^{k-1} \mathbf{w}_i \mathbf{w}_i^T X \tag{7.11}$$

and by substituting this as the new dataset to find a principal component in

$$\mathbf{w}_k = \underset{\|\mathbf{w}\|=1}{\operatorname{argmax}} E\left\{ \left(\mathbf{w}^T \hat{X}_{k-1}\right)^2 \right\}. \tag{7.12}$$

A simpler way to calculate the components $\mathbf{w}_i$ uses the empirical covariance matrix C of the data set X. By finding the eigenvalues and eigenvectors of the covariance matrix C, we find that the eigenvectors with the largest eigenvalues correspond to the dimensions that have the strongest correlation in the dataset. Note that the eigenvectors of C are actually the columns of the matrix V, where $C = ULV^T$ is the singular value decomposition of the empirical covariance matrix C. The original examples are finally projected onto the reduced vector space.

While PCA is a popular technique in pattern recognition and machine learning, it is not optimized for class separability. An alternative is the linear discriminant analysis (LDA), which does take this into account. PCA optimally minimizes the reconstruction error under the L_2 norm.

PCA using the covariance method

Let us have n examples (rows of the observation matrix X) $\mathbf{x}_1 \ldots \mathbf{x}_n$ each of length a (the number of attributes), written as $\mathbf{x}_m = (x_{m,1} \ldots x_{m,a})$, and want to project it into a k dimensional subspace using PCA. The algorithm that describes the steps involved in this procedure is shown in Algorithm 7.2.

Algorithm 7.2 The principal component analysis algorithm.

INPUT: Data organized into a $n \times a$ data matrix D, and
                the desired number of components k.
OUTPUT: The k principal components with largest eigenvalues.

Find the $a \times 1$ empirical mean vector $\mathbf{m}$ along each column (attribute)
Subtract the empirical mean vector $\mathbf{m}$ from each column of the data matrix D.
Store mean-subtracted data $n \times a$ matrix in S.
Find the empirical covariance $a \times a$ matrix C of S: $C = S \cdot S^T$
Compute and sort by decreasing eigenvalue, the eigenvectors V of C.
Store the mean vector $\mathbf{m}$.
Store the first k columns of V as P. P will have dimension $a \times k$, $1 \le k \le a$.

When different dimensions of the input data have different measuring units, by using matrix C we are computing linear combinations of data of different scales. In such cases it makes more sense to use normalized data. After computing the matrix C with elements

$$C_{ij} = \sum_{m=1}^{n} x_{m,i} x_{m,j} \tag{7.13}$$

we can also compute the correlation matrix R with elements

$$R_{ij} = C_{ij}/(\sigma_i \cdot \sigma_j) \tag{7.14}$$

The matrix R is symmetric (like the covariance matrix), its values are between -1 and 1, and the diagonal elements are $C_{ii} = 1$. For this case the Algorithm 7.2 is modified by replacing the matrix C with R in the last three steps, as well as by storing the values of $\sigma = (\sigma_1, \ldots, \sigma_a)^T$.

After k principal components are found, they are used for projecting new examples into the k-dimensional component space. Let us have an a-dimensional example $\mathbf{e}$. Then the k-dimensional projected vector is

$$\mathbf{v} = P^T(\mathbf{e} - \mathbf{m}) \qquad (7.15)$$

for the non-normalized PCA. If the correlation matrix R has been used instead of the covariance matrix C, the elements of the input vector should be normalized:

$$\mathbf{z} = (\mathbf{e} - \mathbf{m}) \cdot \sigma^{-1} \qquad (7.16)$$

Then the projected vector is

$$\mathbf{v} = P^T \cdot \mathbf{z} \qquad (7.17)$$

7.7.4 Independent component analysis

Independent component analysis (ICA) is a higher-order method that, similarly to PCA, seeks linear projections, although not necessarily orthogonal to each other. However, the used projections should be as nearly statistically independent as possible. Statistical independence is much stronger than uncorrelatedness, since it involves higher-order statistics instead of second-order. Formally, random variables $\mathbf{x} = \{x_1, \ldots, x_a\}$ are said to be *uncorrelated* if $\forall i \neq j, 1 \leq i, j, \leq a$ we have

$$\text{Cov}(x_i, x_j) = E((x_i - \mu_i)(x_j - \mu_j)) = E(x_i x_j) - E(x_i)E(x_j) = 0 \qquad (7.18)$$

On the other hand, random variables $\mathbf{x}$ are *independent* if the corresponding multivariate probability density f factorizes, and can be rewritten as

$$f(x_1, \ldots, x_a) = f_1(x_1) f_2(x_2) \ldots f_a(x_a) \qquad (7.19)$$

Independence always implies uncorrelatedness, but in general the reverse does not hold. Only if the distribution $f(x_1, \ldots, x_a)$ is multivariate normal, are the two equivalent. Therefore, for Gaussian distributions, the principal components are independent components.

Different types of ICA can be characterized by the type of components (linear or non-linear), and whether the noise is explicitly included (noisy or noise-free). The most popular noise-free linear ICA model for the a-dimensional random vector $\mathbf{x}$ seeks to estimate the components of the k-dimensional vector s and the $a \times k$ full column rank mixing matrix A (7.7):

$$(x_1, \ldots x_a)^T = A \cdot (s_1, \ldots, s_k)^T \qquad (7.20)$$

such that the components of $\mathbf{s}$ are as independent as possible, according to some definition of independence. The noisy linear ICA contains an additive random noise component:

$$(x_1, \ldots x_a)^T = A \cdot (s_1, \ldots, s_k)^T + (u_1, \ldots u_a)^T \qquad (7.21)$$

While noise-free ICA is just a special case of noisy ICA, nonlinear ICA is usually considered as a separate case.

As originally intended, independent component analysis (ICA) was designed for separating a multivariate signal into additive subcomponents supposing the mutual statistical independence of the non-Gaussian source signals. The independence assumption is correct in most cases so the blind ICA separation of a mixed signal gives very good results. Besides blind source separation, ICA has been applied to many different problems, including exploratory data analysis, blind deconvolution, and feature extraction. In the feature extraction context, the columns of the matrix A represent features in the data, and the components s_i give the coefficient of the i-th feature in the data. Several authors have used ICA to extract meaningful features from natural images. It must however be noted that ICA is not able to extract the actual number of source signals, the order of the source signals, nor the signs or the scales of the sources.

Linear ICA algorithms

In linear ICA, the data matrix X is considered to be a linear combination of non-Gaussian (independent) components, i.e. $X = SA$ where columns of S contain the independent components and A is a linear mixing matrix. In short, ICA attempts to "un-mix" the data by estimating an un-mixing matrix W where $XW = S$. Under this generative model the measured "signals" in X tend to be "more Gaussian" than the original source components (in S) due to the Central limit theorem. Thus, in order to extract the independent components/sources we search for an un-mixing matrix W that maximizes the non-Gaussianity of the sources.

In contrast with PCA, the goal of ICA is not necessarily dimensionality reduction. To find $k < a$ independent components, one needs to first reduce the dimensionality of the original data from a to k, by a method such as PCA. There is no order among the independent components. Once they are estimated, they can be ordered according to the norms of the columns of the mixing matrix (similar to the ordering in PCA), or according to some non-Gaussianity measure.

Statistical ICA algorithms therefore find the independent components (also called factors, latent variables or sources) by maximizing the statistical independence of the estimated components. Non-Gaussianity, motivated by the Central limit theorem, is one method for measuring the independence of the components. Non-Gaussianity can be measured, for instance, with kurtosis[2], or with approximations of negative normalized entropy (neg-entropy).

The estimation of the noise-free ICA model in (7.20) consists of two parts: specifying the objective function (also called the contrast, the loss function, or the cost function), and the algorithm to optimize the objective function. Objective functions can be categorized into two groups:

- multi-unit contrast functions that estimate all k independent components at once,

---

[2]Kurtosis (the fourth standardized moment) is defined as the ratio of the fourth cumulant and the square of the second cumulant of the probability distribution: $\gamma_2 = \kappa_4/\kappa_2^2 = \mu_4/\sigma^4 - 3$.

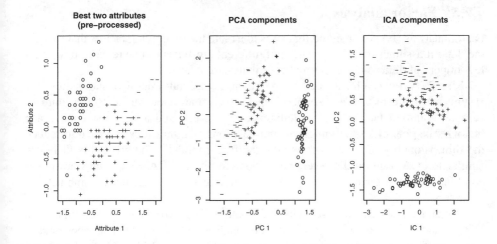

Figure 7.15: Dimensionality reduction for a three-class problem..

such as the likelihood of the noise-free ICA model, and mutual information between random variables (Kullback-Leibler divergence),

- one-unit contrast functions that estimate a single independent component at a time, such as various approximations of negative normalized entropy (neg-entropy).

There exist several algorithms for ICA, among them the most popular are infomax, FastICA and JADE. Typical algorithms for ICA use centering (subtracting the mean of each variable of the data matrix X), whitening (projecting the data onto its principle component directions, i.e. $X \longrightarrow XK$ where K is a pre-whitening matrix), and dimensionality reduction as preprocessing steps in order to simplify and reduce the complexity of the problem for the actual iterative algorithm. Whitening and dimensionality reduction can be achieved with the principal component analysis or the singular value decomposition. First, the data is centered by subtracting the mean of each column of the data matrix X. The data matrix is then "whitened" by projecting the data onto its principle component directions i.e. $X \to XK$. The ICA algorithm then estimates an un-mixing matrix W so that $XKW = S$. W is chosen so as to maximize the non-Gaussianity approximation.

Figure 7.15 shows a comparison of dimensionality reduction techniques for a three-class problem. Compared are the filtering approach (two best attributes selected), PCA and ICA, both with two best components. Both PCA and ICA clearly outperform filtering in terms of class separability (although they are not designed to maximize it). Note that PCA and ICA result in almost the same components, where ICA components are determined up to their sign.

7.7.5   Factor analysis

Factor analysis (FA) is a method that aims to isolate the underlying factors that explain the data. It assumes that all the values of different attributes can be reduced down to a few important dimensions because the attributes are related.

Like PCA, FA is a linear method, based on the second-order data summaries. FA assumes that the measured variables depend on some unknown, and often unmeasurable, common factors (e.g. intelligence test results and a common intelligence factor). The goal of FA is to uncover such relations, and thus it can be used to reduce the dimensionality of datasets following the factor model. The process is therefore similar to PCA, only in the reverse direction. While in PCA components are linear combinations of original attributes, in FA the original attributes are linear combinations of factors.

Factor analysis can be used either for knowledge extraction by examining the factors and their loadings, or for dimensionality reduction. For dimensionality reduction, factor analysis does not offer any advantages over PCA in terms of captured information from original attributes. However, there might be significant contributions when the factor interpretability allows for identification of common causes, a simple explanation, and knowledge extraction.

The factor model

The zero-mean a-dimensional random vector $\mathbf{x}$ with covariance matrix Σ satisfies the k-factor model if

$$\mathbf{x} = \Lambda \mathbf{f} + \mathbf{u} \qquad (7.22)$$

where Λ is a $a \times k$ matrix of constants (loadings), and $\mathbf{f}$ and $\mathbf{u}$ are the random common factors and specific factors, respectively. In addition, the factors are all uncorrelated and the common factors are standardized to have unit variance. Under these assumptions, the diagonal covariance matrix of $\mathbf{u}$ can be written as $\mathrm{Cov}(u) = \Psi = diag(\psi_{11}, \psi_{22}, \ldots, \psi_{aa})$. If the data covariance matrix can be decomposed as

$$\Sigma = \Lambda \Lambda^T + \Psi, \qquad (7.23)$$

then it can be shown that the k-factor model holds. Since x_i can be written as

$$x_i = \sum_{j=1}^{k} \lambda_{ij} f_j + u_i, \quad i = 1, \ldots, a \qquad (7.24)$$

its variance may be decomposed as

$$\sigma_{ii} = \sum_{j=1}^{k} \lambda_{ij}^2 + \psi_{ii} = h_i^2 + \psi_{ii} \qquad (7.25)$$

where the first part $h_i^2 = \sum_{j=1}^{k} \lambda_{ij}^2$ is called the communality and represents the variance of x_i common to all variables, while the second part ψ_{ii} is called the specific or unique variance and represents the contribution in the variability of x_i due to its specific u_i part, not shared by the other variables. The term λ_{ij}^2 measures the magnitude of the dependence of x_i on the common factor f_j. If several variables x_i have high loadings λ_{ij} on a given factor f_j, the implication is that those variables measure the same unobservable quantity, and are therefore redundant. Unlike PCA, the factor model does not depend on the scale of the variables. However, the factor model also holds for orthogonal rotations of the factors. Given the orthogonal matrix G and the model (7.22), the new model

$$\mathbf{x} = (\Lambda G)(G^T \mathbf{f}) + \mathbf{u} \tag{7.26}$$

also holds, with new factors $G^T f$ and corresponding loadings ΛG. Therefore, the factors are generally rotated to satisfy some additional constraints, such as

$$\Lambda^T \Psi^{-1} \Lambda \quad \text{is diagonal} \tag{7.27}$$

$$\Lambda^T D^{-1} \Lambda \quad \text{is diagonal} \quad D = \text{diag}(\sigma_{11}, \ldots, \sigma_{aa}) \tag{7.28}$$

where the diagonal elements are in decreasing order. There are techniques, such as the *varimax* method, to rotate the factors to obtain a parsimonious representation with few significantly non-zero loadings (i.e. sparse matrix Λ). Independent component analysis (Section 7.7.4) can be thought of as a factor rotation method, where the goal is to find rotations that maximize certain independence criteria. Parameter estimates for Λ and Ψ can also be derived by using different techniques; two most popular are the principle factor analysis and the maximum likelihood factor analysis.

7.7.6 Random projections

The method of random projections is a simple yet powerful dimensionality reduction technique that uses random projection matrices to project the data into lower dimensional spaces. The original data $X \in \mathbb{R}^a$ is transformed to the lower dimensional $S \in \mathbb{R}^k$ with $k \ll a$ via

$$S = RX \tag{7.29}$$

where the columns of R are realizations of independent and identically distributed (i.i.d.) zero-mean normal variables, scaled to have the unit length. The method was proposed in the context of clustering text documents, where the initial dimension a can be in the order of 10^5, and the final dimension k is still relatively large, of the order of 100. Under such circumstances, even PCA, the simplest of the discussed dimensionality reduction techniques, can be computationally too expensive. It has been shown empirically that results with the random projection method are comparable with results obtained with PCA, and take a fraction of the time required by PCA. To even further reduce the computational burden of the random projection method, at a slight loss in accuracy, the random projection matrix R may be simplified by thresholding its values to -1 and $+1$, or by matrices whose rows have a fixed number of $1s$ (at random locations) and the rest $0s$.

There exist some encouraging theoretical results for random projections. For example, if the similarity between two feature vectors is measured by their inner product (giving the cosine of their angle for unit-length vectors), it can be shown that if the dimension of the reduced space k is large, random projection matrices preserve the similarity measure: on the average, the distortion of the inner products is zero, and its variance is at most $1/2k$.

7.8   **FORMAL DERIVATIONS AND PROOFS

Anything that has real and lasting value is always a gift from within.

— *Franz Kafka*

In this section we sketch the proof of the theorem concerning the boundaries between intervals for discretization. It states that if in discretization the expected impurity reduction is used to estimate the discretized attribute's quality, the candidates for interval boundaries are only boundaries between examples that belong to different classes.

Proof. Let $\phi(P(C_1), ..., P(C_{m_0}))$ be an impurity measure for a given class probability distribution. If, for estimation of attribute quality $q(A)$ the expected impurity reduction is used, we get, for a boundary that defines two intervals V_1 and V_2, the following quality criterion:

$$q(A) = \phi(P(C_1), ..., P(C_{m_0})) - \sum_{j=1}^{2} P(V_j)\, \phi\left(P(C_1|V_j), ..., P(C_{m_0}|V_j)\right) \quad (7.30)$$

For this quality criterion it can be shown that q has its maximum either at the beginning, or at the end of each sequence of examples belonging to the same class. This can be proved by showing that the second derivative of q is always positive with respect to the boundary change. Since the function q is convex, its maximum is either at the beginning, or at the end of the interval.

The impurity measure ϕ is actually not a function of m_0 arguments, m_0 being the number of classes, but a function of $m_0 - 1$ arguments. Since the class probabilities sum to 1, the probability of the last class is unambiguously determined by probabilities of other $m_0 - 1$ classes. Therefore,

$$q(A) = \phi(P(C_1), ..., P(C_{m_0-1})) - \sum_{j=1}^{2} P(V_j)\phi(P(C_1|V_j), ..., P(C_{m_0-1}|V_j)) \quad (7.31)$$

Let us find in the learning set a sequence of Max examples that all belong to the same class C_{m_0}, ordered by values of the continuous attribute. Let $x \in 0...Max$ be possible boundaries between these examples (including the lowermost and the uppermost boundaries). The lowermost boundary is at the beginning of the sequence ($x = 0$). We use the following notation:

n	=	total number of learning examples
$n(C_k)$	=	number of learning examples from the class C_k,
$n(V_1)$	=	number of learning examples left of the boundary $x = 0$
$n(C_k, V_1)$	=	number of learning examples from the class C_k left of the boundary $x = 0$
$n(C_k, V_2)$	=	number of learning examples from the class C_k right of the boundary $x = 0$

$p_{k.}$	=	$n(C_k)/n$
$p_{.1}$	=	$(n(V_1) + x)/n$
$p_{.2}$	=	$1 - (n(V_1) + x)/n = (n - n(V_1) - x)/n$
$p_{k|1}$	=	$n(C_k, V_1)/(n(V_1) + x)$
$p_{k|2}$	=	$n(C_k, V_2)/(n - n(V_1) - x)$

We can now derive:

$$\frac{\partial q}{\partial x} = -\frac{\phi(p_{1|1}, ..., p_{m_0-1|1})}{n} + \frac{n(V_1) + x}{n(n(V_1) + x)^2} \sum_{k=1}^{m_0-1} n(C_k, V_1) \frac{\partial \phi(p_{1|1}, ..., p_{m_0-1|1})}{\partial p_{k|1}} +$$
$$\frac{\phi(p_{1|2}, ..., p_{m_0-1|2})}{n} - \frac{n - n(V_1) - x}{n(n - n(V_1) - x)^2} \sum_{k=1}^{m_0-1} n(C_k, V_2) \frac{\partial \phi(p_{1|2}, ..., p_{m_0-1|2})}{\partial p_{k|2}}$$

$$(7.32)$$

$$\frac{\partial q}{\partial x} = -\frac{\phi(p_{1|1}, ..., p_{m_0-1|1})}{n} + \frac{1}{n(n(V_1) + x)} \sum_{k=1}^{m_0-1} n(C_k, V_1) \frac{\partial \phi(p_{1|1}, ..., p_{m_0-1|1})}{\partial p_{k|1}} +$$
$$\frac{\phi(p_{1|2}, ..., p_{m_0-1|2})}{n} - \frac{1}{n(n - n(V_1) - x)} \sum_{k=1}^{m_0-1} n(C_k, V_2) \frac{\partial \phi(p_{1|2}, ..., p_{m_0-1|2})}{\partial p_{k|2}}$$

$$(7.33)$$

$$\frac{\partial^2 q}{\partial x^2} = \frac{2-2}{n(n(V_1) + x)^2} \sum_{k=1}^{m_0-1} n(C_k, V_1) \frac{\partial \phi(p_{1|1}, ..., p_{m_0-1|1})}{\partial p_{k|1}} -$$
$$-\frac{1}{n(n(V_1) + x)^3} \sum_{k=1}^{m_0-1} n(C_k, V_1)^2 \frac{\partial^2 \phi(p_{1|1}, ..., p_{m_0-1|1})}{\partial p_{k|1}^2} +$$
$$+\frac{2-2}{n(n - n(V_1) - x)^2} \sum_{k=1}^{m_0-1} n(C_k, V_2) \frac{\partial \phi(p_{1|2}, ..., p_{m_0-1|2})}{\partial p_{k|2}} -$$
$$-\frac{1}{n(n - n(V_1) - x)^3} \sum_{k=1}^{m_0-1} n(C_k, V_2)^2 \frac{\partial^2 \phi(p_{1|2}, ..., p_{m_0-1|2})}{\partial p_{k|2}^2} \qquad (7.34)$$

After simplifications of the above equations it becomes clear that the second derivative is always positive, since ϕ is concave and thus its second derivative is always negative:

$$\frac{\partial^2 q}{\partial x^2} = -\frac{1}{n(n(V_1) + x)^3} \sum_{k=1}^{m_0-1} n(C_k, V_1)^2 \frac{\partial^2 \phi(p_{1|1}, ..., p_{m_0-1|1})}{\partial p_{k|1}^2} -$$
$$-\frac{1}{n(n - n(V_1) - x)^3} \sum_{k=1}^{m_0-1} n(C_k, V_2)^2 \frac{\partial^2 \phi(p_{1|2}, ..., p_{m_0-1|2})}{\partial p_{k|2}^2} \qquad (7.35)$$

Thus q is convex

$$\frac{\partial^2 q}{\partial x^2} > 0 \qquad (7.36)$$

and its maximum is at its extreme boundaries: $x = 0$ or $x = Max$.

$\square$

7.9   SUMMARY AND FURTHER READING

It should be our care not so much to live a long life as a satisfactory one.

— Seneca

- Data preprocessing is used for representing complex structures with attributes, discretization of continuous attributes, binarization of attributes, converting discrete attributes to continuous, and dealing with missing and unknown attribute values. Various visualization techniques provide valuable help in data preprocessing.

- Complex structures, such as text documents, images, and graphs cannot directly be used as inputs for machine learning algorithms. They have to be described by derived attributes, such as bag of words (for text documents), various statistics (for images and graphs), or with the help of dimensionality reduction techniques, such as principal component analysis.

- Discretization of continuous attributes is a necessary step when using machine learning methods that cannot deal with continuous attributes. Continuous attribute values are replaced with indices of corresponding non-overlapping subintervals. Discretization algorithms need to determine both the optimal number of subintervals and the optimal boundaries between them.

- Binarization of attributes is necessary when using machine learning methods that can deal only with two-valued (binary) attributes. Continuous attributes are binarized by applying two-interval discretization. Discrete attributes are binarized either by generating a binary attribute for each original attribute value, or by generating a binary attribute for each possible different split of attribute values into two disjunct subsets.

- Several machine learning methods (different regression models, discriminant functions, and also neural networks) cannot deal with discrete attributes, and assume that all attributes are continuous. Multi-valued discrete attributes used within such methods are binarized, and each binary attribute is subsequently treated as a continuous attribute.

- In practice, it often happens that values of some attributes are missing. Missing values can either be ignored, supplanted by the most probable attribute value, or treated as a probability distribution of attribute values.

- Single attributes are usually visualized with histograms. For this purpose, continuous attributes need to be discretized. For visualization of pairs of attributes, scatterplot visualization techniques are used. Scatterplots are useful for detecting mutual dependence between pairs of attributes. Several attributes are visualized at the same time by pairwise scatterplots, parallel plots, star glyphs, or Chernoff faces. Similar sets of attribute values produce similar figures.

- Results of machine learning can be visualized by depicting the structure of generated models, by depicting class-boundary hypersurfaces in attribute space, or their projections.

- Dimensionality reduction techniques are used to reduce the dimensionality of data representation by selecting a subset of relevant attributes (features), or by transforming a set of attributes into a smaller set of relevant attributes. There exist two fundamentally different approaches to dimensionality reduction: feature subset selection techniques (e.g., filtering), and feature extraction techniques (e.g., principal component analysis, independent component analysis, and many others).

Julesz et al. (1973) discuss image parameterization by using first and second order statistics. Principal component analysis (PCA) has first been used in image processing by Sirovich and Kirby (1987). Luo (1998) discusses image processing techniques for pattern recognition. Turk and Pentland (1991) use PCA for face recognition. Rushing et al. (2001) and Bevk and Kononenko (2006) describe the use of association rules for image parameterization. Korotkov (1998) and Kononenko et al. (2004) use domain-tailored image description for analysis of GDV images. Brank and Leskovec (2003) describe various complex graphs that have been successfully described with attributes and subsequently used for machine learning.

The proof from Section 7.8 is due to Breiman et al. (1984). Fayyad (1993) and Dougherty et al. (1995) describe several supervised and unsupervised methods for attribute discretization. Kononenko (1993) discusses benefits of fuzzy discretization for Bayesian classifiers.

Spence (2001) describes general principles of data visualization and several techniques of visualizing attribute values. Hand et al. (2001) discuss how various anomalies in data collection can be detected by visualizing attributes. They also describe the study, qualitatively reconstructed in Figure 7.5. Možina et al. (2004) developed a method for visualization of the naive Bayesian classifier with nomograms. Demšar (2006) discusses visualization of results of statistical tests.

A collection of works edited by Liu and Motoda (1996) is a comprehensive overview of feature subset selection techniques. Kira and Rendell (1992a) describe the filtering approach, and Kohavi and John (1996) discuss the wrapper approach.

Pearson (1901) invented the principal component analysis and introduced it as a dimensionality reduction technique. Hyvarinen et al. (2001) is an excellent source on independent component analysis both for theoretic and algorithmic aspects. Lawley and Maxwell (1971) and Mardia et al. (1979) are comprehensive sources on factor analysis. Kaski (1998) discusses the use of random projections for dimensionality reduction.

Chapter 8

*Constructive Induction

Knowledge without action is useless. Action without knowledge is dangerous.

— Sai Baba

The choice of the appropriate attribute space (for propositional learning) or the predicate space (for relational learning) is crucial for the success of machine learning algorithms. Attribute values are collected from the learning set and comprise all information that is available to the learning algorithm. It is left to the learning algorithm to decide how to use it.

While building a model (hypothesis), dependencies between independent variables (attributes) and the dependent variable (class) have to be accounted for. Dependencies between attributes, as well as the utilized model space determine whether the chosen attribute space is appropriate for a given learning problem. If not, attributes have to be transformed either in advance, or during the learning process. The mapping from the original attribute space to the transformed attribute space, more suitable for machine learning, is often called *constructive induction*. The appropriateness of new attributes can be evaluated according to several criteria:

- quality of new attributes,

- complexity of new attributes,

- comprehensibility of new attributes,

- performance of learned models,

- complexity of learnt models,

- comprehensibility of learnt models, and

- acceleration of the learning process.

The relative importance of the above criteria may vary depending on what the results of machine learning will be used for. Frequently, the most important criterion is

213

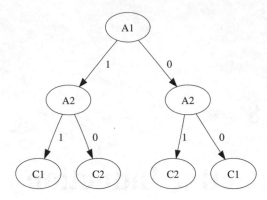

Figure 8.1: A decision tree for the original XOR problem.

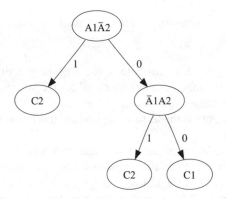

Figure 8.2: A decision tree for the XOR problem with two new attributes, obtained by using conjunction and negation operators on original attributes from Figure 8.1.

the performance of learned models. In real-time applications, such as control of dynamic processes, it is crucial to minimize the learning time. In many other practical applications we are especially interested in the meaning of new attributes; here the model performance serves just as a constraint.

An example of constructive induction used within decision trees is shown in Figures 8.1, 8.2 and 8.3. Figure 8.1 depicts the solution of the XOR problem using the original attributes, Figure 8.2 the solution with attributes obtained by using conjunction and negation operators, and Figure 8.3 the solution with an attribute obtained by using the equivalence operator. Both types of constructive induction contribute to reduction of the decision tree size. The latter decision tree is certainly the best of the batch: it is the smallest as well as the most comprehensible.

Constructive induction can be performed either manually by utilizing the background knowledge of domain experts, or automatically by using methods similar to those described in this chapter. We first define the notion of dependencies between attributes and describe approaches for their measuring and visualization. Then we

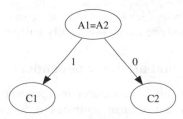

Figure 8.3: A decision tree for the XOR problem with a new attribute, obtained by using the equivalence operators on original attributes from Figure 8.1.

describe approaches to constructive induction with pre-defined operators, and finally we discuss approaches to constructive induction of discrete (or discretized) attributes without pre-defined operators.

8.1   DEPENDENCE OF ATTRIBUTES

A healthy social life is found only, when in the mirror of each soul the whole community finds its reflection, and when in the whole community the virtue of each one is living.
                                                                    — Rudolf Steiner

In the probability calculus terminology an attribute is a *random variable*, and an attribute value is an *event*. By observing dependencies between two (or more) attributes, we actually observe dependencies between their values, that is, between events.

8.1.1   Dependence of events

Events A and B are *mutually independent* if the probability of the joint event factorizes:

$$P(A, B) = P(A)P(B) \qquad (8.1)$$

If, at the same time, the outcome C is known, this may or may not change the shape of relation (8.1). If it does not change, events A and B are *conditionally independent*.

$$P(A, B|C) = P(A|C)P(B|C) \qquad (8.2)$$

Otherwise, even if (8.1) holds, the events are conditionally dependent. An extreme example of conditional dependence is an XOR function, shown in Table 6.1. The correct model for this function is

$$C = (A_1 \neq A_2) = (A_1 \ \text{XOR} \ A_2) \qquad (8.3)$$

Although the values of attributes A_1 and A_2 are independent, they are strongly conditionally dependent.

Alternatively, two events may be dependent, and information of event C makes them independent. An extreme case is when $A \equiv B \equiv C$. Since A and B are identical, they are completely dependent. However, when the value of C is known, both A and B are completely determined and thus conditionally independent.

8.1.2 Bias, variance and attribute dependence

Attributes can be conditionally dependent or independent for a given value of the dependent variable. For independent attributes it is sufficient (and optimal in terms of computational performance) to use linear algorithms, such as the naive Bayesian classifier, linear regression, logistic regression, two-layered perceptron, linear discriminant function, and support vector machines with linear kernel functions. However, if attributes are conditionally dependent, learning algorithms must account for dependence, and therefore linear algorithms are unsuitable because of their *bias*.

On the other hand, when attributes are conditionally independent, algorithms that assume attribute dependence do not perform well. For example, while growing decision and regression trees, the trees by themselves account for dependencies between attributes already in the tree, and new attributes that are included into the tree. If attributes are conditionally independent, learning examples are unnecessarily shattered. This results in small example sets in tree nodes that consequently cause unreliable generalizations and larger errors due to *variance* in data as well as in the tree.

8.1.3 Measuring attribute dependence

In classification problems attribute dependence can be estimated with *entropy* by measuring the average dependence between attribute values. In Chapter 6 we define class entropy H_C, attribute entropy H_A, joint class-attribute entropy H_{CA} and conditional class entropy given the value of attribute A. We define dependence between the class C and the attribute A with information gain:

$$Gain(A) = H_C + H_A - H_{CA} = H_C - H_{C|A} = H_A - H_{A|C} \qquad (8.4)$$

It can be shown that the normalized information gain is a proximity measure (1-distance):

$$1 - D(C, A) = \frac{H_C + H_A - H_{CA}}{H_{CA}} = \frac{H_C + H_A}{H_{CA}} - 1 \qquad (8.5)$$

The same measures can be used for measuring the dependence between any two attributes. The more dependent the attributes are, the smaller is the distance between them. If they are identical, the distance is $D(A, A) = 0$. If they are completely independent, the distance is maximal, that is $D(A, B) = 1$.

Information gain can be generalized to an arbitrary number of attributes. In this context, information gain is called *mutual information*. It is defined as

$$I(A_1; A_2) = H_{A_1} + H_{A_2} - H_{A_1 A_2} = H_{A_2} - H_{A_2|A_1} = H_{A_1} - H_{A_1|A_2} \qquad (8.6)$$

Mutual information is actually the average mutual dependency between the values of two attributes. The larger the mutual information, the more dependent the attributes are.

The conditional mutual information given the class C is defined with

$$I(A_1; A_2|C) = H_{A_1|C} + H_{A_2|C} - H_{A_1 A_2|C} = H_{A_1 C} + H_{A_2 C} - H_C - H_{A_1 A_2 C} \quad (8.7)$$

It is always nonnegative and equals 0 if and only if attributes A and B are conditionally independent for the given value C of the class.

For three attributes an *interaction gain* can be defined:

$$I(A_1; A_2; A_3) = I(A_1; A_2|A_3) - I(A_1; A_3) - I(A_2; A_3) \quad (8.8)$$

or alternatively

$$I(A_1; A_2; A_3) = H_{A_1 A_2} + H_{A_2 A_3} + H_{A_1 A_3} - H_{A_1} - H_{A_2} - H_{A_3} - H_{A_1 A_2 A_3} \quad (8.9)$$

Interaction gain amounts to the quantity of information common to all three attributes that is not present in any of their subsets. Interaction gain is symmetric, that is

$$I(A_1; A_2; A_3) = I(A_1; A_3; A_2) = I(A_2; A_1; A_3) = \dots$$

According to its sign, interaction gain can either be:

- positive: this means that the joined attributes provide new information that cannot be obtained from single attributes (as in the case of the XOR problem).

- negative: in this case there exists redundant information that can, if attributes are treated individually, mislead the learning process. This can be avoided if the attributes are joined. An extreme case is where multiple copies of an attribute exist; here all copies (except the original) can be rejected.

- equal to 0: this indicates that all attributes are mutually independent, or one attribute is independent of the other two. There however exist some rare cases where interaction gain is 0 although the three attributes are in a three-way interaction.

Interaction gain can be generalized to an arbitrary number of attributes. Let S be a set of k attributes, $|S| = k$. A *k-way interaction gain* is defined with

$$I(S) = \sum_{T \subseteq S} (-1)^{|S| - |T|} H(T) = I(S \setminus X | X) - I(S \setminus X), \quad X \in S \quad (8.10)$$

Reliability of higher-order interaction estimations is much dependent on the number of available learning examples. A simple rule of thumb suggests using the learning set of at least ten times the cardinality of Cartesian product of attributes. For two binary-valued attributes this means at least $2 \cdot 2 \cdot 10 = 40$ learning examples. Usually at most three- or four-way interactions are estimable in practice.

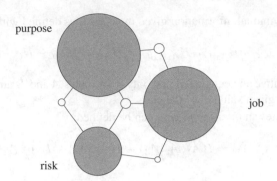

Figure 8.4: An example of a 3-way positive interaction between three variables: the risk of a loan, the client's job and the purpose of a loan.

8.1.4 Visualization of attribute dependence

Visualization of the interaction gain is a very useful tool that aids in analysis of attribute dependencies. When we are interested in attribute interactions regardless of the class attribute (or the class attribute is treated as an ordinary attribute), we visualize three-way interaction gains. They can be either positive or negative. We may visualize several attributes at the same time; however in planar graphs only three-way interactions can be visualized. For higher-order interactions, higher-dimensional graphs are required.

Figure 8.4 depicts an example of a positive interaction gain between three variables (attributes). Variables are represented by gray circles; their size is proportional to each variable's entropy. White circles on edges between variables represent positive mutual information. Their size is proportional to the amount of mutual information. As shown in Figure 8.4, in our example mutual information is rather small. The white circle in the middle that connects all variables represents a 3-way positive interaction that is larger then either pairwise mutual information.

Figure 8.5 depicts an example of negative interaction gain between three variables (attributes). Pairwise mutual information is much larger than in the previous example. The gray circle in the middle that connects all variables represents a 3-way negative interaction. It represents an amount of redundant information shared by all three variables.

Conditional information gains $I(A_1; A_2|C)$, $I(A_1; A_2; A_3|C)$, ..., with respect to the given value of dependent variable (class) C can be represented with a graph such as depicted in Figure 8.6. Attributes are represented by gray circles positioned in the bottom row. White circles in the middle row depict conditional interactions between pairs of attributes – except where they are negligibly small. The size of circles is proportional to the strength of interaction with respect to the given class value. The figure clearly shows that there exist several significant interactions; this makes the use of linear methods impracticable. The grey circle in the topmost row represents a negative conditional 3-way interaction that suggests a certain amount of redundancy

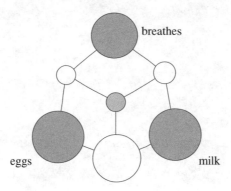

Figure 8.5: An example of a 3-way negative interaction between three variables: animal lays eggs, breathes, and has milk.

in the rightmost three attributes. Other 3-way interactions are negligible.

8.2 CONSTRUCTIVE INDUCTION WITH PRE-DEFINED OPERATORS

If you don't break your ropes while you're alive do you think ghosts will do it after?
                                                              — Kabir

The main purpose of constructive induction is to reshape the attribute space into a more useful representation for machine learning. Since it is difficult to anticipate what kind of new attributes are bound to be best, constructive induction is actually performed as a part of the learning process. The task of the learning algorithm is therefore also to construct new attributes, which form a part of the generated knowledge and thus a result of the learning process.

Candidates for new attributes can be constructed by using various pre-defined sets of operators. They can either be constructed in a data pre-processing step before learning, or during the learning process, for example while building a decision or regression tree. Since the space of new attributes is huge, it must be constrained by various heuristics. The quality of candidate attributes is estimated with appropriate quality measures. Only the best new attributes are retained; they either supplement or supplant the original attributes.

Let $\mathcal{A} = \{X_1, X_2, ..., X_n\}$ be a set of attributes. Candidates for new attributes can be constructed in several ways:

Linear combination of continuous attributes: The set of candidate attributes consists of all possible linear combinations of continuous or binary attributes. For each subset of continuous or binary attributes $A_c \subseteq \mathcal{A}$ the possible candidates

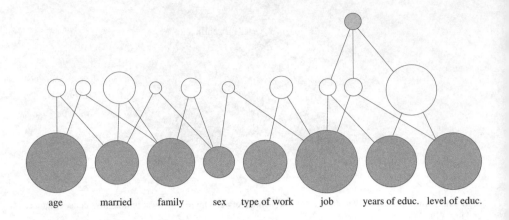

Figure 8.6: Visualization of conditional interaction gains for eight attributes and fixed class value. Conditional two-way interactions between pairs of attributes are positive, whereas the conditional 3-way interaction is negative.

for new continuous attributes are

$$\sum_{X_k \in A_c} a_k X_k \tag{8.11}$$

Possible candidates for new binary attributes are

$$\sum_{X_k \in A_c} a_k X_k > t \tag{8.12}$$

In both cases the attribute quality has to be optimized with respect to the values of coefficients a_k; for new binary attributes optimization also includes the threshold value t.

Products of continuous attributes: For each subset of continuous or binary attributes $A_c \subseteq \mathcal{A}$ the possible candidates for new continuous attributes are

$$\prod_{X_k \in A_z} X_k \tag{8.13}$$

The product space is normally bounded with the cardinality of A_c so that $A_c \leq t$. Threshold t is usually set to 2 or 3.

Boolean combinations of discrete attributes: For a given set of Boolean operators (say, conjunction $\wedge$ and disjunction $\vee$) we define all possible new binary attributes. If we are limited to conjunction only, then for each subset of binary attributes $A_b \subseteq \mathcal{A}$ the candidates for new attributes are

$$\bigwedge_{X_k \in A_b} X_k \tag{8.14}$$

If an attribute is defined as a conjunction of original attributes, say

$$X = X_1 \wedge X_2 \wedge X_3 \qquad (8.15)$$

we must be aware that one value of the new attribute is a conjunction of the original attribute values

$$X_1 = 1 \wedge X_2 = 1 \wedge X_3 = 1 \Rightarrow X = 1 \qquad (8.16)$$

while the other value is a disjunction of negated original values

$$X_1 = 0 \vee X_2 = 0 \vee X_3 = 0 \Rightarrow X = 0 \qquad (8.17)$$

In such logical expressions we can also include binarized discrete attributes (one discrete value is represented by one binary attribute) and continuous attributes (discretized to two intervals).

Special operators: Special operators are defined in accordance with the background knowledge of a given problem. Some examples of special operators are:

- for each subset of continuous attributes a new attribute can be maximal, minimal, or mean value of the original continuous attributes;

- m-of-k binary attributes: for each subset consisting of k binary attributes we define a new binary attribute that has the value 1 only if (at least) m original attributes have value 1;

- x-of-k continuous attributes: for each subset consisting of k binary attributes we define a new (whole numbered) continuous attribute that tells the count x of the original attributes that have value 1;

- continuous attributes defined by using various arithmetic expressions on subsets of continuous or binary attributes, by using operators (e.g., +, -, *, /) and functions (e.g., sin, cos, exp, log);

- binary attributes defined by comparing ($=$, $>$, ...) attribute values of different attributes;

- one binary attribute defined for each continuous attribute so that its value is 1 when the value of the respective continuous attribute falls to a certain interval (say, if the value lies within $k = 1, 2$, or 3 times standard deviation of the attribute's mean value).

Since the space of all possible new attributes is often much too large to be exhaustively searched, heuristic algorithms are used for this purpose. They are usually based on greedy search with iterative improvements. Besides computational complexity, we must also account for the danger of overfitting the learning set. For this purpose usually simpler new attributes, consisting of fewer original attributes are preferred.

8.3 CONSTRUCTIVE INDUCTION WITHOUT PRE-DEFINED OPERATORS

Reason is powerless in the expression of Love.

— *Jellaludin Rumi*

If the operators are not defined in advance, construction of new operators takes part in the learning process. Thus the operators become a result of machine learning and hence a part of generated knowledge. Such approaches to constructive induction can be divided into hypothesis-based constructive induction and constructive induction based on Cartesian products.

8.3.1 Hypothesis-based constructive induction

Generally speaking, for any learned function we can always define a new attribute whose values are equal to the learned function. In this sense every machine learning algorithm performs constructive induction. However, from a practical point of view parts of a function (hypothesis) are more interesting than the complete function.

A hypothesis (theory, model) or its parts are results of machine learning that represent potentially new and useful knowledge. The resulting hypothesis or its parts can be used for altering data encoding. For example, if a learning algorithm produces a rule

```
if A and B and C then D
```

we can define a new binary attribute with value 1 when A and B and C is true, and 0 if false. In decision trees useful new attributes can represent frequently recurring subtrees. In discriminant and regression functions, parts of a function (e.g., linear combinations) consisting of attributes with larger coefficients can be used as new continuous attributes. In learned multi-layered feedforward neural networks a function calculated by a particular hidden neuron can be used as a new continuous attribute.

The semi naive Bayesian classifier (described in Section 9.6) explicitly searches for dependencies between values of different attributes and joins them into new binary attributes.

8.3.2 Constructive induction based on Cartesian products

A new discrete attribute can also be constructed as a Cartesian product of two or more original attributes. Such an attribute has as many values as the product of the original attributes' cardinalities:

$$|A_1 \times A_2 \times ... \times A_k| = |A_1| \cdot |A_2| \cdot ... \cdot |A_k| \tag{8.18}$$

The problem of such an attribute is in its fragmentation of learning examples: for each value of the new attribute there are much fewer examples available than there were for the respective original attributes' values. The same statement holds for multi-valued discrete attributes, or too finely discretized continuous attributes. In such cases it is often beneficial to reduce the number of attribute values. Iterative methods, analogous to that of bottom-up or top-down discretization, can be used for this purpose. In each iteration we join two attribute values that are, according to some criterion, most similar to each other, into a single value. The process terminates when the attribute quality becomes too low. In an extreme case, when an attribute has only two values left, and joining them would render the attribute useless, some methods (such as functional decomposition, described below) detect and remove such attributes, either because they are useless or because they are redundant.

A criterion that determines which two values to join is, similarly to discretization and binarization, normally one of the attribute quality measures. In one iterative step we join attribute values so as to maximize the attribute quality. As described in Section 7.2 we can, for this purpose, use any impurity measure. Since it holds that the expected impurity reduction q increases with increasing number of attribute values, measures that overestimate multi-valued attributes, such as information gain and Gini index, are not suitable for joining attribute values. It is more advisable to use measures that do not overestimate multi-valued attributes: proximity measure $1 - D$, *MDL* and *ReliefF*. These measures stop the process when a locally optimal number of values is determined. Of the above measures, ReliefF has a decided advantage because it uses the context of other attributes for joining values.

Functional decomposition

A context of other attributes can be explicitly utilized by the method of *functional decomposition*. From the original target function (learning problem) functional decomposition builds a hierarchy of learning problems. By using constructive induction it defines intermediate problems that correspond to new attributes. Such an intermediate step of functional induction is best illustrated by an example.

Table 8.1 shows a three-class learning problem with attributes A_1, A_2 in A_3. Attributes A_1 and A_2 have each three possible values, whereas the attribute A_3 has only two. After building a Cartesian product of attributes A_2 and A_3, we can, by using the context of the attribute A_1, join the values of original attributes into a new attribute $A_{2,3}$ as shown in Table 8.2. A new attribute changes the learning problem as shown in Table 8.3. In this case constructive induction has constructed a new attribute $A_{2,3}$ as the minimum of the original attribute values. The original learning problem is now transformed to calculating the maximum of attributes A_1 and $A_{2,3}$. This example clearly illustrates how constructive induction based on Cartesian products can define a useful new operator which is a result of the learning process and thus a part of the generated knowledge.

When MDL or $1 - D$ measure are used for joining values of Cartesian products, they completely ignore the context of other attributes. On the other hand, if ReliefF measure is used, the context is implicitly included. Functional decomposition explicitly accounts for the context within the *partitioning matrix*. The partitioning matrix is an alternative representation of the learning set. Its columns correspond to the values of Cartesian products of attributes being joined. Its rows correspond to the values of

A_1	A_2	A_3	C
1	1	1	1
1	1	3	1
1	2	1	1
1	2	3	2
1	3	1	1
1	3	3	3
2	2	1	2
2	3	1	2
2	3	3	3
3	1	1	3
3	3	1	3

Table 8.1: A simple three-class learning problem with three attributes and 11 learning examples.

A_2	A_3	$A_{2,3}$
1	1	1
1	3	1
2	1	1
2	3	2
3	1	1
3	3	3

Table 8.2: Construction of a new attribute by joining values of two original attributes from Table 8.1. The new attribute can be explained as the minimum of the original attributes' values.

A_1	$A_{2,3}$	C
1	2	2
1	3	3
1	1	1
2	3	3
2	1	2
3	1	3

Table 8.3: A modified learning problem from Table 8.1; after joining two attributes the new learning problem is calculating the maximum of attributes A_1 and $A_{2,3}$.

A_1	A_2 A_3	1 1	1 3	2 1	2 3	3 1	3 3
1		1	1	1	2	1	3
2		-	-	2	-	2	3
3		3	-	-	-	3	-
$A_{2,3}$		1	1	1	2	1	3

Table 8.4: A partitioning matrix for learning examples from Table 8.1.

Cartesian products of other attributes. The values in the partitioning matrix correspond to class labels (or more generally, to distributions of class labels). A partitioning matrix for learning examples from Table 8.1 is shown in Table 8.4. Within the partitioning matrix we search for compatible or almost compatible columns. Two columns are compatible either if they are identical or if any mismatch occurs where one column has an empty value (-). The last row in the partitioning matrix names each column with a value of the new attribute, all compatible columns having the same name. The smaller the set of compatible columns is, the fewer values the new attribute will have.

For joining the values of the Cartesian product in noise-free problems, the complexity criteria that minimize the number of new attribute values can be used. For real-world noisy data (when a more general scenario for joining partially compatible columns is used), it is more advisable to use robust criteria that minimize the classification error.

The problem of searching for optimal constructs is of combinatorial nature: it is not known in advance how many and which attributes are to be joined. Since exhaustive search is obviously out of question, heuristic approaches are frequently used for this purpose. Here, the non-myopic algorithm ReliefF that estimates the attribute quality in the context of other attributes can serve as a useful tool. We can observe the difference between attribute quality estimations obtained with a non-myopic and a myopic (Eq. 6.19) ReliefF. If, for a particular attribute, this difference is large, this means that the attribute carries information that, in combination with other attributes, can yield positive interaction information. Such an attribute is therefore a potentially good candidate for constructive induction methods.

8.4   SUMMARY AND FURTHER READING

Why do you want to read others' books when there is the book of yourself?
                                                              — Jiddu Krishnamurti

- Constructive induction is a mapping from the original attribute space to the transformed attribute space, that is more suitable for machine learning.

- Dependence (interaction) between attributes can be used to guide constructive induction. Interacting attributes (or their values) can be joined. Interaction between attributes can be either positive (signifying new information) or negative (signifying redundant information).

- Constructive induction can be performed by using an arbitrary set of pre-defined operators, such as linear combination and product of continuous attributes, Boolean combinations of binary attributes, and various threshold operators.

- Constructive induction can also be performed without pre-defined operators. It can be based on earlier hypotheses, or on the Cartesian product of all attributes. For the latter approach, an efficient method is the functional decomposition.

Michalski et al. (1983) introduced constructive induction in machine learning. Han (1980) discusses interactions between two and more attributes and defines a generalization of interaction gain to an arbitrary number of attributes. Jakulin and Bratko (2003) study dependencies between attributes. They discuss approaches for determining mutual information and interaction gain. They also show several methods for visualizing attribute interactions. Breiman et al. (1984) discuss constructive induction with pre-defined operators. They argue that the space of candidate attributes is too large for exhaustive search and suggest some approaches for dealing with this problem. Ragavan and Rendell (1993) suggest using lookahead to construct new features with pre-defined operators. Zupan (1997) was the first to use the functional decomposition in machine learning and to show its usefulness. Zupan et al. (1999) further developed the described approach that builds a hierarchy of learning problems. Demšar et al. (2001) uses the ReliefF algorithm for constructive induction.

Chapter 9

Symbolic Learning

When you manipulate you are divided ... heaven and hell are created immediately;
then there is vast distance between you and the truth. Don't manipulate, allow things
to happen.

— Osho

In this chapter we describe symbolic learning methods: decision trees and rules, association rules, regression trees, inductive logic programming, naive and semi-naive Bayesian classifiers, and Bayesian belief networks.

9.1 LEARNING OF DECISION TREES

If you judge people, you have no time to love them.

— Mother Theresa

For building decision trees, learning examples are normally described with attributes and labelled with a discrete class. Each learning example is represented as a vector of attribute values. Attributes can be either discrete or continuous, and their number is given in advance. A more thorough discussion of representation with attributes can be found in Section 4.1.1.

9.1.1 Building and using decision trees

Decision tree (Figure 4.1) consists of internal nodes – corresponding to attributes, edges – corresponding to subsets of attribute values, and terminal nodes (leaves) – corresponding to discrete class labels. Each path, starting in a tree root (topmost node) and ending in a tree leaf, corresponds to a decision rule. The conditions (pairs of attribute names and corresponding sets of attribute values) evaluated in each internal node along the path are conjunctively connected. An example of a decision tree for a three-class problem is shown in Figure 9.1. The basic algorithm for building decision trees is shown in Algorithm 9.1.

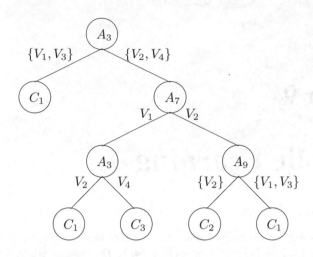

Figure 9.1: An example decision tree for a three-class problem. The root node is labelled with A_3, and leaves with classes C_1 (twice), C_2 and C_3. A path from the root node to the leaf labelled C_3 implements the decision rule if $(A_3 = V_2 \vee A_3 = V_4) \wedge (A_7 = V_1) \wedge (A_3 = V_4)$ then class $= C_3$

The key factor of a decision tree building algorithm is the choice of the best attribute. For this purpose, impurity measures such as information gain, information gain ratio, Gini-index, and ReliefF are frequently used. They are discussed in more detail in Chapter 6.

Decision tree is the symbolic representation of a classification function that summarizes some regularities from a given problem domain. For domain experts it is usually interesting to review the tree structure because it often conforms to their knowledge of the problem or even provides new insights.

Once a decision tree is built, it can be used for classification (labelling) of new examples. From the root node we traverse along the edges according to each new example's attribute values until we reach a leaf. A leaf contains local information of the class frequencies; they are used to estimate the class probability distribution in the leaf. For this purpose, probability estimates such as the m-estimate (Section 3.1.5) are used. The total number of learning examples in a leaf indicates the reliability of this estimation.

A special kind of a leaf is an empty (null) leaf. It is a leaf to which there exists a valid path, but which has no corresponding learning examples, and therefore cannot make any speculations about the class labels. In null leaves, classification is normally evaluated by using the naive Bayesian classifier that uses only attributes from the path leading to the respective null leaf. The class probability distribution is calculated by the naive Bayesian classifier during the learning process and is fixed for classification.

Algorithm 9.1 The basic decision tree learning algorithm.

INPUT: A set of learning examples.
OUTPUT: A decision tree.

   if the stopping criterion is satisfied **then**
      create a leaf that corresponds to all remaining learning examples
   else
      choose the best (according to some criterion) attribute A_i
      label the current tree node with A_i
      for each value V_j of the attribute A_i **do**
         label an outgoing edge with value V_j
         recursively build a subtree by using a corresponding subset of learning examples
      end for
   end if

where the stopping criterion is:

- the learning set is pure enough (e.g., all examples or most of them are labelled with the same class label), or
- there are not enough learning examples, or
- there are no good attributes left.

9.1.2   Building binary decision trees

Since the reliability of class probability estimations in decision tree leaves is highly dependent on the number of learning examples, it is not advisable to shatter the learning set into too small subsets of examples. Many learning algorithms build binary decision trees by extending the basic decision tree learning algorithm (Algorithm 9.1) so as to binarize the attributes prior to quality estimation (Algorithm 9.2).

The number of all possible binary versions of a discrete attribute with n values is $2^n - 1$ (Section 7.3). Such a combinatorial explosion can be avoided by using a greedy algorithm (Algorithm 7.1) that locally optimizes the binary attribute's quality. Continuous attributes are discretized to two intervals and treated as binary.

Binary attributes in decision trees allow for using attribute quality measures that otherwise over-estimate multi-valued attributes, such as information gain and Gini-index. Binary decision trees are usually smaller than the ordinary ones, thus providing better generalization and better performance (e.g., classification accuracy). Our example in Figure 9.1 is a binary decision tree. We can see that the same attribute (A_3) may appear several times on the same path from the root to the leaf.

9.1.3   Pruning decision trees

Because the lower levels of a decision tree are frequently unreliable due to small numbers of learning examples, they must be handled with special care. Various stopping criteria are used to stop building the tree when its lower levels become

---

Algorithm 9.2 The binary decision tree learning algorithm.

INPUT: A set of learning examples.
OUTPUT: A binary decision tree.

   if the stopping criterion is satisfied **then**
      create a leaf that corresponds to all remaining learning examples
   else
      generate all binary versions of all attributes
      choose the best (according to some criterion) binary attribute A_i
      label the current tree node with A_i
      for each value $B_j \in \{B_1, B_2\}$ of the binary attribute A_i **do**
         label an outgoing edge with value B_j
         recursively build a subtree by using a corresponding subset of learning examples
      end for
   end if

---

unreliable or irrelevant. However, since it is difficult to estimate (un)reliability in advance, building frequently proceeds regardless of the nodes' reliability. The tree is reduced in size (*post-pruned*) after the building phase. The basic post-pruning algorithm   is shown in Algorithm 9.3.   For estimating the expected errors, the m-estimate can be used (Section 3.1.5).

Algorithm 9.3 The basic decision tree post-pruning algorithm.

INPUT: A decision tree.
OUTPUT: A pruned decision tree.

   for all internal nodes in a bottom-up manner **do**
      estimate the expected classification error in subtrees E_S
      estimate the expected classification error in the current node E_N
      if $E_S \geq E_N$ **then**
         prune the subtrees and convert the node into the leaf
      end if
   end for

Alternatively, the MDL principle can be used for post-pruning. Instead of classification error, the encoding length of a decision tree and class distributions in leaves is estimated. This process is similar to attribute estimation with the MDL principle, as described in Chapter 6. The length of class distribution encoding is calculated by using the *Prior_MDL* formula (Equation 6.7).

    For each internal node the encoding length of the class distribution of learning examples is compared with the encoding length of its subtrees. Subtrees are pruned if the encoding length of the class distribution of learning examples in the node is less than or equal to the encoding length of its subtrees.

    Nodes are reviewed in a bottom-up manner (from leaves to the root). Encoding length of a leaf is equal to the encoding length of the class distribution of learning examples in a leaf. An important advantage of MDL for post-pruning is that it does not require tuning any parameters and works almost optimally. This pruning method therefore results in a useful approximation of the optimal tree. By experimenting with different parameter values (such as m in m-estimate) for other post-pruning methods the end-user can subsequently adjust the tree size.

9.1.4 Missing and "don't care" values

In real-life domain problems it frequently happens that, for some examples, one or more attribute values are missing. While building a decision tree we can, if an example is missing a value of a chosen attribute, estimate the conditional probability that, given the class label C_j, the example corresponds to the edge labelled with the attribute value V_i. In this case the m-estimate looks as follows:

$$P(V_i|C_j) = \frac{n(V_i, C_j) + mP(C_j)}{n(C_j) + m} \tag{9.1}$$

where $P(C_j)$ is the estimated prior probability of the class C_j. The example is then propagated along all edges, in each edge weighted with the corresponding conditional probability $P(V_i|C_j)$. Examples with no unknown attribute values have a unit weight. For continuous attributes, the values V_i correspond to open intervals below or above the chosen boundary.

This principle can be generalized to "don't care" values. If there exist learning examples where some discrete attribute values have "don't care" values, they are weighted with a product of number of attribute values for all attributes with "don't care" values. This is done before building the tree. Thus an example is effectively multiplied into as many copies as there are possible combinations of values for "don't care" attribute values. For continuous attributes, example weights have to be determined heuristically.

For instance, if a learning example has "don't care" values for one binary and one ternary attribute, its weight is $2 \cdot 3 = 6$. If a ternary attribute is chosen in some node, the example is propagated with weight $6/3 = 2$. If both attributes are chosen, the example is propagated with weight 1.

9.2   LEARNING OF DECISION RULES

The problem after the war is with the victor. He thinks he has just proved that war and violence pay. Who will now teach him a lesson?

— A.J.Muste, peace activist

Every decision tree can be transformed into a set of decision rules. Each path from the root to a leaf corresponds to a single decision rule. On the other hand, not every set of decision rules can be transformed into a decision tree. Sets of decision rules are therefore more flexible than decision trees.

9.2.1 Generating a single rule

For generating a single rule, the J-measure (described in Chapter 6) is most appropriate for evaluating its quality. Learning a single rule usually proceeds in a general to specific manner. At the beginning the rule is empty and covers all learning examples from all classes (or both positive and negative examples). The consequent part of such a rule is a class distribution equivalent to the class distribution of the learning set. In one step the rule is specialized in all possible ways so that the antecedent part is conjunctively extended by a single condition of the type $(attribute = value)$ for discrete attributes, or $(attribute > value)$ or $(attribute < value)$ for continuous attributes.

Then, a heuristic rule quality estimation (such as J-measure) is used on all rule extensions to evaluate the candidate rules according to the number of covered examples and their class distribution. If the beam search (described in Chapter 5) is used, we keep as much best rules as is the beam size. If the greedy search is used, we keep a single best rule (equivalent to the beam size 1).

Specialization is repeated until the stopping criterion is satisfied. This may be either a sufficiently high rule accuracy, or an insufficient number of learning examples covered by the rule. Finally, from all candidate rules a single best rule is selected.

9.2.2 Generating a set of rules

Rules can be generated either separately for each class (so that all the examples from one class are positive and others negative), or simultaneously for all classes. Rule learning algorithms frequently use some variant of the *covering algorithm*, shown in Algorithm 9.4. The majority rule, that is eventually included as the last rule of the

---

Algorithm 9.4 The basic covering algorithm for induction of decision rules.

INPUT: A set of learning examples.
OUTPUT: An ordered set of decision rules.

> **while** learning set is not empty **do**
>> generate a decision rule
>> from the learning set remove all examples correctly classified by this rule
>> **if** the generated rule is not good **then**
>>> generate the majority rule **and** empty the learning set
>> **end if**
> **end while**

---

set, classifies all the remaining learning examples, not covered by any other rule, to the majority class. Thus we get an ordered set of rules, where rules are used for classification in the order of their generation.

Another possibility is to generate *redundant rules*, that is, the rules that may cover the same learning examples. This can be achieved by randomly generating an initial set of rules and subsequently improving it by some optimization method. A set of redundant rules is used for classification so that answers of all rules covering the new example are combined in order to produce the final answer – classification. Answers of single rules can be combined with various methods, such as voting, weighted voting, or the naive Bayesian classifier (see Section 3.5.1).

9.3 LEARNING OF ASSOCIATION RULES

You have power over your mind – not outside events. Realize this, and you will find strength.

— Marcus Aurelius

Association rules are used for finding potentially interesting and important relations between attributes in (possibly huge) collections of data. Association rules have originally been used in the *market basket analysis* With their help, merchants can plan arrangement of items on the shelves in their shops, sales strategies, and special discounts. For example, a rule may say that there is a high probability that a customer buying the item A, will also buy the item B. Such a rule suggests that it is beneficial to lower the price of item A while keeping or even raising the price of the item B. Merchants may organize items on shelves so that items A and B are in close proximity, thus easing the customers' shopping. Alternatively, items A and B may be placed far from each other so that customers are forced to review several other shelves and possibly buy something else.

In the market basket analysis a learning example represents a single customer's purchase (contents of his/her market basket). Originally, all attributes were binary, indicating presence (1) or absence (0) of an item. This representation can be generalized so that, instead of indicating the item's presence, the attribute counts its quantity. Since the number of attributes is potentially huge (often more than 10^5), and purchases rarely exceed few tens of items, data matrices are necessarily very sparse. Learning examples are therefore most often represented as lists of items whose counts are greater than zero.

Since the number of all possible association rules is huge – much larger than the number of all possible classification rules – the rule space needs to be sensibly reduced.

9.3.1 Support and confidence

Usually we are interested only in association rules that cover enough learning examples (say, more than 1% of purchases), and are sufficiently accurate (say, over 80%). Measures that define these two criteria are *support* and *confidence*. For a rule

$$A \longrightarrow B$$

where A and B are conjunctions of *(attribute=value)* conditions, they are defined as follows:

$$support \; = \; \frac{n(A \wedge B)}{n} = P(A \wedge B) \qquad (9.2)$$

$$confidence \; = \; \frac{n(A \wedge B)}{n(A)} = P(B \mid A) \qquad (9.3)$$

Here, n is the number of all examples and n_X the number of examples that satisfy the condition X. Support is therefore the probability that, for a randomly chosen example, both the antecedent and the consequent conditions are satisfied. Confidence is the actual accuracy of the rule when the antecedent condition is satisfied.

Since databases where association rules are generated are typically huge – much too large to fit in the primary (fast) computer memory, the most important part in design of algorithms for mining association rules is to minimize the number of passes through the entire database.

9.3.2   APriori algorithm

APriori is one of the first efficient algorithms for generating all association rules that satisfy the given conditions on support and confidence. APriori generates association rules in two steps. In the first step attributes are ordered according to some criterion (e.g., alphabetically); this eases checking for set equivalence. The algorithm then generates all i-tuples of conditions with sufficiently high support. These i-tuples (also called *frequent itemsets*) are subsequently used to generate rules that exceed the given confidence threshold.

Generation of frequent itemsets (i-tuples) starts with 1-tuples, that is, with a single pass through the entire database where the algorithm searches for all conditions with sufficiently high support. From i-tuples, $(i + 1)$-tuples are generated such that all the subsets of size i of their conditions have sufficiently high support. It is not necessary to pass through the database for this step – all highly supported i-tuples have already been collected and stored in the previous step. Support for the new $(i + 1)$-tuples is checked in another pass through the database. For each i it is necessary to traverse the database only once. Since, by increasing the number of conditions i, support of the itemsets quickly decreases, the set of $(i + 1)$-tuples quickly becomes empty. This concludes the first step of the APriori algorithm.

In the second step, frequent itemsets (i-tuples) are used to generate all possible association rules that are subsequently checked for their confidence. Typically, there are too many candidate rules for exhaustive checking. For three conditions A, B and C all possible rules are

$$
\begin{array}{lll}
A \wedge B \longrightarrow C & \quad & C \longrightarrow A \wedge B \\
A \wedge C \longrightarrow B & \quad & B \longrightarrow A \wedge C \\
B \wedge C \longrightarrow A & \quad & A \longrightarrow B \wedge C
\end{array}
$$

Again we have to deal with a combinatorial explosion; this however can be avoided by introducing the following constraint. If rule

$$A \longrightarrow B \wedge C$$

exceeds the threshold values of the minimal support and confidence, the same holds for rules

$$
\begin{array}{lll}
A \wedge B & \longrightarrow & C \\
A \wedge C & \longrightarrow & B
\end{array}
\tag{9.4}
$$

Therefore, once we have the first of the above rules, the others need not be considered at all. This constraint is very useful because it suggests an efficient strategy for generating association rules by incrementally extending their consequent parts. We start with all rules that have only a single conjunction in the consequent part, and keep only those with sufficiently high confidence. Then we use these rules to obtain the rules with the consequent part consisting of two conjunctions by extending the rules in the manner that does not violate the constraint (9.4). Again, only rules with sufficiently high confidence are kept. The process incrementally continues until there are no more sufficiently confident rules available for extension. In practice it often turns out that the number of conjunctions in consequent parts is rather low – usually 2 or 3. This concludes the second part of the APriori algorithm.

For rule generation the access to the database is no longer required. For confidence calculation only support of itemsets that constitute the antecedent part is necessary. They, however, were all calculated in the first part of the APriori algorithm and are normally stored in a hash table.

9.3.3 Improving APriori

There exist several variations of the original APriori algorithm. Most of them are intending to speed-up the original algorithm. To achieve this purpose they aim to minimize the number of passes through the database, the number of candidate rules that need reviewing, or the time needed for the calculation of itemset frequencies.

The number of passes through the databases can be reduced by checking all possible i-tuples as well as $(i + 1)$-tuples in the same pass. The $(i + 1)$-tuples are generated from (as yet) unchecked i-tuples; thus their number is considerably larger than necessary. Such an approach is acceptable only if the passes through the database are adequately time-consuming.

Another approach to achieve significant reduction of database traversals is sampling. Since association rules are typically mined from large databases, sampling can, in a single pass, produce a representative set of examples, that can be stored in fast primary memory. This sample is used to generate all i-tuples with a slightly relaxed support criterion. Their support is subsequently checked by another pass through the entire database, and only i-tuples with sufficiently high support are kept. This approach requires only two database traversals. Rarely, if there exists an i-tuple with too low support on a sample, but all $(i - 1)$-tuples that comprise this i-tuple have sufficiently high support, a third pass through the database is necessary. In this pass all such i-tuples are verified on the entire database.

To reduce the time necessary for calculation of itemset frequencies, candidate itemsets are represented with tree structures. Since attributes in itemsets (i-tuples) are ordered, all candidate itemsets can be represented with trees where a root or any internal node has as many outgoing edges as there are possible attributes in the first part of the itemset. Each subtree therefore consists of all itemsets that share the same attribute in their first part. Each itemset corresponds to a tree leaf. When a new example is read from the database, the algorithm traverses from the root towards the leaves according to the example's attributes. When a leaf is reached, its frequency is incremented by one.

In practice, the computational complexity of association rule mining is largely dependent on threshold values for support and confidence. Normally, only a limited number of best association rules is desired. However, for a new database it is difficult to choose suitable threshold values in advance. Improper threshold settings result either in an empty set of association rules, or in a too large set of rules; the latter is usually reflected in unacceptably slow computation and incomprehensible (lengthy) rules. This can be avoided by starting with conservatively high values for support and confidence thresholds. The learning process is repeated several times by slowly decreasing the threshold values for support and confidence, until a sufficiently large set of rules is generated.

9.4 LEARNING OF REGRESSION TREES

In times like these, it is helpful to remember that there have always been times like these.

— *Paul Harvey*

For building *regression trees* the learning examples are described with attributes and labelled with continuous values of the target variable. Each learning example is represented as a vector of attribute values. Attributes can be either continuous or discrete, and their number is given in advance.

9.4.1 Building and using regression trees

A regression tree consists of internal nodes – corresponding to attributes, edges – corresponding to subsets of attribute values, and terminal nodes (leaves) – corresponding to functions mapping from attribute space to the continuous target value. The simplest and most popular function is a constant function. Another popular function is a linear function of a subset of attributes. Each path starting in a tree root and ending in a tree leaf corresponds to a regression rule. Conditions (pairs of attribute names and corresponding sets of attribute values), evaluated in each internal node, are conjunctively connected. An example of a regression tree is shown in Figure 9.2.

The basic algorithm for building regression trees (Algorithm 9.5) is similar to that for building decision trees (Algorithm 9.1). The stopping criterion of Algorithm 9.5 has to account for the quality of the function that models classes of learning examples in a leaf. The model in a leaf can be one of the following functions:

Constant function: the mean value of the target values of learning examples in a leaf is calculated.

Linear function: target values of learning examples in a leaf are modeled with a straight line (see Section 10.3).

Arbitrary function: target values of learning examples in a leaf are modeled with an arbitrary function. Here the function complexity with respect to the number

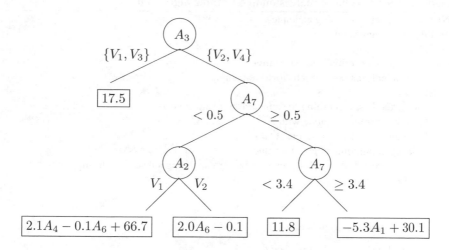

Figure 9.2: An example regression tree. Note the linear functions in some leaves.

of learning examples in a leaf has to be be accounted for in order to avoid overfitting.

Similarly to decision trees, the key factor of the regression tree building algorithm is the choice of the best attribute. For this purpose, measures such as the change of variance and regressional ReliefF (RReliefF) are frequently used. They are discussed in more detail in Chapter 6. Besides, the quality of the attribute in a current node can also be estimated with the quality of a function model in the current node's successors.

Analogously to decision trees, regression trees can also deal with missing and "don't care" values. However, since the target variable is continuous, conditional probabilities of the missing value cannot be directly calculated. This problem can be easily resolved by discretizing the target variable.

A regression tree is a symbolic representation of a function that summarizes some regularities from a given problem domain. Its structure is usually interesting for domain experts because it often conforms to their background knowledge and even provides new insights. The generated regression tree is used for calculation of the continuous target values for new examples. From the root node we traverse along the edges according to the new example's attribute values until we reach a leaf. Each leaf contains a function that predicts the target value of examples falling in the leaf.

As in the case of decision trees, reliability of the target value estimations in regression tree leaves is highly dependent on the number of learning examples. It is not advisable to shatter the learning set into small subsets of examples. Therefore many regressional learning algorithms build binary regression trees. The basic algorithm is modified so that all attributes are binarized before the best attribute is chosen.

Binary regression trees allow for using the change of variance as an attribute quality

---

Algorithm 9.5 The basic regression tree learning algorithm.

INPUT: A set of learning examples.
OUTPUT: A regression tree.

    if the stopping criterion is satisfied **then**
        create a leaf that corresponds to all remaining learning examples
    else
        choose the best (according to some criterion) attribute A_i
        label the current tree node with A_i
        for each value V_j of attribute A_i **do**
            label an outgoing edge with value V_j
            recursively build a subtree by using a corresponding subset of learning examples
        end for
    end if

where the stopping criterion is either

- the model quality in a leaf is good enough
- there are not enough learning examples, or
- there are no good attributes left.

---

measure because binarization compensates for their overestimation of multi-valued attributes. Binarization frequently provides more compact and more precise regression trees. Our example in Figure 9.2 is a binary regression tree.

9.4.2   Pruning of regression trees

Because the lower levels of regression trees are frequently unreliable due to small numbers of learning examples, they are handled with special consideration. Various criteria are used to stop building the tree when its lower levels become unreliable or irrelevant.

As in the case of decision trees, it is difficult to estimate node (un)reliability in advance; therefore tree building frequently proceeds as long as possible, regardless of the nodes' reliability. The tree is reduced in size (*post-pruned*) after the building phase. The basic post-pruning algorithm is the same as for decision trees (Algorithm 9.3). For estimating the expected error e of a node, the modified m-estimate (see Section 3.1.5 for the original definition) can be used:

$$e = \frac{n}{n+m}e_v + \frac{m}{n+m}e_k \qquad (9.5)$$

Here n is the number of learning examples in a node, e_v is the average error of the node model (function) on the same examples, and e_k is the average error of the same model on all learning examples. As in decision trees, we compare the expected error in the current node and the expected error in its subtrees. If the expected error of subtrees is greater, they are pruned and the node is converted into the leaf. The process is repeated in a bottom-up manner, starting with leaves and ending with a root node.

Alternatively, the MDL principle can be used for post-pruning. Instead of the model error, the encoding length of the regression tree and errors on learning examples in leaves are estimated. Since we are dealing with real numbers, it is crucial to select a suitable encoding and its parameters, such as the precision of number representations that can significantly influence the degree of pruning.

9.5 *INDUCTIVE LOGIC PROGRAMMING

Laughter is the shortest distance between two people.

— *Victor Borge*

As discussed in Chapter 4, in *inductive logic programming* (ILP) the task of the learning algorithm is to induce, given the background knowledge B, the set of positive learning examples E^+ and the set of negative examples E^-, as simple a target relation (hypothesis) H as possible, covering all positive learning examples $e \in E^+$ while not covering any negative example $e \in E^-$:

$$\forall e \in E^+ : \ B \wedge H \vDash e \tag{9.6}$$

$$\forall e \in E^- : \ B \wedge H \nvDash e \tag{9.7}$$

Learning examples are presented as a set of facts. The set of positive learning examples E^+ consists of n-tuples that are elements of the n-ary target relation. The set of negative learning examples E^- consists of n-tuples that are not elements of the target relation.

Background knowledge B is a set of relations that can be used by the learning algorithm for inferring a definition of the target relation. In background knowledge, relation is given either *extensionally* – as a set of facts not including any variables, or *intensionally* – as an ordered set of prolog clauses.

A hypothesis space $\mathcal{H}$ is a set of all possible definitions (valid prolog programs) of the target relation. In Chapter 4 the reader can find a description of logical programs in the first-order predicate calculus and operators that are used in ILP.

9.5.1 Generating a set of rules in FOIL

In this section we describe a top-down, general-to-specific approach for learning logic programs with a *covering algorithm*, as used in the FOIL system. The basic FOIL algorithm is shown in Algorithm 9.6. Its stopping criterion depends on the number of covered positive learning examples, the number of covered negative learning examples, and the complexity of the generated clause.

For estimating the quality of a clause or a literal, FOIL uses the adjusted *information gain*. It is adjusted so as to favor clauses that cover many positive and few negative learning examples. This is because the basic information gain is

---

Algorithm 9.6 The basic FOIL learning algorithm.

INPUT: A set of positive and a set of negative examples.
OUTPUT: A set of rules (prolog program).

   while the learning set has some positive examples left **do**
      {Build a rule (prolog clause)}
      Start with a fact (a rule without the body) whose head consists only of variables so that it covers all learning examples.
      while the stopping criterion is not satisfied **do**
         Add a literal in the clause's body so as to maximize its quality
      end while
      Remove from the learning set all positive learning examples covered by the new rule.
   end while

---

symmetric, and would equally estimate clauses that cover few positive and many negative examples. This property is acceptable when learning propositional rules because the rules are generated for all classes. However, in ILP the rules are generated only for the positive class. Information gain is modified as shown in Equation (9.8).

$$\text{gain}(L|Clause) = -N(+|Clause, L) \cdot$$
$$\cdot \left(\log_2 P(+|Clause) - \log_2 P(+|Clause, L) \right) \quad (9.8)$$

Here, L is a new literal, $Clause$ is the current clause, $(Clause, L)$ is the current clause extended with literal L, $N(+|Clause, L)$ is the number of positive learning examples covered by the extended clause, $P(+|Clause)$ is the probability that an example covered by the clause is positive, and $P(+|Clause, L)$ the probability that an example covered by the extended clause is positive. The adjusted information gain can also be negative; this happens when

$$P(+|Clause) > (P + |Clause, L)$$

Candidate literals can be of the form

$$X_i = X_j$$
$$X_i = constant$$
$$Q(V_1, ..., V_k)$$

and their negations. X_i is an existing variable, V_i is either an existing or a newly introduced variable (of which at least one must already exist in the clause), and Q is a predicate from the background knowledge, or the target predicate. In the latter case FOIL produces a recursive definition of the target predicate. In recursive call, the arguments are strictly limited so as to prevent endless recursion.

For example, let the target predicate be $grandmother(X, Y)$ and let the background knowledge comprise relations $mother(X, Y)$ and $female(X)$. The FOIL learning process starts building the target predicate with an unconditional clause

$$grandmother(X, Y).$$

that covers all positive and negative learning examples. FOIL then generates all possible literals that can be used as an extension of the (so far empty) body clause:

$$
\begin{array}{lll}
mother(X,Y), & mother(X,Z), & mother(Y,Z), \\
mother(Y,X), & mother(Z,X), & mother(Z,Y), \\
female(X), & female(Y), & X = Y
\end{array}
\qquad (9.9)
$$

and their negations. If this example would allow recursive clauses, candidate literals would also comprise the clauses $grandmother(Y,X)$, $grandmother(Z,X)$, ..., where Z is a new variable. Only the best candidate literal is kept in the clause's body, and learning proceeds with generating new candidate literals.

The stopping criterion depends on the number of covered positive learning examples, the number of covered negative learning examples, and the complexity of the generated clause. By including the complexity of the generated clause we penalize the generation of overly complex clauses that overfit learning examples. For this purpose, measures based on the MDL principle or some other heuristic can be used.

9.5.2   ReliefF for ILP

Instead of modifying the myopic quality measures such as the information gain, the non-myopic quality measure ReliefF can be adapted for use in ILP. Equivalently to information gain, ReliefF is also symmetric with respect to positive and negative examples. While this is acceptable in propositional learning, it is not in ILP where we are interested only in clauses covering positive examples.

ReliefF is adapted for ILP so that, when increasing the quality W of a literal L for nearest misses, an asymmetric diff function is used. It calculates, for a given literal L, the difference between the coverage of the given learning example I and the nearest miss M. $L(X) = 0$ means that literal L does not cover example X, and $L(X) = 1$ means that literal L covers example X.

$$
\mathrm{diff}(L,I,M) = \begin{cases}
 & \quad L(I) \quad\ L(M) \\
0, & \quad 0 \qquad\ 0 \\
0, & \quad 0 \qquad\ 1 \\
1, & \quad 1 \qquad\ 0 \\
0, & \quad 1 \qquad\ 1
\end{cases}
\qquad (9.10)
$$

The quality W of literal L increases only if the literal covers the given positive example while not covering the nearest negative example (nearest miss). All other cases fail to increase the quality W of literal L in the following formula from the ReliefF algorithm:

$$
W[L] = W[L] + \mathrm{diff}(L,I,M)
$$

9.6 NAIVE AND SEMI-NAIVE BAYESIAN CLASSIFIER

You may say I'm a dreamer, but I'm not the only one.

— *John Lennon*

9.6.1 Naive Bayesian classifier

The naive Bayesian classifier assumes conditional independence of attributes with respect to the class. Derivation of the basic formula (9.11) of the naive Bayesian classifier from the Bayes rule is provided in Section 4.4.

$$P(C_k|V) = P(C_k) \prod_{i=1}^{a} \frac{P(C_k|v_i)}{P(C_k)} \qquad (9.11)$$

The task of the learning algorithm is to use learning examples to estimate unconditional probabilities $P(C_k)$, $k = 1...m_0$, and conditional class probabilities $P(C_k|v_i)$, $k = 1...m_0$ given the value v_i of attributes A_i, $i = 1...a$. For estimation of prior (unconditional) class probabilities, Laplace's law of succession is used:

$$P(C_k) = \frac{n(C_k) + 1}{n + m_0} \qquad (9.12)$$

where $n(C_k)$ is the number of learning examples from the class C_k, n is the total number of learning examples, and m_0 the number of classes (values of the A_0 attribute). For estimation of conditional class probabilities, the m-estimate is used

$$P(C_k|v_i) = \frac{n(C_k, v_i) + mP(C_k)}{n(v_i) + m} \qquad (9.13)$$

where $n(C_k, v_i)$ is the number of learning examples from the class C_k and with value v_i of the attribute A_i, and $n(v_i)$ is the total number of learning examples with value v_i of the attribute A_i.

In the naive Bayesian classifier, learning is reduced to calculating prior and conditional class probabilities. If an example is missing a value for a given attribute, this example is not used when calculating probabilities for that attribute. For classification, the naive Bayesian classifier can use all available attributes. If a new example is missing an attribute value for some attribute, this attribute is simply ignored when calculating the formula (9.11).

The naive Bayesian classifier can readily be used with discrete attributes; continuous attributes need to be discretized first. In the naive Bayesian classification it is best to use *fuzzy discretization* (Section 7.2.3). In fuzzy discretization each learning example has, for a newly discretized attribute, its values given as a distribution of memberships to different intervals. This approach preserves both the learning set and the order of intervals, and the "fuzziness" parameter is used to control the continuous attributes' fragmentation.

Although the conditional independence is a fairly strong assumption, in practice the naive Bayesian classifier usually performs very well.

- In medical diagnosis problems, symptoms depend on the underlying illness (diagnosis), however, given the diagnosis (class), they are relatively independent. This is the reason why the naive Bayesian classifier is one of the most successful learners in medical diagnostics.

- There exist several artificial problems that were developed for evaluating specific aspects of machine learning algorithms. One of them is the problem of the numeric LED display. Each digit (0–9) is displayed with a subset of seven segments. The noise level determines the probability of the failure of each segment. The task of the learning algorithm is to determine the digit given the subset of switched-on segments. Since the failure of a single segment is independent of the failures of other segments, each attribute's value (1 or 0) is, given the class, independent of the values of other attributes. Therefore in this problem the naive Bayesian classifier achieves the optimal performance (classification accuracy).

In the naive Bayesian classifier, all probability estimations are rather reliable and thus the danger of overfitting is relatively small. Another point in favor of the naive Bayesian classifier is that, even when the conditional independence assumption is not entirely met, the class probability estimations usually differ enough that the independence assumption error does not change their order.

The naive Bayesian classifier therefore performs well even in problems where the conditional independence assumption is not entirely true. However in problems with strong dependencies between attributes, the naive Bayesian classifier miserably fails. In such cases, the *semi-naive Bayesian classifier* (Section 9.6.3) often performs well.

9.6.2 Explaining decisions

By applying the logarithm to the original formula (9.11) of the naive Bayesian classifier, and multiplying both sides with -1, we get

$$- \log_2 P(C_k|V) = - \log_2 P(C_k) - \sum_{i=1}^{a} \big(\log_2 P(C_k|v_i) - \log_2 P(C_k) \big) \quad (9.14)$$

The minus logarithm of the event probability is interpreted as the amount of information (in bit) necessary to find out whether the event has occurred. The factor $\log_2 P(C_k|v_i) - \log_2 P(C_k)$ is interpreted as a difference between prior and posterior amount of information necessary to determine whether an example belongs to class C_k. In other words, this factor represents the information gain contributed by the value v_i in favor of the class C_k.

The entire formula (9.14) is interpeted as the prior amount of information, necessary to label an example with label C_k minus the sum of information gains of all attributes. A decision of the naive Bayesian classifier can therefore be explained

A	B	C
1	1	0
1	0	1
0	1	1
0	0	0

Table 9.1: The XOR problem.

with the sum of information gains in favor of a particular class (if the attribute's information gain is positive), and the sum of information gains against a particular class (if the attribute's information gain is negative). Such explanations are closely related to nomograms (Section 7.6.4). In many problems, domain experts praise such explanations as very comprehensible.

9.6.3 Semi-naive Bayesian classifier

The aim of the *semi-naive Bayesian classifier* is to account for strong dependencies between values of different attributes. Events A and B are said to be *independent* when $P(AB) = P(A)P(B)$. Dependence between A and B is proportional to the difference between $P(A)P(B)$ and $P(AB)$. In extreme cases we have $A = B$ where $P(AB) = P(A) = P(B)$ or $A = \overline{B}$, where $P(AB) = 0$. We are interested in conditional dependence of events A and B with respect to the event C. Events A and B are independent with respect to C if:

$$P(AB|C) = P(A|C)P(B|C) \tag{9.15}$$

Dependence between A and B with respect to C is proportional to the difference between $P(A|C)P(B|C)$ and $P(AB|C)$. The extreme cases are the XOR problem $C = A \underline{\vee} B = (A \neq B)$ where $P(AB|C) = 0$, and the equivalence problem $C = (A = B)$ where $P(AB|C) = P(A|C) = P(B|C)$.

The XOR (exclusive or) problem (Table 9.1) is a classical nonlinear problem, that can be solved neither by the naive Bayesian classifier nor by a two-layered perceptron. The multi-layered perceptron using a generalized delta rule is able to solve the XOR problem at the cost of a suitable network topology and several hundred passes through the learning set. The XOR problem can be solved in several different ways:

- Learning examples are stored. Such a solution is appropriate only if XOR is known in advance to be present in the data and only in exact domains.

- Classes are split into subclasses and the problem is implicitly simplified to learning a disjunction. This solution has similar drawbacks as the previous one.

- Attributes are joined in a manner similar to the multi-layered perceptrons, where hidden-layer neurons represent new concepts defined by neurons from the previous layer. Besides, instead of joining whole attributes, single values of different attributes can also be joined, which is more flexible.

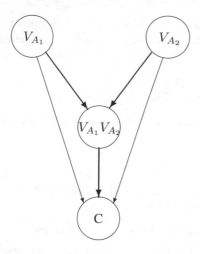

Figure 9.3: Joining two dependent attribute values in the semi-naive Bayesian classifier.

For the semi-naive Bayesian classifier, the latter approach (joining attribute values) is the most appropriate. If the values of two attributes V_{A_1} and V_{A_2} are found to be dependent with respect to the class C, these values can be joined as shown in Figure 9.3.

Joining attribute values

It remains to define the formula for detecting the dependencies between attributes. From the following formulae that are valid for every attribute A_1, A_2 and C (here C stands for the class attribute):

$$H(A_1|A_2C) + H(A_2|C) \;=\; H(A_1A_2|C) \tag{9.16}$$
$$H(A_1|C) \geq H(A_1|A_2C) \tag{9.17}$$

we get

$$H(A_1|C) + H(A_2|C) - H(A_1A_2|C) \geq 0 \tag{9.18}$$

The above formulae are suitable for detecting dependencies between attributes. Equality in (9.18) holds only if the attributes A_1 and A_2 are independent with respect to class C. The dependence of attributes A_1 and A_2 with respect to C is proportional to the value of the left-hand side of (9.18).

Equation (9.18) cannot be used to detect dependencies between *single values* of attributes, because it could join values of the same attribute. Since a learning example cannot hold two different values of the same attribute, such a join is senseless. Besides, (9.18) needs a threshold above which it is useful to join attributes without losing the reliability of approximations of probabilities. On the other hand, by joining two attribute values, the probability estimation of the joint event becomes less reliable. It is therefore necessary to find a compromise between non-naivety and reliability of probability estimations. This, however is not possible without changes in (9.18).

Let us calculate the probability of the class C_k when attributes A_1 and A_2 have respective values V_{A_1} and V_{A_2}. If the attributes A_1 and A_2 are mutually independent (or treated as such), their joint influence is a product of two independent factors:

$$\frac{P(C_k|V_{A_1})}{P(C_k)} \cdot \frac{P(C_k|V_{A_2})}{P(C_k)} \tag{9.19}$$

However, when A_1 and A_2 are treated as mutually dependent, their joint influence is represented with the factor

$$\frac{P(C_k|V_{A_1}V_{A_2})}{P(C_k)} \tag{9.20}$$

In this case they are actually treated as if their values were joined. Generally, for joining two attribute values, two conditions need to be satisfied:

- values of (9.19) in (9.20) should be sufficiently different, and
- the approximation of $P(C_k|V_{A_1}V_{A_2})$ with relative frequency should be sufficiently reliable.

For reliability estimation of the probability approximation, the Chebyshev theorem (9.21) can be used. This theorem gives the lower bound on the probability, that the relative frequency f of an event after n trials differs from the factual prior probability p for less than ε:

$$P(|f - p| \le \varepsilon) > 1 - \frac{p(1-p)}{\varepsilon^2 n} \tag{9.21}$$

The lower bound is proportional to n and to ε^2. In our case we are interested in the reliability of the following approximation:

$$P(C_k|V_{A_1}V_{A_2}) \approx \frac{n(C_k, V_{A_1}V_{A_2})}{n(V_{A_1}V_{A_2})} \tag{9.22}$$

Therefore, the number of trials n in (9.21) is equal to the number of examples when both $A_1 = V_{A_1}$ and $A_2 = V_{A_2}$, that is, $n(V_{A_1}V_{A_2})$. As the prior probability p is unknown, the worst case for p is assumed, i.e. $p = 0.5$.

It remains to determine the value of ε. As we are interested whether the values of (9.20) and (9.19) are significantly different, it makes sense for ε to be proportional to the difference between these two values. Since the joint value $V_{A_1}V_{A_2}$ will influence all classes, ε is the average difference between (9.19) and (9.20) over all classes:

$$\varepsilon = \sum_{C_k} P(C_k) \left| P(C_k|V_{A_1}V_{A_2}) - \frac{P(C_k|V_{A_1})P(C_k|V_{A_2})}{P(C_k)} \right| \tag{9.23}$$

It is necessary to determine the threshold τ for the probability (9.21) above which it is useful to join two values of two attributes. Experiments have shown that the semi-naive Bayesian classifier performs best when $\tau \in [0.5, 1]$.

Therefore, the rule for joining attribute values V_{A_1} and V_{A_2} states: join two values V_{A_1} and V_{A_2} if the probability is greater than τ that the actual (unknown) influence of the new value $V_{A_1}V_{A_2}$ differs, in average over all classes, from the used influence by less than the difference between the used influence and the influence of the values V_{A_1} and V_{A_2} without joining them:

$$1 - \frac{1}{4\varepsilon^2 n(V_{A_1} V_{A_2})} \geq \tau \qquad (9.24)$$

The values can be iteratively joined so that more than two values can be joined together until probability estimations are sufficiently reliable. In this manner we get a multi-layered Bayesian classifier, as shown in Figure 9.4.

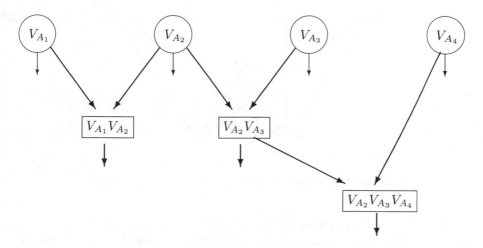

Figure 9.4: An example of the semi-naive Bayesian classifier depicted as a multi-layered Bayesian neural network.

Since reliability of probability estimations quickly decreases with an increasing number of joint values, in most cases exhaustive search is efficient enough. The number of passes through the learning set is in practice roughly proportional to the number of attributes. The algorithm using the exhaustive search strategy is shown in Algorithm 9.7.

Algorithm 9.7 The semi-naive Bayesian classifier learning algorithm.

INPUT: A set of learning examples.
OUTPUT: A semi-naive Bayesian classifier.

  Learn the naive Bayesian classifier from entire learning set.
  for each attribute value V_{A_1} **do**
    for each attribute value V_{A_2} of different attributes **do**
      join V_{A_1} and V_{A_2}
    end for
    From learning set determine the relative frequencies for joint values.
    Discard the pairs for which $\frac{1}{4\varepsilon^2 n(V_{A_1} V_{A_2})} > \tau$.
  end for

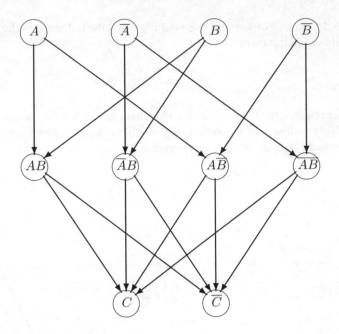

Figure 9.5: The XOR problem solved with the semi-naive Bayesian classifier.

The XOR problem, as shown in Table 9.1 is solved by Algorithm 9.7 as shown in Figure 9.5. In order to improve reliability of probability approximations, the number of learning examples is doubled (from 4 to 8).

9.6.4   Practical considerations

The learning algorithm of the semi-naive Bayesian classifier balances between the non-naivety and the reliability of probability estimations. By increasing the non-naivety, it decreases the reliability of probability estimations, and vice versa. By decreasing the threshold τ (that usually defaults to 0.5), the algorithm decreases the reliability of probability estimations and increases the non-naivety in exact problem domains.

A crucial point in Bayesian learning is the estimation of probabilities. Experimental evaluations show that prior probabilities estimated with Laplace's law of succession and conditional probabilities estimated with the m-estimate and parameter m set to 2 provide almost optimal performance.

Bayesian classifiers can easily be implemented as Bayesian neural networks (see Section 11.4.3). Due to their efficiency, simplicity, and good performance, Bayesian classifiers (both naive and semi-naive) are among the most popular learners, rivalled only by decision trees. It is thus interesting to compare the two approaches.

Decision trees (Section 9.1), due to their non-naivety and less reliable probability estimations, are more suitable for exact problems, while Bayesian classifiers, due to their naivety and reliable probability estimations, are suitable for soft, inexact, noisy problems. Several problem analyses have shown that human experts typically define attributes in a relatively independent manner due to easier (linear) reasoning. Since the attribute independence assumption is not violated, in such problems the naive Bayesian classifier tends to perform optimally.

An important advantage of the naive and the semi-naive Bayesian classifier over decision trees is also in handling of missing attribute values. When an example misses a decision tree attribute value, its classification immediately becomes less reliable. On the other hand, the naive and the semi-naive Bayesian classifier simply ignore such an attribute and still use all others to produce the final classification. For example, let us consider a problem with 50 attributes, and a decision tree of depth at most 5, so that there are at most 5 conditions on each path from the root to a leaf. If for one of the five attributes a value is missing, only four of them are used for classification, and even for these four it is not certain whether they are all correct. On the other hand, the naive and the semi-naive Bayesian classifier use all other 49 attributes to produce the final classification! Especially in problems of medical diagnostics, domain experts (physicians) complain that decision trees comprise too few attributes to reliably describe the patient, and this makes their classifications (diagnoses) inherently unreliable.

9.7 BAYESIAN BELIEF NETWORKS

Put your hand on a hot stove for a minute, and it seems like an hour. Sit with a pretty girl for an hour, and it seems like a minute. THAT'S relativity.

— Albert Einstein

Bayesian belief networks are a generalization of the naive Bayesian classifier. In Bayesian belief networks, a directed acyclic graph is used to explicitly express dependencies between attributes. Bayesian belief networks can also be used for modeling probability distribution of problems, described with attributes, but without class labels (unsupervised learning).

A Bayesian belief network is a directed acyclic graph where each node corresponds to a single attribute (or the class), and each edge represents a direct correlation between two nodes (attributes). Each node is assigned a table of conditional probabilities of all corresponding attribute values with respect to the values of *parent* attributes – nodes that are sources of edges that sink in the current node. If a node has no parents, it is assigned a table of prior probabilities of all corresponding attribute values.

A Bayesian belief network graph represents conditional independencies between attributes in the following sense: given the values of the parent nodes (attributes), each node (attribute) is conditionally independent of its non-successors in the graph. In practice, dependencies in the graph often correspond to causal relations.

A Bayesian belief network describes the probability distribution of all possible combinations of attribute values for a given problem domain. Its structure (topology) can either be given in advance as a part of background knowledge, or it can be constructed according to attribute (in)dependence estimations from learning examples.

Prior and conditional probabilities are calculated in the same way. Unsupervised learning of a Bayesian belief network from data is therefore the search for such a network that best describes the target probability distribution.

9.7.1   Bayesian belief networks for classification

Not every Bayesian belief network topology is suitable for classification. Only such graphs, where the class is the parent of (all) attributes and itself has no parent, can be used for this purpose. For example, in medical diagnosis problems, the diagnosis (illness) is the source of all symptoms; thus the class (diagnosis) is the parent of all attributes (symptoms). An illustration of the Bayesian belief networks for classification is shown in Figure 9.6. In this case, the Bayesian belief network enforces the following conditional independencies:

- attribute A_1 is conditionally independent of attributes A_3, A_4 and A_5 given the value C_k of class C, i.e., for arbitrary values v_1, v_3, v_4, v_5 of attributes A_1, A_3, A_4 in A_5 and for any class C_k it holds:

$$P(A_1 = v_1 | A_3 = v_3, A_4 = v_4, A_5 = v_5, C = C_k) = P(A_1 = v_1 | C = C_k)$$

or shorter
$$P(A_1 | A_3, A_4, A_5, C) = P(A_1 | C)$$

Obviously, all similar equations, based on subsets of values of attributes A_3, A_4 and A_5, also hold, e.g.:

$$P(A_1 | A_3, A_4, C) = P(A_1 | C)$$

and
$$P(A_1 | A_5, C) = P(A_1 | C)$$

- attribute A_2 is conditionally independent of attributes A_4 and A_5 given the values of class C, and given the values of attributes A_1 and A_3:

$$P(A_2 | A_1, A_3, A_4, A_5, C) = P(A_2 | A_1, A_3, C)$$

- attribute A_3 is conditionally independent of attributes A_1 and A_5 given the value of class C;

- attribute A_4 is conditionally independent of attributes A_1, A_2 and A_5 given the value of class C, and given the value of attribute A_3;

- attribute A_5 is conditionally independent of all other attributes (A_1, A_2, A_3, A_4) for the given value of class C.

Besides defining the network topology that determines dependencies between attributes, we have to assign a table of conditional probabilities of all corresponding attribute values with respect to the values of parent to each node in the network. For our example in Figure 9.6 we therefore need the following:

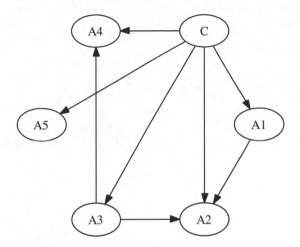

Figure 9.6: A simple example of a Bayesian belief network for classification.

- for class attribute C the prior probabilities $P(C = C_k)$ for each label $C_k \in C$;

- for attribute A_1 a table of conditional probabilities of its values v_1, given the class label C_k: $P(A_1 = v_1|C = C_k)$ or shorter $P(A_1|C)$;

- for attribute A_2 a table of conditional probabilities given the class C and values of attributes A_1 and A_3: $P(A_2|C, A_1, A_3)$;

- for attribute A_3 a table of conditional probabilities given the class C: $P(A_3|C)$;

- for attribute A_4 a table of conditional probabilities given the class C and the values of attribute A_3: $P(A_4|C, A_3)$;

- for attribute A_5 a table of conditional probabilities given the class C: $P(A_5|C)$.

Once the topology of a Bayesian belief network is determined, a table of conditional probabilities can be computed for each node from the learning set. It is beneficial to use the m-estimate to compute conditional probabilities, and Laplace's law of succession for prior probabilities. Considering their reliability, probability estimations in nodes with more parents (A_2 in Figure 9.6) are less reliable than those in nodes with fewer parents. For the class (C in Figure 9.6) only prior probabilities have to be estimated. Of all the attributes, the most reliable probability estimations are for those with only a single parent (A_1, A_3 and A_5 in Figure 9.6).

A special case of the Bayesian belief network is the *naive Bayesian classifier*. Since in the naive Bayesian classifier all attributes are conditionally independent with respect to the class, the graph of the corresponding Bayesian belief network takes the shape of a flattened two-layered tree. Its root is the class, and all second-layer nodes (leaves) are the attributes. An example of the Bayesian belief network topology for the naive Bayesian classifier is shown in Figure 9.7.

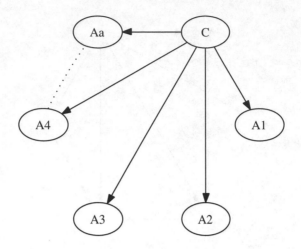

Figure 9.7: A topology of the Bayesian belief network that corresponds to the naive Bayesian classifier.

Since the edges in a Bayesian belief network correspond to (causal) dependencies between its nodes (attributes and the class), the edges in Figure 9.7 are directed from the cause (the class) towards consequences (attributes). On the other hand, directed edges in Figures 9.3, 9.4 and 9.5 show the direction of influence for calculated conditional probabilities and are therefore directed from attributes towards the class.

Independence of attributes greatly simplifies the calculation of tables assigned to the nodes of a Bayesian belief network. To complete the network for the naive Bayesian classifier it is sufficient to estimate prior class probabilities $P(C = C_k)$ and for each attribute A_j conditional probabilities for each value of this attribute given the class label C_k: $P(A_j = v_j | C = C_k)$.

9.7.2 Classification with Bayesian belief networks

After a Bayesian belief network is learned (all prior and conditional probabilities for the given network topology are calculated), it can be used for classification of new examples. In the network, attribute values are set to the known new example's values (unknown values are ignored). With given attribute values, conditional probabilities for all values C_k of class C need to be calculated:

$$P(C = C_k | A_1 = v_1, A_2 = v_2, ..., A_a = v_a) \qquad (9.25)$$

It can be shown that for the purpose of calculating (9.25) tables assigned to network nodes are sufficient. By Bayes' rule it holds

$$P(C = C_k | A_1 = v_1, A_2 = v_2, ..., A_a = v_a) =$$
$$P(C = C_k) \frac{P(A_1 = v_1, A_2 = v_2, ..., A_a = v_a | C = C_k)}{P(A_1 = v_1, A_2 = v_2, ..., A_a = v_a)} \qquad (9.26)$$

Since the denominator in (9.26) is independent of the class, it can be treated as a normalizing factor. The numerator is expanded by successive applications of the chain rule:

$$P(A_1 = v_1, A_2 = v_2, \ldots, A_a = v_a | C = C_k) =$$
$$P(A_1 = v_1 | C = C_k) \cdot P(A_2 = v_2 | A_1 = v_1, C = C_k) \cdot \ldots \qquad (9.27)$$
$$\ldots \cdot P(A_a = v_a | A_1 = v_1, \ldots, A_{a-1} = v_{a-1}, C = C_k)$$

Since the order of attributes in the expanded rule is arbitrary, and since a Bayesian belief network for classification requires conditional independence for each node A_j with respect to its parent nodes C, A_{j1}, ..., A_{jk_j}:

$$P(A_j = v_j | A_1 = v_1, \ldots, A_{j-1} = v_{j-1}, C = C_k) =$$
$$P(A_j = v_j | A_1^j = v_{j_1}, \ldots, A_{k_j}^j = v_{jk_j}, C = C_k) \qquad (9.28)$$

Equation (9.27) can be simplified so that in the right-hand side of the product for each attribute A_j we use the factor

$$P(A_j = v_j | A_{j1} = v_{j_1}, \ldots, A_{jk_j} = v_{jk_j}, C = C_k) \qquad (9.29)$$

determined with the Bayesian belief network, and stored in the node corresponding to the attribute A_j. By using the above formulae, for our example in Figure 9.6 we get:

$$P(A_1 = v_1, A_2 = v_2, A_3 = v_3, A_4 = v_4, A_5 = v_5 | C = C_k) =$$
$$P(A_1 = v_1 | C = C_k) \cdot P(A_2 = v_2 | A_1 = v_1, A_3 = v_3, C = C_k) \cdot$$
$$\cdot P(A_3 = v_3 | C = C_k) \cdot P(A_4 = v_4 | A_3 = v_3, C = C_k) \cdot \qquad (9.30)$$
$$\cdot P(A_5 = v_5 | C = C_k)$$

For the naive Bayesian classifier, Equation (9.27) can be simplified even further:

$$P(A_1 = v_1, A_2 = v_2, \ldots, A_a = v_a | C = C_k) =$$
$$P(A_1 = v_1 | C = C_k) \cdot P(A_2 = v_2 | C = C_k) \cdot \ldots \cdot P(A_a = v_a | C = C_k) \qquad (9.31)$$

9.7.3   Learning the Bayesian network topology

For learning the Bayesian belief network's structure (topology) from data, one needs to define a suitable optimization criterion that should be satisfied by the learned topology. As in many other machine learning methods, the basic underlying principle is the minimum description length (MDL) principle: the sum of description lengths of the network and data has to be minimal in the sense of Equation (3.6). By introducing new edges to the network topology, we increase the network description length and simultaneously decrease the data description length. The task of the learning algorithm is to find a network topology that, for a given learning set, minimizes the MDL

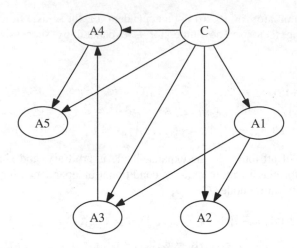

Figure 9.8: An example tree-augmented naive Bayesian classifier.

criterion. It can be shown that for a fixed network topology, optimal (in the MDL sense) values of network parameters (prior and conditional probabilities) are those estimated from the given learning set. As a consequence, learning reduces to determining optimal network structure (topology), since optimal network parameters (probability estimations) are uniquely determined by the learning set.

However, since the number of possible network structures is typically much too large to allow for exhaustive search, structures are either restricted to the certain subclass, or an optimization algorithm that finds approximately optimal structures is applied. In the latter case, greedy search is frequently used. In a single step the algorithm either introduces a new edge, removes an existing edge, or reverses one existing edge's direction so as not to introduce a cycle. The algorithm can start with different initial structures: an empty graph, a fully connected graph, a randomly connected graph, or a graph generated with an efficient algorithm for searching in a restricted network subclass.

For classification purposes, network topologies are limited to graphs where the class is the parent of all attributes and itself has no parents. The optimization algorithm has only to determine the edges of the attribute subgraph. A trivial – empty – attribute subgraph with no edges between attributes corresponds to a naive Bayesian classifier (Figure 9.7).

A well-analyzed network topology subclass is the *tree-augmented naive Bayesian classifier*. Here, the attribute subgraph is a tree: each attribute has only one parent attribute, with an exception of the root attribute which has none. An example of a tree-augmented naive Bayesian classifier is shown in Figure 9.8; its attribute subgraph is depicted in Figure 9.9. An efficient algorithm for learning of the tree-augmented naive Bayesian classifier topology is described in Section 9.7.4. A tree-augmented naive Bayesian classifier network topology is a good starting point for greedy optimization algorithms. They may result in general (non-tree) attribute subgraphs that have fewer

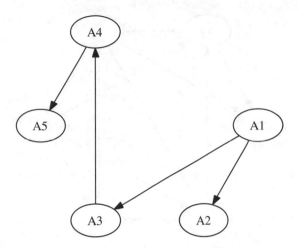

Figure 9.9: An attribute subgraph of the Bayesian belief network from Figure 9.8.

(Figure 9.6) or more (Figure 9.10) edges than the original graph (Figure 9.8).

Instead of learning a single Bayesian belief network for all classes, we can learn for each class a separate Bayesian belief network, adapted to the probability distribution. Only examples from that class are used to build a network structure. However, the complete learning set, where all examples from other classes are considered as "negative" classes, is used to calculate probability tables. By this approach we get as many binary classifiers as is the number of classes. The advantage of using many binary Bayesian belief networks is that network structures are more adapted to corresponding class distributions. A potential drawback of this approach is the danger of overfitting to learning examples.

9.7.4   Learning tree-augmented naive Bayesian classifiers

An optimal tree-augmented naive Bayesian classifier can be constructed so that edges in a full attribute subgraph are labelled with conditional mutual information of the two connecting attributes given the class label. The algorithm then searches for a maximum spanning tree (Algorithm 9.8).

If there is no available information on causal relations, the choice of the maximum spanning tree root can indeed be arbitrary. For finding the maximum spanning tree, one of the existing efficient algorithms for finding minimum spanning trees can be used with only slight modifications. Their computational complexity[1] is $O(m \log n)$ where n is the number of nodes and m the number of edges. In the case of Bayesian belief networks $n = a$ (the number of attributes) and $m = a(a - 1)/2$, so the computational complexity is $O(a^2 \log a)$.

---

[1] For definition of O-notation see Section A.2 in the appendix.

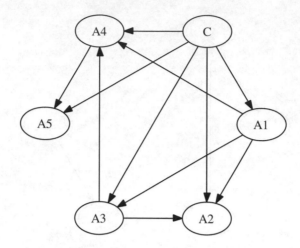

Figure 9.10: An example Bayesian belief network for classification without its subgraphs restricted to trees. If edges are treated as undirected, it contains cycles.

9.8   SUMMARY AND FURTHER READING

Stop talking and thinking, and there is nothing you will not be able to know.

— *Sosan*

- Symbolic learning methods are those that represent the generated knowledge in a symbolic way, such as a tree or a set of rules.

- Decision trees consist of internal nodes (corresponding to attributes), edges (corresponding to subsets of attribute values), and terminal nodes – leaves (corresponding to discrete class labels). Each path, starting in a tree root

---

Algorithm 9.8 The algorithm for learning the optimal structure of a tree-augmented naive Bayesian classifier.

INPUT:	A set of learning examples.
OUTPUT:	A tree augmented naive Bayesian classifier.

Compute conditional mutual information $I(A_i; A_j|C)$ given the class label C between all pairs of attributes A_i and A_j (see Equation (8.7)).

Build a full undirected attribute subgraph and label the edges between all pairs of attributes A_i and A_j with corresponding conditional mutual information $I(A_i; A_j|C)$.

Find a maximum spanning tree in the attribute subgraph.

Transform the undirected maximum spanning tree in a directed graph so that an arbitrary node is selected as the root, and all edges are directed away from it.

In the attribute subgraph (a tree) include the class and edges connecting the class with each attribute.

(topmost node) and ending in a tree leaf, corresponds to a decision rule. Decision trees are usually built in a top-down manner. The learning algorithm selects the best attribute for the root node, and then recursively builds its subtrees. Since fully grown decision trees often generalize badly, they are usually pruned by removing some of the lower nodes.

- Decision rules are usually conjunctions of pairs of attribute names and corresponding sets of attribute values. Rules are generated in sets – either for each (discrete) class separately, or for all classes at the same time.

- Association rules are used for finding potentially interesting and important relations between attributes in huge collections of data. They are often used in business (especially marketing) applications. Association rules are essentially an unsupervised learning technique. One of the first efficient (and definitely best known) algorithms for generating association rules is APriori.

- Similarly to decision trees, regression trees consists of internal nodes – corresponding to attributes, edges – corresponding to subsets of attribute values, and terminal nodes (leaves) – corresponding to functions mapping from attribute space to the continuous target value. The simplest and most popular function is a constant function. Another popular function is a linear function of a subset of attributes. Regression rules are generated similarly to decision rules; for better generalization they also often need to be pruned.

- Inductive logic programming (ILP) is a first-order (relational) machine learning approach that, given the background knowledge and sets of positive and negative examples, generates relations (described with logical programs). Logical programs need to be as simple as possible while covering all positive learning examples, and no negative ones. One of the best known ILP algorithms is FOIL.

- The naive Bayesian classifier assumes conditional independence of attributes with respect to the class. Although this is a seemingly very restrictive assumption, the naive Bayesian classifier often performs excellently in real-world problems. The semi-naive Bayesian classifier accounts for strong dependencies between pairs of values of different attributes.

- Bayesian belief networks are a generalization of the naive Bayesian classifier. In Bayesian belief networks, a directed acyclic graph is used to explicitly express dependencies between attributes. Besides classification, Bayesian belief networks can also be used for modeling probability distribution of problems, described with attributes, but without class labels (unsupervised learning).

Hunt et al. (1966) describe the basic algorithm for inductive learning of decision trees. Quinlan (1979), Kononenko et al. (1984), Cestnik et al. (1987), Quinlan (1993), Breiman et al. (1984), Kononenko et al. (1997), and many others analyze the use of different impurity measures for evaluation of attribute quality while building decision trees. These measures are discussed in more detail in Chapter 6. Cestnik and Bratko

(1991) study post-pruning methods for decision trees. Clark and Niblett (1987a) and Smyth and Goodman (1990) discuss generation of decision rules, and introduce J-measure for evaluation of their quality. Clark and Niblett (1987b,a) describe the use of covering algorithms for induction of rule sets. Smyth and Goodman (1990) and Kononenko and Kovačič (1992) describe benefits of redundant rules. The seminal paper by Agrawal and Srikant (1994) is the primary source of the APriori algorithm for mining of association rules.

Breiman et al. (1984) analyze several attribute quality measures for classification and regression. They introduce measures based on the change of variance for attribute evaluation in regression problems. One alternative non-myopic measure for attribute evaluation in regression problems is RReliefF (Robnik-Šikonja and Kononenko, 1997).

The FOIL algorithm (Quinlan, 1990) was one of the first inductive logic programming programs. The field of inductive logic programming is summarized in a book by Lavrač and Džeroski (1994). Kononenko et al. (1996) describe the adaptation of the ReliefF algorithm for use in inductive logic programming.

Kononenko (1993) advocates the use of the naive Bayesian classifier in medical diagnostics. He discusses explanation of its decisions with sums of information scores, and describes domain experts' favorable reviews of such explanations. Pirnat et al. (1989) compare decision trees and Bayesian classifiers in medical diagnostics and review their advantages and disadvantages.

Kononenko (1991b) discusses the background and motivations for the semi-naive Bayesian classifier and illustrates its use for problems with attribute dependencies. Numerous recently developed techniques have sought to improve the accuracy of the naive Bayesian classifier by alleviating the attribute interdependence problem. Zheng and Webb (2005) summarize the semi-naive Bayesian methods into two groups: those that apply the conventional naive Bayesian classifier with a new attribute set, and those that alter the basic method by allowing inter-dependencies between attributes.

In his influential book, Pearl (1988) introduces Bayesian belief networks. Friedman et al. (1997) describe Bayesian classifiers based on Bayesian belief networks. In this context they analyze benefits of different methods for probability estimation, and algorithms for learning network topologies (including the tree-augmented naive Bayesian classifier) from data. A book by Cormen et al. (1990) is a comprehensive reference to algorithms in general, and algorithms on graphs (including that for finding the minimum spanning trees) in particular.

Chapter 10

Statistical Learning

Those who know all, but are lacking in themselves, are utterly lacking.
— Gospel of Thomas, 67

In this chapter we describe some basic statistical learning methods: nearest neighbors, discriminant functions, linear regression, and support vector machines.

10.1 NEAREST NEIGHBORS

We ought to do good to others as simply as a horse runs, or a bee makes honey, or a vine bears grapes season after season without thinking of the grapes it has borne.
— Marcus Aurelius

Learning with nearest neighbor methods is different from other machine learning methods in the sense that it is just storing all or a subset of learning examples. When a new example is presented to the nearest neighbor predictor, a subset of learning examples *similar* to the new example is used to make a prediction. Since learning almost does not take place, nearest neighbor methods are often characterized as *lazy learning* methods. The main burden of calculation is transferred to prediction of the target variable value of a new example; thus for nearest neighbor methods the computational complexity of a prediction is considerably higher than for other machine learning methods.

Nearest neighbor methods are used for solving classification and regression problems. We describe the basic k-nearest neighbors, distance-weighted k-nearest neighbors, and locally weighted regression.

10.1.1 K nearest neighbors

The simplest of nearest neighbor algorithms, k-nearest neighbors (k-NN) simply uses the stored learning examples to make a prediction. When predicting the target value c_x of a new example t_x, the k learning examples nearest (most similar) to the new example are collected. For classification problems, the prevalent class from the set of nearest neighbors is predicted:

$$c_x = \operatorname*{argmax}_{c \in \{C_1, \dots, C_{m_0}\}} \left\{ \sum_{i=1}^{k} \delta(c, c_i) \right\} \tag{10.1}$$

where $\{C_1, \dots, C_{m_0}\}$ is the set of possible class labels and

$$\delta(a, b) = \begin{cases} 1, & a = b \\ 0, & a \neq b \end{cases} \tag{10.2}$$

For regression problems, the mean target variable value from the set of nearest neighbors is predicted:

$$c_x = \frac{1}{k} \sum_{i=1}^{k} c_i \tag{10.3}$$

k is a user-specified parameter that is usually set to some odd number (e.g., 1, 5, 7, 15). If there is no noise in attributes and class values, the best nearest neighbor algorithm is 1-NN. However, if the noise is present, we can, by increasing the value k, average the results and thus reduce the probability of an erroneous prediction. On the other hand, by increasing k we increase the probability that examples quite different from the new example, contribute to the final prediction. Thus, for each learning problem, the estimation of the parameter k needs to be established separately.

The parameter k does not determine the size of the neighborhood in terms of its diameter, but in terms of its cardinality. Thus the diameter of the neighborhood changes from example to example with respect to density of examples in a given region of the attribute space. By fixing the neighborhood diameter, we could get in some regions too many near examples, and none in the others. Using the cardinality to determine the size of the neighborhood, the k-nearest neighbors algorithm elegantly deals both with sparsely and densely populated regions of the attribute space.

The k-nearest neighbors algorithm is sensitive to the chosen distance measure for determining which learning examples are nearest to the new example. For continuous attributes, the Euclidean distance metric is usually used. All continuous attributes are scaled to the $[0, 1]$ interval. The distance between two attribute values of the same attribute is thus equal to their absolute difference. For discrete attributes, the distance is 1 for two different values, and 0 if the two values are equal. The distance between two examples is thus given by

$$D(t_l, t_j) = \sqrt{\sum_{i=1}^{a} d(v_{i,l}, v_{i,j})^2} \tag{10.4}$$

where for all continuous attributes the distance d between two attribute values $v_{i,l}$ and $v_{i,j}$ is defined by

$$d(v_{i,l}, v_{i,j}) = |v_{i,l} - v_{i,j}| \tag{10.5}$$

For discrete attributes, the distance d is defined by

$$d(v_{i,l}, v_{i,j}) = \left\{ \begin{array}{ll} 0, & v_{i,l} = v_{i,j} \\ 1, & v_{i,l} \neq v_{i,j} \end{array} \right. \tag{10.6}$$

The above computations assume that all attributes equally contribute to distance calculation. However, it is often the case that more important attributes should have greater impact on the distance measure than the unimportant ones. For this purpose, attributes are first evaluated with some attribute quality measure q, and then the weighted distance is calculated by

$$D(t_l, t_j) = \sqrt{\sum_{i=1}^{a} q(A_i) d(v_{i,l}, v_{i,j})^2} \tag{10.7}$$

10.1.2   Weighted k-nearest neighbors

The main problem of the basic k-nearest neighbors method is setting the parameter k. This problem can be addressed by using a more robust weighted k-NN method. Each learning example's impact on the final prediction is weighted proportionally to its distance to the new example. The impact of the distance can be determined by a linear, polynomial, exponential, or by some other function. Such a function is also called a *kernel function*. For quadratic function, we get for classification problems

$$c_x = \operatorname*{argmax}_{c \in \{C_1, \ldots, C_{m_0}\}} \left\{ \sum_{i=1}^{k} \frac{\delta(c, c_i)}{D(t_x, t_i)^2} \right\} \tag{10.8}$$

and for regression problems

$$c_x = \frac{\sum_{i=1}^{k} c_i / D(t_x, t_i)^2}{\sum_{i=1}^{k} 1 / D(t_x, t_i)^2} \tag{10.9}$$

If learning examples are weighted, the parameter k actually becomes redundant. It is not necessary to limit the cardinality of the neighborhood to k, since the distant examples only negligibly contribute to the final prediction, whereas the near examples contribute most.

10.1.3   Locally weighted regression

The basic nearest neighbor idea can be generalized for regression so that instead of averaging (Equation 10.9) a general regression function of k nearest neighbors is used (e.g., linear or quadratic function, neural networks). Locally weighted regression produces a local approximation of the target function in the neighborhood of the new example. A local approximation is subsequently used to predict the target function value for the new example. In practice, linear locally weighted regression is most frequently used. This is actually just the basic linear regression (Section 10.3), performed on k nearest neighbors of the new example. Since the value of the parameter k is usually rather small (in the order of 10), the number of learning examples (k) used for local regression is also small. Thus, the use of more complex local models would increase the danger of overfitting the learning examples. Since for each new example the nearest neighbors have to be found anew, and the local model created, the whole procedure is rather time-consuming and this also discourages the use of complex models.

10.2   DISCRIMINANT ANALYSIS

Take your life in your own hands and what happens? A terrible thing: no one to blame.

— Erica Jong

In discriminant analysis we seek for discriminant functions that can be used for solving a given classification problem. As described in Section 4.3, discriminant functions implicitly describe boundary surfaces between classes in a-dimensional space (a is the number of attributes). Linear and quadratic discriminant functions, ϕ functions, and neural networks are most frequently used for this purpose. We discuss in more depth linear discriminant functions for solving two-class problems. Besides the analytical solution presented in this section, the delta rule for learning of the two-layered perceptron (Section 11.5) can be used for function approximation. One of the most successful discriminant analysis methods, support vector machines, is described separately.

Let $\mathbf{v}^T = \langle v_1, \ldots, v_a \rangle$ be the vector of all values of attributes $A_1, \ldots, A_a$. For a two-class problem we need only a single discriminant function of a arguments

$$g(v_1, \ldots, v_a) = w_0 + \sum_{i=1}^{a} w_i v_i = w_0 + \mathbf{w}^T \mathbf{v} \qquad (10.10)$$

that maps a-dimensional attribute space into a real number. A boundary surface between the two classes is defined by the following equation

$$g(\mathbf{v}) = 0 \qquad (10.11)$$

The task of the learning algorithm is to find a function g that minimizes the classification error of learning examples. This task can be decomposed into two parts. In the first part we seek for a function g_d that maximizes the distance between the two classes. In the second part we define a decision function

$$g(\mathbf{v}) = g_d(\mathbf{v}) + w_0 \qquad (10.12)$$

and thus we finally get

$$g_d(v_1, \ldots, v_a) = \sum_{i=1}^{a} w_i v_i = \mathbf{w}^T \mathbf{v}. \qquad (10.13)$$

10.2.1 Optimal discriminant function

Let us define a distance measure between examples from both classes. For each learning example from the first class $\mathbf{t}_{1;j}, j = 1 \ldots n(C_1)$, described with an attribute vector $\langle v_{1;1,j}, \ldots, v_{1;a,j} \rangle$,

$$\mathbf{t}_{1;j}^T = \langle v_{1;1,j}, \ldots, v_{1;a,j} \rangle \tag{10.14}$$

we get the function value

$$z_{1;j} = g_d(\mathbf{t}_{1;j}) = g_d(v_{1;1,j}, \ldots, v_{1;a,j}) = \sum_{i=1}^{a} w_i v_{1;i,j} \tag{10.15}$$

or (in vector form)

$$z_{1;j} = \mathbf{w}^T \mathbf{t}_{1;j} \tag{10.16}$$

Analogously, for each learning example from the second class $\mathbf{t}_{2;j}, j = 1 \ldots n(C_2)$

$$\mathbf{t}_{2;j} = \langle v_{2;1,j}, \ldots, v_{2;a,j} \rangle \tag{10.17}$$

we get the function value

$$z_{2;j} = g_d(\mathbf{t}_{2;j}) = g_d(v_{2;1,j}, \ldots, v_{2;a,j}) = \sum_{i=1}^{a} w_i v_{2;i,j} \tag{10.18}$$

or (in vector form)

$$z_{2;j} = \mathbf{w}^T \mathbf{t}_{2;j} \tag{10.19}$$

The number of all learning examples is $n = n(C_1) + n(C_2)$. The average function value over all examples from the first class is

$$\bar{z}_1 = \frac{1}{n(C_1)} \sum_{j=1}^{n(C_1)} z_{1;j} = \mathbf{w}^T \bar{\mathbf{t}}_1 \tag{10.20}$$

where $\bar{\mathbf{t}}_1$ is an average learning example (vector) from the first class:

$$\bar{\mathbf{t}}_1 = \frac{1}{n(C_1)} \sum_{j=1}^{n(C_1)} \mathbf{t}_{1;j}$$

$$\bar{\mathbf{t}}_1^T = \langle \bar{v}_{1;1}, \ldots, \bar{v}_{1;a} \rangle \tag{10.21}$$

Here $\bar{v}_{j;i}$ stands for the average value of attribute A_i over all examples belonging to the class C_j. The average function value over all examples from the second class is

$$\bar{z}_2 = \frac{1}{n(C_2)} \sum_{j=1}^{n(C_2)} z_{2;j} = \mathbf{w}^T \bar{\mathbf{t}}_2 \tag{10.22}$$

where $\bar{t}_2$ is an average learning example (vector) from the second class:

$$\bar{t}_2 = \frac{1}{n(C_2)} \sum_{j=1}^{n(C_2)} t_{2;j} \tag{10.23}$$

The average function value over all examples (regardless of their class) is

$$\bar{z} = \frac{1}{n} \left(\sum_{j=1}^{n(C_1)} z_{1;j} + \sum_{j=1}^{n(C_2)} z_{2;j} \right) \tag{10.24}$$

Variance of all learning examples is given by

$$s_z^2 = \frac{1}{n-1} \left(\sum_{j=1}^{n(C_1)} (z_{1;j} - \bar{z})^2 + \sum_{j=1}^{n(C_2)} (z_{2;j} - \bar{z})^2 \right) \tag{10.25}$$

It can also be expressed in terms of a covariance matrix $\mathbf{S}$:

$$\mathbf{S} = \frac{1}{n-1} \sum_{j=1}^{n} (\mathbf{t}_{*j} - \bar{\mathbf{t}})(\mathbf{t}_{*j} - \bar{\mathbf{t}})^T \tag{10.26}$$

where $\mathbf{t}_{*j}$ is any learning example (regardless of its class), and $\bar{\mathbf{t}}$ is an average example.

We wish to maximize the squared standardized difference between the two averages $\bar{z}_1$ and $\bar{z}_2$. It can be calculated with

$$\frac{(\bar{z}_1 - \bar{z}_2)^2}{s_z^2} = \frac{\left(\mathbf{w}^T (\bar{t}_1 - \bar{t}_2) \right)^2}{\mathbf{w}^T \mathbf{S} \mathbf{w}} \tag{10.27}$$

The squared standardized difference has its maximum not only at

$$\mathbf{w} = \mathbf{S}^{-1} (\bar{t}_1 - \bar{t}_2) \tag{10.28}$$

but also where $\mathbf{w}$ equals to the above expression multiplied by an arbitrary scalar value. The necessary condition for existence of $\mathbf{S}^{-1}$ is obviously that $n - 2 > a$. Thus, the discriminant function g_d is defined with

$$g_d(\mathbf{v}) = (\bar{t}_1 - \bar{t}_2)^T \mathbf{S}^{-1} \mathbf{v} \tag{10.29}$$

10.2.2   Classification with discriminant function

In order to facilitate classification, a threshold w_0 of a discriminant function g needs to be determined, so that

$$g(\mathbf{v}) = g_d(\mathbf{v}) + w_0 \tag{10.30}$$

According to Fisher's linear classification rule, a new example is labeled with a class label such that the average value of g_d for learning examples of this class (calculated from (10.20) and (10.22)) is closest to the value of g_d for the new example. Since $\mathbf{w}$ is determined by Eq. (10.28), it holds that $\bar{z}_1 > \bar{z}_2$. The threshold w_0 is therefore calculated as

$$w_0 = \frac{1}{2}(\bar{z}_1 + \bar{z}_2) \tag{10.31}$$

and the function g is

$$g(\mathbf{v}) = (\bar{\mathbf{t}}_1 - \bar{\mathbf{t}}_2)^T \mathbf{S}^{-1}\mathbf{v} + \frac{1}{2}(\bar{z}_1 + \bar{z}_2) \tag{10.32}$$

The new example $\mathbf{v}$ is labelled with the first class label if

$$g(\mathbf{v}) \geq 0, \tag{10.33}$$

and with the second class label if

$$g(\mathbf{v}) < 0. \tag{10.34}$$

10.3   LINEAR REGRESSION

Be yourself, who else is better qualified?

— Frank J. Giblin

As opposed to discriminant analysis where we assign discrete class labels, in regression we are determining a function that maps the attribute space into a real value. All attributes must be continuous (or treated as continuous). Besides the methods described in this section, other methods can be used to solve regression problems: regression trees, nearest neighbor methods, neural networks, and support vector machines.

Let $\mathbf{v}^T = \langle 1, v_1, \ldots, v_a \rangle$ be a vector of all attribute values, extended with the constant value 1. In linear regression, we search for a function that is a linear combination of all attributes, or of their subset:

$$
\begin{aligned}
\hat{c} &= g(v_1, \ldots, v_a) = \\
&= w_0 + \sum_{i=1}^{a} w_i v_i = \mathbf{w}^T \mathbf{v}
\end{aligned}
\tag{10.35}
$$

The task of the learning algorithm is to determine the vector $\mathbf{w}$ of parameters w_i, $i = 0 \ldots a$, so as to minimize the sum of squared errors (SSE) of predicted target values over all learning examples:

$$
\begin{aligned}
SSE &= \sum_{j=1}^{n} (c_j - \hat{c}_j)^2 = \\
&= \sum_{j=1}^{n} \left(c_j - w_0 - \sum_{i=1}^{a} w_i v_{i,j} \right)^2
\end{aligned}
\tag{10.36}
$$

Besides the analytical solution given below, various approximate methods (such as the two-layered perceptron, described in Section 11.5) can be used for determining the regression function.

Let $\mathbf{V}$ be the matrix of all learning examples (extended with leading $1s$):

$$\mathbf{V} = \begin{bmatrix} 1 & v_{1,1} & \cdots & v_{a,1} \\ 1 & v_{1,2} & \cdots & v_{a,2} \\ \vdots & \vdots & \ddots & \vdots \\ 1 & v_{1,n} & \cdots & v_{a,n} \end{bmatrix} \tag{10.37}$$

and $\mathbf{c}$ the vector of their respective target values:

$$\mathbf{c}^T = \langle c_1, \ldots, c_n \rangle. \tag{10.38}$$

It can be shown that SSE is minimal when it holds:

$$\mathbf{w} = (\mathbf{V}^T \mathbf{V})^{-1} \mathbf{V} \mathbf{c} \tag{10.39}$$

A prerequisite for calculating $(\mathbf{V}^T \mathbf{V})^{-1}$ is that $n > a + 1$ and that no learning example is a linear combination of any other learning examples.

10.4   LOGISTIC REGRESSION

If you don't know where you are going, any road will get you there.

— Lewis Carroll

Although the name suggests that it is used for *regression*, in fact the logistic regression is a *classification* method, used when the dependent (target) variable is dichotomous (two-class). It is used to predict the likelihood (the odds ratio) of the outcome based on the attributes (called *covariates* in logistic regression). Logistic regression is a special case of *generalized linear models* (GLM), that itself is a generalization of linear regression, described in the previous section. In GLM, Equation (10.35) is generalized so that on its right-hand side an arbitrary function $f(c)$ (link function) of the dependent variable c can be used:

$$\begin{aligned} \widehat{f(c)} &= g(v_1, \ldots, v_a) = \\ &= w_0 + \sum_{i=1}^{a} w_i v_i = \mathbf{w}^T \mathbf{v} \end{aligned} \tag{10.40}$$

Commonly used link functions are $f(c) = c$ for linear regression, $f(c) = 1/c$, $f(c) = \log(c)$, and $f(c) = \log(c/(1 - c))$ (the *logit link function*). Generalized linear models can be easily adopted for use in discrete two-class problems. For this purpose, the independent variable estimates the probability of the first of the two classes, $c = P(C_1)$. When using together with the logit link function, we get logistic regression:

$$\log \frac{P(C_1)}{1 - P(C_1)}) = \mathbf{w}^T \mathbf{v} \tag{10.41}$$

Removing the logarithm and rearranging the terms we get the *sigmoid function*:

$$y = P(C_1) = \frac{1}{1 + e^{-\mathbf{w}^T \mathbf{v}}} \tag{10.42}$$

To determine the weights $\mathbf{w}$, we are given a set of learning examples $\mathcal{T} = \{\langle t_l, d(l) \rangle\}$, $l = 1 \ldots n$, where $d(l) = 1$ if the correct class of t_l is C_1, and $d(l) = 0$ if the correct class of t_l is C_2. We assume that $d(l)$ given t_l follows the Bernoulli distribution with probability $y(l) = P(C_1|t_l)$, as calculated in Equation (10.42):

$$d(l)|t_l \sim Bernoulli(y(l)) \tag{10.43}$$

The sample likelihood is

$$l(\mathbf{w}|\mathcal{T}) = \prod_l y(l)^{d(l)} \left(1 - y(l)\right)^{1-d(l)} \tag{10.44}$$

By taking the negative logarithm of the likelihood, we obtain the error function E, in our case the *cross entropy* function:

$$
\begin{aligned}
E(\mathbf{w}|\mathcal{T}) &= -\log l(\mathbf{w}|\mathcal{T}) \\
&= -\sum_l d(l) \log y(l) + (1 - d(l)) \log(1 - y(l)) \tag{10.45}
\end{aligned}
$$

To minimize the cross entropy (thus maximizing the sample likelihood) we can use the gradient descent method. For the sigmoid function in Equation (10.42), we get the following weight update equation:

$$
\begin{aligned}
\Delta w_j &= -\eta \frac{\partial E}{\partial w_j} = \\
&= \eta \sum_l (d(l) - y(l)) v_{j,l} \tag{10.46}
\end{aligned}
$$

This update equation directly corresponds to the batch updates of the delta learning rule for the two-layered perceptron (Equation (11.29)). The logistic regression model can therefore be seen as a feedforward neural network with no hidden units. When the weights are determined, logistic regression is used for classification so that the class label C_k, $k \in \{1, 2\}$, with highest likelihood $P(C_k)/(1 - P(C_k))$ is predicted.

10.5 *SUPPORT VECTOR MACHINES

Until he extends his circle of compassion to include all living things, man will not himself find peace.

— Albert Schweitzer

Support vector machines (SVM) are among the most successful machine learning methods – both for solving regression and classification problems. Most machine algorithms tend to minimize the number of attributes used in their prediction function. On the other hand, SVM methods tend to use all the available attributes, even if they are not of much importance. They are used – in linear combinations – for prediction of the target variable, either discrete or continuous. In SVM methods it is therefore important how to combine the attributes and not how to choose the appropriate ones.

SVM methods are suitable for learning with large sets of examples, described with large numbers of possibly less important attributes. While SVM methods achieve high predictive performance, the interpretation of the learned knowledge as well as of particular predictions is usually difficult.

In the following we discuss SVM methods for classification in more detail. In essence, SVMs are designed for dichotomization between two classes. If there are more classes, the problem is divided into subproblems where one class is discriminated from the rest of classes. A new example is labelled with the class label that maximizes the decision function (the value of $\mathbf{w}_0 \cdot \mathbf{t} - b_0$ from Equation (10.52)).

10.5.1   Basic SVM principle

The basic idea of SVM methods is to place an optimal class separating hyperplane in the space of original (or transformed) attributes. If the learning examples are linearly separable, then in general there exist several possible separating hyperplanes (Figure 10.1).

An optimal hyperplane is equally (and therefore most) distant from the nearest examples from both classes. Learning examples nearest to the optimal hyperplane are called *support vectors*. The distance between the hyperplane and its support vectors is called the *margin*. The optimal hyperplane is therefore selected so as to maximize the margin (Figure 10.2).

Let n be the number of learning examples, and a the number of attributes. The set of learning examples is given with pairs $(\mathbf{t}_j, y_j)$, $j = 1 \ldots n$, where $y_j = 1$ if the corresponding learning example belongs to the first class, and $y_j = -1$, if the corresponding learning example belongs to the second class. We assume that all attributes are continuous, or they are treated as such, therefore $\mathbf{t}_j \in \mathbb{R}^a$, $j = 1 \ldots n$. The hyperplane equation is given by

$$(\mathbf{w} \cdot \mathbf{t}) - b = 0 \qquad (10.47)$$

An optimal hyperplane should correctly classify all learning examples

$$\forall j \in 1 \ldots n : \quad y_j(\mathbf{w} \cdot \mathbf{t}_j - b) \geq 1 \qquad (10.48)$$

as well as minimize its own complexity measure $\frac{1}{2}(\mathbf{w} \cdot \mathbf{w})$. By minimizing the magnitudes of coefficients we minimize the complexity of the solution. The stated problem of constrained optimization can be transformed to the functional maximization:

$$W(\alpha) = \sum_{j=1}^{n} \alpha_j - \frac{1}{2} \sum_{i,j}^{n} \alpha_i \alpha_j y_i y_j (\mathbf{t}_i \cdot \mathbf{t}_j) \qquad (10.49)$$

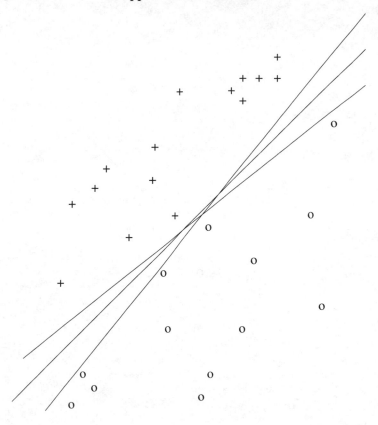

Figure 10.1: For a linear two-class classification problem there exist several hyperplanes that exactly dichotomize between examples belonging to the first class (labeled with +) and examples belonging to the second class (labeled with o).

with constraints

$$\forall j \in 1 \ldots n : \; \alpha_j \geq 0 \tag{10.50}$$

and

$$\sum_{j=1}^{n} \alpha_j y_j = 0 \tag{10.51}$$

This is a quadratic optimization problem that can be solved by using fast existing algorithms.

Let $\alpha_0 = (\alpha_1^0, \ldots, \alpha_n^0)$ be the solution of the above optimization problem. The only non-zero coefficients α_j are those that correspond to support vectors. A classification rule of the optimal hyperplane is thus defined with

$$
\begin{aligned}
Y(\mathbf{t}) &= \operatorname{sign} \left(\mathbf{w}_0 \cdot \mathbf{t} - b_0 \right) \\
&= \operatorname{sign} \left(\sum_{\text{support vectors } \mathbf{t}_j} y_j \alpha_j^0 (\mathbf{t}_j \cdot \mathbf{t}) - b_0 \right) \tag{10.52}
\end{aligned}
$$

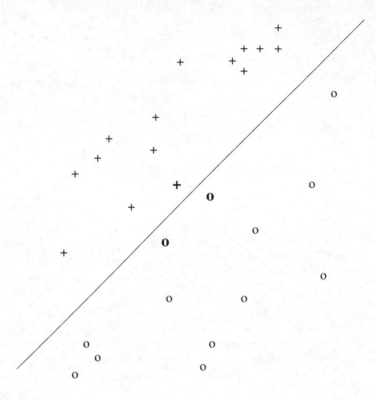

Figure 10.2: An optimal hyperplane for the classification problem from Figure 10.1. All three support vectors are emphasized.

The threshold value b_0 is given by

$$b_0 = \frac{1}{2}(\mathbf{w}_0 \cdot \mathbf{t}_*(1) + \mathbf{w}_0 \cdot \mathbf{t}_*(-1)) \qquad (10.53)$$

where $\mathbf{t}_*(1)$ and $\mathbf{t}_*(-1)$ respectively denote an arbitrary support vector from the first or the second class. The coefficient vector $\mathbf{w}_0$ of the optimal hyperplane is thus determined with its support vectors:

$$\mathbf{w}_0 = \sum_{\text{support vectors } \mathbf{t}_j} y_j \alpha_j^0 \mathbf{t}_j \qquad (10.54)$$

The solution complexity of the optimal hyperplane is determined with the number of support vectors. This number is rather small when compared with the number of learning examples – in practice, the ratio is usually between 3% and 5% – and therefore the solution complexity is also relatively small. Since the solution complexity depends solely on the number of support vectors, the result would be exactly the same if all non-support vectors were removed from the learning set. The optimization criterion also minimizes the magnitude of $\frac{1}{2}(\mathbf{w} \cdot \mathbf{w})$, thus minimizing the magnitude of coefficients in linear combinations of attributes.

10.5.2 Inexact classification

In inexact classification the constraints (10.48) that require correct classification of each learning example are relaxed, so as to allow the error of magnitude ξ_j in classification of the j-th learning example:

$$\forall j \in 1 \ldots n: \ y_j(\mathbf{w} \cdot \mathbf{t}_j - b) \geq 1 - \xi_j \tag{10.55}$$

The optimization problem now minimizes

$$\frac{1}{2}(\mathbf{w} \cdot \mathbf{w}) + C \sum_{j=1}^{n} \xi_j \tag{10.56}$$

where C is the constant parameter and its value is given in advance. The parameter C balances between the solution complexity $(\mathbf{w} \cdot \mathbf{w})$ and the solution error $(\sum_{j=1}^{n} \xi_j)$. The problem is again transformed to functional maximization, where constraints (10.50) change to

$$\forall j \in 1 \ldots n: \ C \geq \alpha_j \geq 0 \tag{10.57}$$

while the constraint (10.51) remains unchanged.

Similarly to the exact solution, in inexact solution the only non-zero coefficients α_j are those that correspond to support vectors.

10.5.3 SVM method

Besides the use of support vectors, the main idea of the SVM method is the use of an implicit transformation of the attribute space to a more complex one. In the original space, classes often cannot be satisfactorily separated by a linear hyperplane. However, by applying a non-linear transformation, in a higher-dimensional attribute space the classes may become linearly separable. The transformation is chosen in advance and may vary between different problems.

The true power of the SVM method lies in the fact that transformations are not performed explicitly. In machine learning methods that use explicit attribute transformations, the number of attributes may be considerably increased. For example, when the product transformation of the original attributes is used, the number of transformed attributes is a polynomial of the degree of the length of the product function. The problem of having to deal with too many attributes is also called the *curse of dimensionality*.

For SVM methods it is sufficient to calculate the dot products of support vectors with a new example in the transformed attribute space. Let $\mathbf{t}_j$ be the j-th learning example (vector) in the original attribute space, and $\mathbf{z}_j$ its higher-dimensional transformation. The dot product is calculated with the help of the *kernel function* K that facilitates an implicit transformation:

$$\mathbf{z}_j \cdot \mathbf{z} = K(\mathbf{t}, \mathbf{t}_j) \tag{10.58}$$

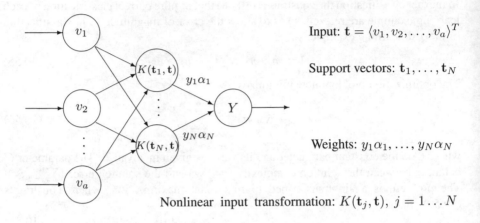

Input: $\mathbf{t} = \langle v_1, v_2, \ldots, v_a \rangle^T$

Support vectors: $\mathbf{t}_1, \ldots, \mathbf{t}_N$

Weights: $y_1\alpha_1, \ldots, y_N\alpha_N$

Nonlinear input transformation: $K(\mathbf{t}_j, \mathbf{t})$, $j = 1 \ldots N$

Figure 10.3: The classification rule of the SVM method. N is the number of support vectors.

Thus, instead of a dot product, a convolution of dot products is used. The maximization functional is therefore

$$W(\alpha) = \sum_{j=1}^{n} \alpha_j - \frac{1}{2} \sum_{i,j}^{n} \alpha_i \alpha_j y_i y_j K(\mathbf{t}_i, \mathbf{t}_j) \qquad (10.59)$$

with the same constraints for coefficients α_j^0 as described in Sections 10.5.1 and 10.5.2. The classification rule for classification of new examples $\mathbf{t}$ is

$$Y(\mathbf{t}) = \text{sign}\left(\sum_{\text{support vectors } \mathbf{t}_j} y_j \alpha_j^0 K(\mathbf{t}_j, \mathbf{t}) - b_0 \right) \qquad (10.60)$$

for given coefficients α_j^0 – solutions of the optimization problem. Figure 10.3 graphically depicts the classification rule of the SVM method.

Different kernel functions yield different transformations of the attribute space and consequentially different SVM methods. Some popular kernel functions are:

Linear function. It preserves the original attribute space:

$$K(\mathbf{t}_j, \mathbf{t}) = \mathbf{t} \cdot \mathbf{t}_j \qquad (10.61)$$

Polynomial function For a given polynomial degree d we use the following dot
product convolution:

$$K(\mathbf{t}_j, \mathbf{t}) = [(\mathbf{t} \cdot \mathbf{t}_j) + 1]^d \qquad (10.62)$$

Radial function. For a given value of the parameter γ the dot product convolution is
determined by:

$$K(\mathbf{t}_j, \mathbf{t}) = e^{-\gamma|\mathbf{t}-\mathbf{t}_j|^2} \qquad (10.63)$$

Sigmoid function. For a given sigmoid function S (say, $S = \tanh$) we get a kernel
function of parameters v and c:

$$K(\mathbf{t}_j, \mathbf{t}) = S(v(\mathbf{t} \cdot \mathbf{t}_j) + c) \qquad (10.64)$$

If a sigmoidal kernel function is chosen, SVM performs similarly to the
three-layered perceptron. However, as opposed to the three-layered perceptron
(described in more detail in Section 11.5), SVM determines the optimal topology
by itself (the number of hidden neurons equals the number of support vectors).
Perceptron's first-layer weights correspond to attribute values of support vectors,
and second-layer weights to the calculated coefficients α_j^0 (see Figure 10.3).

It has been experimentally shown that for the same classification problem, even wildly
different kernel functions provide mostly (about 80%) the same support vectors.

10.6   SUMMARY AND FURTHER READING

*God cannot be explained, He cannot be argued about, He cannot be theorized, nor can
He be discussed and understood. God can only be lived.*

— Meher Baba

- Learning with nearest neighbor methods consists merely of storing all or a subset
  of learning examples. When a new example is presented to the nearest neighbor
  predictor, a subset of learning examples similar to the new example is used to
  make a prediction. Nearest neighbor methods are often named lazy learning
  methods.

- In discriminant analysis we seek for discriminant functions that can be used for
  solving a given classification problem. Discriminant functions implicitly describe boundary surfaces between classes in high-dimensional space. Frequently
  used discriminant functions are linear and quadratic discriminant functions, ϕ
  functions, and neural networks.

- In linear regression we are searching for a linear function that maps the attribute
  space into a real value. All attributes must be continuous (or treated as
  continuous). Besides linear function, more complex (non-linear) functions can
  also be used for regression.

- Logistic regression is a classification method that can be used exclusively in two-class problems. It is used to predict the likelihood of the classes based on the attribute values.

- Support vector machines (SVMs) place class-separating hyperplanes in the original (or transformed) attribute space. An optimal hyperplane is equally (and therefore most) distant from the nearest examples from both classes. Learning examples nearest to the optimal hyperplane are called support vectors. Support vector machines are among the most successful machine learning methods – both for solving regression and classification problems.

An excellent book by Duda et al. (2001) is a comprehensive reference to statistical learning from a pattern recognition perspective. It includes nearest neighbor methods, discriminant analysis and support vector machines. Rencher (1995) discusses discriminant functions as well as linear regression and provides derivations of analytical solutions for both methods as described in this chapter. Mardia et al. (1979) is a comprehensive reference for multivariate statistical methods that, among others, also covers regression methods and discriminant analysis. The book by Hosmer (2000) includes a discussion on theoretical and practical aspects of logistic regression. Alpaydin (2005) discusses extensions of logistic regression to multi-class problems. Hastie and Loader (1993) study local regression methods. Vapnik (1995) is the principal author of the support vector machine method. The book by Cristianini and Shawe-Taylor (2000) is a comprehensive reference to this topic.

Chapter 11

Artificial Neural Networks

Intelligence emerges from the interaction of large numbers of simple processing units.
— David Rumelhart and John McClelland

This chapter introduces the field of artificial neural networks (ANN), overviews various approaches, and provides a detailed description of some ANN models: Hopfield's and Bayesian neural network, two-layered and multi-layered perceptron, and radial basis function networks. The last section gives pointers to literature where the reader can find descriptions of other models of this wide and heterogeneous field. Recall that the symbol $\diamond$ indicates that the proof of the assertion can be found at the end of the chapter (in Section 11.7).

11.1   INTRODUCTION

You are nothing perceivable, or imaginable. Yet, without you there can be neither perception nor imagination.

— Sri Nisargadatta Maharaj

To illustrate the abilities of ANN, we start with a simple example of the matrix calculus which can be implemented by an artificial neural network. Then we overview interesting properties of ANN and fields of applications, describe analogies with the brain, and relate ANN with symbolic artificial intelligence methods.

11.1.1   Simple example

Consider a simple matrix calculus which can be implemented by an artificial neural network. The task is to recognize the following two patterns (learning examples):

$$\mathbf{t}_1 = (1, 1, 1)^T$$

and

$$\mathbf{t}_2 = (1, -1, -1)^T$$

The task can be solved by the following matrix calculus. Let us construct a (memory) matrix as a sum of outer products of the target patterns:

$$M = \mathbf{t}_1 \mathbf{t}_1^T + \mathbf{t}_2 \mathbf{t}_2^T = \begin{bmatrix} 2 & 0 & 0 \\ 0 & 2 & 2 \\ 0 & 2 & 2 \end{bmatrix}$$

Let us further introduce a decision (threshold) function:

$$f(x) = \begin{cases} 1, & x > 0 \\ 0, & x = 0 \\ -1, & x < 0 \end{cases}$$

By generalizing the threshold function to vectors:

$$f(\mathbf{t}) = (f(v_1), f(v_2), f(v_3))^T$$

we get the following equations:

$$f(M\mathbf{t}_1) = f((2,4,4)^T) = (1,1,1)^T = \mathbf{t}_1$$

$$f(M\mathbf{t}_2) = f((2,-4,-4)^T) = (1,-1,-1)^T = \mathbf{t}_2$$

The product of the memory matrix with one of the input vectors normalized with the threshold function returns the same input vector.

Let us try the same procedure when the input vectors are only partially known. The zero indicates an unknown value:

$$\mathbf{t}_1^u = (1,1,0)^T$$

$$\mathbf{t}_2^u = (1,0,-1)^T$$

$$f(M\mathbf{t}_1^u) = f((2,2,2)^T) = (1,1,1)^T = \mathbf{t}_1$$

$$f(M\mathbf{t}_2^u) = f((2,-2,-2)^T) = (1,-1,-1)^T = \mathbf{t}_2$$

We see that the memory matrix is able to reconstruct the missing values of input vectors. Let us try also with a wrong value:

$$\mathbf{t}_1^w = (1,1,-1)^T = \mathbf{t}_2^w$$

$$f(M\mathbf{t}_1^w) = f((2,0,0)^T) = (1,0,0)^T$$

In this case the answer is nondecisive. In fact the spoiled input vector is equally distant to both original input vectors.

The above principles can be under certain conditions (such as orthogonality of input vectors) generalized to larger dimensionalities and to larger numbers of input vectors. It is interesting that besides input vectors also their complements are memorized. For example, if we use vector $(1,-1,-1)$ for learning then also its complement $(-1,1,1)$ is automatically memorized.

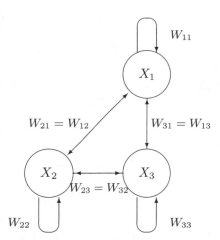

Figure 11.1: A simple auto-associative artificial neural network.

The above calculus can be implemented by a simple artificial neural network depicted in Figure 11.1. Each vector component v_i is associated with one neuron X_i: $X_i = v_i$. Therefore, in this case the number of neurons N is equal to the number of (binary) attributes: $a = N$. Each neuron has two possible states, $X_i = 1$ or $X_i = -1$, and is connected to all the neurons, including itself. The connections, called *synapses*, are associated with weights that correspond to memory matrix elements. The connections are bi-directional, therefore the matrix is symmetric. The diagonal elements correspond to weights of connections of neurons to themselves.

Initially, all the weights are set to zero. In the learning phase for each input vector the state of each neuron is set to the corresponding component value and each weight is increased or decreased by 1, depending on whether the two connected neurons are in the same or in different states (this learning rule is called the generalized Hebbian learning rule). When all the input vectors are "shown" to the network, the learning finishes and the weight values become fixed. Note that for changing the value of a weight all the necessary information is locally available – only the states of two connected neurons are needed.

Processing of a new example starts by setting the state of each neuron to the corresponding component value of the example. The output signal of a neuron corresponds to its state. Each neuron then simultaneously calculates its new (updated) state from the signals, obtained from all other neurons, using the rule:

$$X_i{}^{NEW} = f(\sum_j W_{ji} X_j)$$

where S_j is the (current) state of the j-th neuron, W_{ji} is the weight of the synapse between the j-th and the i-th neurons, and $X_i{}^{NEW}$ is the new state of the i-th neuron.

Therefore, each neuron is a simple processing unit, able to calculate the weighted

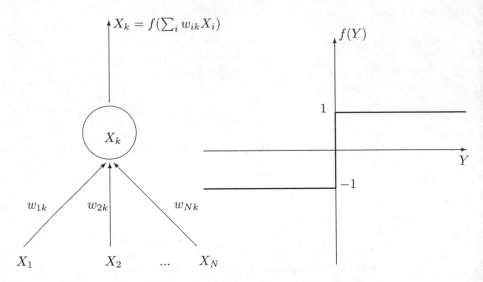

Figure 11.2: An artificial neuron and a combination function.

sum of its inputs and, by using a threshold function, to transform the obtained sum into one of two possible output values (see Figure 11.2). The weighted sum is called the *activation function*, and the threshold function f is called the *output function*. An output function can return more than two different values, as described below. An activation and an output function together are called the *combination function*.

Figure 11.2 represents an artificial neuron with a typical combination function. Such a neuron can be in two different states: 0 (inactive) and 1 (active). Sometimes, as in the above example, values –1 and 1 are used instead. The combination function can be generalized in order to get continuous neuron states with values from a given interval (e.g. [0,1]).

In the above example all the neurons were processing in parallel and synchronously. If the processing is repeated once more, none of the neurons changes its state. We say that the neural network has reached a *fixed point* or an *equilibrium*. In general, such a neural network repeats the processing stage until it *converges* into a fixed point. With synchronous processing it is possible that a network never converges. A network can, however, process *asynchronously* (at a time only one neuron changes its state).

If the weight of a synapse is positive, the synapse is *excitatory*. If the weight of a synapse is negative, the synapse is *inhibitory*. A weight equal to 0 corresponds to a missing synapse. Usually, the weights of the synapses are represented with a matrix.

11.1.2   Distributed memory

The basic characteristic of ANN is distributed memory. The memory elements are the weights on the synapses. Each neuron has access to memory weights on the synapses which connect that neuron with others (in general a neuron is connected only to a subset of neurons). We can interpret this as a large number of constraints that simultaneously influence the network behavior.

In a distributed memory each datum is partially stored in a number of memory elements and the recall from the memory is not always exact. The returned value can be only an approximation of the true datum as each memory element (weight) takes a part in memorizing a number of different data. The distributed memory has the following interesting properties:

Automatic generalization: each memory element (weight) represents a kind of correlation between activities of two connected neurons (an average over all situations – learning examples). Such knowledge can be used for an approximation of missing values or for correcting wrong values.

Adaptability to changing environment: in a changing environment a network can incrementally change its weights in order to adapt to the environmental changes. Forgetting the old knowledge can be controlled with certain parameters.

Distributivity and storage accuracy: by increasing the level of distributivity we can improve the storage accuracy. This can be achieved by different coding, i.e. instead of using one neuron to code one vector component, several neurons can be used to code several components of input vectors. Each component is stored in connections with several other components which enables more accurate recall.

Constructive character: each processing element – neuron – represents a novel micro-attribute which combines several basic attributes and, therefore, describes the given domain from a new perspective. The novel attribute is, however, hard to interpret.

Robustness: as each datum is coded with several neurons and each neuron contributes to the storage of several data, the removal of one neuron does not lead to complete loss of a single datum but rather partially decreases the storage accuracy of several data.

Spontaneous recollection of forgotten data: spontaneous recollection without re-learning of forgotten data can appear during learning of new data. This interesting property appears also with human learning.

In computers the data are stored locally, each datum having an exact address. With distributed representation in ANN a datum is addressed with the datum itself (in an autoassociative ANN) or with another datum (in a hetero-associative ANN). If the "address" is accurate, the network returns the exact answer, otherwise it returns an approximate answer (which is in a certain way similar to the corresponding exact answer). This kind of storage is called the *content addressable memory*. Therefore, in principle, in an ANN there is no difference between a datum and its address. For representing completely different data or data on completely different levels of abstractions a distributed memory requires different modules.

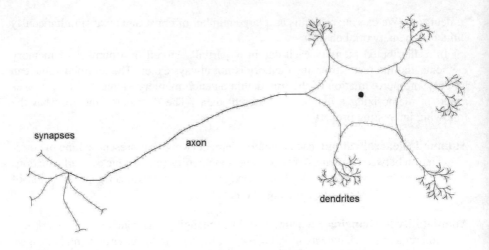

Figure 11.3: Schema of a biological neuron.

11.1.3   Properties of ANN

Nice properties of artificial neural networks are similarity to biological systems, high level of parallelism, possibility of asynchronous processing, multidirectional execution, real-time adaptability, robustness with respect to damages and to missing data, ability to learn and automatic generalization, no need for additional software, no need for a fixed configuration, no difference between data and addresses, and, last but not least, well developed mathematical foundation. The most important deficiency of ANN is the inability to explain its decisions. Note however, that only a subset of properties holds for any ANN and currently there is no ANN for which all these properties hold.

Similarity to biological systems: the field of ANN imitates the human brain functioning and at the same time tries to achieve better performance in hard problem solving. An ANN is an abstraction and a simplification of biological neural networks.

There are different biological neurons in different parts of the brain, however, their basic structure is the same (see Figure 11.3). Dendrites transmit input signals to the neuron and an axon transmits the output signal over the synapses towards the dendrites of other neurons. Although highly simplified, ANN models suffice for useful modeling and analyses which enable better understanding of processes in the brain.

Learning and operating in ANN use only *local information*. For example, during learning, for changing the weight of a synapse only the states of two connected neurons are needed. The *locality principle* makes ANN more biologically plausible.

Parallelism: a high degree of parallelism in ANN is caused by the fact that each neuron operates relatively independently of other neurons. In principle, this enables very fast overall execution. That is why neural networks are able to adapt to a complex environment in real time. However, most of today's ANN applications are simulated on sequential computers. A technology development of the future should provide large-scale parallel implementations. Note that an implementation is easier if neurons are allowed to operate asynchronously.

Multidirectional execution: certain ANN topologies in principal make no difference between input and output. Each neuron can be used either for input, output or both. In one case one subset of neurons can represent an input and another subset an output, while in another case they can switch their roles. Our example network in Figure 11.1 has this property.

Robustness: due to distributed representation, ANN are robust with respect to damages of single neurons and synapses. As already stated, the removal of one neuron or synapse does not lead to complete loss of a single datum but rather partially decreases the storage accuracy of several data. The accuracy of an ANN gradually decreases with the number of destroyed neurons or synapses. The same is true for biological neural networks.

ANN are robust also with respect to the incomplete (missing) data. Missing data are approximated by the use of a number of stored correlations in a memory matrix. Therefore, a loss of data can be to some extent compensated with a distributed memory. The less complete are the data, the worse is the approximation.

Learning: learning in ANN is a kind of "spontaneous" weight change on a synapse. One memory element (synapse) represents a kind of correlation between activities of two connected neurons.

Relation between hardware and software: a neural network does not run any software in a classical sense. The only algorithm is the one used by each neuron. All the other execution can be interpreted as spontaneous. By introducing a neural hardware, we can hardly speak about computers or inference machines – a better term is a "relaxator". Neural hardware can be static or dynamic – old synapses can be eliminated and new ones can emerge. For certain tasks the topology of a network can be randomly generated. The only requirement is that the number of synapses is much larger than the number of neurons, which is analogous to the brain.

Mathematical foundation: the field of ANN has a well developed theoretical background in linear algebra. Well known and well investigated terms apply to ANN, such as linearity, linear and inverse transformation, orthogonality, eigenvalue, eigenvector, fixed point, and convergence.

Explanation of decisions: the biggest deficiency of ANN is the inability to explain the decisions. Each decision is obtained by a complex process of simultaneous execution of a large number of neurons which is usually very hard to interpret.

In domains where the transparency of decisions is of crucial importance ANN are not appropriate. Note that when solving complex tasks (such as medical diagnosis), human experts are also mostly unable to explain their decisions.

11.1.4   Applications

Nowadays it is rather easy to develop applications with standard models of ANN. There are many commercial software packages available that provide user-friendly definition of an ANN's topology and the use of several common ANN models, such as Hopfield's, Boltzmann's, Grossberg's, Kohonen's models, and the most widely used multi-layered perceptron. Fields of application include:

- quality control in various production processes,

- medical diagnosis from various measurements and medical images,

- recognition and classification of images,

- recognition of manually written text and signatures,

- time series analysis and prediction,

- recognition of voice and speech,

- identification of objects with sonar,

- dimensionality reduction etc.

In image recognition it is important to obtain rotational and size invariant processing, which can be achieved with special ANN topologies. The basic idea is to try several transformations in parallel and compare the results with stored patterns. With iterative repetition of transformations a pattern is reinforced that best corresponds to the input pattern. For classification problems with large numbers of different classes self-organizing ANN are used where each neuron specializes for one particular class.

Another field of application is combinatorial optimization. For large problems, where many constraints have to be simultaneously taken into account, only parallel approaches are feasible due to the huge time complexities of sequential algorithms. Neural architecture can sometimes lead to very efficient combinatorial optimization where standard methods fail. Note however, that the number of neurons has to be proportional to the number of parameters of the target problem.

Another application area is cognitive modeling. ANN are able to model a variety of cognitive processes. They enable simulation, empirical evaluation, and formal analysis of various models.

11.1.5   Analogy with brain

The brain is content-addressable, as is the case also with ANN. Mental processes use the brain as a whole. It is not possible to locally separate the memory function from processors, as we can do with classical digital computers. The memory in cortex is distributed. In neurophysiology it is known that synaptic connections contribute significantly to human memory.

The speed of neurons is measured in milliseconds and is much slower than that of contemporary computer processors. As perception, language processing, intuitive thinking and the access to the memory require about 100 milliseconds, we can conclude that "the algorithm" cannot be longer than about 100 steps. Therefore, to implement such a short algorithm for solving such complex tasks we need an extremely high level of parallelism.

In the brain as well as in ANN the performance gradually decreases with the number of destroyed neurons. There is no single neuron of crucial importance whose damage would collapse the whole system. In the cortex there is no single part on which all the other parts depend. Also, no part of the brain is irreplaceable. For example, with children born without one of the hemispheres, the other hemisphere takes over the functions of the missing hemisphere and children grow up normally.

Human perception is to a certain extent invariant to height, translation, and rotation. The brain is able to automatically generate a reduced representation. Different cortex regions have specialized for different sensorial signals while preserving the topology of spatial signals. The same principle can be simulated with ANN. There exists much neurophysiological evidence that brain neurons use self-organization which can be modeled by a certain kind of ANN.

For efficient processing it is not necessary to fully interconnect the neural network. For a certain statistical accuracy it suffices that the number of interconnections is much larger than the number of neurons. If the human brain (with 10^{10} neurons and on average with 10^4 synapses per neuron) would operate by the principle of a simple threshold function and if the only memory would be that of the synapses, then it can be shown that we have enough capacity to memorize every experience we can encounter in 100 years! There is a lot of psychological evidence that the brain indeed memorizes just every experience throughout the whole life.

A genetic code cannot determine all the connections in the brain and obviously a part of them is randomly (or at least independently from the gene code) generated. In the brain there is no "hardware" in the strict sense of the word, nor is there any software in the usual sense of the word. The brain is not an appropriate medium for recursive processing, and recursive statements are hard to understand by (untrained) humans.

ANN models do not strictly follow the analogy with the brain. The majority of biological neurons have either excitatory or inhibitory synapses. On the other hand, an ANN can have both types of synapses with single neuron. Besides, as opposed to ANN, the size of the signal in a biological neuron is given with the impulse frequency. Another major difference is that currently known ANN models do not use global communication between the neurons, while in the brain the global communication is not only present but seems to be of crucial importance.

Symbolic Artificial Intelligence	Artificial Neural Networks
symbolic level	subsymbolic level
transparent decisions	only sometimes
explicitly stored rules	dynamically created rules
sequential processing	parallel processing
logic, conscious level	intuitive, subconscious level
psychological analogy	also
no similarity to biological systems	similarity to biological systems
left hemisphere	right hemisphere

Table 11.1: Relation between symbolic AI methods and ANN models.

11.1.6   Relation to symbolic AI methods

The most important deficiency of ANN is their inability to explain the decisions. This makes them less attractive in situations where transparency of a decision process is required. Symbolic artificial intelligence aims to develop (expert) systems that are able to explain their decisions and sometimes also argue about alternative possibilities. Table 11.1 gives an overview of the relation between symbolic AI methods and ANN models.

The goal of AI research is to develop methods and tools in order to provide the computers with more intelligent behavior. One of the basic requirements is the transparency of reasoning – an AI system has to be able to explain its decisions. The ideas for developing AI methods come from analogies with human ways of reasoning, however, those analogies are at a high, symbolic and logic level. AI researchers are concerned with what the brain can do and not with how it is able to do it. Most of the computer models in AI research are far from biological similarity and analogy. Symbolic learning generates explicit rules based on a set of solved problems (learning examples).

On the other hand, ANN models are based on analogy with the human brain on a relatively low, subsymbolic level. ANN researchers are interested also in how the brain operates. ANN models take into account the similarity to biological systems. The rules in an ANN are not explicitly stored but are rather dynamically created during problem solving. Stored patterns, gained with experience, can be dynamically combined in a completely novel way, corresponding to a new rule, which was never explicitly encountered. The network acts as if it "knows" the rules but cannot represent them in an explicit and symbolic way.

Consider the analogy with humans. Unexperienced humans use deep knowledge, gathered in schools and from books, and try to apply the general rules to solve specific problems from their domain. They consciously apply the rules on a logical, symbolic level. With experience a human expert gathers more specific rules which are, however, not explicitly stored. Those rules can be automatically applied without reconsidering the background general rules from the domain theory. The expert becomes more efficient and the problem solving becomes subconscious.

We could, in a highly simplified manner, say that ANN execute functions of the right hemisphere, which is usually specialized more for parallel, subconscious (intuitive) processing. On the other hand, symbolic AI methods are executing the functions of the left hemisphere, which is usually specialized for sequential, conscious, logical reasoning. We can speculate that by an appropriate combination of both approaches we can expect a huge leap in possibilities and efficiency of computer problem solving.

11.2 TYPES OF ARTIFICIAL NEURAL NETWORKS

To know is to be.

— *Sri Nisargadatta Maharaj*

Artificial neural networks can be classified by various criteria:

- topology of ANN,
- application purpose,
- learning rule, and
- combination function.

11.2.1 Topology

When defining an ANN, a variety of topologies can be used. Most frequent topologies are without layers, two-layered and multi-layered feedforward ANN, and bi-directional two-layered ANN.

ANN without layers: a general form of ANN has a topology without layers – each neuron is connected to every other neuron in both directions (see example in Figure 11.1). The processing starts by setting the state of each neuron. Each neuron then simultaneously, synchronously or asynchronously, calculates its new (updated) state from the signals, obtained from all other neurons. The process iterates until a certain condition is met (such as a fixed point). Due to feedback loops such a network needs a mechanism to control or prevent cycling.

Two-layered feedforward ANN: two-layered ANN have an input layer and an output layer of neurons. Each input neuron is connected with each output neuron with a directed connection (see Figure 11.4). The processing starts by setting the state of each input neuron. Each output neuron then only once calculates its output from the signals, obtained from all the input neurons. As input neurons do not calculate their state – they only distribute a value to all the output neurons – some authors call such an ANN a single-layered feedforward ANN. If each neuron uses a linear combination function, as shown in Figure 11.2, a two-layered feedforward ANN can solve only linear problems.

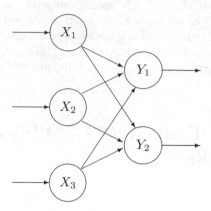

Figure 11.4: A two-layered feedforward ANN with three input and two output neurons.

Multi-layered feedforward ANN: if we add one or more additional (hidden) layers of neurons between the input and the output layer we get a multi-layered feedforward ANN. They operate similarly to two-layered ANN and the number of calculation steps is equal to the number of hidden layers plus one. The calculation begins with the first hidden layer and ends with the output layer. Although they use linear activation function, the multi-layered feedforward ANN can solve also nonlinear problems. A simple three-layered ANN that solves a hard nonlinear problem is shown in Figure 11.5.

Bi-directional two-layered ANN: bi-directional two-layered ANN has two layers. Each neuron from one layer is connected with each neuron from the other layer with a bi-directional connection (a connection that works in both directions). Processing starts by setting the state of all neurons in one layer. Then in each iteration each neuron of the opposite layer calculates its new (updated) state. The iterations stop when a certain condition is met (such as a fixed point). Like in NN without layers, due to feedback loops such a network needs a mechanism to control or prevent cycling.

11.2.2   Application purpose

With respect to the purpose of the application we distinguish the following ANN types: auto-associative memory, hetero-associative memory, temporal associative memory, classifiers and regressors, and ANN for clustering.

Auto-associative memory: the task is for a given partial and/or noisy pattern (example) to complete and/or correct the pattern. An auto-associative memory is usually implemented on a feedback topology without layers.

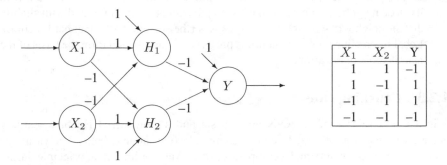

Figure 11.5: A three-layered ANN for calculating XOR. Two hidden neurons and the output neuron have additional constant inputs with weights equal to 1 (constant input is called a threshold or a bias).

Hetero-associative memory: it is a special case of an auto-associative memory, where a pattern (example) is divided into several subpatterns. Input to the network is one subpattern or a subset of subpatterns and the task is to reconstruct the missing subpatterns. A special case is a bi-directional topology, where we have only two subpatterns.

Temporal associative memory: it is a special case of a hetero-associative memory, where each subpattern is a pattern (example) from another time interval. Usually, the task is to predict the pattern of the next time interval given the patterns from the current time interval and from several past time intervals.

Classification and regression: for classification we have input neurons, where descriptions of examples are provided, and output neurons, which determine the class values. Most often a multi-layered feedforward topology is used. For regression we need only one output neuron with continuous output values.

Clustering: with clustering (described in detail in the next chapter) the task is to divide a set of examples into a number of (usually disjoint) subsets, called clusters, so that each cluster contains examples, that are similar to each other. An ANN's structure should enable each output neuron to eventually specialize for one of the clusters – the neuron triggers (becomes active) if the input neurons represent a member of the corresponding cluster. Therefore an ANN has to have an input layer, where the number of neurons is determined with the number of attributes, and an output layer, where the number of neurons corresponds to the number of clusters. Each output neuron is connected to all the other output neurons with inhibitory synapses, so that only one output neuron can be active at a time.

Self-organization: for efficient representation it is sometimes necessary to appropriately order neurons so that each corresponds to a certain value interval of the input parameter (e.g. the sound frequency). With an appropriate topology the neurons sort themselves so that close neurons respond to similar values of the input signal. The idea is that in the output layer each neuron is connected with its close neighbors from the same layer with excitatory synapses and with slightly distant neighbors with inhibitory synapses (the so called Mexican hat function). Local interactions between neurons preserve continuity and form the basis of the neural self-organization.

11.2.3 Learning rule

Basic learning rules used in ANN are a basic and a generalized Hebbian learning rule, a basic and a generalized delta learning rule (the latter is better known as the backpropagation of errors), and a competitive rule. Another important principle during learning is unlearning – forgetting out-of-date data in order to emphasize recently encountered data.

Hebbian learning rule: a basic rule, known also from neurophysiology, is the Hebbian learning rule. It states that the connection weight is proportional to the frequency of simultaneous activity of both connected neurons. The rule is incremental – the weight is slightly increased each time both neurons are active during the learning phase. All the necessary information is locally available.

The generalized Hebbian learning rule states that the connection weight is proportional to the correlation of states of two connected neurons. The rule is incremental – the weight is slightly increased each time both or none of two connected neurons are active during the learning phase, and slightly decreased each time when only one of two connected neurons is active. As with the basic Hebbian rule, here all the necessary information is also locally available.

Delta learning rule: a simple rule that enables learning in a two-layered feedforward ANN (with an input and an output layer of neurons) is a delta learning rule. At the beginning all the weights are set randomly. For each learning example the output values are computed and compared to expected output values (determined with the target value of the learning example). The difference (error) is used to correct the weights in a direction that decreases the difference. The direction of correction is determined by a derivative of the error function and the amplitude of correction is controlled with a special parameter called the learning rate. The process is iteratively repeated over all learning examples until a stopping criterion is met (for example, when all the differences fall below a certain threshold).

A generalized delta rule, better known as the backpropagation of errors, enables learning in multi-layered feedforward ANN. The rule uses the same basic principle as the basic delta rule. At the beginning all the weights are set randomly and for each learning example the output values are computed and compared to expected output values. The difference is used to correct the weights in a direction that decreases the difference – the weight update process proceeds backwards from the output towards the input layer. Firstly, the weights of the output layer are updated. Then the differences between the actual and the expected values of the second last layer are calculated and the weights are appropriately updated. The process is repeated until the input layer is reached.

As opposed to Hebbian learning, the backpropagation learning rule is much less biologically plausible – currently there is no neurophysiological evidence that would support a hypothesis that certain parts of the brain use such a learning rule.

Competitive learning rule: with this rule only one neuron in a layer is allowed to be active – when one neuron wins, all the other competitors are eliminated with inhibitory connections. Only the winner is allowed to change its weights. It slightly increases weights which helped it to win, and slightly decreases all the other weights. There is a lot of neurophysiological evidence that the brain uses various kinds of competitive learning.

Forgetting: forgetting is useful in problems where fresh data is more important than old ones (out-of-date). When new data is encountered, the update process gives larger influence to the new data and decreases the influence of the stored knowledge. Forgetting is sometimes implemented by gradual decreasing of all weight values, where the decrease is proportional to the size of the weight. Such a process also prevents the weights to become overly large.

11.2.4 Combination function

A combination function has two parts: an activation function (A) and an output function (f). An activation function combines the input values into an intermediate value. An output function is typically a kind of threshold function that maps an activation into a neuron's state which corresponds to an output value of that neuron.

Activation function: the most frequently used activation function is the linear activation function, implemented as a weighted sum:

$$A(X_j) = \sum_i W_{ij} X_i + C_j$$

where W_{ij} is a weight between i-th and j-th neuron, X_i the state of the i-th neuron, and C_j a constant activation of the j-th neuron, called also a *threshold* or a *bias*. If we represent the states of N neurons with a vector:

$$X = (X_1, X_2, ..., X_N)^T$$

and the weights W_{ij} with a weight matrix

$$M = \begin{bmatrix} W_{11} & W_{12} & ... & W_{1N} \\ W_{21} & W_{22} & ... & W_{2N} \\ ... & & ... & \\ W_{N1} & W_{N2} & ... & W_{NN} \end{bmatrix}$$

we can describe the output Y of a network layer X (after one iteration) with

$$Y = MX$$

As matrix M represents a linear transformation, the activation function $Y = A(X)$ is linear.

Rarely used is a more general *sigma-pi* function with a general form:

$$sp(X_1, ..., X_N) = \sum_{S_i \in P} W_i \prod_{k \in S_i} X_k$$

where P is a powerset of the set of all indices of neurons. S_i is a set of neuron indices whose outputs are multiplied and the result is weighted with W_i. It can be shown that with sigma-pi threshold elements we can implement any monotonous Boolean function. A single neuron is not enough as the number of subsets S_i increases with the number of input neurons. Each neuron can use a number of weights, equal to the number of input neurons. By combining several neurons any monotonous function can be implemented.

Output function: an output function can be deterministic binary, deterministic continuous, or stochastic (which is usually binary). With a deterministic function the output of a neuron is exactly determined with its input, while with a stochastic function it is determined only probabilistically.

A binary deterministic function is usually a threshold function (see Figure 11.2). Output values are usually 0 and 1 or –1 and 1. A threshold can be fixed or can change through learning.

A continuous deterministic function is usually a sigmoid function that maps an arbitrary real value into a real value on the interval $(0, 1)$. A commonly used continuous output function is (see Figure 4.5):

$$f(X) = \frac{1}{1 + e^{-X}}$$

The main advantage of such a continuous function is that it is a derivable function that enables the implementation of the gradient search (described in Section 5.7). A continuous function also highly increases the memory capacity of an ANN. For example, an auto-associative ANN with N neurons and with a continuous combination function has up to 3^N fixed points.

In order to avoid local optima, some ANN models use stochastic output functions that enable probabilistic search – a function returns the probability of each of (usually two) possible outputs and then one is selected according to the probability distribution. Learning is slower, which enables the network to avoid many local optima and to increase the probability of reaching a global optimum. As in simulated annealing (Section 5.8) a temperature is used to control the level of stochastic behavior.

11.3   *HOPFIELD'S NEURAL NETWORK

For every action there is an equal and opposite reaction.

— Albert Einstein

A simple example of ANN described at the beginning of the chapter and depicted in Figure 11.1 is in fact the Hopfield's neural network. It uses a fully connected graph. We shall separately describe a discrete and a continuous variant of Hopfield's models.

11.3.1   Discrete model

A discrete Hopfield's model uses the usual weighted sum:

$$A_j = \sum_{X_i=1, i\neq j} T_{ji} + I_j = \sum_{i\neq j} X_i T_{ji} + I_j \tag{11.1}$$

Here T_{ji} represent an element of the memory matrix T, obtained during the learning phase as the sum of outer products of n learning examples $\mathbf{t}_k$ which are a-dimensional vectors :

$$T = \sum_{k=1}^{n} h(\mathbf{t}_k)h(\mathbf{t}_k)^T$$

I_j stands for a threshold (a bias) which can also be learned. However, for simplicity, we assume for each j that $I_j = 0$. Learning examples $\mathbf{t}$ are vectors (each learning example is described with a binary attributes). Each component corresponds to one neuron which can have a state value 0 or 1. Therefore, the number of neurons N is equal to the number of attributes: $N = a$. Before learning, a preprocessing step transforms each learning example $\mathbf{t}$ so that values 0 are changed into -1:

$$\mathbf{t} = (v_1, \ldots, v_N), \quad v_i \in \{0, 1\}$$

$$h(v_i) = \begin{cases} 1, & v_i = 1 \\ -1, & v_i = 0 \end{cases}$$

We distinguish two topologies: one without and one with feedback connections from each neuron to itself. A model without feedback connections has a memory matrix with zero diagonal ($T_{ii} = 0$ for all $i = 1 \ldots N$). X_i is a state of the i-th neuron with possible values 0 and 1 (although learning uses values -1 and 1).

The Hopfield's model uses the generalized Hebbian learning rule. Therefore a weight corresponds to the number of learning examples with the same state value of two connected neurons minus the number of learning examples with different state values. The network learns by setting the values of all neurons with a given learning example ($X_i = v_i$) and by appropriate updating of all connection weights:

$$T_{ij}^{NEW} = T_{ij} + h(v_i)h(v_j)$$

When the network "meets" all the learning examples, the learning phase finishes and the weights do not change any more.

In the execution phase, neurons are set to the values that correspond to a new example (which can be incomplete and/or noisy) and the task is to complete and/or correct the example. The neurons operate in parallel and asynchronously. Each neuron calculates its activation level A_j from locally available information using Equation (11.1). Then it updates its state value using a threshold function:

$$X_j^{NEW} = f(A_j) = \begin{cases} 1, & A_j > 0 \\ X_j, & A_j = 0 \\ 0, & A_j < 0 \end{cases}$$

Note that if $A_j = 0$ the neuron does not change its state.

As neurons operate asynchronously only one neuron at a time changes its state. This process is guaranteed to converge in a finite number of iterations into a stable state (a fixed point) where none of the neurons can change its state any more. A fixed point is a result of the execution phase.

The proof of stability of the execution phase is based on an energy function which measures the difference between the current state of each neuron and its activation level:

$$E(X_1, ..., X_N) = -\frac{1}{2} \sum_j \sum_{i \neq j} X_j X_i T_{ji} \tag{11.2}$$

Energy of the network has a lower bound and with each iteration the energy decreases. As the network can be in a finite number of different states the process is guaranteed to converge into a fixed point in a finite number of iterations. In a fixed point energy reaches its local minimum. A formal proof is provided in Section 11.7.1.

$\diamondsuit$

11.3.2 Continuous model

Hopfield's continuous model uses the same topology as the discrete model – each neuron is connected with each other neuron. The combination function of the continuous model is analogous to Equation (11.1). The dynamics is described with the following two equations:

$$C_j \frac{du_j}{dt} = \sum_{i, i \neq j} T_{ji} X_i - \frac{u_j}{R_j} + I_j = A_j - \frac{u_j}{R_j} \tag{11.3}$$

$$X_j = g_j(u_j) \tag{11.4}$$

Here X_i is the state (and the output) of the i-th neuron, u_j the input (activation level) of the j-th neuron and I_j, R_j, C_j constants. An output function g_j defines the relation between input and output. It is derivable and sigmoidal with asymptotes 0 and 1. From Equation (11.3) it follows that the speed of change u_j is proportional to the difference between the current and new u_j, calculated with Equation (11.1). The condition $i \neq j$ is omitted, as for the learning rule it holds $T_{ii} = 0$.

The learning rule for the continuous model is the same as for the discrete one. After learning the memory matrix T is fixed. The execution phase starts by setting the neurons' states to values that correspond to a new, possibly incomplete and/or noisy example. The neurons operate in parallel and *continuously* change their states with dynamics, described with the above equation. It is guaranteed that such a network always converges onto a fixed point (which is the result of the execution).

The stability of the continuous model can be proven by defining the energy of the network's state:

$$E = -\frac{1}{2} \sum_j \sum_{i, i \neq j} X_j X_i T_{ji} - \sum_j I_j X_j$$

$$+ \sum_j \frac{1}{R_j} \int_0^{X_j} g_i^{-1}(X) dX \qquad (11.5)$$

which monotonously decreases. The proof is provided in Section 11.7.1.

◇

11.4 *BAYESIAN NEURAL NETWORK

People take different roads seeking fulfillment and happiness. Just because they're not on your road doesn't mean they've gotten lost.

— H. Jackson Brown, Jr.

This section briefly overviews several variants of Bayesian neural networks (BNN) which combine the idea of the Hopfield's auto-associative model with the naive Bayesian classifier (NB), described in Section 9.6.1. Bayesian neural networks can be, among others, used as efficient implementations of the naive and the semi-naive Bayesian classifier (see Section 11.4.3).

It is interesting that in BNN the basic Hebbian learning rule is used, while in Hopfield's models the generalized Hebbian rule is used. BNN models use for an activation function two variants of NB: the basic NB, based on probabilities, and the one based on odds. As with Hopfield's models, we distinguish discrete and continuous BNN.

11.4.1 Topology and learning rule

The topology of the BNN is the same as that of the Hopfield's model. Also with BNN we distinguish two topologies: one without and one with feedback connections of each neuron to itself. For brevity, we shall assume only topologies without feedback connections.

Each synapse has an associated weight. Besides, each neuron contains two additional weights that enable the network to use NB for an activation function. Learning examples are binary vectors. One neuronal weight corresponds to the number of learning examples and the other to the number of learning examples with the corresponding component value equal to 1. The state of a neuron corresponds to its output. For a discrete model it can be either 0 (inactive) or 1 (active). For a continuous model it can have any real value on the interval $[0, 1]$.

Before learning all weights are set to 0. In the learning phase for each learning example the state of each neuron is set to the value of the corresponding input vector component. Each synapse weight is increased if the two connected neurons' states are active (the basic Hebbian learning rule). Besides, for each neuron the first neuronal weight is increased (counting the learning examples) and the second weight is increased if the neuron's state is active. When the learning phase is completed the weights do not change any more. The learning rule guarantees that the synapse weight matrix is symmetric.

In the execution phase the neurons are set to the component values of a new, possibly incomplete and/or noisy example. The execution phase proceeds as in Hopfield's models – all the neurons operate in parallel. In a discrete model they calculate and update their output asynchronously and in a finite number of steps the network converges onto a fixed point which corresponds to the result. In the continuous model the neurons gradually change their outputs until a stable state is reached.

11.4.2 Discrete models

A BNN model with probabilities uses for a combination function an NB formula which takes into account only active neurons. Let $X_i, i = 1...N$ be current states of all neurons and $P(X_j = 1)$ the prior probability of an active state of the j-th neuron. The updated state X_j^{NEW} of the j-th neuron is calculated as follows:

$$X_j^{NEW} = D_j(P(X_j = 1|X_1, \ldots, X_N))$$ (11.6)

where

$$P(X_j = 1|X_1, \ldots, X_N) = P(X_j = 1) \prod_{X_i = 1, i \neq j} \frac{P(X_j = 1|X_i = 1)}{P(X_j = 1)}$$ (11.7)

is the probability that the j-th neuron is active, and

$$D_j(X) = \begin{cases} 1, & \text{if } X > P(X_j = 1) \\ X_j, & \text{if } X = P(X_j = 1) \\ 0, & \text{if } X < P(X_j = 1) \end{cases}$$ (11.8)

is a threshold function. If the calculated probability is greater than the prior probability, the new state becomes 1, if it is equal, the neuron doesn't change its current state, and if it is lower, the new state becomes 0.

Only active neurons ($X_i = 1$) influence the calculation. Therefore we can interpret state 1 that an event occurred and state 0 that it didn't occur or that is is not known whether it occurred or not. The examples should be coded accordingly. Each neuron corresponds to one attribute value. Therefore each attribute is represented with a number of neurons equal to the number of attribute values. For a given attribute value, the corresponding neuron is set to 1 and all the others to 0. If the value of the attribute is unknown, all the neurons for that attribute are set to 0. Therefore, the number of neurons is equal to:

$$N = \sum_{i=1}^{a} m_i$$

where m_i is the number of values of the i-th attribute.

The probabilities in Equation (11.7) can be approximated by using frequencies stored in network weights. $P(X_j = 1)$ is calculated with a quotient between the second and first weight of the j-th neuron. $P(X_j = 1 | X_i = 1)$ is calculated with a quotient between the weight of the synapse connecting the i-th and j-th neurons and the second weight of the i-th neuron (one can use the m-estimate of probabilities instead, see Section 3.1.5).

The discrete BNN model is guaranteed to converge to a fixed point in a finite number of iterations. In order to prove the stability we define, analogously to Hopfield's energy function, a similarity function that measures the similarity between the current neuronal states and their activation levels:

$$Sim(X_1, \ldots, X_N) = \prod_{X_i=1} \frac{P(X_i = 1 | X_1, \ldots, X_N)}{P(X_i = 1)} \qquad (11.9)$$

The similarity monotonously increases which guarantees the stability. The proof is provided in Section 11.7.2.

$\diamond$

Another variant of the BNN model uses odds instead of probabilities ($odds = P/(1 - P)$). Here all the neurons contribute to the calculations of activation levels and not only those with states values equal to 1. The combination function that calculates the updated state X_j^{NEW} of the j-th neuron is:

$$X_j^{NEW} = Dq_j(odds(X_j = 1 | X_1, \ldots, X_N)) \qquad (11.10)$$

where

$$odds(X_j = 1 | X_1, \ldots, X_N) = odds(X_j = 1) \prod_{i \neq j} \frac{odds(X_j = 1 | X_i)}{odds(X_j = 1)} \qquad (11.11)$$

is the odds of the activity of the j-th neuron and

$$Dq_j(X) = \begin{cases} 1, & \text{if } X > odds(X_j = 1) \\ X_j, & \text{if } X = odds(X_j = 1) \\ 0, & \text{if } X < odds(X_j = 1) \end{cases} \qquad (11.12)$$

is a threshold function and $odds(X_j = 1)$ is a prior odds of state 1 for the j-th neuron. The proof of stability of this model is also provided in Section 11.7.2.

$\diamond$

Note that the same learning rule can be used for this model as for the BNN model which uses probabilities. However, with this model the interpretation of states 0 and 1, is symmetric. The examples should be coded in such a way that each neuron represents one binary attribute with values 0 and 1 and the number of neurons N is equal to the number of attributes: $N = a$. Therefore, all the attributes have to be binary (or have to be transformed into several binary attributes). For coding unknown values we need a special value that prevents influencing other neurons.

Relation between BNN and Hopfield's model

By using the logarithm on Equation (11.7) we get:

$$\log P(X_j = 1 | X_1, \ldots, X_N) = \log P(X_j = 1) +$$

$$+ \sum_{X_i = 1, i \neq j} \log \frac{P(X_j = 1 | X_i = 1)}{P(X_j = 1)} \tag{11.13}$$

For brevity, we omit the base of the logarithm which is always 2. By appropriate renaming we get a combination function used by Hopfield's model:

$$A_j = \sum_{X_i = 1, i \neq j} T_{ji} + I_j = \sum_{i \neq j} X_i T_{ji} + I_j \tag{11.14}$$

The major difference between the two models is in the learning rule. While Hopfield's model uses a generalized Hebbian rule the BNN model uses the basic Hebbian learning rule. It was empirically shown that BNN extracts more information and has better performance.

The proof of stability of Hopfield's model is based on the energy function (11.2) while for the stability of the BNN model we use the similarity function (11.9). With appropriate renaming as above we can show the following relation (see Section 11.7.2):

$$E(X_1, \ldots, X_N) = -\frac{1}{2} \log Sim(X_1, \ldots, X_N) \tag{11.15}$$

¿From relation (11.15) it follows that we could interpret the energy also as the *entropy* or the *information content* of a network state. Namely, the negated Equation (11.13) can be interpreted as the sum of information gains of active neurons towards the conclusion that other active neurons are indeed active. Due to symmetry, each information gain appears twice which is appropriately modified with the normalization constant $1/2$. A fixed point can be interpreted as a network state with locally minimal information content.

11.4.3   Implementation of Bayesian classifiers

The naive Bayesian classifier can be implemented in a directional two-layered or multidirectional single-layered Bayesian neural network (BNN). Similarly, the semi-naive Bayesian classifier can be implemented in a directional or multidirectional multi-layered Bayesian neural network.

A directional BNN is actually the naive Bayesian classifier implemented as a directed acyclic graph. Input neurons correspond to all possible (discrete or discretized) attribute values, and output neurons to class labels. The network gets as an input the values of input neurons, and computes in one step the activation values for output neurons. Thus the question of stability during execution does not need to be raised, as opposed to multidirectional neural networks.

A multidirectional BNN is analogous to *Hopfield's neural network*, and a directional BNN is analogous to the *perceptron*. Hopfield's neural network uses the generalized Hebbian learning rule, while BNN uses the basic Hebbian learning rule. In both cases the learning complexity is proportional to the number of learning examples. In BNN learning is incremental and a single pass through the learning set is sufficient, as opposed to the perceptron that uses the delta learning rule and iterates through the learning set several times. With respect to naivety, a directional BNN is analogous to a two-layered perceptron, as they can both compute only linear functions.

When compared to symbolic learning methods, one of the most serious disadvantages of neural networks is their inability to comprehensibly explain their decisions (classifications). This problem is most aggravating when considering hidden layer neurons of multi-layered neural networks. As opposed to Hopfield's neural networks, two-layered and multi-layered perceptrons, all BNN can comprehensibly explain their decisions exactly as described in Section 9.6.2. While the interpretation of neurons from hidden layers of multi-layered neural networks is particularly difficult, in multi-layered BNN it is straightforward.

11.4.4 Continuous models

The contribution of the i-th neuron for activity of the j-th neuron in a discrete BNN model that uses probabilities is given with $\log \frac{P(X_j|X_i)}{P(X_j)}$. A more general definition of the information gain is given with:

$$X_i \times \log \frac{P(X_j|X_i)}{P(X_j)}$$

where X_i is the current state of the i-th neuron. In a continuous model X_i can have any real value from the interval [0,1] and can be interpreted as the probability that the i-th neuron is active. The generalized formula (11.13) contains a sum over all neurons (and not only active ones):

$$\log P(X_j|X_1,\ldots,X_N) = \log P(X_j) + \sum_{i \neq j} \left(X_i \times \log \frac{P(X_j|X_i)}{P(X_j)} \right) \quad (11.16)$$

¿From this we get the combination function for continuous BNN which is a generalization of Equation (11.7):

$$P(X_j|X_1,\ldots,X_N) = P(X_j) \prod_{i \neq j} \left(\frac{P(X_j|X_i)}{P(X_j)} \right)^{X_i} \quad (11.17)$$

If in Equation (11.16) we replace $\log P(X_j|X_1,\ldots,X_N)$ with A_j, $\log P(X_j)$ with I_j, and $\log \frac{P(X_j|X_i)}{P(X_j)}$ with T_{ji}, we get the combination function of Hopfield's model.

Therefore, for the description of the dynamics of the continuous BNN model we can use Equations (11.3) and (11.4). The proof of stability is analogous to that of Hopfield's continuous model and a similarity function (11.9) generalized to continuous states is therefore:

$$Sim(X_1, \ldots, X_N) = \prod_j \left(\frac{P(X_j | X_1, \ldots, X_N)}{P(X_j)} \right)^{X_j} \qquad (11.18)$$

In a similar way we can generalize the discrete BNN model that uses odds by generalizing the discrete weight of evidence:

$$\log \frac{odds(X_j = 1 | X_i)}{odds(X_j = 1)}$$

to

$$X_i \times log_2 \frac{odds(X_j = 1 | X_i = 1)}{odds(X_j = 1)} + (1 - X_i) \times log_2 \frac{odds(X_j = 1 | X_i = 0)}{odds(X_j = 1)}$$

Here X_i represents the current state of the i-th neuron that can have any real value from the interval $[0, 1]$. A generalized combination function is the following:

$$odds(X_j | X_1, \ldots, X_N) =$$

$$= odds(X_j = 1) \prod_{i \neq j} \left[\left(\frac{odds(X_j = 1 | X_i = 1)}{odds(X_j = 1)} \right)^{X_i} \left(\frac{odds(X_j = 1 | X_i = 0)}{odds(X_j = 1)} \right)^{1 - X_i} \right]$$

$$(11.19)$$

and an appropriate generalization of the similarity function for this BNN model is:

$$Sim(X_1, \ldots, X_N) =$$

$$= \prod_j \left[\left(\frac{P(X_j = 1 | X_1, \ldots, X_N)}{P(X_j = 1)} \right)^{X_j} \left(\frac{P(X_j = 0)}{P(X_j = 0 | X_1, \ldots, X_N)} \right)^{1 - X_j} \right]$$

$$(11.20)$$

Section 11.7.2 describes dynamics and provides a proof of stability for a continuous BNN model that uses odds.
◇

11.5 PERCEPTRON

To know the world you forget the Self – to know the Self you forget the world.
— Sri Nisargadatta Maharaj

Perceptron is a feedforward neural network with an input layer of neurons that are used only to distribute the input signals to the next layer, and an output layer. A perceptron with no other layers is called two-layered (some authors call it single-layered as the input layer does no calculation) and a perceptron with one or more additional – hidden – layers of neurons is called multi-layered.

11.5.1   Two-layered perceptron

A two-layered perceptron consists of N input neurons X_1, ..., X_N and of M output neurons Y_1, ..., Y_M. Each input neuron is connected with a directed connection (synapse) with each output neuron (see Figure 11.6). Each synapse has an associated weight. The execution starts by assigning the component values of the input $t = (v_1, ..., v_a, 1)$ to the corresponding input neurons: $X_i = v_i$. The last component is a constant – the corresponding weights are interpreted as thresholds θ_i of output neurons. All attributes are continuous or binary and the number of attributes a is equal to the number of neurons N in the input layer: $a = N$. All the output neurons simultaneously and independently calculate their output values:

$$Y = WX \qquad (11.21)$$

where W is the weight matrix. Therefore each output neuron calculates the function:

$$Y_i = \sum_{j=1}^{N} W_{ji} X_j + \theta_i \qquad (11.22)$$

W_{ji} is the weight on the connection between the j-th input and the i-th output neuron and θ_i is a threshold of the i-th output neuron.

Learning rule for classification

Two layered feedforward networks that for the combination function use a weighted sum can solve only linear problems – each output neuron describes with Equation (11.22) a hyperplane that is able to classify input examples into two classes. Therefore, a two-layered perceptron is not able to solve an XOR problem. For two-class problems we have only one output neuron ($M = 1$), while for multi-class problems we have one output neuron for each class ($M = m_0$).

As output neurons calculate their output independently of each other we can limit our discussion to a single output neuron. In such a case the weights can be represented with a vector W and the output is defined with:

$$Y = W^T X \qquad (11.23)$$

If $Y \geq 0$, then the input example is classified to the first class, and if $Y < 0$, it is classified to the second class (or, for multi-class problems, to the subset of remaining classes).

The learning task is to appropriately set the weight vector W so that it correctly classifies learning examples. An iterative learning rule is defined as follows. Learning starts with random weights (alternatively they can all be set to 0). The learning proceeds by iteratively presenting learning examples to the network by appropriately setting the input neurons. Using Equation (11.23) the output is calculated. If the l-th learning example $t_l = X(l)$ is correctly classified, the weights are not modified. If it is, however, incorrectly classified, the weights are modified according to the following two rules:

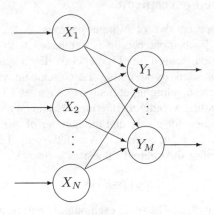

Figure 11.6: A two-layered feedforward artificial neural network (perceptron).

1) If the correct class is the first one and $W^T X(l) < 0$:

$$W^{NEW} = W + \eta X(l) \qquad (11.24)$$

2) If the correct class is the second one and $W^T X(l) \geq 0$:

$$W^{NEW} = W - \eta X(l) \qquad (11.25)$$

The learning rate η determines the speed of learning. It can be shown that if the target function is linear, the above learning is guaranteed to converge to a consistent and complete classifier.

Equations (11.24) and (11.25) can be described with a single equation:

$$W^{NEW} = W + \eta \left(d(l) - \text{sign}(Y(l)) \right) X(l) \qquad (11.26)$$

where $d(l)$ is the target output value:

$$d(l) = \begin{cases} +1 & \text{if } \mathbf{t}_l \text{ belongs to the first class} \\ -1 & \text{if } \mathbf{t}_l \text{ belongs to the second class} \end{cases}$$

and $\text{sign}(\cdot)$ is a sign function:

$$\text{sign}(x) = \begin{cases} +1 & x \geq 0 \\ -1 & x < 0 \end{cases}$$

Delta learning rule

A more general variant of the learning rule (11.26), that can be used for classification as well as for regression, is a *delta learning rule*. For regression and for two-class problems we have only one output neuron ($M = 1$). The delta learning rule takes into account the difference between the actual output and the target output:

$$W^{NEW} = W + \eta \left(d(l) - Y(l) \right) X(l)$$

$$W^{NEW} = W + \eta \left(d(l) - W^T X(l) \right) X(l) \tag{11.27}$$

The delta rule uses a *gradient search* (described in Section 5.7) – the weight vector is changed in a direction of smaller error which is equal to a direction of the negative derivative. Namely, the squared error $E(l)$ is given with:

$$E(l) = \left(d(l) - W^T X(l) \right)^2$$

and its derivative is:

$$\frac{dE(l)}{dW} = -2 \left(d(l) - W^T X(l) \right) X(l)$$

Therefore the delta learning rule of Equation (11.27) can be rewritten in a general form:

$$W^{NEW} = W - \eta \frac{dE(l)}{dW} \tag{11.28}$$

The delta learning rule is called also the *least-mean-squared-error rule* because in the limit, provided the learning rate η is small enough, it converges to an optimal solution by the least-mean-squared-error criterion.

Often instead of sequential learning a *batch* delta learning rule is used. Instead of calculating the differences between actual and target values and updating the weights separately for each learning example, we first calculate the difference for all learning examples $t_1 = X(1)$, ..., $t_n = X(n)$, and only then do we update the weights in a direction of negative derivative. For batch learning the error is defined with:

$$E = \sum_{l=1}^{n} \left(d(l) - W^T X(l) \right)^2$$

and its derivative is:

$$\frac{dE}{dW} = -2 \sum_{l=1}^{n} \left(d(l) - W^T X(l) \right) X(l)$$

Therefore, the batch delta learning rule is given with:

$$W^{NEW} = W - \eta \frac{dE}{dW} = W + \eta \sum_{l=1}^{n} \left(d(l) - W^T X(l) \right) X(l) \tag{11.29}$$

Note that constant 2 is subsumed within η. The batch rule takes into account more information at once and usually converges faster. However, as the algorithm requires the calculation of errors over all learning examples before updating the weights, a local information does not suffice and therefore the batch learning rule is not appropriate for an implementation with a neural network hardware.

11.5.2   Multi-layered perceptron

If between an input and an output layer we add one or more *hidden layers* of neurons we obtain a multi-layered feedforward ANN, also called a multi-layered perceptron (see Figure 11.7). With a multi-layered perceptron we can calculate any nonlinear function. An example perceptron with one hidden layer that solves the XOR problem is depicted in Figure 11.5. The number of input neurons is determined by the classification or the regression problem in the same way as for the two-layered perceptron. However, the appropriate number of hidden layers and the number of hidden neurons for each hidden layer has to be determined empirically.

The execution is similar to that of a two-layered perceptron except that the number of calculation steps increases with the number of hidden layers. The calculation begins with the first hidden layer and continues sequentially through layers towards the output layer. At each layer, neurons simultaneously and independently of each other calculate their outputs and transmit them to every neuron of the next layer.

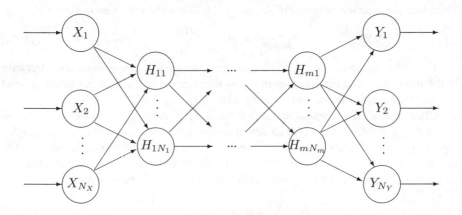

Figure 11.7: Multi-layered feedforward artificial neural with m hidden layers network.

Let $m > 0$ represent the number of hidden layers, each consisting of N_k hidden neurons, $1 \leq k \leq m$. Let there be N_X input and N_Y output neurons. For simplicity, in the following derivation we omit the bias (threshold) terms.

A neuron from the first hidden layer calculates its output for a given learning example $\mathbf{t}_l = X(l)$ as follows:

$$H_{1i}(l) = f\left(\sum_{j=1}^{N_X} W_{ji}^{(1)} X_j(l) \right) \qquad (11.30)$$

Here $W^{(k)}$ represents a weight matrix of synapses that lead to the k-th hidden layer.

Let us define also the activation levels of the first hidden layer:

$$A_{1i}(l) = \sum_{j=1}^{N_X} W_{ji}^{(1)} X_j(l)$$

On the k-th hidden layer, for $1 < k \leq m$, neurons calculate their outputs as follows:

$$H_{ki}(l) = f\left(A_{ki}(l)\right) \qquad (11.31)$$

where their activation levels are calculated from outputs $H_{k-1,j}$ of the preceding layer:

$$A_{ki}(l) = \sum_{j=1}^{N_k} W_{ji}^{(k)} H_{k-1,j}(l)$$

The output neurons calculate their outputs as follows:

$$Y_i(l) = f\left(A_i(l)\right) \qquad (11.32)$$

where the activation levels of output neurons are defined with:

$$A_i(l) = \sum_{j=1}^{N_m} W_{ji}^{(m+1)} H_{m,j}(l)$$

In order to derive the generalized delta learning rule we need to calculate the errors of output neurons. The error of the i-th output neuron for the given l-th learning example is given with:

$$e_i(l) = d(l) - Y_i(l)$$

For the error of the whole network we use the following formula:

$$E(l) = \frac{1}{2} \sum_{i=1}^{N_Y} e_i^2(l) \qquad (11.33)$$

A multi-layered perceptron can be trained for solving classification and regression problems with a *generalized delta learning rule*, better known as the *backpropagation of errors*. The idea of backpropagation is the same as with the basic delta learning rule. We start with random weights (setting all weights to 0 is not appropriate). A learning example is used to set appropriately the values of input neurons, and the network (with a forward propagation) calculates its output. Then the difference from the target output is calculated and the weights are modified in order to decrease the difference. The modification starts with weights of the output layer. Then the error is propagated back to the last hidden layer and its weights are appropriately modified. The process continues backwards until it reaches and modifies the weights of the first hidden layer (note that input neurons have no weights).

As we need to calculate derivatives of errors also for hidden neurons, the output (threshold) function has to be continuous and continuously derivable. For that purpose we use a sigmoid function, depicted in Figure 4.5:

$$f(X) = \frac{1}{1 + e^{-X}}$$

Its derivative is:

$$f'(X) = \frac{e^{-X}}{(1 + e^{-X})^2} = f(X)(1 - f(X)) \qquad (11.34)$$

The weights should be updated in order to minimize the error E, i.e. they are changed in a direction of the negative derivative:

$$W^{NEW} = W - \eta \frac{dE}{dW} \qquad (11.35)$$

Therefore, the backpropagation of errors uses *gradient search*. The main problem is how to calculate the derivatives for hidden layers. The idea is to back-propagate errors from the output layer towards the hidden layers. The derivatives needed to calculate the updated weights in Equation (11.35) are calculated using the chain rule. We start with the output layer, and the calculated derivatives on each layer are used for calculation of derivatives on the preceding layer. Here we give only results, and the complete derivation of the generalized delta learning rule is provided in Section 11.7.3.
◇
The weights $W^{(m+1)}$ of output neurons are updated as follows:

$$W_{ji}^{NEW\ (m+1)} = W_{ji}^{(m+1)} - \eta \frac{\partial E(l)}{\partial A_i(l)} H_{mj}(l)$$

where partial derivatives are given with:

$$\frac{\partial E(l)}{\partial A_i(l)} = -e_i(l) f'(A_i(l))$$

The weights of the last (m-th) hidden layer are updated as follows:

$$W_{ji}^{NEW\ (m)} = W_{ji}^{(m)} - \eta \frac{\partial E(l)}{\partial A_{mi}(l)} H_{m-1,j}(l)$$

where partial derivatives are given with:

$$\frac{\partial E(l)}{\partial A_{mi}(l)} = f'(A_{mi}(l)) \sum_{j=1}^{N_Y} \frac{\partial E(l)}{\partial A_j(l)} W_{ij}^{(m+1)}$$

For hidden layers with index k, $1 < k < m$, we have:

$$W_{ji}^{NEW\ (k)} = W_{ji}^{(k)} - \eta \frac{\partial E(l)}{\partial A_{ki}(l)} H_{k-1,j}(l)$$

where partial derivatives are given with:

$$\frac{\partial E(l)}{\partial A_{ki}(l)} = f'(A_{ki}(l)) \left(\sum_{j=1}^{N_{k+1}} \frac{\partial E(l)}{\partial A_{k+1,j}(l)} W_{ij}^{(k+1)} \right)$$

Finally, for the first hidden layer ($k = 1$) we have:

$$W_{ji}^{NEW\ (1)} = W_{ji}^{(1)} - \eta \frac{\partial E(l)}{\partial A_{1i}(l)} X_j(l)$$

where partial derivatives are given with:

$$\frac{\partial E(l)}{\partial A_{1i}(l)} = f'(A_{1i}(l)) \left(\sum_{j=1}^{N_2} \frac{\partial E(l)}{\partial A_{2,j}(l)} W_{ij}^{(2)} \right)$$

11.5.3 Problems with backpropagation

The generalized delta learning rule has several deficiencies:

1. The learning process does not always converge to an optimal network – it can get stuck into a local optimum (which is the case for any gradient search). Which local optimum will be found largely depends on the initial random setting of the network weights. If the solution reached is not satisfactory the whole learning process has to be repeated.

2. Only the number of input and the number of output neurons is known in advance; however, we cannot be sure about the appropriate number of hidden layers and about the appropriate number of hidden neurons at each hidden layer. Therefore, the selection of an appropriate topology has to be done empirically.

3. In order to overcome overfitting, the learning process has to be stopped when the error on an independent validation set starts to grow – this happens before the error on the learning set stops decreasing. The determination of the right moment to stop requires an additional validation set and additional testing time, which increases the overall time complexity.

4. Learning requires a large number of passes through the set of learning examples – typically the number of passes is several tens or even hundreds of thousands. The network in Figure 11.5 was trained with only 4 learning examples and it still needed over 500 passes to learn a correct classifier.

5. The learning rate η influences the convergence of the learning process and has to be empirically determined.

6. The generalized delta learning rule has no biological analogy – current neurophysiological evidence does not support biological plausibility of the backpropagation of errors learning in the brain.

The first three problems can be partially solved with appropriate improvements of the generalized delta learning. The last three problems, however, cannot be avoided and if they become unacceptable, some other type of ANN or some other machine learning method has to be used.

The problem of local optima can be overcome to some extent if the learning rule

$$W_{ji}^{NEW} = W_{ji} - \Delta W_{ji}$$

is extended with a *momentum term* – the updating process takes into account the last update $\Delta W_{ji\ OLD}$:

$$W_{ji}^{NEW} = W_{ji} - \Delta W_{ji} - \alpha \Delta W_{ji}^{OLD}$$

Parameter α determines the influence of the old update to the new one. The learning process becomes more conservative, which enables it to persist in a direction determined by previous iterations, and to eventually get out of relatively small local optima.

The other two problems (selecting an appropriate topology and avoiding overfitting) can be overcome using various approaches. An interesting approach is the weight elimination method that adds to the error function (11.33) a term that penalizes large weights. This forces the updating process to keep the weights small. If the weight of a synapse becomes small enough, the synapse is eliminated. The process eventually eliminates redundant hidden neurons. This way we solve both problems:

- The learning starts with an overly large network and the learning process itself eliminates redundant neurons.
- By automatically finding an appropriate topology the network avoids overfitting.

However, the method introduces additional parameters which cannot be easily set.

11.6 RADIAL BASIS FUNCTION NETWORKS

Everything that irritates us about others can lead us to an understanding of ourselves.
— Carl Gustav Jung

Radial basis function networks (RBF networks) build upon an older pattern recognition technique – radial basis functions. The radial basis function approach is based on Cover's theorem on the separability of patterns. This theorem states that nonlinearly separable patterns can be separated linearly if the pattern is cast nonlinearly into a higher dimensional space. Therefore an RBF network converts the input to a higher dimension after which it can be classified using only one layer of neurons with linear activation functions.

The RBF network is a popular alternative to the multi-layered perceptron. Although it is not quite as well suited to larger applications, it can offer advantages over the multi-layered perceptron in some applications, as it can be easier to train. The RBF network has a similar form to the multi-layered perceptron in that it is a multi-layered,

Input neurons

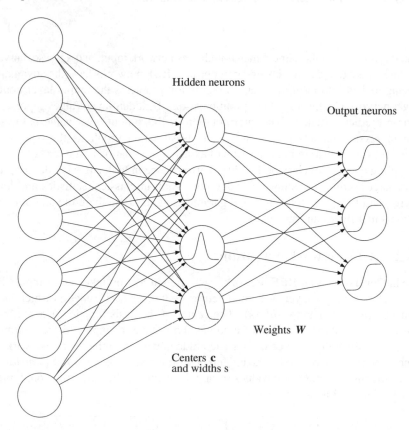

Figure 11.8: A typical topology of an RBF network for classification.

feed-forward network. However, unlike the multi-layered perceptron, the hidden neurons in the RBF are different from the neurons in the input and output layers: they contain the radial basis function, a non-linear transformation from which the neural network's name is derived. Like multi-layered perceptrons, RBF networks are suited to applications such as pattern discrimination and recognition, classification and regression, interpolation, prediction and forecasting, and process modeling.

11.6.1   Topology of RBF networks

The topology of an RBF network (Figure 11.8) is simple. It contains an input layer, a hidden layer with *nonlinear* activation functions, and an output layer with linear activation functions. The most popular choice for the nonlinear activation function B

is the Gaussian with parameters center (**c**) and width (s).

$$B(t) = e^{-\|\mathbf{t}-\mathbf{c}\|^2/(2s^2)} \tag{11.36}$$

Center **c** is a vector of the same dimensionality as network input, and s is a scalar value.

With respect to the multi-layered perceptrons, RBF networks have the advantage of not being locked into local minima. In regression problems the output layer contains a single neuron which uses a linear combination of hidden layer values representing the mean predicted output. The interpretation of this output layer value is the same as for regression models in statistics. In classification problems the output layer neurons use typically a sigmoid function of a linear combination of hidden layer values, representing a posterior class probability. Performance in both cases is often improved by shrinkage techniques, known as ridge regression in classical statistics and known to correspond to a prior belief in small parameter values (and therefore smooth output functions) in a Bayesian framework.

11.6.2   RBF network execution

In the hidden layer of an RBF network, each hidden neuron takes as an input all the outputs (**t**) of the input layer. A hidden neuron contains a basis function which has the parameters *center* (**c**) and *width* (s). The center of the basis function is a vector **c** of numbers c_j. The dimensionality of **c** equals the number of inputs to the neuron and there is normally a different center for each hidden neuron in the neural network. The first computation performed by the hidden neuron is to compute the *radial distance d*, between the input vector **t** with values v_j and the center of the basis function, typically by calculating the Euclidean distance:

$$d = \|\mathbf{t} - \mathbf{c}\| = \sqrt{(v_1 - c_1)^2 + (v_2 - c_2)^2 + \cdots + (v_a - c_a)^2}$$

The neuron output o is then computed by applying the basis function B to this distance divided by the width s:

$$o = B(d/s)$$

The basis function is a curve – typically a Gaussian function – which has a peak at zero distance and which falls to smaller values as the distance from the center increases. As a result, the neuron gives an output of 1.0 when the input is centered, but which reduces as the input becomes more distant from the center. There are three sets of variables that affect each hidden neuron's contribution to the network's output: its position (center) and extent (width), and the weights on connections to the output layer.

11.6.3   RBF network training

Training occurs by adjusting the centers (**c**) and widths (s) in hidden-layer neurons, and weights (**W**) between the hidden and the output layer, so as to improve the modeling accuracy of the network. Training can be accomplished in a number of ways, from self-organizing techniques to supervised techniques as used in feedforward networks.

The centers **c** are initialized randomly. Then, for each learning example t_l, the learning algorithm associates it with its closest center:

$$\|t_l - c_j\| = \min_{k=1}^{h} \|t_l - c_k\| \qquad (11.37)$$

where h is the number of hidden neurons. The center is updated as follows:

$$c_j = c_j + \eta(t_l - c_j) \qquad (11.38)$$

where η is the learning rate parameter. η is normally selected as the inverse of the total number of examples associated with (closest to) a particular hidden neuron.

Once the centers are known it is easy to calculate the corresponding widths **s**. For each center, say c_j we merely have to find the farthest learning example, say t_l, associated with this center. The width s_j is then set proportionally to the distance between c_j and t_l:

$$s_j = \frac{\|t_l - c_j\|}{2} \qquad (11.39)$$

Note that centers and widths are computed in an unsupervised manner (i.e., the target variable is not used).

The weights **W** in the RBF networks are found through optimization of an objective function E. The most common objective function is the mean squared error. The simplest learning algorithm used in RBF networks is gradient descent. In gradient descent learning, the weights are adjusted at each time step by moving them in a direction opposite from the gradient of the objective function

$$\mathbf{W}^{NEW} = \mathbf{W} - \nu \frac{dE(\mathbf{W})}{d\mathbf{W}} \qquad (11.40)$$

where ν is another learning rate parameter and E is the objective function (e.g., the mean squared error).

11.6.4 Some properties of RBF networks

RBF networks have the advantage of not suffering from local minima in the same way as multi-layered perceptrons. This is because the only parameters that are adjusted in the learning process are linear mappings (weights) from the hidden layer to the output layer. Linearity ensures that the error surface is quadratic and therefore has a single easily found minimum. In regression problems this can be found in one matrix operation. In classification problems the fixed non-linearity introduced by the sigmoid output function is most efficiently dealt with using iterated re-weighted least squares.

RBF networks have the disadvantage of requiring good coverage of the input space by radial basis functions. RBF network centers are determined with reference to the distribution of the input data, but without reference to the prediction task. As a result, representational resources may be wasted on areas of the input space that are irrelevant to the learning task. A common solution is to associate each data point with its own center, although this can cause the linear system to be solved in the final layer to be rather large, and requires shrinkage techniques to avoid overfitting.

Associating each input datum with an RBF leads naturally to kernel methods such as Support Vector Machines and Gaussian Processes (the RBF is the kernel function). All three approaches use a non-linear kernel function to project the input data into a space where the learning problem can be solved using a linear model. Like Gaussian Processes, and unlike SVMs, RBF networks are typically trained in a Maximum Likelihood framework by maximizing the probability (minimizing the error) of the data under the model. SVMs take a different approach to avoiding overfitting by maximizing a margin. In most classification applications RBF networks are outperformed by SVMs. In regression applications they can be competitive when the dimensionality of the input space is relatively small.

11.7 **FORMAL DERIVATIONS AND PROOFS

Tenacity of purpose and honesty in pursuit will bring you to your goal.
                                                   — *Sri Nisargadatta Maharaj*

11.7.1 Stability of Hopfield's models

Discrete model: the discrete Hopfield's model converges in a finite number of iterations into a fixed point.

Proof. Let us define the energy function which measures the difference between the current state of each neuron and its activation level:

$$E(X_1, ..., X_N) = -\frac{1}{2} \sum_j \sum_{i \neq j} X_j X_i T_{ji} \qquad (11.41)$$

It suffices to prove that with each iteration the energy decreases. As the network can be in a finite number of different states the process is guaranteed to converge into a fixed point in a finite number of iterations.

Let us suppose that in a current iteration the j-th neuron changes its state: $X_j \rightarrow \overline{X}_j$. There are two possible cases:

1. If $A_j = \sum_{i \neq j} X_i T_{ji} > 0$, then $X_j = 0$, $\overline{X}_j = 1$ and the change of energy is as follows:

$$E(X_1, ..., \overline{X}_j, ..., X_N) - E(X_1, ..., X_j, ..., X_N) = -\frac{1}{2} \sum_{i \neq j} X_i T_{ji} < 0 \quad (11.42)$$

2. If $A_j = \sum_{i \neq j} X_i T_{ji} < 0$, then $X_j = 1$, $\overline{X}_j = 0$ and the change of energy is as follows:

$$E(X_1, ..., \overline{X}_j, ..., X_N) - E(X_1, ..., X_j, ..., X_N) = +\frac{1}{2} \sum_{i \neq j} X_i T_{ji} < 0 \quad (11.43)$$

In both cases the energy decreases.   □

Continuous model: the continuous Hopfield's model converges onto a fixed point.

Proof. Let us define the energy of the network's state:

$$E = -\frac{1}{2} \sum_j \sum_{i,i \neq j} X_j X_i T_{ji} - \sum_j I_j X_j$$

$$+ \sum_j \frac{1}{R_j} \int_0^{X_j} g_i^{-1}(X) dX \tag{11.44}$$

$$= -E1 + \sum_j \frac{1}{R_j} \int_0^{X_j} g_i^{-1}(X) dX \tag{11.45}$$

It suffices to prove that the energy monotonously decreases:

$$\frac{dE}{dt} \leq 0 \tag{11.46}$$

and observing the fact that

$$\frac{dE}{dt} = 0 \rightarrow \forall j : \frac{dX_j}{dt} = 0$$

Therefore we only have to prove the inequality (11.46). Because

$$\frac{d(X_i X_j)}{dt} = X_j \frac{dX_i}{dt} + X_i \frac{dX_j}{dt}$$

the derivative of the first part of the right-hand side of Equation (11.44) is equal to:

$$-\sum_j \left(\sum_{i,i \neq j} X_i T_{ji} \right) \frac{dX_j}{dt}$$

Due to

$$g_j^{-1}(X_j) = u_j$$

we have the complete derivative:

$$\frac{dE}{dt} = -\sum_j \left(\sum_{i,i \neq j} X_i T_{ji} - \frac{u_j}{R_j} + I_j \right) \frac{dX_j}{dt}$$

¿From Equation (11.3) it follows:

$$\frac{dE}{dt} = -\sum_j C_j \left(\frac{du_j}{dt} \right) \frac{dX_j}{dt}$$

and because

$$g_j^{-1}(X_j) = u_j$$

we get:

$$\frac{dE}{dt} = -\sum_j C_j \left(\frac{d}{dt} g_j^{-1}(X_j) \right) \frac{dX_j}{dt}$$

or equivalently

$$\frac{dE}{dt} = -\sum_j C_j \left(\frac{d}{dX_j} g_j^{-1}(X_j) \right) \left(\frac{dX_j}{dt} \right)^2 \qquad (11.47)$$

Because g_j is a sigmoidal and derivable function it holds for each j:

$$\frac{d}{dX_j} g_j^{-1}(X_j) \geq 0$$

The other two factors of the sum in Equation (11.47) are also positive. This concludes the proof of $\frac{dE}{dt} \leq 0$. ☐

11.7.2 Stability of BNN models

Discrete BNN model that uses probabilities: the discrete BNN model that uses probabilities is guaranteed to converge to a fixed point in a finite number of iterations.

Proof. Let us define the similarity function which measures the similarity between the current neurons' states and their activation levels:

$$Sim(X_1, \ldots, X_N) = \prod_{X_i=1} \frac{P(X_i = 1 | X_1, \ldots, X_N)}{P(X_i = 1)} \qquad (11.48)$$

We show that due to asynchronous operation the similarity monotonously increases. Due to a finite number of different states the similarity has an upper bound which guarantees the stability.

The j-th neuron changes its state in two cases:

a)

$$X_j = 1, P(X_j = 1 | X_1, \ldots, X_N) < P(X_j = 1), \overline{X}_j = 0 \qquad (11.49)$$

Here it holds that the quotient between the previous and the new similarity is equal to:

$$Sim(X_1, \ldots, \overline{X}_j, \ldots, X_N) / Sim(X_1, \ldots, X_j, \ldots, X_N) =$$

$$= \frac{P(X_j = 1)}{P(X_j = 1 | X_1 \ldots X_j \ldots X_N)} \prod_{X_i=1} \frac{P(X_i = 1 | X_1 \ldots \overline{X}_j \ldots X_N)}{P(X_i = 1 | X_1 \ldots X_j \ldots X_N)}$$

$$= \frac{P(X_j = 1)}{P(X_j = 1 | X_1 \ldots X_j \ldots X_N)} \prod_{X_i=1, i \neq j} \frac{P(X_i = 1) P(X_j = 1)}{P(X_i = 1 \wedge X_j = 1)}$$

$$= \left(\frac{P(X_j = 1)}{P(X_j = 1 | X_1 \ldots X_j \ldots X_N)} \right)^2 > 1 \quad \text{(due to 11.49)} \qquad (11.50)$$

b)

$$X_j = 0, P(X_j = 1 | X_1, \ldots, X_N) > P(X_j = 1), \overline{X}_j = 1 \qquad (11.51)$$

Here it holds that the quotient between the previous and the new similarity is equal to:

$$Sim(X_1, \ldots, \overline{X}_j, \ldots, X_N)/Sim(X_1, \ldots, X_j, \ldots, X_N) =$$

$$= \frac{P(X_j = 1|X_1 \ldots X_j \ldots X_N)}{P(X_j = 1)} \prod_{X_i=1, i \neq j} \frac{P(X_i = 1|X_1 \ldots \overline{X}_j \ldots X_N)}{P(X_i = 1|X_1 \ldots X_j \ldots X_N)}$$

$$= \frac{P(X_j = 1|X_1 \ldots X_j \ldots X_N)}{P(X_j = 1)} \prod_{X_i=1, i \neq j} \frac{P(X_i = 1 \wedge X_j = 1)}{P(X_i = 1)P(X_j = 1)}$$

$$(11.52)$$

Due to $P(X_j = 1|X_1 \ldots X_j \ldots X_N) = P(X_j = 1|X_1 \ldots \overline{X}_j \ldots X_N)$ we get

$$= \left(\frac{P(X_j = 1|X_1 \ldots X_j \ldots X_N)}{P(X_j = 1)} \right)^2 > 1 \quad (\text{due to } 11.51) \qquad (11.53)$$

$\square$

Discrete BNN model that uses odds: the discrete BNN model that uses odds is guaranteed to converge to a fixed point in a finite number of iterations.

Proof. The proof is analogous to the above proof of the discrete BNN model that uses probabilities. We use the same similarity measure defined with Equation (11.48) modified by replacing the condition $X_i = 1$ (only active neurons) with X_i (i.e. the product runs over all neurons).

Let X_j be the current state of the j-th neuron. Let the new state of the j-th neuron be $\overline{X}_j$, due to $odds(X_j|X_1, \ldots, X_N) < odds(X_j)$, which is equivalent to $odds(\overline{X}_j|X_1, \ldots, X_N) > odds(\overline{X}_j)$. Then the quotient between the previous and the new similarity is equal to:

$$Sim(X_1, \ldots, \overline{X}_j, \ldots, X_N)/Sim(X_1, \ldots, X_j, \ldots, X_N) =$$

$$= \frac{odds(X_j)}{odds(X_j|X_1 \ldots X_j \ldots X_N)} \prod_{i \neq j} \frac{P(X_i|X_1 \ldots \overline{X}_j \ldots X_N)}{P(X_i|X_1 \ldots X_j \ldots X_N)}$$

$$= \frac{odds(X_j)}{odds(X_j|X_1 \ldots X_j \ldots X_N)} \prod_{i \neq j} \frac{odds(X_j)}{odds(X_j|X_i)}$$

$$= \left(\frac{odds(X_j)}{odds(X_j|X_1 \ldots X_j \ldots X_N)} \right)^2 > 1 \text{ (from initial condition) } (11.54)$$

$\square$

Relation between energy and similarity: from definitions of energy with Equation (11.41) and similarity with Equation (11.48), and with an appropriate renaming, the following relation holds:

$$E(X_1, \ldots, X_N) = -\frac{1}{2} \log Sim(X_1, \ldots, X_N) \qquad (11.55)$$

Proof. Let us use the following renaming:

$$\log \frac{P(X_j = 1|X_i = 1)}{P(X_j = 1)} = T_{ji}$$

Then we can write the following:

$$
\begin{aligned}
\log Sim(X_1, ..., X_N) &= \sum_{X_j=1} \log \frac{P(X_j|X_1, ..., X_N)}{P(X_j)} \\
&= \sum_j X_j \log \frac{P(X_j|X_1, ..., X_N)}{P(X_j)} \\
&= \sum_j X_j \sum_{i \neq j} X_i T_{ji} \\
&= \sum_j \sum_{i \neq j} X_i X_j T_{ji}
\end{aligned}
\tag{11.56}
$$

□

Continuous BNN model that uses odds: the continuous BNN model that uses odds uses the following combination function:

$$
odds(X_j|X_1, ..., X_N) =
$$

$$
= odds(X_j = 1) \prod_{i \neq j} \left[\left(\frac{odds(X_j = 1|X_i = 1)}{odds(X_j = 1)} \right)^{X_i} \left(\frac{odds(X_j = 1|X_i = 0)}{odds(X_j = 1)} \right)^{1-X_i} \right]
\tag{11.57}
$$

Using logarithm of Equation (11.57) and replacing $\log odds(X_j|X_1, ..., X_N)$ with A_j, $\log odds(X_j)$ with I_j, and $\log \frac{P(X_j=Y|X_i=Z)}{P(X_j=Y)}$ with T_{ji}^{YZ} we get:

$$
A_j = I_j + \sum_{i \neq j} (X_i(T_{ji}^{11} - T_{ji}^{01}) + (1 - X_i)(T_{ji}^{10} - T_{ji}^{00}))
\tag{11.58}
$$

If we use the activation level A_j above in Equation (11.3) we get a description of the dynamics of the continuous BNN model that uses odds. We now show the stability.

The continuous BNN model that uses odds converges onto a fixed point.

Proof. ¿From the proof of the stability of the Hopfield's continuous model, it follows that for the stability a sufficient condition in Equation (11.45) is the following:

$$
\frac{dE_1}{dt} = \sum_j \left(\frac{dX_j}{dt} A_j \right)
\tag{11.59}
$$

If in Equation (11.45) we use for E_1 the following expression:

$$
E_1(X_1, ..., X_N) = \sum_j I_j X_j +
$$

$$
+ \frac{1}{2} \sum_j \sum_{i \neq j} (X_j X_i T_{ji}^{11} + X_j(1 - X_i)T_{ji}^{10} + (1 - X_j)X_i T_{ji}^{01} + (1 - X_j)(1 - X_i)T_{ji}^{00})
\tag{11.60}
$$

then the condition (11.59) holds due to:

$$\frac{dE_1}{dt} = \sum_j \left(\frac{dE_1}{dX_j} \frac{dX_j}{dt} \right)$$

$$= \frac{1}{2} \sum_j \left(\frac{dX_j}{dt} A_j \right) + \frac{1}{2} \sum_i \left(\frac{dX_i}{dt} A_i \right)$$

$$= \sum_j \left(\frac{dX_j}{dt} A_j \right) \tag{11.61}$$

□

11.7.3 Backpropagation of errors

The backpropagation of errors changes the weights in a direction of the negative derivative:

$$W^{NEW} = W - \eta \frac{dE}{dW} \tag{11.62}$$

where the error for the given l-th learning example is defined with:

$$E(l) = \frac{1}{2} \sum_{i=1}^{N_Y} e_i^2(l)$$

The error of the i-th output neuron is given with:

$$e_i(l) = d(l) - Y_i(l)$$

We use partial derivatives with respect to weights $W_{ji}^{(m+1)}$, calculated with the chain rule:

$$\frac{\partial E(l)}{\partial W_{ji}^{(m+1)}} = \frac{\partial E(l)}{\partial e_i(l)} \frac{\partial e_i(l)}{\partial Y_i(l)} \frac{\partial Y_i(l)}{\partial A_i(l)} \frac{\partial A_i(l)}{\partial W_{ji}^{(m+1)}}$$

Particular partial derivatives are:

$$\frac{\partial E(l)}{\partial e_i(l)} = e_i(l) \tag{11.63}$$

$$\frac{\partial e_i(l)}{\partial Y_i(l)} = -1 \tag{11.64}$$

$$\frac{\partial Y_i(l)}{\partial A_i(l)} = f'(A_i(l)) \tag{11.65}$$

$$\frac{\partial A_i(l)}{\partial W_{ji}^{(m+1)}} = H_{mj}(l) \tag{11.66}$$

Note that f' is a derivative of the output function and is defined with Equation (11.34).
We are ready to derive the rule for updating the weights $W^{(m+1)}$ of output neurons:

$$W_{ji}^{NEW\ (m+1)} = W_{ji}^{(m+1)} - \eta \frac{\partial E(l)}{\partial W_{ji}^{(m+1)}} \tag{11.67}$$

$$= W_{ji}^{(m+1)} - \eta \frac{\partial E(l)}{\partial A_i(l)} H_{mj}(l) \tag{11.68}$$

$$= W_{ji}^{(m+1)} + \eta e_i(l) f'(A_i(l)) H_{mj}(l) \tag{11.69}$$

as partial derivatives are given with:

$$\frac{\partial E(l)}{\partial A_i(l)} = -e_i(l)f'(A_i(l))$$

For updating the weights of the hidden layers we cannot directly calculate errors e_i. Therefore, we back-propagate errors of the output neurons by calculating partial derivatives with respect to the activation levels. We start with:

$$\frac{\partial E(l)}{\partial A_{mi}(l)} = \frac{\partial E(l)}{\partial H_{mi}(l)} \frac{\partial H_{mi}(l)}{\partial A_{mi}(l)}$$

The second factor is equal to:

$$\frac{\partial H_{mi}(l)}{\partial A_{mi}(l)} = f'(A_{mi}(l))$$

For the first factor we use the chain rule:

$$\frac{\partial E(l)}{\partial H_{mi}(l)} = \sum_{j=1}^{N_Y} \frac{\partial E(l)}{\partial A_j(l)} \frac{\partial A_j(l)}{\partial H_{mi}(l)} \tag{11.70}$$

$$= \sum_{j=1}^{N_Y} \frac{\partial E(l)}{\partial A_j(l)} \frac{\partial \left(\sum_{p=1}^{N_m} W_{pj}^{(m+1)} H_{m,p}(l) \right)}{\partial H_{mi}(l)} \tag{11.71}$$

$$= \sum_{j=1}^{N_Y} \frac{\partial E(l)}{\partial A_j(l)} W_{ij}^{(m+1)} \tag{11.72}$$

Therefore for the last (m-th) hidden layer we get:

$$\frac{\partial E(l)}{\partial A_{mi}(l)} = f'(A_{mi}(l)) \sum_{p=1}^{N_Y} \frac{\partial E(l)}{\partial A_p(l)} W_{ip}^{(m+1)}$$

As the partial derivative is equal to:

$$\frac{\partial A_{mi}(l)}{\partial W_{ji}^{(m)}} = H_{m-1,j}(l)$$

we can write the rule for updating the weights $W_{ji}^{(m)}$ of the last hidden layer:

$$W_{ji}^{NEW\ (m)} = W_{ji}^{(m)} - \eta \frac{\partial E(l)}{\partial W_{ji}^{(m)}} \tag{11.73}$$

$$= W_{ji}^{(m)} - \eta \frac{\partial E(l)}{\partial A_{mi}(l)} H_{m-1,j}(l) \tag{11.74}$$

$$= W_{ji}^{(m)} - \eta f'(A_{mi}(l)) \left(\sum_{p=1}^{N_Y} \frac{\partial E(l)}{\partial A_p(l)} W_{ip}^{(m+1)} \right) H_{m-1,j}(l) \tag{11.75}$$

For other hidden layers with index k, $1 < k < m$, it holds:

$$\frac{\partial A_{ki}(l)}{\partial W_{ji}^{(k)}} = H_{k-1,j}(l)$$

and

$$\frac{\partial E(l)}{\partial A_{ki}(l)} = f'(A_{ki}(l)) \left(\sum_{p=1}^{N_{k+1}} \frac{\partial E(l)}{\partial A_{k+1,p}(l)} W_{ip}^{(k+1)} \right)$$

Therefore, the updating rule for these hidden layers is:

$$W_{ji}^{NEW\ (k)} = W_{ji}^{(k)} - \eta \frac{\partial E(l)}{\partial A_{ki}(l)} H_{k-1,j}(l) \tag{11.76}$$

$$= W_{ji}^{(k)} - \eta f'(A_{ki}(l)) \left(\sum_{p=1}^{N_{k+1}} \frac{\partial E(l)}{\partial A_{k+1,p}(l)} W_{ip}^{(k+1)} \right) H_{k-1,j}(l)$$

For the first hidden layer ($k = 1$) it holds:

$$\frac{\partial A_{1i}(l)}{\partial W_{ji}^{(1)}} = X_j(l)$$

and

$$\frac{\partial E(l)}{\partial A_{1i}(l)} = f'(A_{1i}(l)) \left(\sum_{p=1}^{N_2} \frac{\partial E(l)}{\partial A_{2,p}(l)} W_{ip}^{(2)} \right)$$

Therefore the updating rule for the first hidden layer is as follows:

$$W_{ji}^{NEW\ (1)} = W_{ji}^{(1)} - \eta \frac{\partial E(l)}{\partial A_{1i}(l)} X_j(l) \tag{11.77}$$

$$= W_{ji}^{(1)} - \eta f'(A_{1i}(l)) \left(\sum_{p=1}^{N_2} \frac{\partial E(l)}{\partial A_{2,p}(l)} W_{ip}^{(2)} \right) X_j(l) \tag{11.78}$$

11.8   SUMMARY AND FURTHER READING

There is no way to Peace. Peace is the Way.

— *Thich Nhat Hanh*

- In *artificial neural networks* (ANN) each *neuron* is a simple processing unit, able to calculate the *activation function* on its inputs and, by using an *output function*, to transform the obtained results into output values. Both functions together are called the *combination function*.

- In *distributed memory* the memory elements are the weights on the synapses. Each datum is partially stored in a number of memory elements. The returned value can be only an approximation of the true datum, as each memory element (weight) takes part in memorizing a number of different data. The properties of distributed memory are robustness, automatic generalization, adaptability to changing environment, spontaneous recollection of forgotten data; larger distributivity increases the storage accuracy, and the memory has constructive character.

- ANN have several nice properties: similarity to biological systems, high level of parallelism, possibility of asynchronous processing, multidirectional execution, real-time adaptability, robustness with respect to damages and to missing data, ability to learn and automatic generalization, no need for additional software, no need for a fixed configuration, no difference between data and addresses, and a well developed mathematical foundation. The most important deficiency of ANN is the *inability to explain its decisions*.

- With respect to *topology*, ANN can be without layers, two-layered and multi-layered feedforward ANN, and bi-directional two-layered ANN. With respect to *the purpose of the application* we distinguish auto-associative memory, hetero-associative memory, temporal associative memory, classifiers and regressors, and ANN for clustering. *Learning rules* are the basic and the generalized Hebbian learning rule, the basic and the generalized delta learning rule (backpropagation of errors), the competitive rule, and forgetting. The *activation function* can be a weighted sum, naive Bayes or a sigma-pi function. The *output function* can be deterministic or stochastic, and binary (threshold) or continuous (sigmoid).

- *Hopfield's neural network* can be a discrete or a continuous associative memory. It uses a fully connected network, trained with the generalized Hebbian learning rule. All neurons simultaneously and asynchronously calculate the weighted sum and update their states until a fixed point is reached. The proof of stability is based on the energy function, which monotonously decreases.

- The *Bayesian neural network* is analogous to Hopfield's NN, however, it is trained with the basic Hebbian learning rule and the activation function is the naive Bayesian formula. Instead of the energy function, the entropy of the network's state is used.

- *Perceptron* can be two-layered or multi-layered. The two-layered perceptron uses the basic delta-learning rule and can solve only linear problems. The multi-layered perceptron uses the generalized delta learning rule (backpropagation of errors) and in principle is able to learn any (nonlinear) function. It has several deficiencies: it can get stuck in a local optimum, the appropriate number of hidden neurons is not known in advance, the network may overfit the learning data, requires a large number of passes through the learning examples, the learning rate has to be empirically determined, and it has no biological analogy.

- *Radial basis function networks* (RBF) are multilayered feedforward NN that convert the input to a higher dimension, after which it can be classified using only one layer of neurons with linear activation functions. The hidden neurons contain the radial basis functions. Training in an unsupervised manner adjusts the center and width parameters in hidden-layer neurons, and using a gradient descent adjusts the weights between the hidden and the output layer. RBF networks have no problem with local minima, however, the appropriate number of hidden neurons is crucial and often the shrinkage techniques are required to avoid overfitting.

There are many general textbooks on artificial neural networks. A good starting point is a book by Haykin (1998). A thorough collection of early scientific papers related to ANN is described by Anderson and Rosenfeld (1988). An inspiring collection that besides backpropagation describes several different ANN models and provides interesting discussions on brain analogy is a book edited by Rumelhart and McClelland (1986). In the same volume Hinton et al. (1986) discuss interesting properties of the distributed representation and a spontaneous recollection (Hinton and Sejnowski, 1986). Smolensky (1986) relates the symbolic and the subsymbolic learning by humans and by ANN. Rumelhart and Zipser (1986) introduce an ANN model for clustering which uses competitive learning. Williams (1986) has shown that with sigma-pi activation functions and using the threshold output functions one can implement any monotonous Boolean function. A complementary edition (McClelland and Rumelhart, 1986) describes various ANN approaches to cognitive modeling. An excellent book by Kohonen (1984) discusses several interesting statistical properties of ANN with respect to their (random) topology and the number of synapses per neuron, and the relation between ANN and the brain. An inspiring book by Russell (1979) discusses the limitless potentials of the human brain.

The field of ANN became attractive with a biological learning rule discovered by Hebb (1949). Rosenblatt (1962) introduced the first concrete neural model, a two-layered perceptron. Minsky and Papert (1969) have shown that the basic delta rule converges if the target function is linear, and that it cannot solve nonlinear problems. They also proved that a universal computing machine can be simulated with an ANN. In the seminal works by Hopfield (1982; 1984) the associative neural networks were defined, which provoked an increasing interest in the field, soon resulting in new models, such as the Boltzmann machine (Hinton and Sejnowski, 1986), and a bi-directional and a temporal associative memory (Kosko, 1987, 1988). For some models which use an asymmetric weight matrix the convergence was shown empirically (Wong, 1988). Several authors studied the memory capacity of the Hopfield models (Kohonen, 1984; McEliece et al., 1987; Wong, 1988; Guez et al., 1988). Hopfield and Tank (1985) showed how associative ANN models can be used for an efficient solving of combinatorial problems. Early ANN models for image recognition are described by Hinton (1981), Fukushima (1988), and Widrow and Winter (1988). Bayesian neural networks were defined by Kononenko (1989a; 1989b).

The backpropagation algorithm for learning multi-layered perceptrons was independently invented by several researchers, but made popular by a seminal work by Rumelhart et al. (1986b). Weigend et al. (1991) introduced a weight elimination principle into the backpropagation learning. Wassermann and Schwartz (1987,1988) discuss the biological implausibility of the backpropagation learning rule. The radial basis function (RBF) networks were introduced by Broomhead and Lowe (1988). Two comprehensive references to radial basis function networks are books by Yee and Haykin (2001) and Buhmann (2003).

There exist several important ANN models, not covered by this chapter. Adaptive resonance theory (ART) was first introduced by Cohen and Grossberg (1983) and was further developed by Carpenter and Grossberg (1987a; 1987b; 1990). A unique kind of network model used for unsupervised learning is the Self-Organizing Map introduced by Kohonen (1982; 1984). Barto et al. (1983) use a small number of complex artificial neurons for learning to control dynamic systems.

Chapter 12

Cluster Analysis

If something is in me which can be called religious then it is the unbounded admiration for the structure of the world so far as our science can reveal it.

— Albert Einstein

As opposed to the rest of the book, this chapter is not concerned with supervised learning, but with unsupervised learning, that is, learning without a teacher. Clustering is by far the most popular unsupervised learning method. In this chapter we review several approaches to clustering and discuss their properties and relations to their supervised learning counterparts.

12.1   INTRODUCTION

There is nothing more difficult to take in hand, more perilous to conduct or more uncertain in its success than to take the lead in the introduction of a new order of things.

— Niccolo Machiavelli

Clustering is considered as the most important unsupervised learning problem. It aims to find some structure in a collection of unlabeled data. Informally, clustering is the process of organizing examples into groups whose members are similar in some way. A *cluster* is a collection of examples which are similar to each other and are dissimilar to examples from other clusters. A slightly different kind of clustering is conceptual clustering: two or more examples belong to the same cluster if it defines a concept common to all those examples. In other words, examples are grouped according to their fit to descriptive concepts and not according to simple similarity measures.

The goal of clustering is to determine an intrinsic grouping in a set of unlabeled data. But how to decide what constitutes a good clustering? There is no absolute best criterion which would be independent of the final aim of the clustering. Consequently, domain knowledge has to be used to define this criterion in such a way that the results of the clustering suit end-user's needs. For instance, we could be interested in finding representatives for homogeneous groups (data reduction), in finding natural clusters and describing their unknown properties, in finding useful and suitable groupings or in finding unusual data examples (outlier detection).

Historically, the problem of clustering has been addressed in many contexts in many application areas. Its usefulness has a broad appeal as one of the key steps in exploratory data analysis. In its essence, clustering is a combinatorially difficult problem. Unfortunately, the widespread use of many fundamentally different techniques utilizing significantly different assumptions and contexts in different application areas has slowed down the emergence of useful generic concepts and methodologies.

In the following sections we discuss several approaches to clustering. In some cases we graphically illustrate the difference between different clustering methods. For this purpose we use the *swiss* dataset. It consists of 6 continuous attributes describing a standardized fertility measure and socio-economic indicators for each of 47 French-speaking provinces of Switzerland at about 1888. This dataset is a part of R statistical package, and can also be found at `opr.princeton.edu/archive/eufert/switz.html`.

12.1.1 Clustering and classification

It is very important to be aware of differences between clustering and classification because the process of clustering is sometimes also called classification. In the context of machine learning and data mining this contradicts the usual meaning of classification: we speak of supervised classification where classes (groups) are known in advance. On the other hand, in clustering, the number (and labels) of groups are not known in advance, therefore we speak of unsupervised classification. A useful clustering algorithm should satisfy several criteria:

- scalability;
- dealing with different types of attributes;
- discovering clusters with arbitrary shape;
- minimal requirements for domain knowledge to determine input parameters;
- ability to deal with noise, outliers, and missing data;
- insensitivity to order of input records;
- high dimensionality;
- interpretability and usability.

There are a number of problems with clustering methods:

- current clustering techniques do not address all the requirements adequately (and concurrently);
- dealing with a large number of dimensions and a large quantity of data items can be problematic because of time complexity;

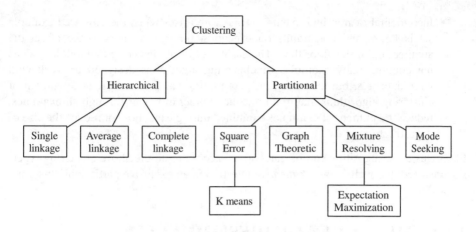

Figure 12.1: One possible taxonomy of clustering algorithms.

- the effectiveness of the method depends on the definition of (dis)similarity measures (e.g., Euclidean distance);
- if an obvious distance measure doesn't exist we must define it, which is not always easy, especially in multi-dimensional spaces;
- the result of the clustering algorithm can be interpreted in different ways.

12.1.2 Taxonomy of clustering algorithms

Clustering algorithms may be classified in several different ways:

- Hierarchical or partitional. An (agglomerative) hierarchical clustering algorithm is based on the union between the two nearest clusters. An initialization sets every example as a cluster. After a few iterations of joining clusters the final clusters are obtained. In partitional clustering examples are divided into clusters. A detailed taxonomy of clustering algorithm based on this criterion is shown in Figure 12.1.

- Exclusive or overlapping. In exclusive clustering methods examples are grouped in an exclusive way, so that if a certain example belongs to one cluster then it cannot be included in another cluster. On the other hand, in overlapping methods (such as fuzzy clustering), each example may belong to several clusters with different degrees of membership. In this case, each example is associated with a list of appropriate membership values.

- Deterministic or stochastic. This issue is most relevant to partitional approaches designed to optimize a squared error function. Optimization can be accomplished using traditional techniques or through a random search of the state space consisting of all possible labelings.

- Incremental or non-incremental. This issue arises when the clustered example set is large, and constraints on execution time or memory space affect the architecture of the algorithm. The early history of clustering methodology does not contain many examples of clustering algorithms designed to work with large data sets, but the advent of data mining has fostered the development of clustering algorithms that minimize the number of passes through all examples, reduce the number of examples examined during execution, or reduce the size of data structures.

Each clustering algorithm can be categorized according to the above clustering types. For instance, the well-known *k-means* algorithm is an exclusive partitional clustering algorithm.

12.2   MEASURES OF DISSIMILARITY

Perception is strong and sight weak. In strategy it is important to see distant things as if they were close and to take a distanced view of close things.

— *Miyamoto Musashi*

Many clustering algorithms assume that the relationship in a set of n examples is described with an $n \times n$ matrix containing a measure of dissimilarity for each pair of examples. Therefore, an important component of a clustering algorithm is the dissimilarity (distance) measure between examples. If values of all attributes are in the same units then it is possible that a simple Euclidean distance metric is sufficient to successfully group similar data instances. However, even in this case the Euclidean distance can sometimes be misleading because of different attribute scalings. Therefore, domain knowledge must be used to guide the formulation of a suitable distance measure for each particular application.

Since dissimilarity is fundamental to the definition of a cluster, a measure of the dissimilarity between two examples drawn from the same attribute space is essential to most clustering procedures. Because of the variety of attribute types and scales, the distance measure must be chosen carefully. It is most common to calculate the dissimilarity between two examples using a distance measure defined on the attribute space. Usually (although not always) a pairwise dissimilarity d_{ij} between examples with indices i and j is chosen such that

1. $d_{ij} \geq 0$,

2. $d_{ii} = 0$, and

3. $d_{ij} = d_{ji}$.

A distance measure is said to be *metric* if it satisfies the above three criteria as well as the triangle inequality $d_{ij} \leq d_{ik} + d_{kj}$ for all triplets of example indices (i, j, k). The third criterion excludes asymmetric distance measures. It is however, sometimes relaxed, and asymmetric distance measures have their use in practice. The most popular asymmetric measure is the Kullback-Leibler distance (see Equation 3.92).

With respect to the attribute types there exist several different dissimilarity measures, for homogeneous as well as for heterogeneous attribute types.

12.2.1   Dissimilarity measures for discrete data

When all attributes are binary they belong to only one of two possible states, denoted by 1 and 0. For a pair of examples (t_i, t_j) we define the following four quantities:

- a: the number of attributes that are 1 for both examples
- b: the number of attributes that are 1 for example t_i and
  0 for example t_j
- c: the number of attributes that are 0 for example t_i and
  1 for example t_j
- d: the number of attributes that are 0 for both examples

	1	0	j
1	a	b	
0	c	d	
i			

Two common dissimilarity measures for binary attributes are the simple matching coefficient and the Jaccard's coefficient.

Simple matching coefficient

$$d_{ij} = \frac{b+c}{a+b+c+d} \tag{12.1}$$

Jaccard's coefficient

$$d_{ij} = \frac{b+c}{a+b+c} \tag{12.2}$$

They are both members of a larger group of dissimilarities, described by

$$d_{ij} = \frac{b+c}{\alpha a + b + c + \delta d} \quad \text{where } \alpha > 0, \ \delta \geq 0 \tag{12.3}$$

The multitude of possible measures with respect to varying the values of parameters α and δ is due to apparent uncertainty as to how to deal with the count d of 0-0 matches.

General discrete dissimilarity

For multi-valued and ordinal discrete attributes, each attribute value can be considered as a binary attribute. This approach is however unattractive because of the large number of negative (0-0) matches. A superior approach is to calculate a matching score δ_{klm} that measures the disagreement between the l-th and the m-th value of the k-th attribute. For nominal (unordered) discrete attributes, δ_{klm} is calculated so as

$$\delta_{klm} = \begin{cases} 1, & l \neq m \\ 0, & l = m \end{cases}$$

For ordinal (correctly ordered) discrete attributes, the set $\{\delta_{klm}\}$ should satisfy the monotonicity conditions:

$$\delta_{klm} < \delta_{klr}, \text{ if } l > m > r \text{ or } l < m < r$$

A contribution to dissimilarity d_{ij} between i-th and j-th example is defined by $d_{ijk} = \delta_{klm}$ if the k-th attribute has a value l for the i-th example, and value m for the j-th example. The overall measure of dissimilarity is defined by

$$d_{ij} = \frac{1}{a} \sum_{k=1}^{a} d_{ijk} \qquad (12.4)$$

where a is the number of discrete attributes. By division with a it is ensured that d_{ij} lies between 0 and 1.

12.2.2 Dissimilarity measures for continuous data

Dissimilarity measures for continuous attributes can be broadly divided into distance-type measures and correlation-type measures. Distance-type measures are formulated so as to allow for different weighting of continuous attributes. Let v_{ik} be the value that the k-th continuous attribute takes for the i-th example ($i = 1 \dots n$, $k = 1 \dots a$), and let w_k, $k = 1, \dots, a$ be non-negative weights associated with attributes, allowing standardization and weighting of the original attributes.

Minkowski metrics
This is a family of dissimilarity measures, determined by a parameter λ:

$$d_{ij} = \left(\sum_{k=1}^{a} w_k^{\lambda} \, |v_{ik} - v_{jk}|^{\lambda} \right)^{\frac{1}{\lambda}} \qquad (\lambda \geq 1) \qquad (12.5)$$

Minkowski metrics are most frequently used with $\lambda = 1$ or 2.

City block (manhattan) metric

$$d_{ij} = \left(\sum_{k=1}^{a} w_k \, |v_{ik} - v_{jk}| \right) \qquad (12.6)$$

This is the case of Minkowski metric with $\lambda = 1$.

Euclidean distance

$$d_{ij} = \left(\sum_{k=1}^{a} w_k^2 \, |v_{ik} - v_{jk}|^2 \right)^{\frac{1}{2}} \qquad (12.7)$$

This is the case of Minkowski metric with $\lambda = 2$.

Canberra metric

$$d_{ij} = \begin{cases} 0, & \text{for } v_{ik} = 0 = v_{jk} \\ \sum_{k=1}^{a} \frac{|v_{ik} - v_{jk}|}{|v_{ik}| + |v_{jk}|}, & \text{otherwise} \end{cases} \qquad (12.8)$$

The Canberra metric is very sensitive to small changes close to $v_{ik} = 0 = v_{jk}$; this makes it an appropriate generalization of dissimilarity measures for binary attributes. This measure is frequently normalized by dividing it with the number of attributes a.

The correlation-type measures of dissimilarity provide information about the relative magnitude of different attributes. Learning examples take the form of a vector with a components and the measure is restricted to the comparison of the directions of the vectors. Two frequently used correlation-type measures are the *angular separation* and the *correlation coefficient*. They both measure the cosine between two vectors, but differ in the way the vectors are measured, respectively from the origin and from the mean of the data. For this purpose, the cross-product (12.9) and the Pearson correlation index (12.10) are used.

Angular separation

$$\phi_{ij} = \frac{\sum_{k=1}^{a} v_{ik} v_{jk}}{\sqrt{\sum_{k=1}^{a} v_{ik}^2 \sum_{k=1}^{a} v_{jk}^2}} \qquad (12.9)$$

$$d_{ij} = \frac{1 - \phi_{ij}}{2}$$

Correlation coefficient

$$\overline{v}_i = \frac{1}{a} \sum_{k=1}^{a} v_{ik}$$

$$\phi_{ij} = \frac{\sum_{k=1}^{a} (v_{ik} - \overline{v}_i)(v_{jk} - \overline{v}_j)}{\sqrt{\sum_{k=1}^{a} (v_{ik} - \overline{v}_i)^2 \sum_{k=1}^{a} (v_{jk} - \overline{v}_j)^2}} \qquad (12.10)$$

$$d_{ij} = \frac{1 - \phi_{ij}}{2}$$

Since for both angular separation and correlation coefficient we have

$$-1 \le \phi_{ij} \le 1$$

with the value 1 reflecting the strongest positive relationship and the value -1 the strongest negative relationship, these coefficients are mapped into the $[0, 1]$ interval by taking $d_{ij} = (1 - \phi_{ij})/2$.

12.2.3 Dissimilarity measures for mixed data

Each of the previously mentioned dissimilarity measures is particularly appropriate for examples described by a single type of attribute. Frequently the attributes are of several different types: continuous, ordered discrete (ordinal) and unordered discrete (nominal). A general measure, which is relevant to all attribute types and hence can be used to compare examples described by attributes of mixed type is the general dissimilarity coefficient.

General dissimilarity coefficient

$$d_{ij} = \frac{\sum_{k=1}^{a} w_{ijk} d_{ijk}}{\sum_{k=1}^{a} w_{ijk}} \tag{12.11}$$

Here d_{ijk} denotes the dissimilarity contribution provided by the k-th attribute. w_{ijk} is usually 1 or 0 depending on whether or not the comparison is valid for the respective attribute. Dissimilarity contributions d_{ijk} can be defined for different attribute types in the spirit of measures (12.1) – (12.10).

12.2.4 Dissimilarity measures for groups of examples

Thus far, we have reviewed only dissimilarity measures between two individual examples. However, in clustering applications it is occasionally necessary to measure the (dis)similarity between groups of examples (clusters). Two basic approaches to define such an inter-group dissimilarity are based either on a summary of intra-group dissimilarities, or on a dissimilarity between representatives of each group, constructed by choosing a suitable summary statistic for each attribute.

There are several possibilities for deriving inter-group dissimilarities from the dissimilarity matrix. If we take the smallest dissimilarity between any two examples, one from each group, we speak of the *nearest neighbour dissimilarity* that is the basis for the *single linkage clustering* techniques. The opposite approach where we take the largest dissimilarity between any two examples, one from each group, we speak of the *furthest neighbour dissimilarity* which is the basis for the *complete linkage clustering* techniques. Instead of using extreme values, an inter-group dissimilarity can be defined also as the average dissimilarity between examples from both groups. This dissimilarity measure is used in the *average linkage clustering*.

For continuous data we can construct inter-group dissimilarity measures simply by substituting the attribute values with the group means. For example, for groups $\mathcal{A}$ and $\mathcal{B}$ we get by using the Euclidean distance measure:

$$d^2(\mathcal{A}, \mathcal{B}) = \sqrt{\sum_{k=1}^{a} \left(\overline{v}_k^{(\mathcal{A})} - \overline{v}_k^{(\mathcal{B})} \right)^2} \tag{12.12}$$

It is, however more appropriate to use measures which incorporate the knowledge of the within-group variation, such as the Mahalanobis distance D^2 given in a matrix form:

$$D^2(\mathcal{A}, \mathcal{B}) = (\overline{v}^{(\mathcal{A})} - \overline{v}^{(\mathcal{B})})^T \mathbf{W}^{-1} (\overline{v}^{(\mathcal{A})} - \overline{v}^{(\mathcal{B})}) \tag{12.13}$$

where $\mathcal{A}$ and $\mathcal{B}$ are groups, $\overline{v}^{(\mathcal{A})}$ and $\overline{v}^{(\mathcal{B})}$ the group mean vectors, and $\mathbf{W}$ is the pooled within-group covariance matrix[1] for the two groups.

12.2.5   Construction and choice of measures

As we can see from the previous sections, one can select from a vast number of dissimilarity measures. Unfortunately, there are no definitive rules on which measure to choose for a particular problem. A measure should have some favorable properties, such as scale of data, metric and Euclidean properties. Although they are not conclusive, since measures should be considered in the context of the study where they are used, including the nature of data and the type of analysis, there do exist some general guidelines.

- The nature of data should strongly influence the choice of dissimilarity measure. For example, when continuous attributes are noisy, or some relevant threshold values exist, it is best to discretize such attributes and use them as ordinal discrete attributes.

- The choice of dissimilarity measure should depend on the scale of the attribute values.

- The clustering method should influence the choice of dissimilarity measure.

There are also several practical considerations that need to be accounted for when constructing or modifying existing dissimilarity measures.

- *Weighting of attributes.* All the distance measures are constructed so as to enable a differential weighting of attributes, thus reflecting their importance in dissimilarity measures. But how should the weights be chosen? One common approach is to define the weights from the learning set of examples where the weight w_k of the k-th attribute is inversely proportional to some measure of variability in this attribute. Setting $w_k = 0$ effectively excludes the attribute from the process.

- *Standardization.* Often the attributes are not measured on the same scale, and even not in the same units. It is therefore insensible to use the original attribute values in dissimilarity measures. For continuous attributes the usual solution is to standardize each attribute to unit variance by using standard deviations calculated from the set of all examples, or to standardize each attribute by division with its sample range. Standardization is a special case of weighting where each weight is a reciprocal of the measure chosen to quantify the variability of an attribute.

- *Missing attribute values.* Such problems are common to all branches of data mining. They can occur for a variety of reasons and may be dealt with in a number of ways. The simplest way is to use only examples with a complete set of attribute values. However, this can considerably reduce the number

---

[1] For the definition of covariance matrix see Section A.4 in the appendix.

of examples available for clustering. Alternatively, one can use dissimilarity measures that can deal with missing values, such as the general dissimilarity coefficient (12.11). Another possibility is to estimate the missing values, e.g., by using an appropriate summary statistics.

12.3 HIERARCHICAL CLUSTERING

Divide and rule, the politician cries; unite and lead, is watchword of the wise.
— *Johann Wolfgang von Goethe*

Hierarchical algorithms can be agglomerative (bottom-up) or divisive (top-down). Agglomerative algorithms begin with each example as a separate cluster and merge them in successively larger clusters. Divisive algorithms begin with the whole set of examples and proceed to divide it into successively smaller clusters. Both approaches yield a hierarchy of clusters.

The traditional representation of cluster hierarchy is a *dendrogram* (Figure 12.2(a)), that is, a binary tree with individual examples at the leaves and a single cluster including all examples at the root. The height of the node corresponds to the value of the clustering criterion at this node. Agglomerative algorithms begin at the bottom of the tree, whereas divisive algorithms begin at the top.

Cutting the tree at a given height will give a clustering at a selected precision. Cutting higher in a tree gives a coarse clustering – one gets a few larger clusters, while by cutting lower one gets smaller clusters.

A dendrogram is usually accompanied by a *banner plot* (Figure 12.2(b)). A banner plot summarizes the hierarchy of clusters depicted by a dendrogram. The lengths of the bars correspond to the respective heights of internal nodes in the clustering hierarchy. Particularly for large datasets, such plots can assist the end user in the rapid identification of the membership of each cluster.

12.3.1 Agglomerative hierarchical clustering

Agglomerative hierarchical clustering methods build a hierarchy from individual elements by progressively merging clusters. The first step is to determine which elements to merge in a cluster. Usually, we want to take the two closest elements, therefore we must define a distance d_{ij} between examples with indices i and j and generalize it to clusters – sets of examples. Usually, distance measure $d(\mathcal{A}, \mathcal{B})$ between two clusters $\mathcal{A}$ and $\mathcal{B}$ is one of the following:

- the minimum distance between elements of each cluster (also called the single linkage clustering):

$$d(\mathcal{A}, \mathcal{B}) = \min_{i \in \mathcal{A}, \, j \in \mathcal{B}} d_{ij}$$

The dendrogram and the banner plot of the single linkage hierarchical clustering on the *swiss* dataset in shown in Figure 12.2.

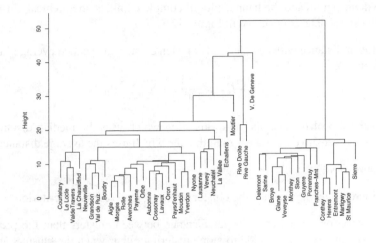

Agglomerative Coefficient = 0.77

(a) Dendrogram.

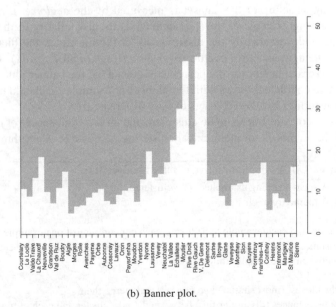

(b) Banner plot.

Figure 12.2: Results of the agglomerative hierarchical clustering (single linkage) on the swiss dataset.

- the maximum distance between elements of each cluster (complete linkage clustering):

$$d(\mathcal{A}, \mathcal{B}) = \max_{i \in \mathcal{A}, \, j \in \mathcal{B}} d_{ij}$$

The dendrogram and the banner plot of complete linkage hierarchical clustering on the *swiss* dataset in shown in Figure 12.3.

- the mean distance between elements of each cluster (also called average linkage clustering):

$$d(\mathcal{A}, \mathcal{B}) = \frac{1}{|\mathcal{A}|\,|\mathcal{B}|} \sum_{i \in \mathcal{A}} \sum_{j \in \mathcal{B}} d_{ij}$$

A variation of the average-link clustering which uses the median distance, is much less sensitive to outliers than the one which uses the average distance.

- the sum of all intra-cluster variance;

- the increase in variance for the cluster being merged (the Ward criterion).

Each agglomeration occurs at a greater distance between clusters than the previous agglomeration, and one can decide to stop clustering either when the clusters are too far apart to be merged (the distance criterion) or when there is a sufficiently small number of clusters (the number criterion).

Clustering structure of the dataset is measured by the *agglomerative coefficient*. For each learning example t_i, $m(i)$ is defined as its dissimilarity to the first cluster it is merged with, divided by the dissimilarity of the merger in the final step of the algorithm. The agglomerative coefficient is the average of all $1 - m(i)$. It can also be seen as the average height (or the percentage grayed) of the banner plot. Because the agglomerative coefficient grows with the number of examples, it should not be used to compare clusterings between datasets of very different sizes.

Given a set of n examples to be clustered, and an $n \times n$ distance (or dissimilarity) matrix, the basic process of hierarchical clustering is shown in Algorithm 12.1.

Algorithm 12.1 Basic agglomerative clustering algorithm.

INPUT: A set of learning examples to be clustered.
OUTPUT: A hierarchy of clusters.

Start by assigning each example to a cluster, each containing just one example.
Let the distances (dissimilarities) between the clusters be the same as the distances (dissimilarities) between the examples they contain.
repeat
   Find the closest (most similar) two clusters and merge them
   Compute distances (dissimilarities) between the new cluster and each of the old clusters.
until all examples are clustered into a single cluster.

The complete linkage clustering produces tightly bound or compact clusters. The single linkage algorithm, by contrast, has a tendency to produce elongated clusters (it suffers from a chaining effect – compact clusters connected by bridges of noisy examples). This can be clearly seen from dendrograms in Figures 12.2 and 12.3 both by visual inspection and by the agglomerative criterion (0.77 vs. 0.89).

Otherwise, the single linkage algorithm is more versatile than the complete linkage algorithm and has several desirable theoretical properties. However, from a pragmatic viewpoint, it has been observed that the complete linkage algorithm often produces more useful hierarchies than the single linkage algorithm.

Although agglomerative strategies are well studied and easy to implement, they have some weaknesses that limit their usefulness in practice:

- they do not scale well: their time complexity[2] is at least $O(n^2)$, where n is the number of examples;

- they can never undo what was done previously, so the algorithm could not repair a mistake it made in an earlier phase even when it would detect it.

12.3.2 Divisive hierarchical clustering

Divisive hierarchical clustering does the reverse of the agglomerative by starting with all examples in one cluster and subdividing them into smaller clusters. Divisive methods are significantly less popular than agglomerative. They are computationally demanding if all $2^{n-1} - 1$ possible divisions of a cluster of n examples into two sub-clusters are considered in each step. However, for data consisting solely of binary attributes, relatively simple and computationally effective *monothetic divisive methods* are available. The term monothetic refers to the use of a single attribute that is used to split at a given step. On the other hand *polythetic divisive methods* use all attributes at each step. While divisive methods are less commonly used than agglomerative methods, they have an important advantage. Most users are interested in the main structure in their data, and this is revealed in the beginning (first few partitions) of a divisive method.

Monothetic divisive methods

In monothetic divisive methods a split of a cluster is made by choosing the attribute that optimizes a criterion reflecting either the cluster homogeneity or the association with other attributes, thus minimizing the number of cluster splits. An example of the homogeneity criterion is the *information content* C (that in our case signifies disorder or *chaos*), defined by a attributes and n examples:

$$C = a\,n \log n - \sum_{i=1}^{a} \left(n_i \log n_i - (n - n_i) \log(n - n_i)\right) \qquad (12.14)$$

where n_i is the number of examples having attribute i equal to 1. If a cluster $\mathcal{A}$ is to be split into clusters $\mathcal{B}$ and $\mathcal{C}$, the reduction in C is $C_{\mathcal{A}} - C_{\mathcal{B}} - C_{\mathcal{C}}$. The ideal set of clusters

---

[2]For definition of O-notation see Section A.2 in the appendix.

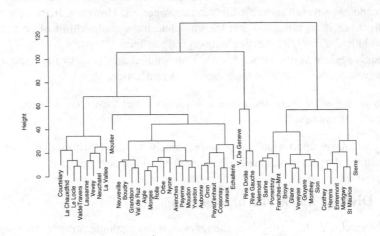

Agglomerative Coefficient = 0.89
(a) Dendrogram.

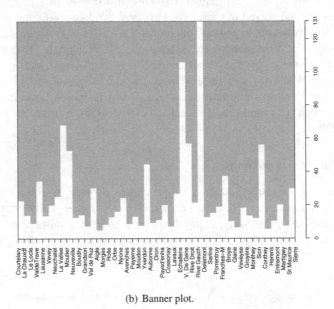

(b) Banner plot.

Figure 12.3: Results of the agglomerative hierarchical clustering (complete linkage) on the swiss dataset.

would have members with identical attribute values and $C = 0$. Therefore, at each step clusters are split according to an attribute that leads to the greatest reduction in C. This approach closely resembles building decision trees in machine learning (compare with Section 9.1).

Instead of measuring the cluster homogeneity, an overall association within attributes can be considered in each step. Let the observed frequencies be defined as in Table 12.1.

	1	0	A_j
1	a	b	
0	c	d	
A_i			

Table 12.1: Observed frequencies used for calculating the association criteria between attributes (for example, a is the number of all examples with value 1 for both attributes A_i and A_j). The number of all examples is $n = a + b + c + d$.

Some frequently used measures of association, summed over all pairs of attributes, are:

$$|ad - bc| \tag{12.15}$$

$$(ad - bc)^2 \tag{12.16}$$

$$\frac{(ad - bc)^2 n}{(a + b)(a + c)(b + d)(c + d)} \tag{12.17}$$

$$\sqrt{\frac{(ad - bc)^2 n}{(a + b)(a + c)(b + d)(c + d)}} \tag{12.18}$$

$$\frac{(ad - bc)^2}{(a + b)(a + c)(b + d)(c + d)} \tag{12.19}$$

At each step, the cluster split is made according to the values of an attribute whose association with the others is maximal. Of the above criteria, (12.15) and (12.16) have the advantage that there is no danger of numerical problems (division by zero) if any of the frequencies from Table 12.1 is zero. Criteria (12.17), (12.18) and (12.19) are related to the χ^2 statistic, squared root of χ^2 statistic, and the Pearson correlation coefficient, respectively.

Monothetic divisive methods possess several appealing features. Among them are easy classification of new examples, and handling of examples with missing attribute values by utilizing association between attributes. An important advantage is also their transparency; it is easy to see which attribute has produced a cluster split. They are therefore most popular in areas such as medical diagnostics, where the transparency is of utmost importance.

Polythetic divisive methods

Polythetic divisive methods are similar to agglomerative methods in the sense that they produce splits according to all attributes, and can work with a dissimilarity matrix. As all divisive methods, they work around the potential problem of considering all possible splits by using heuristic methods. Algorithm 12.2 describes a basic polythetic divisive clustering algorithm. The dendrogram and the banner plot of polythetic divisive hierarchical clustering on the *swiss* dataset in shown in Figure 12.4.

Algorithm 12.2 Polythetic divisive clustering algorithm.

INPUT: A set of learning examples to be clustered.
OUTPUT: A hierarchy of clusters.

    Let all examples be elements of the same cluster $\mathcal{A}$
    Let $C = \{\mathcal{A}\}$ (set of clusters)
    repeat
        Let cluster $\mathcal{X} \in C$ be largest in diameter (defined by the largest dissimilarity between two elements)
        Find an example $s \in \mathcal{X}$ that is farthest away from all other examples within the cluster $\mathcal{X}$
        Let s be the seed element for a new cluster $\mathcal{S}$ (splinter cluster), i.e. $\mathcal{S} = \{s\}$.
        for each example $e \in \mathcal{X}$ **do**
            if e is closer to $\mathcal{S}$ than to $\mathcal{X}$ -$\{e\}$ **then**
                move e from $\mathcal{X}$ to $\mathcal{S}$
            end if
            Let $C = C \cup \{S\}$
        end for
    until all clusters consist of single examples

Clustering structure of the dataset is measured by the *divisive coefficient*. For each learning example t_i, $d(i)$ is defined as the diameter of the last cluster to which it belongs (before being split off as a single observation), divided by the diameter of the whole dataset. The divisive coefficient is the average of all $1 - d(i)$. Just like the agglomerative coefficient, the divisive coefficient can also be seen as the average width (or the percentage grayed) of the banner plot. Because the divisive coefficient grows with the number of observations, it should not be used to compare clusterings between datasets of very different sizes.

12.3.3   Practical considerations

Hierarchical methods form the backbone of cluster analysis in practice. They are widely available in statistical software packages and easy to use. However the user has to select the measure of dissimilarity, the clustering method, and (implicitly) the number of clusters, explicitly specified by the clustering level. In practice the main problem is that no particular clustering method can be recommended in advance, since methods with favorable mathematical properties (e.g, single linkage) often do not produce empirically interpretable results. In addition, to use the results one must

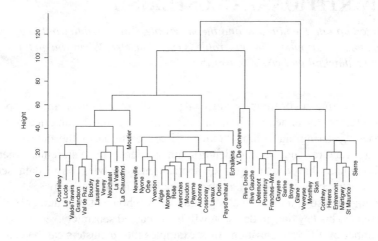

Divisive Coefficient = 0.88
(a) Dendrogram.

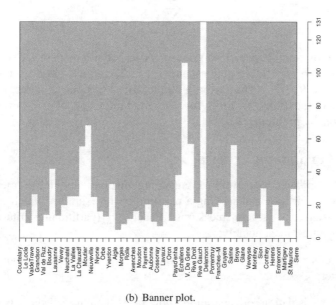

(b) Banner plot.

Figure 12.4: Results of the divisive hierarchical clustering on the swiss dataset.

choose the partition, and the best way of doing this is unclear (often left to the end user). When there is no underlying hierarchy it is often better to use partitional methods.

12.4   PARTITIONAL CLUSTERING

Life is divided up into the horrible and the miserable. The horrible would be terminal cases, blind people, cripples. The miserable is everyone else. When you go through life you should be thankful that you're miserable.

— Woody Allen

Partitional clustering algorithms produce a partition of examples into a specified number of clusters by either minimizing or maximizing some numerical criterion. A partitional clustering algorithm obtains a single partition of the data instead of a clustering structure, such as the dendrogram produced by hierarchical methods. Partitional methods have advantages in applications involving large data sets for which the construction of a dendrogram is computationally prohibitive. A problem accompanying the use of a partitional algorithm is the choice of the number of desired output clusters. This key design decision will be discussed separately.

The number of different partitions of n examples into g clusters can be calculated by applying the following formula:

$$N(n, g) = \frac{1}{g!} \sum_{m=1}^{g} (-1)^{g-m} \binom{g}{m} m^n \qquad (12.20)$$

The number of possible partitions grows very fast. For a moderately small clustering problem with $n = 100$ examples and $g = 5$ required clusters, this number is $N(100, 5) \approx 6.6 \cdot 10^{67}$. Thus, even with the fastest computers, combinatorial search of the set of possible labelings for an optimum value of a criterion is clearly computationally prohibitive.

12.4.1   Partitioning criteria

A general approach to partitional clustering involves defining a measure of the adequacy of a partition and seeking a partition of the examples which optimizes that measure. There exist several measures of adequacy (partitioning criteria), based on cluster properties, most notably:

- cluster's compactness: how dissimilar are examples that lie within the same cluster;

- cluster's isolation, or separation: how far is the cluster from other clusters (or from the rest of examples).

Some clustering criteria can be used only when all attributes are continuous, whereas others can use a dissimilarity matrix. We review them separately, after defining an overall clustering criterion.

Having chosen a measure $h(\mathcal{C})$ of the cluster's compactness or isolation, an overall clustering criterion can be defined by a suitable aggregation over all clusters. Let C be the current partition consisting of g clusters: $C = \{\mathcal{C}_1, \ldots \mathcal{C}_g\}$. There are several possibilities for defining an aggregation function:

$$c(n, g) = \sum_{\mathcal{C} \in C} \frac{h(\mathcal{C})}{|\mathcal{C}|} \tag{12.21}$$

$$c(n, g) = \max_{\mathcal{C} \in C} h(\mathcal{C}) \tag{12.22}$$

$$c(n, g) = \min_{\mathcal{C} \in C} h(\mathcal{C}) \tag{12.23}$$

Criterion (12.21) reflects the average compactness, whereas criteria (12.22) and (12.23) reflect the compactness of the worst and the best cluster, respectively. When dealing with compactness criteria (12.24–12.28), a partitioning that either minimizes or maximizes the chosen aggregate criterion $c(n, g)$ is sought. When considering isolation criteria (12.29–12.30), the aim is to maximize $c(n, g)$.

Partitioning criteria for continuous data

The most commonly used partitioning criterion for continuous data (all attributes are continuous) is the *sum of squares*. This is a measure of cluster compactness based on the squared Euclidean distance measured from the cluster center (centroid) defined with mean attribute values of all examples:

$$h(\mathcal{C}) = \sum_{k \in \mathcal{C}} \sum_{i=1}^{a} (v_{ki} - \bar{t}_i^{(\mathcal{C})})^2 \tag{12.24}$$

Here $\bar{t}_i^{(\mathcal{C})}$ is the mean value for the i-th attribute for cluster $\mathcal{C}$:

$$\bar{t}_i^{(\mathcal{C})} = \frac{1}{|\mathcal{C}|} \sum_{k \in \mathcal{C}} t_{ki}$$

Another frequently used partitioning criterion for continuous data is L_1 *measure* (12.25). It is a measure of cluster compactness based on the manhattan distance measured from the cluster center (centroid) defined with median attribute values of all examples:

$$h(\mathcal{C}) = \sum_{k \in \mathcal{C}} \sum_{i=1}^{a} |x_{ki} - m_i^{(\mathcal{C})}| \tag{12.25}$$

Here $m_i^{(\mathcal{C})}$ is the median value for the i-th attribute for the cluster $\mathcal{C}$ in question:

$$m_i^{(\mathcal{C})} = \underset{k \in \mathcal{C}}{\text{median}} \{x_{ki}\}$$

Partitioning criteria derived from the dissimilarity matrix

The *diameter* criterion is a measure of cluster compactness that measures the dissimilarity between the most dissimilar pair of examples from the same cluster:

$$h(\mathcal{C}) = \max_{i,j \in \mathcal{C}} d_{ij} \tag{12.26}$$

The *star* criterion is a measure of cluster compactness named by the shape of the graph formed by linking together all pairs of examples whose pairwise dissimilarities are included in the sum:

$$h(\mathcal{C}) = \min_{i \in \mathcal{C}} \sum_{j \in \mathcal{C}} d_{ij} \tag{12.27}$$

The *sum of distances* criterion is a measure of cluster compactness calculated as the sum of all pairwise dissimilarities (the elements of the lower triangular matrix):

$$h(\mathcal{C}) = \sum_{\substack{i,j \in \mathcal{C} \\ j < i}} d_{ij} \tag{12.28}$$

The *split* criterion is a measure of cluster isolation that measures the smallest dissimilarity between an example in the cluster and an example outside the cluster:

$$h(\mathcal{C}) = \min_{i \in \mathcal{C}, j \notin \mathcal{C}} d_{ij} \tag{12.29}$$

The *cut* criterion is a measure of cluster isolation that measures the sum of the dissimilarities between examples in the cluster and examples outside the cluster:

$$h(\mathcal{C}) = \sum_{i \in \mathcal{C}} \sum_{j \notin \mathcal{C}} d_{ij} \tag{12.30}$$

12.4.2 Partitional algorithms

The problem of infeasible exhaustive search of all possible partitions has led to design of *iterative relocation* algorithms that perform the search by local optimization (see Section 5.6). These algorithms involve a specification of an initial partition of examples into g clusters and a set of allowable transformations for changing a partition into another partition.

An initial partition can be obtained in several ways. It may be given as a part of the background knowledge, it may be a result of other clustering methods, or it may be chosen at random. Allowable transformations move either a single example, or all applicable examples simultaneously, from their original cluster to another cluster whose mean or median is closest to them. The basic iterative relocation algorithm is sketched in Algorithm 12.3 and can be repeated several times with different initial partitions.

Algorithm 12.3 The basic iterative relocation algorithm

INPUT: A set of learning examples to be clustered, and the number g of desired clusters.
OUTPUT: Partition of learning examples into g clusters.

Find some partition of n examples into g clusters
  repeat
      Calculate the change in the clustering criterion produced by applying allowable transformations
      Make the change which leads to the greatest improvement of the clustering criterion
  until the clustering criterion stops improving

K-means

By far the most popular partitional algorithm is the *k-means*. This is a squared error algorithm, meaning that it uses a squared Euclidean distance (sum of squares) for the optimization criterion. It is also one of the simplest and the fastest clustering algorithms. It assigns each example to the cluster whose center (centroid) is the nearest. The center is the mean of all the examples in the cluster, i.e. its coordinates are the arithmetic mean for each dimension separately for all the examples in the cluster. For the data set with a attributes and the cluster with two examples $x = (x_1, \ldots, x_a)$ and $y = (y_1, \ldots, y_a)$, the centroid z is calculated as $z = (z_1, \ldots, z_a)$, where $z_i = (x_i + y_i)/2$, $i = 1 \ldots a$. Because of its nature, the k-means algorithm can be used only if all attributes are continuous (or treated as such).

The basic structure of the k-means algorithm is shown in Algorithm 12.4. It is similar to (yet more specific than) that of the more general iterative relocation algorithms. The main advantages of the k-means algorithm are its simplicity and speed,

---

Algorithm 12.4 The k-means algorithm.

INPUT: A set of learning examples to be clustered, and the number k of desired clusters.
OUTPUT: Partition of learning examples into k clusters.

Randomly generate k clusters and determine the cluster centers or directly generate k seed examples as cluster centers
  repeat
      Assign each example to the nearest cluster center
      Recompute the new cluster centers
  until no example has changed from one cluster to another.

---

which allows it to run it on large datasets. Because of a random initial clustering it does not yield the same result with each run of the algorithm. It is very important how initial centroids are placed, because different locations cause significantly different results. Often it is best to place them as far away from each other as possible.

While the k-means algorithm maximizes inter-cluster (or equivalently, minimizes intra-cluster) dissimilarity, it does not ensure that the obtained solution is a global minimum. There exist some approaches such as *global k-means* that aim to alleviate this problem.

Global k-means

The global k-means is an initialization independent deterministic clustering method that initially starts with one centroid and sequentially adds one centroid at a time until a maximum number of clusters max_k is reached. A solution with k centroids is obtained by exploiting the solution with $k-1$ centroids using a search algorithm that consists of a series of executions of the k-means algorithm from suitable candidate initial positions of the k centroids. An interesting byproduct of the approach is that it provides solutions for every number of clusters $k = 1, \ldots, M$. Its drawback is that it is computationally expensive for large datasets.

Partitioning around medoids

The partitioning around medoids (PAM) algorithm is based on the search for k representative examples or medoids (star centers, see Section 12.4.1). These examples represent the structure of the data. After finding a set of k medoids, k clusters are constructed by assigning each example to its nearest medoid. The goal is to find k representative examples which minimize the sum of dissimilarities of all examples to their closest representative examples.

When compared with the k-means algorithm, PAM has the following advantages:

- It is more general because it can deal with all types of attributes and all dissimilarity measures. It operates on a dissimilarity matrix of the given data set.

- It is more robust, because it minimizes a sum of dissimilarities instead of a sum of squared Euclidean distances.

- It assists the user in selecting the optimal number of clusters because it provides an alternative graphical technique – the silhouette plot, described below and depicted in Figure 12.5(b).

Algorithm 12.5 shows the structure of the PAM algorithm. It consists of two phases: a build phase and a swap phase. If medoids are not specified as a part of the background knowledge, the algorithm first looks for a good initial set of medoids (build phase). Then it finds a local optimum for the clustering criterion function, that is, a solution such that there is no single swap of a non-medoid example with a medoid that will improve the criterion (swap phase).

Silhouette plots

Silhouette plots summarize for each example how appropriate its cluster is. A silhouette of a cluster is a plot of "suitability values" $s(i)$ ranked in decreasing order for all the examples in the cluster. The plot of an example is a horizontal line, with the length proportional to $s(i)$. The silhouette shows which examples lie well within the

---

Algorithm 12.5 Partitioning around medoids algorithm

INPUT: A set of learning examples to be clustered, and the number k of desired clusters.
OUTPUT: Partition of learning examples into k clusters.

{ Build phase }
Sequentially select k centrally located examples, to be used as initial medoids
{ Swap phase }
repeat
    Assign each example to the cluster represented by the most similar medoid
    for each medoid i **do**
        for each non-medoid example j **do**
            calculate the change in clustering criterion C_{ij} when swapping j and i
            if C_{ij} has improved **then**
                swap i and j
            end if
        end for
    end for
until there is no change in clusters

---

cluster and which ones are merely somewhere in between clusters. A wide silhouette indicates large $s(i)$ values and hence a pronounced cluster. The height of a cluster is simply equal to the number of examples in the cluster (see Figure 12.5(b)).

The entire silhouette plot shows the silhouettes of all clusters next to each other, so that the quality of clusters can be compared. The overall average silhouette width of the silhouette plot is the average of $s(i)$ over all examples in the data set.

The silhouette plot is quite useful for deciding the number of clusters. One can run a clustering algorithm (e.g. partitioning around medoids) several times, each time for different values of k and then compare the resulting silhouette plots. The average silhouette width can be used to select the best number of clusters (by choosing that k which yields the highest average silhouette width). Average silhouette width values can be interpreted as follows:

$0.70 - 1.00$	A strong structure has been found.
$0.50 - 0.70$	A reasonable structure has been found.
$0.25 - 0.50$	The structure is weak and could be artificial.
< 0.25	No substantial structure has been found.

While silhouette plots were developed in conjunction with partitioning algorithms, they can easily be used in other clustering methods and adapted by a suitable definition of the suitability values $s(i) \in [-1, 1]$. When the i-th example has a value of $s(i)$ close to 1, it is nearer to its own cluster than to the neighboring clusters, and is therefore well clustered. When an example has $s(i)$ close to -1, the opposite holds, and the example is taken to be badly clustered.

Originally, $s(i)$ is defined as the standardized difference between $a(i)$ and $b(i)$, where $a(i)$ is the average dissimilarity between the i-th example and all other examples from its own cluster, and $b(i)$ is is the average dissimilarity between the i-th example and all examples from the nearest cluster.

For partitional methods, clusters can be visualized by reducing the attribute space to two dimensions (e.g., with the principal component analysis (PCA) by selecting the largest two components), and accompanied by silhouette plots. An example of partitioning the *swiss* datasets into three clusters is shown in Figure 12.5.

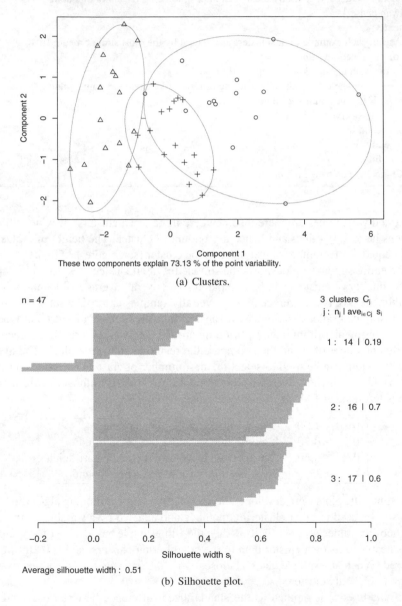

(a) Clusters.

(b) Silhouette plot.

Figure 12.5: Results of the partitioning around medoids clustering on the *swiss* dataset. Low silhouette widths for the first cluster suggest that this cluster might be artificial.

12.4.3   Number of clusters

A crucial parameter in the partitional clustering is the number of clusters which has to be given in advance. It may be given as a part of the background knowledge or chosen by the end user. A variety of methods have been suggested which may be helpful in particular situations. Most are relatively informal and essentially work by visualizing the value of the clustering criterion against the number of clusters. Large bumps in the plot are usually considered as indicators for an appropriate number of clusters. Obviously, these methods are highly subjective. Several more formal techniques have been suggested which try to overcome the subjectivity problem. However, there have been only limited investigations of their properties.

The most common approach is to obtain a complete hierarchy of clusterings using an agglomerative approach. The set of partitions is then examined for all numbers of clusters $1 \leq g \leq n$ in an attempt to determine the most appropriate value for g by utilizing some *stopping rule*. Two categories of stopping rules exist: global and local.

Global stopping rules

Global rules evaluate a criterion function $G(c)$ based on the within-cluster and between-cluster variability, and identify the optimal value for the number of clusters. They are based on the complete set of available examples.

Let $G(c)$ be the criterion function calculated for the fixed value of the number (c) of clusters in a given hierarchy. The optimal number of clusters is obtained by maximizing its value over all possible values of c:

$$g = \underset{c \in \{1...n\}}{\operatorname{argmax}} \{G(c)\} \qquad (12.31)$$

The optimal clustering from the clustering hierarchy is subsequently used as an initial clustering in a partitional clustering algorithm with g clusters. Since some criterion functions display distracting behaviour for large values of c, the value of c is usually restricted only to smaller values. An example of a global criterion function is

$$G(c) = \frac{B}{c-1} \bigg/ \frac{W}{n-c} \qquad (12.32)$$

where B and W respectively denote the total within-cluster sum of squared distances to the centroids, and the total between-cluster sum of squared distances.

Local stopping rules

Local rules involve examining whether a pair of smaller clusters should be amalgamated (or a single cluster should be subdivided). Unlike global rules, they are based only on a partial set of examples and can assess only hierarchically-nested partitions.

Local stopping rules are frequently based on statistical tests. For example, a local stopping rule can be based on comparing the within-cluster sum of squared distances (W_1) with the sum of within-cluster sum of squared distances when the cluster was optimally divided into two (W_2). If the cluster contains m examples described by a attributes, the hypothesis that the cluster is homogeneous (and should not be subdivided) is rejected if

$$\frac{W_2}{W_1} < 1 - \frac{2}{\pi \, a} - \alpha \sqrt{\frac{2(1 - \frac{8}{\pi^2 a})}{m \, a}} \qquad (12.33)$$

where α is the significance level of the test.

12.5   MODEL-BASED CLUSTERING

I don't know half of you half as well as I should like; and I like less than half of you half as well as you deserve.

— J. R. R. Tolkien

One possible taxonomy of clustering algorithms, based on partitional vs. hierarchical clustering dichotomy, is shown in Figure 12.1. There is, however, also a fundamental distinction between discriminative (or dissimilarity-based) approaches and generative (or model-based) approaches to clustering. In discriminative approaches, one computes a distance or a dissimilarity function between pairs of examples and then groups similar examples together into clusters. Parametric, model-based approaches, on the other hand, attempt to learn generative models from the data, with each model representing one particular cluster. The number of required clusters must often be specified in advance.

For model-based clustering approaches, the model type is specified a priori, such as a Gaussian or a hidden Markov model (HMM). The model structure (e.g., the number of hidden states in an HMM) can be determined by model selection techniques and parameters estimated by using some maximum likelihood algorithm, e.g., the expectation-maximization (EM) algorithm. Probabilistic model-based clustering techniques have shown promising results in a corpus of applications. Gaussian mixture models are the most popular models used for vector data. Multinomial models have been shown to be effective for high-dimensional text clustering. For clustering more complex data such as time sequences, the dominant models are Markov chains and hidden Markov models.

Compared to similarity-based methods, the model-based methods offer better interpretability since the resulting model for each cluster directly characterizes the cluster. The model-based partitional clustering algorithms often have a computational complexity that is linear in the number of examples under certain practical assumptions. By far the most popular are models based on finite mixture models. Other advantages of model-based clustering include the flexibility in choosing the component distribution, the availability of a soft cluster membership, the availability of well-studied statistical inference techniques, and the availability of a density estimation for each cluster.

12.5.1   Finite mixture models

In (finite) mixture models, each cluster is represented by a parametric distribution, like a Gaussian (continuous) or a Poisson (discrete) distribution. The entire data set is therefore modeled by a mixture of these distributions. An individual distribution used to model a specific cluster is often referred to as a component distribution.

A mixture model with high likelihood tends to have the following traits:

- component distributions have high peaks (data in one cluster are tight),

- the mixture model covers the data well (dominant patterns in the data are captured by component distributions).

Finite mixture densities are a family of probability density functions of the form

$$f(t; p, \theta) = \sum_{j=1}^{c} p_j g_j(t; \theta_j) \tag{12.34}$$

where t is an a-dimensional random variable (whose instantiations are learning examples), $p = (p_1, \ldots, p_c)^T$ is a vector of mixing proportions ($p_i \geq 0$, $\sum_i p_i = 1$), $\theta = (\theta_1, \ldots, \theta_c)^T$ is a vector of density parameters, with density g_j being parameterized with θ_j and weighted with p_j, and c is the number of components forming the mixture and ultimately corresponds to the number of clusters.

Finite mixtures are a suitable model for cluster analysis under the assumption that each group of examples suspected of containing clusters comes from a population with a different probability distribution. These probability distributions may come from the same family, but differ in values of distribution parameters. For example, when the component densities are Gaussian (multivariate normal), they may have different mean vectors and possibly different covariance matrices. The parameters of the assumed mixture distributions are estimated so as to maximize their likelihood, by utilizing the *expectation-maximization* (EM) algorithm.

Having estimated the parameters $\hat{p}$ and $\hat{\theta}$, an example (t_i) can be associated with a particular cluster ($\mathcal{C}_k$) on the basis of the maximum value of the estimated posterior probability:

$$P(\mathcal{C}_k | t_i) = \frac{\hat{p}_k g_k(t_i; \hat{\theta}_k)}{\sum_{j=1}^{c} \hat{p}_j g_j(t_i; \hat{\theta}_j)} \quad \text{for } k = 1, 2, \ldots, c \tag{12.35}$$

12.5.2   Maximum likelihood estimation and EM algorithm

In the maximum-likelihood estimation problem we have a density function $f(t|\theta)$ that is governed by the set of parameters θ. We also have a learning set of n examples, drawn from the same distribution, i.e., $\mathcal{T} = \{t_1, \ldots, t_n\}$. We assume that these data vectors are independent and identically distributed (*iid*) with respect to distribution f. The resulting density for the examples is therefore

$$f(\mathcal{T}|\theta) = \prod_{l=1}^{n} f(t_l|\theta) = \mathcal{L}(\theta) \tag{12.36}$$

The function $\mathcal{L}(\theta)$ is called the *likelihood* of the parameters given the data, or just the likelihood function. The likelihood is thought of as a function of the parameters θ where the data $\mathcal{T}$ is fixed. In the maximum likelihood problem, our goal is to find the θ that maximizes $\mathcal{L}$. That is, we wish to find θ^* which maximizes the likelihood $\mathcal{L}$

$$\theta^* = \underset{\theta}{\operatorname{argmax}} \{\mathcal{L}(\theta)\} \tag{12.37}$$

or (because it is analytically easier)

$$\theta^* = \underset{\theta}{\operatorname{argmax}} \{\log \mathcal{L}(\theta)\} \tag{12.38}$$

that maximizes the *log-likelihood*. Since in many cases the maximization of $\mathcal{L}(\theta)$ (or $\log \mathcal{L}(\theta)$) cannot be performed analytically, more elaborate techniques have to be deployed, and the *EM algorithm* (expectation-maximization algorithm) is one of them.

EM algorithm

Expectation-maximization (EM) is a description of a family of related algorithms, not a specific algorithm. Therefore, EM is a meta-algorithm which is used to devise particular algorithms. The EM algorithm for fitting a mixture density model is one particular example from this family. Another example, applied to hidden Markov models, is the Baum-Welch algorithm.

There are two main applications of the EM algorithm. The first is when the data indeed has missing values, due to problems with or limitations of the observation process. The second (more frequent) is when optimizing the likelihood function is analytically intractable but can be simplified by assuming the existence of additional but missing (or unobservable) variables.

We assume that data $\mathcal{T}$ is observed and is generated by some distribution. We call $\mathcal{T}$ the incomplete data. We also assume that a complete data set exists $\mathcal{X} = (\mathcal{T}, \mathcal{Z})$ and that its joint density function is:

$$f(\mathcal{X}|\theta) = f(\mathcal{T}, \mathcal{Z}|\theta) = f(\mathcal{Z}|\mathcal{T}, \theta)f(\mathcal{T}|\theta) \tag{12.39}$$

With this new density function, we can define a new likelihood function,

$$\mathcal{L}(\theta|\mathcal{X}) = \mathcal{L}(\theta|\mathcal{T}, \mathcal{Z}) = f(\mathcal{T}, \mathcal{Z}|\theta) \tag{12.40}$$

called the *complete-data likelihood*. Note that this function is in fact a random variable since the missing information $\mathcal{Z}$ is unknown, random, and presumably governed by an underlying distribution. That is, we can think of $\mathcal{L}(\theta|\mathcal{T}, \mathcal{Z}) = h_{\mathcal{T},\theta}(\mathcal{Z})$ for some function $h_{\mathcal{T},\theta}(\cdot)$ where $\mathcal{T}$ and θ are constant and $\mathcal{Z}$ is a random variable. The original likelihood $\mathcal{L}(\theta|\mathcal{T})$ is referred to as the *incomplete-data likelihood* function.

The EM meta-algorithm is a general method of finding the maximum-likelihood estimate of the parameters of an underlying distribution from a given data set when the data is incomplete or has missing values or unobservable (latent) variables. EM is frequently used for data clustering, especially in machine learning and computer vision.

It alternates between taking an expectation (E-step), which computes the expected value of the latent variables, and performing a maximization (M-step), which computes the maximum likelihood estimates of the parameters given the data and setting the latent variables to their expectation.

E-step: since the $\mathcal{Z}$ values are unobservable, the EM first finds the expected value of the complete-data log-likelihood for $\log f(\mathcal{T}, \mathcal{Z}|\theta)$ with respect to the unobservable data $\mathcal{Z}$ given the observed data $\mathcal{T}$ and the current parameter estimates. This expectation is usually denoted as $\mathcal{Q}$:

$$Q(\theta|\theta^{(i)}) \quad = \quad E\left[\log \mathcal{L}(\theta|\mathcal{T}, \mathcal{Z})\,\Big|\,\mathcal{T}, \theta^{(i)}\right] \tag{12.41}$$

In the first step only the fixed, data-dependent parameters of function $\mathcal{Q}$ are calculated. Once the parameters of $\mathcal{Q}$ are known, it is fully determined and maximized in the second (M) step.

M-step: in this step EM iteratively improves the initial estimate θ_0 and constructs new estimates $\theta^{(1)}, \ldots, \theta^{(N)}$. An individual re-estimation step that derives $\theta^{(i+1)}$ from $\theta^{(i)}$ takes the following form (shown for the discrete case; the continuous case is similar):

$$\theta^{(i+1)} = \underset{\theta}{\mathrm{argmax}}\left\{Q(\theta|\theta^{(i)})\right\} \tag{12.42}$$

In other words, $\theta^{(i+1)}$ is the value that maximizes the expectation of the complete data log-likelihood with respect to the conditional distribution of the latent data under the previous parameter value $\theta^{(i)}$.

These two steps are repeated as necessary. It can be proved that each iteration is guaranteed to increase the log-likelihood, that the algorithm is guaranteed to converge to a local maximum of the likelihood function, and that the only stationary points of the iteration are the stationary points of the observed data likelihood function. In practice, this means that the EM algorithm will always converge to a local maximum of the observed data likelihood function.

EM algorithm is particularly useful when the maximum likelihood estimation of a complete data model is easy. A classic example is maximum likelihood estimation of a finite mixture of Gaussians, where each component of the mixture can be readily estimated from data.

If the j-th component destiny is Gaussian (multivariate normal) with mean vector

$$\mu_j = \left(\mu_j^{(1)}, \mu_j^{(2)}, \ldots, \mu_j^{(a)}\right)^T$$

and covariance matrix

$$\Sigma_j = \left[\sigma_j^{(i,k)}\right] \quad \text{where } i = 1 \ldots a, \; k = 1 \ldots a,$$

the maximum likelihood results in the following equations:

$$\hat{p}_j \;=\; \frac{1}{n} \sum_{i=1}^{n} P(\mathcal{C}_j|t_i) \tag{12.43}$$

$$\hat{\mu}_j \;=\; \frac{1}{n\hat{p}_j} \sum_{i=1}^{n} t_i P(\mathcal{C}_j|t_i) \tag{12.44}$$

$$\hat{\Sigma}_j \;=\; \frac{1}{n} \sum_{i=1}^{n} (t_i - \hat{\mu}_j)(t_i - \hat{\mu}_j)^T P(\mathcal{C}_j|t_i) \tag{12.45}$$

Here, $P(\mathcal{C}_j|t_i)$ are the estimated posterior probabilities from Equation 12.35. Initial posterior probabilities are calculated from given initial parameter estimates which are subsequently iteratively optimized with the EM algorithm until some suitable convergence criterion is satisfied. Initial parameter estimates for $\hat{\mu}_j$, $\hat{\Sigma}_j$, and $\hat{p}$ can be obtained with k-means clustering.

12.6　OTHER CLUSTERING METHODS

All animals are equal but some animals are more equal than others.

— George Orwell

12.6.1　Fuzzy clustering

One of the problems of the usual (crisp) clustering algorithms is that they give a hard partitioning of the data, that is to say that each example is attributed to one and only one cluster. But examples on the edge of the cluster, or near another cluster, may not be as much in the cluster as examples in the center of the cluster.

This problem is addressed by the fuzzy clustering algorithms. In fuzzy clusters, an example does not belong to a given cluster, but has a degree of belonging to the cluster, as in fuzzy logic. For each example t we have a coefficient giving the degree $u_k(t)$ of membership to the k-th cluster. Normally, the sum of those coefficients is 1, so $u_k(t)$ may denote a probability of an example t belonging to a certain cluster:

$$\forall t : \sum_{k=1}^{c} u_k(t) = 1 \tag{12.46}$$

Most non-fuzzy (crisp) clustering algorithms can easily be fuzzified.

Fuzzy c-means clustering

The fuzzy c-means is a fuzzy variant of the k-means partitional algorithm. With fuzzy c-means, the centroid (also called a prototype) of a cluster is computed as being the mean of all examples, weighted by their degree (u_k) of belonging to the cluster C_k:

$$center_k = \frac{\sum_t u_k^m(t) \cdot t}{\sum_t u_k(t)}. \tag{12.47}$$

The degree of being in a certain cluster is related to the inverse of the distance to the center of the cluster:

$$u_k(t) \propto \frac{1}{d(center_k, t)} \tag{12.48}$$

The coefficients are fuzzified with a real parameter $m > 1$ and normalized so that their sum equals to 1:

$$u_k(t) = \frac{1}{\sum_j \left(\frac{d(center_k, t)}{d(center_j, t)}\right)^{(2/(m-1))}} \tag{12.49}$$

For $m = 2$ this is equivalent to normalizing the coefficient linearly to make their sum 1. When m is close to 1, the cluster center closest to the example is given a much larger weight than the others, and the algorithm is most similar to k-means.

The fuzzy c-means algorithm (Algorithm 12.6) is similar to the crisp k-means algorithm (Algorithm 12.4). It minimizes the intra-cluster variance, but has the same problems as the k-means: it may get stuck in a local minimum, and its results depend on the initial choice of cluster centers.

Algorithm 12.6 The fuzzy c-means algorithm
___
INPUT: A set of learning examples to be clustered, and the number k of desired clusters.
OUTPUT: Partition of learning examples into k clusters and their membership values u_k.

     Randomly generate k clusters and determine the cluster centers or directly generate k prototypes as cluster centers
     Assign to each example t coefficients $u_k(t)$ for being in the clusters
     repeat
         Recompute the new cluster centers using Equation (12.47)
         For each example t calculate its coefficients $u_k(t)$ of being in a cluster C_k using Equation (12.48)
     until the cumulative change of coefficients between two iterations is no more than the sensitivity threshold ϵ, chosen in advance

---

12.6.2   Conceptual clustering

Conceptual clustering was proposed as a means of discovering understandable patterns in data. In conceptual clustering methodology, an explicit definition of properties that are more or less satisfied by members of each cluster is derived during the clustering process. Early conceptual clustering approaches were based on monothetic divisive clustering algorithms.

Monothetic clustering algorithms successively split the data into a larger number of clusters by dividing one of existing clusters into two sub-clusters. At each split they consider only divisions specified by the values of a single binary attribute. The process is repeated until an appropriate number of clusters has been obtained. This approach is similar to that used for binary decision trees; however the process of obtaining the hierarchical structure is unsupervised (example labels are not known in advance).

Similarly to the monothetic divisive clustering, conceptual clustering algorithms build a structure out of the data successively by trying to subdivide a group of observations into subclasses. The result is a hierarchical structure known as the concept hierarchy. Each node in the hierarchy subsumes all the nodes underneath it, with the whole data set at the root of the hierarchy tree. Each cluster can readily be described by the presence or absence of attribute values along the path from the root of the hierarchy to the node that represents the cluster.

More recent approaches to conceptual clustering generally define a measure of the adequacy of clustering and require iterative search strategies for its optimization. Both in adequacy measures and in search strategies the heuristic techniques can be used. Such approaches are usually oriented towards clustering of examples described solely with discrete attributes; continuous attributes need to be discretized in advance.

CLUSTER/2

The algorithm CLUSTER/2 bases its adequacy (criterion) function on measures of common attribute values within a cluster, non intersecting attribute values between clusters, and simplicity of the conjunctive expression for describing a cluster. It is based on a combination of features, including the fit between data and clustering, as well as the simplicity, accuracy and distinctness of the cluster descriptions, and also provides a hierarchical clustering tree.

Informally, the CLUSTER/2 algorithm works as follows. A set of c seeds is specified around which a partition into c clusters is to be specified. Associated with each seed is a set of maximal *complexes* that describe (cover) it while covering no other seed. A complex is a logical conjunction of "attribute=value" pairs. Each set of complexes (also called a *star*) associated with a seed generally covers also other examples from the data set. Each star is reduced and simplified as far as possible, as long as it continues to cover its cluster. Examples covered by more than one star are removed and new stars are calculated from the reduced data set. For each of the removed examples a cluster is optimally selected, and new stars are calculated. New seeds are then selected – one from each cluster. The process is repeated until no further improvements in the clustering are obtained. The final stars provide a conceptual description of the clusters.

COBWEB

While conceptual clustering discovers "understandable" patterns in data, its definition does not specify a performance task that improves with learning. On the other hand, the algorithm COBWEB uses for this purpose the prediction of unobserved properties. As such, the COBWEB system forms classification trees that are intended to yield "good" prediction along many attributes, rather than optimal prediction along a single teacher-defined attribute (the class) as in supervised learning from examples. In many cases prediction with a single COBWEB classification tree approximates predictions obtained from multiple special-purpose decision trees.

An important distinction between COBWEB and earlier conceptual clustering systems such as CLUSTER/2 is that it is incremental - COBWEB integrates an example into an existing classification tree by classifying the example along a path of "best" matching nodes. Probabilistic summaries of previous examples are stored at each node. For the matching function and the criterion used for subtree revision, COBWEB uses the category utility CU function to guide the classification and the tree formation:

$$CU(\mathcal{C}) = P(\mathcal{C}) \left(\sum_k \sum_s P(v_{ks}|\mathcal{C})^2 - \sum_k \sum_s P(v_{ks})^2 \right) \qquad (12.50)$$

Here, v_{ks} denotes the event that the k-th attribute has the s-th value. The quality of the partitioning into clusters $C = \{\mathcal{C}_1 \dots \mathcal{C}_c\}$ can be measured by

$$Q(C) = \frac{1}{c} \sum_{i=1}^{c} CU(\mathcal{C}_i) \qquad (12.51)$$

The category utility bases its evaluation on all of the example's attribute values rather than a single one, making COBWEB a polythetic classifier as opposed to monothetic classifiers (such as ordinary decision trees). Similarly, COBWEB's subtree revisions are triggered by considering the prediction ability over all attributes. However, the concern for multiple attributes complicates the subtree revision. In ordinary decision trees a subtree is simply deleted, but in COBWEB a deletion that benefits one attribute may be inappropriate for others. In response, the system identifies points in the tree for cost-effective prediction of individual attributes. These points are marked by normative or default values that COBWEB dynamically maintains during incremental clustering.

COBWEB maintains a knowledge base that coordinates many prediction tasks, one for each attribute. This is in sharp contrast to learning from examples systems where a knowledge base needs only to support one task. However, despite the COBWEB's greater knowledge base complexity, its tree structure is still too restrictive; it has been shown that more general structures, such as directed acyclic graphs yield better classification performance.

12.6.3 Evolutionary clustering

Evolutionary algorithms (such as genetic algorithms described in Section 5.9) can be used to perform broad searches over the space of possible clustering solutions and thus automatically estimate the number of clusters. In such algorithms, data partitions, initially sampled from the search space, evolve through probabilistic rules. Better partitions (i.e., those with higher objective function values) have a higher probability of being put forward during the evolutionary search, thus favoring an efficient search for good data partitions. Moreover, evolutionary approaches can be used to optimize clustering algorithms widely used in practice, such as the popular k-means, as well as its extensions to the fuzzy domain (e.g., fuzzy c-means). These algorithms (discussed in sections 12.4.2 and 12.6.1, respectively) suffer from two common problems, namely:

- the user needs to define the number of clusters, and
- the possibility of getting trapped into local optimal solutions.

Evolutionary algorithms that eliminate, split, and merge clusters may overcome these drawbacks, allowing the evolution of better partitions in terms of both the number of clusters and positions of their centroids (or alternatively, prototypes). Concerning computational efficiency, evolutionary clustering algorithms are often more efficient than multiple runs of the stand-alone application of k-means (or fuzzy c-means) on initial partitions randomly generated over a predetermined range of values for the number of clusters.

12.6.4   Knowledge-based clustering

Machine learning and data mining aim at finding interesting concepts, patterns, relationships, regularities, and structures in a given dataset. However, in practice it is rather atypical to be faced with data about which nothing is known in advance. More typically, some knowledge has already been acquired in the past, possibly through precedent knowledge discovery processes. This knowledge can be used to guide the clustering process in order to obtain better, or more interesting clusters. There exist several fundamentally different approaches to incorporating the background knowledge into the clustering process.

Clustering with constraints

Sometimes a part of the background knowledge are restrictions (constraints) on the membership of clusters. Most often, the examples and clusters need to retain their spatial relationship. This is a common situation in geographical, geological, and all image processing applications. Spatial constraints are usually two-dimensional, but can be also three- or four-dimensional (when time is included), or one-dimensional (temporal constraints in retrieval of multimedia documents).

There exist several approaches for obtaining constrained clusters. Hierarchical clustering methods can be modified so as to constrain the topology of the clustering tree (dendrogram). Constraints can also be accounted for in clustering dissimilarity measures by incorporating the actual distance between examples. Standard hierarchical or partitional methods can then be applied, using a modified dissimilarity matrix. This approach has a problem in that it is difficult to determine the weight of the spatial distance. Especially for spatial constraints, a more commonly used method is by using the concept of contiguity via the *contiguity matrix*.

The contiguity matrix is a binary $n \times n$ matrix indicating which of n examples are contiguous (i.e., they have a natural mutual boundary in space). Each example is unambiguously assigned to a spatial region (e.g., a *Voronoi diagram*), and examples whose regions share a boundary are said to be contiguous. With the use of a contiguity matrix, standard partitional or hierarchical methods can be applied with appropriate modifications. The modified algorithm should ensure that only contiguous examples are clustered. A drawback of this approach is that the modified algorithms only rarely retain all the properties of the original methods.

Semi-supervised clustering

In many data mining problems there is a large supply of unlabeled examples, but only a limited supply of labeled examples, that can be expensive to obtain. Consequently, the *semi-supervised learning*, learning from a combination of both labeled and unlabeled data, has become a topic of significant interest. Similarly, the *semi-supervised clustering* uses a small amount of supervised data in the form of class labels or pairwise constraints on some examples to aid unsupervised clustering. Semi-supervised clustering can be either constraint-based or metric based.

In constraint-based approaches, the clustering algorithm itself is modified so that user-provided labels or constraints are used to get a more appropriate clustering. This is achieved by modifying the clustering objective function so that it includes a term for satisfying specified constraints and enforcing constraints to be satisfied during the cluster assignment in the clustering process.

In metric-based approaches, an existing clustering algorithm that uses a particular dissimilarity measure is employed; however, the measure is first modified (learned) to satisfy the labels or constraints in the supervised data. Several dissimilarity measures, such as the Jensen-Shannon divergence, the Euclidean distance, and the Mahalanobis distances, have been used for the metric-based semi-supervised clustering, and modified (learned) by using different approaches, such as the gradient descent, the shortest-path algorithm, and the convex optimization.

For example, the standard k-means clustering algorithm can be modified as follows. Labeled examples are transformed into constraints, so that between examples known to belong to different clusters the dissimilarity is larger than a given threshold. A modified dissimilarity function is constructed so as to minimize the distance between examples in the data set that are known to be similar with respect to these constraints using classical numerical methods (e.g., the shortest path algorithm is used to modify the Euclidean distance function). The standard k-means clustering algorithm in conjunction with the modified dissimilarity function is then used to generate clusters.

Supervised clustering

Unlike traditional clustering, *supervised clustering* methods assume that the examples are labeled (classified). The goal of supervised clustering is to identify class-uniform clusters that have high probability densities. *Discriminative clustering* is a very general approach that minimizes dissimilarity within clusters. Labels are represented as an additional (auxiliary) attribute. Dissimilarity represents the loss of mutual information between the auxiliary attribute (e.g. class) and the clusters caused by representing each cluster by a prototype. The technique seeks to produce clusters that are internally as homogeneous as possible in conditional distributions $P(c\ell|t \in C)$ ($c\ell$ being a class and t being an example) of the auxiliary attribute, i.e., belong to a single class. Similarly, the *information bottleneck algorithm* is an agglomerative clustering algorithm, that minimizes the information loss with respect to $P(c\ell|A)$ with $c\ell$ being a class and A being an attribute. Supervised clustering techniques have been successfully used for creating summaries of datasets and for enhancing existing classification algorithms.

Non-redundant clustering

Data may often contain multiple plausible clusterings. In order to discover a clustering which is useful to the user, the constrained clustering techniques are frequently used. These techniques assume the background knowledge in the form of explicit information about the desired clustering. By contrast, in *non-redundant clustering* the background knowledge is about an undesired (existing) clustering. The problem is then to find a novel, somehow orthogonal clustering in the data. The non-redundant clustering algorithm addresses this problem in an information-theoretic framework that makes use of the concept of the conditional mutual information as its cornerstone. The information or knowledge gained by a clustering process is quantified in terms of how much new information it adds about relevant aspects of the data, conditioned on the already available knowledge.

12.7 SUMMARY AND FURTHER READING

That which is static and repetitive is boring. That which is dynamic and random is confusing. In between lies art.

— *John A. Locke*

- Clustering is the process of organizing examples into groups whose members are similar in some way. A cluster is a collection of examples which are similar to each other and are dissimilar to examples from other clusters. Clustering is considered as the most important unsupervised learning approach.

- Since dissimilarity is fundamental to the definition of a cluster, a measure of the dissimilarity between two examples drawn from the same attribute space is essential to most clustering procedures. Because of the variety of attribute types and scales, the dissimilarity measure must be chosen carefully. There exist several dissimilarity measures for various attribute types and their combinations.

- Hierarchical clustering algorithms are either agglomerative (bottom-up) or divisive (top-down). Agglomerative algorithms begin with each example as a separate cluster and merge them in successively larger clusters. Divisive algorithms begin with the whole set of examples and proceed to divide it into successively smaller clusters. Both approaches yield a hierarchy of clusters. Cluster hierarchy is often visually represented as a dendrogram, and accompanied with a banner plot. Hierarchical clustering algorithms are computationally very demanding and therefore inappropriate for clustering large datasets.

- Partitional clustering algorithms produce a partition of examples into a spec-ified number of clusters by either minimizing or maximizing some numerical criterion. A partitional clustering algorithm obtains a single partition of the data instead of a clustering structure, such as the dendrogram produced by hierarchical methods. Partitional methods have advantages over hierarchical in applications involving large data sets for which the construction of a dendrogram is computationally prohibitive. Their main problem is that the number of desired output clusters needs to be chosen in advance. The most well-known partitional clustering algorithm is k-means.

- In model-based clustering algorithms, the cluster model is specified a priori, such as a mixture of Gaussians, or a hidden Markov model (HMM). The model structure (e.g., the number of hidden states in an HMM) can be determined by model selection techniques and parameters estimated by using some maximum likelihood algorithm, e.g., the expectation-maximization (EM) algorithm.

- Expectation-maximization (EM) is a meta-algorithm which is used to devise particular algorithms. The EM algorithm for fitting a mixture density model is one particular example from this family. EM-family algorithms are usually used for optimizing the likelihood function parameters, or filling missing values in data.

- An emerging subfield of cluster analysis comprises knowledge-based clustering approaches that utilize available background knowledge on the clustering prob-lem.

Books by Gordon (1999) and Everitt et al. (2001) are excellent and comprehensive references for clustering algorithms, sometimes covering a wealth of details. A paper by Jain et al. (1999) is a detailed overview of clustering algorithms with several illustrative examples. Gower (1971, 1985) has made a thorough overview and analysis of dissimilarity measures. The result on the number of different partitions of n examples into g clusters is due to Liu (1968). The k-means algorithm is due to MacQueen (1967). Likas et al. (2003) discuss the global k-means algorithm. The book by Kaufman and Rousseeuw (1990) is an excellent reference for partitional and hierarchical clustering algorithms. The taxonomy of clustering algorithms shown in Figure 12.1 was inspired by Jain et al. (1999). Milligan and Cooper (1985) studied the criteria for determining the most appropriate number of clusters. The expectation-maximization (EM) algorithm was developed by Dempster et al. (1977), who also proved that it always converges to a local optimum. The introduction of conceptual clustering in machine learning as well as the algorithm CLUSTER/2 are due to Michalski et al. (1983). The incremental conceptual clustering algorithm COBWEB is due to Fisher (1987, 1996). Gordon (1999) is an excellent reference to constrained clustering. Hruschka and Ebecken (2003); Hruschka et al. (2004a,b, 2006) discuss the use of evolutionary algorithms for finding globally almost optimal cluster partitions.

Wagstaff et al. (2001) constrained the k-means clustering algorithm with the back-ground knowledge. Demiriz et al. (1999) used genetic algorithms for semi-supervised clustering. Klein et al. (2002) studied how to make use of background knowledge by modifying clustering constraints. Xing et al. (2003) studied distance metric learning in the context of semi-supervised learning. Tishby et al. (1999), Sinkkonen et al. (2002) and Slonim and Tishby (2000) made significant contributions to supervised clustering. Gondek and Hofmann (2004) discussed the use of background knowledge as a negative guideline in non-redundant clustering.

Chapter 13

**Learning Theory

*Believe nothing, no matter where you read it, or who said it, no matter if I have said it,
unless it agrees with your own reason and your own common sense.*

— Buddha

This chapter describes the formal learning theory and its basic results. The theory aims
to give a formal basis for discussing natural and machine learning. The basic theorems
determine exact learnability bounds for certain learning problem classes. The theory
studies a basic question:

*Is there an algorithm that is able to learn, after a finite reading from an infinite
sequence of words from a target language, a rule that differentiates between the words
from the target language and all other words?*

The task of the learning algorithm is therefore to read a sequence of words and
to generate a hypothesis – a rule for classification of words – after each new word
is encountered. After a finite number of guesses the algorithm eventually ends up
with a correct guess which does not change with further reading of words. If such
an algorithm exists we say that the target language is *learnable*. Usually, instead of
learning a single language, we are interested in the learnability of various classes of
languages.

The results of the theory constrain the learnability of certain classes of languages
with respect to various characteristics of the learning algorithms, the target languages,
the classification rules, the time and space complexities etc. An illustrative result of
the theory is the following:

*An algorithm, that is able to learn sufficiently simple classification rules, can
learn only finitely many languages (Theorem 13.16).*

The basic notation used in this chapter is the following:

$\mathbb{N}$	a set of natural numbers $\{0, 1, 2, ...\}$
$\mathcal{F}$	a set of all functions $f : \mathbb{N} \rightarrow \mathbb{N}$
$\varphi, \psi, ...$	functions (partial or total) from $\mathcal{F}$
$\varphi(x) \downarrow$	$\varphi \in \mathcal{F}$ is defined on $x \in \mathbb{N}$
$\varphi(x) \uparrow$	$\varphi \in \mathcal{F}$ is not defined on $x \in \mathbb{N}$
$\mathcal{F}^P$	$= \{\varphi \in \mathcal{F} \mid \varphi \text{ has property } P\}$
$\subseteq$	subset
$\subset$	proper subset
$t, t', ...$	infinite sequences of natural numbers (texts)
$\overline{t_n}$	first n numbers of text t
t_n	n-th number of text t
$\mathcal{T}$	a set of all texts
SEQ	$= \{\overline{t_n} \mid t \in \mathcal{T} \wedge n \in \mathbb{N}\}$
	a set of all finite sequences of numbers
$\sigma, \tau, ...$	elements of SEQ
$rng(\sigma)$	a (finite) set of numbers in sequence σ
$rng(t)$	$= \{t_i \mid i \in \mathbb{N} - \{0\}\}$
	a set of all numbers (words) in text t
$lh(\sigma)$	the length of the sequence of numbers σ
$\sigma\hat{\ }\tau$	sequence σ extended with sequence τ
σ^-	$\sigma \in SEQ$ without the last number
$\sigma^- n$	a sequence of last n numbers from sequence σ

The learning theory is based on the computability theory and the theory of recursive functions. After a brief introduction to these two fields, Section 13.2 provides basic definitions and theorems of the basic learnability paradigm together with formal proofs. The succeeding sections provide some generalizations of the learnability paradigm and important results with intuitive interpretation. However, the formal proofs are omitted (indicated with symbol $\diamond$ at the end of the theorem).

Section 13.3 studies the learnability with respect to the learning function properties (the basic paradigm, described in Section 13.2 is a special case where the learner can be any function). We provide results for different interesting subsets of learning functions, such as recursive, total, time-limited, memory-limited, reliable, consistent functions, and functions with a restriction of the hypothesis space to sufficiently simple hypotheses.

Section 13.4 studies a further generalization of the learnability with respect to the properties of input data (learning examples). We describe results for different interesting input data properties, such as incomplete and noisy data. Therefore, the basic paradigm, described in Section 13.2 is a special case where the learner can be any function and the input data are complete and noiseless.

Section 13.5 generalizes the learning success criterion. The usual criterion allows the convergence to a single language index. One modification is that learning may converge to a set of indices of the same language. Another one is that learning should converge to a sufficiently simple hypothesis.

Finally Section 13.6 discusses implications of the learning theory for designing the machine learning algorithms.

13.1 COMPUTABILITY THEORY AND RECURSIVE FUNCTIONS

Without work, all life goes rotten. But when work is soulless, life stifles and dies.
— Albert Camus

We begin with the computability theory which derives exact bounds on problems computable by any discrete computer (Turing machine, algorithm). Recursive functions are analogous to algorithms and, like any other known formal system, bear the same undecidability limitations. These formal preliminaries serve to define recursively enumerable sets which represent the (only possible) sets that can possibly be identified – learned by an algorithm.

13.1.1 Computability theory

The computability theory is based on the Church hypothesis:

Everything that can be computed can be computed with a Turing machine.

A *Turing machine* is a simple automaton (see Figure 13.1) that consists of a finite internal memory of the control unit, a read/write (RW) head and an infinite discrete tape which is used as an external memory. A machine M is defined by:

- a finite tape alphabet Γ that contains also a special blank symbol $B \in \Gamma$,

- a finite input alphabet $\Sigma \subset \Gamma$, $B \notin \Sigma$,

- a finite set Q of states of the control unit that contains also an initial state $q_0 \in Q$ and a set of final states $F \subseteq Q$, and

- a partial transition function $\delta : Q \times \Gamma \to Q \times \Gamma \times \{l, r\}$

At the beginning of computation the control unit is in the initial state q_0, the RW head is at the leftmost tape symbol. Initially, the tape contains a finite input word $w \in \Sigma^*$ (Σ^* represents a set of all finite strings of characters from alphabet Σ) and to the right of the input word there is an infinite string of blanks (B). In one computation step (time interval) the control unit, following the rules of the transition function, with respect to the current state and the input symbol (on the tape under the RW head) changes its state, writes a new symbol over the previous input symbol and moves the RW head for one symbol to the left (l) or to the right (r). The computation terminates when in a current state q and with a current input symbol x the transition function δ is not defined: $\delta(q, x) \uparrow$.

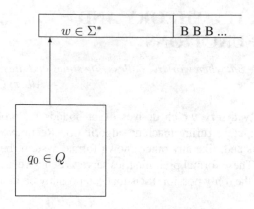

Figure 13.1: Turing machine.

During a computation the current state of the Turing machine is uniquely determined with $w_l q w_r$, where q is the current state of the control unit, w_l is the part of tape to the left of the RW head, and w_r the rest of tape (to the right including the symbol under the RW head) without blanks.

A Turing machine can be interpreted as the language acceptor, the partial function, or as the language generator.

Language acceptor: A language is composed of words, each word being a finite string of characters from an input alphabet. The language of a Turing machine M is a set of words, for which from an initial state after a finite number of steps M terminates in a final state:

$$L(M) = \{w \in \Sigma^* \mid q_0 w \overset{*}{\vdash} w_l q_F x w_r, \; q_F \in F, \; \wedge \, \delta(q_F, x) \uparrow\}$$

With $\overset{*}{\vdash}$ we indicated an arbitrary number of steps performed from the initial state with the given input word. We say that Turing machine M accepts all the words from language $L(M)$.

It can be shown that by restricting the input alphabet to only two symbols, $\Sigma = \{0, 1\}$, the class of languages that can be accepted by Turing machines remains the same. This limitation does not change the computational power (in terms of computability) of Turing machines. Therefore, we can consider the set of possible input words to be a set of natural numbers, $\Sigma^* = \mathbb{N}$, and the language $L(M)$, accepted by a Turing machine M, to be $L(M) \subseteq \mathbb{N}$.

Partial function: *Partial function* is a function that may not be defined for all arguments (as opposed to *total function* which is defined for all arguments). With limited input alphabet $\Sigma = \{0, 1\}$ a Turing machine M defines a partial function $f_M : \mathbb{N} \to \mathbb{N}$:

$$f_M(w) = \begin{cases} xw_r \in \Sigma^*, & q_0 w \vdash^* q_F x w_r, \ q_F \in F \ \wedge \ \delta(q_F, x) \uparrow \\ \uparrow \text{ (undefined)}, & \text{otherwise} \end{cases}$$

Function f_M, defined with some Turing machine M, is called a *Turing computable function*.

Language generator: If we upgrade a Turing machine with an additional output head for writing words (from Σ^* or from $\mathbb{N}$) on an additional infinite output tape, we get a language generator. Initially, the Turing generator has empty input (working) tape and uses it only as an infinite external memory – there is no input word. However, it writes words on the output tape in an arbitrary order. Therefore, the language, generated by a machine M is defined with:

$$L_G(M) = \{w \in \Sigma^* \mid M \text{ writes } w \text{ on the output tape after a finite number of steps}\}$$

Such a Turing generator can be considered as a *grammar* that generates $L_G(M)$.

Note that each Turing machine accepts or generates only one language or computes only one partial function. In addition, with an appropriate coding of Turing machines (with a finite alphabet), we can associate each Turing machine to a natural number ($M \in \mathbb{N}$). Therefore, the number of different Turing machines is equivalent to the number of natural numbers. Note, however, that each Turing machine has an infinite number of equivalent variants which accept/generate the same language (e.g. by adding an arbitrary large number of transitions that do not change the initial state of computation).

It can be shown that the class of languages

$$\mathcal{L}_G = \{L_G(M) \mid M \in \mathbb{N}\} \subset \mathcal{P}(\mathbb{N})$$

that can be generated with Turing machines (generators), is equivalent to the class of languages, that can be accepted by Turing machines:

$$\mathcal{L}_M = \{L(M) \mid M \in \mathbb{N}\}$$

and the latter is equivalent to the class of function domains for functions that can be computed by Turing machines:

$$\mathcal{L}_f = \{L_f(M) \mid M \in \mathbb{N}\}$$

where

$$L_f(M) = \{w \in \mathbb{N} \mid f_M(w) \downarrow\}$$

Therefore, all three classes of languages are equivalent:

$$\mathcal{L}_G = \mathcal{L}_M = \mathcal{L}_f$$

and are called *Turing languages*.

As the number of Turing machines is equal to $|\mathbb{N}| = \aleph_0$ (which corresponds to the countable infinity), we have at most a countably infinite number of Turing languages. On the other hand, the number of all possible languages is $|\mathcal{P}(\mathbb{N})| = 2^{|\mathbb{N}|} = \aleph_1$ (which corresponds to the uncountable infinity, $\aleph_1 \gg \aleph_0$). Therefore, the great majority of languages are not Turing languages, or, if we put it in other terms, the majority of languages (problems) are not computable with Turing machines.

If a Turing machine does not accept an input word, it either terminates in a non-final state or it never terminates. If for a given language L there exists a Turing machine that accepts exactly that language (it accepts all the words from the language and does not accept any other word) and it always terminates after a finite number of steps, we say that the language L is *decidable*. Otherwise it is *undecidable*.

13.1.2　Recursive functions

The theory of computability studies various computational abilities of Turing machines. On the other hand, the theory of recursive functions studies the computability of recursive functions.

The set of all functions (partial and total) $f : \mathbb{N} \to \mathbb{N}$ is denoted with $\mathcal{F}$. $\mathcal{F}$ contains an uncountably infinite number of functions. A set of all total functions (defined on all arguments) is denoted with $\mathcal{F}^{total}$.

The following rules define a set of *primitive recursive functions*:

1. The zero function:

$$Z(x) = 0, \ x \in \mathbb{N}$$

   is primitive recursive.

2. A successor function:

$$S(x) = x + 1, \ x \in \mathbb{N}$$

   is primitive recursive.

3. Projection (identity) functions:

$$I(x_1, ..., x_i, ..., x_n) = x_i; \ \ i, n \in \mathbb{N}, \ i \leq n \wedge 1 \leq j \leq n : \ x_j \in \mathbb{N}$$

   are primitive recursive.

4. The substitution rule: For all $1 \leq k, m \in \mathbb{N}$, if functions f of k arguments and $g_1, ..., g_k$ of m arguments are primitive recursive, then a function of m arguments

$$h(x_1, ..., x_m) = f(g_1(x_1, ..., x_m), ..., g_k(x_1, ..., x_m))$$

   is also primitive recursive.

5. The primitive recursion rule: For $k \geq 1$, if functions g of $k - 1$ arguments and h of $k + 1$ arguments are primitive recursive, then a function

$$
\begin{aligned}
f(0, x_2, ..., x_k) &= g(x_2, ..., x_k) \\
f(y + 1, x_2, ..., x_k) &= h(y, f(y, x_2, ..., x_k), x_2, ..., x_k)
\end{aligned}
$$

is also primitive recursive.

6. Only functions obtained by rules 1-5 are primitive recursive.

Note that all primitive recursive functions are total.

We obtain a set of *partial recursive functions*, or simply *recursive functions*, if we augment the above rules for primitive recursive functions with the minimization operator:

1. All primitive recursive functions are recursive functions.

2. If a function f of $k + 1$ arguments is primitive recursive then the following function is recursive:

$$
g(x_1, ..., x_k) = \mu x [f(x_1, ..., x_k, x) = 0]
$$

where the value $\mu x [Expression]$ equals to the minimal $x \in \mathbb{N}$, for which the *Expression* is true, if such x exists, and is undefined otherwise.

3. Only functions obtained by rules 1-2 are recursive.

It is interesting that, in the second rule above, we can allow function f to be recursive (and not only primitive recursive) and the class of recursive functions does not change. The set of recursive functions is denoted with $\mathcal{F}^{rec}$.

It can be shown that if a Turing machine is interpreted as a partial function, it holds that the class of recursive functions is equivalent to the class of Turing computable functions. A recursive function that corresponds to a Turing machine with index i is denoted with φ_i and its domain with W_i. Therefore, like Turing machines, each function has an infinite number of different indexes: for all $i \in \mathbb{N}$ it holds

$$
\left| \{ j \mid W_j = W_i \} \right| = |\mathbb{N}| = \aleph_0
$$

13.1.3   Undecidability of universal formalisms

It is interesting to note that besides Turing machines and recursive functions, which are considered to be universal formalisms in the sense of computability, the analogous *universality*, in the sense of *descriptive power* and *(un)decidability*, holds also for *grammars of type 0* (i.e. grammars without constraints) and for the *first order predicate calculus*:

- For any given recursive function it holds that for the given argument values it is computable, if it is defined, otherwise the computation may never terminate.

- For any given Turing machine M it holds that on a given input word w it will terminate after a finite number of steps, if the $w \in L(M)$, otherwise it may never terminate.

- For any given grammar of type 0 it holds that if a given expression (word) is from the grammar language, then it can be derived after a finite number of steps, otherwise we may not be able to prove that the expression is not from the grammar language.

- For any given theory described in the first order predicate calculus it holds that if a given logic expression is true (derivable) in that theory, we can prove it in a finite number of steps, otherwise we may not be able to disprove it.

The undecidability holds for all four formalisms:

- There is no universal algorithm which accepts as an input the description of any Turing machine M and its (arbitrary) input word w and computes whether $w \in L(M)$, and which always terminates its computation after a finite number of steps.

- There is no universal algorithm that always terminates its computation after a finite number of steps, and which for any function $\varphi \in \mathcal{F}^{rec}$ and any number $x \in \mathbb{N}$ computes whether $\varphi(x) \downarrow$.

- There is no universal algorithm that always terminates its computation after a finite number of steps, and which for any grammar of type 0 and any input expression computes whether the expression is in the language generated by the grammar.

- There is no universal algorithm that always terminates its computation after a finite number of steps, and which for any theory described in the first order predicate calculus and any input logic expression computes whether the expression is true (derivable) in the given theory.

13.1.4 Recursively enumerable sets

In this section we define some interesting language classes whose learnability is studied in further sections: class RE of partially decidable (recursively enumerable) languages, class RE_{rec} of decidable (recursive) languages, class RE_{fin} of finite languages, and class RE_{svt} of languages that represent total functions (single valued total recursively enumerable languages).

A set $S \subseteq \mathbb{N}$ is *recursively enumerable* if there exists a Turing generator M that generates all words from the set S and no other words. Due to:

$$S = L_G(M) = L(M_a) = L_{\varphi_i}(M_c)$$

for a certain Turing machine – acceptor M_a, and a certain Turing machine M_c that computes function φ_i, we can write

$$S = W_i$$

(i.e., each recursively enumerable set has an associated index).

The class of all recursively enumerable sets is denoted with RE:

$$RE = \{W_i \mid i \in \mathbb{N}\}$$

The class RE is equivalent to the class of all Turing languages. Obviously we have to limit our study to class RE because by definition for other languages there are no algorithmic generators. Therefore, languages outside RE are not learnable.

A collection of all finite sets of natural numbers is denoted with RE_{fin}. A set S is recursive if there exists a Turing machine such that $L(M) = S$ and which always terminates its computation in a finite number of steps. A recursively enumerable set $S \in RE$ is *recursive* if its complement $\overline{S} \in RE$ (by switching the answers yes and no for machine M where $L(M) = S$ we get a machine $\overline{M}$ where $L(\overline{M}) = \overline{S}$). A collection of all recursive sets is denoted with RE_{rec}. It is obvious that if $S \in RE_{rec}$, then $\overline{S} \in RE_{rec}$, therefore we can write:

$$RE_{rec} = \{S \in RE \mid \overline{S} \in RE\}$$

It can be shown that the following holds:

$$RE_{fin} \subset RE_{rec} \subset RE$$

For a certain set $S \subseteq \mathbb{N}$ we say that $f \in \mathcal{F}$ is its *characteristic function*, if it holds:

$$f(x) = \begin{cases} 0, & \text{if } x \in S, \\ 1, & \text{if } x \in \overline{S} \end{cases}$$

Every characteristic function is total. It is obvious that $S \in RE_{rec}$ if and only if $f \in \mathcal{F}^{rec}$. That is, if the characteristic function f is recursive (and therefore also total) then the set S is decidable (recursive), and vice versa.

An interesting subset of recursive sets is the set of all *single valued total recursively enumerable sets*:

$$RE_{svt} = \{S_i = \{\langle x, y \rangle \mid x \in \mathbb{N}, \varphi_i(x) = y\} \in RE \mid i \in \mathbb{N}, \varphi_i \in \mathcal{F}^{total}\}$$

where for each $x, y \in \mathbb{N}$: $\langle x, y \rangle \in \mathbb{N}$, and there exist total recursive functions $\pi_0(x, y) = \langle x, y \rangle$ and $\pi_1(\langle x, y \rangle) = x$ and $\pi_2(\langle x, y \rangle) = y$. Therefore, there exists a bijection (a uniform mapping in both directions): $\mathbb{N} \times \mathbb{N} \leftrightarrow \mathbb{N}$. We say that $S_i \in RE_{svt}$ *represents* some total function φ_i. Such languages are interesting for learning, as together with a language we learn also a function.

For each single valued total set $S \in RE_{svt}$ it holds that $|S| = |\mathbb{N}|$. It can be shown that $RE_{svt} \subset RE_{rec}$, i.e. all single valued total recursively enumerable sets are also recursive (decidable). Therefore, if $S \in RE_{svt}$ then S represents some total recursive function $f \in \mathcal{F}^{rec} \cap \mathcal{F}^{total}$.

13.2 FORMAL LEARNING THEORY

Live as if you were to die tomorrow. Learn as if you were to live forever.
— *Mahatma Gandhi*

The formal learning theory aims to show what languages are algorithmically learnable. Each language is denoted with a recursively enumerable set (which is in turn denoted with a unique natural number – index). The input is an infinite sequence of numbers and the task of the learner (algorithm) is to identify the correct index after a finite number of steps.

13.2.1 Identification

For a formal definition of learning we use the following general scenario. The learner either observes the environment or performs experiments and observes the outcomes of experiments. Therefore, the learner is exposed to a potentially infinite sequence of observations. Let each observation be described with a sentence from a finite alphabet. Then there is an isomorphism between the set of sentences and the set of natural numbers $\mathbb{N}$ – each sentence can be uniquely coded with a natural number. Each infinite sequence of observations can be represented with an infinite sequence of natural numbers which we call *text* and denote it with t. Note that in a text the repetitions of numbers are allowed. First n numbers (observations) from text t are denoted with $\overline{t_n}$, the n-th number is denoted with t_n, and the set of all texts is denoted with $\mathcal{T}$.

Let us define also a set of all finite sequences of numbers:

$$SEQ = \{\overline{t_n} \mid t \in \mathcal{T} \land n \in \mathbb{N}\}$$

The finite sequences of numbers (observations) are denoted with $\sigma \in SEQ$. If text t begins with σ we say that σ *is in* t. The set of numbers in σ is denoted with $rng(\sigma)$ and the length of σ is denoted with $lh(\sigma)$. Therefore, $\sigma \in SEQ$ is in $t \in \mathcal{T}$ if and only if $\sigma = \overline{t_{lh(\sigma)}}$.

If $\sigma, \tau \in SEQ$, we denote with $\sigma^\frown\tau$ a sequence σ extended with sequence τ. For example, if $\sigma = 3, 4, 3, 3, 5$ and $\tau = 5, 7, 1, 1, 3$, then $\sigma^\frown\tau = 3, 4, 3, 3, 5, 5, 7, 1, 1, 3$. $\sigma \in SEQ$, shortened by deleting the last number, is denoted with σ^-. The sequence of last n numbers in sequence $\sigma \in SEQ$ is denoted with σ^-n. For example, if $\sigma = 1, 3, 3, 5, 2, 11$, then $\sigma^- = 1, 3, 3, 5, 2$ and $\sigma^-3 = 5, 2, 11$.

The learning task is to *identify* the language that is composed of all the words in the given text. A language is therefore a nonempty set $S \subseteq \mathbb{N}$ such that $S = rng(t)$, where

$$rng(t) = \{t_i \mid i \in \mathbb{N} - \{0\}\}$$

is the text *rang*, i.e. the set of all numbers from text t. We say that text t is *for* language S. As we are interested only in recursively enumerable languages we can write $S = W_i \in RE$ for some $i \in \mathbb{N}$ (recall that W_i is the language that is generated/accepted by the i-th Turing machine).

The learner has to guess a hypothesis after reading each number from the input text. The hypothesis itself is also a natural number – the index i of language $S =$

W_i. Note that the learner at any time has seen only a finite sequence of numbers (observations). As there exists an isomorphism between SEQ and $\mathbb{N}$ we can encode each finite sequence of numbers (observations) with some natural number. We can define the learner as a function $f \in \mathcal{F}$, $f : \mathbb{N} \to \mathbb{N}$, that for each natural number, interpreted as a finite sequence of observations, returns a natural number that uniquely determines a language – the learner's hypothesis. We say that f is a *learning function*. We are interested only in learners that can be simulated with a computer, therefore we limit learning functions to recursive ones: $f \in \mathcal{F}^{rec}$. However, it is also interesting to compare the class of languages learnable by recursive functions with the one learnable by all functions $f \in \mathcal{F}$.

Although at any time the learner has seen only a finite sequence of numbers, typical hypotheses are infinite languages. None of such hypotheses can be confirmed with a finite number of observations, and each further observation can potentially reject the hypothesis (with the exception of hypothesis $\mathbb{N}$). Therefore each hypothesis needs an infinite number of tests and can never be completely confirmed. The key issue of inductive inference and learning theory is the relation between finite sequences of observations and infinite languages.

Note the following asymmetry of text. For a given text $t \in \mathcal{T}$ and $n \in \mathbb{N}$, if $n \in rng(t)$, then we can confirm it after a finite number of observations (from t). If, however, $n \notin rng(t)$, we cannot confirm it after any finite number of observations.

Definition 13.1. Let $\varphi \in \mathcal{F}$ and $t \in \mathcal{T}$.
i.   We say that φ is *defined on* t, if $\varphi(\overline{t_n}) \downarrow$ for every $n \in \mathbb{N}$.
ii. Let $i \in \mathbb{N}$. We say that φ *converges on* t *to* i, if φ is defined on t and for all but finitely many $n \in \mathbb{N}$ it holds $\varphi(\overline{t_n}) = i$ (therefore there exists $m \in \mathbb{N}$ such that for all $n > m$ it holds $\varphi(\overline{t_n}) = i$).
iii. We say that φ *identifies* t, if there exists $i \in \mathbb{N}$ such that φ converges on t to i and $rng(t) = W_i$. $\diamond$

Note that no finite number of observations suffices to determine the beginning of the convergence. That's why we say that identification is a limiting process in the sense of describing the learning functions behaviors on infinite subsets of their domains.

Definition 13.2. Let $\varphi \in \mathcal{F}$ and $L \in RE$. We say that φ *identifies* L, if φ identifies each text for L. $\diamond$

Definition 13.3. Let $\varphi \in \mathcal{F}$ and let $\mathcal{L} \subseteq RE$ be a collection of languages. We say that φ *identifies* $\mathcal{L}$, if φ identifies each $L \in \mathcal{L}$. We say that $\mathcal{L}$ is *learnable*, if there exists (not necessarily recursive) function $\varphi \in \mathcal{F}$ that identifies $\mathcal{L}$. The collection of languages identified by φ is denoted with $\mathcal{L}(\varphi)$. $\diamond$

¿From the above definitions it follows that each collection of languages that consists of a single language is trivially learnable (with a function that for every $\sigma \in SEQ$ returns the index of that language). That is why we are mostly interested in the learnability of (often infinite) collections of languages.

Consider function h that for every $\sigma \in SEQ$ returns the smallest $i \in \mathbb{N}$ such that $rng(\sigma) \subseteq W_i$. Therefore h always guesses the first language that contains all the words seen so far. It is obvious that h identifies $\{\mathbb{N}\}$ because $\mathbb{N} \in RE$ and therefore has some finite index.

Definition 13.4. Let $\varphi \in \mathcal{F}$, $L \in RE$ and $\sigma \in SEQ$. We say that σ is a *locking sequence* for L and φ, if $rng(\sigma) \subseteq L$, $W_{\varphi(\sigma)} = L$ and for every $\tau \in SEQ$ it holds that if $rng(\tau) \subseteq L$, then $\varphi(\sigma^\frown\tau) = \varphi(\sigma)$. ⋄

13.2.2 Basic theorems

In this section we show for certain language collections whether they are learnable. We begin with the (infinite) set of all finite languages.

Theorem 13.1. RE_{fin} *is learnable.*

Proof. Let f for any $\sigma \in SEQ$ return the smallest index for language $rng(\sigma)$. Therefore f always guesses the finite language that contains exactly the words from σ. Obviously f identifies every finite language. As f identifies RE_{fin}, it holds that RE_{fin} is learnable. □

Note that $f \in \mathcal{F}^{rec}$ therefore RE_{fin} is learnable also if we restrict learners to recursive functions.

The next (infinite) collection of infinite languages is constructed by excluding from the set of natural numbers one number at a time. Therefore, each language contains all natural numbers but one.

Theorem 13.2. $\mathcal{L} = \{\mathbb{N} - \{x\} \mid x \in \mathbb{N}\}$ *is learnable.*

Proof. For any $\sigma \in SEQ$ let x_σ be the smallest $x \in \mathbb{N}$ such that $x \notin rng(\sigma)$. Function g that identifies $\mathcal{L}$ is defined as follows: $g(\sigma) =$ the smallest index for $\mathbb{N} - \{x_\sigma\}$. □

Note that $g \in \mathcal{F}^{rec}$ therefore $\mathcal{L}$ is learnable also if we restrict learners to recursive functions.

The single valued total recursively enumerable sets turn out to be learnable.

Theorem 13.3. RE_{svt} *is learnable.*

Proof. Let for any $\sigma \in SEQ$:

$$h(\sigma) = \begin{cases} \text{the smallest } i: W_i \in RE_{svt} \text{ and } rng(\sigma) \subseteq W_i, & \text{if such } i \text{ exists} \\ 0, & \text{otherwise.} \end{cases}$$

$h \in \mathcal{F}$ always returns the smallest index of a language from RE_{svt} that is consistent with σ. Therefore, h will, given a text for language L, for every $L_s \in RE_{svt}, L_s \neq L$ for some $n \in \mathbb{N}$ discover that $t_n = \langle x, y \rangle \in L$ and that $\langle x, y \rangle \notin L_s$, because such $x \in \mathbb{N}$ exists. □

Later we show that if we restrict learners to recursive functions then RE_{svt} is not learnable (it holds $\mathcal{F}^{rec} \not\ni h$). The above proof uses a special property of single valued total languages. Namely, a finite reading of text t for some language $L \in RE_{svt}$ suffices to conclude whether some word $\langle x, y \rangle$ is or is not in L. In the former case we find for some $n \in \mathbb{N}$ $t_n = \langle x, y \rangle$, and in the latter case we find $t_n = \langle x, y_1 \rangle, y \neq y_1$. As already noted, for texts for other languages from RE the finite reading of a text enables one only to conclude that a certain word is in the corresponding language and does not allow the conclusion that some word is not in the language.

If we augment the set of all finite languages with the (infinite) set of all natural numbers, the obtained collection of languages is not learnable.

Theorem 13.4. $RE_{fin} \cup \{\mathbb{N}\}$ *is not learnable.*

Proof. Assume that some $\varphi \in \mathcal{F}$ identifies $RE_{fin} \cup \{\mathbb{N}\}$. Let σ be a locking sequence for φ and $\mathbb{N}$. Due to $rng(\sigma) \in RE_{fin}$ there exists a text t for language $W_i = rng(\sigma)$, such that $\overline{t_{lh(\sigma)}} = \sigma$. We conclude that φ does not identity $W_i \in RE_{fin}$, because φ converges on t to an index for $\mathbb{N}$. $\qquad\square$

The above theorem can be generalized by replacing $\mathbb{N}$ with an arbitrary infinite recursively enumerable language.

If we augment the collection of languages from Theorem 13.2 with the set of all natural numbers, it becomes nonlearnable.

Theorem 13.5. $\mathcal{L} = \{\mathbb{N} - \{x\} \mid x \in \mathbb{N}\} \cup \{\mathbb{N}\}$ *is not learnable.*

Proof. Like in the previous theorem proof, assume that some $\varphi \in \mathcal{F}$ identifies $\mathcal{L}$. Let σ be a locking sequence for φ and $\mathbb{N}$. Assume some $x \notin rng(\sigma)$. We conclude that for each text t for language $\mathbb{N} - \{x\}$, such that $\overline{t_{lh(\sigma)}} = \sigma$, φ converges on t to an index for $\mathbb{N}$ and not for $\mathbb{N} - \{x\}$. $\qquad\square$

The above theorem can be generalized by replacing sets $\{x\}$ with sets $D \subset \mathbb{N}$ that contain exactly i_0 elements for some fixed $i_0 \in \mathbb{N}$ (in the theorem we have $i_0 = 1$).

It is obvious that the following theorem holds:

Theorem 13.6.
i. *If* $\mathcal{L} \subseteq RE$ *is not learnable then every superset* $\mathcal{L}_S \supseteq \mathcal{L}$ *is also not learnable.*
ii. *RE is not learnable.*
iii. *RE_{rec} is not learnable.* $\qquad\square$

Therefore there is no universal (recursive or nonrecursive) learner that would identify either all recursively enumerable languages or all recursive languages. This result shows that there is no "universal algorithmic learner" which could learn any language that could in principle be learned.

In the next sections the learnability theory is generalized in various directions. We start in Section 13.3 by learnability with respect to various interesting subsets of learning functions. The learnability defined in the previous section is a special case where the learner may be any function, i.e. $\mathcal{S} = \mathcal{F}$. Section 13.4 studies the learnability with respect to various properties of texts, such as incomplete and noisy text. The original learnability is again a special case where text is complete and noiseless. Section 13.5 generalizes the criterion of convergence of the learning function. We study two additional convergence criteria: (a) we allow that a learner does not converge on each text for the target language to a single index but can alternate among different indices of the target language (recall that any language has an infinite number of indices); (b) we require that the learner converges on any text to a correct hypothesis that is sufficiently simple. Finally, Section 13.6 discusses the implications of learning theory for machine learning research.

In the next sections we omit the theorem proofs. Interested readers can find useful references for more advanced study of the learning theory in Section 13.7.

13.3 PROPERTIES OF LEARNING FUNCTIONS

An inferiority complex would be a blessing, if only the right people had it.

— Alan Reed

In this section we study learnability with respect to various interesting subsets of learning functions, which are called properties of learning functions. Learning functions with the following properties are studied: recursive functions, total functions, time-limited functions, memory-limited functions, functions that always return sufficiently simple hypotheses, functions that always return infinite hypotheses, functions that always return single valued total hypotheses, functions that always return learnable hypotheses, consistent functions, conservative functions that do not unnecessarily change their hypotheses, cautious functions that never specialize their hypotheses, decisive functions that never repeat abandoned hypotheses, reliable functions that converge only on identifiable languages, and confident functions which always converge.

13.3.1 Learning strategies

Subsets $S \subseteq \mathcal{F}$ are called *learning strategies*. The class of language collections $\mathcal{L}$ identified by at least one function from strategy S is denoted with $[S]$:

$$[S] = \{\mathcal{L} \subseteq RE \mid some\ \varphi \in S\ identifies\ \mathcal{L}\}$$

With $[S]_{svt}$ we denote classes of collections of single-valued total languages:

$$[S]_{svt} = [S] \cap \mathcal{P}(RE_{svt})$$

For example, from Theorem 13.1 we know that $RE_{fin} \in [\mathcal{F}]$, and from Theorem 13.4 we know that $RE_{fin} \cup \{\mathbb{N}\} \notin [\mathcal{F}]$.

Definition 13.5. We say that the learning strategy S *restricts* strategy S_∞ if $[S \cap S_\infty] \subset [S_\infty]$. ◇

A learning strategy can be considered as a set of functions with a certain property. Therefore, if a subset of functions from S_∞, which are at the same time also in S

(functions have both properties), identifies less collections of languages than the whole function set $\mathcal{S}_\infty$, then the property, represented with $\mathcal{S}$, restricts the learning ability of functions with the property represented with $\mathcal{S}_\infty$.

Theorem 13.7. *Let $\mathcal{S} \subset \mathcal{F}$ be a denumerably infinite set: $|\mathcal{S}| = \aleph_0$. Then $[\mathcal{S}] \subset [\mathcal{F}]$.*
◇

Recursiveness and totality

The basic strategies are recursive functions, computable with Turing machines, and total functions, which are defined for each input.

The direct consequence of Theorem 13.7 is that $\mathcal{F}^{rec}$ restricts $\mathcal{F}$.

Theorem 13.8. $[\mathcal{F}^{rec}] \subset [\mathcal{F}]$. ◇

Therefore, there exist sets of (recursively enumerable) languages which Turing machines cannot learn while some nonrecursive learners (functions from $\mathcal{F} - \mathcal{F}^{rec}$) can.

Theorem 13.9. $RE_{svt} \notin [\mathcal{F}^{rec}]_{svt}$. ◇

Therefore, RE_{svt} is an example of language collections that are not learnable if we restrict learners to recursive functions. However, without that restriction RE_{svt} is learnable (see Theorem 13.3). A direct consequence is the following:

$$[\mathcal{F}^{rec}]_{svt} \subset [\mathcal{F}]_{svt}.$$

The next results are about total learners, denoted with $\mathcal{F}^{total}$. Totality does not restrict either $\mathcal{F}$ or $\mathcal{F}^{rec}$.

Theorem 13.10.
i. $[\mathcal{F}^{total}] = [\mathcal{F}]$.
ii. $[\mathcal{F}^{rec} \cap \mathcal{F}^{total}] = [\mathcal{F}^{rec}]$. ◇

13.3.2   Computational constraints

This section describes three learning strategies that restrict the learning algorithms by time, needed to compute the hypotheses, by the amount of memory available to store the learning examples, and by the hypothesis complexity.

Time-limited functions

Definition 13.6. For each $i \in \mathbb{N}$ we define a partial recursive function

$$\Phi_i(x) = \begin{cases} \text{number of steps performed} \\ \text{by } i\text{-th Turing machine} \\ \text{on input word } x \in \mathbb{N}, & \text{if it halts} \\ \uparrow & \text{if it never halts} \end{cases}$$

The sequence of functions $\Phi_0, \Phi_1, \ldots$ is called a *time complexity measure*. ◇

Definition 13.7. Let h be a recursive and total function: $h \in \mathcal{F}^{rec} \cap \mathcal{F}^{total}$. We say that $\varphi_i \in \mathcal{F}^{rec} \cap \mathcal{F}^{total}$ is *time-limited* with h, if for all but finitely many $x \in \mathbb{N}$ it holds $\Phi_i(x) \le h(x)$. A subset of recursive functions that are time-limited with h is denoted with $\mathcal{F}^{h\text{-}time} \subset (\mathcal{F}^{rec} \cap \mathcal{F}^{total})$. ◇

The following theorem states that for some total recursive function h the set of time-limited functions $\mathcal{F}^{h\text{-}time}$ does not restrict $\mathcal{F}^{rec}$.

Theorem 13.11. *There exists $h \in \mathcal{F}^{rec} \cap \mathcal{F}^{total}$ such that $[\mathcal{F}^{rec}] = [\mathcal{F}^{h\text{-}time}]$.* ◇

Memory-limited functions

A sensible constraint for a learning function is that it is not able to store all so far seen learning examples. We are interested in functions whose current hypothesis depends on the previous hypothesis and a certain number of lastly encountered learning examples. Therefore, the memory-limited functions learn *incrementally*.

Recall the notation: $\sigma \in SEQ$ without the last number is denoted with σ^- and a sequence of last n numbers from sequence σ is denoted with $\sigma^- n$.

Definition 13.8.

i. For each $n \in \mathbb{N}$ we say that $\varphi \in \mathcal{F}$ is *n-memory-limited*, if for each $\sigma, \tau \in SEQ$ it holds that if $\sigma^- n = \tau^- n$ and $\varphi(\sigma^-) = \varphi(\tau^-)$ then $\varphi(\sigma) = \varphi(\tau)$. The class of all n-memory-limited functions is denoted with $\mathcal{F}^{n\text{-}memory\text{-}limited}$.

ii. If for some $n \in \mathbb{N}$ it holds $\varphi \in \mathcal{F}^{n\text{-}memory\text{-}limited}$ we say that φ is *memory-limited*. The class of all memory-limited learning functions is denoted with $\mathcal{F}^{memory\text{-}limited}$. ◇

The first part of the above definition states that if two input sequences have equal last n numbers and have led to equal previous hypotheses then for both sequences any n-memory-bounded function has to return equal current hypotheses (regardless of the differences in these two sequences before last n numbers).

It turns out that there is no difference in learnability between 1-memory-limited and (general) memory-limited functions. Besides, recursive memory-limited functions are able to learn all finite languages.

Theorem 13.12.

i. $[\mathcal{F}^{1\text{-}memory\text{-}limited}] = [\mathcal{F}^{memory\text{-}limited}]$.

ii. $RE_{fin} \in [\mathcal{F}^{rec} \cap \mathcal{F}^{1\text{-}memory\text{-}limited}] = [\mathcal{F}^{rec} \cap \mathcal{F}^{memory\text{-}limited}]$. ◇

However, memory-limited functions restrict both, $\mathcal{F}$ as well as recursive functions. The latter rule holds also the other way around: recursive functions restrict memory-limited functions.

Theorem 13.13.

i. $[\mathcal{F}^{memory\text{-}limited}] \subset [\mathcal{F}]$.

ii. $[\mathcal{F}^{rec} \cap \mathcal{F}^{memory\text{-}limited}] \subset [\mathcal{F}^{rec}] \cap [\mathcal{F}^{memory\text{-}limited}]$. ◇

Therefore, there exist collections of languages that can be learned by some Turing machine but cannot be learned incrementally.

Although by Theorem 13.11 there exists a total recursive function h such that $\mathcal{F}^{h\text{-}time}$ does not restrict $\mathcal{F}^{rec}$, the same conclusion is not valid if the functions are memory-limited.

Theorem 13.14. *For each $h \in \mathcal{F}^{rec} \cap \mathcal{F}^{total}$ it holds*
$$[\mathcal{F}^{h\text{-}time} \cap \mathcal{F}^{memory\text{-}limited}] \subset [\mathcal{F}^{rec} \cap \mathcal{F}^{memory\text{-}limited}]. \diamond$$

Simplicity of hypotheses

To each Turing machine we can associate a measure of complexity proportional to the number of symbols needed to code it – the smaller is the number of symbols needed to code a Turing machine, the smaller is its complexity. Recall that index i of a Turing machine uniquely determines the language W_i accepted (or generated) by that Turing machine.

Definition 13.9.
i. $m(i)$ is the number of symbols needed to code the i-th Turing machine.
ii. $M(L)$ is the number of symbols needed to code the simplest Turing machine with index i that accepts (or generates) L:

$$M(L) = \min_i(m(i) \mid L = W_i)$$

iii.   Let f be a total recursive function $f \in \mathcal{F}^{rec} \cap \mathcal{F}^{total}$. We say that $i \in \mathbb{N}$ is f-simple if it holds $m(i) \leq f(M(W_i))$. $\diamond$

Therefore, hypothesis i is f-simple if the complexity of the i-th Turing machine is no more than "f of the complexity of the smallest Turing machine for language W_i". For example, if $f(x) = 2x$, then i is f-simple, if none of the Turing machines that accept W_i is two times simpler than the i-th Turing machine.

Let us now define also the limits of complexity of the learner's hypotheses.

Definition 13.10.
i.   Let f be a total recursive function $f \in \mathcal{F}^{rec} \cap \mathcal{F}^{total}$. We say that $\varphi \in \mathcal{F}$ is f-simpleminded if it holds for each $\sigma \in SEQ$, that if $\varphi(\sigma) \downarrow$ then $\varphi(\sigma)$ is f-simple. The set of f-simpleminded functions is denoted with $\mathcal{F}^{f\text{-}simpleminded}$.
ii.   If $\varphi \in \mathcal{F}$ is f-simpleminded for some $f \in \mathcal{F}^{rec} \cap \mathcal{F}^{total}$ we say that φ is simpleminded. The set of simpleminded functions is denoted with $\mathcal{F}^{simpleminded}$. $\diamond$

It can be shown that f-simpleminded functions do not restrict $\mathcal{F}$ if $f(x) \geq x$ for all $x \in \mathbb{N}$. However, f-simpleminded functions do restrict recursive functions.

Theorem 13.15.
i. For each $f \in \mathcal{F}^{rec} \cap \mathcal{F}^{total}$ it holds

$$\forall x \in \mathbb{N} : f(x) \geq x \Rightarrow [\mathcal{F}^{f\text{-}simpleminded}] = [\mathcal{F}].$$

ii. $[\mathcal{F}^{rec} \cap \mathcal{F}^{simpleminded}] \subset [\mathcal{F}^{rec}]. \diamond$

For restricting recursive functions with simpleminded functions we can show a stronger result – simplemindedness restricts the recursive learners to be able to learn exactly finite collections of languages.

Theorem 13.16. $\mathcal{L} \subseteq RE$ *is finite if and only if* $\mathcal{L} \in [\mathcal{F}^{rec} \cap \mathcal{F}^{simpleminded}]$. $\diamond$

Therefore, a simpleminded recursive function can learn only a finite number of languages. For infinite collections of languages it holds that by guessing simple hypotheses for some languages no simpleminded recursive learner is able to guess simple hypotheses for other languages. Put it another way, when a learner finds a correct hypothesis for some language the learner is unable to find an equivalent but sufficiently simple hypothesis.

13.3.3 Infinite languages

In this section we discuss strategies that allow only sufficiently general hypotheses. We discuss infinite languages, hypotheses that require at least one inductive inference (cover also unseen examples), and single-valued total languages (where hypotheses represent functions). Recall that texts for single-valued total languages enable finite verifications for checking whether certain words are not included in the target language.

Nontriviality

Often we are interested only in learning of infinite languages. Here we discuss constraints of learners whose hypotheses are always infinite languages.

Definition 13.11. A learning function $\varphi \in \mathcal{F}^{total}$ is said to be *nontrivial* if it always returns a hypothesis for an infinite language:

$$\sigma \in SEQ \Rightarrow |W_{\varphi(\sigma)}| = \aleph_0$$

The class of nontrivial functions is denoted with $\mathcal{F}^{nontrivial}$. $\diamond$

Of course, no nontrivial function can identify finite languages. It is interesting, however, that nontriviality restricts recursive functions when learning infinite languages.

Theorem 13.17. *There exists a collection of infinite languages* $\mathcal{L} \subseteq RE$ *such that it holds* $\mathcal{L} \in [\mathcal{F}^{rec}] - [\mathcal{F}^{rec} \cap \mathcal{F}^{nontrivial}]$. $\diamond$

Therefore, in order to learn some infinite languages an algorithm must occasionally return a hypothesis for a finite language.

Accountability

If we generalize nontriviality in such a way that we allow also finite hypotheses which contain words that were not seen so far, we obtain similar results. The term accountability indicates that each hypothesis needs further verification.

Definition 13.12. A learning function $\varphi \in \mathcal{F}^{total}$ is said to be *accountable* if for every hypothesis it holds:

$$\sigma \in SEQ \Rightarrow W_{\varphi(\sigma)} - rng(\sigma) \neq \{\}$$

The class of accountable functions is denoted with $\mathcal{F}^{accountable}$. ◇

It is obvious that each nontrivial function is also accountable:

$$\mathcal{F}^{nontrivial} \subset \mathcal{F}^{accountable}$$

Of course, like nontrivial functions, accountable functions also cannot identify finite languages. In a similar way as nontriviality, accountability also restricts recursive functions when learning infinite languages.

Theorem 13.18. *There exists a collection of infinite languages* $\mathcal{L} \subseteq RE$ *such that* $\mathcal{L} \in [\mathcal{F}^{rec}] - [\mathcal{F}^{rec} \cap \mathcal{F}^{accountable}]$. ◇

The above result is important – in order to learn some infinite languages an algorithm must occasionally return a hypothesis for a finite language which contains only already encountered input words.

Popperian functions

Nontriviality can be reformulated by limiting the hypotheses to single-valued total languages RE_{svt} (which are also infinite). Such hypotheses can be easily verified with respect to the learning set of examples because languages from RE_{svt} are decidable – for each word we are able to verify whether it belongs to the target language after a finite reading of the input sequence. We name such functions *Popperian* after Karl Popper (1902-1994) who insisted on the falsifiability of scientific practice.

Definition 13.13. We say that the learning function $\varphi \in \mathcal{F}^{total}$ is *Popperian* if for each hypothesis for $\sigma \in SEQ$ it holds that if $\varphi(\sigma) \downarrow$, then $W_{\varphi(\sigma)} \in RE_{svt}$. The class of Popperian functions is denoted with $\mathcal{F}^{Popperian}$. ◇

Function h in the proof of Theorem 13.3 is Popperian.

It holds that each Popperian function is also nontrivial and accountable: $\mathcal{F}^{Popperian} \subset \mathcal{F}^{nontrivial} \subset \mathcal{F}^{accountable}$. Of course, like nontrivial and accountable functions also the Popperian functions cannot identify finite languages. In a similar way as nontriviality and acountability, Popperian functions restrict recursive functions when learning single-valued total languages. However, they do not restrict $\mathcal{F}$ when learning single-valued total languages.

Theorem 13.19.
i. $[\mathcal{F}^{Popperain}]_{svt} = [\mathcal{F}]_{svt}.$
ii. $[\mathcal{F}^{rec} \cap \mathcal{F}^{Popperain}]_{svt} \subset [\mathcal{F}^{rec}]_{svt}.$ ◇

13.3.4   Some sensible learning strategies

In this section we study various sensible learning strategies. A sensible strategy may limit the hypothesis space, e.g hypotheses may be limited to languages, which can be learned by the learner, or to languages that contain all encountered words. A sensible learning strategy may pose the limitations on the sequence of generated hypotheses. The learner may never abandon the consistent hypothesis and therefore should never overgeneralize, or the learner may only generalize (and never specialize) current hypotheses, or the learner may never return to the abandoned hypotheses.

Prudence

Hypotheses of a prudent function are only languages which can be learned by that function.

Definition 13.14. Function $\varphi \in \mathcal{F}$ is said to be *prudent*, if for each hypothesis for given $\sigma \in SEQ$ it holds that if $\varphi(\sigma) \downarrow$ then φ identifies $W_{\varphi(\sigma)}$. The class of prudent functions is denoted with $\mathcal{F}^{prudent}$. $\diamond$

As function f from the proof of Theorem 13.1 is prudent and recursive, it holds:

$$RE_{fin} \in [\mathcal{F}^{prudent} \cap \mathcal{F}^{rec}]$$

Also function g from the proof of Theorem 13.2 is prudent and recursive.
    It turns out that prudence restricts neither $\mathcal{F}$ nor $\mathcal{F}^{rec}$.

Theorem 13.20.
i. $[\mathcal{F}^{prudent}] = [\mathcal{F}]$.
ii. $[\mathcal{F}^{rec} \cap \mathcal{F}^{prudent}] = [\mathcal{F}^{rec}]$. $\diamond$

Consistency

For machine learning, an important property is the consistency of the hypothesis with the learning examples– the hypothesis has to cover all positive examples.

Definition 13.15. We say that the learning function $\varphi \in \mathcal{F}^{total}$ is *consistent* if for every hypothesis it holds that it contains all encountered words:

$$\sigma \in SEQ \Rightarrow rng(\sigma) \subseteq W_{\varphi(\sigma)}$$

The class of consistent functions is denoted with $\mathcal{F}^{consistent}$. $\diamond$

As function f from the proof of Theorem 13.1 is prudent, consistent and recursive it holds:

$$RE_{fin} \in [\mathcal{F}^{prudent} \cap \mathcal{F}^{consistent} \cap \mathcal{F}^{rec}]$$

Also function g from the proof of Theorem 13.2 is prudent, consistent and recursive. Function h from the end of Section 13.2.1 is consistent.

Consistency is analogous to nontriviality which restricts recursive functions when learning infinite languages, although the target is an infinite language. Also consistency restricts recursive functions, although the target has to be consistent with learning examples. However, consistency does not restrict $\mathcal{F}$.

Theorem 13.21.
i. $[\mathcal{F}^{consistent}] = [\mathcal{F}]$.
ii. $[\mathcal{F}^{rec} \cap \mathcal{F}^{consistent}] \subset [\mathcal{F}^{rec}]$. $\diamond$

An even stronger restriction of consistent recursive functions can be shown (Theorem 13.22). They can identify only recursive languages, i.e. languages that are decisive, and they cannot identify all recursive languages. Also when learning single-valued total languages consistency restricts recursive functions.

Theorem 13.22.
i. $[\mathcal{F}^{rec} \cap \mathcal{F}^{consistent}] \subset \mathcal{P}(RE_{rec})$.
ii. $[\mathcal{F}^{rec} \cap \mathcal{F}^{consistent}]_{svt} \subset [\mathcal{F}^{rec}]_{svt}$. $\diamond$

Conservatism

A sensible learning strategy is that the learner does not change its hypothesis until it is not consistent with learning data any more.

Definition 13.16. We say that the learning function $\varphi \in \mathcal{F}$ is *conservative* if for each $\sigma \in SEQ$ it holds that if $rng(\sigma) \subseteq W_{\varphi(\sigma^-)}$, then $\varphi(\sigma) = \varphi(\sigma^-)$. The class of conservative functions is denoted with $\mathcal{F}^{conservative}$. $\diamond$

As function f from the proof of Theorem 13.1 is prudent, consistent, conservative, and recursive it holds:

$$RE_{fin} \in [\mathcal{F}^{prudent} \cap \mathcal{F}^{consistent} \cap \mathcal{F}^{conservative} \cap \mathcal{F}^{rec}]$$

Also function g from the proof of Theorem 13.2 is prudent, consistent, conservative, and recursive. Function h from Section 13.2.1 is consistent and conservative.

Conservatism together with consistency and prudence does not restrict $\mathcal{F}$, however, it does restrict recursive functions.

Theorem 13.23.
i. $[\mathcal{F}^{conservative} \cap \mathcal{F}^{consistent} \cap \mathcal{F}^{prudent}] = [\mathcal{F}]$.
ii. $[\mathcal{F}^{rec} \cap \mathcal{F}^{conservative}] \subset [\mathcal{F}^{rec}]$. $\diamond$

It is interesting that consistency and conservatism together do not restrict memory limited functions.

Theorem 13.24.
$[\mathcal{F}^{conservative} \cap \mathcal{F}^{consistent} \cap \mathcal{F}^{memory\text{-}limited}] = [\mathcal{F}^{memory\text{-}limited}]$. $\diamond$

Caution

Conservative learners never overgeneralize when learning identifiable languages. When a hypothesis is overgeneral they are unable to specialize it. Let us consider learners that never specialize their hypotheses.

Definition 13.17. We say that the learning function $\varphi \in \mathcal{F}$ is *cautious* if for each $\sigma, \tau \in SEQ$ it holds $W_{\varphi(\sigma\hat{\ }\tau)} \not\subset W_{\varphi(\sigma)}$. The class of cautious functions is denoted with $\mathcal{F}^{cautious}$. $\diamond$

As function f from the proof of Theorem 13.1 is prudent, consistent, conservative, cautious, and recursive it holds:

$$RE_{fin} \in [\mathcal{F}^{prudent} \cap \mathcal{F}^{consistent} \cap \mathcal{F}^{conservative} \cap \mathcal{F}^{cautious} \cap \mathcal{F}^{rec}]$$

Also function g from the proof of Theorem 13.2 is prudent, consistent, conservative, cautious, and recursive.

Caution does not restrict $\mathcal{F}$, however, it does restrict recursive functions. But, as one may expect, caution does not restrict conservative recursive functions.

Theorem 13.25.
i. $[\mathcal{F}^{cautious}] = [\mathcal{F}]$.
ii. $[\mathcal{F}^{rec} \cap \mathcal{F}^{cautios}] \subset [\mathcal{F}^{rec}]$.
iii. $[\mathcal{F}^{rec} \cap \mathcal{F}^{cautious} \cap \mathcal{F}^{conservative}] = [\mathcal{F}^{rec} \cap \mathcal{F}^{conservative}]$. $\diamond$

Decisiveness

Conservative learners never overgeneralize when learning identifiable languages. Cautious learners never specialize their hypotheses. Let us consider learners that never return to the hypothesis that was once abandoned.

Definition 13.18. We say that the learning function $\varphi \in \mathcal{F}$ is *decisive* if for each $\sigma, \tau \in SEQ$ it holds that if $W_{\varphi(\sigma-)} \neq W_{\varphi(\sigma)}$ then $W_{\varphi(\sigma\hat{\ }\tau)} \neq W_{\varphi(\sigma-)}$. The class of decisive functions is denoted with $\mathcal{F}^{decisive}$. $\diamond$

As function f from the proof of Theorem 13.1 is prudent, consistent, conservative, cautious, decisive, and recursive it holds:

$$RE_{fin} \in [\mathcal{F}^{prudent} \cap \mathcal{F}^{consistent} \cap \mathcal{F}^{conservative} \cap \mathcal{F}^{cautious} \cap \mathcal{F}^{decisive} \cap \mathcal{F}^{rec}]$$

Also function g from the proof of Theorem 13.2 is prudent, consistent, conservative, cautious, decisive, and recursive.

In fact it holds that every consistent and conservative function is also decisive:

$$\mathcal{F}^{consistent} \cap \mathcal{F}^{conservative} \subset \mathcal{F}^{decisive}$$

Decisiveness does not restrict $\mathcal{F}$. Nor does it restrict recursive functions when learning single-valued total languages.

Theorem 13.26.

i. $[\mathcal{F}^{decisive}] = [\mathcal{F}]$.

ii. $[\mathcal{F}^{rec} \cap \mathcal{F}^{decisive}]_{svt} = [\mathcal{F}^{rec}]_{svt}$. $\diamond$

It is an open problem whether decisiveness restricts recursive functions when learning recursive enumerable languages.

13.3.5   Reliability and confidence

Reliability

It is not necessary for a learning function to converge on an arbitrary text. Even if a function converges on text t it is not necessary that it converges to $i : W_i = rng(t)$. Let us consider reliable learners that never converge to the wrong language.

Definition 13.19. We say that the learning function $\varphi \in \mathcal{F}^{total}$ is *reliable* if for each $t \in \mathcal{T}$ it holds that if φ converges on t then φ identifies t. The class of reliable functions is denoted with $\mathcal{F}^{reliable}$. $\diamond$

As function f from the proof of Theorem 13.1 is prudent, consistent, conservative, cautious, decisive, reliable, and recursive it holds:

$$RE_{fin} \in [\mathcal{F}^{prudent} \cap \mathcal{F}^{consistent} \cap \mathcal{F}^{conservative} \cap \mathcal{F}^{cautious} \cap \mathcal{F}^{decisive} \cap \mathcal{F}^{reliable} \cap \mathcal{F}^{rec}]$$

In fact it holds that reliable functions can identify only finite languages.

Theorem 13.27. $[\mathcal{F}^{reliable}] = \mathcal{P}(RE_{fin})$. $\diamond$

Confidence

Let us consider confident functions that converge on every text.

Definition 13.20. We say that the learning function $\varphi \in \mathcal{F}^{total}$ is *confident* if for each text $t \in \mathcal{T}$ it holds that φ converges on t. The class of confident functions is denoted with $\mathcal{F}^{confident}$. $\diamond$

Neither function f from the proof of Theorem 13.1 nor function g from the proof of Theorem 13.2 is confident.

It turns out that confident functions restrict $\mathcal{F}$ as well as $\mathcal{F}^{rec}$. It also holds that recursive functions restrict confident functions.

Theorem 13.28.

i. $[\mathcal{F}^{confident}] \subset [\mathcal{F}]$.

ii. $[\mathcal{F}^{rec} \cap \mathcal{F}^{confident}] \subset [\mathcal{F}^{rec}] \cap [\mathcal{F}^{confident}]$. $\diamond$

13.4 PROPERTIES OF INPUT DATA

There are no mistakes, no coincidences. All events are blessings given to us to learn from.

— Elizabeth Kubler-Ross

In this section we generalize the learnability paradigm that uses various learning strategies by considering various properties of the input data – texts. We study the learnability from noisy texts and from texts that contain positive and negative learning examples. Finally we consider a scenario with oracles – the learner is allowed to put questions to the teacher (oracle) that provides correct answers.

13.4.1 Evidential relations

Subsets $\mathcal{E} \subseteq \mathcal{T} \times RE$ are called *evidential relations*. Evidential relation $\{(t, L)|rng(t) = L\}$ is called *text*.

Definition 13.21. Let us have an evidential relation $\mathcal{E}$.

i. We say that $\varphi \in \mathcal{F}$ *identifies* $L \in RE$ *on* $\mathcal{E}$ if for each $t \in \{t|(t, L) \in \mathcal{E}\}$ function φ converges on t to an index for L.

ii. We say that $\varphi \in \mathcal{F}$ *identifies* $\mathcal{L} \subseteq RE$ *on* $\mathcal{E}$ if φ identifies every $L \in \mathcal{L}$ on $\mathcal{E}$. In this case we say that $\mathcal{L}$ is *identifiable on* $\mathcal{E}$. ◇

The class of language collections $\mathcal{L}$ identifiable on $\mathcal{E}$ by at least one function from the given strategy $\mathcal{S}$ is denoted with $[\mathcal{S}, \mathcal{E}]$:

$$[\mathcal{S}, \mathcal{E}] = \{\mathcal{L} \subseteq RE \mid some\ \varphi \in \mathcal{S}\ identifies\ \mathcal{L}\ on\ \mathcal{E}\}$$

With $[\mathcal{S}, \mathcal{E}]_{svt}$ we denote the classes of collections of single-valued total languages:

$$[\mathcal{S}, \mathcal{E}]_{svt} = [\mathcal{S}, \mathcal{E}] \cap \mathcal{P}(RE_{svt})$$

Therefore, the learnability paradigm, studied in Section 13.3, is a special case: $[\mathcal{S}, text] = [\mathcal{S}]$ and $[\mathcal{S}, text]_{svt} = [\mathcal{S}]_{svt}$.

13.4.2 Noisy and incomplete texts

In this section we study learning from noisy texts, that contain also incorrect words, and/or from incomplete texts, that lack some words from the target language.

Noisy text

Definition 13.22. The evidential relation
$\{(t, L) \mid for\ some\ finite\ D \subset \mathbb{N}, rng(t) = L \cup D\}$
is called *noisy text*. ◇

As may be expected, noisy texts restrict noise-free texts. It is interesting that the collection of languages, learnable from noisy texts, may contain only languages that differ from each other in an infinite number of words.

Theorem 13.29.
i. $[\mathcal{F}, noisy\ text] \subset [\mathcal{F}, text]$.
ii. $[\mathcal{F}^{rec}, noisy\ text] \subset [\mathcal{F}^{rec}, text]$.
iii. *Let for $L, L_1 \in RE$ be $L \neq L_1$. Then $\{L, L_1\} \in [\mathcal{F}, noisy\ text]$ if and only if the differences $L - L_1$ and $L_1 - L$ are infinite.* ◇

Noisy texts restrict confident and decisive learners so that they are able to learn only a single language.

Theorem 13.30. *Let for $L, L_1 \in RE$ be $L \neq L_1$.*
i. $\{L, L_1\} \notin [\mathcal{F}^{confident}, noisy\ text]$.
ii. $\{L, L_1\} \notin [\mathcal{F}^{decisive}, noisy\ text]$. ◇

Therefore, when learning from noisy texts the learner must be neither confident (should not converge on every text) nor decisive (sometimes it has to repeat some previously abandoned hypotheses).

Incomplete text

Definition 13.23. The evidential relation:
$\{(t, L) \mid \text{for some finite } D \subset \mathbb{N}, rng(t) = L - D\}$
is called *incomplete text*. ◇

Like noisy texts, incomplete texts also restrict usual noise-free texts. Also, the collection of languages, learnable from incomplete texts, may contain only languages that differ from each other in an infinite number of words. Besides, noisy texts restrict incomplete texts; therefore the noise is a more serious restriction than the incompleteness.

Theorem 13.31.
i. $[\mathcal{F}, incomplete\ text] \subset [\mathcal{F}, text]$.
ii. $[\mathcal{F}^{rec}, incomplete\ text] \subset [\mathcal{F}^{rec}, text]$.
iii. *Let for $L, L_1 \in RE$ be $L \neq L_1$. Then $\{L, L_1\} \in [\mathcal{F}, incomplete\ text]$ if and only if the differences $L - L_1$ and $L_1 - L$ are infinite.*
iv. $[\mathcal{F}, noisy\ text] \subset [\mathcal{F}, incomplete\ text]$. ◇

Imperfect text

An imperfect text is noisy and/or incomplete.

Definition 13.24. The evidential relation:
$\{(t, L) \mid \text{for some finite } D_1, D_2 \subset \mathbb{N}, D_1 \neq D_2, rng(t) = (L \cup D_1) - D_2\}$
is called *imperfect text*. ◇

Each incomplete text is imperfect and also each noisy text is imperfect. It turns out that imperfect texts do not restrict the noisy ones when the learner is an arbitrary function from $\mathcal{F}$. As may be expected, imperfect texts restrict usual (perfect) texts when recursive learners learn single-valued total recursive languages.

Theorem 13.32.
i. $[\mathcal{F}, imperfect\ text] = [\mathcal{F}, noisy\ text]$.
ii. $[\mathcal{F}^{rec}, imperfect\ text]_{svt} \subset [\mathcal{F}^{rec}, text]_{svt}$. ◇

It is an open problem whether imperfect texts restrict noisy texts when the learners are recursive.

13.4.3 Texts with positive and negative examples

Definition 13.25. Let $L \in RE$ and $t \in \mathcal{T}$.
i. We say that t is *informant for L* if $rng(t) = \{\langle x, y \rangle \mid x \in L \wedge y = 0 \vee x \notin L \wedge y = 1\}$.
ii. The evidential relation $\{(t, L) \mid t$ is an informant for $L\}$ is called an *informant*. ◇

Therefore an informant contains all positive and all negative learning examples.

Theorems 13.4 and 13.5 show the non-learnability of two language collections when learners are arbitrary functions from $\mathcal{F}$. It turns out that informants provide enough information for the two collections of languages to be learnable also if we restrict the learners to being recursive.

Theorem 13.33.
i. $\{\mathbb{N}\} \cup RE_{fin} \in [\mathcal{F}^{rec}, informant]$.
ii. $\{\mathbb{N}\} \cup \{\mathbb{N} - \{x\} \mid x \in \mathbb{N}\} \in [\mathcal{F}^{rec}, informant]$.
iii. $[\mathcal{F}, text] \subset [\mathcal{F}, informant]$.
iv. $[\mathcal{F}^{rec}, text] \subset [\mathcal{F}^{rec}, informant]$. ◇

Besides, it turns out that informants enable the learnability of the complete collection of recursively enumerable languages RE. However, the latter is not true for recursive learners.

Theorem 13.34.
i. $RE \in [\mathcal{F}, informant]$.
ii. $RE \notin [\mathcal{F}^{rec}, informant]$.
iii. $[\mathcal{F}^{rec}, informant] \subset [\mathcal{F}, informant]$. ◇

It is interesting that informants do not improve the learnability of single-valued total recursive languages, if the learners are recursive.

Theorem 13.35. $[\mathcal{F}^{rec}, informant]_{svt} = [\mathcal{F}^{rec}, text]_{svt}$. ◇

As we already know, a single-valued total recursive language with one positive example in fact provides simultaneously an infinite number of negative examples, which explains the above result.

The next theorem specifies some relations between the learnability from ordinary texts and from informants if the learners have limited memory. It turns out that informants extend the learnability by memory limited learners.

Theorem 13.36.
i. $[\mathcal{F}^{memory\text{-}limited}, text] \subset [\mathcal{F}^{memory\text{-}limited}, informant]$.
ii. $[\mathcal{F}^{memory\text{-}limited} \cap \mathcal{F}^{rec}, text] \subset [\mathcal{F}^{memory\text{-}limited} \cap \mathcal{F}^{rec}, informant]$.
iii. $[\mathcal{F}^{memory\text{-}limited} \cap \mathcal{F}^{rec}, informant] \subset [\mathcal{F}^{rec}, informant]$. ◇

The next results show some relations between the learnability from ordinary texts and from informants when learners use different learning strategies. It turns out that nontriviality, reliability, conservatism, and caution restrict recursive learners when learning from informants.

Theorem 13.37.

i.   *There exists a collection of infinite languages $\mathcal{L} \subseteq RE$ such that $\mathcal{L} \in [\mathcal{F}^{rec}, informant] - [\mathcal{F}^{rec} \cap \mathcal{F}^{nontrivial}, informant]$.*

ii. $[\mathcal{F}^{reliable}, text] \subset [\mathcal{F}^{reliable} \cap \mathcal{F}^{rec}, informant] \subset [\mathcal{F}^{rec}, informant]$.

iii. $[\mathcal{F}^{conservative} \cap \mathcal{F}^{rec}, informant] \subset [\mathcal{F}^{rec}, informant]$.

iv. $[\mathcal{F}^{cautious} \cap \mathcal{F}^{rec}, informant] \subset [\mathcal{F}^{rec}, informant]$. ◇

13.4.4   Texts with oracles

An oracle is a teacher that correctly and in a finite time answers each learner's question about whether some $x \in L$. Let us consider two learning scenarios that include oracles.

Infinite oracle

In the first scenario the learner generates a text by repeatedly posing a question to the oracle for some $x \in \mathbb{N}$. If the oracle returns a positive answer (x is in the target language), the learner constructs index $\langle x, 0 \rangle$ for the input word, and index $\langle x, 1 \rangle$ otherwise. Then the learner constructs a hypothesis. By this scenario, the class of languages, identified by at least one learning function from strategy $\mathcal{S} \subseteq \mathcal{F}$, is denoted with $[\mathcal{S}, oracle]$.

It turns out that an infinite oracle does not extend the learnability with an informant.

Theorem 13.38.

i. $[\mathcal{F}, informant] = [\mathcal{F}, oracle]$.

ii. $[\mathcal{F}^{rec}, informant] = [\mathcal{F}^{rec}, oracle]$. ◇

Finite oracle

In the second scenario the learner has a given text but is allowed to pose finitely many questions to the oracle to verify whether certain words $x \in \mathbb{N}$ are in the target language. By this scenario, the class of languages identified by at least one learning function from strategy $\mathcal{S} \subseteq \mathcal{F}$ is denoted with $[\mathcal{S}, finite\ oracle]$.

It turns out that the finite oracle does not extend the learnability with the ordinary text.

Theorem 13.39.

i. $[\mathcal{F}, text] = [\mathcal{F}, finite\ oracle]$.

ii. $[\mathcal{F}^{rec}, text] = [\mathcal{F}^{rec}, finite\ oracle]$. ◇

13.5 CONVERGENCE CRITERIA

We spend the first twelve months of our children's lives teaching them to walk and talk and the next twelve telling them to sit down and shut up.

— Phyllis Diller

In this section we generalize the learnability paradigm to various learning convergence criteria. The usual criterion that allows the convergence to a single language index is modified in several ways: learning may converge to a set of indices of the same language, to a sufficiently simple hypothesis, or it may converge to an index of the characteristic function of a language.

13.5.1 Convergence

Subsets $C \subseteq RE \times P(\mathbb{N})$ are called *convergence criteria*. A convergence criterion $\{(L, \{n\}) | W_n = L\}$ is said to be *intensional*.

Definition 13.26. Let us have a convergence criterion C and an evidential relation $\mathcal{E}$.

i. We say that $\varphi \in \mathcal{F}$ *C-converges on* $t \in \mathcal{T}$ *to* $L \in RE$ if there exists such $S \subseteq \mathbb{N}$ that $(L, S) \in C$ and φ is defined on t and $\varphi(\overline{t_m}) \in S$ for all but finitely many $m \in \mathbb{N}$.

ii. We say that $\varphi \in \mathcal{F}$ *C-identifies* $L \in RE$ *on* $\mathcal{E}$ if for each $t \in \{t | (t, L) \in \mathcal{E}\}$ function φ *C-converges on* t to L.

iii. We say that $\varphi \in \mathcal{F}$ *C-identifies* $\mathcal{L} \subseteq RE$ *on* $\mathcal{E}$ if φ *C-identifies each* $L \in \mathcal{L}$ *on* $\mathcal{E}$. $\diamond$

The class of languages $\mathcal{L}$ that are *C*-identified on $\mathcal{E}$ by at least one function from $\mathcal{S}$ is denoted with $[\mathcal{S}, \mathcal{E}, C]$:

$$[\mathcal{S}, \mathcal{E}, C] = \{\mathcal{L} \subseteq RE \mid some \; \varphi \in \mathcal{S} \; C\text{-identifies } \mathcal{L} \text{ on } \mathcal{E}\}$$

With $[\mathcal{S}, \mathcal{E}, C]_{svt}$ we denote classes of collections of single-valued total languages:

$$[\mathcal{S}, \mathcal{E}, C]_{svt} = [\mathcal{S}, \mathcal{E}, C] \cap P(RE_{svt})$$

Therefore, the learnability paradigms, studied in Sections 13.3 and 13.4, are special cases, as we have:

$$[\mathcal{S}, text, intensional] = [\mathcal{S}, text] = [\mathcal{S}]$$

and

$$[\mathcal{S}, text, intensional]_{svt} = [\mathcal{S}, text]_{svt} = [\mathcal{S}]_{svt}$$

¿From Theorem 13.10 we know that $[\mathcal{F}^{rec} \cap \mathcal{F}^{total}] = [\mathcal{F}^{rec}]$. It turns out that also a more general relation holds.

Theorem 13.40. *Let us have a convergence criterion C and an evidential relation $\mathcal{E}$. It holds:* $[\mathcal{F}^{rec} \cap \mathcal{F}^{total}, \mathcal{E}, C] = [\mathcal{F}^{rec}, \mathcal{E}, C]$. $\diamond$

13.5.2   Extensional and bounded extensional convergence

Instead of insisting that the learner converges to a single language index we may allow it to converge to a set of indices for the same language.

Extensional convergence

Definition 13.27. The convergence criterion $\{(L, \{n | W_n = L\}) | L \in RE\}$ is called *extensional.* ◇

It turns out that the following relations hold between the learnability with extensional and with intensional convergence criteria: the extensional convergence criterion does not extend the learnability unless the learners are restricted to be recursive.

Theorem 13.41.
$[\mathcal{F}^{rec}, text, intensional] \subset [\mathcal{F}^{rec}, text, extensional] \subset$
$[\mathcal{F}, text, intensional] = [\mathcal{F}, text, extensional].$ ◇

With the intentional convergence criterion, both consistency and conservatism restrict recursive learners (see Theorems 13.21 and 13.23). It turns out that the consistency does not restrict the learnability by recursive learners with the extensional convergence criterion, however, the conservatism restricts it.

Theorem 13.42.
i. $[\mathcal{F}^{rec} \cap \mathcal{F}^{consistent}, text, extensional] = [\mathcal{F}^{rec}, text, extensional].$
ii. $[\mathcal{F}^{rec} \cap \mathcal{F}^{conservative}, text, extensional] \subset [\mathcal{F}^{rec}, text, extensional].$ ◇

The extensional convergence criterion is not sufficient to make all single-valued total languages learnable by recursive learners.

Theorem 13.43. $RE_{svt} \notin [\mathcal{F}^{rec}, text, extensional]_{svt} \subset [\mathcal{F}, text, extensional]_{svt}.$ ◇

Bounded extensional convergence

Definition 13.28. The convergence criterion
$\{(L, D) | L \in RE,\ D = \{n | W_n = L\},\ D$ is nonempty and finite$\}$
is called *bounded* extensional. ◇

It turns out that the following relations hold between the learnability with the bounded extensional, extensional and the intensional convergence criterion: for any learners the convergence criterion does not make the difference, while for recursive learners the intensional criterion is the most restrictive and the extensional is the less restrictive.

Theorem 13.44.
i. $[\mathcal{F}, text, intensional] = [\mathcal{F}, text, bounded] = [\mathcal{F}, text, extensional].$
ii. $[\mathcal{F}^{rec}, text, intensional] \subset [\mathcal{F}^{rec}, text, bounded] \subset [\mathcal{F}^{rec}, text, extensional].$ ◇

While the consistency does not restrict recursive learners with the extensional convergence criterion (Theorem 13.42), it turns out that it does restrict recursive learners with the bounded extensional convergence criterion.

Theorem 13.45. $[\mathcal{F}^{rec} \cap \mathcal{F}^{consistent}, text, bounded] \subset [\mathcal{F}^{rec}, text, bounded]$. $\diamond$

Unlike the extensional convergence criterion, the bounded extensional one does not extend the learnability of single-valued total languages for recursive learners.

Theorem 13.46.
$[\mathcal{F}^{rec}, text, intensional]_{svt} = [\mathcal{F}^{rec}, text, bounded]_{svt} \subset [\mathcal{F}^{rec}, text, extensional]_{svt}$. $\diamond$

13.5.3   Convergence towards simple hypotheses

In a similar way as we defined learning functions $\mathcal{F}^{f\text{-}simpleminded}$ that always guess f-simple hypotheses, we can define a convergence criterion that requires the convergence towards f-simple hypotheses.

Definition 13.29. Let $f \in \mathcal{F}^{total} \cap \mathcal{F}^{rec}$. The convergence criterion
$\{(L, \{n\}|W_n = L$ and n is f-simple $\}$ is called $f\text{-}simple$. $\diamond$

It turns out that the f-simple criterion restricts recursive learners, also when learning only single-valued total languages.

Theorem 13.47. *Let $f \in \mathcal{F}^{total} \cap \mathcal{F}^{rec}$.*
i. $[\mathcal{F}^{rec}, text, f\text{-}simple] \subset [\mathcal{F}^{rec}, text, intensional]$.
ii. $[\mathcal{F}^{rec}, text, f\text{-}simple]_{svt} \subset [\mathcal{F}^{rec}, text, intensional]_{svt}$.
iii. $\bigcup_{g \in \mathcal{F}^{total} \cap \mathcal{F}^{rec}}[\mathcal{F}^{rec}, text, g\text{-}simple]_{svt} \subset [\mathcal{F}^{rec}, text, intensional]_{svt}$. $\diamond$

It is interesting that if the recursive learners are allowed to guess only sufficiently simple hypotheses, then even with the intentional convergence criterion they are unable to learn some language collections, which they would otherwise be able to learn with the more restricted f-simple convergence.

Theorem 13.48. *Let $f \in \mathcal{F}^{total} \cap \mathcal{F}^{rec}$ such that $f(x) \geq x$ for each $x \in \mathbb{N}$. Then it holds* $[\mathcal{F}^{rec} \cap \mathcal{F}^{simpleminded}, text, intensional] \subset [\mathcal{F}^{rec}, text, f\text{-}simple]$. $\diamond$

13.5.4   Convergence towards recursive hypotheses

A sensible restriction of target languages (and therefore hypotheses) is that they should be recursive, i.e. decisive and not only recursively enumerable. Recall that each recursive language has a characteristic function. The problem of learning a recursive language is equivalent to learning of its characteristic function. From Theorem 13.48 we conclude that sometimes it is better not to restrict the hypothesis space but rather to restrict the final hypotheses – hypotheses towards whom the learner converges. Let us consider a convergence criterion that requires that the final hypothesis be the characteristic function of a (recursive) language.

Definition 13.30. The convergence criterion
$\{(L, \{n\}|\varphi_n$ *is a characteristic function for L*$\}$ is called *recursive*. $\diamond$

With $[\mathcal{S},\mathcal{E},\mathcal{C}]_{rec}$ we denote the classes of recursive language collections: $[\mathcal{S},\mathcal{E},\mathcal{C}]\cap \mathcal{P}(RE_{rec})$. Obviously it holds: $[\mathcal{S},\mathcal{E}, recursive] = [\mathcal{S},\mathcal{E}, recursive]_{rec}$. The recursive convergence criterion does not restrict the intensional one, unless the learners are recursive. The same is true for learning from ordinary texts and from informants.

Theorem 13.49.
i. $[\mathcal{F}, text, recursive] = [\mathcal{F}, text, intensional]_{rec}$.
ii. $[\mathcal{F}^{rec}, text, recursive] \subset [\mathcal{F}^{rec}, text, intensional]_{rec}$.
iii. $[\mathcal{F}, informant, recursive] = [\mathcal{F}, informant, intensional]_{rec} = \mathcal{P}(RE_{rec})$.
iv. $[\mathcal{F}^{rec}, informant, recursive] \subset [\mathcal{F}^{rec}, informant, intensional]_{rec}$. $\diamond$

It turns out that if we restrict recursive learners to being either memory-limited, or conservative, or Popperian, then with the recursive convergence criterion some collections of recursive languages become unlearnable.

Theorem 13.50.
i. $[\mathcal{F}^{rec} \cap \mathcal{F}^{memory\text{-}limited}, text, recursive] \subset [\mathcal{F}^{rec}, text, recursive]$.
ii. $[\mathcal{F}^{rec} \cap \mathcal{F}^{conservative}, text, recursive] \subset [\mathcal{F}^{rec}, text, recursive]$.
iii. $[\mathcal{F}^{rec} \cap \mathcal{F}^{Popperian}, text, recursive] \subset [\mathcal{F}^{rec}, text, recursive]$. $\diamond$

13.6 IMPLICATIONS FOR MACHINE LEARNING

When you are no longer attached to anything, you have done your share. The rest will be done for you.

— *Sri Nisargadatta Maharaj*

The learning theory, presented in this chapter, assumes infinite texts and in most cases poses neither time nor space constraints for successful learning. This *learning in the limit* paradigm is therefore more philosophical than practical. However, from the results of the theory we can draw also some useful guidelines for designing the machine learning algorithms.

The basic implications stem from Theorem 13.6 – the set of all recursive (decidable) languages is not learnable – and Theorem 13.8 – the set of all single valued total recursively enumerable sets is not learnable by recursive learners (therefore the set of all total recursive functions is not learnable by recursive learners). This implies that there is no universal algorithmic learner that would be able to learn all recursive languages or all recursive functions. This limitation is analogous to undecidability results from the computational theory (see Section 13.1.3). Therefore, programmers have to take into account that no program can solve all the problems – no machine learning algorithm will ever be able to solve all learning problems. With respect to time and memory restrictions we can state the following. Recall that memory-limited learners are in fact incremental learners. From Theorems 13.11 and 13.14 it follows that time limits are more restrictive for incremental than for non-incremental learners.

¿From Theorems 13.15 and 13.16 it follows that there are no general learners that would be able to always generate simple hypotheses – the learner that always generates simple hypotheses is necessarily specialized for a limited (finite) number of languages.

An interesting general result with practical implications is the following:

If an algorithm uses a restricted hypothesis space that, although restricted, still contains all the target languages, it can happen, due to that restriction, that the algorithm is unable to learn certain target languages (Theorems 13.17, 13.18, 13.19, 13.21, 13.37 and 13.48).

A particular example of the above general constraint is the following:

For machine learning of certain infinite languages the learning algorithm must occasionally put a finite hypothesis which does not cover any so far unseen words (Theorems 13.17 and 13.18).

Another particular example of more practical value is the following:

For machine learning of certain languages the learning algorithm must occasionally put inconsistent hypotheses (Theorems 13.21 and 13.22).

¿From theorems in Section 13.4.2 we can conclude that when learning from noisy texts the learner must be neither confident (should not converge on every text) nor decisive (sometimes it has to repeat some previously abandoned hypotheses). Another important conclusion is that the noise in the input data is a more serious restriction than the incompleteness. Therefore, in data collection it is more important to collect correct data than to collect all the data, or, put it another way, it is better to have a missing datum than a wrong datum. Results from Section 13.4.3 show that collecting negative learning examples is also very important, as negative examples can significantly improve the learnability.

13.7   SUMMARY AND FURTHER READING

The only way to have a friend is to be one.

— *Ralph Waldo Emerson*

- The *learning theory* studies a basic question: Is there an algorithm that is able to learn, after a finite reading from an infinite sequence of words from a target language, a rule that differentiates between the words from the target language and all other words? If such an algorithm exists we say that the target language is *learnable*. The results of the theory constrain the learnability of certain classes of languages with respect to various characteristics of the learning algorithms, the target languages, and the input data.

- The learning theory is based on the computability theory and the theory of recursive functions. The basic result of the computability theory is the undecidability of any universal formalism (such as algorithms, recursive functions, grammars of type 0, and the first order predicate calculus).

- A set is *recursively enumerable* if there exists a Turing generator that generates all words from that set, and no other words. The set is *recursive* (decidable) if it and its complement are recursively enumerable. The task of the learner is to identify the Turing generator for a given input sequence of words.

- By definition, for non-recursively enumerable languages there are no algorithmic generators, therefore they cannot be learnable. Any single recursively enumerable language is *trivially learnable* by a learner, that always outputs the index of the corresponding Turing generator. The set of languages is *learnable*, if there exists a (recursive) learner that is able to learn every language from that set.

- The set of all finite languages is learnable by certain recursive learners. *The set of all recursive languages and the set of all recursively enumerable languages are not learnable.*

- The set of all *single valued total recursively enumerable sets* represents the set of all total recursive functions. It is *not learnable* by any recursive learner, even if the input data contains positive and negative examples (in fact one positive example for such a language simultaneously provides an infinite number of negative examples).

- There exist collections of languages that can be learned by some Turing machines but cannot be learned *incrementally*. *Time limits* are more restrictive for incremental than for non-incremental learners.

- For certain languages from infinite collections of languages it holds that, if any learner finds a correct hypothesis for one such language, the same learner is unable to find an equivalent but sufficiently *simple hypothesis*.

- *If an algorithm uses a restricted hypothesis space that, although restricted, still contains all the target languages, it can happen, due to that restriction, that the algorithm is unable to learn certain target languages.* For machine learning of certain infinite languages the learning algorithm must occasionally put a finite hypothesis which does not cover any so far unseen words. For machine learning of certain languages the learning algorithm must occasionally put inconsistent hypotheses.

- Reliable learners, that never converge to the wrong language, can identify only finite languages.

- The collection of languages, learnable from noisy or incomplete input, may contain only languages that differ from each other in an infinite number of words. When learning from noisy input the learner must not converge on every input sequence and sometimes it has to repeat some previously abandoned hypotheses. *Noise in input data is a more serious restriction than the incompleteness.*

- Sometimes it is better not to restrict the hypothesis space but rather to restrict the final hypotheses – hypotheses towards which the learner converges.

- Extending the input with *negative examples* may significantly improve the learnability.

The identification in the limit paradigm was introduced by Gold (1967). His seminal paper gives an extensive collection of basic results of the learning theory. There are several significant contributions to the field (Solomonoff, 1964; Blum and Blum, 1975; Angluin, 1980; Osherson and Weinstein, 1982; Osherson et al., 1982). We follow the notation and terminology of the excellent book by Osherson et al. (1986) which thoroughly and deeply covers the field of the formal learning theory. It provides also the formal proofs of most of the results mentioned in this chapter. The computability theory is described in classic books by Manna (1974) and Hopcroft and Ullman (1979), and the theory of recursive functions by Rogers (1967). The undecidability paradigm for algorithms is described in detail by Hopcroft and Ullman (1979) and in the context of the first order predicate calculus by Jeffrey (1981).

Although the identification paradigm is interesting as a theoretical framework with more philosophical than practical implications, it motivated the development of the system MIS by Shapiro (1981) which initiated a whole branch of machine learning, called Inductive logic programming (see Section 9.5).

Chapter 14

**Computational Learning Theory

Work expands so as to fill the time available for its completion.
— C. Northcote Parkinson

As opposed to the largely abstract learning theory, described in the previous chapter, computational learning theory is more practically oriented. It formally studies how to design computer programs that are capable of learning, and identifies the computational limits of learning by machines. This chapter provides a review of the field of computational learning theory and emphasizes its most important achievements.

14.1   INTRODUCTION

It's the job that's never started that takes longest to finish.
— J. R. R. Tolkien

When performing experimental and theoretical work in machine learning, one inevitably has to deal with many different problems (domains) of considerably different nature and difficulty. It is natural to start wondering if there exist any general principles that govern machine learning programs (learners). Can we identify learning problems that are more difficult than the others, regardless of applied learning algorithms and the number of provided learning examples? Can a general measure of problem difficulty be defined? Is there a lower bound on how many learning examples (sample complexity) are needed for successful learning? How much computational effort (time complexity) is required for a given sample size for successful learning? These are the questions the computational learning theory aims to answer. While they cannot be answered in general, we can, under certain fairly relaxed restrictions, define learning models for which we can set quantitative bounds for the above and other similar measures.

Computational learning theory is a more practically oriented extension of the

393

formal learning theory described in Chapter 13. It is a branch of theoretical computer science that formally studies how to design computer programs that are capable of learning, and identifies the computational limits of learning by machines. Historically, machine learning researchers have compared learning algorithms empirically, according to their performance on sample problems. While such evaluations provide useful information, it is often difficult to use such evaluations to make meaningful comparisons among competing learning algorithms. Computational learning theory provides a formal framework in which it is possible to precisely formulate and address questions regarding the performance of different learning algorithms. Thus, careful comparisons of both the predictive power and the computational efficiency of competing learning algorithms can be made. Three key aspects that must be formalized are:

- the way in which the learner interacts with its environment,
- the definition of success in completing the learning task,
- a formal definition of efficiency of both data usage (sample complexity) and processing time (time complexity).

It is important to remember that the theoretical learning models are abstractions of real-life problems. Close connections with experimentalists are useful to help validate or modify these abstractions so that the theoretical results reflect empirical performance. The computational learning theory research has therefore close connections to the machine learning research. Besides the model's predictive capability, the computational learning theory also addresses other important features such as simplicity, robustness to variations in the learning scenario, and an ability to create insights to empirically observed phenomena.

The introduction of the first formal definition of learning given by inductive inference researchers also witnessed the first theoretical studies of machine learning (described in more detail in Chapter 13). In early learning models, the learner is required to make a sequence of guesses based on a sequence of learning examples. This sequence should converge at some finite point to a single guess that correctly follows the underlying (unknown) rule. Early approaches did not attempt to capture any notion of efficiency of the learning process (as opposed to modern computational learning theory that emphasizes computational feasibility of a learning algorithm).

A different flavor of the learning theory also surfaced in the field of pattern recognition. Pattern recognition researchers focus only on issues related to the data requirements, as opposed to modern computational learning theory researchers that study both the data (information) requirements for learning as well as the time complexity of learning algorithms.

In this chapter we provide only basic theoretical results of computational learning theory, omitting the proofs as they are mostly well beyond the scope of this book. References to where the proofs can be found are provided in further reading. Section 14.2 describes the basic framework of concept learning and gives notation that we use throughout the chapter. Section 14.3 describes the PAC (distribution-free) model that initiated the field of computational learning theory. Most of the later discussion is based on this model. Section 14.4 discusses an important early result in the field – a demonstration of the relationships between the VC-dimension, a combinatorial measure, and the data requirements for PAC learning. Section 14.5 describes some commonly studied noise models and general techniques for PAC learning from noisy data. Section 14.6 covers some other (non-PAC) well-studied formal learning models – query and on-line learning. Along with having techniques to prove positive results, an important component of the learning theory research are methods for proving that a certain learning problem is hard. Section 14.7 describes some techniques, used to show that some learning problems are hard. Section 14.8 explores a variation of the PAC model, called the weak learning model, and study techniques for boosting the performance of a mediocre learning algorithm. In Section 14.9 we close with a brief summary and an overview of relevant further reading within the field of computational learning theory. In appendix A we review some useful concepts (asymptotic notation and computational complexity classes P, NP, and RP) and tools (union bound and Chernoff bounds) that are frequently used in computational learning theory.

14.2 GENERAL FRAMEWORK FOR CONCEPT LEARNING

Begin at the beginning and go on till you come to the end; then stop.
— Lewis Carroll

For the ease of exposition, we initially focus on binary (two-class) concept learning in which the learner's goal is to infer a description of an unknown target function that classifies (as positive or negative) examples from a given domain. Most of the definitions given here naturally extend to the general setting of learning multi-class or even real-valued target functions.

14.2.1 Basic notation

Let $\mathcal{X}$ be defined as the *example space* (domain), that is, the set of all possible examples (instances, objects) to be classified, either as positive or as negative. In the context of learning, we can think of $\mathcal{X}$ as a set of encodings of examples in the learner's world.

Two well-researched domains are the binary tuple (hypercube) $\{0,1\}^a$, and the a-dimensional continuous space $\mathbb{R}^a$. The former is frequently used when the problem consists of a binary attributes; each example can be then expressed as an element of $\{0,1\}^a$. Similarly, for a real-valued attributes, $\mathbb{R}^a$ can be used. A concept f is a binary (two-class) function over the domain $\mathcal{X}$. Each $\mathbf{x} \in \mathcal{X}$ is referred to as an example. A *concept* over $\mathcal{X}$ is a subset $f \subseteq \mathcal{X}$ of the example space. A *concept class* $\mathcal{C}$ is a collection of concepts on $\mathcal{X}$, or a subset of its power set: $\mathcal{C} \subseteq 2^{\mathcal{X}}$. Typically (but not always), it is assumed that the learner has prior knowledge of $\mathcal{C}$. In learning problems, examples are classified according to membership of a target concept $f \in \mathcal{C}$. Alternatively, a concept can be viewed as a function $f(\mathbf{x})$ that gives the classification (positive or negative) of concept $f \in C$ for each example $\mathbf{x} \in \mathcal{X}$. An example $\mathbf{x} \in \mathcal{X}$

is a positive example (for the given f) if $f(\mathbf{x}) = 1$ (or $\mathbf{x} \in f$), or a negative example if $f(\mathbf{x}) = 0$ (or $\mathbf{x} \notin f$).

Sometimes, $\mathcal{C}$ is decomposed into subclasses $\mathcal{C}_a$ according to some natural size measure a for encoding of examples. Often we refer to a as the size of the problem. For instance, in the domain of binary tuples, a is the number of binary attributes. Similarly, by $\mathcal{X}_a$ we denote the set of examples from $\mathcal{X}$ to be classified for each problem of size a. Obviously we have $\mathcal{C} = \cup_{a \geq 1} \mathcal{C}_a$ and $\mathcal{X} = \cup_{a \geq 1} \mathcal{X}_a$.

14.2.2   Some typical concept classes

Historically, two concept classes have been extensively studied: halfspaces in $\mathbb{R}^n$ and Boolean concepts in $\{0, 1\}^a$.

Halfspaces

A *halfspace* in $\mathbb{R}^a$ is defined with an $a - 1$ dimensional hyperplane dividing $\mathbb{R}^a$ into two subspaces. It is defined by the vector $\vec{a} \in \mathbb{R}^a$ and the scalar $b \in \mathbb{R}$. Let $\mathbf{x} = (x_1, \ldots, x_a)$ be an example $\mathbf{x} \in \mathbb{R}^a$. The halfspace $\mathcal{C}_{\vec{a}, b}$ classifies an example $\mathbf{x}$ as positive if $\vec{a} \cdot \vec{x} \geq b$, and as negative if $\vec{a} \cdot \vec{x} < b$. In $\mathbb{R}^2$ a halfspace is defined by a straight line, and each example is a point on a $\mathbb{R}^2$ plane. For instance, $2x_1 - x_2 \geq 1$ defines a halfspace in $\mathbb{R}^2$. Thus the example $(0, 0)$ is classified as negative, and $(1, 0)$ as positive.

The concept class $\mathcal{C}_{\text{halfspace}}$ is a set of halfspaces in $\mathbb{R}^a$. The concept class $\mathcal{C}_{\text{halfspace}}^{\cap_s}$ is the set of all the intersections of up to s halfspaces in $\mathbb{R}^a$. For $\mathcal{C}_{\text{halfspace}}^{\cap_s}$, an example is positive exactly when it is classified as positive by each of the halfspaces forming the intersection. The set of positive points forms a convex polytope in $\mathbb{R}^a$. Such concept classes have been historically used for introductory and illustrative examples. Of them, the most popular is the class of axis-parallel rectangles in $\mathbb{R}^2$ (Figure 14.1). For this concept class, several nice properties can be proved using only simple and readily comprehensible techniques such as the *union bound*.

Boolean concepts

For Boolean concepts, the domain is $\{0, 1\}^a$. Let $x_1, \ldots, x_a$ denote the values of a binary attributes. A basic building block of a Boolean concept is a *literal*; it is either x_i or $\overline{x_i}$ for $i = 1, \ldots, a$. A *term* (a conjunctive clause) is a conjunction of literals. A *disjunctive normal form* (DNF) formula is a disjunction of terms. One of the open problems of computational learning theory is whether or not the concept class of DNF formulas is efficiently PAC learnable. Since the problem of learning general DNF formulas is a historical open problem, several subclasses have been obtained by making restrictions on how literals can be used and limiting either the size of each term or the number of terms. A *monotone* DNF formula is a DNF formula in which there are no negated variables. A *read-once* DNF formula is a DNF formula in which each variable appears at most once. A *k-term* DNF formula is a DNF formula in which there are at most k terms. A *k-DNF* formula is a DNF formula in which at most k literals

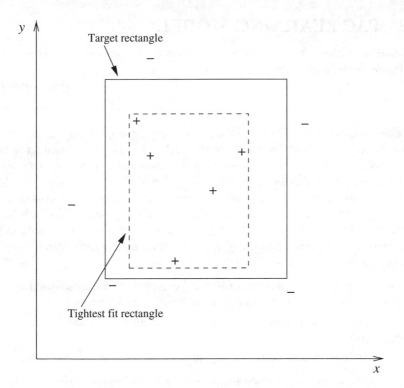

Figure 14.1: Learning axis-parallel rectangles.

are used by each term. A disjunctive clause is a disjunction of literals. A *conjunctive normal form* (CNF) formula is a conjunction of disjunctive clauses. A k-CNF formula is a CNF formula in which at most k literals are used by each clause.

14.2.3 Importance of representation

Both the time and the sample complexity of the learning algorithm obviously depend on the complexity of the underlying target concept. In Chapter 13 we have seen that learnability is often feasible only if the hypothesis space is larger than a subspace containing the target hypothesis. Besides that, the algorithm's efficiency depends heavily on the representation on its hypotheses (that in turn represent concepts). Namely, the complexity of the target concept is dependent on the representation scheme $\mathcal{H}$ used for describing the concepts. Because of the crucial importance of representation, the representation often names the concept class.

The crucial importance of hypothesis representation can be illustrated with the following example. 3-term DNF formulae are not efficiently PAC learnable using a 3-term DNF representation. They are, however efficiently PAC learnable by using a more powerful 3-CNF representation.

14.3   PAC LEARNING MODEL

When you have eliminated all which is impossible, then whatever remains, however improbable, must be the truth.

— Arthur Conan Doyle

Although our exposition of learning models is fairly general, it must be noted that it follows some general guidelines. While the goal of learning is to learn an unknown concept, its concept class is not arbitrary and is assumed in advance. Our learning setting is always such that learning occurs in a probabilistic way since examples are drawn randomly according to a fixed (unknown and unrestricted) distribution. The learner's hypotheses are evaluated in the same probabilistic setting in which learning is performed. There is also an imperative that learning must be efficient both in terms of the sample and the time complexity. Ideally, a learning algorithm should satisfy the following conditions:

- it should require a small number of learning examples, in the sense that this number is bounded by a fixed polynomial in some learning parameters,

- the amount of computation should be small (again, polynomial in some learning parameters),

- the algorithm ultimately outputs a hypothesis h such that its error is small.

The error of the hypothesis h when learning the concept c given the example space $\mathcal{X}$ and the unknown (but fixed) distribution $\mathcal{D}$ is defined with

$$error_{\mathcal{D}}(h) = P_{\mathbf{x} \in \mathcal{D}}(c(\mathbf{x}) \neq h(\mathbf{x})) \tag{14.1}$$

14.3.1   Basic PAC learning model

The field of computational learning theory began with the PAC – probably approximately correct – learning model. In the PAC learning model examples are generated according to an unknown probability distribution $\mathcal{D}$. Therefore the PAC learning model is often referred to as being *distribution-free*. The goal of a PAC learning algorithm is to classify with high accuracy (with respect to the distribution D) any new (unclassified) examples.

Definition 14.1 (Proper PAC learning model)**.** To obtain information about an unknown target concept $c \in \mathcal{C}$, represented by a representation class $\mathcal{H}$ the learner A is provided with labeled (positive and negative) examples of c, drawn randomly according to some unknown target distribution $\mathcal{D}$ over $\mathcal{X}_a$.

The input parameters ϵ and δ are pre-selected such that $0 < \epsilon, \delta < 1$, and k is an upper bound on the representation of c. The learner's goal is to output, with probability at least $1 - \delta$, a hypothesis $h \in \mathcal{H}$ that with probability of at most ϵ disagrees with c on a randomly drawn example from $\mathcal{D}$ (thus, h has error at most ϵ). If such a learning algorithm A exists (that is, an algorithm A meeting the goal for any $a \geq 1$, any target concept $c \in C_a$, any target distribution $\mathcal{D}$, any $0 < \epsilon, \delta < 1$, and any $k > |h|$), then C is PAC learnable.◇

Definition 14.2 (Efficient PAC learning). A PAC learning algorithm is a polynomial-time (efficient) algorithm if the number of examples drawn and the computation time are polynomial in a, k, $1/\epsilon$ and $1/\delta$.◇

Most learning algorithms are really functions from samples to hypotheses (given a sample S the learning algorithm produces a hypothesis h). For the sake of analysis we say that for a given ϵ and δ, the learning algorithm is guaranteed with probability at least $1 - \delta$ to output a hypothesis with error at most ϵ given a sample whose size is a function of ϵ, δ, a and k. In principle, one could run a PAC algorithm on provided data and then empirically measure the error of the final hypothesis. An important exception are statistical query algorithms since they often use ϵ for more than just determining the desired sample size (see Section 14.5.2).

As originally formulated, the PAC learnability also requires the hypothesis to be a member of the concept class C_a. We refer to this more stringent learning model as proper PAC-learnability. A prerequisite for proper PAC learning is the ability to solve the consistent hypothesis problem, which is the problem of finding a hypothesis h describing a concept $c \in C$ that is consistent with a provided sample.

A more general form of learning, in which the goal is to find a polynomial-time algorithm that classifies instances accurately in the PAC sense, is called prediction. In this less stringent variation of the PAC model, the algorithm does not need to output a hypothesis for the concept class C but instead is just required to make its prediction in polynomial time. The idea of prediction in the PAC model is closely related to that of transduction (see Section 3.5.4) in the sense that it also disregards an overall hypothesis in favour of predictions. In general, when referring to the PAC learning model we allow the learner to output any hypothesis that can be evaluated in polynomial time. That is, given a hypothesis h and an example $\mathbf{x}$, we require that $h(\mathbf{x})$ can be computed in polynomial time.

14.3.2 Some variations of the PAC learning model

Many variations of the PAC model are known to be equivalent (in terms of what concept classes are efficiently learnable) to the model defined above. In the definition of the proper PAC model, along with receiving ϵ and δ as input, the learner also receives a (a size of an encoded example), and k (an upper bound on the smallest representation of c in $\mathcal{H}$). It is possible to reduce the parameters to just ϵ and δ. By looking at just one example, the value of a is known. If the demand of polynomial-time computation is replaced with expected polynomial-time computation, then the learning algorithm can estimate the value of the parameter k by a technique called *doubling*.

The doubling technique is used to convert an algorithm A designed to have k as input to an algorithm B that has no prior knowledge of k. Algorithm B begins with an estimate, say 1, for its upper bound on k and runs algorithm A using this estimate to obtain hypothesis h. Then algorithm B uses a hypothesis testing procedure to determine if the error of h is at most ϵ. Since the learner can only gather a random sample of examples, it is not possible to distinguish a hypothesis with error ϵ from one with error slightly greater than ϵ. However, by drawing a sufficiently large sample and looking at the empirical performance of h on that sample, we can distinguish a hypothesis with error at most $\epsilon/2$ from one with error more than ϵ. In particular, given a sample of size $n = \lceil \frac{32}{\epsilon} \ln \frac{2}{\delta} \rceil$ (calculated by using Chernoff bounds), and a hypothesis h that misclassifies at most $\frac{3}{4}\epsilon n$ examples, h is accepted by B. Otherwise, algorithm B doubles its estimate for k and repeats the process.

14.4 VAPNIK-CHERVONENKIS DIMENSION

Silence is argument carried out by other means.

— *Che Guevara*

Although we are concerned with the time complexity of the learning algorithm, an even more fundamental question is the sample complexity (data requirements). A combinatorial parameter (Vapnik-Chervonenkis dimension) is strongly connected to information-theoretic bounds on the sample size needed to have an accurate generalization. However, given a sufficiently large sample the computational problem of finding a "good" hypothesis still remains.

Definition 14.3 (Shattering). A finite set $S \subseteq \mathcal{X}$ is shattered by the concept class $\mathcal{C}$ if for each of $2^{|S|}$ subsets $S' \subseteq S$, there is a concept $f \in \mathcal{C}$ that contains all examples from S' and none from $S - S'$. In other words, for any of $2^{|S|}$ possible labelings of S (where each example $s \in S$ is either positive or negative), there is some $f \in \mathcal{C}$ that realizes the desired labeling (see an example in Figure 14.2). ⋄

Definition 14.4 (Vapnik-Chervonenkis dimension). The Vapnik-Chervonenkis (VC) dimension of concept class $\mathcal{C}$, denoted $\text{VCD}(\mathcal{C})$, is the smallest d for which no set of $d + 1$ examples is shattered by $\mathcal{C}$. Equivalently, $\text{VCD}(\mathcal{C})$ is the cardinality of the largest finite set of points $S \subseteq \mathcal{X}$ that is shattered by $\mathcal{C}$. ⋄

14.4.1 Calculating the VC-Dimension

To prove that $\text{VCD}(\mathcal{C}) \geq d$ it suffices to give d examples that can be shattered. However, to prove $\text{VCD}(\mathcal{C}) \leq d$ one must show that no set of $d + 1$ examples can be shattered. Since the VC-dimension is fundamental in determining the sample complexity required for PAC learning, we sketch through several illustrative computations of the VC-dimension.

Intervals of the real line. It is easy to see that any set of two points can be shattered by an interval, so the VC-dimension is at least 2. However, there exist labelings of any three points on a line (Figure 14.3) that cannot be realized by any interval. The VC dimension for the concept class of intervals of the real line is therefore 2.

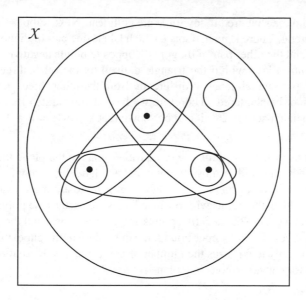

Figure 14.2: Three examples (points in example space $\mathcal{X} = \mathbb{R}^2$) being shattered by the class of two-dimensional convex shapes. All 8 possible ways of labeling the points as positive or negative can be realized.

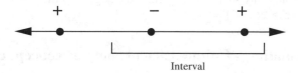

Figure 14.3: Three examples (points on a line) that cannot be shattered by any interval.

Axis-aligned rectangles in the plane. For this concept class the points lying on or inside the target rectangle are positive, and points lying outside the target rectangle are negative (Figure 14.1). Firstly, it is easily seen that there is a set of four points (e.g. $\{(0,1),(0,-1),(1,0),(-1,0)\}$ that can be shattered. Thus $\text{VCD}(\mathcal{C}) \geq 4$. We now argue that no set of five points can be shattered. The smallest bounding axis-parallel rectangle defined by the five points is in fact defined by at most four of the points. Let p be a non-defining point in the set. The set cannot be shattered since it is not possible for p to be classified as negative while also classifying the others as positive. Thus $\text{VCD}(\mathcal{C}) = 4$.

Halfspaces in $\mathbb{R}^a$. Let us first consider the case where $a = 2$, that is, halfspaces in a $\mathbb{R}^2$ plane. Points lying in or on the halfspace are positive, and the remaining points are negative. It is easily shown that any three non-collinear points (e.g. $(0,1),(0,0),(1,0)$) are shattered by $\mathcal{C}$. Thus $\text{VCD}(\mathcal{C}) \geq 3$. We now show that no set of size four can be shattered by $\mathcal{C}$. If at least three of the points are collinear then there is no halfspace that contains the two extreme points but does not contain the middle point. Thus the four points cannot be shattered if any three are collinear. Next, suppose that the points form a quadrilateral. There is no halfspace which labels one pair of diagonally opposite points positive and the other pair of diagonally opposite points negative. The final case is when one point p lays within the triangle defined by the other three. In this case there is no halfspace which labels p differently from the other three. Thus clearly the four points cannot be shattered. Therefore we have demonstrated that $\text{VCD}(\mathcal{C}) = 3$. Generalizing to halfspaces in $\mathbb{R}^a$, it can be shown that $\text{VCD}(\mathcal{C}) = a + 1$.

Convex polygons in the $\mathbb{R}^2$ plane. For convex a-gons in the plane the lower bound on the VC-dimension is induced by showing that any labeling of any $2a + 1$ points on a circle can be realized. For a particular labeling, if there are more examples labeled negative than positive, the points with positive labels are used as the polygon's vertices. Otherwise, the tangents to the negative points are used as edges, and their intersections as polygon's vertices. For the upper bound, it can be shown that choosing the points to lie on a circle actually maximizes the number of points that can be shattered. Thus, the VC-dimension for convex a-gons in a plane is $2a + 1$.

Closed sets in $\mathbb{R}^2$. All points lying in the set or on the boundary of the set are positive, and all points lying outside the set are negative. Any set can be shattered by $\mathcal{C}$, since a closed set can assume any shape in $\mathbb{R}^2$. Thus, the largest set that can be shattered by $\mathcal{C}$ is infinite, and hence $\text{VCD}(\mathcal{C}) = \infty$.

14.4.2   Calculating VC-dimension of complex concept classes

Suppose we wanted to compute the VC-dimension of $\mathcal{C}_{\text{halfspace}}^{\cap_s}$, the class of intersections of up to s halfspaces over $\mathbb{R}^a$. We would like to utilize our knowledge of the VC-dimension of $\mathcal{C}_{\text{halfspace}}$, the class of halfspaces over $\mathbb{R}^a$. For this purpose we can make use of the following theorem:

Theorem 14.1. *Let $\mathcal{C}$ be a concept class with $\text{VCD}(\mathcal{C}) \leq d$. Then the class defined by the intersection of up to s concepts from $\mathcal{C}$ has VC-dimension at most $2ds \log_2(3s)$.* $\diamond$

It can be shown that Theorem 14.1 applies even if we replace intersection with any Boolean function. Thus the concept class $\mathcal{C}_{\text{halfspace}}^{\cap_s}$ of up to s halfspaces, where each halfspace is defined over $\mathbb{R}^d$, has VC-dimension at most $2(d + 1)s \log_2(3s)$.

14.4.3   VC-dimension and PAC learning model

There is a strong connection between the VC-dimension and data requirements of the PAC model. First, an important property is that for $\text{VCD}(\mathcal{C}) = d$, the number of different labelings $\Phi_d(S)$ that can be realized by using $\mathcal{C}$ for a set S, is at most

$$\Phi_d(S) \leq \left(\frac{e|S|}{d}\right)^d = O(|S|^d) \tag{14.2}$$

where constant e is the natural logarithm base[1].

Thus, for a constant $d < |S|$ we have a polynomial growth in the number of labelings versus the exponential growth of the power set $2^{|S|}$ (the number of all possible labelings).

A key result in the PAC model accounts for the VC-dimension of the hypothesis class and gives an upper bound on the sample complexity needed to learn probably (in terms of δ) approximately correct (in terms of ϵ). One can design a learning algorithm A for the concept class $\mathcal{C}$ using hypothesis space $\mathcal{H}$ in the following manner. Any concept $h \in H$ consistent with a sample of size

$$|S| = max \left\{ \frac{4}{\epsilon} \log_2 \frac{2}{\delta}, \frac{8 \, \text{VCD}(\mathcal{H})}{\epsilon} \log_2 13\epsilon \right\} \qquad (14.3)$$

has error at most ϵ with probability at least $1 - \delta$. To obtain an efficient (polynomial-time) PAC learning algorithm, what remains is to solve the algorithmic problem of finding a hypothesis from $\mathcal{H}$ consistent with the labeled sample. Furthermore, there exists an information-theoretic lower bound that learning any concept class $\mathcal{C}$ requires at least

$$|S| = \Omega \left(\frac{1}{\epsilon} \log \frac{1}{\delta} + \frac{\text{VCD}(\mathcal{C})}{\epsilon} \right) \qquad (14.4)$$

examples in the worst case. A key limitation of this technique to design a PAC learning algorithm is that the hypothesis must be drawn from some fixed hypothesis class $\mathcal{H}$. In particular, the complexity of the hypothesis class must be independent of the sample size. However, often the algorithmic problem of finding such a hypothesis from the desired class is *NP*-hard, and hypotheses grow with the size of the sample. In such cases further analysis can be performed through Occam algorithms.

14.4.4   Occam learning

The *Occam learning model* formalizes the famous Occam's razor principle (see also Section 3.1.2) in the sense of the PAC learning model.

As opposed to the PAC learning model, in the Occam learning model we judge the hypotheses not by measuring their predictive power, but by how succinctly they explain the observed data (the learning set of labeled examples). While in PAC learning the learning set is used only as an aid for determining an accurate model of the target concept c and distribution $\mathcal{D}$, in Occam learning we are interested only with a fixed set available for learning.

It can be shown that under appropriate conditions, any algorithm that always finds a succinct hypothesis consistent with a given learning set is also a PAC learning algorithm.

Let $\mathcal{X} = \cup_{a \geq 1} \mathcal{X}_a$ be the example space, let $\mathcal{C} = \cup_{a \geq 1} \mathcal{C}_a$ be the target concept class, and let $\mathcal{H} = \cup_{a \geq 1} \mathcal{H}_a$ be the hypothesis representation class. For a concept $c \in \mathcal{C}$ let $k = |c|$ denote the size (bit length) of the smallest representation (encoding) of c in $\mathcal{H}$

---

[1]For definition of O- and Ω-notations see Section A.2 in the appendix.

Definition 14.5. Let $\alpha \geq 0$ and $0 \leq \beta < 1$ be constants. A is an (α, β)-*Occam algorithm* for C using $\mathcal{H}$ if on a learning set S with cardinality $n = |S|$, labeled according to $c \in C_a$ with size $k = |c|$, A outputs a hypothesis $h \in \mathcal{H}$ such that:

- h is consistent with S (for each learning example **x**, $h(\mathbf{x})$ equals to its true label)
- $|h| \leq (ak)^\alpha n^\beta$ (h is succinct)

A is an *efficient* (α, β)-*Occam algorithm* if its running time is polynomial-bounded in a, n, and k. $\diamond$

By the following two theorems can be shown that any efficient Occam algorithm is also an efficient PAC learning algorithm.

Theorem 14.2. *Let A be an efficient (α, β)-Occam algorithm for C using $\mathcal{H}$. Let $\mathcal{D}$ be the target distribution over the example space $\mathcal{X}$, let $c \in C_a$ be the target concept, and $0 < \epsilon, \delta \leq 1$. There exists a constant $\gamma > 0$ such that if A is given a random sample S of $n = |S|$ examples drawn from $\mathcal{X}$ according to $\mathcal{D}$, so that n satisfies*

$$n = |S| \geq \gamma \left(\frac{1}{\epsilon} \log_2 \frac{1}{\delta} + \left(\frac{nk^\alpha}{\epsilon} \right)^{\frac{1}{1-\beta}} \right)$$

then with probability at least $1 - \delta$ the error of h is less than ϵ.$\diamond$

This result can be rewritten in a more general way.

Theorem 14.3. *Let C be the target concept class. Let $\mathcal{H}_{a,n}$ be the (restricted) hypothesis representation class for C where each example has size a, and the sample size is $|S| = n$. Let $\mathcal{H}_a = \cup_{n \geq 1} \mathcal{H}_{n,a}$ and let $\mathcal{H} = \cup_{a > 1} \mathcal{H}_a$ be the (unrestricted) hypothesis representation class. Let A be an algorithm such that for any a and any $c \in C_a$, if A is given as input a learning set S consisting of n labeled examples of c, then A runs in time polynomial in a, n and k (an upper bound on the shortest representation of c in $\mathcal{H}$), and outputs a hypothesis $h \in \mathcal{H}_{a,n}$ that is consistent with S. There exists a constant $b > 0$ such that for any a, any distribution $\mathcal{D}$ over $\mathcal{X}_a$, and any target concept $c \in C_a$ if A is given a random sample S of $n = |S|$ examples drawn from $\mathcal{X}$ according to $\mathcal{D}$, so that n satisfies*

$$n = |S| \geq b\epsilon n - \log_2 \frac{1}{\delta}$$

then A is guaranteed to find a hypothesis $h \in \mathcal{H}_a$ such that with probability at least $1 - \delta$ its error is less than ϵ. $\diamond$

Theorem 14.3 is more general than Theorem 14.2 as the algorithm A is not required to be an efficient Occam algorithm.

The above results can be used in conjunction with the VC-dimension of a given concept class and its representation class to calculate the sample size lower bounds when the algorithmic problem of finding such a hypothesis from the desired class is *NP*-hard, and hypotheses grow with the size of the sample.

Theorem 14.4. *Let C be a concept class and $\mathcal{H}$ its representation class with* $\text{VCD}(\mathcal{H}) = d$. *Let A be an algorithm that takes as input a learning set S consisting of n labeled examples of $c \in C$, and outputs a hypothesis $h \in \mathcal{H}$ consistent with S. Then A is a PAC learning algorithm for C using $\mathcal{H}$ when given a random sample S of $n = |S|$ examples drawn from X according to $\mathcal{D}$, so that n satisfies*

$$n = |S| \geq \xi \left(\frac{1}{\epsilon} \log \frac{1}{\delta} + \frac{d}{\epsilon} \log \frac{1}{\epsilon} \right)$$

for some constant $\xi \geq 0$. ◇

If we choose a more powerful hypothesis representation (such that $\mathcal{H} \supset C$) it follows that $\text{VCD}(\mathcal{H}) \geq \text{VCD}(C)$. While we may reduce a computation time by choosing a more powerful representation $\mathcal{H}$, this may increase the lower bound of required examples.

There exists also (a significantly more loose) upper bound on the number of learning examples.

Theorem 14.5. *Any algorithm for PAC learning of a concept class C whose VC-dimension is d, must use at most $\Omega(d/\epsilon)$ examples.* ◇

According to Theorems 14.2 and 14.3 we see that by obtaining sufficient data compression we can obtain good generalization. Let $\mathcal{H}_{a,n}$ be the hypothesis space used by algorithm A when each example has size a, the target concept has size k, and the sample size is $n = |S|$. Let A be an Occam algorithm for a concept class C using a hypothesis space $\mathcal{H}_{a,n}$ whose hypothesis size is bounded by some fixed polynomial $p(a, k)$. If $\text{VCD}(\mathcal{H}_{a,n}) \leq p(k, a)(\log_2 n)^\ell$ (and thus $|h| \leq p(k, a)(\log_2 n)^\ell$) for some polynomial $p(k, a) \geq 2$ and $\ell \geq 1$ then the size of h has only a logarithmic dependence on the sample size n. It can be shown that A is a PAC learning algorithm for C using sample size

$$n = |S| \geq \max \left\{ \frac{4}{\epsilon} \log_2 \frac{2}{\delta}, \frac{2^{\ell+4} p(k, a)}{\epsilon} \left(\log_2 \frac{8(2\ell+2)^{\ell+1} p(k, a)}{\epsilon} \right)^{\ell+1} \right\} \quad (14.5)$$

However, only a sub-linear dependence is required to show the following general result. Let A be an Occam algorithm for concept class C that has hypothesis space $\mathcal{H}_{a,n}$. If $\text{VCD}(H_{a,n}) \leq p(k, a)n^\beta$ for some polynomial $p(k, a) \geq 2$ and $\beta < 1$, then A is a PAC learning algorithm for C using sample size

$$n = |S| \geq \max \left\{ \frac{2}{\epsilon} \ln \frac{1}{\delta}, \left(\frac{2 \ln 2}{\epsilon} p(k, a) \right)^{\frac{1}{1-\beta}} \right\} \quad (14.6)$$

14.5   LEARNING IN THE PRESENCE OF NOISE

Always do sober what you said you'd do drunk. That will teach you to keep your mouth shut.

— *Ernest Hemingway*

The basic definition of PAC learning assumes that the input data is drawn randomly from $\mathcal{D}$ and properly labeled according to the target concept. Clearly, for learning algorithms to be of practical use they must be robust with respect to noise in the training data.

14.5.1   Models of noise

In the context of PAC learning several formal models of noise have been proposed.

Random classification noise.   This is the first and most thoroughly studied noise model.   In this model the learner receives the uncorrupted example $(\mathbf{x}, \ell)$ with probability $1 - \eta$. However, the learner receives the example $(\mathbf{x}, \overline{\ell})$ with probability η. So in this noise model, the learner usually gets a correct example, but for some small fraction η of example the labels are inverted.

Malicious classification noise.   In this model the learner receives the uncorrupted example $(\mathbf{x}, \ell)$ with probability $1 - \eta$. However, with probability η, the learner receives the example $(\mathbf{x}, \ell')$ in which $\mathbf{x}$ is unchanged, but the label ℓ' is selected by an adversary who has infinite computing power and knows of the learning algorithm, the target concept, and the distribution $\mathcal{D}$.

Malicious noise.   This is yet another noise model in which the learner receives the uncorrupted example $(\mathbf{x}, \ell)$ with probability $1 - \eta$. However, with probability η, the learner receives an example $(\mathbf{x}', \ell')$ about which no assumptions whatsoever can be made. In particular, this example (and its label) may be maliciously selected by an adversary. Thus in this model, the learner usually gets a correct example, but some small fraction (η) of examples are noisy and the nature of the noise is unknown.

Uniform random attribute noise.   This model is valid only when example space is $\{0, 1\}^a$. Here, an example $(x_1, x_2, \ldots, x_a; \ell)$ is corrupted by a random process that independently flips each bit x_i to $\overline{x}_i$ with probability η for $1 \le i \le a$. The label of the example is never altered. In this noise model, the attributes' values are subject to noise, but that noise is as benign as possible. For example, the attributes' values may be sent over a noisy channel, but not the label.

Product random attribute noise.   In this model, an example $(x_1, x_2, \ldots, x_a; \ell)$ is corrupted by a random process of independently flipping each bit x_i to $\overline{x}_i$ with some fixed probability $\eta_i \le \eta$ for each $1 \le i \le a$. Thus unlike the model of uniform random attribute noise, the noise rate associated with each bit of the example may be different. This model is also valid only when the example space is $\{0, 1\}^a$.

Nasty noise. When the PAC learning algorithm during its execution asks for n examples they are generated by a so-called nasty adversary that works according to the following steps. First, the adversary independently chooses $n = |S|$ examples according to the fixed distribution $\mathcal{D}$ as usual in the PAC model. Upon seeing the specific n examples that were chosen (and using his knowledge of the target function, the distribution $\mathcal{D}$ and the learning algorithm), the adversary is allowed to remove a fraction η of the examples at its choice, and replace these examples by the same number of arbitrary examples of its choice; the n modified examples are then given to the learning algorithm. The only restriction on the adversary is that the number of examples that the adversary is allowed to modify should be distributed according to the binomial distribution with parameters η (the noise rate) and n.

14.5.2   Gaining noise tolerance with random classification noise

The first work on designing noise-tolerant PAC algorithms was done for learning Boolean conjunctions by constructing an algorithm that tolerates random classification noise of a rate approaching the information-theoretic barrier of $1/2$. It makes use of a general technique for finding a hypothesis that minimizes disagreements with a sufficiently large sample and thus allows for handling the random classification noise of any rate approaching $1/2$. However, even the very simple problem of minimizing disagreements (when there are no assumptions about the noise) is NP-hard. The whole approach taken was problem-specific, and it was only with the statistical query learning model that an efficient general approach has emerged.

Statistical query learning model

The first (computationally feasible) tool to design noise-tolerant PAC algorithms was provided by the *statistical query model*. In this model, rather than sampling labeled examples, the learner requests the value of various statistics.

A statistical query model places a restriction on the way in which a PAC learning algorithm can use the learning examples. A statistical query is a tuple of the form $SQ(\chi, \tau)$. Here, χ is a mapping $\mathcal{X} \times \{0, 1\} \rightarrow \{0, 1\}$ and $0 < \tau \leq 1$ is a *tolerance* of the statistical query. χ can be considered as a mapping of a labeled example $(\mathbf{x}, c(\mathbf{x}))$ belonging to the concept c, to 0 or 1, indicating the absence or presence of some property in $(\mathbf{x}, c(\mathbf{x}))$. The choice of both χ and τ is left to the learning algorithm.

For a fixed concept $c \in \mathcal{C}$ and distribution $\mathcal{D}$, we interpret a statistical query $SQ(\chi, \tau)$ as a request for the value

$$P_\chi = P_{\mathbf{x} \in \mathcal{D}} (\chi(\mathbf{x}, c(\mathbf{x})) = 1)) \qquad (14.7)$$

where $P_{\mathbf{x} \in \mathcal{D}}(\cdot)$ suggests that $\mathbf{x}$ is drawn at random from distribution $\mathcal{D}$. However, the result of a query $SQ(\chi, \tau)$ is not a true value P_χ, but an approximation. It can be any value $\hat{P}_\chi$ satisfying $P_\chi - \tau \leq \hat{P}_\chi \leq P_\chi + \tau$.

For example, let us have $\chi_\mathcal{D}(h(\mathbf{x}) = 1) \wedge (c(\mathbf{x}) = 0)$ which is true when $\mathbf{x}$ is a negative example but the hypothesis h classifies $\mathbf{x}$ as positive. The probability that χ is true for a random example is therefore the false positive rate of hypothesis h.

Definition 14.6 (Statistical query model). Let C be the concept class and $\mathcal{H}$ a representation class for C over the example space $\mathcal{X}$. C is efficiently learnable from statistical queries using $\mathcal{H}$ if there exists a learning algorithm A and polynomials $p(\cdot, \cdot, \cdot)$, $q(\cdot, \cdot, \cdot)$ and $r(\cdot, \cdot, \cdot)$ with the property that for any $c \in \mathcal{C}_a$, for any distribution $\mathcal{D}$ over $\mathcal{X}$ and for any $0 < \epsilon < 1/2$ it will produce a hypothesis h such that it holds:

- For every query $SQ(\chi, \tau)$ made by A the predicate χ can be evaluated in time $q(1/\epsilon, a, k)$, and $1/\tau$ is bounded by $r(1/\epsilon, a, k)$.

- A will halt in time bounded by $p(1/\epsilon, a, k)$.

- The output hypothesis $h \in \mathcal{H}$ will have error not greater than ϵ. ◇

Here, a is some natural measure of the concept subclass $\mathcal{C}_a$, and k is an upper bound on the smallest representation size of c in $\mathcal{H}$. We can see that the parameter δ has disappeared from the above definition. As it was used to guard against a small (but non-zero) probability of drawing an unrepresentative learning sample from $\mathcal{D}$, it is not necessary in the statistical query learning, as here the sampling process is completely determined by the query tolerance parameter τ.

The connection between statistical queries and the PAC learning model is evident from the following theorem.

Theorem 14.6. *Let C be the concept class and $\mathcal{H}$ a representation class for C over the example space $\mathcal{X}$. Then if C is efficiently learnable from statistical queries using $\mathcal{H}$, C is efficiently PAC learnable in the presence of random classification noise.* ◇

Relative-error statistical query learning model

A relative-error statistical query model builds upon and extends the original statistical query model. The main difference is that the allowed errors (tolerance) of the approximation of P_χ are now relative – they depend on the magnitude of P_χ – and that there is some threshold for a lower bound of an approximation. Thus, a *relative-error statistical query* takes the form $SQ(\chi, \mu, \theta)$ where χ is a predicate over labeled examples, μ is a relative error bound, and θ is a threshold.

For a target concept c, we define $P_\chi = P_\mathcal{D}(\chi(\mathbf{x}, c(\mathbf{x})))$ where $P_\mathcal{D}$ is again used to denote that $\mathbf{x}$ is drawn at random from distribution $\mathcal{D}$. If $P_\chi \geq \theta$ then $SQ(\chi, \mu, \theta)$ must return an estimate such that $P_\chi(1 - \mu) \leq \hat{P}_\chi \leq P_\chi(1 + \mu)$. Otherwise, the statistical query must return a value indicating that the threshold has been exceeded.

As in the statistical query model there is no confidence parameter δ. Again, this is because statistical queries guarantee that the estimates meet the given requirements. However, when we use random labeled examples to simulate the statistical queries, we can only guarantee that with high probability the estimates meet their requirements. Thus the results on converting a statistical query algorithm into a PAC algorithm reintroduce the confidence parameter δ. It can be shown that by drawing a sufficiently large sample a statistical query can be reliably estimated (within a given tolerance level). More specifically, in the relative-error statistical query model with a set $\mathcal{Q}$ of possible queries, it can be shown that a sample of size

$$|S| = O\left(\frac{1}{\mu^2\theta\log\frac{|\mathcal{Q}|}{\delta}}\right) \qquad (14.8)$$

is sufficient to appropriately answer a relative-error statistical query $SQ(\chi, \mu, \theta)$ for every $\chi \in \mathcal{Q}$ with probability at least $1 - \delta$. For a query set $\mathcal{Q}$ with a known (finite) Vapnik-Chervonenkis dimension $q = \text{VCD}(\mathcal{Q})$ a sample of size

$$|S| = O\left(\frac{q}{\mu^2\theta\log\frac{1}{\mu\theta}} + \frac{1}{\mu^2\theta\log\frac{1}{\delta}}\right) \qquad (14.9)$$

is sufficient.

To handle random classification noise of any rate approaching $1/2$ more complex methods are used for answering the statistical queries. Using knowledge of the noise process and a sufficiently accurate estimate of the noise rate (which must itself be determined by the algorithm), the noise process can be "inverted." The sample complexity required for a query set $\mathcal{Q}$ with a known (finite) Vapnik-Chervonenkis dimension $q = \text{VCD}(\mathcal{Q})$ in the presence of classification noise of rate $\eta \leq \eta_b < 1/2$ is

$$|S| = O\left(\frac{\text{VCD}(\mathcal{Q})}{\mu_*^2\theta_*\rho_*(1-2\eta_b)^2}\left(\log\frac{1}{\mu_*\theta_*\rho_*(1-2\eta_b)} + \log\frac{1}{\delta}\right)\right) \qquad (14.10)$$

where μ_* and θ_* respectively stand for the minimum values of μ and θ across all queries from $\mathcal{Q}$, and $\rho_* \in [\theta_*, 1]$. The amount by which η_b is less than $1/2$ is just $\frac{2}{1-2\eta_b}$. Thus, the above is polynomial as long as $\frac{1}{2} - \eta_b > \frac{1}{p(\cdot)}$ where $p(\cdot)$ is some polynomial.

14.5.3   Some results on more complicated models of noise

Similar results exist for other models of noise. For example, for a fairly general nasty noise model it can be shown that no algorithm can achieve $\epsilon < 2\eta$ in learning any nontrivial class of functions. On the other hand it can be shown that a polynomial (in the usual PAC parameters and in $\epsilon - 2\eta$) number of examples suffices for learning any class of finite VC-dimension with $\epsilon > 2\eta$. Although in this case learning may not always be efficient (in terms of PAC learning) it can be shown that a fairly wide family of concept classes is efficiently PAC-learnable in the presence of nasty noise. There also exist some lower bounds on the sample complexity required to achieve $\epsilon = 2\eta + \Delta$, where $\Delta > 0$ can be arbitrarily small.

14.6   EXACT AND MISTAKE BOUNDED LEARNING MODELS

Freedom is nothing but a chance to be better.

— Albert Camus

The PAC learning model is a batch model – there is a separation between the learning phase and the execution phase. In the learning phase the learner is presented with labeled examples – no predictions are expected. At the end of the learning phase the learner must output a hypothesis h that is used in the execution phase to classify new (unseen) examples. Also, since the learner never finds out the true classification for the unlabeled instances, all learning occurs in the learning phase. However, in computational learning theory several other learning settings have been studied, such as:

- how learning examples are generated (passive observation or active querying),
- the extent of noise in the data (noisy or noiseless),
- criteria for successful learning (exact or probably correct learning),
- learner's assumptions (distribution of examples, concept class known or unknown in advance),
- learning evaluation measures (number of learning examples, time complexity).

In many settings, the learner does not have the luxury of a learning phase but rather must learn as it performs. Two such well-studied models are the on-line learning model, and the query learning model (not to be confused with the statistical query learning model described in Section 14.5.2).

14.6.1   On-line learning model

The on-line model is designed to study learning algorithms that make accurate predictions in circumstances when the learner does not have the learning phase but must learn as it performs. This setting is somewhat similar to the problems addressed by reinforcement learning (Section 1.2.6); however in on-line learning there is always immediate feedback (versus delayed feedback for reinforcement learning).

The most general definition of the on-line learning model is that in which the target function has a real-valued output (without loss of generality, scaled to be between 0 and 1).

Definition 14.7. An on-line learning algorithm for $\mathcal{C}$ is an algorithm that runs under the following scenario. A learning session consists of a set of trials. In each trial, the learner is given an unlabeled example $\mathbf{x} \in \mathcal{X}$. The learner uses its current hypothesis to predict a value $p(\mathbf{x})$ for the unknown (real-valued) target concept $f \in \mathcal{C}$ and immediately after that the learner is told the correct value for $f(\mathbf{x})$. ◇

The goal of the on-line learner is to make predictions so as to minimize the total loss over all predictions. Several loss functions have been proposed to measure the quality of the learner's predictions. Three commonly used loss functions are the following:

- the square loss, defined by
  $$L_2(p(\mathbf{x}), f(\mathbf{x})) = (f(\mathbf{x}) - p(\mathbf{x}))^2$$
- the log loss, defined by
  $$L_{\log}(p(\mathbf{x}), f(\mathbf{x})) = -f(\mathbf{x}) \log p(\mathbf{x}) - (1 - f(\mathbf{x})) \log(1 - p(\mathbf{x}))$$
- the absolute loss, defined by
  $$L_1(p(\mathbf{x}), f(\mathbf{x})) = |f(\mathbf{x}) - p(\mathbf{x})|$$

In the on-line learning model, most often a worst-case model for the environment is assumed. There is some known concept class from which the target concept is selected. An adversary (with an unlimited computing power and the knowledge of the learner's algorithm) selects both the target function and the presentation order for the instances. In this model there is no learning phase; instead the learner receives unlabeled instances throughout the entire learning session. However, after each prediction the learner is shown the correct value. This feedback can then be used by the learner to improve its hypothesis.

For the formal analysis usually a special case is used, where the target function is binary. Correspondingly, predictions must be either 0 or 1. In this special case the most commonly used loss function is the absolute loss. If the prediction is correct then the value of the loss function is 0, and if the prediction is incorrect then the value of the loss function is 1. The total loss of the learner is therefore exactly the number of prediction mistakes. Thus, in the worst-case model we assume that an adversary selects the order in which the instances are presented to the learner and we evaluate the learner by the maximum number of mistakes made during the learning session. Our goal is to minimize the worst-case number of mistakes using an efficient learning algorithm (i.e. each prediction is made in polynomial time). In other words, we are interested in a lower bound for the number of mistakes the learner will make before it learns the target concept. Often the number of mistakes is more important than the total number of learning examples.

Mistake bounds, obtained in such a way, are often quite strong in terms that the order in which examples are presented does not matter. It is however impossible to tell how early the mistakes will occur. It can be shown that in the on-line learning model $\text{VCD}(\mathcal{C})$ is a lower bound on the number of prediction mistakes.

Techniques for designing good on-line learning algorithms

There exist some general techniques for designing good on-line learning algorithms for the special case of concept learning (learning binary functions). Ignoring the issue of computation time, the halving algorithm performs very well.

In the *halving* algorithm all concepts in the concept class $\mathcal{C}$ are initially candidates for the target concept. To make a prediction for example $\mathbf{x}$, the learner takes a majority vote based on all remaining candidates. Then, when the feedback is received, all concepts that disagree with the majority consensus are removed from the set of candidates. It can be shown that at each step the number of candidates is reduced by a factor of at least 2. Thus, the number of prediction mistakes made by the halving algorithm is at most $\log_2 |C|$. Obviously, the halving algorithm will perform poorly if the data is noisy, because once a candidate concept makes a mistake it is irrevocably disregarded.

The *weighted majority* algorithm is a generalization of the halving algorithm constructed for dealing with noisy learning data. It is basically a multiplicative weight-update scheme for the halving algorithm. It provides a simple and effective method for constructing a learning algorithm A that is provided with a pool of "experts" (concepts), one of which is known to perform well, but A does not know which one. Associated with each expert is a weight that gives A's confidence in the accuracy of that expert. When asked to make a prediction, A predicts by combining the votes from its experts based on their associated weights. When an expert suggests the wrong prediction, A passes that information to the given expert and reduces its associated weight using a multiplicative weight-updating scheme in which the weight is multiplied by some weight $0 \leq \beta < 1$. By selecting $\beta > 0$ this algorithm is robust against noise in the data. A sketch of the weighted majority algorithm is shown in Algorithm 14.1.

There exist several learning problems in which the use of the weighted majority algorithm is advantageous. Suppose one knows that the correct prediction comes from some target concept selected from a known concept class. Then one can apply the weighted majority algorithm where each concept in the class is one of the algorithms (experts, concepts) in the pool. For such situations, the weighted majority algorithm is a robust generalization of the halving algorithm – in fact, the halving algorithm corresponds to the special case where $\beta = 0$. As another example, the weighted majority algorithm can often be applied to help in situations in which the prediction algorithm has a parameter whose value must be selected and the best choice for the parameter value depends on the target. In such cases one can build the pool of algorithms by choosing various values for the parameter.

There exist some theoretical results about the performance of the weighted majority algorithm. If the best algorithm in the pool $\mathcal{A}$ makes at most m mistakes, then in the worst case the number of mistakes M made by the weighted majority algorithm is $O(\log |\mathcal{A}| + m)$ where the constant hidden by the $O(\cdot)$ notation depends on β. More specifically, the number of mistakes made by the weighted majority algorithm depends on the quality of several algorithms $A \in \mathcal{A}$:

- if one algorithm in $\mathcal{A}$ makes at most m mistakes

$$M \leq \frac{\log |A| + m \log \frac{1}{\beta}}{\log \frac{2}{1+\beta}} \qquad (14.11)$$

- if there exists a set of k algorithms in $\mathcal{A}$ such that each algorithm makes at most m mistakes:

$$M \leq \frac{\frac{\log |A|}{k} + m \log \frac{1}{\beta}}{\log \frac{2}{1+\beta}} \qquad (14.12)$$

Algorithm 14.1 A weighted majority (generalized halving) algorithm. We obtain the original halving algorithm by setting β to 0.

INPUT: A set of concepts (learned algorithms) A_i, $i = 1 \ldots N$, a set of examples $\mathcal{X}$, and a parameter β

OUTPUT: Weights for the input concepts.

  associate each algorithm A_i with a weight w_i
  for $i = 1$ to N **do**
    let $w_i = 1$
  end for
  for each new example $\mathbf{x} \in \mathcal{X}$ **do**
    let $\mathcal{A}_0$ be the set of algorithms that predicted 0
    let $\mathcal{A}_1$ be the set of algorithms that predicted 1
    let $q_0 = \sum_{A_i \in \mathcal{A}_0} w_i$
    let $q_1 = \sum_{A_i \in \mathcal{A}_1} w_i$
    if $q_0 \geq q_1$ **then**
      predict 0
    else
      predict 1
    end if
    if a prediction is a mistake **then**
      let γ be the prediction
      for $i = 1$ to N **do**
        if A_i's prediction for $\mathbf{x}$ is γ **then**
          let $w_i = w_i \cdot \beta$ {Penalize the mistaken algorithm (concept).}
          inform A_i of the mistake
        end if
      end for
    end if
  end for

- if the total number of mistakes made by a set of k algorithms in $\mathcal{A}$ is m

$$M \leq \frac{\frac{\log |A|}{k} + \frac{m}{k} \log \frac{1}{\beta}}{\log \frac{2}{1+\beta}} \tag{14.13}$$

When $|\mathcal{A}|$ is not polynomial, a directly implemented weighted majority algorithm is not computationally feasible. In this case a virtual weighting technique can be used. It implicitly maintains the exponentially large set of weights so that the time to compute a prediction and then update the "virtual" weights is polynomial. This is achieved by grouping concepts that "behave alike" on seen examples into blocks. For each block only one weight has to be computed and one constructs the blocks so that the number of concepts combined in each block as well as the weight for the block can be efficiently computed. While the number of blocks increases as new counterexamples are received, the total number of blocks is polynomial in the number of mistakes. Thus all predictions and updates can be performed in time polynomial in the number of blocks, which is in turn polynomial in the number of prediction mistakes.

Many variations of the basic weighted majority algorithm have also been studied including how β can be tuned as a function of an upper bound on the noise rate.

14.6.2   Query learning model

A very well-studied formal learning model is the membership and equivalence query model. In this model (often called the exact learning model) the learner's goal is to learn exactly how an unknown (binary) target function f, taken from some known concept class C, classifies all instances from the domain. This goal is commonly referred to as the exact identification. The learner has available two types of queries to find out about f. One is a membership query, in which the learner supplies an example $\mathbf{x}$ from the domain and is told $f(\mathbf{x})$. The other query provided is an equivalence query in which the learner presents a candidate function h and either is told that $h = f$ (in which case learning is complete), or else is given a counterexample $\mathbf{x}$ for which $h(\mathbf{x}) \neq f(\mathbf{x})$. There is a close relationship between this learning model and the on-line learning model (supplemented with membership queries) when applied to classification problems. Algorithms that use membership and equivalence queries can easily be transformed to on-line learning algorithms that use membership queries. Under such a transformation the number of counterexamples provided to the learner in response to the learner's equivalence queries, directly corresponds to the number of mistakes made by the on-line algorithm.

In the query learning model interesting polynomial time algorithms are known for learning deterministic finite automata, Horn sentences, read-once formulae, read-twice DNF formulae, decision trees, and also many others. Membership queries alone are however not sufficient for efficient learning of these classes, and a technique called approximate fingerprints has been developed in order to show that equivalence queries alone are also not enough. In both cases the arguments are information theoretic, and hold even when the computation time is unbounded.

There exist tight bounds on how many equivalence queries are required for a number of these classes, as well as upper and lower bounds on the number of equivalence queries required for learning (when computation time is unbounded), both with and without membership queries. It is known that any class, learnable exactly from equivalence queries, can also be learned in the PAC setting. At a high level the exact learning algorithm is transformed to a PAC algorithm. The learner uses random examples to "search" for a counterexample to the hypothesis of the exact learner. If a counterexample is found, it is given as a response to the equivalence query. Furthermore, if a sufficiently large sample is drawn and no counterexample is found then the hypothesis has error at most ϵ (with probability at least $1 - \delta$). The converse does not hold, because there exist concept classes that are efficiently PAC learnable but cannot be efficiently learned in the exact model.

14.7   INHERENT UNPREDICTABILITY AND PAC-REDUCTIONS

Youth is happy because it has the ability to see beauty. Anyone who keeps the ability to see beauty never grows old.

— Franz Kafka

In Section 14.2.3 we mentioned that a concept class of k-term-DNF formulae is not efficiently PAC learnable using the hypothesis class of k-term-DNF formulae; the same concept class is however efficiently PAC learnable by using a hypothesis class of k-CNF formulas. This motivates an interesting and fundamental question regarding the PAC learning mode: are there concept classes that are hard to learn regardless of the hypothesis class $\mathcal{H}$ used by the learning algorithm? Specifically, we are interested in the existence of *inherently unpredictable* concept classes $\mathcal{C}$ where $\mathrm{VCD}(\mathcal{C}_a)$ is some polynomial in a and thus there is no information-theoretic barrier for their fast and efficient PAC learning.

14.7.1   Hard problems

It can be shown that inherently unpredictable concept classes exist and that several common concept classes are inherently unpredictable. These results show an interesting connection between hardness results for PAC learning and the field of cryptography where the necessary tools were first developed. This connection has roots in some unproven computational assumptions (such as $P \neq NP$ and $RP \neq NP$) that have become widely accepted as standard working assumptions in cryptography and computational complexity.

In order to understand what concept classes are learnable, it is essential to develop techniques to prove when a learning problem is hard. In computational learning theory, there exist two basic types of hardness results that apply to all learning models discussed in this chapter. There are representation-dependent hardness results in which one proves that one cannot efficiently learn $\mathcal{C}$ using a hypothesis class $\mathcal{H}$. These hardness results typically rely on some complexity theory assumption such as $RP \neq NP$. For example, given that $RP \neq NP$, it can be shown that k-term DNF is not learnable using the hypothesis class of k-term DNF. While such results provide some information, what one would really like to obtain is a hardness result for learning a concept class using any reasonable (i.e. polynomially evaluable) hypothesis class.

Representation-independent hardness results meet this more stringent goal. However, they depend on cryptographic (versus complexity theoretic) assumptions. There exist representation-independent hardness results for learning several natural concept classes such as Boolean formulae, deterministic finite automata, and constant-depth threshold circuits (a simplified form of neural networks). These hardness results are based on assumptions regarding the intractability of various cryptographic schemes, such as breaking the RSA function.

14.7.2 Reducibility in PAC learning

Given that we have some representation-independent hardness result (assuming the security of various cryptographic schemes) one would like an easy way to prove that other problems are hard in a similar fashion as one proves a desired algorithm is intractable by reducing a known NP-complete problem to it. We are interested in a notion of reducibility that preserves efficient PAC learnability. For example, if a concept class C reduces to a concept class C' (denoted by $C \leq C'$), and C' is efficiently PAC learnable, then it should follow that C is also efficiently PAC learnable.

Definition 14.8. We say that the concept class C over example space $\mathcal{X}$ *PAC reduces* to the class C' over example space $\mathcal{X}'$ if the following two conditions are met:

- the existence of an efficient example transformation g from $\mathcal{X}$ to $\mathcal{X}'$ and
- the existence of an image concept. ◇

The example transformation g must be polynomial time computable. Hence if $g(\mathbf{x}) = \mathbf{x}'$ then the size of $\mathbf{x}'$ must be polynomially related to the size of $\mathbf{x}$. So for $\mathbf{x} \in \mathcal{X}_a$ it must hold $g(\mathbf{x}) \in \mathcal{X}_{p(a)}$ where $p(a)$ is some polynomial function of a. It is also important that g is independent of the target function. We now define what is meant by the existence of an image concept. For every $f \in C_a$ there must exist some $f' \in C'_{p(a)}$ such that for all $\mathbf{x} \in \mathcal{X}_a$, $f(\mathbf{x}) = f'(g(\mathbf{x}))$ and the number of bits to represent f' is polynomially related to the number of bits needed to represent f.

If $C \leq C'$, what implications are there with respect to learnability? Observe that if we are given a polynomial prediction algorithm A' for C', one can use A' to obtain a polynomial prediction algorithm A for C as follows. If A' requests a labeled example then A can obtain a labeled example $\mathbf{x} \in \mathcal{X}$ from its oracle and give $g(\mathbf{x})$ to A'. Finally, when A' outputs a hypothesis h', A can make a prediction for $\mathbf{x} \in \mathcal{X}$ using $h(g(\mathbf{x}))$. Thus if C is known not to be learnable then neither is C'.

It can be shown that the class of Boolean formulae PAC reduces to the concept class of determinate finite automata (DFAs). Thus since Boolean formulae are inherently unpredictable (under cryptographic assumptions), it immediately follows that DFAs are unpredictable as well. In other words, DFAs cannot be efficiently learned from random examples alone. It is also known (Section 14.5.2) that any algorithm for exact learning using only equivalence queries can be converted into an efficient PAC algorithm. Thus if DFAs are not efficiently PAC learnable (under cryptographic assumptions), it immediately follows that DFAs are not efficiently learnable from only equivalence queries (under cryptographic assumptions). Contrasting this negative result, it can be shown that DFAs are exactly learnable from membership and equivalence queries, and thus are PAC learnable with membership queries.

For $C \leq C'$, the result that an efficient learning algorithm for C' also provides an efficient algorithm for C relies heavily on the fact that membership queries are not allowed. The problem created by membership queries (whether in the PAC or the exact model) is that algorithm A' for C' may make a membership query on an example $\mathbf{x}' \in \mathcal{X}'$ for which $g^{-1}(\mathbf{x}') \notin \mathcal{X}$.

A more restricted type of reduction *without membership queries* (denoted by $C \leq_{wmq} C'$) can be defined. It yields results even when membership queries are allowed. For these reductions, we just add the following third condition to the two conditions (existence of efficient example transformation, existence of image concept):

- for all $\mathbf{x}' \in \mathcal{X}'$, if $\mathbf{x}'$ is not in the image of g (there is no $\mathbf{x} \in \mathcal{X}$ such that $g(\mathbf{x}) = \mathbf{x}'$), then the classification of $\mathbf{x}'$ for the image concept must always be positive or always be negative.

14.8 WEAK AND STRONG LEARNING

With great power comes great responsibility.

— Yoda

As originally defined, the PAC learning model requires the learner to generate, given $\mathcal{X}$, $\mathcal{C}$, and $\mathcal{H}$, with arbitrarily high probability $1 - \delta$, a hypothesis h that is arbitrarily accurate ($error_\mathcal{D}(h) \le \epsilon$ for the target concept). The learning algorithm's running time must be polynomially bounden by $1/\epsilon$ and $1/\delta$, as well as with the size $a = |c|$ of the target concept c being learned, and the size of its smallest representation k in $\mathcal{H}$. PAC learning algorithms are also called *strong learning algorithms*.

While for many problems it is easy to find simple algorithms ("rules-of-thumb") that are often correct, it seems much harder to find a single hypothesis that is highly accurate. A *weak learning algorithm* is one that outputs a hypothesis that has some advantage over random guessing. For instance, we may have a weak learning algorithm A that could achieve the PAC criteria not for all values of ϵ and δ, but for some fixed, constant values ϵ_0 and δ_0. For any concept $c \in \mathcal{C}$, and any distribution $\mathcal{D}$, such an algorithm manages to find a hypothesis h that with probability at least $1 - \delta_0$ has an error less than ϵ_0, and runs in time polynomial just in a and k (as $\epsilon = \epsilon_0$ and $\delta = \delta_0$ are fixed). This motivates some questions. Can we, somehow, use an algorithm A as a subroutine to obtain an improved algorithm A' that achieves PAC criteria for any values of ϵ and δ? Are there concept classes for which there is an efficient weak learner, but there exists no efficient PAC learner?

Somewhat surprisingly, the answer to the second question is no. The technique used to prove this result is to transform a weak learner into a PAC learner. A general method of converting a rough rule-of-thumb algorithm (weak learner) into an arbitrarily accurate strong learner is referred to as the hypothesis boosting. This technique is also a positive answer to the first question.

14.8.1 Weak and strong learnability

If C is strongly learnable, then it is weakly learnable. This can readily be shown by fixing ϵ to any constant less than $1/2$. The converse result — weak learnability implying strong learnability — is not so obvious. If one restricts the distributions under which the weak learning algorithm runs then weak learnability does not imply strong learnability. It can be shown that under a uniform distribution, monotone Boolean functions are weakly, but not strongly, learnable. Only by taking advantage of the requirement that the weak learning algorithm must work for all distributions can it be proven that if concept class C is weakly learnable, then it is strongly learnable.

14.8.2 Boosting the confidence

It is relatively easy to boost the confidence δ by first designing an algorithm A that works for a fixed δ_0, say $\delta_0 = 1/q(a,k)$ where $q(\cdot,\cdot)$ is some fixed polynomial. If we are willing to tolerate a slightly higher hypothesis error $\epsilon_0 + \gamma$ where $\gamma > 0$ is a small additive constant that may be arbitrarily small, we can achieve arbitrarily high confidence $1 - \delta$. A confidence boosting algorithm is sketched in Algorithm 14.2. For an arbitrary $\delta > 0$ the needed number of runs of A is polynomial in $\log_2 \frac{1}{\delta}$.

Algorithm 14.2 Boosting the confidence of the weak algorithm A. We can get rid of the parameter γ (an additive constant for ϵ by using a smaller error bound $\epsilon' = \epsilon/2$ as the error parameter for *WeakLearn*, and set $\gamma = \epsilon/2$.

INPUT: A parameter γ.
OUTPUT: A (strongly) learned hypothesis.

> let $l = \lceil (1/q(a,k)) \log(2/\delta) \rceil$, where $q(\cdot,\cdot)$ is some fixed polynomial
> **for** $i = 1$ to l **do**
>   draw a random sample S from $\mathcal{X}$ according to $\mathcal{D}$
>   run *WeakLearn* on S to obtain a hypothesis h_i
> **end for**
> let $n = (c_0/\gamma^2) \log(2K/\delta)$, where $c_0 > 0$ is some appropriate constant
> draw a random sample S' of size n from $\mathcal{X}$ according to $\mathcal{D}$
> return the hypothesis h_i such that it makes fewest mistakes on S'

14.8.3 Boosting the accuracy

Proving that weak learnability implies strong learnability has also been called the hypothesis boosting problem, because a way must be found to boost the error of slightly-better-than-random hypotheses to be arbitrarily close to 0. This has been achieved by constructing an algorithm that uses a weak learner and as a whole fulfills the PAC criteria.

The original boosting (strong learning by utilizing a weak learner) algorithm is shown in Algorithm 14.3. The key to forcing a weak learner to output hypotheses that can be combined to create a highly accurate hypothesis is to create different distributions on which the weak learner is trained. Since the original work, several variants of boosting algorithms have been proposed. Figure 14.4 describes AdaBoost, a boosting algorithm that has been widely used in practice. The input to AdaBoost is a sequence $\langle (\mathbf{x}_1, c_1), \ldots, (\mathbf{x}_n, c_n) \rangle$ of labeled examples where each label comes from the set $C = \{c^{(1)} \ldots (m_0)\}$, and a parameter T, the number of rounds.

Some of the practical advantages of AdaBoost are that is is fast, simple and easy to program, requires no parameters to tune (besides T, the number of rounds), no prior

---

Algorithm 14.3 Boosting the accuracy by an algorithm that transforms a weak learner into a strong one.

INPUT: A parameter α and a distribution $\mathcal{D}'$
OUTPUT: A (strongly) learned hypothesis.

   let $h_0 = \text{WeakLearn}(\mathcal{D}')$
   if $\alpha \geq 1/2 - 1/p(a, k)$ **then**
      return h_0
   end if
   let $\beta = g^{-1}(\alpha)$
   let $h_1 = \text{StrongLearn}(\beta, \mathcal{D}')$
   compute $\hat{e}_1$
   if $e_1 \leq 2\alpha/3$ **then**
      return h_1
   end if
   let $\mathcal{D}'_2$ be a distribution created by filtering $\mathcal{D}'$ according to h_1 such that it gives the weight of exactly $1/2$ to those examples on which h_1 errs
   let $h_2 = \text{StrongLearn}(\beta, \mathcal{D}'_2)$
   compute $\hat{e}_2$
   if $e_1 \leq \alpha - \tau$ **then**
      return h_2
   end if
   let $\mathcal{D}'_3$ be a distribution created by filtering $\mathcal{D}'$ according to h_1 and h_2, such that it gives the weight of exactly $1/2$ to those examples on which h_1 and h_2 disagree
   let $h_2 = \text{StrongLearn}(\beta, \mathcal{D}'_3)$
   let h = majority(h_1, h_2, h_3)
   return h

---

knowledge is needed about the weak learner, it is provably effective, and it is flexible since you can combine it with any classifier that finds weak hypotheses.

Several early experiments performed with AdaBoost by using some simple rules of thumb or decision trees as the weak learners have shown that the obtained strong learner often outperforms the best known algorithms on some standard benchmarks. Since its introduction, AdaBoost has widely gained in popularity, and has been a cornerstone of many approaches of boosting. It has been extended to handle situations in which predictions are multi-valued or real-valued (the original AdaBoost could handle only binary predictions).

Algorithm 14.4 The algorithm AdaBoost to boost the accuracy of a better-than-random hypothesis (created by a weak learner) to a very accurate hypothesis.

INPUT: A sequence of labeled examples $\langle (\mathbf{x}_1, c_1), \ldots, (\mathbf{x}_n, c_n) \rangle$, a set of labels
            $C = \{c^{(1)} \ldots (m_0)$, and parameter T (the number of rounds).

OUTPUT: A (strongly) learned hypothesis.

for $i = 1$ to n **do**
  let $D_1(i) = 1/n$
end for
for $t = 1$ to T **do**
  call a weak learner providing it with the distribution D_t to obtain the hypothesis h_t
  calculate ϵ_t, the error of h_t: $\epsilon_t = \sum_{i:h_t(\mathbf{x}_i) \neq c_i} D_t(i)$
  if $\epsilon_t \geq 1/2$ **then**
    let $t = t - 1$
    abort the loop
  end if
  let $\beta_t = \epsilon_t / (1 - \epsilon_t)$
  update distribution D_{t+1}:
  let Z_t be a normalization constant so D_{t+1} is a valid probability distribution
  if $h_t(\mathbf{x}_i) = c_i$ **then**
    let $D_{t+1} = \frac{D_t(i)}{Z_t} \cdot \beta_t$
  else
    let $D_{t+1} = \frac{D_t(i)}{Z_t}$
  end if
end for
output the final hypothesis:
$h_{fin}(\mathbf{x}) = \mathrm{argmax}_{c \in C} \sum_{t:h_t(\mathbf{x})=c} \log \frac{1}{\beta_t}$

14.9   SUMMARY AND FURTHER READING

A box without hinges, key, or lid, yet golden treasure inside is hid.

— *J. R. R. Tolkien*

- Computational learning theory formally studies how to design computer programs that are capable of learning, and identifies the computational limits of learning by machines.

- The Vapnik-Chervonenkis (VC) dimension of a concept class $\mathcal{C}$, denoted $\mathrm{VCD}(\mathcal{C})$, is the smallest d for which no set of $d + 1$ examples is shattered by $\mathcal{C}$. Equivalently, $\mathrm{VCD}(\mathcal{C})$ is the cardinality of the largest finite set of points $S \subseteq \mathcal{X}$ that is shattered by $\mathcal{C}$. The Vapnik-Chervonenkis dimension is strongly connected to information-theoretic bounds on the sample size necessary for an accurate generalization.

- In the PAC (distribution-free) learning model, examples are generated according to an unknown probability distribution. The goal of a PAC learning algorithm is to classify with arbitrary accuracy (with respect to the unknown distribution) all new (unclassified) examples. PAC is a batch learning model. The basic definition of PAC learning assumes that the input data are properly (noise-free) labeled according to the target concept. Since practical learning algorithms necessarily have to be robust with respect to noise in the learning data, in the context of PAC learning several formal models of noise have been proposed.

- The on-line learning model is designed to study learning algorithms that make accurate predictions in circumstances when the learner does not have the learning phase but must learn as it performs. There exist some general techniques for designing good on-line learning algorithms for the special case of concept learning (learning binary functions), such as halving and weighted majority.

- A very well-studied formal learning model is the membership and equivalence query model. In this model (often called the exact learning model) the learner's goal is to learn exactly how an unknown (binary) target function taken from some known concept class, classifies all instances from the domain. The learner has available two types of queries to find out about the target function: a membership query and an equivalence query.

- Inherently unpredictable concept classes are those that are not efficiently PAC-learnable, although their VC-dimension is polynomial in the number of attributes, and thus there is no information-theoretic barrier for their fast and efficient PAC learning. An example of an inherently unpredictable concept class is learning k-term DNF formulae. Several important practical problems can be reduced to inherently unpredictable concept classes, and thus it can be shown that there exist no efficient PAC algorithms for those problems.

- Any better-than-random (weak) learning algorithm can be transformed into a strong (PAC) learning algorithm by using the boosting technique. Descendants of this technique, such as the AdaBoost algorithm, have found widespread acceptance in practice and are the most important practical result of computational learning theory.

The first formal definition of learning was introduced by Gold (1967). It is discussed in more detail in Chapter 13. The field of modern computational learning theory began with the seminal work in PAC learning by Valiant (1984). Angluin and Smith (1987) present an overview of early learning theory. Duda and Hart (1973) discuss the pattern recognition approach to the learning theory. Early important results in PAC learning were obtained by Pitt and Valiant (1988), Pitt and Warmuth (1990), and Haussler et al. (1991, 1994).

Vapnik and Chervonenkis (1971) defined the VC-dimension and provided basic results that were subsequently used for proving its connections to the learning theory (Blumer et al., 1987, 1989). Theorems 14.2 and 14.3 are due to Blumer et al. (1987), whereas Theorems 14.1 and 14.4 are due to Blumer et al. (1989). The closely related Theorem 14.5 is due to Ehrenfeucht and Haussler (1989).

Valiant (1985), Angluin and Laird (1988), Sloan (1988), Goldman and Sloan (1995), and Bshouty et al. (1999) studied the impact of different kinds of noise to the PAC learning model. Kearns (1993) introduced a statistical query model and proved the Theorem 14.6. His work was later improved by Aslam and Decatur (1997).

Littlestone (1988) has shown the connection between VC-dimension and the lower bound on the number of prediction mistakes for the on-line learning model. Basic techniques for designing good on-line algorithms have been analyzed and extended by Maass and Warmuth (1995) and Cesa-Bianchi et al. (1993).

Angluin (1988, 1990), Littlestone (1988) and Blum (1990) studied the membership and equivalence query model and its relationship to the on-line learning model and the PAC learning model. Several interesting polynomial time algorithms for well-known concept classes in the query learning model are due to Angluin (1987) (finite automata), Angluin et al. (1992) (Horn sentences), Angluin et al. (1993) (read-once formulae), Aizenstein and Pitt (1991) (read-twice DNF formulae), Bshouty and Mansour (1995) (decision trees), and many others.

Bounds for the number of equivalence queries were studied by Maass and Turán (1992) and Bshouty et al. (1996). Many results on inherent unpredictability and reducibility in PAC learning are due to Angluin (1987), Pitt and Warmuth (1990) and Kearns and Valiant (1989). Perhaps the most practically useful product of the computational learning theory is the equivalence of weak and strong learning. Several early results have been published by Kearns and Valiant (1989) and Schapire (1990). Their results have been further extended by Freund and Schapire (1996), who proposed the AdaBoost boosting algorithm that has been widely used in practice.

Good general introductions to computational learning theory (along with pointers to relevant literature) can be found in textbooks by Kearns and Vazirani (1994) and Natarajan (1991). Shorter, yet very instructive expositions are presented by Goldman (1998) and Mitchell (1997).

There are many interesting research directions besides those discussed here. One general direction of research is in defining new, more realistic models, and models that capture different learning scenarios. For probabilistic target concepts Kearns and Schapire (1990) introduced the p-concepts model. There has been a lot of work in extending the VC theory to real-valued domains (Haussler, 1992). Blum et al. (1995) have addressed the problem of learning with membership queries in the presence of noise. Some researchers have studied also the connections of the computational learning theory results with other fields, such as inductive logic programming, information retrieval, expert systems, neural networks, computational complexity, and many others.

Appendix A

*Definitions of some lesser known terms

It's a poor sort of memory that only works backwards.

— *Lewis Carroll*

In several chapters we either mention or use various tools and results from probability calculus and algorithmic theory. Here we briefly review the most important of them.

A.1 COMPUTATIONAL COMPLEXITY CLASSES

Any sufficiently advanced technology is indistinguishable from magic.

— *Arthur C. Clarke*

After the theory explaining which problems can be solved and which cannot be, it was natural to ask about the relative computational difficulty of computable functions. This is the subject matter of computational complexity.

The time complexity of a problem is the number of steps that it takes to solve an instance of the problem as a function of the size of the input (usually measured in bits), using the most efficient algorithm. To understand this intuitively, consider the example of an instance that is n bits long that can be solved in n steps. In this example we say the problem has a time complexity of n. Of course, the exact number of steps will depend on exactly what machine or language is being used. To avoid that problem, we generally use the *O-notation*. If a problem has time complexity $O(n^2)$ on one typical computer, then it will also have complexity $O(n^2)$ on most other computers, so this notation allows us to generalize away from the details of a particular computer.

For proving some results from computational learning theory, most relevant are the complexity classes P, RP, and NP, although several other complexity classes exist. Interesting relations hold between different complexity classes – P is a subset of RP, which is a subset of NP:

$$P \subseteq RP \subseteq NP \qquad (A.1)$$

It is not known whether any of these subsets are strict. However, it is believed that $P \neq RP$ or $RP \neq NP$, since otherwise $P = NP$, which is widely believed (although not proven) to be false.

A.1.1 Complexity class P

In computational complexity theory, P is the complexity class containing problems which can be solved by a deterministic Turing machine using a polynomial amount of computation time, or polynomial time.

P is known to contain many natural problems, including linear programming, calculating the greatest common divisor, and finding a maximum matching. Recently it was shown that the problem of determining if a number is prime is in P.

P is often taken to be the class of computational problems which are *efficiently solvable* or *tractable*, although there are potentially larger classes that are also considered tractable such as RP. Also, there exist problems in P (for instance, they may at least require $n^{1000000000}$ operations) which are intractable in practical terms, although their computational complexity is polynomial.

A.1.2 Complexity class NP

The complexity class NP is the set of problems that can be solved by a non-deterministic Turing machine in polynomial time. This class contains many problems that people would like to be able to solve effectively. Equivalently, it is the set of problems for which, if a solution is *guessed*, it can be verified by a deterministic Turing machine in polynomial time. All the problems in this class have the property that their solutions can be checked effectively.

A.1.3 Complexity class RP

In complexity theory, RP (randomized polynomial time) is the complexity class of problems for which a probabilistic Turing machine exists with these properties:

- It gives its answers according to the following table:

Correct answer	RP algorithm (1 run) Answers produced		Correct answer	RP algorithm (k runs) Answer produced	
	YES	NO		YES	NO
YES	$\geq 1/2$	$\leq 1/2$	YES	$\geq 1 - (1/2)^k$	$\leq (1/2)^k$
NO	0	1	NO	0	1

- It always runs in polynomial time in the input size.
- If the correct answer is NO, it always returns NO.
- If the correct answer is YES, then it returns YES with probability at least $1/2$.

In other words, the algorithm is allowed to flip a truly-random coin while it is running. The only case in which the algorithm can return YES is if the actual answer is YES; therefore if it returns YES, then the correct answer is definitely YES, and the algorithm terminates. However, the algorithm can return NO, no matter what the actual answer is. If it returns NO, it might be wrong.

If the correct answer is YES and the algorithm is run k times then it will return YES at least once with probability at least $1 - (1/2)^k$. So if the algorithm is run 100 times, then the chance of it giving the wrong answer every time is lower than the chance that cosmic rays corrupted the memory of the computer running the algorithm. The definition of RP therefore says that the answer YES is always right and NO is usually right. In this sense, if a source of random numbers is available, most algorithms in RP are highly practical. The fraction $1/2$ in the definition is arbitrary. The set RP will contain exactly the same problems, even if the $1/2$ is replaced by any constant nonzero probability less than 1.

An alternative characterization of RP that is sometimes easier to use is the set of problems recognizable by nondeterministic Turing machines where the machine accepts its input if and only if at least some constant fraction of the computation paths, independent of the input size, accept the input. NP on the other hand, needs only one accepting path, which could constitute an exponentially small fraction of the paths. This characterization makes the fact that RP is a subset of NP obvious.

A.2   ASYMPTOTIC NOTATION

The only way to discover the limits of the possible is to go beyond them into the impossible.

— Arthur C. Clarke

In mathematical analysis, and in particular in the analysis of algorithms, to classify the growth of functions one has recourse to asymptotic notations. In the 19th century, the German mathematician P. Bachman had proposed the *O-notation* that had been later extended to four other notations $(o, \Omega, \omega, \Theta)$.

- The *O-notation* means that the function f has an asymptotic upper bound g:

$$f(x) \in O(g(x)) \iff (\exists c > 0)(\exists x_0)(\forall x > x_0)|f(x)| \leq c|g(x)| \quad \text{(A.2)}$$

  or equivalently,

$$f(x) \in O(g(x)) \iff \lim_{x \to \infty} \left| \frac{f(x)}{g(x)} \right| < \infty \quad \text{(A.3)}$$

- The *o-notation* restricts the *O*-notation to mean that the function is bounded from above but that the bound must not be tight, i.e., the function must grow strictly slower than its *o*-reference.

$$g(x) \in o(f(x)) \iff (\forall c > 0)(\exists x_c)(\forall x > x_c) |g(x)| < c|f(x)| \quad \text{(A.4)}$$

or equivalently,

$$f(x) \in o(g(x)) \iff \lim_{x \to \infty} \frac{g(x)}{f(x)} = 0 \qquad \text{(A.5)}$$

- The Ω-notation is the counterpart of O-notation for functions bounded from below.

$$f(x) \in \Omega(g(x)) \iff (\exists c > 0)(\exists x_0)(\forall x > x_0) \, c|g(x)| \le |f(x)| \qquad \text{(A.6)}$$

or equivalently,

$$f(x) \in \Omega(g(x)) \iff \lim_{x \to \infty} \left| \frac{f(x)}{g(x)} \right| > 0 \qquad \text{(A.7)}$$

- The ω-*notation* is the counterpart of o-notation for functions bounded from below without converging towards their reference.

$$f(x) \in \omega(g(x)) \iff (\forall c > 0)(\exists x_c)(\forall x > x_c) \, c|g(x)| < |f(x)|. \qquad \text{(A.8)}$$

or equivalently,

$$f(x) \in \omega(g(x)) \iff \lim_{x \to \infty} \frac{f(x)}{g(x)} = \infty \qquad \text{(A.9)}$$

- The Θ-*notation* means there is an asymptotically tight-bound, i.e., that the function really behaves like its reference function:

$$f(x) \in \Theta(f(x)) \iff (\exists c_0, c_1 > 0)(\exists x_0)(\forall x > x_0) \, c_0 g(x) \le f(x) \le c_1 g(x). \qquad \text{(A.10)}$$

or equivalently,

$$f(x) \in \Theta(g(x)) \iff 0 < \lim_{x \to \infty} \left| \frac{f(x)}{g(x)} \right| < \infty \qquad \text{(A.11)}$$

More simply put, we could say that

- $f \in O(g)$ means that f has order at most g,

- $f \in \Omega(g)$ means that f has order at least g, and

- $f \in \Theta(g)$ means that f has order exactly g.

For computational learning theory (Chapter 14), the most relevant are O and Ω notations.

A.3 SOME BOUNDS FOR PROBABILISTIC ANALYSIS

Wisdom sets bounds even to knowledge.

— Friedrich Nietzsche

A.3.1 Union bound

In probability theory, the union bound (also known as the Boole's inequality) says that for any finite or countable set of events, the probability that at least one of the events happens is no greater than the sum of the probabilities of the individual events.

Formally, for a countable set of events $A_1, A_2, A_3, \ldots$, we have

$$P\left(\bigcup_i A_i\right) \le \sum_i P[A_i]. \tag{A.12}$$

A.3.2 Chernoff bounds

In probability theory, the Chernoff bound gives a lower bound for the success of majority agreement for n independent Bernoulli trials (coin flips). The Chernoff bound is a special case of Chernoff's inequality.

Let $X_1, \ldots, X_n$ be a sequence of independent Bernoulli trials each having probability $P(X_i = 1) = p$ and $P(X_i = 0) = 1 - p$. Let $S = \sum_{i=1}^{n} X_i$ be a random variable, counting the total number of successes. Then, for $0 \le \gamma \le 1$ the following bounds hold:

- Additive (Chernoff) form

$$P(S > (p + \gamma)n) \le e^{-2n\gamma^2}$$

and

$$P(S < (p - \gamma)n) \le e^{-2n\gamma^2}$$

- Multiplicative (Hoeffding) form

$$P(S > (1 + \gamma)pn) \le e^{-np\gamma^2/3}$$

and

$$P(S > (1 - \gamma)pn) \le e^{-np\gamma^2/2}$$

Chernoff bounds are frequently used in analysis of randomized algorithms (or in computational devices such as quantum computers) to calculate a bound on the number of runs necessary to determine some value by majority agreement, up to a specified probability.

A.4 COVARIANCE MATRIX

I never had to choose a subject - my subject rather chose me.

— *Ernest Hemingway*

The *covariance matrix* is a matrix of covariances between elements of a vector. It is the natural generalization of the concept of the variance of a scalar-valued random variable to higher dimensions.

Let $\mathbf{x}$ be a vector with m scalar random variable components, and μ_k the expected value of the k-th element of $\mathbf{x}$, i.e., $\mu_k = E[x_k]$. Then, the corresponding covariance matrix W is defined as:

$$
\begin{aligned}
W &= E\left[(\mathbf{x} - E[\mathbf{x}])\,(\mathbf{x} - E[\mathbf{x}])^\top \right] \\[2mm]
&= \begin{bmatrix}
E[(x_1 - \mu_1)(x_1 - \mu_1)] & \cdots & E[(x_1 - \mu_1)(x_m - \mu_m)] \\
E[(x_2 - \mu_2)(x_1 - \mu_1)] & \cdots & E[(x_2 - \mu_2)(x_m - \mu_m)] \\
\vdots & \ddots & \vdots \\
E[(x_m - \mu_m)(x_1 - \mu_1)] & \cdots & E[(x_m - \mu_m)(x_m - \mu_m)]
\end{bmatrix}
\end{aligned}
$$

$$(A.13)$$

The ij-th element of the covariance matrix W is the covariance between x_i and x_j.

References

R. Agrawal and R. Srikant. Fast algorithms for mining association rules in large databases. In *Proc. 12th International Conference on Very Large Data Bases VLDB'94*, pages 487–499, 1994.

D. W. Aha, D. Kibler, and M. K. Albert. Instance-based learning algorithm. *Machine Learning*, 6:37–66, 1991.

A.V. Aho, J.E. Hopcroft, and J.D. Ullman. *Data Structures and Algorithms*. Addison-Wesley, Reading, MA, Menclo Park, CA, London, Amsterdam, 1983.

H. Aizenstein and L. Pitt. Exact learning of read-twice DNF formulas. In *Proc. 32th Annu. IEEE Sympos. Found. Comput. Sci.*, pages 170–179. IEEE Computer Society Press, 1991.

E. Alpaydin. *Introduction to Machine Learning*. MIT Press, Cambridge, Massachussetts, 2005.

J. A. Anderson and E. Rosenfeld, editors. *Neurocomputing: Foundations of Research*. Cambridge-London: MIT Press, 1988.

J.A. Anderson. *Learning and Memory*. John Wiley and Sons, New York, 1995. 3rd Extended Edition.

P. J. Angeline and K. E. Kinnear, editors. *Advances in Genetic Programming 2*. MIT Press, Cambridge, MA, 1996.

D. Angluin. Inductive inference of formal languages from positive data. *Information and Control*, 45:117–135, 1980.

D. Angluin. Learning regular sets from queries and counterexamples. *Inform. Comput.*, 75(2): 87–106, 1987.

D. Angluin. Queries and concept learning. *Machine Learning*, 2:319–342, 1988.

D. Angluin. Negative results for equivalence queries. *Machine Learning*, 5:121–150, 1990.

D. Angluin and P. Laird. Learning from noisy examples. *Machine Learning*, 2:343–370, 1988.

D. Angluin and C. Smith. Inductive inference. In *Encyclopedia of Artificial Intelligence*, pages 409–418. J. Wiley and Sons, New York, NY, 1987.

D. Angluin, M. Frazier, and L. Pitt. Learning conjunctions of Horn clauses. *Machine Learning*, 9:147–164, 1992.

D. Angluin, L. Hellerstein, and M. Karpinski. Learning read-once formulas with queries. *Journal of ACM*, 40:185–210, 1993.

J. A. Aslam and S. E. Decatur. Specification and simulation of statistical query algorithms for efficiency and noise tolerance. *Journal of Computer and System Sciences*, 1997.

J. D. Bagley. *The behavior of adaptive systems which employ genetic and correlation algorithms*. PhD thesis, University of Michigan, 1967.

A. G. Barto, R. S. Sutton, and C. W. Anderson. Neuronlike adaptive elements that can solve difficult learning control problems. *IEEE Trans. on Systems, Man, and Cybernetics*, SMC-13 (5):834–846, 1983.

G. P. Beaumont. *Probability And Random Variables*. Horwood Publishing, Chichester, 2004.

J. M. Bernardo and A. F. M. Smith. *Bayesian Theory*. John Wiley, 2000.

M. Bevk and I. Kononenko. Towards symbolic mining of images with association rules: Preliminary results on textures. *Intelligent Data Analysis*, 2006. (in press).

A. Blum. Separating distribution-free and mistake-bound learning models over the Boolean domain. In *Proc. of the 31st Symposium on the Foundations of Comp. Sci.*, pages 211–218, Los Alamitos, CA, 1990. IEEE Computer Society Press.

A. Blum, P. Chalasani, S. A. Goldman, and D. K. Slonim. Learning with unreliable boundary queries. In *Proc. 8th Annu. Conf. on Comput. Learning Theory*, pages 98–107, New York, NY, 1995. ACM Press.

L. Blum and M. Blum. Towards a mathematical theory of inductive inference. *Information and Control*, 28:125–155, 1975.

A. Blumer, A. Ehrenfeucht, D. Haussler, and M. K. Warmuth. Occam's razor. *Inform. Proc. Lett.*, 24:377–380, 1987.

A. Blumer, A. Ehrenfeucht, D. Haussler, , and M. K. Warmuth. Learnability and the Vapnik-Chervonenkis dimension. *Journal of ACM*, 36(4):929–965, 1989.

R. Borger and A.M. Seaborne. *The Psychology of Learning*. Penguin Books, Harmondsworth, 1966.

Z. Bosnić and I. Kononenko. Estimation of prediction reliability in regression based on a transductive approach. In B. Prasad, editor, *Proc. 2nd Indian International Conference On Artificial Intelligence IICAI-05*, pages 3502–3516, Pune, India December 20-22, 2005.

Z. Bosnić, I. Kononenko, M. Robnik Šikonja, and M. Kukar. Evaluation of prediction reliability in regression using the transduction principle. In B. Zajc and M. Tkalčič, editors, *Proceedings of The IEEE Region 8 EUROCON 2003*, volume 2, pages 99–103, 2003.

R. R. Bouckaert and E. Frank. Evaluating the replicability of significance tests for comparing learning algorithms. The University of Waikato, New Zealand, 2004.

R. J. Brachman and T. Anand. The process of knowledge discovery in databases. In *Advances in Knowledge Discovery and Data Mining*, pages 37–57. MIT Press, 1996.

J. Brank and J. Leskovec. The download estimation task on KDD Cup 2003. *SIGKDD Explorations*, 5(2):160–162, 2003.

I. Bratko. *Prolog Programming for Artificial Intelligence*. Addison-Wesley, 2000. (3rd Edition).

L. Breiman. Random forests. *Machine Learning*, 45(1):5–32, 2001.

L. Breiman. Bagging predictors. *Machine Learning*, 24(2):123–140, 1996.

L. Breiman, J. H. Friedman, R. A. Olshen, and C. J. Stone. *Classification and Regression Trees*. Wadsforth International Group, 1984.

D. S. Broomhead and D. Lowe. Multivariable functional interpolation and adaptive networks. *Complex Systems*, 2:321–355, 1988.

N. H. Bshouty and Y. Mansour. Simple learning algorithms for decision trees and multivariate polynomials. In *Proc. 36th Annual Symposium on Foundations of Computer Science*, pages 304–311, Los Alamitos, CA, 1995. IEEE Computer Society Press.

N. H. Bshouty, S. A. Goldman, T. Hancock, and S. Matar. Asking questions to minimize errors. *Journal of Computer and System Sciences 52*, pages 268–286, 1996.

N. H. Bshouty, N. Eiron, and E. Kushilevitz. PAC learning with nasty noise. In *Algorithmic Learning Theory, 10th International Conference, ALT '99, Tokyo, Japan, December 1999, Proceedings*, volume 1720, pages 206–218. Springer, 1999.

M. D. Buhmann. *Radial Basis Functions: Theory and Implementations*. Cambridge University Press, 2003.

T. Buzan. *Make the Most of Your Mind*. Colt Books Ltd, 1977.

F. Capra. *The Tao of Physics*. Flamingo, GB, 1983.

G. A. Carpenter and S. Grossberg. A massively parallel architecture for a self-organizing neural pattern recognition machine. *Computer Vision, Graphics, and Image Processing*, 37:54–115, 1987a.

G. A. Carpenter and S. Grossberg. ART 2: Self-organization of stable category recognition codes for analog input patterns. *Applied Optics*, 26:4919–4930, 1987b.

G. A. Carpenter and S. Grossberg. ART 3: Hierarchical search using chemical transmitters in self-organizing pattern recognition architectures. *Neural Networks*, 3:129–152, 1990.

N. Cesa-Bianchi, Y. Freund, D. P. Helmbold, D. Haussler, R. E. Schapire, and M. K. Warmuth. How to use expert advice. In *Proc. 25th Annu. ACM Sympos. Theory Comput.*, pages 382–391, New York, NY, 1993. ACM Press,.

B. Cestnik. Estimating probabilities: A crucial task in machine learning. In *European Conf. on Artificial Intelligence 90*, pages 147–149, August 1990.

B. Cestnik and I. Bratko. On estimating probabilities in tree pruning. In Y. Kodratoff, editor, *European Working Session on Learning*, pages 138–150. Springer Verlag, March 1991.

B. Cestnik, I. Kononenko, and I. Bratko. Assistant 86: A knowledge elicitation tool for sophisticated users. In I.Bratko and N. Lavrač, editors, *Progress in Machine Learning*. Sigma Press, Wilmslow, England, 1987.

J. P. Changeux. *Neuronski čovek (L'Homme Neuronal)*. Nolit, Beograd, Yugoslavia, 1986.

W. Chase and F. Bown. *General Statistics*. John Wiley & Sons, 1986.

P. Clark and R. Boswell. Rule induction with CN2: recent improvements. In Y. Kodratoff, editor, *Proc. European Working Session on Learning*, pages 151–163, Porto, March 1991, 1991. Springer Verlag.

P. Clark and T. Niblett. Learning *if-then* rules in noisy domains. In B. Phelps, editor, *Interactions in Artificial Intelligence and Statistical Methods*. Technical Press, Hampshire, England, 1987a.

P. Clark and T. Niblett. Induction in noisy domains. In I. Bratko and N. Lavrač, editors, *Progress in Machine learning*. Sigma Press, Wilmslow, England, 1987b.

M. A. Cohen and S. Grossberg. Absolute stability of global pattern formation and parallel memory storage by competitive neural networks. *IEEE Transactions on Systems, Man, and Cybernetics*, SMC-13:815–826, 1983.

T. H. Cormen, C. E. Leiserson, and R. L. Rivest. *Introduction to algorithms*. The MIT Press, 1990.

T. M. Cover and P. E. Hart. Nearest neighbor pattern classification. *IEEE Trans. on Information Theory*, IT-13:21–27, 1967.

N. Cristianini and J. Shawe-Taylor. *An Introduction to Support Vector Machines and other kernel-based learning methods*. Cambridge University Press, 2000.

H. de Garis. Genetic programming: Evolutionary approaches to multistrategy learning. In R. Michalski and G. Tecuci, editors, *Machine Learning: A Multistrategy approach*, volume IV. Morgan Kaufmann, 1994.

A. Demiriz, K. P. Bennett, and M. J. Embrechts. Semi-supervised clustering using genetic algorithms. In *Artificial Neural Networks in Engineering (ANNIE-99)*, pages 809–814, 1999.

A. P. Dempster, N. M. Laird, and D.B. Rubin. Maximum likelihood from incomplete data via the EM algorithm. *Journal of the Royal Statistical Society*, 39(1):1–38, 1977.

J. Demšar. Statistical comparisons of classifiers over multiple data sets. *Journal of Machine Learning Research*, 7:1–30, 2006.

J. Demšar, B. Zupan, and I. Bratko. Transformation of attribute space by function decomposition. In G. Della Riccia, H. J. Lenz, and R. Kruse, editors, *Data fusion and perception*, pages 237–247, New York, 2001. Springer.

P. Diaconis and B. Efron. Computer-intensive methods in statistics. *Scientific American*, 248: 96–108, 1983.

T. G. Dietterich. Learning and inductive inference. In P. Cohen and E.A. Feigenbaum, editors, *The Handbook of Artificial Intelligence*, volume 3. Pitman Books Ltd, 1982.

T. G. Dietterich. Approximate statistical tests for comparing supervised classification learning algorithms. *Neural Computation*, 10(7):1895–1924, 1998.

T. G. Dietterich and G. Bakiri. Solving multiclass learning problems via error-correcting output codes. *Journal of Artificial Intelligence Research*, 2:263–286, 1995.

P. Domingos. Metacost: A general method for making classifiers cost-sensitive. In *Proc. of KDD-99*, pages 155–164. New York: ACM Press, 1999.

J. Dougherty, R. Kohavi, and M. Sahami. Supervised and unsupervised discretization of continuous features. In *Proc. ICML'95*, pages 194–202. Morgan Kaufmann, 1995.

H. L. Dreyfus. *What Computers Can't Do*. New York: Harper & Row, 1972.

M.P. Driscoll. *Psychology of Learning for Instruction*. Allyn and Bacon, London, 1994.

R. O. Duda and P. E Hart. *Pattern Classification and Scene Analysis*. John Wiley and Sons, 1973.

R. O. Duda, P. E. Hart, and D. G. Stork. *Pattern Classification*. Wiley Interscience, New York, 2001.

J. P. Egan. Signal detection theory and ROC analysis. *Series in Cognition and Perception*, 1975.

A. Ehrenfeucht and D. Haussler. A general lower bound on the number of examples needed for learning. *Inform. Comput.*, 82(3):247–251, 1989.

A. Eiben and J.E. Smith. *Introduction to Evolutionary Computing*. Springer, Berlin, 2003.

A. Einstein. Science and religion. *Nature*, 146:605–607, 1940.

B. S. Everitt, S. Landau, and M. Leese. *Cluster Analysis*. Arnold Publishers, 4th edition, 2001.

U. M. Fayyad. *On the induction of decision trees for multiple concept learning*. PhD thesis, The University of Michigan, 1991.

U. M. Fayyad. Multi-interval discretization of continuous-valued attributes for classification learning. In *Proc. IJCAI 1993*, pages 1022–1027. Morgan Kaufmann, 1993.

U. M. Fayyad. Sky image cataloging and analysis tool. In *Proc. IJCAI-95*, pages 2067–2068, 1995. Montreal.

U. M. Fayyad and R. Uthurusamy. Data mining and knowledge discovery in databases (editorial). *Communications of the ACM*, 39(11):24–26, 1996.

D. H. Fisher. Knowledge acquisition via incremental conceptual clustering. *Machine Learning*, 2:139–172, 1987.

D. H. Fisher. Iterative optimization and simplification of hierarchical clusterings. *Journal of Artificial Intelligence Research*, 4:147–180, 1996.

D. B. Fogel. *Evolutionary Computation: Toward a New Philosophy of Machine Intelligence*. Piscataway, NJ, IEEE Press, 1995.

A.A. Freitas. *Data Mining and Knowledge Discovery with Evolutionary Algorithms*. Springer, Berlin, 2002.

Y. Freund and R. Schapire. Experiments with a new boosting algorithm. In *Proceedings of the Thirteenth International Conference on Machine Learning*, pages 148–156, San Mateo, CA., 1996. Morgan Kaufmann.

N. Friedman, D. Geiger, and M. Goldszmidt. Bayesian network classifiers. *Machine Learning*, 29:131–163, 1997.

K. Fukushima. A neural network for visual pattern recognition. *IEEE Computer*, pages 65–75, 3 1988.

A. Gammerman, V. Vovk, and V. Vapnik. Learning by transduction. In *Proceedings of 14th Conference on Uncertainty in Artificial Intelligence*, pages 148–155, 1998.

M. Gams, M. Paprzycki, and X. Wu, editors. *Mind Versus Computer*. IOS Press, Amsterdam, 1997.

G. Giacinto and F. Roli. Dynamic classifier selection based on multiple classifier behaviour. *Pattern Recognition*, 34:1879–1881, 2001.

E. M. Gold. Language identification in the limit. *Information and Control*, 10(5):447–474, 1967.

D. E. Goldberg. *Genetic Algorithms in Search, Optimization and Machine Learning*. Addison-Wesley, 1989.

S. A. Goldman. Computational learning theory. In M. J. Atallah, editor, *Algorithms and Theory of Computation Handbook*, chapter 30. CRC Press, 1998.

S. A. Goldman and R. Sloan. Can PAC learning algorithms tolerate random attribute noise? *Algorithmica*, 14(1):70–84, 1995.

D. Goleman. *Emotional Intelligence: Why It Can Matter More Than IQ*. Bantam, 1997.

D. Gondek and T. Hofmann. Non-redundant data clustering. In *Proceedings of the Fourth IEEE International Conference on Data Mining*, pages 75–82, 2004.

I. J. Good. *Probability and the Weighing of Evidence*. Charles Griffin, London, 1950.

I. J. Good. *The Estimation of Probabilities – An Essay on Modern Bayesian Methods*. The MIT Press, Cambridge, 1964.

A. D. Gordon. *Classification*. Chapman & Hall/CRC, 2nd edition, 1999.

J. C. Gower. A general coefficient of similarity and some of its properties. *Biometrics*, 27: 857–72, 1971.

J. C. Gower. Measures of similarity, dissimilarity and distance. In S. Kotz, N. L. Johnson, and C. B. Reed, editors, *Encyclopaedia of statistical sciences*, volume 5. John Wiley & Sons, New York, 1985.

R. Grossman, M. Hornick, and G. Meyer. Data mining standards initiatives. *Communications of the ACM*, 45-8:59–61, 2002.

A. Guez, V. Protopopsecu, and J. Barhen. On the stability, storage capacity and design of nonlinear continuous neural networks. *IEEE Trans. on Systems, Man, and Cybernetics*, 18 (1):80–87, 1988.

T. S. Han. Multiple mutual informations and multiple interactions in frequency data. *Information and Control*, 46(1):26–45, 1980.

D. Hand, H. Mannila, and P. Smyth. *Principles of Data Mining*. MIT Press, 2001.

T. Hastie and C. Loader. Local regression: automatic kernel carpentry. *Statistical Science*, 8: 120–143, 1993.

D. Haussler. Decision theoretic generalizations of the PAC model for neural net and other learning applications. *Inform. Comput.*, 100(1):78–150, 1992.

D. Haussler, M. Kearns, N. Littlestone, and M. K. Warmuth. Equivalence of models for polynomial learnability. *Inform. Comput.*, 95(2):129–161, 1991.

D. Haussler, N. Littlestone, and M. K. Warmuth. Predicting $\{0, 1\}$ functions on randomly drawn points. *Inform. Comput.*, 115(2):284–293, 1994.

S. Haykin. *Neural Networks: A Comprehensive Foundation*. Prentice Hall, 2nd edition, 1998.

D. O. Hebb. *The Organization of Behavior*. Wiley, New York, 1949.

S. Hettich, C.L. Blake, and C.J. Merz. UCI repository of machine learning databases, 1998. URL http://www.ics.uci.edu/~mlearn/ MLRepository.html.

G. E. Hinton. A parallel computation that assigns canonical object based frames of reference. In *Proc. 7th Int. Joint Conf. on AI IJCAI-81*, 1981.

G. E. Hinton and T. J. Sejnowski. Learning and relearning in Boltzmann machines. In D.E. Rumelhart and J.L. McClelland, editors, *Parallel Distributed Processing, Foundations*, volume 1. Cambridge: MIT Press, 1986.

J. H. Holland. *Adaptation in Natural and Artificial System*. University of Michigan Press, Ann Arbor, 1975.

J. H. Holland. Escaping brittleness: The possibilities of general-purpose learning algorithms applied to parallel rule-based systems. In R. S. Michalski, J. G. Carbonell, and T. M. Mitchell, editors, *Machine Learning: An Artificial Intelligence approach*, volume 2, pages 593–623. Morgan Kaufman., Los Altos, 1986.

J. E. Hopcroft and J. D. Ullman. *Introduction to Automata Theory, Languages, and Computation*. Addison-Wesley, 1979.

J. J. Hopfield. Neural networks and physical systems with emergent collective computational abilities. *National Academy of Sciences*, 79:2554–2558, 1982.

J. J. Hopfield. Neurons with graded response have collective computational properties like those of two-state neurons. *National Academy of Sciences*, 81:4586–4590, 1984.

J. J. Hopfield and D. W. Tank. Neural computation of decisions in optimization problems. *Biological Cybernetics*, 52:141–152, 1985.

D. Hosmer. *Applied Logistic Regression*. John Wiley & Sons, New York, 2000.

E. R. Hruschka and N. F. F. Ebecken. A genetic algorithm for cluster analysis. *Intell. Data Anal.*, 7(1):15–25, 2003.

E. R. Hruschka, R. J. G. B. Campello, and L. N. de Castro. Evolutionary search for optimal fuzzy c-means clustering. In *Proceedings of the IEEE International Conference on Fuzzy Systems*, volume 2, pages 685–690, 2004a.

E. R. Hruschka, L. N. de Castro, and R. J. G. B. Campello. Evolutionary algorithms for clustering gene-expression data. In *Proc. ICDM'04*, pages 403–406, 2004b.

E. R. Hruschka, R. J. G. B. Campello, and L. N. de Castro. Evolving clusters in gene-expression data. *Information Sciences*, 176(13):1898–1927, 2006.

E. Hunt, J. Martin, and P. Stone. *Experiments in Induction*. Academic Press, New York, 1966.

A. Hyvarinen, J. Karhunen, and E. Oja. *Independent Component Analysis*. Series on Adaptive and Learning Systems for Signal Processing, Communications and Control. Wiley, 2001.

R. L. Iman and J. M. Davenport. Approximations of the critical region of the Friedman statistic. *Communications in Statistics*, pages 571–595, 1980.

C. Jacob. Stochastic search methods. In M. Berthold and D.J. Hand, editors, *Intelligent data analysis: An Introduction*. Springer, 2003. 2nd Edition.

A. K. Jain, M. N. Murty, and P. J. Flynn. Data clustering: A review. *ACM Computing Surveys,*, 31(5):264–323, 1999.

A. Jakulin and I. Bratko. Analyzing attribute dependencies. In *Proc. PKDD 2003*, pages 229–240, Berlin, 2003. Springer Verlag.

R. Jeffrey. *Formal Logic: Its Scope and Limits*. McGraw-Hill, 1981.

T. Joachims. Transductive inference for text classification using support vector machines. In *Proceedings 16th International Conference on Machine Learning*, pages 200–209, 1999.

K. De Jong. Genetic-algorithms-based learning. In Y. Kodratoff and R. S. Michalski, editors, *Machine Learning, An Artificial Intelligence Approach*, volume 3. Morgan Kaufmann, 1990.

B. Julesz, E. N. Gilbert, L. A. Shepp, and H. L. Frisch. Inability of humans to discriminate between visual textures that agree in second-order-statistics. *Perception*, 2:391–405, 1973.

S. Kaski. Dimensionality reduction by random mapping: fast similarity computation for clustering. In *Proc. IEEE International Joint Conference on Neural Networks*, pages 413–418, 1998.

L. Kaufman and P. J. Rousseeuw. *Finding Groups in Data: an Introduction to Cluster Analysis*. John Wiley & Sons, New York, 1990.

M. Kearns. Efficient noise-tolerant learning from statistical queries. In *Proc. 25th Annu. ACM Sympos. Theory Comput.*, pages 392–401, New York, 1993. ACM Press.

M. Kearns and L. G. Valiant. Cryptographic limitations on learning Boolean formulae and finite automata. In *Proc. of the 21st Symposium on Theory of Computing*, pages 433–444, New York, 1989. ACM Press.

M. J. Kearns and R. E. Schapire. Efficient distribution-free learning of probabilistic concepts. In *Proc. of the 31st Symposium on the Foundations of Comp. Sci. (1990)*, pages 382–391, Los Alamitos, CA, 1990. IEEE Computer Society Press,.

M. J. Kearns and U. V. Vazirani. *An Introduction to Computational Learning Theory*. The MIT Press., 1994.

R. King, S. Muggleton, R. Lewis, and M. Sternberg. Drug design by machine learning: The use of ILP to model the structure-activity relationship of trimethoprim analogues binding to dihydrofolate reductase. *National Academy of Sciences*, 1992.

R. King, K. Whelan, F. Jones, P. Reiser, C. Bryant, S. Muggleton, D. Kell, and S. Oliver. Functional genomic hypothesis generation and experimentation by a robot scientist. *Nature*, 427:247–252, 2004.

K. Kinnear, editor. *Advances in Genetic Programming*. MIT Press, Cambridge, MA, 1994.

K. Kira and L. Rendell. A practical approach to feature selection. In D. Sleeman and P. Edwards, editors, *Proc. Intern. Conf. on Machine Learning*, pages 249–256, Aberdeen, UK, 1992a. Morgan Kaufmann.

K. Kira and L. Rendell. The feature selection problem: traditional methods and new algorithm. In *AAAI-92*, 1992b. San Jose, CA.

S. Kirkpatrick, C. D. Gelatt, and M. P. Vecchi. Optimization by simulated annealing. *Science*, 220:671–680, 1983.

D. Klein, S. D. Kamvar, and C. Manning. From instance-level constraints to space-level constraints: Making the most of prior knowledge in data clustering. In *Proc. of 19th Intl. Conf. on Machine Learning (ICML-2002)*, pages 307–314, 2002.

Y. Kodratoff and R. S. Michalski, editors. *Machine Learning, An Artificial Intelligence Approach*, volume 3. Morgan Kaufmann, 1990.

R. Kohavi and G. John. The wrapper approach. In H. Liu and H. Motoda, editors, *Feature Extraction, Construction and Selection : A Data Mining Perspective*, pages 33–50. Springer Verlag, Berlin, 1996.

T. Kohonen. *Self-Organizing Maps*. Springer, Berlin, Heidelberg, New York, 2001. 3rd Extended Edition.

T. Kohonen. Clustering, taxonomy, and topological maps of patterns. In *Proc. Sixth Int. Conf. on Pattern Recognition*, pages 1148–1151, Munich, Germany, 1982.

T. Kohonen. *Self-Organization and Associative Memory*. Berlin: Springer-Verlag, 1984.

I. Kononenko. Bayesian neural networks. *Biological Cybernetics*, 61:361–370, 1989a.

I. Kononenko. ID3, sequential Bayes, naive Bayes and Bayesian neural networks. In *4th European Working Session on Learning*, pages 91–98, Montpellier, France, 1989b.

I. Kononenko. Bayesian neural network based expert system shell. *International Journal on Neural Networks*, 2:43–47, 1991a.

I. Kononenko. Semi-naive Bayesian classifier. In Y. Kodratoff, editor, *European Working Session on Learning'91*, pages 206–219. Springer-Verlag, 1991b. Porto, March 4–6.

I. Kononenko. Inductive and Bayesian learning in medical diagnosis. *Applied Artificial Intelligence*, 7:317–337, 1993.

I. Kononenko. Estimating attributes: Analysis and extensions of RELIEF. In L. De Raedt and F. Bergadano, editors, *European Conf. on Machine Learning*, pages 171–182, Catania, Italy, 1994. Springer Verlag.

I. Kononenko. On biases in estimating multivalued attributes. In *Int. Joint Conf. on Artificial Intelligence IJCAI-95*, pages 1034–1040, 1995. Montreal, August 20–25.

I. Kononenko. Science and spirituality. Technical report, FRI, 2002. URL `lkm.fri.uni-lj.si/xaigor/eng/sas.htm`.

I. Kononenko and I. Bratko. Information based evaluation criterion for classifier's performance. *Machine Learning*, 6:67–80, 1991.

I. Kononenko and S. J. Hong. Attribute selection for modeling. *Future Generation Computer Systems*, 13(2-3):181–195, 1997.

I. Kononenko and M. Kovačič. Stochastic generation of multiple rules. In *Proc. Machine Learning Conf*, Aberdeen, Scotland, 1992.

I. Kononenko and N. Lavrač. *Prolog Through Examples*. Sigma Press, Wilmslow, Cheshire, UK, 1988.

I. Kononenko, I. Bratko, and E. Roškar. Experiments in automatic learning of medical diagnostic rules. In *Proc. International School for the Synthesis of Expert's Knowledge Workshop*, Bled, Slovenia, 1984.

I. Kononenko, B. Cestnik, and I. Bratko. *Assistant Professional User's Guide*. Jožef Stefan Institute, Ljubljana, 1988.

I. Kononenko, M. Robnik-Šikonja, and U. Pompe. ReliefF for estimation and discretization of attributes in classification, regression, and ILP problems. In A. Ramsey, editor, *AIMSA-96*, pages 31–40. IOS Press, 1996. Sozopol, Bulgaria.

I. Kononenko, E. Šimec, and M. Robnik. Overcoming the myopia of inductive learning algorithms. *Applied Intelligence*, 7:39–55, 1997.

I. Kononenko, M. Bevk, A. Sadikov, and L. Šajn. Classification of different types of coronas using parametrization of images and machine learning. In K. Korotkov, editor, *Measuring energy fields : state of the science*, volume 1, pages 193–208. Fair Lawn: Backbone, 2004. GDV bioelectrography series.

K. Korotkov. *Aura and Consciousness*. State Editing & Publishing Unit "Kultura", 1998. St.Petersburg, Russia.

B. Kosko. Constructing an associative memory. *Byte*, pages 137–144, 1987.

B. Kosko. Bidirectional associative memories. *IEEE Trans. on Systems, Man, and Cybernetics*, 18(1):49–50, 1988.

M. Kovačič. Markovian neural networks. *Biological Cybernetics*, 64:337–342, 1991.

J. R. Koza. *Genetic Programming: On the Programming of Computers by Means of Natural Selection*. MIT Press, Cambridge, MA, 1992.

M. Kubat and S. Matwin. Addressing the curse of imbalanced training sets: One sided selection. In *Proc. Fourteenth Intl. Conf. Machine Learning*, pages 179–186. Morgan Kaufmann, 1997.

M. Kukar. Transductive reliability estimation for medical diagnosis. *Artif. intell. med.*, pages 81–106, 2003.

M. Kukar. Quality assessment of individual classifications in machine learning and data mining. *Knowledge and Information Systems*, 9(3):364–384, 2006.

M. Kukar and I. Kononenko. Reliable classifications with machine learning. In T. Elomaa, H. Mannila, and H. Toivonen, editors, *Proc. 13th European Conference on Machine Learning*, pages 219–231. Springer, 2002. Helsinki, Finland, August 19-23.

M. Kukar and I. Kononenko. Cost-sensitive learning with neural networks. In *Proc. European Conference on Artificial Intelligence ECAI'98*, pages 445–449, Brighton, UK, 1998.

W. Langdon, L. Spector, U. M. O'Reilly, and P. J. Angeline, editors. *Advances in Genetic Programming 3*. MIT Press, Cambridge, MA, 1998.

E. Lausch. *Manipulation – Der Griff nach dem Gehirn*. Deutsche Verlags-Anstalt, Stuttgart, 1972.

N. Lavrač and S. Džeroski. *Inductive logic programming: techniques and applications*. Ellis Horwood, 1994.

N. Lavrač, A. Varšek, M. Gams, I. Kononenko, and I. Bratko. Automatic construction of the knowledge base for a steel classification expert system. In *The 6th Int. Workshop on Expert Systems and Their Applications*, pages 727–740, 1986. Avignon.

N. Lavrač, E. Keravnou, and B. Zupan. Intelligent data analysis in medicine. In N. Lavrač, E. Keravnou, and B. Zupan, editors, *Proc. Intelligent Data Analysis in Medicine and Pharmacology (IDAMAP-97)*, pages 33–39, Nagoya, Japan, 1997.

D. N. Lawley and A. E. Maxwell. *Factor Analysis as a Statistical Method*. Butterworths, 2nd edition, 1971.

D. B. Lenat. The role of heuristics in learning by discovery: Three case studies. In R. Michalski, J.G. Carbonell, and T.M. Mitchell, editors, *Machine Learning, An Artificial Intelligence Approach*. Tioga, 1983.

D. B. Lenat and J. S. Brown. Why AM and EURISKO appear to work. *Artificial Intelligence*, pages 269–294, 1984.

D. B. Lenat and E. A. Feigenbaum. On the thresholds of knowledge. In *Proc. 10th International Joint Conference on Artificial Intelligence*. Morgan-Kaufmann, 1987.

M. Li and P. Vitanyi. *An Introduction to Kolmogorov Complexity and its Applications*. Springer Verlag, 1993.

A. Likas, N. A. Vlassis, and J. J. Verbeek. The global k-means clustering algorithm. *Pattern Recognition*, 36(2):451–461, 2003.

R. Lindsay, B. Buchanan, E. Feigenbaum, and J. Lederberg. DENDRAL: A case study of the first expert system for scientific hypothesis formation. *Artificial Intelligence*, 61(2):209–261, 1993.

N. Littlestone. Learning when irrelevant attributes abound: A new linear-threshold algorithm. *Machine Learning*, 2:285–318, 1988.

G. L. Liu. *Introduction to the combinatorial mathematics*. McGraw Hill, New York, 1968.

H. Liu and H. Motoda. *Feature Extraction, Construction and Selection : A Data Mining Perspective*. Springer Verlag, Berlin, Heidelberg, New York, 1996.

J. W. Lloyd. *Foundations of Logic Programming*. Springer Verlag, 1984.

D. Lorimer, editor. *The Spirit of Science*. Floris Books, Edinburgh, 1998.

D. Luo. *Pattern Recognition And Image Processing*. Horwood Publishing, Chichester, 1998.

W. Maass and G Turán. Lower bound methods and separation results for on-line learning models. *Machine Learning*, 9:107–145, 1992.

W. Maass and M. K. Warmuth. Efficient learning with virtual threshold gates. In *Proc. 12th International Conference on Machine Learning*, pages 378–386, San Mateo, CA., 1995. Morgan Kaufmann.

J. MacQueen. Some methods for classification and analysis of multivariate observations. In *Proceedings of the Fifth Berkeley Symposium on Mathematical Statistics and Probability*, pages 281–297, 1967.

Sri Nisargadatta Maharaj. *I am That*. Chetana, Mumbai, India, 1973.

Z. Manna. *Mathematical Theory of Computation*. McGraw-Hill, 1974.

R. L. Mantaras. ID3 revisited: A distance based criterion for attribute selection. In *Int. Symp. Methodologies for Intelligent Systems*, Charlotte, North Carolina, U.S.A, 1989.

K. V. Mardia, J.T. Kent, and J.M. Bibby. *Multivariate Analysis*. Probability and Mathematical Statistics. Academic Press, 1979.

J. L. McClelland and D. E. Rumelhart, editors. *Parallel Distributed Processing: Psychological and Biological Models*, volume 2. Cambridge: MIT Press, 1986.

R. J. McEliece, E. C. Posner, E. R. Rodemich, and S. S. Venkatesh. The capacity of the Hopfield associative memory. *IEEE Trans. on Information Theory*, IT-33(4):461–482, 1987.

R. Michalski and G. Tecuci, editors. *Machine Learning: A Multistrategy approach*, volume IV. Morgan Kaufmann, 1994.

R. Michalski, J. G. Carbonell, and T. M. Mitchell, editors. *Machine Learning, An Artificial Intelligence Approach*. Tioga, 1983.

R. Michalski, J. G. Carbonell, and T. M. Mitchell, editors. *Machine Learning, An Artificial Intelligence Approach*, volume 2. Morgan Kauffman, 1986.

R. S. Michalski and R. L. Chilausky. Learning by being told and learning from examples: An experimental comparison of the two methods of knowledge acquisition in the context of developing an expert system for soybean disease diagnosis. *Int. Journal of Policy Analysis and Information Systems*, 4:125–161, 1980.

R. S. Michalski, I. Bratko, and M. Kubat, editors. *Machine Learning, Data Mining and Knowledge Discovery: Methods and Applications*. John Wiley & Sons, 1998.

D. Michie. Personal models of rationality. *Journal of Statistical Planning and Inference*, 21, 1989. Special Issue on Foundations and Philosophy of Probability and Statistics.

D. Michie and R. A. Chambers. BOXES: An experiment in adaptive control. In E. Dale and D. Michie, editors, *Machine Intelligence 2*. Edinburgh: Oliver and Boyd, 1968.

D. Michie and R. Johnston. *The Creative Computer: Machine Intelligence and Human Knowledge*. New York: Viking, 1984.

G. W. Milligan and M. C. Cooper. An examination of procedures for determining the number of clusters in a data set. *Psychometrika*, pages 159–179, 1985.

M. Minsky and S. Papert. *Perceptrons*. Cambridge, MA: MIT Press, 1969.

T. M. Mitchell. *Machine Learning*. McGraw-Hill, 1997.

M. Možina, J. Demšar, M. Kattan, and B. Zupan. Nomograms for visualization of naive Bayesian classifier. In *ECML-04*. Springer Verlag, 2004. Pisa, Italy.

S. Muggleton. *Inductive Logic Programming*. Academic Press, 1992.

C. Nadeau and Y. Bengio. Inference for the generalization error. *Machine Learning*, 52:239–281, 2003.

B. K. Natarajan. *Machine Learning: A Theoretical Approach*. Morgan Kaufmann, San Mateo, CA., 1991.

R. Neapolitan and K. Naimipour. *Foundations of Algorithms*. D.C. Heath and Company, Lexington,MA, Toronto, 1996.

T. Niblett and I. Bratko. Learning decision rules in noisy domains. In *Expert Systems 86*, 1986. Brighton, UK.

N. Nilsson. *Learning Machines*. McGraw-Hill, 1965.

D. Osherson and S. Weinstein. Criteria of language learning. *Information and Control*, 52: 123–138, 1982.

D. Osherson, M. Stob, and S. Weinstein. Learning strategies. *Information and Control*, 53: 32–51, 1982.

D. N. Osherson, M. Stob, and S. Weinstein. *Systems That Learn.* Bradford Book, The MIT Press, 1986.

A. Paterson and T. Niblett. *The ACLS User Manual.* Intelligent Terminals Ltd, Glasgow, 1982.

M. Pazzani, C. Merz, P. Murphy, K. Ali, T. Hume, and C. Brunk. Reducing misclassification costs: Knowledge-intensive approaches to learning from noisy data. In *Proc. Eleventh Intl. Conf. Machine Learning*, pages 217–225. Morgan Kaufmann, 1994.

J. Pearl. *Probabilistic Reasoning in Intelligent Systems: Networks of Plausible Inference.* San Mateo, CA: Morgan Kaufmann Publishers, 1988.

K. Pearson. Principal components analysis. *The London, Edinburgh, and Dublin Philosophical Magazine and Journal of Science*, page 559, 1901.

R. Penrose. *The Emperor's New Mind.* Oxford University Press, 1989.

V. Pirnat, I. Kononenko, T. Janc, and I. Bratko. Medical estimation of automatically induced decision rules. In *2nd Europ. Conf. on Artificial Intelligence in Medicine*, pages 24–36, 1989. City University, London, August 29–31.

L. Pitt and L. Valiant. Computational limitations on learning from examples. *Journal of ACM 35*, pages 965–984, 1988.

L. Pitt and M. K. Warmuth. Prediction preserving reducibility. *J. of Comput. Syst. Sci. 41(3)*, pages 430–467, 1990.

W. H. Press, S. A. Teukolsky, W. T. Vettering, and B. P. Flannery. *Numerical recipes in C: The art of scientific computing.* Cambridge University Press, 1988.

F. Provost and T. Fawcett. Robust classification for imprecise environments. *Machine Learning*, 42:3:203231, 2001.

F. Provost, T. Fawcett, and R. Kohavi. The case against accuracy estimation for comparing induction algorithms. In *Proc. Fifteenth Intl. Conf. Machine Learning*, pages 445–553. Morgan Kaufmann, 1998.

J. R. Quinlan. Discovering rules from large collections of examples. In D. Michie, editor, *Expert Systems in the Microelectronic Age*. Edinburgh University Press, 1979.

J. R. Quinlan. Induction of decision trees. *Machine Learning*, 1:81–106, 1986.

J. R. Quinlan. Learning logical definitions from relations. *Machine Learning*, 5(3):239–266, 1990.

J. R. Quinlan. *C4.5: Programs for Machine Learning.* Morgan Kaufmann, 1993.

H. Ragavan and L. Rendell. Lookahead feature construction for learning hard concepts. In *Proc. 10th Intern. Conf. on Machine Learning*, pages 252–259, Amherst, MA, 1993. Morgan Kaufmann.

C. Rajski. A metric space of discrete probability distributions. *Information and Control*, 4: 373–377, 1961.

A. C. Rencher. *Methods of Multivariate Analysis*. John Wiley & Sons, 1995.

J. Rissanen. Modeling by the shortest data description. *Automatica-Journal IFAC*, 14:465–471, 1978.

J. Rissanen. A universal prior for integers and estimation by minimum description length. *The Annals of Statistics*, 11(2):416–431, 1993.

M. Robnik-Šikonja and I. Kononenko. An adaptation of Relief for attribute estimation in regression. In *Proc. Int. Conf. on Machine Learning ICML-97*, pages 296–304, Nashville, 1997.

M. Robnik-Šikonja and I. Kononenko. Theoretical and empirical analysis of ReliefF and RReliefF. *Machine Learning*, 53:23–69, 2003.

H. Rogers. *Theory of Recursive Functions and Effective Computability*. McGraw-Hill, 1967.

F. Rosenblatt. *Principles of Neurodynamics*. Spartan Books, Washington, DC, 1962.

D. E. Rumelhart and J. L. McClelland, editors. *Parallel Distributed Processing: Foundations*, volume 1. Cambridge: MIT Press, 1986.

D. E. Rumelhart and D. Zipser. Feature discovery by competitive learning. In D.E. Rumelhart and J.L. McClelland, editors, *Parallel Distributed Processing: Foundations*, volume 1. Cambridge: MIT Press, 1986.

D. E. Rumelhart, G. E. Hinton, and J. L. McClelland. A general framework for parallel distributed processing. In D. E. Rumelhart and J. L. McClelland, editors, *Parallel Distributed Processing: Foundations*, volume 1. Cambridge: MIT Press, 1986a.

D. E. Rumelhart, G. E. Hinton, and R. J. Williams. Learning internal representations by error propagation. In D. E. Rumelhart and J. L. McClelland, editors, *Parallel Distributed Processing: Foundations*, volume 1. Cambridge: MIT Press, 1986b.

J. A. Rushing, H. S. Ranagath, T. H. Hinke, and S. J. Graves. Using association rules as texture features. *IEEE Transactions on Pattern Analysis and Machine Intelligence*, pages 845–858, 2001.

P. Russell. *The Brain Book: Know Your Own Mind and How to Use It*. Routledge and Kegan Paul, London & Hawthorne, New York, 1979.

O. Sacks. *The Man Who Mistook His Wife for a Hat and other Clinical Tales*. Harper & Row Pub, 1985.

S. L. Salzberg. On comparing classifiers: Pitfalls to avoid and a recommended approach. *Data Mining and Knowledge Discovery*, 1:317–328, 1997.

A. L. Samuel. Some studies in machine learning using the game of checkers. *IBM Journal*, 3 (3), 1959.

R. E. Schapire. The strength of weak learnability. *Machine Learning*, 5(2):197–227, 1990.

P. Schauer. *Interferon*. DDU Univerzum, Ljubljana, 1984.

H. P. Schwefel. *Numerical Optimization of Computer Models*. Wiley, Chichester, 1981.

J.R. Searle. *The rediscovery of the Mind*. MIT Press, Cambridge, MA, 1992.

C. E. Shannon and W. Weaver. *The Mathematical Theory of Communications*. Urbana: The University of Illinois Press, 1949.

E. Shapiro. Inductive inference of theories from facts. Research report 192, Dept. of Computer Sc., Yale University, New Haven, 1981.

J. W. Shavlik and T. G. Dietterich, editors. *Readings in Machine Learning*. Morgan Kaufmann, 1990.

J. Sinkkonen, S. Kaski, and J. Nikkila. Discriminative clustering: Optimal contingency tables by learning metrics. In T. Elomaa, H. Mannila, and H. Toivonen, editors, *Proc. European Conf. on Machine Learning (ECML-2002)*, pages 418–430. Springer, 2002.

L. Sirovich and M. Kirby. A low-dimensional procedure for the characterisation of human faces. *Journal of the Optical Society of America*, pages 519–524, 1987.

R. Sloan. Types of noise in data for concept learning. In *Proc. 1st Annu. Workshop on Comput. Learning Theory*, pages 91–96, San Mateo, CA., 1988. Morgan Kaufmann.

A. Sloman. The emperor's real mind: review of Roger Penrose's The Emperor's New Mind: Concerning computers, minds and laws of physics. *Artificial Intelligence*, 56:355–396, 1992.

N. Slonim and N. Tishby. Document clustering using word clusters via the information bottleneck method. In *Research and Development in Information Retrieval*, pages 208–215, 2000.

P. Smolensky. Information processing in dynamical systems: Foundations of harmony theory. In D.E. Rumelhart and J.L. McClelland, editors, *Parallel Distributed Processing: Foundations*, volume 1. Cambridge: MIT Press, 1986.

P. Smyth and R. M. Goodman. Rule induction using information theory. In G. Piatetsky-Shapiro and W. Frawley, editors, *Knowledge Discovery in Databases*. MIT Press, 1990.

R. J. Solomonoff. A formal theory of inductive inference: Parts 1 and 2. *Information and Control*, 7:122 and 224254, 1964.

R. J. Solomonoff. Complexity-based induction systems: Comparisons and convergence theorems. *IEEE Transaction on Information Theory*, 24:422432, 1978.

R. Spence. *Information Visualization*. Addison-Wesley, 2001.

R. S. Sutton and A. G. Barto. *Reinforcement Learning: An Introduction*. MIT Press, 1998.

M. Taube. *Computers and Common Sense: The Myth of Thinking Machines*. New York: Columbia University Press, 1961.

G. Tesauro. Temporal difference learning of backgammon strategy. In *Int. Machine Learning Conf*, 1992. Aberdeen.

G. Tesauro. Temporal difference learning and td-gammon. *Communications of the ACM*, 38(3), 1995.

N. Tishby, F. C. Periera, and W. Bialek. The information bottleneck method. In *Proc. 37th Allerton Conference on Communication and Computation*, 1999.

E. Tolle. *The Power of NOW*. Namaste Publishing Inc., Canada, 1997.

M. Turk and A. Pentland. Eigenfaces for recognition. *Journal of Cognitive Neuroscience*, pages 71–86, 1991.

P. Turney. Cost-sensitive classification: empirical evaluation of a hybrid genetic decision tree induction algorithm. *Journal of Artificial Intelligence Research*, 2:369–409, 1995.

T. Urbančič and I. Bratko. Constructing control rules for dynamic system: probabilistic qualitative models, lookahead and exaggeration. *Int. J. Syst. Sci.*, 24(6):1155–1164, 1993.

H. Vafie and K. DeJong. Improving a rule induction system using genetic algorithms. In R. Michalski and G. Tecuci, editors, *Machine Learning: A Multistrategy approach*, volume IV. Morgan Kaufmann, 1994.

L. G. Valiant. A theory of the learnable. *Commun. ACM 27*, pages 1134–1142, 1984.

L. G. Valiant. Learning disjunctions of conjunctions. In *Proc. 9th International Joint Conference on Artificial Intelligence,*, pages 560–566, 1985.

V. Vapnik. *The nature of Statistical Learning*. Springer Verlag, 2nd edition, 2000.

V. Vapnik. *The nature of Statistical Learning*. Springer Verlag, 1st edition, 1995.

V. Vapnik. *Statistical Learning Theory*. John Wiley, New York, USA, 1998.

V. N. Vapnik and A. Y. Chervonenkis. On the uniform convergence of relative frequencies of events to their probabilities. *Theory of Probab. and its Applications*, 16(2):264–280, 1971.

A. Varšek. Qualitative model evolution. In *Proc. 12th Int. Joint Conf. on Artificial Intelligence IJCAI-91*, pages 1311–1316. Morgan Kaufmann, 1991.

V. Vovk. Asymptotic optimality of transductive confidence machine. In N. Cesa-Bianchi, M. Numao, and R. Reischuk, editors, *Proc. Thirteenth International Conference on Algorithmic Learning Theory*, pages 336–350, Berlin, Heidelberg, New York, 2002. Springer Verlag.

K. Wagstaff, C. Cardie, S. Rogers, and S. Schroedl. Constrained k-means clustering with background knowledge. In *Proc. of 18th Intl. Conf. on Machine Learning (ICML-2001)*, pages 577–584, 2001.

B.A. Wallace. *The Taboo of Subjectivity: Towards a New Science of Consciousness*. Oxford University Press, 2000.

M. P. Wand and M. C. Jones. *Kernel Smoothing*. Chapman and Hall, London, 1995.

P. D. Wasserman and T. Schwartz. Neural networks: What are they and why is everybody so interested in them now. part 1: Winter 1987, pp. 10–12, part 2: Spring 1988, pp. 10–15. *IEEE Expert*, 1987,1988.

A.S. Weigend, D.E. Rumelhart, and B.A. Huberman. Generalization by weight-elimination with application to forecasting. In R.P. Lippmann, J.E. Moody, and D.S. Touretzky, editors, *Advances in Neural Information Processing Systems 3*, pages 875–882. San Mateo,CA: Morgan Kaufmann, 1991.

S. M. Weiss and C. Kulikowski. *Computer Systems that Learn*. Morgan Kaufmann, 1991.

A. P. White and W. Z. Liu. Bias in information-based measures in decision tree induction. *Machine Learning*, 15:321–329, 1994.

B. Widrow and R. Winter. Neural nets for adaptive filtering and adaptive pattern recognition. *IEEE Computer*, pages 25–39, 1988.

R. J. Williams. The logic of activation functions. In D.E. Rumelhart and J.L. McClelland, editors, *Parallel Distributed Processing: Foundations*, volume 1. Cambridge: MIT Press, 1986.

I. Witten and E. Frank. *Data Mining: Practical Machine Learning Tools and Techniques with Java Implementations*. Morgan Kaufmann, 2000.

I. H. Witten and E. Frank. *Data Mining: Practical Machine Learning Tools and Techniques*. Morgan Kaufmann, 2nd edition, 2005.

A. J. W. Wong. Recognition of general patterns using neural networks. *Biological Cybernetics*, 58(6):361–372, 1988.

K. Woods, W. P. Kegelmeyer, and K. Bowyer. Combination of multiple classifiers using local acuracy estimates. *IEEE Transactions on PAMI*, 19(4):405–410, 1997.

E. P. Xing, A. Ng, M. Jordan, and S. Russell. Distance metric learning with applications to clustering with side information. *Advances in Neural Information Processing*, 15, 2003.

P. V. Yee and S. Haykin. *Regularized Radial Basis Function Networks: Theory and Applications*. Wiley, Chichester, 2001.

F. Zheng and G.I. Webb. A comparative study of semi-naive Bayes methods in classification learning. In *Proceedings of the 4th Australasian Data Mining Workshop (AusDM05)*, pages 141–156, 2005.

B. Zupan. *Machine Learning with Functional Decomposition*. PhD thesis, University of Ljubljana, Faculty of Computer and Information Science, 1997. (in Slovene).

B. Zupan, M. Bohanec, J. Demšar, and I. Bratko. Learning by discovering concept hierarchies. *Artificial Intelligence*, 109:211–342, 1999.

Index

PROBABILITY AND RANDOM VARIABLES

G.P. BEAUMONT, Senior Lecturer, Department of Statistics and
Computer Science, Royal Holloway & Bedford New College
ISBN 1-904275-19-2 350 Pages

This undergraduate text distils the wisdom of an experienced teacher and
yields, to the mutual advantage of students and their instructors, a sound and
stimulating introduction to probability theory. The accent is on its essential
role in statistical theory and practice, built on the use of illustrative examples
and the solution of problems from typical examination papers.
Mathematically-friendly for first and second year undergraduate students, the
book is also a reference source for workers in a wide range of disciplines who
are aware that even the simpler aspects of probability theory are not simple.

DIGITAL IMAGE PROCESSING:
Mathematical and Computational Methods, Software Development, Applications

JONATHAN M. BLACKLEDGE, Loughborough University
ISBN 1-898563-49-7 824 pages

This authoritative text provides mathematical methods required to describe
images, image formation and different imaging systems, coupled with the
principle techniques used for processing digital images. It is based on a
course for postgraduates reading physics, electronic engineering,
telecommunications engineering, information technology and computer
science. This book relates the methods of processing and interpreting digital
images to the 'physics' of imaging systems. Case studies reinforce the
methods discussed, with examples of current research themes.

Contents: Part 1: Mathematical and Computational Background • Vector
Fields • 2D Fourier Theory • The 2D DFT, FFT and FIR Filter • Field and
Wave Equations • Green Functions Part 2: Imaging Systems Modelling •
Scattering Theory • Imaging of Layered Media • Projection Tomography •
Diffraction Tomography • Synthetic Aperture Imaging • Optical Image
Formation Part 3: Digital Image Processing Methods • Image Restoration
and Reconstruction • Reconstruction of Band-Limited Images • Bayesian
Estimation Methods • Image Enhancement Part 4: Pattern Recognition and
Computer Vision • Segmentation and Edge Detection • Statistical
Modelling and Analysis • Fractal Images and Image Processing • Coding
and Compression

Readership: Postgraduate students in applied mathematics, physics,
electrical and electronic engineering and applied computing • Research
scientists in areas including telecommunications, medical physics,
astrophysics, control engineering, defence and IT security.
This book forms the second part of a complete MSc course in an area that is
fundamental to the continuing revolution in information technology and
communication systems.

DIGITAL SIGNAL PROCESSING Mathematical and Computational Methods, Software Development and Applications
SECOND EDITION
Professor JONATHAN M. BLACKLEDGE, Department of Electronic & Electrical Engineering, Loughborough University
ISBN 1-904275-26-5 813 pages

This book forms the first part of a complete MSc course in an area that is fundamental to the continuing revolution in information technology and communication systems. Massively exhaustive, authoritative and comprehensive and reinforced with software, this is an introduction to modern methods in the developing field of Digital Signal Processing (DSP). The focus is on the design of algorithms and the processing of digital signals in areas of communications and control, providing the reader with a comprehensive introduction to the underlying principles and mathematical models.
Contents: Part I: Mathematical Methods For Signal Analysis: Introduction to complex analysis • Delta function and Green's function • Fourier series; the Fourier transform, convolution and correlation, sampling theorem, Laplace transform • The Hilbert transform and quadrature detection, modulation and demodulation, the Wavelet transform, the Z-transform, the Wigner transform • Part II: Computational Techniques In Linear Algebra: Basic linear algebra, types of linear systems, formal methods of solution • Direct methods of solution and iterative improvement • Vector and matrix norms, conditioning and the condition number, the least squares method • Iterative methods of solution • The conjugate gradient method • Computation of eigen values and eigen vectors • Part III: Programming and Software Engineering: Number systems and numerical error, programming languages, software design methods, structured and modular programming • Software engineering for DSP in C • Part IV: Digital Signal Processing: Methods Algorithms and Building a Library Digital frequency filtering, the DFT and FFT, computing with the FFT, spectral leakage and windowing • Inverse filters, the Wiener filter, the matched filter, constrained deconvolution, homomorphic filtering; noise and chaos • Bayesian estimation methods, the maximum entropy method, spectral extrapolation • FIR and IIR filters, non-stationary signal processing • Random fractal and multi-random-fractal signals.

PATTERN RECOGNITION AND IMAGE PROCESSING

DAISHENG LUO, Institute of Biomedical and Life Science, Glasgow University
ISBN 1-898563-52-7 245 pages

This book delivers a course module for advanced undergraduates, Postgraduates and researchers of electronics, computing science, medical imaging, or wherever the study of identification and classification of objects by electronics-driven image processing and pattern recognition is relevant. Object analysis first uses image processing to detect objects and extract their features, then identifies and classifies them by pattern recognition. Its manifold applications include recognition of objects in satellite images which enable discrimination between different objects, such as fishing boats, merchant ships or warships; machine spare parts e.g. screws, nuts etc. (engineering); detection of cancers, ulcers, tumours and so on (medicine); and recognition of soil particles of different types (agriculture or soil mechanics in civil engineering).
Contents: Image processing and pattern recognition • Orientation analysis • Object detection • Arrangement analysis • Shape analysis • Conclusions • Analysis of roundness/sharpness.

GAME THEORY: Mathematical Models of Conflict

A.J. JONES, Professor of Computing Science, University of Cardiff
ISBN 1-898563-14-4 286 pages

Reprinted in 2006, this modern, up-to-date text for senior undergraduate and graduate students, teachers and professionals in mathematics, operational research, economics, sociology; and psychology, defence and strategic studies, and war games. Engagingly written with agreeable humour, the book can also be understood by non-mathematicians. It shows basic ideas of extensive form, pure and mixed strategies, the minimax theorem, non-cooperative and co-operative games, and a "first class" account of linear programming, theory and practice. The text is selfcontained with comprehensive source references. Based on a series of lectures given by the author in the theory of games at Royal Holloway College; it gives unusually comprehensive but concise treatment of cooperative games, an original account of bargaining models, with a skilfully guided tour through the Shapely and Nash solutions for bimatrix games and a carefully illustrated account of finding the best threat strategies.
Choice (American College Library Association): "Begins with saddle points and maximax theorem results. Readers should be able to solve simple two-person zero-sum games. It analyses non-cooperative games (Nash equilibrium), linear programming and matrix games, and cooperative games (Edgeworth trading model). Detailed solutions are provided to all problems. For undergraduates." (*American College and Research Libraries: D. Robbins, Trinity College*).